Jefferson Davis, Confederate President

Jefferson Davis, Confederate President

HERMAN HATTAWAY

AND

RICHARD E. BERINGER

University Press of Kansas

© 2002 by the University Press of Kansas
All rights reserved

Published by the University Press of Kansas (Lawrence, Kansas 66049), which was
organized by the Kansas Board of Regents and is operated and funded by Emporia
State University, Fort Hays State University, Kansas State University, Pittsburg State
University, the University of Kansas, and Wichita State University

Library of Congress Cataloging-in-Publication Data

Hattaway, Herman.
Jefferson Davis, Confederate president / Herman Hattaway and Richard E. Beringer
p. cm.
Includes bibliographical references (p.) and index.
ISBN 0-7006-1170-3 (cloth : alk. paper)
1. Davis, Jefferson, 1808–1889.   2. Presidents—Confederate States of
America—Biography.   3. Confederate States of America—Politics and government.
4. United States—History—Civil War, 1861–1865—Campaigns.
5. Confederate States of America—Biography.   6. Statesmen—United States—
Biography.   I. Beringer, Richard E., 1933–.   II. Title.
E467.1.D26 H38 2002
973.7'13'092—dc21   2001007131

British Library Cataloguing in Publication Data is available.

Printed in the United States of America

10 9 8 7 6 5 4 3 2 1

To Archer Jones

But a very few attempts and reflections thoroughly convince me how futile (from a high point of view) are all efforts either at a full statement of the war in its origins or for writing its history—not only its military history, but what may be, with its vast complications, civil and domestic, diplomatic and social byplay, not less important than its military history . . . with results of greatest importance for scores, centuries of years to come."

—Walt Whitman, as quoted in Walter Lowenfels, ed.,
Walt Whitman's Civil War

CONTENTS

PREFACE

The story of Jefferson Davis's life and career is a great although ultimately tragic one. The man himself has been written about by myriad biographers and other historians.[1] Yet despite knowing the basic facts concerning Davis's life, there still remains much to be explained about him and especially about his presidency. Even after the many myths and lies about him have been stripped away, a residual tinge of mystery lingers. Davis the man was a potent mixture of triumph and tragedy, although he sometimes gets lost in the confusion, excitement, and bureaucratic routine of war. In some measure, he has become the most misunderstood figure of the Civil War. By focusing on his presidency and administration, we hope to dispel some of that misunderstanding and provide a clearer image of Davis as leader of the Confederacy. Thus, assuredly, this is not a biography; otherwise, we would have included a great deal more about Davis's life before and after the Civil War. For a full look at his life, we refer readers to the works of William C. Davis, Felicity Allen, and William J. Cooper Jr. We do, however, believe that we have superseded some of what they had to say about Davis's Civil War career. This is a long book, longer than we originally intended or expected. But the story is complex and justifies length.

We present a lot of narrative military history, but of course we do not intend for this book to be comprehensive in that genre. For that, we refer readers to Herman Hattaway and Archer Jones, *How the North Won,* Hattaway's *Shades*

---

1. See Herman Hattaway, "Jefferson Davis and the Historians," in *The Civil War High Command,* ed. Roman J. Heleniak and Lawrence L. Hewitt (Shippensburg, Pa.: White Maine, 1991); William C. Davis, *Jefferson Davis: The Man and His Hour* (New York: HarperCollins, 1991), and reviews by David Herbert Donald, in *New York Times Book Review,* January 12, 1992, and Herman Hattaway, in *Journal of American History* 79 (December 1992): 1178–79; Felicity Allen, *Unconquerable Heart: Life of Jefferson Davis* (Columbia: University of Missouri Press, 2000); and William Cooper Jr., *Jefferson Davis: American* (New York: Knopf, 2000).

of Blue and Gray, and Russell Weigley, *A Great Civil War.*[2] We do feel it is necessary to include enough specifics about certain campaigns and battles so as to show how they affected Davis and how he reacted to them.

Similarly, we include a lot of biographical data about a goodly number of individuals. Again, those who are expecting a simple and straightforward political/administrative narrative may be inclined to fault us for going so far afield. But again, such information is crucial to show how Davis felt about the capabilities and worth of various individuals and why he felt that way—both when he was discerning and when his eyes and judgment were beclouded by biases, misapprehensions, and just plain wrong assessments, responses that led to egregiously flawed decisions and actions.

---

2. (Urbana: University of Illinois Press, 1983); (Columbia: University of Missouri Press, 1999); and (Indianapolis: University of Indiana Press, 2000).

ACKNOWLEDGMENTS

We have been under contract to do this book for seventeen years. During that time countless numbers of people helped us in one way or another. To all whom we do not now mention by name, we apologize and do say a heart-felt "thanks."

While much of this work is based on our research in original sources, also much of it is a synthesis of what we regard as the best and most appropriate scholarship (both old and new) that illuminates understanding of the Civil War South. We are grateful to all writers whose works we used.

Beringer acknowledges the valuable assistance of Sandy Slater, head, Elwyn B. Robinson Department of Special Collections, Chester Fritz Library, University of North Dakota. He also thanks her staff and the many other staff members of that library (most notably the interlibrary loan workers) for their unfailing patience and assistance.

We both acknowledge the influence and friendship of Archer Jones. He has been a co-author with each of us on previous works. Now retired and living in Richmond, Virginia, he was the dean of humanities and social sciences at North Dakota State University. A long-time acquaintance, critic, and source of encouragement for both of us, we hope that our admiration and respect for him is reflected by the dedication of this book.

We also acknowledge the assistance of the following libraries, archives, and private individuals for the reproduction of images that are duly credited where they appear: the Eleanor S. Brockenbrough Library at The Museum of the Confederacy; the Prints and Photographs Division, Library of Congress; the Madison Bay Company; the Georgia Department of Archives and History; the Archives and Records Section, North Carolina Department of Cultural Resources; the Valentine Museum / Richmond History Center; the Archives Division, State Historical Society of Wisconsin; the United States Civil War Center, Louisiana State University (also the Special Collections Department there and Jules D'Hemecourt); the Special Collections Department at Transylvania University Library; John L. Kimbrough, M.D., Benbrook Texas; the

Chicago Historical Society; the Filson Historical Society, Louisville, Kentucky; and Felicity Allen, Auburn, Alabama. Much technical assistance was provided by Wanda M. Weber, photographer, Division of Biomedical Communications, University of North Dakota School of Medicine and Health Sciences.

We owe a special note of thanks to Lynda Lasswell Crist, Mary Seaton Dix, and other members of the editorial staff of the Papers of Jefferson Davis at the Jefferson Davis Association, Rice University, Houston, Texas. Since the 1960s they and their associates and predecessors have been preparing the absolutely essential and finely wrought published edition of the *Papers of Jefferson Davis*. With the tenth of a projected fifteen volumes now complete, we have found this series absolutely essential to understanding the South in the Civil War era. Additionally, Ms. Crist and Ms. Dix also provided us access to photocopy and microfilm primary sources in the files of the Jefferson Davis Association. The designation of JDA in many of our footnotes designate some of the material from other repositories of the association.

Hattaway thanks his dear friends Albert Castel and James Rawley, both of whom read the entire transcript in an earlier form and made many useful suggestions for emendation. Archer Jones also helped with composing a few of the passages on strategy and on General Leonidas Polk. All of Hattaway's graduate students have at one time or another been exposed to various parts of this book, and their reactions have been beneficial. He wishes to particularly thank his doctoral graduates and students: Mark Snell, Ethan Rafuse, Michael J. C. Taylor (who did quite a lot of footnote double-checking), Ron Machion, and Nola Sleevi. A good many of Hattaway's friends who hold professorships around the country have looked at and commented on various parts of the typescript.

We both also thank the readers engaged by the Kansas University Press for their advice, suggestions, and in some cases blurbs that we much appreciate. Thanks, too, to Melinda Wirkus, the senior production editor; Michael Briggs, the editor in chief (and a special friend); Claire Sutton, the copyeditor; and Edythe C. Porpa, the indexer.

Our wives, Margaret and Louise, have been, as ever, our best friends, comforters, and sources of encouragement.

Of course, everything that remains faulty or wrong in this book is entirely our fault.

Prologue

A MOMENTOUS STEP

Jefferson Davis appeared on the floor of the U.S. Senate chamber for the last time on January 21, 1861, arising from a sickbed to do so. His head ached mightily. His speech was full of emotion, "graceful, grave, and deliberate," and delivered in an atmosphere of "profound silence, broken only by repeated applause." Davis was resigning from the Senate because his home state, Mississippi, had proclaimed its secession from the Union on January 9. Senator James G. Blaine later observed that "no man gave up more than Mr. Davis," because "for several years he had been growing in favor with a powerful element in the Democracy of the free States, and, but for the exasperating quarrel of 1860, he might have been selected as the Presidential candidate of his party."[1]

Davis's farewell Senate speech painstakingly delineated his hair-splitting philosophical attitude toward the nature of the Union and the pending crisis. "Secession," he asserted, "is to be justified upon the basis that the States are sovereign. There was a time when none denied it. I hope the time may come again." But here was the unfortunate reality: "A State finding herself in the condition in which Mississippi has judged she is, in which her safety requires that she should provide for the maintenance of her rights out of the Union," fully justified such a step, but it was also tragic for the departing state because she "surrenders all the benefits (and they are known to be many,) deprives herself of the advantages (they are known to be great,) severs all the ties of affection (and they are close and enduring)."[2]

Referring to the time when the Declaration of Independence had first been created, Davis recalled that "the communities were declaring their independence; the people of those communities were asserting that no man was born— to use the language of Mr. Jefferson—booted and spurred to ride over the rest of mankind; that men were created equal—meaning the men of the political community." Davis suggested that one of the reasons for the Declaration had been that King George III had "endeavored to do just what the North has been endeavoring of late to do—to stir up insurrection among our slaves."[3]

Davis then drew his conclusion: "We recur to the compact which binds us together; we recur to the principles upon which our Government was founded; and when you deny them, and when you deny to us the right to withdraw from a Government which thus perverted threatens to be destructive of our rights, we but tread in the path of our fathers when we proclaim our independence, and take the hazard."[4]

Many senators, including prominent Northerners such as John P. Hale and Simon Cameron, surrounded Davis to shake hands and say goodbye; they liked him in spite of their philosophical differences. Despite the conviviality of the moment, however, Davis's wife Varina thought him "inexpressibly sad." That night she heard him praying aloud: "May God have us in His holy keeping, and grant that before it is too late peaceful councils may prevail."[5]

Davis's home state had been the second to proclaim secession, South Carolina having done so on December 17, 1860. Florida followed suit on January 10, Alabama the next day, and Georgia on the nineteenth. Four other U.S. senators joined Davis in formal withdrawal from the legislative body on January 21. Louisiana became the sixth state to secede, on January 26, and a convention in Texas voted for secession on February 1. On February 4, delegates from the first six states to proclaim separation from the Union began meeting in Montgomery, Alabama, to deliberate the formation of a new country: the Confederate States of America.

The Davises had departed Washington the day following his farewell speech, arriving in Jackson, Mississippi, on January 28. There they learned that he had been appointed the major general of "the Army of Mississippi." A lover of things military, he took delight in this appointment; perhaps it fulfilled his most cherished desire of the moment. But there already was much talk among the delegates in Montgomery concerning the ultimate role Davis would play. Some people urged that he become secretary of war; others thought he should be general in chief, and still others spoke of him as the most likely president. Davis expressed his own view in a letter to Mississippi congressman Alexander M. Clayton on January 30: "The post of Presdt. of the provisional government is one of great responsibility and difficulty, I have no confidence in my capacity to meet its requirements. I think I could perform the functions of genl." Yet he also wrote, "I would prefer not to have either place, but in this hour of my country's severest trial will accept any place to which my fellow citizens may assign me."[6] He was, of course, to be elected president of the Confederacy.

How did Jefferson Davis meet the problems that he was chosen to solve? To what degree did he in fact solve them at all? One way to consider the Davis presidency is to apply the same terms that some political scientists have used to examine the presidents of the United States. To do this, we shall examine Davis's leadership both in light of the traditional evidence and with regard to a modern theory of presidential leadership. One of the most promising models, and one that seems to offer keen insight into Davis's leadership, is that posed by James David Barber.[7] We employ his ideas with a light hand in our text, but we present a somewhat elaborate discussion of them in an appendix.

Barber believes that "a President's personality is an important shaper" of his decisions and that the "character, world view, and style" of a president may be understood in psychological terms. A president's "personality interact[s] with the power situation he faces and the national 'climate of expectations.' " The core of Barber's argument is that the character of a president may be "defined according to (a) how active he is, and (b) whether or not he gives the impression he enjoys political life."[8] How does he "feel about his experience— is his effort in life a burden to be endured or an opportunity for personal enjoyment"?[9] This orientation is closely related to his self-esteem: "Does he find himself superb, or ordinary, or debased, or in some intermediate range?"[10]

Accordingly, Barber has analyzed the American presidency since Theodore Roosevelt and has derived four styles of presidential leadership: active-positive, active-negative, passive-positive, and passive-negative. The active-positive president enjoys an active life and has "relatively high self-esteem and relative success in relating to the environment."[11] The active-negative president also pursues an active life, but he lacks enjoyment in what he does. His activity is "compulsive," and for all his work there is little "emotional reward." He may seem ambitious and power hungry, and he has a problem keeping his "aggressive feelings" in check. For the active-negative leader, "life is a hard struggle to achieve and hold power, hampered by the condemnations of a perfectionistic conscience."[12]

The passive-positive president, on the other hand, is receptive and compliant, an "other-directed character whose life is a search for affection as a reward for being agreeable and cooperative." His self-esteem is low, and he possesses a "superficial optimism" that allows him to overcome doubt.[13] The passive-negative president does little and enjoys it less than the other types. Oriented toward "dutiful service," he withdraws from ineffectiveness and uncertainty "by emphasizing vague principles . . . and procedural arrangements."[14] Of course, these are not hard-and-fast categories but only "tendencies."

Clearly, Davis was an active-negative president, desiring power, yet melded in was a hint of passive-negative that underlined his "civic virtue."[15] He poured a great deal of energy and commitment into his work, but we suspect that he did not enjoy it much. Although he tried, he ultimately could not adequately inspire his people. Recognizing that a significant number of them were reluctant Confederates, he still proved incapable of swaying many of them. Perhaps he was hampered by an ignorance of public relations as we know them in our own time.

The Southern populace wanted to maintain their extant way of life as they interpreted it. But Davis wanted independence more than anything else, and he himself was willing to accept what the populace regarded as unthinkable burdens and alternatives to achieve it. In the end, Southerners were less ardent about attaining independence at any price than was Davis. Thus, the Southern people were unwilling to fight long enough and hard enough and to accept drastic changes in their society and ways of life to achieve an ultimate victory. Such a victory would have come at too great a price. But Davis, with his active-negative leadership style, did want that victory.

Jefferson Davis was intelligent and experienced, by all appearances having the qualities that quite fit the task of being Confederate president. A likeable person and popular with a significantly large segment of his constituency, he had a goodly array of warm and supportive friends. Although hard working (perhaps too hard), he was also temperamental, prone to flare out in inopportune moments. He was a sickly individual (perhaps this reality hampered his performance). And he was too much influenced by proximate events, i.e., circumstances in the East, which induced him to rely too much on the discretion of his friends in the West: Leonidas Polk, Albert Sidney Johnston, Braxton Bragg, John C. Pemberton, and (finally) John B. Hood. Indeed, Davis was probably detached from reality by the last three or four months of the Civil War.

Despite this complexity, we wish to delineate Jefferson Davis as an American president. True, of course, he was president of a new and rival would-be nation, one that was trying to form itself under crisis circumstances and defending its own idea of nationhood. But it is crucial to remember that the Confederacy was very much akin to the older nation out of which it had been carved; it was an outgrowth of a part of it and was residually part of the American heritage. The ultimate essence of America is, we think, paradox. Somehow, functioning under conditions of paradox has proved workable in the United States, yet it was unworkable in the Confederacy. Perhaps then it was the concept of Confederate government, rather than Davis himself, that failed.

Davis was a competent man. But as Confederate president, he showed an egregiously flawed ability to assess higher generalship. Making his old friend Leonidas Polk a general officer was a horrible error, and Polk's performance proved that from the outset. For the sake of popular will and morale, Davis should have relieved Braxton Bragg from army command much earlier than he finally did. Late in the war Davis was correct in his decision to relieve Joseph E. Johnston from army command but could not bring himself to appoint the most logical (and best) alternative, P. G. T. Beauregard, because, as the historian Grady McWhiney has observed and we agree, Davis and Beauregard hated each other. Davis was blinded by this hatred; driven by that and other unfolding factors, he named the utterly incompetent John Bell Hood to army command. Polk, Bragg, and Hood—these three—committed a mass of scale-tipping errors that collectively were enough to doom the Confederacy.

Davis in earlier contexts had been a good administrator, but as Confederate president this was not so. Forced into the presidential office by a strong sense of duty rather than by a genuine desire to continue his prewar political career, he failed to keep a sufficiently firm grip on civil administration. He did not press for adequate taxation until it was too late; he did not press Congress to regularize impressment until it was too late; and he was inadequately involved in military subsistence problems. This last was exacerbated by his having another old crony, Lucius B. Northrop, serve far too long as commissary general of subsistence—a job Northrop simply could not at all perform well (once Davis took someone to his bosom, that individual could never do enough wrongs to change his mind-set).

Further undermining his efforts, Davis frequently suffered illnesses during the Civil War, which were probably exacerbated by heavy mental stress, some of them quite likely psychosomatic. In any event, he did not look forward to the momentous task at hand. Varina wrote that when Davis was notified of his election as president of the Confederacy, "he looked so grieved that I feared some evil had befallen our family." He told her the news "after a few minutes' painful silence . . . [and] as a man might speak of a sentence of death."[16] Against such dark moods, Davis strove valiantly to secure legitimacy and true nationhood for his beleaguered homeland. That he ultimately failed says as much about the enormous obstacles he confronted as it does about his flaws as presidential leader.

Jefferson Davis,
Confederate President

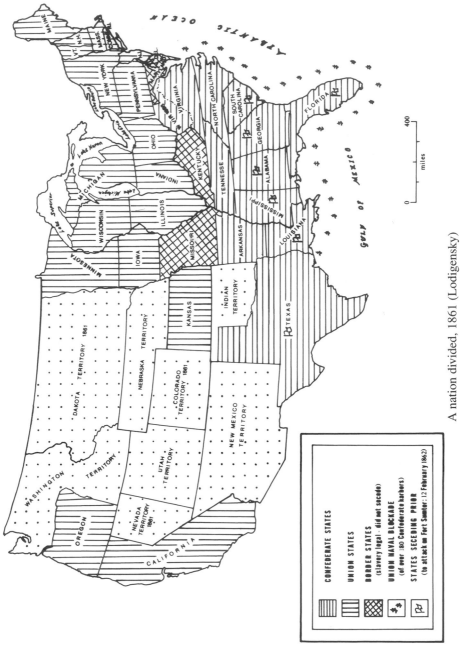

A nation divided, 1861 (Lodigensky)

CONFEDERATE STATES

UNION STATES

BORDER STATES
(slavery legal – did not secede)

UNION NAVAL BLOCKADE
(of over 180 Confederate harbors)

STATES SECEDING PRIOR
(to attack on Fort Sumter: 12 February 1862)

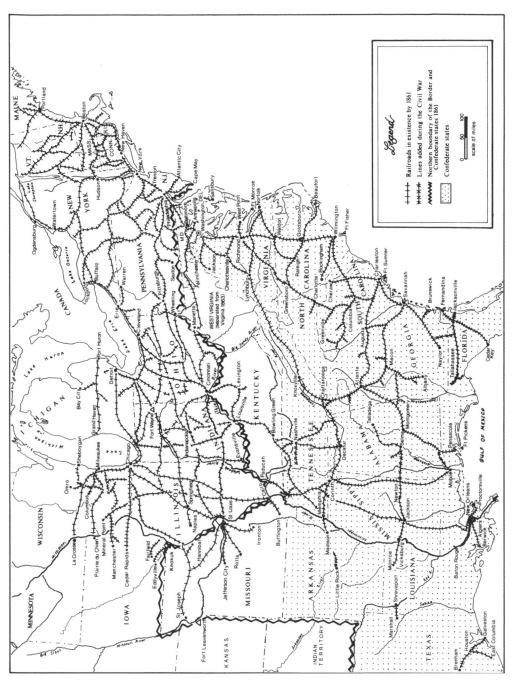

Railroads of the North and South, 1861–1865 (Lodigensky)

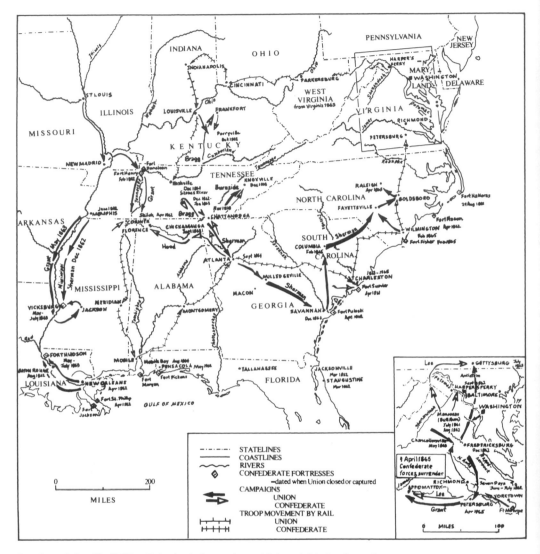

Battles of the Civil War: Principal Campaigns, 1861–1865 (Lodigensky)

1

WHAT MANNER OF MAN?

Jefferson Davis was a Welshman by paternal ancestry, and his mother was from a Scotch-Irish family. Born in Kentucky on June 3, 1808, Davis was the tenth and last child of his parents. They prospered rather well, though never did they become truly wealthy. By 1810 they had relocated to the Mississippi Territory, and "there my memories begin," Jefferson wrote in his last year, recalling life in and around the towns of Woodville and Poplar Grove. He remembered vividly the wound inflicted on his brother Samuel's horse, for example, in the January 1815 Battle of New Orleans. Jefferson's young life was spent on a farm verging on the edge of the American wilderness. His parents were loving; his older siblings, and particularly certain slaves, doted on him. And always there were slaves.[1]

When he was but a young boy, Jefferson Davis had met Andrew Jackson, and he thought then and perhaps forever after that Old Hickory was the greatest man he ever met. As one of Davis's recent biographers, Felicity Allen, puts it, he had an "unusual view of Jackson through the honest eyes of a child."[2] Davis primarily remembered Jackson's "unaffected and well-bred courtesy." Davis was much impressed that "the hero always said grace at the table." More than seven decades later he wrote, "in me he inspired reverence and affection that has remained with me through my whole life."[3]

A Jeffersonian in political and social philosophy, perhaps Davis, unlike his hero Jackson, was a purer version, in fact as well as in namesake. (Abraham Lincoln, whose presidency Davis, as head of the Confederacy, was to rival, was quite the opposite: Lincoln rejected Jeffersonianism and all that grew from it.)[4]

The young Davis spent two years of formal schooling under the Roman Catholic friars of St. Thomas in Springfield, Kentucky. The school rightly enjoyed a fine reputation, and students came from Indiana, Louisiana, Michigan, Mississippi, and Missouri as well as from Kentucky.[5] There he not only learned a great deal, he also became enamored with Catholics—so much so that, as Felicity Allen opines, "he remained prejudiced in their favor."[6] Although far from home, he kept in touch through letters from his parents, none of which survives.[7]

Davis's true scholarly bent, nurtured at St. Thomas, was clearly recognized by the faculty at Transylvania University, where he spent three years.[8] This first institution of higher learning west of the Appalachians was well endowed by doting planters and enjoyed a sterling reputation in much of the region. The impressive city of Lexington was the center of the rich Bluegrass region. "Poetry cannot paint groves more beautiful, or fields more luxuriant," wrote one enthusiastic observer. Lexington was a cosmopolitan town, and as Davis's most recent biographer, William J. Cooper Jr., points out, "The Athenaeum stocked newspapers and periodicals from East Coast cities. The public library held 6,000 books; in addition, the library at Transylvania contained more than 5,500 volumes, and the two debating societies owned another 1,000."[9]

Davis encountered difficulty in mathematics while taking the entrance examinations. He had hoped to enter as a sophomore, but instead he was put in classes with younger boys; always before he had been grouped with older ones. He was "quite disappointed," and as he put it, "I felt my pride offended." Davis apparently made his feelings known, and the mathematics professor agreed to tutor him privately; and after the remainder of the first session and through the ensuing summer, he had mastered the deficiency and was admitted to the junior class. Afternoons were mostly free, and while many other students participated in athletics, Davis took private lessons in French and dance.[10]

Davis made many friends at Transylvania; some he later worked with in Congress. At the end of his junior year he was given honors and chosen to give an address at a class exhibition, which he entitled "An Address on Friendship." A local newspaper noted that "Davis on friendship made friends of the hearers." Beyond doubt Davis was well liked. Fellow student George W. Jones, a future senator from Iowa who remained a devoted friend until Davis's death (admittedly no unbiased observer), recalled that Davis "was considered the best looking as he was the most intelligent and best loved student in the University."[11]

In June 1824 all seemed well in the world to the sixteen-year-old Jefferson Davis. But in July he learned that his father had died. As Cooper observes, this "had a profound impact on the youthful Jefferson." Sixteen was of course an impressionable age, and his brother Joseph, twenty years older, became profoundly influential as a surrogate father. Joseph was, and forever remained, quite ambitious for Jefferson. At this moment, Transylvania did not measure up to Joseph's hopes, and he decided that Jefferson should go to the U.S. Military Academy. He secured an appointment through the good offices of Secretary of War John C. Calhoun.[12]

"It was no desire of mine to go," Davis asserted to his sister Amanda. But Jefferson was a dutiful lad who much respected the wishes of his oldest brother-cum-father-figure. Jefferson admitted to his sister, "as Brother Joe evinced some anxiety for me to do so, I was not disposed to object."[13] At the Military Academy Jefferson became a lifelong friend and admirer of both Albert Sidney Johnston and Leonidas Polk. He also doubtless knew two Virginians who were in the class behind him, Robert E. Lee and Joseph E. Johnston, but he did not become close to either of them.[14]

The West Point Davis knew was virtually the creation of the superintendent, Brevet Lieutenant Colonel Sylvanus Thayer. A keen admirer of Napoleon Bonaparte, a believer in high standards, and an advocate of a modified Socratic teaching system, Thayer had shaped the institution into a first-rate engineering school with high standards and a demanding schedule. As Cooper has put it: "Only on Sunday afternoons, the Fourth of July, Christmas Day, and New Year's Day did the cadets have any respite from their mandated regimen"; indeed, Cooper suggests, it was a "military monastery."[15]

Nevertheless, the young man was something of a risk taker, and as Cooper points out, "Davis willingly and knowingly challenged the system in both small and large matters. His brother Joseph worried that Jefferson might end up in the guard house." There were three occasions when Jefferson tempted fate and did jeopardize his survival at the academy. Each incident involved alcohol. Still, in this forbidden imbibing, Davis managed to impress his peers as being convivial. One miserable youth, Edgar Allan Poe, who remained a cadet for less than one year, called Davis "the sole congenial soul in the entire God-forsaken place."[16]

Never adept at mathematics, Davis struggled with that subject, but he persevered and ultimately graduated twenty-third in a class of thirty-three. This standing put him into the Infantry Corps. He never later spoke favorably about any of his West Point instructors. Nothing survives of his opinions about Thayer, but Cooper suggests that since Davis obviously disliked the system Thayer had imposed, "it is most unlikely that he would have had much positive to say." Thayer certainly had little regard for Davis. In 1855, when Davis was secretary of war, Thayer declared, "Neither [Davis] nor my opinion of him have changed since I knew him as a cadet. If I am not deceived, he intends to leave his mark in the Army & also at West Point & a *black* mark it will be I fear. He is a recreant and unnatural son, would have pleasure in giving his Alma Mater a kick & would disclaim her, if he could."[17]

Nevertheless, "In one fundamental sense Thayer was absolutely wrong . . . ; [Davis] absolutely prized West Point. Its imprint never left him. His lifelong military bearing he acquired there."[18] For Davis, the experience at West Point was the beginning of a military dimension of his life that he seemed destined to exit, reenter, and exit—on and on—until after the Civil War. In many respects he seems to have been standing at attention throughout all his years. Still, he had a love-hate relationship with the military: he loved it most only when he was out of it.

Davis graduated from the Military Academy on July 1, 1828. His frontier services were rather uneventful. During his first assignment, at Fort Winnebago, Wisconsin Territory, he became something of a construction superintendent. When he got there the fort consisted of "only log huts connected by a stockade." Davis set to work improving the officers' quarters, and in the process also became a furniture maker. Seeking to create an edifice that would provide universal storage from clothes to china, according to Mrs. John H. Kinze, the wife of the Indian agent at the fort, he and his helpers "exhausted all of their architectural skill." She described the "structure" as "timbers [that] had been grooved and carved," forming pillars that "swelled in and out in a most fanciful manner"; not only paneled, the doors also "radiated out in a way to excite the imagination of all unsophisticated eyes." She and the wife of Major David E. Twiggs, the post commander, "christened the whole affair, in honor of its projector, a 'Davis.'"

It was, however, on this duty tour that Davis suffered his first grave illness, a severe case of pneumonia, which commenced in March 1831. It probably was brought on by arduous labors in the harsh outdoors, overseeing the building of a sawmill. Allen cites a source that indicates he had been "often wet to the skin for hours," in intense cold, and suggests that these "lumbering days came close to being his last." Davis's second wife, Varina, later wrote in her memoirs that "he became so emaciated that his servant, James Pemberton, used to lift him like a child from the bed to the window." But Pemberton in good time at last managed to nurse the patient back to health.[19]

Davis occasionally ruminated upon his present duties and his apparent place in the world. In a long letter to his sister Lucinda, written during his first summer in the army, he admitted that he did not find the army exciting, but he also confessed, "I know of nothing else that I could do which I would like better." He found some compatriots with "genteel" manners, and he liked that. Furthermore, "as far as morality is deemed necessary in the intercourse of men in the world it is strictly observed." "Dissipation," he noted, was "less common than among the citizens of Mississippi," and if drunkards did appear, "they are dismissed from the service." Most revealingly, he asserted that West Point "made me a different creature from that which nature had designed me to be." Cooper suggests that the twenty-one-year-old Davis was both evincing pride in his profession, and "at the same time he obviously struggled with his emotional state." He had essentially been on his own since the age of fourteen. The kind of self-examination in which he was indulging "in those circumstances could lead to an enveloping sadness, which he clearly confronted." He shared with his siblings the news about this confrontation, and in 1833 a loving niece, Joseph's oldest daughter and Jefferson's contemporary, warned him against "that ever preying *viper* melancholy." She suggested that he would "cherish ambition, cherish pride, and run from excitement to excitement." Cooper asserts that "Lieutenant Davis clung to his family," which was large and extended, and that "all cared enormously for him"; indeed, "home never strayed too far from Jefferson's mind." Moreover, Joseph counseled him that in charting "a plan of life, we should look to the end and take not the shortest route but the surest, that which is beset with the fewest difficulty [*sic*] and the most pleasant to travel."[20]

Apparently, Jefferson generally tried to heed his brother's and his other relatives' advice. His army career was fairly uneventful, but on one occasion he did get into some trouble and was court-martialed for insolence, disrespect toward a senior officer, and dereliction of duty. He was acquitted, but it had been a narrow scrape. One of his fellow junior officers, Lieutenant Lucius B. Northrop, testified in his behalf, thereby gaining Davis's highest esteem for the rest of his life. Davis had taken the court-martial very seriously. He felt that not only had the accusation threatened his army career, it also had maligned his public reputation and challenged his sense of himself. His honor had been questioned. He longed to "wipe away the discredit which belongs to my arrest," asserting that "the humble and narrow reputation which a subaltern can acquire by years of the most rigid performance of his duty, is little worth in the wide world of Fame, but yet is something to himself." Cooper suggests that "this classic combining of the public and private dimensions of reputation formed the fundamental underpinning to the idea of honor in Jefferson Davis's own mind and in the South."[21]

Otherwise, Davis was a good soldier and officer: "Unlike Cadet Davis, Lieutenant Davis was not constantly at war with rules and regulations." Events allowed him to demonstrate that he was both physically strong and courageous. Several accounts reveal his ability to defend himself. On horseback he could dazzle. And as Cooper observes, "His personality along with a 'gay laugh' charmed many of his compatriots." He much enjoyed the company of his old West Point chums whenever their assignments brought them together, especially that of his dearest friend Albert Sidney Johnston. And Davis met new people, with whom he formed mutual friendships, including Captain William S. Harney, a fellow officer at Fort Winnebago. Eight years Davis's senior, Harney became "a boon companion whom Davis would admire into old age."[22]

Not all went well for Davis, however. During an eventful winter at Camp Jackson (soon renamed Fort Gibson), Oklahoma Territory, for the second time in his twenty-five years he became seriously ill. He was plagued with bronchial difficulties and even toyed with trying to get a medical discharge. Bronchial and respiratory problems thereafter remained constants throughout what proved to be Davis's long life.[23]

Then Davis managed to meet and to fall in love with Sarah Knox Taylor, the daughter of Zachary Taylor, his commanding officer. And the attraction was mutual. Indeed, as Allen observes, "It must have been love at first sight."[24] Born at Fort Knox, in Vincennes, Indiana Territory, on March 6, 1814, "Knox," as she was known, was eighteen when she and Davis met. Cooper tells us that "the only extant likeness of her is a stylized portrait of a girlish teenager with long flowing hair, a rounded chin, and a prominent forehead framing luminous eyes. Her winsome personality charmed her contemporaries, who commented on her intelligence and wit."[25] On March 2, 1835, Davis resigned his military commision, having decided to give up his army career in order to become a cotton planter.[26] He and Knox were married on June 17. However, while on a honeymoon in Mississippi both newlyweds contracted either yellow fever or malaria: she died of it on September 15, 1835, after suffering only a short while; he was left to suffer occasional residual ailments for his remaining fifty-four years.

Davis grew up in a slave society and was steeped in its ideology. Indeed, "Race and the place of African-Americans in American society were central in Davis's life. . . . For his entire life he believed in the superiority of the white race."[27] But as Cooper rightly points out, we should strive to understand Davis as a man of his time, not condemn him for not being a man of our time. Further, Davis's mind-set was a bit unusual; he was something of a maverick. When in 1858 abolitionists were predicting slave revolts, Davis replied to them in a speech in New York City: "Our doors are unlocked at night. . . . We lie down to sleep trusting to them for our defence, and the bond between the master and the slave is as near as that which exists between capital and labor anywhere." He returned to this idea late in his Confederate presidency when contemplating the military manpower problem. Davis's slave James Pemberton accompanied him throughout his army career. When Davis began his career as a planter, he placed Pemberton in charge of the land clearing; later, he made Pemberton his overseer. Although Mississippi law did not recognize the legitimacy of slave marriages, Cooper observes that "probably the great majority of slaveowners recognized alliances between slaves, as did the Davises."[28] The abolitionist, Davis scornfully suggested, "knows literally nothing" of these relations.[29]

Allen contends that "Southerners were never very good at seeing people abstractly." But what Davis "saw abstractly was servitude: 'Chattel slavery never existed in this country,' " he asserted, " ' it was merely a term used to excite prejudice.' " In his hair-splitting reasoning, what a slave owner purchased was "a lifelong right to service and labor," but since there were laws that rendered it illegal to kill or maim a slave, the enslaved "were therefore not chattels." Slaves, Davis declared, enjoyed a "double identity 'as a person and as property.' " Slavery on Jefferson Davis's plantation, and also on Joseph's, was interestingly unusual: "The Davis slave families had garden plots and peach trees and chickens, which they fed from the unlocked corncrib and were free to sell. Both brothers had literate slaves."[30] But ultimately there was in Davis's mind a paradoxical duality: "He perceived no contradiction between his faith in liberty and the existence of slavery. From at least the time of the American Revolution white southerners defined their liberty, in part, as their right to own slaves and to decide the fate of the institution without outside interference."[31]

In the early winter 1837–1838 Davis visited Washington, D.C., there renewing his friendship with his old companion of Transylvania and Fort Crawford days, George W. Jones, a delegate to Congress from Wisconsin Territory. Jones introduced Davis to President Martin Van Buren, no doubt a heady experience, but on the same visit he was introduced to Franklin Pierce, and the two became firm friends for life. Allen suggests that "simplicity and spiritual affinity bound them together," but there was more. Pierce was fiercely committed to a political career, and Davis began to reveal that he too was keenly interested in politics. Pierce was thirty-three, the youngest member of the U.S. Senate, and a Yankee; Davis was intrigued that he could find one whose intelligence impressed him. Moreover, Pierce was a state-rights Democrat, which further endeared him to Davis. They could and did agree on what Davis "had held for a long time" as "his basic belief" in "our novel and admirable form of government, in which the States are independent though united, and the general government supreme in its functions, though devoid of all power except that which has been delegated to it by the States."[32]

On one occasion during this visit to Washington, D.C., a serious accident occurred. Davis went to a large party with Jones and two other senators, Warren Allen of Ohio and Lewis Linn of Missouri. They indulged in much eating and drinking and had a good time generally. About midnight they all decided to leave—Davis and Allen in a carriage with Senator John J. Crittenden of Kentucky. After reaching Crittenden's home, Davis and Allen decided to go the rest of the way on foot so as to "digest our supper and wine." Somehow they missed the bridge spanning Tiber Creek (which then flowed just beyond First Street not far up Capitol Hill) and plunged into the darkness below. In Warren Allen's words, "Davis fell headforemost upon the stones and was nearly killed." Although inebriated himself, Allen managed to get Davis back to Jones's room. Cooper suggests that "in all likelihood the fall resulted in a concussion as well as lacerations." Clearly in this instance Davis had been perilously drunk. However, in later years both Jones and Varina Davis insisted that he never again drank to excess. Davis did "in the future . . . seem to keep his drinking under control, though always taking pleasure in a glass of whiskey. Relishing his pipes and cigars throughout his life, Davis never gave up smoking despite his recurring bronchial problems."[33]

Joseph introduced his youngest brother to Varina Banks Howell, and they married on February 26, 1845. He was eighteen years older than she: her birthday was May 7, 1826. Despite some occasional, mostly early, marital difficulties—probably owing mostly to the age difference—they proved a good match. She was well educated, witty, and outspoken. He adored her. "Laughter filled the air at Brierfield," the plantation he and his slaves developed on land given him by Joseph. Jefferson and Varina enjoyed a wonderful, lighthearted, and learned lifestyle: "There was always a book at hand, a poem on the tongue." "A lover of guns," Jefferson hunted birds, bear, and deer. Varina excelled at gardening, particularly at growing roses; indeed her "gardens became her hallmark wherever she lived."[34]

Given his makeup and predilections, it perhaps was inevitable that Jefferson Davis would seek public office. In part, it was pure unbridled ambition, but he later asserted that he regarded political activism as his duty: "Man is not born for himself alone, or for his family only," he said; rather—and especially in this land of self-government—"no one has a right to wholly withdraw himself from connection with public affairs."[35] Davis first was elected to the U.S. House of Representatives, where he much impressed the venerable John C. Calhoun with his oratorical abilities.[36] Indeed, Cooper has found a comment by one of Davis's political opponents describing his voice as a distinct asset, "musical and well-modulated."[37] Perhaps the most prophetic comment came when, after one of Davis's early speeches, the former president and subsequently the great crusader for free speech, John Quincy Adams, remarked, "That young man, gentlemen, is no ordinary man. He will make his mark yet, mind me."[38]

Even before Davis secured his first nomination to Congress, his neighbors demonstrated their admiration for him by inviting him to give the eulogy during the ceremonies held in Vicksburg to commemorate Andrew Jackson, who had died June 8, 1845. After a typical expression of self-deprecation, Davis agreed to memorialize the man whom he so idolized and idealized. "From my childhood I was attached to General Jackson," he communicated to a friend. And later, Davis asserted that "my confidence and respect for him increased," and "my affection and admiration followed him to the grave, and cling to his memory."[39]

Davis seems to have gone from good to better and best as a politician and speaker. On at least two occasions friends and associates called on him to mediate grave differences between notable Mississippi Democrats. In other contexts, even his Whig opponents spoke of him as "a handsome speaker." The *Vicksburg Sentinel* boasted: "We predict that he becomes the Calhoun of Mississippi."[40]

When the Mexican War came, Davis grasped his chance to gain fame: he resigned from Congress and took the command of a regiment of Mississippi Riflemen (volunteers). He had both the clout and the foresight to see that his men were armed with newly devised rifles, the invention of Eli Whitney's son. These .54-caliber weapons, which used percussion caps instead of unreliable flint and powder, could propel their bullets nearly one thousand yards. They were safer and faster to load and fire, vastly superior to the old flintlock smoothbores then in use in the army. Davis showed obvious enjoyment of his command, and it "proved him an organizer, a leader, and, above all, a fighter."[41] In the battle reports, prepared almost immediately afterward, Davis's officers and men often "noted his effectiveness as a combat commander and his leadership qualities. They found him cool, decisive, and always in their midst taking every risk other soldiers took."[42]

Davis became a hero during the Battle of Buena Vista, his mounted men charging at a crucial moment. Deployed in supposedly now outmoded V formation, they turned the tide toward an American victory. Davis did, however, suffer a painful wound during the bloody fighting. A musket ball pierced his right foot near the ankle, driving shards of brass from his shattered spur and bits of his sock into his flesh. Yet he refused to leave the field and remained on horseback while his wound was wrapped. For two years he had to use crutches, and for three more the afflicted foot at times caused him extreme pain. During that period the bone exfoliated, and the shattered pieces either worked themselves out or were removed surgically, each generating intense pain. The wound caused him recurrent pain and discomfort for the rest of his life.[43]

Most important for Davis's long-term political career, his Mexican War service provided him fame. And although Mississippians hailed his entire regiment, Davis the commander received special accolades. A publically announced "spontaneous project" called for funds to be raised to present him with a special commemorative sword. "Davis is one of those brilliant meteors that shoots alone and illuminates the military horizon of the world, at intervals, long and far between," exclaimed an eastern newspaper.[44]

The resultant fame catapulted Davis into a seat in the U.S. Senate early in 1848. And except for the seventeen months spent on his plantation after he lost the 1851 gubernatorial race in Mississippi and the four years he served as secretary of war in the Pierce administration, there he served most prominently, until his dramatic resignation in January 1861.

His first few years in public life were marred by acutely strained relations between him and Varina. Indeed, he did not let her accompany him when he first moved to Washington. "I cannot expose myself to such conduct as your's when with me here," he declared. "I cannot bear constant harassment, occasional reproach, and subsequent misrepresentation." But time heals almost all wounds, and this breech proved no exception. Davis's ill-feeling gradually waned. Meanwhile, he could feel secure in the reality that Brierfield was thriving. While he tended to senatorial duties, he could, as Cooper put it, "rest assured that capable and loyal men, one black, the other white, watched over the major source of his financial well being."[45]

Davis was an active, prominent, and involved senator. And he was able to play starring roles because his party enjoyed a comfortable majority and his fellows held him in high esteem. The biggest, and also most controversial, issue with which he perennially wrestled was the question of expanding slavery into the territories. Davis wrote and spoke a great deal with both intelligence and passion on the subject. After John C. Calhoun's death in 1850, Davis succeeded him as the principal spokesman for state rights and Southern prerogatives. He was consistent and adamant: "In his reading, the U.S. Constitution had nowhere authorized Congress to prohibit slavery in any territory." As for popular sovereignty: "Congress could not turn over any decision regarding slavery to the settlers in a territory because they had no claim to sovereignty; only the states were sovereign."[46]

As Cooper observes, "Davis did not believe that destruction of the Union and fraternal bloodletting were inevitable." He asserted that the three-fifths provision in the Constitution offered a quintessential solution to how diametrically opposed sections of the country could compromise. Cooper points out that "he was willing, he told his listeners, to adhere to that honorable practice of finding a middle way." But there were limits: "Davis enunciated clearly that he would make a deal, but only if the other side evinced a willingness to meet him at least partway."[47]

Two joyful events entered the Davises' lives in 1852. On July 30, their first child was born, Samuel Emory Davis, named for his grandfather Davis. And Davis's dear friend, Franklin Pierce, won the presidency in November. Davis was Pierce's choice to be secretary of war, and he proved outstanding in that office; he was perhaps the second greatest to that time, inferior only to his other hero, John C. Calhoun. As Cooper observes, "Secretary Davis strove mightily to reform the organization and structure of the army, aiming toward greater efficiency, enhanced professionalism, and a clearly unified chain of command. . . . Technology had always fascinated him . . . [and] inventors found a ready welcome in his office. . . . [He also] participated actively in the governance of the Military Academy. . . . [But] Davis made his chief concern the great American West."[48]

If it had not already long before been amply demonstrated, Davis's performance in this office revealed that by nature he was a hard worker. Furthermore, he was rather a perfectionist. He wanted to know everything about whatever interested him. Cooper has identified a significant facet of Davis's administrative style: "Davis started out and remained a hands-on secretary, seeking involvement in all aspects of his department's operations."[49] Many people noted his "encyclopedic erudition."[50] Allen insightfully observes that "Davis has been called 'innovative,' and in details, he was, but he was also devoted to tradition and prerogative."[51]

Davis might begin work somewhat late in the day, but he would frequently labor until the wee hours of the morning. Sometimes he would bring home to dinner his dear friend, Colonel Samuel Cooper, the adjutant general of the army, whom Varina thought "looked ready to faint." She sometimes sent nice luncheons for them to the office, with wine, but Davis typically forgot to eat or to offer any to the colonel, either. Cooper admitted that he had "the greatest affection and admiration" for Davis, but "another four years would have killed me."[52]

Davis's years as war secretary were for the most part happy ones for him and his family, save for the stunning loss in summer 1854 of little Sam. Some hideous illness, possibly measles, claimed his life, the child not yet two, on June 13. But despair was eased by new joy: Varina's second baby arrived on

February 25, 1855. Margaret Howell Davis ("Maggie") was named for her maternal grandmother. And on January 16, 1857, Varina gave birth to Jefferson Davis Jr. Then, following the conclusion of his tour as war secretary, Davis was again returned to the Senate.

In the Senate Davis became the great spokesman for state-rights ideology and a champion of things military. He served on the committees on military affairs, library, and pensions. And he applied tortuous logic to the antislavery question. If blacks should be forced into "responsibilities" unprepared, he argued, then "instead of a blessing, liberty would be their greatest curse." He maintained that their present situation in the Southern states was bringing them "immense improvement" by "association with a more elevated race," and this could be clearly seen by contrasting them "with recently-imported Africans" in the West Indies and "with the free blacks of the northern States," who he suggested were "miserable, impoverished, loathsome from the deformity and disease which follows after penury and vice; covering the records of the criminal court, and filling the penitentiaries."[53]

Certainly the vexing and unresolved problem of the 1850s proved to be the question of expansion of slavery into new western territory. A new political party, the Republican, was formed in 1854, its primary platform plank being opposition to such expansion. To Davis, the right was utterly fundamental. As he pointed out, "The political heresy [is] that ours is an union of the people," as a whole, rather than of states, and that the federal government has supreme, rather than delegated, power. Unless all are equals in the compact of states originally formed, having equal access to territories, "it ceases to be the Union," and becomes "despotism."[54]

Davis went on to reveal some of his own peculiarities concerning the nature of slavery, which was under much criticism and attack from abolitionists and other antislavery people. He regarded as "fictions" the charges that slave marriages were not recognized, that families often were broken up and separated, that the slaves were sometimes put in "fetters," and that they were not exposed to the Bible. "What could be more ridiculous," he asserted, "than the idea of prohibiting the Bible to our slaves?" In its "sacred pages," they would learn "submission and faithful, not eye service, to masters" and how to avoid the newspeak of the day "whereof cometh envy, strife, railings, evil surmising" (he was citing 1 Timothy 6: 4–5). "We rely on the Bible as authority for the establishment of slavery among men, and on the Constitution for its recognition throughout the United States."[55]

Davis deeply believed that secession was constitutional, but most of his writings concerning the nature of the U.S. Constitution came after the Civil War, when he was attempting to justify what had been done. He believed that he was in agreement with the Framers of the Constitution. He began his justification for secession with a restatement of the social compact theory of John Locke. Davis believed that the federal Constitution was a social compact among the states to form the central government. He assumed that since each state entered into the Union voluntarily, then each could, whenever it chose, leave. He came to believe that a Northern cabal had broken that original compact, in a similar way that Great Britain had broken the social compact in the 1700s. He believed that the Articles of Confederation and the U.S. Constitution were coequal documents—both of them manifestations of social compact. Unlike the Articles, the Constitution delineated clear powers for the legislative, executive, and judicial branches, and it gave the government broader powers in the domestic sphere. The Framers and politicians in later antebellum decades subsequently debated the exact nature of these powers.

Davis's argument that the Constitution, like the Articles, was a compact was twofold: first, the language had evolved, and in the 1800s "compact" did not have the same meaning as it had had in the 1700s; second, the absence of the word "compact" in the Constitution did not negate the fact that it was one. Davis believed that the evolution of "compact" had begun in the 1830s, when people looked at the Constitution and declared that it was not a compact because the word did not appear in the document. Nationalists claimed that the term applied only to the Confederation period. Davis responded that the Constitution was implicitly a compact and that there was no need to call itself such, any more than a painting of a horse needed to be titled "this is a horse."[56]

The problem was that "divided sovereignty" seemed an oxymoron. Davis knew this, so the problem became one of asserting where true sovereignty resided in the structure of the U.S. government. The viewpoint of Alexander Hamilton, espoused by the Federalists, and ultimately by Abraham Lincoln, was that when the people ratified the Constitution, they gave their sovereignty to the government. Davis denied this: the only powers justly exercised by the federal government were those delegated to it.[57] He believed that the Tenth Amendment ensured state sovereignty, declaring what he believed already was obvious in the Constitution. Since the states had ordained and authorized the Constitution, therefore there was no ultimate power over the states. The final authority, to be sure, rested with the people. And, in essence, "the states *are* the people."[58]

Jefferson Davis deeply believed that secession was not only "within the stream of the American tradition" but that it was the very "heart of the American idea of government."[59] Secession could take place whenever an individual state exercised its sovereign right to dissolve the current social compact and to create a new one. Although the right of secession was not explicit in the Constitution, it was implicit since the Constitution was a contract between the central government and the states.

Davis argued that the Constitution was no different from any other contract, and he applied basic contract law to prove his point. If a contract was perpetual, or had no specific end, then either party retained the right to terminate the contract. Davis's analogy was faulty, however, since contract law courts interpreted contracts without provisions for termination or perpetuity by a standard of reasonableness. He argued that the social compact was as breakable as any contract made between individuals. Davis stressed the American-ness of Southern separation from the old Union: "We have changed the constituent parts, but not the system of our government. The Constitution formed by our fathers is that of these Confederate States," he proclaimed in his presidential Inaugural Address.[60]

Davis's ideas were not those of a collective South but were his deeply held personal beliefs. Yet those beliefs were not, as he presumed, based on mindsets that had prevailed in 1789. They were, rather, ideas that had taken form beginning in the 1820s, revolving around John C. Calhoun's doctrine of Nullification. What Davis failed adequately to perceive was that his great mentor did not propound a formula to guarantee secession; instead, he offered one that might provide an avenue to maintain union and at the same time maintain the rights of the slaveholding minority. In this case, as the historian Richard Hofstadter observes, Calhoun was "the Marx of the master class."[61]

But "The South [Davis] cried, *was American*."[62] And as Cooper emphasizes, Davis was American.[63] In 1857, however, "denying that he intended to alarm anyone, Davis predicted that 1860 would bring 'the monster crisis,' what he termed 'the ordeal of fire' for American patriotism. He hoped for the best, but charged Mississippians to prepare for the worst."[64]

The amazing truth is, however, that in playing so major a role as he did in the coming of secession, Davis eliminated himself as a possible candidate for the presidency of the United States. He gave lip service, after secession, to having preferred a military role in the Confederacy, but before secession he probably had seen himself as the man who could unite the two quarreling sections of the country. More likely, though, he simply did not know just what he really wanted, or what would be needed—such is the conclusion of one of his biographers, William C. Davis.[65] Surely we could say that of most other Southerners on the eve of the Civil War.

Secession was the final and tragic result of two unfortunate flaws in the makeup of the United States of America. First, human slavery—which had existed quite nearly throughout the entirety of the English colonial period—had at the time of the Revolution and in its aftermath become a sectionally divisive factor. Seven of the new Northern states eliminated the institution while the six Southern ones clung to it. Then, in the ensuing decade, it grew enormously in those states because it proved increasingly profitable, particularly in the burgeoning cotton kingdom, made possible as a result of Eli Whitney's invention of the cotton gin in the 1790s. Different fundamental ways of life developed within the two sections, the South characterized by the dominant "large landed unit," the plantation. Even if only a fraction, some one-fourth actually, of the Southern whites belonged to slave-owning families, the lifestyle of most Southerners depended on the continuance of the system and the majority of them knew that. Besides, many nonslaveholders held hopes of owning some slaves one day, and over time many of them did indeed acquire some.

Second, a cloudy and unresolved dichotomy existed between strict constructionists and loose constructionists. Simply stated, the former wished for the central government to be quite circumscribed and limited in power and function; the latter wished for a wide latitude in governmental functioning so that whatever seemed most desirable at any given later moment might be reconciled as being "constitutional." Put another way, as the political parties emerged, there was a tension between Jeffersonianism and Hamiltonianism. The followers of Thomas Jefferson wished for strict limitations on the government's prerogatives; the followers of Alexander Hamilton wanted a strong government that would stimulate American growth and protect the nation from foreign competition.

These tensions were never fully resolved. As time elapsed, both sections wished for their particular self-interests to be nurtured. The South's peculiar institution made that region keenly sensitive to any kind of limitation that might be imposed. And from the outset, indeed there had been limitations: even in the Confederation period slavery was banned in the Northwest Territory (later Ohio, Indiana, Illinois, Wisconsin, and Michigan). The international slave trade was, by compromise, allowed to continue for two decades following ratification of the Constitution and thereafter forever banned. And the "three-fifths compromise" in the Constitution allowed that for the purposes of a per capita tax (which originally had been envisioned as perhaps the main source of federal revenue), as well as for determining the population base to decide the numbers of seats in the House of Representatives, three-fifths of the total numbers of slaves would be counted, no more and no less.

Each section clearly wanted the government to act in ways that the leaders of the sections perceived as advantageous. Southerners by and large were adamantly opposed to protective tariffs (one of the several mainstays in Hamilton's grand economic plan for the new nation) because the South was principally an exporter of staple agricultural products and an importer of nearly all its manufactured needs. In the 1830s John C. Calhoun proposed the doctrine of Nullification, whereby a single state, or preferably a coalition of states still constituting a minority, could nullify within their borders any federal law that they considered contrary to their fundamental rights within the Union. Nullification was first directed toward the tariff, but it clearly could be refashioned later and applied to any antislavery legislation.

White Southerners zealously asserted that they had a fundamental right to take their slaves into the western territories. If they could not do this, then they reasoned that a first step was being taken toward someday forcing the obliteration of their peculiar institution. But even for those who might be discomfited by the existence of this labor system, there was another vexing problem: all the slaves were black. With only a relatively few exceptions, the whites of both the North and the South did not anticipate simply freeing the nearly 4 million souls held in bondage on the eve of the Civil War and integrating them wholly and without prejudice into American society.

To be sure, there were some whites who created organizations dedicated to full emancipation of the blacks. But they remained a small minority. Still, they managed to persuade a goodly majority of Northern whites that slavery was unfortunate, if not absolutely wrong, and ought to be eliminated in the United States. A first step in what might be a long, drawn-out process would be to limit slavery's further expansion. In 1854 the Republican Party emerged with a platform that successfully melded a number of coalitions into a viable new major party, dedicated primarily to prohibiting slavery in the new territories. They won the presidency in 1860. For Jefferson Davis, and white Southerners who thought as he did, this was a final design in a long pattern of usurpation of Southern rights and the justification for leaving the Union.

Slavery was not the sum total of the cultural differences between the North and South, however. Grady McWhiney has stressed the cultural differences that were the legacies of the North's supposedly predominant Anglo-Saxon heritage as opposed to the South's Celtic sanguinity.[66] Several historians have delineated potent differences in the kinds of Christianity that predominated, leading Samuel H. Hill to go so far as to assert that the churches in the two regions were like "third cousins alienated" by the eve of the Civil War.[67] The historian Bertram Wyatt-Brown has concluded that Southern white men needed slaves as well as their "code of honor" to fulfill their concept of manhood; and Edward Ayers has observed that Northern middle-class men felt a deep need to have a "culture of dignity," in which institutions figured more prominently than notions of honor or community. Most profoundly, Nina Silber asserts that "on the eve of the Civil War, the two societies rested on two completely different patterns of behavior and codes of morality."[68]

These differences may have had a potent impact on politics. "The Republican press, for example, attributed the economic panic of 1857 not to the forces of the market but to 'ruinous habits' and 'luxurious living,' personal failings which exemplified a lack of moral restraint."[69] Thus, when the Republicans came to power with the 1860 election of Abraham Lincoln, here was still another reason why the two sections might opt to go their separate ways.

The argument that state rights was the true justification for secession by and large appeared after the Civil War.[70] Antebellum white Southerners strongly believed in state rights up to a point, but they cared more about their specific and peculiar interests and desires—even if that meant national power was required to step in and preserve them. The South had become a minority, and the people knew it; nothing could be done to alter that. And white Southerners would not have wanted it altered if it had been possible. Above all, white Southerners were satisfied with things as they were. Indeed, some historians, notably George Rable and James McPherson, have contended that the war was a revolution against change, an attempt to restore the pristine Republic of an earlier time.[71]

But the moment finally came when enough white Southerners, those who were men of power and influence, concluded that their desires and interests were no longer safe within the old Union. So they seceded and formed the Confederacy. Actually, the process had deep historical roots, and it followed somewhat different pathways in the various states,[72] but it coalesced with the election of Abraham Lincoln—an avowed opponent of any further spread of slavery into new territory—as president of the United States. This of course explains only secession and the formation of the Confederacy; it does not explain why nearly 1 million Southerners eventually fought a bitter war trying to create a Confederate nation. They did so primarily because their homeland was invaded, and they displayed great courage and ideological commitment.

Other factors were clearly significant, too. Secession and Civil War were the ultimate results of a fullness of time, a zeitgeist. Much has been written on the subject, and many persons today still argue vehemently that factors other than slavery were the most important. A fairly good summation of recent scholarship on the matter can be found in Gabor S. Boritt's *Why the Civil War Came*.[73]

Virtually all participants in the war blamed the people on the other side. Boritt himself suggests that "to see the individual as a mere victim is unbearably pessimistic." He has concluded that Abraham Lincoln bears a measure of blame for precipitating the war: Lincoln was committed to a policy that the South regarded as contrary to its elemental rights and safety within the Union. Glenna Matthews shows that women who took active roles in public life had much to do with the coming of the war. David Blight argues that the black abolitionists played a significant role, indeed that among American blacks generally there had grown a "culture of expectation," and as one escaped slave put it, black people "knew what time it was." William Gienapp analyzes political processes—the dangerous ambiguities in the Constitution inevitably had to be resolved. And the creation of the Republican Party was possibly the crucial link in bringing the war. William Freehling subtly suggests a dual reality: in the late antebellum United States, republicanism had progressed so far that, on the one hand, the extant system of government increasingly threatened slavery; on the other hand, that same system gave proslavery Southerners the confidence to secede. Adding to the zeitgeist theory, Mark Summers finds "national mission, sectional pride, paranoid fears, and just plain cussedness" leading to an eagerness for a civil war. As to why the North wanted a war, Summers echoes Phillip Paludan, asserting that a profound determination to preserve law and order—as each side perceived it—lay behind the motivation to fight.[74]

Thus, for perhaps myriad reasons, Jefferson Davis found himself at the head of a would-be nation. The problems that lay before him were so numerous and hugely difficult that he could only scarcely have perceived just how vast a challenge he faced. Was he up to the tasks ahead? What manner of man, indeed, was he?

2

THE ESTABLISHMENT OF GOVERNMENT

Shortly before the eve of secession, two events punctuated the lives of the Jefferson Davis family. Jefferson's friends urged him to collect his New England speeches and publish them in book form, and this he did, issuing a fifty-six-page work in April 1859. Davis worked hard to distribute the book, and it proved to be quite in demand, not only in Mississippi but nationally, too. This added even more to Davis's name recognition and political prominence. Then, on April 18, Jefferson and Varina welcomed the birth of another child. Varina had planned to name him William Howell Davis for her father, but Jefferson had a different intention. The child was named Joseph Evan Davis, to honor Jefferson's brother, who was by this time Varina's nemesis. She was also unhappy that the baby looked like a Davis, and she prayed that it would outgrow that resemblance. But otherwise the family was filled with joy, for as Cooper points out, "father and mother certainly delighted in their children."[1]

The initial preference of a majority of the Montgomery delegates for Confederate president probably was Robert Toombs, a longtime U.S. senator from Georgia. But circumstances—mainly, the personal dislike of a few Georgia delegates and his having become a Constitutional Unionist, which angered many of the Democrats—ruined his chances for the post, which indeed he wanted. A widely known drinking problem did not help his candidacy, either. Many observers have speculated since that Toombs could have been a better president than Davis, but Toombs's ablest biographer, William Y. Thompson, shows fairly convincingly that this was unlikely.[2]

Toombs had enjoyed the initial advantage, truly wanted the position, and did all he could to get it, but his several negative qualities prompted the delegates to strive mightily to find a more desirable alternative. Davis had been on virtually everyone's shortlist, because of his great prominence as a political leader and his image as a moderate who could appeal to the Upper South. Besides Toombs, the only other possibilites were Howell Cobb, Robert M. T. Hunter, Robert B. Rhett, William L. Yancey, and the long shot Joseph Brown, all mentioned as possible choices; but in truth, the only other viable contender was Cobb. In many respects Cobb was a logical choice, but he, like Toombs, lacked solid support from his home state's delegation. Perhaps more important, Cobb was a member of the convention and did not seek the position; possibly he did not even want it.[3]

Perhaps most significant for Davis's chances, in addition to his presecession national stature, he had not been among the fire-eaters; that is, he was not a radical on the issue of secession. He was fully supportive of the right to secede, but he had not urged that the step be taken when it was. Davis, like his previous mentor Calhoun, had hoped to devise effective mechanisms and means whereby the rights of the Southern states might be adequately preserved and protected, short of leaving the Union. But if that were not possible, then there existed every right to take that drastic step.

So Jefferson Davis became the designated provisional Confederate president to lead the would-be nation, which then consisted of seven states. When he saw the messenger approaching on February 10, 1861, with the news, he was taking rose cuttings in the garden. The messenger dismounted and handed over the telegram, doubtlessly expecting to see elation on Davis's face as he read. Varina saw something else: a look of dreadful anguish. After a few moments of ominous silence, he told her the news.[4] He reacted as the active-negative president he proved to be: he would do his duty, but he would find no fulfillment in the job. In this ominous mood, he resigned his major generalship (that perhaps pained him deeply: he loved his military persona) and set out for Montgomery.[5]

Illustrative of the flawed physical infrastructure within the Confederacy, Davis's train ride from his home in Mississippi to Montgomery, Alabama, had almost comic dimensions. The absence of any trackage between Meridian and Montgomery necessitated that he go first from Vicksburg to Jackson, then north to the Memphis and Charleston Railroad in Tennessee (which was still in the Union), east to Chattanooga, back south to Atlanta and the Confederacy, and finally west to Montgomery. This long trip, which took five days, gave Davis the opportunity to introduce himself to masses of the citizenry. At some Tennessee stops he received a chilly reception, but within the Confederacy, at every station they turned out, shooting off guns by day and burning bonfires at night. He made at least twenty-five short speeches, well received by enthusiastic audiences. Cooper tells us that one "reporter characterized the entire trip as 'one continuous ovation.' "[6] While waiting in a depot he was asked by the chief justice of Mississippi if there would be a war, and Davis told him frankly that "there would be war, long and bloody." And he was from the outset resolved on an aggressive strategy when and if it commenced. "There will be no war in our territory," he said. "It will be carried into the enemy's territory."[7]

Who, if anyone, might have been a better choice? One has to remember that the Confederacy then comprised only the seven Deep South states. Perhaps the best man for the job would have been the incumbent vice president of the United States, John C. Breckinridge, but—despite pretensions later manifested by the Confederacy—his state, Kentucky, never became a Confederate state. Possibly James Mason of Virginia could have done a better job, but Davis was chosen before Virginia seceded. And Davis was a highly placed political leader for good reason; prior to secession there were many people within the Democratic Party who sought to have him nominated to run for U.S. President in 1860, none more supportive than former president Franklin Pierce. As William L. Yancey said on the occasion of Davis's inauguration, "The man and the hour have met." Less certain was what Yancey said just afterward: "Prosperity, honor and victory await his administration."[8]

Davis was firm and resolute. He hoped for peace, but not at any price. He was resolved on Southern independence, and if war must come, it would be accepted. He exuded optimism in his quaint turning of phrases: "It may be that our career shall be ushered in, in the midst of storms," adding that "it may be that as this morning opened with clouds, mist and rain, we shall have to encounter inconveniences at the beginning; but as the sun rose, lifted the mist, dispersed the clouds, and left a pure sunlight, Heaven will so prosper the Southern Confederacy, and carry us safe from sea to the safe harbor of constitutional liberty."[9] And he already was thinking about principal military command. He was asked by Thomas Watts, a member of the Alabama delegation to Montgomery, who Davis thought ought to be the "chief commander" in the field. "There is one man above all others—he is now in California—I have written to him—I believe he is with us," said Davis: "Albert Sidney Johnston."[10]

Given his active-negative personality, could Davis be a successful revolutionary leader? He was stiff and formal—and this inhibited his popular appeal. He lacked both the passion and eloquence that seems necessary in revolutionary leaders. Some observers also believed that his lack of the common touch would inhibit his capacity to move the people with his words and to inspire great willingness to sacrifice. He was, though, intelligent and hardworking. He had a wide variety of experiences and was distinguished in things military. He seemed to love abstraction and legalism. Above all, he believed in the rightness of the Confederacy with every fiber of his being; but did he truly believe in it with all his heart?

For along with his stiff formality, Davis was a perfectionist, compulsive and aggressive. His "rigid self-control" often served him well and led to "superior achievement." But in an active-negative personality "success does not produce joy." He would work hard, but he would follow his own course and refuse to compromise because compromise was "not only mistaken but evil." He would call for loyalty, but whether (in his own judgment) he would always receive it, only time could tell. As James David Barber has put it, the active-negative president is "a man under orders, required to concentrate, to produce, to follow out his destiny as he sees it." "Extraordinarily capable," Davis became "extraordinarily rigid, becoming more and more closed to experience, including the advice of his ardent allies."[11] Whether he could make the people as a whole feel that Confederate survival was their cause, and not just "a rich man's war and a poor man's fight," as many of them quickly came to believe, was also a question for the future.[12]

As soon as Davis took office he began conducting public business in a hotel parlor. Thomas Cooper DeLeon wrote that Davis received both high officials and casual visitors "without ceremony." He arrived at nine each morning and returned home at six each evening—by his wife's account—"exhausted and silent." He slept but little and ate less. He pushed himself to exhaustion. Usually he sat at a desk, writing correspondence and often rummaging in the jumble of books, maps, papers, and even samples of uniform fabric, hats, feathers, and epaulettes. Sometimes he sat on a sofa, "rising up with the stately grace that never deserted him" to meet one visitor after another, attempting to get along with each—a difficult task for anyone in his position.[13]

Even Varina Davis perceived that her husband was compulsive in his drive and also hypersensitive to any criticism. (This is one of the stark differences between Davis and his Northern counterpart, Abraham Lincoln; the latter could work well with people who blatantly disliked him.) Nonetheless, the Davises tried to present a pleasant public facade. They entertained often. To anyone "who complained that this house was too costly for the public purse, Varina reportedly quipped that before long she expected to be . . . in another Executive Mansion, in Washington."[14]

John Brawner Robbins's "Confederate Nationalism: Politics and Government in the Confederate South, 1861–1865" is a work of profound significance that receives far less attention than it deserves because he apparently never chose to publish it. What, after all, is Confederate nationalism? In Robbins's words,

It is the desire to create and sustain a central government, the ability to think in larger than local terms and, in general, the conviction that Southern independence is of paramount importance. It is Jefferson Davis, Clement C. Clay, Albert G. Brown, Louis T. Wigfall, Ethelbert Barksdale, John Milton, Francis R. Lubbock, Thomas O. Moore, and a host of lesser-known public figures and plain citizens throughout the length and breadth of the Confederacy. It is tampering with—and at times violating—constitutional rights, property rights, and social codes which all Southerners held most sacred.[15]

Too often overlooked, Robbins has asserted, is that the antebellum South had some sense of nationalism, too, and that it was not un-American at all. In studying the struggle to ensure its survival, one is struck by how often the phrase reoccurs: "to preserve our way of life." Thus, primarily, state rights was a surface issue, not the "foundation stone" of the Southern way of life or politics.[16]

It is interesting as well as significant that the South that formed the Confederacy and its first permanent government was not as politically united then, or even at the time of the November 1861 elections, as it became after suffering defeat in the war and enduring the subsequent Reconstruction. The electorate that created the Confederacy comprised slightly more than 40 percent of voters, outside of Texas and South Carolina, who had been members of the Whig Party. And yet, generally, the early Confederate elections were relatively devoid of issues and excitement. In 1861 Southerners were determined to try to present a united front to the world, and this they thought precluded contentious political contests.[17] Political rivalry did become more apparent in 1861 when it came to the selection of Confederate senators and in high-level appointments in the new government. Thomas R. R. Cobb of Georgia, a representative in the Provisional Congress who had been an early advocate of secession, complained to his wife; "The best claim to distinction under the existing regime—seems to be either to have opposed secession or have done nothing for it."[18]

We have suggested in *Why the South Lost the Civil War* that the Confederacy lacked a genuine nationalism, "a feeling of oneness, that almost mystical sense of nationhood." It "functioned as a nation . . . only in a technical, organizational sense, and not in a mystical or spiritual sense."[19] Drew Gilpin Faust has probed the creation of Confederate nationalism and disagrees to a considerable degree with us, and therefore we with her; but she does offer some good insights, taking as her point of departure that "if we examine other nationalist movements, it is clear that the 'creation' of culture has almost always been a necessary and self-conscious process."[20]

Secession came, and Southerners were compelled to confront the ideological paradoxes that had long been implicit in their civilization. The white South collectively, its myriad people, labored to build a consensus, to secure a necessary foundation of popular support for the new would-be nation: both the powerful and the comparatively powerless were fused into a collective effort to render the Confederate cause one that stirred patriotic loyalties. Politicians, clergymen, journalists, educators, and many other groups of individuals tried to formulate an agenda for nationhood and to infuse the minds and hearts of the populace with it.

Confederates early equated their struggle for independence with other successful nationalist movements, none more vociferously so than with that of the French Revolution. The "Marseillaise" was published in the South on several occasions during the war, with pro-Confederate variations of the words; and the music was played on many an occasion. Indeed, the song became so firmly identified as a Confederate anthem that when a troupe of French actors visiting in New York sang it, they were slapped into jail, accused of being Southern sympathizers.[21]

From the very beginning, Confederate apologists tried to equate their struggle with the struggle of 1776.

> *Rebels* before,
> Our fathers of yore,
> *Rebel's* the righteous name
> *Washington* bore.
> Why, then, be ours the same.

Thus, Confederates argued, they were the legitimate heirs of the American Revolution, restoring the proper inheritance that had been distorted within the old Union. From the earliest days of declared Southern independence, as Faust asserts, "there existed a widespread and self-conscious effort" to lay claim to "American nationalism as their own, to give themselves at once an identity and history."[22] Such conscious behavior was a fatal confession that they indeed lacked what they sought to achieve with such determination.

But it was an iffy procedure; as Benedict Anderson has put it, nationalism assumes that a group of strangers must come to believe that they have some close, even intimate, relationship. And what realities limited the possible in this instance? Communication was severely hampered by scant capacity to produce and disseminate the printed word. Southerners had not been, and could not speedily become, a well-read people. (The Southern humorist Roy Blount suggests that "it was easier for a person to enter heaven through the eye of an onion ring than it was to sell a book in the South.") Indeed, a significantly large portion of Southerners were illiterate. The postal rates, which soon rose to be two and three times higher than those in the North, inhibited widespread dissemination of propaganda by mail. There was not even an engraver available within the South to make the new National seal: it had to be devised abroad, transported across the Atlantic, and run through the naval blockade.[23]

But one avenue was wide open, and that was through music and song. Songbooks and sheet music proved to be the most popular printed matter published in the Confederacy. Indeed, so many songs were written by ordinary folk in the South that, as Faust has observed, the process reached and stirred huge numbers of women, particularly in remote locations, and so "many well-received ballads stimulated direct popular responses" that there was created "a kind of singing dialogue throughout the South."[24]

Clergy, too, possessed an enormous power. The authority that the common folk so willingly accorded to them and to their weekly sermons (which quite often were printed and disseminated widely) rendered them equally as influential as any of the politicians. Early on they began delineating an ideological underpinning for a theory of "just war." Sermons, tracts, and religious newspapers were printed and distributed in abundance. Both the soldiers and the populace at home were exhorted concerning the war's origins and purposes. Thus, the ultimate essence of the clerical effort at generating nationalism came to be, as Faust put it, "to involve more than simply establishing a new political status for the South; it required the location of the Confederacy not only within the world but within eternity, as an instrumental part of God's designs."[25]

On February 4, 1861, representatives from the first six states to secede began their work (the Texas delegation was delayed, not arriving until March 2). Montgomery was a pleasant and unassuming country town situated on the Alabama River, founded only forty years earlier. Still, its streets were unpaved; and there were but two hotels, one of them dirty and unpleasant. After the Texas delegation arrived, the total of fifty men present organized themselves into the Provisional Congress of the Confederate States of America.

Although the numbers of delegates from the various states reflected the particular state's previous representation in the U.S. Congress, the totals were irrelevant because in the Provisional Congress, each state was sovereign and had only one vote. Nine of the delegates had been members of the U.S. Senate, and eighteen had served in the House of Representatives. Four had been at times in both bodies. One had been Speaker of the House and secretary of the treasury; another had served as a senator and secretary of war.

A committee composed of two members from each state was appointed to serve as a constitutional convention, with Robert W. Barnwell of South Carolina as chairman. These Southern statesmen included some remarkably bright and insightful constitutional theorists. Primarily, they believed they were the legitimate inheritors, and now the restorers, of the original principles upon which the old nation had been founded. In July 1861, Alexander H. Stephens, the vice president of the Confederacy, claimed that "we simply wish to govern ourselves as we please. We simply stand where our revolutionary fathers stood in '76. We stand upon the great fundamental principle announced on the 4th of July, 1776, and incorporated into the Declaration of Independence— that great principle announced that governments derive their just power from the consent of the governed."[26] Because the Confederate Constitution mirrors the U.S. Constitution in so much of its text, scholars generally have been misled into disregarding the several truly significant differences. The Confederate Framers knew what they were trying to do: embrace a conservatism that they correctly perceived to have been eroding in the old Union.[27] The committee completed its work on February 8, and near midnight on that same day the provisional constitution was adopted. Davis later asserted that "the conservative temper of the people of the Confederate States was conspicuously exhibited in [this] the most important product of the early labors of their representatives in Congress assembled."[28]

The following day, on the motion of Robert Barnwell Rhett, a committee of twelve was appointed to produce a draft of the permanent Constitution of the Confederate States of America. As before, each state was represented by two delegates: Alabama, Richard W. Walker and Robert H. Smith; Florida, Jackson C. Morton and James B. Owens; Georgia, Thomas R. R. Cobb and Robert Toombs; Louisiana, Alexander De Clouet and Edward Sparrow; Mississippi, Alexander M. Clayton and Wiley P. Harris; South Carolina, Robert B. Rhett and James B. Chesnut Jr.[29] This committee met as a constitutional convention each night, from seven to eleven, and sometimes later. Beginning on February 28, 1861, by March 11 it had a completed document.[30] Rather little debate ensued, for the delegates were in considerable agreement concerning what they wanted. As Robert Barnwell Rhett put it, they wanted "to make the Constitution of the Confederate States simply the Constitution of the United States, as the South had always interpreted its powers, with only such alterations as would remove ambiguity, and better carry out its plain intents."[31] The first words of the new Preamble reflected that: "We, the People of the Confederate States, each state acting in its sovereign and independent character." The Preamble also included an invocation of "the favor and guidance of Almighty God," and it omitted the general welfare clause.[32]

The Confederate Constitution did not establish slavery. It left that matter to the states. It did, however—and interestingly—contain a stronger prohibition against the African slave trade than did the U.S. Constitution. And, more important, it guaranteed the right of property in slaves: not once but three times. Article 1, section 8, provided, "No . . . law denying or impairing the right of property in negro slaves shall be passed." Article 4, section 2, stated that "the citizens of each State . . . shall have the right of transit and sojourn in any State of this Confederacy, with their slaves . . . ; and the right of property in said slaves shall not be thereby impaired." Article 4, section 3, concerning the possible acquisition of new territory, established that "in all such territory, the institution of negro slavery, as it now exists in the Confederate States, shall be recognized and protected by Congress and by the territorial government."

The essential differences between the new and the old came in two areas: the relationship between the executive and legislative branches of government and the relationship between the states and the central government. The essences of the main differences were of two types: those that spelled out the federal nature of the system to be established and those that made adjustments to the functioning of the federal government, particularly the presidency. The Confederate Constitution made explicit what had been intended by the Tenth Amendment: all powers not delegated to the central government by the Constitution, nor prohibited by it to the states, are reserved to the states, or to the people. It also put significant limits on the power of taxation and expenditure. It expressed a genuine bias in favor of a free market and limited government to correct the sectional and class favoritism that the Framers perceived had been carried out by congressional majorities in the Union.[33] More important, Davis had more power over the purse than Lincoln did. The Confederate president had a line-item veto on appropriation bills, meaning a check against irrelevant riders. There were limits on the degree to which the Congress could exceed the president's spending recommendations.

Even more interesting were the changes in the executive and the judicial branches. The Confederate Constitution made the president a stronger officer than he had been under the U.S. Constitution. Clearly the Framers wanted him to be the high and honorable chief magistrate that they felt had been intended by the U.S. Constitution, rather than the party leader he had come to be in fact. The president was to serve one six-year term, thus abolishing the reelection question and the second-term impasse. On April 19, 1862, a presidential succession bill passed by the Confederate Congress became law. It provided for the succession, after the vice president, through the president pro tempore of the Senate and the Speaker of the House.[34] The president could remove cabinet members and diplomats from office at his pleasure and will. Other civil officers, however, could be removed only for dishonesty, incapacity, inefficiency, misconduct or neglect of duty or when their services had become unnecessary. Thus did the Confederacy establish a rudimentary civil service system, which predated that of the U.S. Civil Service by twenty-two years.

Cabinet members were to be allowed the right to speak in Congress on matters pertaining to their departments, if the Congress specifically provided for it (which it ultimately did not). This action would have enhanced the process of deliberation well beyond the formal exchange of messages or informal conferences, and it would have saved much time and confusion. Although cabinet members would have no vote, enough members of Congress were concerned about this departure from American practice that this chance to increase accountability and economy failed.

Protective tariffs were outlawed. The national government was forbidden to grant bounties or to engage in financing internal improvements except to provide beacons, buoys, "and other aid to navigation" along coasts, rivers, and harbors and to remove obstructions from waterways. States were permitted to enter into agreements with other states to improve the navigation of a river that divided or flowed through two or more states. The amending process was simplified. Any three states could call a convention for the purpose, and ratification would require only two-thirds of the states, rather than the three-fourths needed under the U.S. Constitution.

Concerning the judiciary, the right of judicial review was concurrent—to be shared by both state and federal courts. But the strongest element of state rights within the judiciary was a clause that allowed any judicial officer or other officer exercising his function solely within the limits of any particular state to be impeached by a two-thirds vote of both houses of the state legislature—a trial then to be conducted by the Confederate Senate. And to underline the point, all Confederate judicial districts were confined by Congress to the territory of a single state. The Constitution also provided for the creation of a Confederate supreme court, but for fear of recreating the strong judiciary of the United States, the Congress never passed a judiciary act to create one. Such measures were introduced from time to time, debated, and amended, but they always floundered on the issue of appellate jurisdiction. Davis asked the first session of the permanent Congress to pass such a law, but the legislature balked. On that occasion, Senator Louis T. Wigfall of Texas told the Senate that John Marshall and the U.S. Supreme Court had split the Union and that if Marshall "had been a man of inferior intellect, the old Union would still have been in existence. But his unimpeachable character, his great intellect enabled him to fasten his principles of nationality upon our institutions." Senator Clement C. Clay of Alabama agreed: the problem of whether to allow appeals from state courts to the proposed Confederate supreme court was the point that prevented agreement on the issue of the creation of the high court.[35]

The most basic principle embodied by the Confederate Constitution was that ultimately the people ruled—government had to rest upon the consent of the governed. And this did not mean simply whatever temporary majority might gain control of the presidency, the Congress, or the Supreme Court. It meant instead the consent of the governed acting through all branches of both state and federal governments. It was Jeffersonianism pure and simple; it was a final rejection of Hamiltonianism. And it was more than that, for it "reinvigorated the states with the spirit of the [Federal] Tenth Amendment's reserved-powers provision as interpreted by its Antifederalist sponsors."[36] Significantly, though, the Confederate Constitution was silent on the subject of secession; that right was regarded as so utterly elemental as not to require mentioning. As Robbins has noted, if inserted, it would imply that perhaps the U.S. Constitution did not sanction secession after all. This was a thought that might undermine the legitimacy of the Confederacy.[37]

Other differences between the Confederate and U.S. Constitutions are also significant. Thomas R. R. Cobb had led the push to include reference to the Deity, but he also wanted a prohibition of Sunday mails, and in that he failed. The base of representation in the House of Representatives was raised from thirty thousand to fifty thousand; thus the Confederate House would be smaller than the U.S. House, reflecting the reality that the South wished to be less democratic. The first twelve Amendments to the U.S. Constitution (the only ones adopted at that time) were incorporated within the body of the Confederate Constitution. No law could relate to more than one subject, and that subject had to be clearly expressed in the title. Unlike in the Union, voting was strictly limited to citizens of the Confederacy. The Post Office Department would have to be self-sustaining after March 1, 1863. New states could be admitted only by a vote of two-thirds of the House of Representatives and of the Senate. Free states (without slavery) were not prohibited, although there was a strong fight to ban them, led by Robert B. Rhett and William P. Miles of South Carolina and Thomas R. R. Cobb.

The permanent Constitution of the Confederate States of America was adopted by the Provisional Congress by a unanimous vote on March 11, 1861. The Constitution was submitted to the various states, and each state adopted it, either by a vote of the secession convention if it was still sitting, or by their legislatures. Some ratified it unanimously, as did Georgia, and some fought over it intensely, as was the case in South Carolina. Nowhere was it submitted to the people for a vote.

The Provisional Congress also opted for relative conservatism, indeed even more rigorously than in its selection of Davis, in choosing a vice president. The mantle fell upon the widely respected former Whig, Alexander H. Stephens of

Georgia. Possessed of enormous intelligence but physically quite frail, Stephens seemed to be perpetually melancholy. William C. Davis observes that

> Stephens's ailments and . . . melancholy aged him prematurely. He had been what people call 'sickly' from the day of his birth. . . . Much of his life he weighed under eighty pounds, and never did he top one hundred. . . . His head was too small, his hair already thinning into wisps and clumps, and his ears too large, sticking out to make him look like an elf. . . . [His] melancholy nature almost homeric in its breadth and impact on him . . . [combined with] recurring bouts of pain and illness left him with an outlook on life and the human condition that was gloomy at best and that did not improve when he underwent a religious awakening that made him a lifelong Calvinist.[38]

Stephens was, nevertheless, both sharp-tongued and witty. The most crucial element in his selection is that he had been a cooperationist, one of those Southerners who asserted a right of secession but who opposed it when it came, preferring that if Georgia left the Union (and he hoped it would not), it would leave in cooperation with the other slave states. Choosing him was clearly aimed at pleasing unionists and other cooperationists and eliciting their support of the Confederacy. It was also, ultimately, an office that Stephens clearly earned by playing so large and significant a leadership role in the drafting of the Confederate Constitution.[39]

It was not, however, a choice likely to produce warm and harmonious relations between the president and vice president. Enmity, ill will, and political disagreements between Davis and Stephens had deep roots, even though Toombs, Stephens, and Davis had shared a mess while living at the same hotel in Washington, D.C. At least then, W. C. Davis observes,

> They were a convivial group, though Davis himself seemed stern and aloof and was always rather formal, at least with Toombs. . . . Davis's vivacious wife Varina entered much more into the social spirit of the mess, however, and especially enjoyed the hearty, bluff Georgian [Toombs] and his wife. . . . She also could not help but observe in their months together at the same table that Toombs genuinely loved Stephens. . . . Varina Davis was also perceptive enough to see in Little Aleck "a virile mind sustained by an inflexible will."[40]

In a speech on October 25, 1849, Davis had called Stephens's vote in Congress to defeat the Clayton compromise bill, "treason of that *little pale star* from Georgia, . . . and seven other calculating demagogues from six different southern States, and representing strong whig districts."[41] Davis had believed that passage of the bill "would have forever ended the quarrel between the North and South."[42]

Stephens converted to the Democrat Party in 1855. At least after that he and Davis managed on occasion to relate civilly. But they were prone to disagreement: they exchanged a number of letters while Davis was secretary of war, in January 1856, clashing over the War Department's action in the case of an army surgeon who had been acquitted in a murder case and wanted either for his rank to be restored or to be allowed to resign with honor.[43]

Despite their propensity to disagree, Davis and Stephens had apparently amicable visits on April 22 and 23, 1858, to discuss the Lecompton compromise in Kansas (which, had it been affirmed, would have brought Kansas into the Union as a slave state).[44] In 1860, after the Democratic Party had taken the initial moves to split into two factions, in a condemnatory reply to a speech made by Stephen A. Douglas, Davis read with obvious approval from a letter written by Stephens that asserted the "constitutional impossibility" of squatter sovereignty. Douglas supported it, and Davis, Stephens, and others condemned it because they wanted free and unfettered rights for slaveholders to take their chattel into the territories.[45] But their harmony over the Lecompton issue was an anomaly: except for that, until the Confederacy was formed, Davis and Stephens had been "at odds on every important political measure since 1845."[46]

From the outset of their collaboration as the principal Confederate officials, Stephens and Davis seemed to be working in harmony and for common goals. There was, both men could clearly see, a lot that needed to be done, and Davis welcomed Stephens warmly at this time. They met daily, Davis earnestly seeking Stephens's help and counsel, and Stephens "thoroughly relished his privileged status."[47]

Stephens meanwhile delivered a speech in Savannah at the invitation of the Georgia convention, on March 21, 1861, which became notorious as his Cornerstone speech. He expounded at great length on how he found excellence in the Confederate Constitution; how patriotic and conservative he believed the congressmen to be; how vile the U.S. government had become; and how "our new government is founded upon exactly the opposite idea; its foundations are laid, its cornerstone rests upon the great truth, that the negro is not equal to the white man; that slavery—subordination to the superior race—is his natural and normal condition." It proved most helpful to the Northern abolitionists, who seized on its content to goad Lincoln into instituting draconian measures. One Yankee newspaper later estimated that Stephens's speech had been "of incalculable value to us."[48]

Stephens was then sent to Virginia, arriving on April 22, 1861, to contact various officials and to try to secure Virginia's loyalty to the Confederacy. His efforts gave early promise of bearing fruit, and they did: long before Virginia left the Union it was clearly leaning toward the Confederacy.[49]

Since Davis was full of confidence in himself but had little faith in the capabilities of others, his selection of cabinet officers was an agonizing task. The problem was compounded by the reality that most of the public men of the South whom he knew well had been in the Senate, and he knew little or nothing of their administrative capacity.[50] Guessing games concerning whom he might pick took place at the Exchange Hotel. Some suspected it would be this particular man; others emphatically claimed it would be that. One wag set them straight: "You are all wrong," he said. It will be "for Secretary of State, Hon Jeff. Davis of Miss.; War and Navy, Jeff. Davis of Miss.; Interior, ex-Senator Davis, of Miss.; Treasury, Col. Davis, of Miss.; Attorney General, Mr. Davis, of Miss."[51]

Vice President Stephens had "somewhat self-importantly told friends that he intended to use his influence on Davis to persuade him toward the best possible cabinet appointments." Thus he was both amazed and deeply disappointed that Davis cared little or nothing about Stephens's opinions of the choices.[52] Taking his initial cue from the absence of political parties, Davis concluded that each state should be represented (at first this included Mississippi, because Texas joined late; after Texas entered the Confederacy, then Mississippi was not to have a cabinet officer, being adequately honored by having the president among its sons). Davis was guided in his first choices, though without admitting it, by favoring former Democrats and prosecessionists. To his credit, he gave fair consideration to potential political rivals. Hence he chose the influential Robert Toombs for secretary of state. Unfortunately, that put "the right man in the wrong position." Toombs proved to be inadequate for any task even partially related to international diplomacy. He was a blustering, crude, bluntly outspoken proponent of slavery (which hurt the Confederacy abroad), and sometimes he drank to excess. He lacked even the necessary tact to get along with Davis, and it was said that "Bob Toombs disagrees with himself between meals."[53]

Actually, Davis had wanted Toombs to be secretary of the treasury, and for that post he would have been better qualified. Davis had intended his old and esteemed friend, Robert W. Barnwell of South Carolina, to be secretary of state. But the South Carolina delegation hastily pressed Davis to name Christopher G. Memminger secretary of the treasury. If, however, Memminger were to be the cabinet member from South Carolina, he had to be secretary of the treasury, for that was all he was qualified to be. So, by force of Davis's rule of thumb, Toombs had to become secretary of state, and the job he could have done better went to Memminger.[54] Born in Germany, Memminger at least had had some training in finance during his political career in South Carolina. E. Merton Coulter has observed that Memminger was "a man of sound instincts but weak will power." He was antagonistic, and this made many of his dealings with others difficult and often futile. He became an easy target, as faultfinders blamed him for what Congress did rather than for what he had recommended that they do. Louis T. Wigfall later suggested that Memminger was so naive that he "seemed to think he could finance the Confederacy by passing around the hat."[55]

The office of secretary of war went to a political hack, Leroy Pope Walker of Alabama. He had no military training and was not a soldier, but he held a commission as brigadier general in the Alabama militia. His early correspondence clearly indicates that he did not believe there would be a war, and he not only announced publicly that there was not going to be one, but he also promised that he would wipe up with his pocket handkerchief any blood that eventually might be spilled over secession. Considering Davis's own prediction of a long war, Walker's perspective made him a dubious choice. Politically astute observers assumed that Davis probably planned to run this department himself. The famous diarist, Mary Boykin Chesnut, wife of Senator James Chesnut of South Carolina, wrote that Joe Davis Jr. had said, " 'Would heaven only send us a Napoleon.' . . . Not one bit of use, if heaven did," she asserted, "Walker would not give him a commission!"[56]

But the quaintly colorful Walker, addicted to chewing tobacco with obvious relish, followed by unusually profuse spitting, at least was a man possessed of considerable energy. As late as March 29 he still remained complacent, but when it at last became evident that hostilities probably were inevitable, he became much more active with war preparations.[57] Nonetheless, he was inadequate for the job, and he was gone from the cabinet by fall. He and Davis disagreed about the occupation of Columbus, Kentucky, by Confederate forces, and he resigned on September 16. (He was appointed a brigadier general the next day but served as such for only a few months owing to obvious unsuitability. Late in the war he took the rank of colonel and functioned as a military court judge in north Alabama.)

A relatively little-known Floridian, Stephen R. Mallory, was Davis's pick for secretary of the navy. Before the Union proclaimed a blockade of the Confederate coastline, few people paid much attention to him or his job, although he had served on the naval affairs committee in the U.S. Senate. He proved to be an excellent choice. But the enormous task of building a navy from virtually nothing later made him a target for sniping criticism. Rumored to be a rake, he was convivial and witty.[58]

Judge John H. Reagan of Texas became the postmaster general. He proved to be exceptionally able in performing this job, but he apparently exerted little influence in cabinet meetings, and he quarrelled with several other cabinet members. Because the Congress gave him the daunting task of rendering the postal service self-supporting by 1863, he had to do some early financial structuring. In May 1861, he persuaded the Congress to double the postal rates on newspapers. But this led to an outcry from the opposition and claims that the Davis administration was trying to undermine the civil liberties by silencing them. Reagan never became popular while the war was on, but he did his job strikingly well; and at least happily for him later in life, after the Civil War he was probably by far the most popular of the former Confederate civil officials.[59]

The selection of an attorney general seemed to be of no significance; the spot was the least important in the cabinet. Davis's choice fell on Judah P. Benjamin of Louisiana, who proved to be the most intelligent and capable member of the cabinet. He was a Jew who had married a Roman Catholic, from whom he was separated. He had a weakness for gambling. A skilled attorney and a wise and experienced politician, he was a thoroughly charming man and loved all the comforts of the good life: fine food, wine, Havana cigars, and witty conversation. Although eventually he served throughout the war in three different cabinet posts, it may be correct to say that he never threw himself completely into supporting the Confederacy. Sometimes it seemed that he was conducting himself with somewhat of a bemused objectivity.[60]

Burton J. Hendrick has suggested that too much pork barrel principle went into Davis's initial cabinet selections. Nevertheless, the cabinet members established their offices in a commercial building in Montgomery while the president continued to transact his business in the Exchange Hotel. Only one of the cabinet sessions that occurred during the approximately three months that the administration remained in Montgomery was of any significance, but that meeting was of truly great import. At that point the members decided to agree with Davis that the moment was propitious to justify opening fire on Fort Sumter. Only one man in the cabinet, according to Hendrick, understood that Lincoln was maneuvering the Confederacy into firing the first shot, and that was Robert Toombs. Despite exerting all the influence he possessed to dissuade Davis and the rest, he could not achieve his goal.[61]

The Confederate Congress quickly and easily confirmed Davis's cabinet selections; but immediately a bitter and tawdry struggle for lower-echelon positions in the new government began. Montgomery was turned into a den of aging political hacks who wanted jobs. Mary Chesnut suggested that "there never was such a resurrection of the dead and forgotten."[62] Howell Cobb remarked that it seemed half of Georgia was present, seeking office, and "the other half were at home writing letters on the same subject." Mary Chesnut commented that "a War of Secession . . . will end a War for the Succession of Places." William Howard Russell, the English war correspondent, who had gained international fame for his dispatches from the war in the Crimea, described Montgomery as filled with "placemen with or without places, and a vast number of speculators, contractors, and the like, attracted by the embryo government."[63]

It seemed too that nearly every appointment or commission granted would be followed by a whining complaint that the rank was too low. It proved to be a bitterly difficult task for the active-negative president. "I hope you will not have occasion to take the field," David Yulee of Florida wrote to Davis on March 1, "but if there is a war, . . . you have the example of Napoleon before you." Did Napoleon, Davis mused, have to endure all the paperwork that he was enduring and the endless fretting by ambitious men?[64]

The Confederacy, even after four more states later seceded and joined it, had many physical disadvantages that made maintaining its independence at best an iffy proposition. It was overwhelmingly rural, with few cities of significance, and it had a poor infrastructure. There was far less railroad trackage than in the North. Most roads were poor. There was scant industrial development. By any material measure, the South was much weaker than the North.

But the weaker side sometimes can prevail. To do so, it must have wise leadership and firm determination among its people. If war comes, as indeed it did, there must be superior strategic decisions efficiently and effectively executed. Most important, the people's will to continue the struggle must be maintained. Did Davis have the charisma necessary to lead this would-be country that was so dominated by elite agricultural concerns? Could the common folk, the masses, be adequately stirred? What would happen if the going got tough, even bitter?

3

PROVISIONAL ADMINISTRATION

As Confederate first couple, Jefferson and Varina Davis from the outset made strong and generally positive impressions. The English journalist William Howard Russell depicted Varina as "a comely, sprightly woman, verging on matronhood, of good figure and manners, well-dressed, ladylike and clever." Any number of folk noted her quick mind and wit. Mary Boykin Chesnut, who became one of Varina's closest and dearest friends, recorded in her diary, "She is awfully clever—always." Varina gave her first levee on March 6 at the Exchange Hotel. It proved such a success that she continued giving them regularly, and Jefferson attended most of them.[1]

Mary Chesnut observed that Varina found "playing Mrs. President of this small Confederacy slow work after leaving . . . Washington." Indeed Varina privately called Montgomery "a strange community," depicting the Confederate Congress as "the Botany Bay, no I am too polite to say that, but bear garden of the South," and she complained about the poor sanitation. Judah Benjamin informed a Northern friend, and Varina did not totally disagree with his sentiment, that "we will show you what a true Republican government is— no pate, no champagne, no salmon, no nothing—people don't give dinners here: but only nice tea parties."[2]

There were three distinct Confederate Congresses during Davis's administration: the Provisional Congress, which met in five sessions between February 4, 1861, and February 17, 1862; the First Congress, which met in four sessions from February 18, 1862, to February 17, 1864; and the Second Congress, which had two sessions between May 2, 1864, and March 18, 1865, its life cut short by the end of the war. If one goes by the number of states subject to Reconstruction after the war, the final official count of seceded states was eleven. But rump groups in Kentucky and Missouri acted to secede, so both the United States and the Confederacy claimed those two states. Both the

U.S. and Confederate Congresses included representatives from them, too, elevating the number of Confederate states to thirteen. In addition, the Arizona Territory and the Indian Nations of the Cherokee, Choctaw, Creek, Seminole, and Chickasaw had the right of representation in the Confederate Congress, but no vote.

Confederate congressman Robert Eden Scott's headstone notes that he was "killed by a Yankee deserter" and bears a quotation from Shakespeare's *Julius Caesar,* but it does not mention his service in the Provisional Confederate Congress. The same omission holds concerning a strikingly large number of other Southern legislators; such evidence indicates the post–Civil War South was much more fascinated by things military than by things political. Few Confederate congressmen, their relatives, or historians attached much importance to their Civil War office in the final assessments of their lives.[3]

Most Confederate congressmen were in the prime of their lives; 39 percent were in their forties in 1860, but they ranged widely from the youngest (sixteen were thirty or younger) to the oldest, seventy-one-year-old Thomas Fearn of Alabama. Age had only minor correlation with a congressman's behavior or voting propensity, although younger congressmen were more likely to have been lifelong Democrats. Too, they were more likely to have been secessionists in the crisis of 1860–1861. The majority, two hundred six of the two hundred sixty-seven, were lawyers, though one hundred seven of these also engaged in farming or planting. Sixty-two members owned fifty or more slaves, including twenty-five who owned at least one hundred fifteen; a mere twenty-two could be identified as nonslaveowners, and another eight had only one. This was a striking contrast to the majority of the men who became Confederate generals, who owned no slaves themselves; most of them also belonged to nonslaveholding families. The holdings of another twenty-five members could not be determined, but the median holding was sixteen slaves.[4]

Numerous entertaining morsels of information can be obtained from Ezra J. Warner and Wilfred Buck Yearns's *Biographical Register of the Confederate Congress.* Warren Akin "gained considerable renown for being audible a mile away." Nathan Bass owned so much land and so many slaves in two counties that he "is sometimes supposed to have been two different men, and enjoys the unusual distinction of having been enumerated twice in the 1860 federal census." John Bullock Clark was denied reappointment by his governor because of "alleged extracurricular activities in Richmond, which were said to include mendacity, drunkenness, and the attempted seduction of General Albert Pike's mistress." Reuben Davis wanted early in life "to become a lawyer, but his father, who felt that it was impossible for a lawyer to enter the kingdom of Heaven, persuaded him to study medicine." James Farrow won enduring distaff gratitude by championing a law by which "asking for the ages of clerks should not apply to lady clerks." Thomas Marsh Forman "bore the name of Thomas Forman Bryan until 1846," when he had it changed so that he could profit from the provisions of his grandfather's will. This change resulted in his five eldest children being surnamed Bryan and the two youngest Forman.[5]

Newspaperman E. A. Pollard, editor of the *Richmond Examiner,* once described Benjamin Harvey Hill—the true Talleyrand of the Confederacy—as "the very picture of a smooth and plausible mediocrity." Although some people held William Hamilton MacFarland in high esteem, others "found him pompous and overbearing, and he was once characterized as 'the curly-headed poodle . . . nearly overcome with dignity and fat.'" William (Extra Billy) Smith "moved to California in 1849 and would have become its first United States senator had that not entailed giving up his Virginia citizenship." Hugh French Thomason suggested that the Confederate "troops be armed with pikes, lances, spears, and shotguns." George Graham Vest enjoyed the dubious "distinction of having been the sole member of the Congress to be publicly horsewhipped." In 1879 he became a member of the U.S. Senate, and "as late as 1900 the *Chicago Journal,* a Republican newspaper, acknowledged him to have been 'half the brains on the Democratic side of the Senate.'" And one almost wishes to have had the honor of knowing John William Clark Watson, reputed to have been "the smartest man who ever lived in Holly Springs, Mississippi."[6]

Two striking factors stand out about the Confederate congressmen. First, a goodly number of soldiers served in the Congress—some of them officers but quite a few of them privates. In one instance a private won election over his company commander. Second, a surprisingly large percentage of the congressmen later returned to prominent public lives following the war's conclusion—on both the state and national levels. More than a few subsequently served in the U.S. Congress, some held cabinet posts, and large numbers of them received appointments to other important federal jobs. Quite obviously, they were capable public servants and administrators whom the electorate found appealing.[7]

Not only did the membership of the Congress change at elections, but it also changed between them. In terms of bringing about shifts in voting patterns, the former phenomenon was considerably the more profound. In the U.S. Congresses of the 1960s, the turnover at election time ranged from 15 percent to 20 percent. A century earlier, the 1861 Confederate elections brought about a two-thirds turnover, and those in 1863 caused a one-third replacement rate. In 1861, the new congressmen tended to be Democrats and Secessionists, but in 1863 about two-thirds of the fifty newly elected representatives were former Unionists and three-fourths of them former Whigs.

Former political affiliation was among the most important determinants of congressional behavior. The Whig Party had died, North and South, but many Whigs moved into other parties while keeping their Whiggish attitudes.[8]

There had been a dichotomous antebellum Southern political economy; it was a meld of that which concerned the market-oriented planters and the subsistence-farming upcountry folk. Both were linked by racial attitudes and a belief in relatively limited government, but Whig sentiments tended toward approval of a greater activism in government and purposeful regulation of the economy; planters tended to be Whigs. They wanted government to do things, but only if those things gave them some benefit or advantage: for example, they were adamantly opposed to protective tariffs while upcountry folk had less concern about those. The ensuing wartime experiences created pressures on both elements.

Most congressmen were well-informed, publicly active men. Only 10 percent had no discoverable prior political experience. No less than two-thirds of them had sat in state legislatures, and one-third had served in the U.S. Congress. Eighty-six Confederate congressmen had been delegates to their state secession conventions (or the equivalent legislature in Kentucky).[9]

The Confederate Congress was far from being an assemblage of strangers: on the contrary, many of these men had known one another for years. Southerners historically have tended to be keenly aware of their far-flung genealogical relationships, and there were many family ties that linked numerous congressmen. And family ties were not the only significant linkages: there were eight sets of law partners, and the law teachers of several congressmen also were present. Other occasional business dealings had occurred at times among various congressmen.[10]

There were no official political party organizations in the Confederacy. Eventually there was a discernible pro-Davis and an anti-Davis faction, and had the Confederacy endured long enough, these factions might have evolved into parties. But the main motivations for coalescence of anti-Davis sentiment had to do with state rights and localism. Some of those who became aggrieved with Davis believed state rights were being unduly trampled by the increasingly centralizing policies that war realities forced on the Confederate government. And others objected to the special interests engendered by the geographic location of a politician's constituency. Anti-Davis manifestations never took as distinct a party orientation as did anti-Lincoln sentiment in the North, however.

Yet in the Confederacy, there was continuing party antagonism well after 1861, depending on one's prewar affiliation. One telling illustration was the frequent denial by congressmen and other civil officials that such affiliations existed, or that they themselves were responsible for any party's actions if they did. In trying to perceive how these antagonistic groupings might be motivated to oppose one another, it appears that less emphasis was attached to one's stand on secession than on one's particular prewar party membership.

Ultimately, because of the essential lack of meaningful sectional or party directives in the traditional sense, the Confederate congressman was left almost entirely to individual decision making. Hence, personal characteristics and individual circumstances, as well as the current situation within one's constituency, were significant. A large number of the many roll-call votes in the Confederate Congress produced sharply close divisions. Such circumstances indicate that much was done by the Confederate Congress without even approximate consensus. It is a complicated matter: careful analysis seems to indicate that "congressmen were split, not by a single attribute, but by a number of them working sometimes at cross-purposes and at other times in concert."[11]

In many respects the Provisional Congress deviated from the norms of legislative bodies in America. In the first place it was unicameral. For a very brief time, it was the de facto executive and legislative branch of government. Its membership varied, ranging from the scant number of original delegates to the eventual hundred-plus representatives from thirteen states and a territory. Voting was by states, not by individuals. When the body was at work on the Confederate Constitution, it was also a constitutional convention, rather more than a legislature. Most important for analytical purposes, its early months were the only time during the existence of any Confederate Congress when a significant amount of effort could be devoted to the formulation of peacetime legislation.

Nation building dominated the first half of 1861. But gradually circumstances forced the Provisional Congress to devote more and more of its time and effort to the problem of trying to win the war that had erupted. This was perhaps the most chronic malady of the Confederate Congress: nation building took second place to the evermore pressing problems of national survival.

No decisive differences can be traced to slaveholding. Although almost none of the Confederate congressmen was really poor, wide gaps did exist. The relatively poorer legislators showed tendencies, in contrast to their wealthier colleagues, to support expanded compensation benefits from sequestration receipts—for example, when it was deemed necessary for the government to take private property for some apparently necessary purpose, such as to support the war effort—lower assessments of land and slaves for the War Tax, choosing army officers by election, and payment of bounties to soldiers.

The first national flag of the Confederacy was raised on a staff at 3:30 P.M. on March 4, 1861, above the capitol in Montgomery by Miss L. T. Tyler, a granddaughter of the venerable former president John Tyler, who was a member of the Provisional Congress. Cannon thundered a salute, and the assembled crowds gave shouts of welcome to the ensign, or so asserted the *Mobile Daily Advertiser.*[12] Mary Boykin Chesnut noted the occasion differently in her diary: "We stood on the balcony to see our Confederate Flag go up. Roar of cannon, &c&c. Miss Saunders complained—so said Captain Ingraham—of the deadness of the mob. 'It was utterly spiritless,' she said. 'No cheering— or so little—no enthusiasm.' "[13]

Banners symbolic of secession had been flying at various places throughout the South for some months previous, especially so as each state left the Union. Many of these flags, most notably the palmetto flag of South Carolina, later were adopted as state flags. "The bonnie blue flag," a banner with a single large white star on a solid blue background, endearingly famous, had been the national flag of the short-lived Republic of West Florida. An Irish minstrel, Harry McCarthy, in 1861 toured the cotton states singing the immediately popular song, "The Bonnie Blue Flag." It came as close as any other to being the unofficial national anthem of the Confederacy:

> We are a band of brothers
>   And native to the soil
> Fighting for the property
>   We gained by honest toil;
> And when our rights were threatened,
>   The cry rose near and far—
> Hurrah for the Bonnie Blue Flag
>   That bears the single star!
>
> Hurrah! Hurrah!
>   For Southern rights hurrah!
> Hurrah for the Bonnie Blue Flag
>   That bears the single star.
>
> As long as the Union
>   Was faithful to her trust,
> Like friends and like brothers
>   Both kind were we and just;
> But now, when Northern treachery
>   Attempts our rights to mar,
> We hoist high the Bonnie Blue Flag
>   That bears the single star.

Within one week after the first meeting of the Provisional Congress the Committee on Flag, Seal, Coat of Arms, and Motto was appointed. It quickly became evident that there was a public clamor for a flag that was much like the old U.S. flag—indeed, some people even asserted that they had more right to the old one than the Union did and that it ought to come up with a new design. On March 4 the committee adopted a design by Professor Nicola Marschall, and the convention approved it at once. It had a canton of blue with a circle of stars to correspond in number to the states. The field was covered with three broad strips—actually bars, too wide to be considered stripes—of equal width, the top and bottom bars red and the middle bar white. It was immediately nicknamed the Stars and Bars and remains officially designated so to this day. The committee had hoped to have the flag hoisted for the first time over the capitol at the very moment that President Lincoln was delivering his Inaugural Address, but the flag raising had to be delayed until late in the day because whoever was the first Betsy Ross of the Confederacy did not get the banner done in time.

The first bills passed by the Provisional Congress were to provide for the procurement of munitions of war and for authorizing Davis's executive secretary. A prominent citizen of Montgomery, Alexander B. Clitherall, had been serving temporarily in that capacity, but Davis had at hand an old friend, Robert Josselyn. Fifty years old, he was a native of Massachusetts but had spent the past twenty-five years as a resident of Mississippi. He had served in Davis's regiment during the Mexican War. According to William C. Davis, "Fat, jolly, graying, a bit too fond of the bottle, he added poetry to his other talents." It was with a bit of self-promotion that he, a private in the Mexican War, was addressed now as captain.[14]

Bonds were destined to play an inglorious part in the financial history of the Confederacy. The Treasury ultimately issued so many of them that the people eventually lost confidence that the government could ever repay them and thereafter ceased to buy them. But this was far from the case at the outset. On February 28, 1861, the Confederate Congress authorized the president to borrow not over $15 million in 8 percent bonds, generating both interest and principal by a cotton export tax of one-eighth of a cent a pound. At first the Treasury planned to offer only $5 million, but the banks oversubscribed the issue to the tune of an additional $3 million within two days.[15]

In any civil war, manpower is an essential need and a continuing problem. And it was also one of those problems that led Davis and the Confederate government to exercise more power than the citizenry had anticipated, eventually causing people like William Waters Boyce to accuse Davis of usurpation. It is clear that to have any success at all, Davis and the government had to exercise every bit of the power they could be granted—or that they could seize—especially on manpower questions.

Initially, Confederates relied on militia; it was militia (or mobs, for it was often difficult to tell the difference) who seized federal installations throughout the South and constituted the force that compelled the surrender of Fort Sumter, albeit under the command of a regular officer in the Confederate Army, Pierre Gustave Toutant Beauregard. Davis pointed out in his Inaugural Address as provisional president, however, that "under ordinary circumstances" the Confederacy could "rely mainly upon the militia." However, the first half of 1861 was not ordinary, and Davis recommended that "in the present condition of affairs . . . there should be a well-instructed and disciplined army, more numerous than would usually be required on a peace establishment."[16] He suggested formation of "a provisional army . . . on which we must, in any early necessity, expect mainly to rely."[17] In the American military tradition, conscription had been mentioned but never implemented, so it was quite natural that initial legislation pertained to volunteers.

Congress had already acted along these lines, for on February 28, 1861, it passed "An Act to raise Provisional Forces for the Confederate States of America, and for other purposes." This provisional army would be composed of the existing forces of the states plus subsequent volunteers. The forces received would be considered "a part of the Provisional Army of the Confederate States." Quite wisely, the Congress required that all volunteers agree to serve for at least one year,[18] in contrast to the situation within the United States, where the national government was limited to calling out militia for no more than ninety days. This provision gave a significant initial advantage to the Confederacy, for the Union, which called for troops for as little as three months, had a difficult time organizing and training and having troops on hand when the fighting started. For the first year, at least, the South had a stability of force that lent significant strength to its army. Congress soon proposed to raise an army of one hundred thousand men, a figure that seems pitifully small in retrospect but that seemed gigantic in early 1861. This initial legislation was supplemented by a more comprehensive law just one week later.[19]

The supplemental bill passed on March 6 provided the basis for future expansion and organization of the Provisional Army of the Confederate States; much of the future legislation pertaining to raising troops was in the form of amendments to this law. Volunteers should come with their own clothes, and if in the cavalry, horses, and would receive a clothing allowance. Their pay would be the same as that of the regular army, and cavalrymen would receive forty cents per day for their horses. Officers were to be appointed according to the law of the states from which they came, which meant that they would be elected, but the president reserved prerogative to appoint general officers. All such troops would be part of the Army of the Confederate States and not of any individual state.[20]

On February 26, President Davis signed a bill creating the general staff of the regular army, which provided the basic administrative agencies for the conduct of war.[21] It created the Adjutant and Inspector General's Department, the Quartermaster's Department, the Subsistence Department, and the Medical Department. The initial structure of these departments consisted of a colonel, four to eight assistants ranked variously from lieutenant colonel to captain, and a few clerks. Within a month all bureaus were expanded somewhat, but even with that they subsequently proved to be inadequate for the tasks they soon faced.[22]

The rickety staff organization created by Congress continued the U.S. Army's prior practice of dividing two essential supply functions. Instead of a supply service, as in the subsequent modern American military establishment, there were to be separate departments of Quartermaster General and Commissary General. The number of personnel assigned to these vital military functions, however, was hopelessly inadequate and reflected both premodern notions of organization and a false belief that the war was going to be a short one.

Additional changes were made later, and in 1863, for example, the Quartermaster and Commissary functions were combined at the regimental level.[23] In much the same way, on March 15, 1861, the Congress created the Office of Second Auditor within the Treasury Department to audit War Department accounts. On May 21 the second auditor was given a staff of eleven clerks, and in February 1862 he got thirty-six more, as the bureaucracy grew to match the growing war effort.[24]

On March 6, 1861, the legislation to create a regular army and a provisional army reached Davis. To the already extant staff departments now were added a Corps of Engineers, a Corps of Artillery, eight regiments of artillery, and two of cavalry. Enlisted men were to receive one ration per day, in kind if possible, and a yearly allowance of clothing. Privates were to receive eleven dollars per month; corporals thirteen; buck sergeants seventeen; first sergeants twenty; and engineer sergeants thirty-four. The quartermasters and commissaries were to be bonded.[25]

Congress was at work on all sorts of other legislation: issues such as the postal service, rail transportation, acquisition of light ships, creation of a lighthouse bureau, liquor control, registration of vessels, naming of Indian agents, and so on. The Congress worked long and hard, and many of the sessions were held in secret.

Quite a number of candidates jockeyed for positions in the Staff Departments. One man particularly stood out in his quest for appointment: Abraham C. Myers. Born in South Carolina, he was a West Point graduate. In 1839 he had been appointed a captain in the Quartermaster Department and performed brilliantly in the Mexican War as a division supply officer, becoming by the end of that war the chief quartermaster of the army in Mexico. When secession came, he was chief quartermaster of the Southern Department, with headquarters in New Orleans. At the same time that he handed in his resignation from the army, on January 28, he turned over to the government of Louisiana all the stores that were in his possession. He immediately was named quartermaster general of Louisiana. He subsequently became the quintessential political manipulator in order to secure the job as quartermaster general of the Confederate States. His manipulations, combined with his obvious qualifications, led to his being given the post, albeit in an acting capacity, confirmed by the Congress on March 16, 1861. Myers proved generally satisfactory as Confederate quartermaster general, although he became involved in political controversy and resigned in August 1863. He opposed impressment, yet he nonetheless was forced to adopt the system.

In contrast to Myers, the future Confederate chief of ordnance had to be coaxed. This was Josiah Gorgas, a Pennsylvania native and West Point graduate who had seen service in the Mexican War and subsequently had married into the prominent Gayle family of Alabama politicians. Congress did not actually authorize an Ordnance Department, but the obvious need for one led to its de facto existence. Gorgas at first refused the post, but on April 8, 1861, a special order announced that "Major Josiah Gorgas, of the Corps of Artillery and Ordnance, is assigned to duty as Chief of the Bureau of Ordnance." Davis wrote to him: "Men must be fed, next armed, and even clothing must follow these; for if they are fed and have arms and ammunition they can fight."[26]

Although Myers and Gorgas proved to be excellent choices for their posts, the selection of the commissary general of subsistence was bungled. Lucius Bellinger Northrop of South Carolina had been a plebe at West Point the same year that Davis had been a senior. Later as junior officers in the U.S. Army, they served at the same post, and Northrop had testified in Davis's defense at his court-martial. But Northrop's military career foundered: he accidentally shot himself in the knee in 1839 and subsequently was subject to chronic sickliness, spending many years on sick leave, even long enough to allow him to complete medical studies and become a physician. When dropped from the rolls in 1848, he appealed to Davis, who had him restored to the army with a promotion to captain, his sole duty being to send in periodic reports indicating the state of his disability. In 1861 Davis incorrectly believed that his old friend was well qualified to be commissary general of subsistence, with the rank of colonel.[27]

Eventually it was determined that Northrop's department should furnish to each trooper a daily ration based on the then standard U.S. Army ration: three-fourths pound of pork or bacon or one and one-fourth pounds fresh and/or salt beef; eighteen ounces of bread or flour or twelve ounces of hard bread or one and one-fourth pounds of corn meal. Additionally, each hundred men collectively should receive eight quarts of peas or beans or ten pounds of rice; six pounds of coffee; twelve pounds of sugar; four quarts of vinegar; one and one-half pounds of tallow or one and one-fourth pounds of adamantine or one pound of sperm candles; four pounds of soap; and two quarts of salt. These allowances could be adjusted for troops on the march or if they faced other special conditions.[28]

The uniform issue of the regular army was a blue-flannel shirt, four pairs of gray-flannel trousers, three red-flannel undershirts, four pairs of cotton drawers, three pairs of wool stockings, two pairs of boots, blanket, leather stock, and cap. The total cost of all this was $26.95 per set, issuing to be semi-annual. Orders for five thousand sets of such uniforms went out to contractors in New Orleans by mid-April. Volunteers who furnished their own uniforms were allowed a $21.00 commutation payment semiannually. But Myers quickly perceived that of the huge number of volunteers streaming into the ranks, especially after Fort Sumter's fall in April, only a scant few would provide themselves with the necessary clothing. Soon the New Orleans contractors were called upon to supply fifteen hundred uniform sets per week. Myers arranged with mills in Georgia and Virginia to add to the streams of incoming supplies for volunteers, but he failed to arrange for any supply from Europe, even though he suggested the idea.[29]

Myers established a series of quartermaster depots, where supplies would be collected and held, subject to need. Depots in Montgomery, San Antonio, Charleston, New Orleans, and Mobile were later supplemented by additional ones in Nashville, Lynchburg, and Richmond, after the second wave of secession.[30]

Impressment was an issue that linked a number of other Confederate problems. It was most frequently applied in the context of taking supplies of food and forage for the army, but it also involved taking slave labor, railroad equipment, and even taking over railroads themselves. Impressment turned out to be intertwined with the entire economy, including tax laws, currency issues, loan policies, the regulation of foreign commerce, railroad construction and regulation, price controls, and even regulations specifying what crops could be grown. Its scope was so wideranging that it is a good point from which to examine the battle of necessity versus property rights in the Confederacy. Not even conscription, which came in 1862, involved so many other issues, even though conscription asserted the truly awful power of taking a man's body against his will and placing him where he did not want to go and where hostile bullets were extremely likely to kill or maim him. Conscription, when it came, involved grave necessity; impressment, on the other hand, involved not only necessity but also one of the bedrocks of Confederate nationalism: the sanctity of property rights.

When, much later in the war, South Carolina congressman William Waters Boyce accused Davis of despotism, impressment was one of the issues he mentioned.[31] And he was justified, even though Davis's messages said less about impressment than about many other issues, and the Congress legislated less on impressment than on any of the other major issues of the war. This was so because the necessity had been so obvious, the abuses so many and so frequent, and the alternatives so few. There was really only one alternative to impressment: to let the army go without. Although the Confederate leaders tried to argue around this reality, few of them were willing to let the army forgo needed supplies, so they were forced to let impressment continue.

Even tinkering with the system was mainly a quest for alternatives that did not exist; whatever changes were made, abuses nonetheless continued because the imperative of Confederate existence was that the army must survive. And survive it did, for four years, without effective hindrance to its collection of supply. Impressment, as much as anything else, underlined the subordinate position of the liberty that Confederates assumed was truly theirs. It stood in second place to the brutal requirements of military necessity, but not because Jefferson Davis wanted it that way. The Confederates began the Civil War in great innocence of what modern warfare requires of its citizens. The army was not just a large body of men fighting on some distant front. The need for supply required tentacles that reached into virtually every locality, and yet the war began without an effective supply system.

If some of the fledgling nation's citizenry clung to naive hopes that there might be no war, Davis was not among them. In February he commented on a Union senator who had said that "without a little blood-letting," the Union would not be "worth a rush." As Davis much later soberly observed, "With such unworthy levity did these leaders of sectional strife express their exultation in the prospect of the conflict, which was to drench the land with blood and enshroud thousands of homes in mourning!"[32]

4

To Sumter

Davis perceived from the outset that he would have to build a Confederate States Army and that this would be a daunting undertaking. He concentrated his efforts, as William Cooper observes, "on three major tasks, . . . [including] a lengthy enlistment policy," and in this "he failed."

> Davis's pleas did get twelve-month enlistments, but no more. . . . Davis courted officers from the U.S. Army . . . [and] in this area he experienced success. . . . In addition, Davis knew his country faced a perilous shortage of military equipment, especially weapons. He dispatched agents to both the United States and Europe. . . . Although the tasks, both civilian and military, were unending, to Davis one [area] seemed foremost [in importance]: diplomacy. He identified three diplomatic fronts, though he realized their interconnection: the slave states still in the Union; Europe, especially Great Britain; and the United States.[1]

As to the continuing Federal presence in various U.S. forts within the Confederacy; two were in the Florida Keys; there was Fort Pickens in Pensacola, Florida; and the most visible, Fort Sumter, was in the harbor of Charleston, South Carolina. Davis bluntly told a visitor, "The North means to compel us into a political servitude we disown and spurn."[2]

The first session of the Provisional Congress adjourned on March 16, 1861, its work rather well done. On the same day, President Davis, following urging from the congressmen, appointed William Lowndes Yancey, Pierre A. Rost, and A. Dudley Mann as commissioners to Britain to attempt negotiating for recognition. In opting for these men and subsequently in his other diplomatic choices, Davis "revealed both his ignorance of foreign affairs, and his penchant for correlating commitment to the Confederacy with suitability for important assignments." Yancey was a "voluble Alabama fire-eater. . . .

Mann, who had considerable experience in the old Union, . . . was a Confederate and Davis loyalist, but also an ineffectual lightweight."[3]

In Texas, on March 18, 1861, the aging hero and governor of that state, Sam Houston, refused to take an oath of allegiance to the Confederacy; he did not believe that secession necessarily meant adherence to the would-be new nation, whose existence he opposed. This proved to be his last major act in public life. And in stark contrast to Houston's inaction and his alienation from the Confederacy, the commander of the U.S. forces in the Department of Texas, seventy-one-year-old Brevet Major General David E. Twiggs, surrendered his entire command to Colonel Ben McCulloch, who represented the new Confederate state of Texas. For this, Twiggs, who became the oldest officer of the old army to take up arms for the Confederacy, was dismissed from U.S. service on March 1 and on May 22 was appointed major general in the provisional Army of the Confederacy, the senior officer of that grade, and assigned to command the District of Louisiana. The Confederacy gained substantially in getting Texas, but not in getting Twiggs as an acceptable general officer; his various infirmities soon compelled his retirement, and he died on July 15, 1861.

The initial diplomatic outreach of the Confederacy was to the border states. Many Confederate leaders cherished the hope that the conservative nature of the new Constitution would appeal to persons there, thus motivating them to secede. Various congressmen traveled through Arkansas, Tennessee, Virginia, and North Carolina trying to persuade these states to join the new government. Toombs virtually begged Vice President Stephens to go to Arkansas, but, typically, he refused. George Sanders unofficially but forcefully prevailed upon Governor Beriah Magoffin of Kentucky. Davis and War Secretary Leroy Pope Walker both tried to persuade Virginia, Walker even sending a spy to Richmond to encourage any secessionist sentiments that might be openly or even privately expressed. He suggested that offices in the government would be found for prominent Virginians, especially for John Tyler, if Virginia seceded.[4]

As required by Congress, Howell Cobb ordered all acts and resolutions of the first congressional session to be printed, and as a prospectus of sorts he sent copies of the resulting 131-page booklet to all the Southern governors. He also began to study the U.S. statutes with a view to revising them appropriately to meet Confederate needs.[5]

For his part, Secretary of State Robert Toombs could do little except to send Yancey, Rost, and Mann to Europe to beg for recognition of their fledgling nation. They carried copies of their Constitution; letters of introduction to Belgium, France, England, and Russia; reprints of federal laws that had been adopted by the Confederacy; a treatise on international law; and a generous allowance for expenses of one thousand dollars per month. They were instructed to study science, commerce, finance, the arts, and any other subject that might be useful. They were to purchase books, maps, political tracts—any materials that they might imagine and deem to be helpful to the Confederate State Department. Toombs would have liked to have given them leave to promise anything the foreign powers wanted in exchange for recognition, but he was constrained from doing so. Their commissions stated that they had authority to "agree, treat, consult, and negotiate on and concerning all matters and subjects interesting to both nations; and to conclude and sign a treaty or treaties, convention or conventions, touching the premises."[6] But their powers were circumscribed by the Constitution and by Davis's specific wishes. In reality they had little latitude in negotiating and were to explain Davis's constitutional theories by way of justifying a request for recognition. They were to inform the British government that the Confederates had "by act of their people in convention assembled, severed their connection with the United States, [having] assumed the powers which they delegated to the Federal Government for certain specified purposes under the compact known as the Constitution of the United States" and were now "endowed with every attribute of sovereignty and power necessary to entitle them to assume a place among the nations of the world." Yancey, Rost, and Mann were to assure their listeners—assuming the listeners cared—that secession had not been a hasty decision. They were to "allude to some of the more prominent of the causes" that led to secession, including the tariff and bounty issues and the Northern attempt "to overthrow the constitutional barriers [protecting] our property, our social system, and our right to control our own institutions."[7]

This appeal to the justice of the Confederate position on slavery was poorly calculated to win British enthusiasm for the South's independence, but Yancey, Rost, and Mann were also to point out tactfully but forcefully that the other slave states were expected to join the Confederacy (at this date including only the seven states of the Deep South) and that the Southern states produced about 95 percent "of all the cotton grown in the States which recently constituted the United States." The cotton from the Confederacy was worth at least $600 million to Great Britain, and the envoys were to ensure that "the British ministry will comprehend fully the condition to which the British realm would be reduced if the supply of our staple should suddenly fail or even be considerably diminished." After making this not so subtle allusion to the King Cotton theory, the envoys would presumably "negotiate treaties of friendship, commerce, and navigation" and after their successful completion would go on to Paris, Brussels, and St. Petersburg to play the game again.[8]

In reality Yancey, Rost, and Mann could ask for recognition, hoping to get it by their reliance on American constitutional tradition and by the threat of potential damage to British interests if there were a significant interruption in the flow of raw cotton. Everything would be in accord with the Constitution and Davis's approving or disapproving eyes. Any diplomatic success thus would take months.[9]

On the domestic front, there was more to be hoped for. Davis sent Martin Crawford, John Forsyth, and Andre B. Roman on a mission to Washington, D.C., with a message to President-elect Abraham Lincoln that they came with "an earnest desire to unite and bind together our respective countries by friendly ties."[10] Although neither Lincoln nor his choice for secretary of state, William H. Seward, would meet with them officially, they did succeed in gathering a lot of useful gossip (and some not so useful), which they dutifully and regularly telegraphed to Davis. Most encouragingly, they were greeted with friendliness by various foreign ministers to the United States, especially the Russian ambassador.[11] They became so bold as to propose foreign policy to Toombs: they specifically suggested that the Confederacy deny any designs on Cuba (a lie), in order to gain a sympathetic ear from the Spanish foreign minister. Toombs ignored them.

Crawford thought little of the new president of the United States, whom he called "a poor miserable stupid ass, having no opinions of his own, drifting from one place to another." Crawford nonetheless thought that he, Forsyth, and Roman were having a good effect and was encouraged that Seward indirectly promised that there would be no confrontation over Fort Sumter. But all too soon, the signs that the Confederate emissaries discerned from activities in the War and Navy Departments seemed ominous. On April 6, 1861, Roman learned of rumors that the United States would forcefully resupply either Fort Sumter or Fort Pickens within a few days. This they immediately reported to Davis, who in turn began preparing his fledgling nation for war.[12]

The U.S. postal system within the seceded states was the last among the federal agencies to be taken over by the Confederate government.[13] Indeed, the United States continued handling mail in the seceded states until after the firing on Fort Sumter. At every turn, in every facet, the Rebel mail system grew under the watchful eyes and careful guidance of the capable postmaster general, Judge John H. Reagan. His selection proved fortuitous, for President Davis had offered the position first to George Ellet and then to Wirt Adams, Mississippians who both refused, and twice to Reagan before he could be persuaded to accept. As a member of the Provisional Congress, Reagan had fought the selection of Davis as president: he had wanted him to be named commanding general. Davis regarded this as a major compliment. The two became close friends.

Reagan played a key role as one of the Confederacy's top statesmen. He later said that he twice refused the postmaster generalship because he thought it would be a thankless task, the people expecting more and faster results than possible: "I did not desire to become a martyr." But this self-made man had a keen and independent mind, and he dedicated himself completely once he made the leap. Reagan personally oversaw the conversion and fitting of the postal offices, and by the end of March 1861, he had filled all the jobs in his organization. To his great good fortune, and that of the Confederacy, he had been successful in securing the services of a great many former U.S. postal workers, in what was practically a coup d'etat. Reagan's secret agents garnered not only experienced people but also induced them to bring a supply of forms, postal maps, contract copies, books of instructions, and other necessary information. Local printers provided the additional forms, blanks, and record books. He began conducting an informal school, the experienced postal workers serving as teachers for the new ones. Almost all other postal personnel across the South, postmasters, clerks, carriers, and local or district officials, retained the same jobs they had held under the U.S. government.

Reagan relegated specific tasks to various bureaus. The Contract Bureau negotiated mail contracts and made arrangements for carrying the mail. The Appointment Bureau handled the establishment and discontinuance of post offices, changes of their sites and names, appointment and removal of postmasters and other agents, and the procurement and distribution of supplies. The Finance Bureau watched over monies, kept accounts, and distributed postage stamps and official envelopes. An Inspection Office oversaw the performance of mail contractors and route agents and to some extent that of postmasters. An Office of Military Telegrams administered the employment of officers of the various Southern telegraph companies as government agencies.

By April 1, Reagan issued a call for the printing of the first Confederate postage stamps and postal envelopes. He personally oversaw the selection of the grade of paper and the style of printing to be used. When the first stamp designs arrived, he engaged still more draftsmen to prepare postal maps for the new, and greatly truncated, delivery routes. Advertisements were published, soliciting bids for everything from mail sacks to wrapping paper, twine to sealing wax. The deadline for everything to be on hand was May 1. Reagan would oversee 1,305 routes operated by 1,087 contract carriers and 71 route agents, all at a cost of $56,000 per annum. Even the critical *Charleston Mercury* complimented him on his achievements.

That the U.S government continued mail service for so long a time after secession benefited the Confederacy greatly, although actually there had been sound reasons: many business houses in the North had financial accounts to settle with Southern customers, the U.S. Post Office hoped to collect the monies still owed to it by Southern postmasters, and the Federal War Department received much valuable information by mail from loyal citizens and secret agents. Moreover, intercepted mail from known Southern sympathizers and prosecession groups in the North led to many arrests.

In a brisk reaction to the seriousness of the situation after war broke out, the federal mail system in seceded states officially ceased to operate on May 28, 1861, and the United States declared postal intercourse between the two sections to be unlawful. Nevertheless, for several months postal matter passed between the North and South through Louisville and Nashville. The two post offices in those cities, one in the Union and the other in the Confederacy, were managed by persons who, sympathetic to continued international mail service, made use of the rail connection between them. The United States soon "demonetized" all stamps in Southern possession, but the Louisville Post Office let northbound letters mailed in the South go postage due, marking them with a special cancel: "Southn. Letter Unpaid." This continued until about mid-July 1861.

Despite a good start in establishing a system, recruiting people, and obtaining necessary material, and even with help from some federal officials, the Confederate postal system found itself rather suddenly on its own. Scant or nonexistent supplies necessitated a number of expedients. Until the appearance of official Confederate postage stamps, postmasters throughout the South prepared temporary substitutes known as "provisionals." These varied in almost every way imaginable, and so there are huge numbers of such relics today, in innumerable colors and designs. Some offices even produced provisional (postage-paid) envelopes. By and large the provisional system worked quite well until official stamps could be secured.

Christopher Memminger was among those who failed egregiously to foresee a long war; thus, the initial proposals concerning the Treasury were more suited for the first year of a young nation at peace. Making no plans for raising a large revenue, he called for a few minor taxes, a small bond issue, and the issue of a uniform paper currency. His first office was in an unswept room in Montgomery, with no desk or chair or writing paper. His chief clerk, Henry D. Capers, was authorized to draw on Memminger's own private bank account to assemble necessary furnishings because he had no funds, either. Like Reagan,

Memminger successfully enticed a number of important Treasury officials to leave Washington, and they brought with them instruction books and printed forms.[14] Secretary Memminger went about forming his department in an efficient but sometimes abrasive manner. He tended to be abrupt in his dealings with other people, and he sometimes manifested a rather sanctimonious attitude. He quickly managed to antagonize various staff members. Edward C. Elmore became treasurer, Alexander Clitherall recorder and later registrar, Lewis Cruger controller, Bolling Baker auditor, and Commander Raphael Semmes, recently resigned from the U.S. Navy, took charge of the Lighthouse Bureau. Philip Clayton became assistant secretary of the treasury. Twelve clerks assisted them, headed by Chief Clerk Capers.[15]

No modern government could possibly function financed solely by specie, and in any case, there was only $26 million of it in the entire Confederacy in early 1861, about one-half of that in New Orleans banks, that city being by far the largest center of commerce in the South. Over the course of the war, the Confederate government managed to obtain only $27 million in specie, including a melange of most issues circulating at the time, but mostly Spanish dollars, quarter- and half-dollars, English sovereigns, napoleons, and U.S. coins. Specie was required for two major reasons: to pay interest on certain kinds of bonds that were ultimately issued and to pay for foreign expenses. The Confederacy did plan to coin its own money because there was a considerable amount of bullion on hand, and there was hope of mining more in Georgia and North Carolina. Four sample half-dollars eventually were struck at the New Orleans mint; but lacking the needed skilled workers, the Treasury abandoned its plans for Confederate coinage. Paper proved necessary.[16] Thus, at the outset, Treasury notes were issued. The first shipment arrived in Montgomery on April 2, 1861, and several high officials made something of a show accepting their pay in notes. Alexander B. Clitherall took the first. A leading Montgomery citizen, he had first emerged as a valuable supporter of the Confederacy by providing the Congress with an original Gilbert Stuart portrait of George Washington (on loan from Clitherall's mother) to hang behind the rostrum. When legislation was passed authorizing Davis's secretary, Clitherall had temporarily filled that job, until he was relieved by Robert Josselyn.[17]

The first Confederate notes, totaling only $1 million in denominations of $50 or more, were in fact bonds, because they had to be endorsed each time they passed hands. Moreover, they bore a small amount of interest, which would tend to slow their circulation because people would often opt to hold them for that increase. There were, of course, also many state bank notes in circulation, but they did not possess the uniformity of value that the Confederate notes did.[18]

The first Confederate tax was the current U.S. tariff, incorporated into Confederate law when the first session of the Provisional Congress continued in force all laws of the United States not inconsistent with the Provisional Constitution. E. Merton Coulter has noted that the tariff became an instrument of commercial and industrial policy rather than a source of revenue. Douglas Ball, reviewing the difficulty of collecting the tariff under blockade circumstances, more accurately calls it "an exercise in abstract philosophy [rather] than a serious effort to raise revenue under war conditions." For practical purposes the tariff ceased to be an effective tax, and no more than $3.5 million was raised from that source during the entire war, most of that during the first year.[19]

The first touch of taxation was embodied in legislation passed on February 28, 1861, which authorized a $15 million issue of ten-year, 8 percent bonds. It provided for one-eighth of a cent per pound on all cotton exported to service the interest and principal. It was not a bad idea and in fact was uniquely innovative in American history, but it embittered many of the cotton planters, who believed correctly that they were being singled out from all other producers of wealth to bear this particular burden. Only $11 million of this loan was ever subscribed, however.[20]

Secretary of War Walker, despite his hunch that there would be no war, nevertheless worked hard. He was either at his desk or conferring with Davis, sometimes for hours at a time. Davis would ring a little bell on his table, and like Pavlov's dog, Josselyn would fetch Walker. But Walker carried out some tasks in a rather silly manner. On March 8, he sent out a troop requisition to the states, but instead of using the telegraph he had it sent by mail. Thus, Mississippi governor John Pettus, only two hundred miles away in Jackson, did not get his message for eight days; it took eleven to reach Governor Milton F. Perry in Florida. William C. Davis suggests that Walker "repeatedly forgot to think about the fastest ways of doing important things."[21]

The general staff organization was completed by late March, with Samuel Cooper appointed adjutant and inspector general of the Confederate army. Other staff officers included Abraham Myers (quartermaster general), and Lucius Northrop (commissary general). John Withers, the assistant adjutant general, arrived on April 3. A few days later the chief of the Ordnance Bureau, Josiah Gorgas, arrived. On August 31, 1861, Congress confirmed the appointment of full generals: Cooper, Albert S. Johnston, Robert E. Lee, Joseph E. Johnston, and P. G. T. Beauregard, in that order of rank. Cooper was given a date of rank from May 16.[22]

Davis made the selections for commissions as generals in the provisional army, but Walker handled the paperwork. On March 15 he sent word to Virginia that Robert E. Lee and Joseph E. Johnston had been commissioned brigadiers, although neither had yet resigned from the U.S. Army, as their state was still in the Union. Lee and Johnston had sound military credentials, but their commissions were also part of the early Confederate endeavor to induce more states to secede.

Walker was not a very diplomatic man, and he had poor relations with various state governors. Perhaps the worst were the dealings between Walker and the governors of Georgia and South Carolina over the matter of raising regiments and the granting of rank: the governors did not feel that their states were getting an adequate share of military and naval rank whenever their militia officers and regiments transferred into the Confederate army.[23]

The most confusing matter was the distinction among the regular army (which soon disappeared and became a theoretical paper force for all practical purposes), the provisional army, and the volunteers who were militia. Utterly at loose ends, Walker asked Attorney General Judah Benjamin for an official interpretation, which clarified the situation logically but did little to satisfy the governors (or Walker). The difficulty created by law and necessity so mixed up volunteers and provisionals that Walker could not determine which appropriations laws to apply to which troops. Attorney General Benjamin tried to explain which troops were in the provisional army and which in the volunteer army, but as he noted, "State troops, and volunteer companies and battalions are all fused into one force that is called the 'Provisional Army' . . . [and] under the law neither of the appropriations [about which Walker inquired] is applicable to your whole Provisional army as now constituted." In the end Benjamin could suggest only that Walker estimate the proportion of troops who were in each category and apply appropriations in corresponding proportion. This was no way to run an army.[24]

Despite bickering from various governors, however, a steady flow of volunteers did pour in. Governor Andrew B. Moore of Louisiana sent several hundred men; Pettus provided nearly forty companies from Mississippi; even some Indians trekked in from western Texas to become Confederate warriors. A considerable number of men from outside the Confederacy also attempted to enlist, including the National Volunteers from the District of Columbia, a company from Memphis, and huge numbers of Kentuckians. These non-Confederate citizens were turned down for the time being, because to take them might hurt diplomacy. Walker was convinced, and Davis concurred, that for the present there were more than enough soldiers coming in from the seven Rebel states.[25]

The comprehensive bill for raising military forces, which had been passed on March 6, proved to be a success, and Davis reported to Congress at the end of April that "requisitions for troops have been met with such alacrity that the numbers tendering their services have in every instance greatly exceeded the demand."[26] The law depended on local enthusiasm and leadership, for the usual procedure was that some local notable would announce his intention to raise a company or a regiment of volunteers. If he was held in high regard by his neighbors, he would be successful in securing sufficient individuals to fill the announced company or regiment, although some might have been embarrassed to find that in attempting to raise a regiment, they secured only enough volunteers for a company. In that event the would-have-been colonel might settle for a captaincy and go off to war with what he had, or he might continue to recruit, or he might let someone else take charge while he went home to sulk. At any rate, the men had the right to elect their own officers, but it was generally understood that the one who raised the company or regiment would be entitled to election as its commander.

The laws did create some confusion. In June 1861, after Virginia had joined the Confederacy, Davis requisitioned the states for troops. Virginia governor John Letcher complied but complained that Davis had no right to organize the men called for and appoint their officers and staff. He claimed that the Confederate Constitution reserved the right to appoint officers of the militia to the states. Since the troops Davis had called for were not to be regulars, Letcher assumed that they must be militia and that the governors could not justly be deprived of their appointment powers.[27]

In the following days, Congress enacted and the president signed several pieces of legislation designed to promote mobilization. Provision was made to receive volunteers without a call on the states, and on May 16 Davis signed a bill increasing the size of the army. Three additional regiments were authorized for the regular army, and the brigadier generals previously authorized were to become full generals. Bureaus were enlarged, and a few days later the president was authorized to assign regular officers to command and staff duty with volunteers.[28]

The Confederate military operated as the American military traditionally had, making contracts and purchasing whatever supplies might be needed. And even before there was a Quartermaster's Bureau, Davis began to authorize seizure of necessary war material. An immediate fuss was created when the president ordered that some vitally needed saltpeter be taken for use by the Confederate government. The prices demanded for such necessities were too high, admitted Robert Barnwell Rhett Sr., but he was nevertheless angered because the president had no authority to issue such an order. The president was, he thought, guilty of "military usurpation."[29] The Congress partially remedied this problem when it authorized the president to contract for munitions and the machines to make them,[30] though this did not meet the need. But over the next weeks legislation provided appropriations for the regular purchase of subsistence, munitions, and medical supplies.[31] Furthermore, the Confederacy supplemented traditional practice when states appropriated money and sent supplies not only to state units on home duty but also to its regiments on active duty with the provisional army. And from time to time private individuals made donations.

Sometimes the usual system was too slow, or the supplies were located at an inconvenient distance from where they were needed. In that case the army resorted to impressment, a method of supply sanctioned by such a long tradition in warfare that few people in the Confederate government gave it a second thought, until it began to create a problem. Most Confederates had no particular objection to this practice, especially if it was infrequent and their own property was not seized; but otherwise, the system inevitably created resentment. Still, it seemed like one of the ordinary powers of government in warfare. "It is a right inherent in the very nature of Governments," wrote the editor of the *Augusta (Georgia) Chronicle,* "whose duty it is to provide for the public defense at any sacrifice to private rights."[32] The Confederate Ordnance chief Josiah Gorgas declared in 1864 that "in such a war as this—a war for national existence—the whole mass of the nation must be engaged. It must be divided into those who go into the field and fight, and those who stay at home and support the fighting portion—supplying food and materials of war."[33]

The Confederate government used three sources of military supply: the conversion of internal agricultural and industrial production to war uses; overseas procurement; and the trade that developed and flourished through the enemy lines from Union territory. By the end of the war, the government controlled virtually all aspects of the Southern economy. This was accomplished, however, amid constant general bitterness and public hostility. The expansion of governmental administration proceeded slowly, nonetheless, dictated by a crisis psychology and with grudging tolerance.

On May 3, 1861, the Confederate Congress established the office of chaplain.[34] The president could appoint any number of chaplains, and they would be paid eighty-five dollars per month. The pay issue was destined to be a problem. Less than three weeks later, the Congress reduced chaplains' pay to fifty dollars per month because, as the main sponsor of the bill argued, they would have to work only one day out of seven and should surely not be recompensed at the same level as a lieutenant. (The congressmen also were somewhat concerned that unworthy ministers might seek appointment for pecuniary reasons.) But many protests ensued, and on April 19, 1862, the chaplains' pay was raised to eighty dollars per month.[35] In August 1861, the Congress allowed chaplains to draw the same rations as privates. In response, however, the Commissary General then ruled that chaplains could not buy family supplies from the Commissary, as other commissioned officers were allowed to do. It became increasingly difficult, and often impossible, for chaplains to live on their pay. Throughout the war, Confederate chaplains were always in short supply. The poor pay was a large part of the reason but not the whole: quite a few able ministers served well as officers in staff or even command positions, and many of them even served as combatants in the ranks.

The law implied that the chaplain would be a commissioned officer, but it did not designate any specific rank. Chaplains often were thought of, both among the public and among the soldiery, as captains and typically were deferred to as such. One of them wrote that "a good many of the men incorrectly suppose us to rank as 'captain' and frequently salute as such. Many address us as 'Preacher,' and more say 'Chaplain,' while not a few ring the charges as 'Parson' and 'Passon.' . . . I received a unique welcome as follows: 'We are glad to see you. We have long wanted a Chapel.'"

What a chaplain should wear was usually left to his own choosing. Some of them elected a regular military outfit, and some wore some special ornamentation, such as a feather in their hat, and still others wore their usual clerical garb. One showed himself to Brigadier General Theophilus T. Holmes, who deemed him to look too much like a military staff officer: "Go back, sir, this is no place for you; take off that sash, retire to the grove, and besiege a Throne of Grace."

As to denominational affiliation, the recommendations of regimental commanders carried much weight. There were occasional infelicitously selected individuals, such as one writer complained about in the *Confederate Baptist,* a contemporary periodical: "We have known of a post at which one of the Chaplains was a papal priest, where not more than a half a dozen out of six hundred soldiers are of his persuasion; and another, where two Episcopal clergymen were set over an equal number of men who were about exclusively Baptist and Methodists, with a few Presbyterians." Situations such as these, of course, were best avoided. On rare occasion a regiment might have the prospective chaplain give them a sample sermon. In some regiments, such as those of Tennessee (where state law required it), the men might choose their chaplain by popular election.

What exactly a chaplain should do was always an uncertainty: hold services, to be sure, but how often? And in what format? It was to be worked out on an individual basis. Chaplains also served as medical aides and as hospital attendants. Many of them provided soldiers with religious literature and served as counselors and confessors.

The U.S. military establishment on the brink of war was rather small. The pro-Southern elements soon detached themselves and joined the Confederacy. But when the conflict proved to be long lasting, the extant prewar establishment had to be supplemented extensively by nonprofessional personnel. The amateur officer—a farmer; a small-town lawyer; a grocer suddenly in command of a company or possibly even a regiment, studying *Hardee's Tactics* by night trying to learn what to do with his men the next morning—was a stereotype that rang true on both sides, especially during the war's first year. Both armies, North and South, were officered, sometimes even at quite high levels, by amateur warriors. Thomas J. (Stonewall) Jackson named a clergyman as his chief of staff; Braxton Bragg's chief had been head of the New Orleans waterworks before the war. Some few of the amateurs transcended their status and eventually become professionals themselves; more often, they did not. Nevertheless, a great many of them did manage to do fairly good jobs.

Northerners more typically had had previous job experiences in civilian life that rendered them capable soldiers; many regiments possessed within their ranks as many as sixty different occupations, and rarely was there a unit that did not have experienced individuals who could perform all manner of repairs. This was not so in the Southern army. But there was a crucial factor that matched the North's occupational advantage: the antebellum South had established a great many military schools throughout the region.[36]

In *The Militant South,* historian John Hope Franklin has suggested that support for the Southern military schools reflected a distinctly Southern martial spirit—that antebellum Southerners had been growing increasingly militant with the passage of time.[37] More recently, Bruce Allardice has found that the schools often lacked much support in public monies because the prewar South had an egalitarian bias against higher education, and the schools were popularly looked on as playgrounds for the sons of wealthy planters.[38] But there were lots of military schools in the South. And if having attended one of them did not render a lad fit to command an army, it assuredly made him far superior fodder for a growing military establishment. If someone already knew how to drill, how to shoot, and had some discipline and familiarity with military organization, he clearly was more able to step into the lower ranks than those who did not. Then, when occasion opened the way, they rose in the hierarchy.

By far the greatest academy in this genre was the Virginia Military Institute, founded in 1839; indeed, other military schools around the South were fashioned in tune with VMI. Often its graduates became the teachers in the other military schools. By 1843 South Carolina had converted its Columbia Arsenal and Charleston Citadel into interconnected military schools. In 1847 Kentucky chartered the privately organized Kentucky Military Institute at Frankfort. Alabama had several private military schools, which the state aided with public monies. Mississippi loaned muskets to the Brandon State Military College. Georgia loaned one hundred muskets and one hundred light cavalry swords to Bowden College. Florida furnished arms both to the West Florida Seminary and the Quincy Military Academy. Arkansas provided six cannons for use at the Arkansas Military Institute.

Huge numbers of graduates from military schools eventually joined the Confederate army. Allardice points out that the previous studies on West Point and the Confederate Army focused on graduates, but there were large numbers of Southerners who became Rebel soldiers who attended the Academy for a time and did not graduate. That is true as well of attendees who did not graduate from the other military schools. While 304 West Point graduates joined the Confederate Army, there were at least 12,000 men, and possibly many more, signing up who had matriculated at one or another of ninety-six Southern military schools. (By contrast, there have been identified only fifteen military schools in the free states during the period from 1827 to 1860.)[39]

These men from the various military schools, however, found their ways into one—and only one—of the field armies the Confederacy eventually created, as Richard McMurry has observed. This was the one Robert E. Lee took command of early in 1862, remaining at its head to the end of the war: the Army of Northern Virginia.[40] Allardice suggests that "a look at the numbers for just one military school, VMI, bears out McMurry's thesis. No fewer than 180 field officers of Lee's army had attended VMI—enough to officer an entire army corps."[41]

Eventually the Confederacy named 8 men to be full generals, 17 as lieutenant generals, 72 to the rank of major general, and 328 as brigadier generals.[42] Some of them, to be sure, were woeful substitutes for qualified general officers. Some were good at lower levels but finally reached—or surpassed—their levels of incompetence. A few of them proved to be great. Sometimes, though quite rarely, the great ones were untutored geniuses. Most of the greats were well-trained and experienced professionals.

In mid-March 1861 the Congress adjourned. No one lamented this, save the keepers and staffs of the hotels and rooming houses in Montgomery. "I am delighted to leave this place," wrote William Dorsey Pender to his wife. He had only been there for three days, seeking appointment as a captain in the army. "It is not pleasant to loaf in a large city much less a small one."[43] And a South Carolinian, who was in part venting his displeasure with the secret sessions that had been held, commented, "The Congress is not of much use, and may just as well adjourn as not."[44]

The drive for ratification of the permanent Constitution continued. South Carolina ratified it on April 3; and Florida, the last of the original seven states to do so, acted on April 22. Meanwhile, many congressmen traveled through the border states, spreading the good news about their new Constitution and gushing about its conservative nature, which they hoped would appeal to those who might be suspicious of the motives of the first seceders. Soon there came pouring back to Montgomery cheery predictions of more new Confederate states.[45]

Memminger meanwhile notably addressed the collection of customs duties and the designation of ports of entry along the Confederacy's then northern border and elsewhere. In late March he declared a port of entry at Hernando, Mississippi, supposedly on the Mississippi Central Railroad, though, alas, the town was situated more than thirty miles from the track. One Natchez editor, upset because his city had been passed over, suggested that "a little more geographical attention would not hurt the Department."[46]

Of those who remained in Montgomery, no one seemed to be working harder than Secretary of War Walker. Unfortunately, however, his intense preoccupation with his labors tended to render him sometimes confused, thus delaying the accomplishment of his desires through his lack of mental acuity and the application of good sense.[47]

Relations with other slave states were at the time an important foreign policy issue. Despite Secretary of State Toombs's occasional bluster, in truth he would have forced himself to adopt nearly any facade in order to bring about both expansion of the seven-state Confederacy and its recognition by foreign powers. Indeed, observers in Montgomery soon perceived a degree of constrained harmony between Toombs and Davis, despite their history of clashing with each other (a few years previously they had come close to facing each other in a duel). Though never becoming intimate friends, they now worked together.[48]

Everyone in Montgomery was anxious for positive word from the Yancey-Rost-Mann delegation, but progress in Europe took months to develop. Meanwhile, the most anticipated telegrams in the Confederate capital were from the other diplomatic mission in Washington, D.C. Crawford, Forsyth, and Roman, however, had conferred only with Seward through an intermediary, John A. Campbell, a member of the U.S. Supreme Court from Alabama.[49]

Apparently Seward gave the three Southerners the impression that he, not Lincoln, would be able to set policy. He refused to see them personally, but he led them to believe—or perhaps they were led by wishful thinking—that Fort Sumter would be evacuated on March 20. But the day came and went and nothing happened; Seward begged for more time. Meanwhile, the commissioners were somewhat coddled by a Russian diplomat, who assured them that Seward was favorably inclined toward their desires. Seward then consented to an "accidental" meeting with them at the Russian's home on the evening of March 28. Again, though, there was only more delay.[50]

The commissioners kept sending upbeat messages back to Montgomery. To some there, including Davis, the delay merely confirmed what they already believed: that war was inevitable. Davis pushed on more firmly with war preparations,[51] but the situation deteriorated rapidly. On April 6 Lincoln sent South Carolina a message that he would send a fleet to resupply Fort Sumter but promised that if the fleet were unmolested he would not attempt a military reinforcement. The next day he set in motion plans to land troops at the fort. The commissioners learned of these plans and felt their mission was being forced to an end. On the evening of April 7 they sent Seward a demand that he reply to their earlier memorandum of March 12, in which they had asked for a formal statement of Union intent. At two o'clock in the afternoon of April 8, Frederick Seward, acting as his father's secretary, handed the commissioners a memorandum that had been written three weeks before, on March 15. It declared that Seward could not meet with the Confederate emissaries; their mission was over, and they promptly telegraphed Toombs to that effect.[52]

Secretary of War Walker quickly decided that he could use John Forsyth's services since his usefulness to Toombs was over. Walker telegraphed him, telling him to start looking around for guns. Within two days he managed to buy up ninety tons of cannon powder and ten tons of rifle powder, which a New York firm had offered for sale. Trying to keep his good fortune a secret, Forsyth referred to his purchase as "rope." He also managed to buy two thousand pistols and several thousand rifles.[53]

Newly resigned U.S. Army men began streaming into Montgomery, and one by one Walker commissioned them and sent them to the various fortifications taken over by the Confederate states. Some of the men were famous, like the Texan Indian fighter Ben McCulloch, who was assigned command of a new regiment intended for service on the frontier. Davis's fellow Mississippian Earl Van Dorn was given command in Texas. Davis walked with him down to the river bluff, where Van Dorn boarded a steamboat and lifted his hat in salute to the gathered crowd, while the calliope played the "Marseillaise." Thus he and many other young men began marching off to near-certain war. "They were stalwart, handsome fellows, and had intelligent faces," wrote one Virginian then visiting in Montgomery. "They will make the best fighting material in the world."[54]

Whenever he thought of the coming events at Charleston President Davis was equally confident. "Our people are a gallant, impetuous and determined people, worthy, in all respects, of their heroic sires," he told Charles E. L. Stuart, a prosecession New York journalist. "What they resolve to do, that, they most assuredly, mean to persevere in doing." Davis said that he abhorred violence, but the fact was that throughout his life his hair-trigger temper often had made him quick to resort to action.[55]

At this time Stuart had no job, but he spent much of his time with the other journalists and was hoping for an appointment, possibly a generalcy from Davis. "That vile Bohemian," one of Davis's official family termed him, "a free lance of a fellow." Nevertheless, he had a bit of self-deprecating wit, calling himself one of the "conviction-burdened nobodies" who then were streaming into Montgomery looking for some kind of billet. He managed to become well acquainted with Davis, who confided many of his own convictions to him and which he recorded.[56]

Within the cabinet, only Toombs stood adamant against opening fire at Sumter and thus beginning a war. On April 9, in a heated session, he later claimed that he had warned, "The firing upon that fort will inaugurate a civil war greater than any the world has yet seen." He paced to and fro in the cabinet room and alluded to the words of Henry Wadsworth Longfellow: "The shot that is fired at Fort Sumter will reverberate 'round the world.'" The Confederates should move slowly and deliberately, he cautioned. "At this time, it is suicide, murder, and will lose us every friend at the North. You will wantonly strike a hornet's nest which extends from mountains to ocean, and legions, now quiet, will swarm out and sting us to death. It is unnecessary; it puts us in the wrong; it is fatal."[57] His words fell on deaf ears.

There were to be sure potent arguments that supported the contention that the Confederacy should indeed take Fort Sumter. As Cooper sums them up, "The Union occupation mocked the independence of the Confederacy. . . . Zealots in South Carolina might strike against the fort on their own initiative . . . [and thus] undermine the authority of the Confederate government. . . . [the attack probably] would mobilize the citizens behind their government and, perhaps more important, bring the Upper South, especially Virginia, within the Confederate fold." Thus, "The weight of these considerations . . . directed Davis's course."[58]

Until the formation of the Confederacy, all the seceded states, but especially South Carolina, functioned as separate nations. Even following establishment of the new central government, the Palmetto State maintained its own army. Beginning in February 1861 the numerous professional and quasi-professional soldiers in the Army of South Carolina assumed various duties, particularly in and around Charleston, relieving cadets from the Citadel and other volunteers who had been on duty since the unarmed U.S. merchant ship the *Star of the West* had been fired upon and forced away on January 9.

The Federal commander in Charleston was Major Robert Anderson. After South Carolina had seceded, Anderson moved his force of eighty-five soldiers and forty-three civilians from Fort Moultrie on the coast into Fort Sumter, the strongest of several military installations in the harbor. South Carolina officials demanded that Anderson evacuate his command of "foreign troops" from Confederate soil, but Anderson refused, and an impasse developed.

As the Sumter crisis simmered, President Davis decided to send a general officer to assume command of operations there, Brigadier General P. G. T. Beauregard, whom many persons thought looked like Napoleon in a gray uniform. He arrived in Charleston on March 3 and three days later appointed a personal staff: recently resigned U.S. Army captain and South Carolina native Stephen D. Lee (who held a commission in the Army of South Carolina), and several high luminaries, former-governors, and senators.[59]

During the ensuing five weeks, both Confederate and Union authorities moved closer to war. Attitudes hardened; and in the first week of April, Beauregard stopped allowing provisions and mail to enter Sumter. Since the Confederate emissaries in Washington had reported rumors that Lincoln had decided at the same time both to hold the fort by force if necessary and to send a naval relief expedition with supplies, the Confederates decided to capture the place before the Unionists could make it any stronger. "The first blow must be successful, both for its moral and physical consequences," Davis told South Carolina governor Francis Pickens. "A Failure would demoralize our people and injuriously affect us in the opinion of the world as reckless and precipitate."[60]

On Thursday, April 11, Beauregard believed he was ready to make his move. The relief expedition ordered by Lincoln was in sight, although a heavy swell was keeping the Federal steamer *Baltic* from approaching Fort Sumter. Beauregard drafted his formal demand that the Federals surrender or he would open fire. He called several aides to his office: Lee, Colonel James Chesnut Jr., and an aide-de-camp to Governor Pickens. They shoved off from Charleston wharf at 2:40 P.M. in a small rowboat, flying a white flag. They arrived, the Federal officer of the day met them, and they were escorted into the guardroom, where Major Anderson awaited them.[61]

Anderson finally produced a written reply about 4:30 P.M. He would not surrender. The aides accepted the answer and spent a few brief moments in courteous conversation with Anderson as they walked together toward the wharf. There Anderson threw a new light on the situation when he asked if Beauregard would open fire at once, with no further notice. Colonel Chesnut, although in truth he did not know, said no—there would be further warning before fire was opened. Anderson then said that if his command were "not hacked to pieces" by the Confederate batteries, he would be "starved out in a few days." Not at first realizing that the fort might thus be taken without a fight, the aides got into their boat; then Chesnut did a double take and quickly asked Anderson to repeat his remark, asking him for permission to quote it in their report to Beauregard.[62]

Learning of Anderson's comment, Beauregard at once telegraphed the government in Montgomery. The War Department answered with orders to ask Anderson to state a specific time when he would evacuate; if Anderson replied unsatisfactorily, then Beauregard was authorized to take the fort by force. The aides quickly began readying for another boat trip.[63] Beauregard carefully instructed them to deliver the ultimatum to Anderson and to decide themselves whether or not the Union commander's answer was satisfactory. If it was not, then the aides should go at once to Fort Johnson on James Island and give the command for a signal gun to be fired. On the way to the barge, they were joined by Roger Pryor, a hot-tempered and loose-tongued Virginia congressman, who was there with one purpose in mind—to help force striking a blow. Their barge slipped off silently into the foggy night and reached Sumter forty-five minutes after midnight.[64] Major Anderson received the message and again called his officers into a private conference while the Confederates waited.

The Federals debated so long that the Southerners grew impatient. Finally, at 3:15 A.M., April 12, 1861, Anderson gave his answer. He would evacuate on April 15, four days thence. But he added so many "ifs" to his answer that it became no answer at all—if he were not fired upon, if he were not resupplied, and if he received no orders to the contrary. The Confederate officers took but five minutes to decide and to declare that the reply was unsatisfactory. Sitting in one of the casemates of the fort, Colonel Chesnut dictated a note, which Captain Lee inscribed, and the governor's aide made a copy. The Confederacy would open fire on Fort Sumter one hour from that moment; it then was 3:20 A.M.[65] The Confederates rowed over to Fort Johnson in the thickening haze and fog, and the aides informed the commander there to open fire at the appointed time.

The bombardment continued all day. "Tolerable good firing on our side," Lee noted; "rather wild from Sumter." Actually neither side did any real damage to the other. There was much noise, but it was a bloodless conflict. A dull drizzle that fell all day added the only touch of gloom to the scene. Hot shot fired from Fort Moultrie landed within the walls of Sumter and caused the barracks to burst into flames.

Suddenly, near midday, the fort's flag went down. Beauregard dispatched Lee, Roger Pryor, and William Porcher Miles, a Charlestonian and member of the Confederate Congress for the duration of the war, to ask Anderson if the Federals wanted any help—a subtle way of asking if they were ready to surrender.[66]

The flag had come down once because it had been shot down. The Federals then improvised a new pole and remounted their colors. But then Louis T. Wigfall, who had been on Morris Island, reached the fort in a small rented boat, announced that he was from Beauregard's headquarters, and demanded surrender of the fort. Anderson was interested, and Wigfall promised generous terms, so they reached an agreement. Then the white flag was hoisted. Soon after that Wigfall left, and Lee, Pryor, and Miles arrived. They announced their mission, whereupon Anderson told them of Wigfall's visit. The aides responded that Wigfall's action was unofficial, that even they did not have the authority to negotiate terms. Anderson then threatened to resume fire, but he was dissuaded.

By agreement with Anderson, the aides returned to Beauregard with a written statement explaining the arrangement with Wigfall. Anderson would not fire in the meantime and would surrender if Beauregard agreed to the stated terms. He did, and thus fell Fort Sumter. Lee remembered that "Major Anderson, his officers, and men were blackened by smoke and cinders, and showed signs of fatigue and exhaustion." The officers engaged in a little friendly conversation, and each revealed to the other that they had sustained no personnel casualties whatever during the entire bombardment of nearly forty hours. Lee recalled that "congratulations were exchanged on so happy a result." It was war, but many of the opposing soldiers still liked each other.[67]

"There has been no blood spilled more precious than that of a mule," Davis declared on first hearing the news. There were celebrations in the streets of Montgomery, but Davis did not participate; he soberly reflected on the ominous future. He confessed to intimates that he feared the North would not take the episode lightly. Sumter's fall, he told them, was "either the beginning of a fearful war, or the end of a political contest." One observer thought Davis seemed to be neither "elated or depressed," just as one might expect in an active-negative personality.[68] He did, however, try his hand at both poetry and pun—not his forte: "With mortar, Paixhan and petard, we tender old Abe our Beauregard."[69]

The only death of the entire episode took place during the surrender ceremonies the next day. Major Anderson had his guns fire a salute to the Union flag, and some shells accidentally exploded, instantly killing Yankee private Daniel Hough—the war's first casualty. Several other persons, one of whom died soon after, sustained serious wounds; and the Charleston women who tended to them became the Civil War's first nurses.

Later, Beauregard, Governor Pickens, and various other Southern notables toured the fort. Anderson was supposed to have been gone by this time, but the Federals elected to stay and bury their dead soldier inside the fort with full military honors. The Confederates witnessed the ceremony, a "very impressive scene" and an "impressive prayer by the sailor's chaplain from the city." Then Anderson and his men marched out, in full-dress uniforms, carrying their arms, the Federal band playing "Yankee Doodle." The Southerners hoisted the Confederate and Palmetto flags, and all batteries in the harbor fired salutes. The South had acquired a new fort and celebrated the victory. Soon after the popular "Beauregard Victory March" was written.[70]

The Fort Sumter episode had tremendous results. For the North the response was much like that of the United States after Pearl Harbor in 1941. The mass of the populace on both sides now embraced the reality that war had come. Charles Royster recalls the words of the British military historian, Basil Henry Liddell Hart: "That vast human sigh of relief [is] one of the most recurrent phenomena in history, marking the outset of every great conflict."[71]

The decision at Sumter was a controversial issue then and remains so today. The suggestion, formally articulated by the historian Charles W. Ramsdell, has been that Lincoln carefully forced the Confederacy to fire the first shot in order to place it in the position of aggressor.[72] To his contemporaries who so asserted, Davis replied, "If that notion is correct, then Lincoln was not only a shrewd manager of events, he was actually the aggressor himself." Later historians, notably Richard N. Current, believe that Lincoln did expect that the South might fire the first shot at Sumter, but he rather hoped that it would not.[73] James M. McPherson believes the latter interpretation most plausible, but of course there is no certainty. There were a number of Confederate leaders who believed that if the South struck a blow it would bring in the border states that were still standing aloof, and as events turned out, they were correct. "Therefore," writes McPherson, "to Abraham Lincoln's challenge, Shall it be Peace or War? Jefferson Davis replied, War," and issued the fateful order to Beauregard to fire before the Union garrison could be reinforced.[74] And yet, Sumter was an accidental beginning. As Grady McWhiney has shown, Davis and General Braxton Bragg had schemed to take the Union garrison at Fort Pickens near Pensacola, but plans went awry; "thus war came at Fort Sumter only because the Confederates were neither subtle enough nor strong enough to begin it at Fort Pickens."[75]

Until war came, the North had not really been gearing up for it; and in the South, too, there followed a much keener commitment to preparation. There was a stark contrast between a mood of anxious uncertainty, which had prevailed before Sumter's fall, and the purposeful action that followed it. One Southerner, Mary Tucker Magill, later recalled the months that ensued as "the holiday times of the war." A Northern minister, the Reverend Henry Clay Fish, indicated that God had given the war in order to awaken the national pride and the moral sense that had almost been lost in the secession winter. Once given the war, the people not only proved equal to accepting it, but they indeed seemed to thrive on it. The war thus must be prosecuted to the fullest—quite simply, because it had begun.[76]

Jefferson Davis. (Courtesy National Archives.)

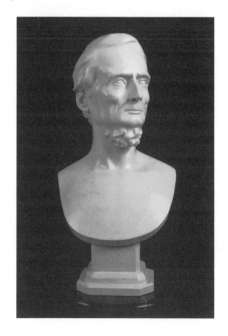

Jefferson Davis bust by Frederick Volck. Frederick Volck, 1833–1891, was a Maryland-based artist living in Richmond in 1862 when he did this bust of Davis. He used pictures and visual observations of Davis, but there was no formal sitting. (Courtesy The Museum of the Confederacy, Richmond, Virginia. Photography by Katherine Wetzel.)

Varina Davis with Winnie Davis as a baby. Varina Davis, 1826–1906, was Jefferson Davis's second wife. They married in 1845. Winnie Davis, 1864–1898, whose proper name was Varina Anne, was nicknamed "pie-cake" and became known after the war as "The Daughter of the Confederacy." (Courtesy Transylvania University Library, Special Collections and Archives.)

The White House of the Confederacy. The Davis family lived in the Confederate White House in Richmond. The picture is of the south portico. Today the building is part of The Museum of the Confederacy. (Courtesy The Museum of the Confederacy, Richmond, Virginia. Photography by Katherine Wetzel.)

Robert E. Lee. Lee's first year as a
Confederate general was undistinguished,
but after taking command of the Army of
Northern Virginia in June 1862 his impres-
sive success made him the leading hero of
the Confederacy. (Courtesy Library of
Congress, Prints and Photographs
Division, LC-B8172-0001 DLC.)

Joseph E. Johnston. J. E. Johnston,
along with Pierre G. T. Beauregard,
was in command at First Manassas.
However, he and Davis soon quarreled
over his rank. Their mutual dislike
degenerated into lifelong hatred that
impaired the effectiveness of both
men. Johnston held several important
commands, including the defense of
Richmond until his wound in May
1862, but most notably the Army of
Tennessee in defense of Atlanta after
Bragg's resignation in December 1863.
(From Francis Trevelyan Miller, editor
in chief, *The Photographic History of
the Civil War in Ten Volumes* [New
York: The Review of Reviews,
1911–1912], vol. 10, *Armies and
Leaders,* 1912, 241.)

Pierre G. T. Beauregard. Beauregard's most important commands were at Charleston during the Fort Sumter crisis; at First Manassas; at Shiloh, after the death of Albert Sidney Johnston; at the Union siege of Charleston; and in support of Lee during the Petersburg campaign. Relations between Beauregard and Jefferson Davis deteriorated to the point of intense mutual dislike. (Courtesy Madison Bay Company.)

James Longstreet. Most of Longstreet's significant service was under the command of Lee, who called him "my old warhorse." He disagreed with Lee's tactics at Gettysburg; for generations, former Confederates blamed him for Lee's defeat there. (From Francis Trevelyan Miller, editor in chief, *The Photographic History of the Civil War in Ten Volumes* [New York: The Review of Reviews, 1911–1912], vol. 10, *Armies and Leaders,* 1912, 245.)

Albert Sidney Johnston. A. S. Johnston was an old friend of Davis since their days together at West Point. Davis expected much from Johnston, but he was killed at Shiloh before his abilities were fully tested. (From Francis Trevelyan Miller, editor in chief, *The Photographic History of the Civil War in Ten Volumes* [New York: The Review of Reviews, 1911–1912], vol. 9, *Poetry and Eloquence of Blue and Gray,* 1912, 93.)

Braxton Bragg. Bragg became one of Davis's early favorites and was appointed to command of the Army of Tennessee after Beauregard's dismissal. He resigned his command after his disastrous defeat at Missionary Ridge in November 1863. (From Benson J. Lossing, *A History of the Civil War, 1861–65, and the Causes That Led up to the Great Conflict* [New York: The War Memorial Association, 1912], 126.)

Leonidas Polk. Polk was another friend of Davis from West Point days. An Episcopal bishop in 1861, he was appointed a major general by Davis and was killed in 1864. (From Francis Trevelyan Miller, editor in chief, *The Photographic History of the Civil War in Ten Volumes* [New York: The Review of Reviews, 1911–1912], vol. 10, *Armies and Leaders,* 1912, 247.)

John Bell Hood. Hood lost the use of his left arm at Gettysburg and his right leg at Chickamauga. He was promoted to full general and led the Army of Tennessee to virtual destruction at the Battle of Nashville in 1864. (Courtesy Madison Bay Company.)

Stephen D. Lee. Stephen Dill Lee served as an aide to General Beauregard during the Fort Sumter crisis and later served with distinction in both the eastern and western theaters. He ended the war as a lieutenant general. (Courtesy Madison Bay Company.)

John C. Pemberton. Pemberton surrendered his army of thirty thousand to General Ulysses S. Grant on July 4, 1863, to end the siege of Vicksburg. A Pennsylvanian by birth and upbringing, Pemberton never regretted his decision to side with the Confederacy. (From Benson J. Lossing, *A History of the Civil War, 1861–65, and the Causes That Led up to the Great Conflict* [New York: The War Memorial Association, 1912], 348.)

Alexander H. Stephens. Stephens was a reluctant secessionist in 1861 but was elected to the vice presidency of the Confederacy in order to preserve the appearance of Confederate unity. He and Davis soon disagreed on several vital issues. Disgusted, Stephens spent much of the war at his home in Georgia. He was one of the delegates Davis sent to the unsuccessful peace conference at Hampton Roads in February 1865. (Courtesy Library of Congress, Prints and Photographs Division, LC-B8172-1430 DLC.)

Robert Toombs. Toombs had support for the presidency of the Confederacy but lost the backing of his own state's delegation. He served briefly as secretary of state and then went into the army. He resigned his commission after the Battle of Antietam. (From Benson J. Lossing, *A History of the Civil War, 1861–65, and the Causes That Led up to the Great Conflict* [New York: The War Memorial Association, 1912], 36.)

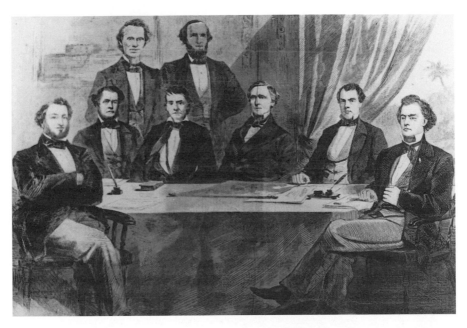

The cabinet of the Confederate States at Montgomery. The first cabinet, 1861, *left to right*: Attorney General Judah P. Benjamin, Secretary of the Navy Stephen R. Mallory, Secretary of the Treasury Christopher G. Memminger, Vice President Alexander H. Stephens (not actually a cabinet member), Secretary of War Leroy P. Walker, President Jefferson Davis, Postmaster General John H. Reagan, Secretary of State Robert Toombs. (From *Harpers Weekly,* June 1, 1861, 340. Courtesy Elwyn B. Robinson Department of Special Collections, Chester Fritz Library, University of North Dakota.)

Joseph E. Brown. Governor Brown of Georgia was quick to object to several Confederate policies, most notably conscription, and did his best to obstruct their enforcement. But he exerted much energy to ensure proper supply of Georgia troops and to provide relief for needy families at home. (Courtesy Georgia Department of Archives and History.)

Zebulon B. Vance. Governor Vance of North Carolina was originally a Unionist, but he entered the army after the fall of Fort Sumter. He resigned his colonel's commission to run for governor in 1862. He was often viewed as an obstruction to the war effort by Jefferson Davis, although both Davis and Vance tried to smoothe over their differences. (Courtesy North Carolina Division of Archives and History, Raleigh.)

5

THE WAIT FOR LAND BATTLES

In the immediate aftermath of Fort Sumter, President Abraham Lincoln called for seventy-five thousand volunteers to put down what he termed a "combination of forces too strong to be put down by ordinary course of law," and he announced a blockade of Southern coasts. President Jefferson Davis countered by announcing the licensing of privateers. Davis did not sanction government sponsorship of blockade runners, however; not until late in the war did he consider blockade running anything but a private affair.[1] Lincoln responded on April 19, 1861, with a proclamation of a blockade by the North of all Southern ports, and he threatened that any captured privateers would be hanged. The blockade started immediately but was weak at first, and never total, although it grew stronger as each year of the war unfolded.

Lincoln's call for volunteers and the proclaimed blockade clearly indicated to Davis the war he had both long feared and anticipated was imminent. Judah Benjamin told one of his friends that the Confederate leadership definitely regarded Lincoln's proclamation "an unmistakable declaration of war."[2] Davis called the Provisional Congress back to Montgomery to convene in a special session beginning on April 29.

He delivered a message, acknowledging that hostilities had begun, but he insisted that the war had been forced on the Confederacy. Secession, he argued, did not mean that the Confederacy had wanted war. What about the commission he had sent to Washington in pursuit of peace? He asserted that the Confederates had not been treated fairly: "The crooked paths of diplomacy can scarcely furnish an example so wanting in courtesy, in candor, and directness as was the course of the United States Government toward our commission in Washington." And so now war would come. "We feel that our cause is just and holy. . . . We protest solemnly in the face of mankind that we desire peace at any sacrifice save that of honor and independence; we seek no conquest, no aggrandizement, no concession of any kind from the States with which we were lately confederated; all we ask is to be let alone."[3] Ensuing events and assertions soon proved that Davis did not quite precisely mean what he said.

At three o'clock in the afternoon on the day that Fort Sumter surrendered, General Braxton Bragg arrested Lawrence H. Mathews, a newspaper correspondent in Pensacola, Florida, for publishing an article that suggested that Bragg had given him some sensitive information about sand batteries soon to be raised on the island of Santa Rosa. Mathews was expelled from Pensacola and soon was writing letters from the capital in Montgomery, apparently under house arrest. He was the first of an untold many Confederate citizens who were incarcerated and held without due process of law. Historian Mark Neely has discovered the records of 4,108 civilian prisoners held by military authority, records that were preserved but filed in such a confusing manner as to keep them hidden from researchers until recently. According to Neely, "There would *never* be a day during the Civil War when Confederate military prisons did not contain political prisoners." Quite simply, "the Confederate government curtailed many civil liberties and imprisoned troublesome citizens." And though some individuals might from time to time protest, this continued for the entirety of the Confederacy's existence.[4]

Civil liberties were further curtailed in the Confederacy by the War Department's establishment of a domestic passport system. Every time citizens wished to travel, they were obliged to obtain a government document authorizing the trip. This applied to all railroad passage for most of the war. It also imposed restrictions on all other modes of travel, variously, but throughout the would-be nation. Passports were required in some places as early as summer 1861 and nearly everywhere by summer 1864. Neely tells us that "the passport system interfered with religion, business, journalism, and government itself. It could [even] keep dying Catholics from receiving last rites and government assessors from appraising property for vital taxation."[5]

Neely suggests that Davis, specifically, as his memoirs show, and postwar white Southerners, generally, wanted to paint a picture of much greater solidarity of support for the war than was the actuality. We have long known that the Lincoln administration on numerous occasions curtailed civil liberties for the good of the cause.[6] But Neely asserts that in truth the presidents of both sides essentially did the same things—they bent the laws for the sake of greater security and stability. "The political prisoners on both sides seem much alike," Neely observes. "They came mostly from border areas—in the Confederacy, especially Tennessee and Virginia," but North Carolina's coastlines, too, and "many prisoners came from areas near the military fronts." As Neely puts it: "Lincoln was no 'dictator,' and Jefferson Davis was no 'constitutionalist.'"[7]

We believe that, to an extent, Neely potentially distorts the true portrait of Davis by putting it this way, for Davis was a constitutionalist to an extreme degree. Neely's assessment leaves no room for ambiguity and paradox—both always operative in any American governmental functioning. Yet he offers a new and correct perspective, which we too are trying to reveal here, that Davis was an American president and a tangible forerunner of presidents to come. Otherwise, we agree with Neely: "What really happened: the Confederate government restricted civil liberties as modern democratic nations did in war."[8]

A phrase that frequently appears in the Confederate records of civilian prisoners is "Union man." Indeed, over 13 percent of the civilian prisoners were incarcerated because of their political opinions. Neely tells us that "there was never a moment in Confederate history when pro-Union opinions could be held without fear of government restraint."[9] And yet there were great numbers of instances when Southerners did express pro-Union sentiments. Jon Wakelyn has recently provided a book-length compendium of pro-Union Confederate pamphlets.[10] Generally, the populace in all the highland regions of the Confederacy either was unenthusiastic about the new government or outright hostile to it. The people in fifty-five counties of western Virginia actually broke away and were admitted to the Union in 1863 as the last slave state, West Virginia.

The same would have happened in eastern Tennessee except that there the Confederate military force prevailed sufficiently long to prevent what occurred in western Virginia, where the Union early established predominance. Even so, squelching the populace's pro-Union leanings in the highlands regions occupied much of the Confederate government's time and resources. Neely chides previous general historians of the Confederacy for having paid so little attention to the troubles in Tennessee, where in November 1861 a revolt erupted that was "the largest internal uprising against Confederate authority during the Civil War." East Tennesseans made up over 16.5 percent of the known civilian prisoners incarcerated by the Confederacy.[11]

Antebellum white Southerners had been anxious that the black populace, slave and free alike, posed a danger to stability and safety. These fears in no way subsided after the war came; if anything, they intensified. And some blacks in the Confederacy did indeed act in ways that endangered national security; they were almost always willing to aid Union forces by providing information and assisting as guides. As Neely has observed, many blacks who proved troublesome to the Confederacy had their liberties suppressed: "Among the 4,108 [known] civilian prisoners, at least 345 (about 8 percent) were African American. They are surely under-reported."[12]

Although the vast bulk of the refugees from the European radical revolutionary movements who came to the United States stayed in the North, some of them went to the South, and conservative Southerners feared that their ideals might impel them to act in a way contrary to the Confederacy's good. On August 8, 1861, the Congress passed the Alien Enemies Act of the Confederate States of America. It proclaimed that "all natives, citizens, denizens or subjects of the hostile nation or government, being males of fourteen years of age and upward, who shall be within the Confederate States and not citizens thereof . . . [are] liable to be apprehended, restrained or secured and removed as alien enemies."[13] Such acts are common in modern nations at war, though perhaps also shameful; Neely, however, chides all Civil War historians for having so underemphasized or ignored this reality.[14]

The citizens of the states that constituted the Upper South were less impulsive than those in the seven original Confederate States: for the former, the mere election of Abraham Lincoln to the U.S. presidency had not been a sufficient catalyst to induce secession. But once the South had been fired upon, the situation was altered; Lincoln stood resolute in his insistence that there could be no legitimate secession. When he issued his proclamation declaring that an insurrection existed and called for seventy-five thousand militia to be supplied from the various states, immediately the strongly pro-Union states telegraphed their compliance, but the Southern states still in the Union as quickly refused.[15]

Davis later assessed Lincoln's proclamation, measuring it against his own conception of state rights and the legitimacy of the Confederacy: "President Lincoln [has introduced] his farce 'of combinations too powerful to be suppressed by the ordinary course of judicial proceedings.' . . . It can but surprise any one in the least degree conversant with the history of the Union, to find States referred to as 'persons composing combinations,' and that the sovereign creators of the Federal Government, the States of the Union, should be commanded by their agent to disperse. The levy of so large an army could only mean war; but the power to declare war did not reside in the President."[16] Lincoln did not "declare war," and in any case what else could he do to deal with "combinations too powerful to be suppressed by the ordinary course of judicial proceedings"?

While Union governors were clogging the wires with queries about the number of troops they should provide, and when, and by what route, and whether they could send more, the border-South governors clearly indicated their sympathies. In North Carolina, state troops seized unoccupied Fort Macon, and Governor John W. Ellis told the U.S. Secretary of War that he doubted the call was genuine, "which its extraordinary character leads me to doubt," and that he regarded the "levying of troops . . . for the purpose of subjugating the States of the South as in violation of the Constitution and a gross usurpation of power. I can be no party to this wicked violation of the laws of the country and to this war upon the liberties of a free people."[17] He then ordered the seizure of the other two Federal forts in North Carolina and called on his state to raise troops for the Confederacy—all before North Carolina had seceded. In May North Carolina called its convention and passed a unanimous ordinance of secession.[18]

On April 16, Governor John Letcher of Virginia informed the new Union Secretary of War Simon Cameron that he too doubted the genuineness of the call and replied that Virginia militia "will not be furnished to the powers at Washington for any such use. . . . Your object is to subjugate the Southern States. . . . You have chosen to inaugurate civil war."[19] The day after Letcher's reply, the Virginia state convention voted for secession, with a referendum scheduled for May 23.

When Lincoln's call reached Arkansas, Governor Henry M. Rector indignantly replied in much the same terms as had Letcher: "The people of this Commonwealth are freemen, not slaves, and will defend to the last extremity their honor, lives, and property against Northern mendacity and usurpation."[20] On May 6 the Arkansas convention passed an ordinance of secession with only one dissenting vote.

The governor of Tennessee, Isham G. Harris, informed Lincoln that "Tennessee will not furnish a single man for purpose of coercion, but 50,000 if necessary, for the defense of our rights and those of our Southern brethren."[21] On May 1 the Tennessee legislature authorized Harris to appoint commissioners to negotiate with the Confederacy—though the state was still in the Union—and declared Tennessee independent, a position ratified by popular referendum on June 8.

Within the Confederacy, "every thing is moving on steadily and energetically," a delighted Howell Cobb reported on May 3.[22] The Congress voted its official thanks to Beauregard for his achievement at Fort Sumter.[23] On May 5, it passed by unanimous voice vote a resolution "recognizing the existence of war between the United States and the Confederate States." The timing of the resolution was intentional, since Lincoln's twenty-day grace period expired the next day.[24] Clearly, what had moved the Confederate States, and many individual Southern citizens, to accept war was not the abstract issue of slavery but Lincoln's decision to hold the Union together, by force if necessary.

It was a bitter disappointment to the Southerners that Delaware, Maryland, Kentucky, and Missouri, slave states all, did not officially secede. There were serious internal divisions in these states, and significant numbers of men from Maryland, Kentucky, and Missouri eventually served in the armies of one side or the other. Kentucky tried to be officially neutral, but that proved impossible. On April 17 Claiborne F. Jackson of Missouri labeled Lincoln's call "illegal, unconstitutional, and revolutionary in its object, inhuman and diabolical," an "unholy crusade" that he would not support.[25] The Rebels eventually established pro-Confederate regimes in Kentucky and Missouri, but these states never made officially legitimate resolutions of secession in the way that the other eleven Confederate states did.

Border state hesitancy was less severe in Maryland and Delaware. In Maryland Governor Thomas H. Hicks was forced to walk a fine line in his divided state. He asked for and received assurances that troops from Maryland would be used only to protect the District of Columbia and government property in Maryland itself, and by his order volunteers were drawn from the state militia to fill the Maryland regiments.[26] In Delaware Governor William Burton tried to evade the issue. He claimed he had no authority to call out troops and that in any case Delaware had no organized militia. Volunteer companies were being formed, he said, but he had no authority to call them; it was up to them to offer their own service. Robert Patterson, a Pennsylvania major general of militia, asked War Secretary Cameron for permission to go to Delaware to muster troops there and received permission to go to both Delaware and Maryland for that purpose.[27]

There were stars for Kentucky and Missouri in the Confederate flag and they were represented during the war in both the U.S. and Confederate Congresses; further, there were self-proclaimed regimes operating in exile, but that is as far as it went. Because of the inability to establish pro-Confederate governments in their own territory, Kentucky and Missouri experienced much of the war but little of Confederate governance. Conditions were much more unstable and violent in Missouri, however, and in that state guerrilla warfare and its depredations often erupted. In his memoirs Davis wrote, "Missouri had refused to engage in war against her sister States of the South; therefore she was first to be disarmed, and then to be made the victim of an invasion characterized by such barbarous atrocities as shame the civilization of the age. The wrongs she suffered, the brave efforts of her unarmed people to defend their hearthstones and the liberties against the desecration and destruction of both, form a melancholy chapter in the history of the United States."[28] There was some truth but also much hyperbole in his reflections.

On April 29, Davis delivered a lengthy message to the newly seated second session of the Provisional Congress. The gallery was packed with ladies and gentlemen waving handkerchiefs and calling out good wishes. He spoke not so much to his audience but to the entire Western world. He reviewed the creation of the Confederate government and termed Lincoln's proclamation of April 15 to have been a declaration of war. He followed with a long explanation of the justifications for secession and a summary of the efforts to negotiate with the Northerners. He charged the United States with acting in bad faith during the pre-Sumter period. He reported on the activities of the various Confederate governmental departments. He claimed "that in every portion of our country there has been exhibited the most patriotic devotion to our common cause." Then he concluded with his statement "that our cause is just and holy; . . . all we ask is to be left alone." The floor and the gallery burst into applause.[29]

Never, however, was it true that the Confederacy wanted only "to be left alone." In the first place, contrary to Davis's concept, the Confederacy was not yet a sovereign nation. For that status to have been legitimate, it would have been necessary that other sovereign nations recognize it as such. The South's true task was not to maintain its independence but to secure it. The South indeed had three related but clear cut-war aims: independence, territorial integrity, and the acquisition of all the slave states, plus a share in the western territories of the United States. The South regarded this last as their "just share of the inheritance," given the Southern contributions to their acquisition.[30]

Thus, a mental parsing was involved. What was meant by seeking "no aggrandizement" was that the Confederacy would not seek to acquire any of the free states or any "unfairly large" share of the western territories; otherwise, the South intended to be aggressive and acquisitive from the outset. "By April 11, 1861, Southerners had seized nineteen forts, sixteen ships, eight arsenals and depots, three army barracks, one payroll, one mint, one hospital, and numerous customhouses and post offices."[31] But as Davis said, "He who makes the assault, is not necessarily he that strikes the first blow or fires the first gun." The Confederate mind-set held that the Civil War had opened not with the firing on Fort Sumter but when Lincoln on April 15 called for seventy-five thousand militia, the announcement by a "foreign power" of its intention to "invade" the South.[32]

Proclaiming the South's military strategy to be "offensive-defensive" seems to be another concept, like state rights, which Davis continued to refine within his mind more after than before or during the war. Indeed, he studied Antoine-Henri Jomini and tried semantically to harmonize with the Napoleonic master after the fact. The Confederacy's military strategy was not primarily defensive but precisely the other way around.[33] The actual Confederate war policy and grand strategy evolved, almost always in response to unfolding circumstances. Consequently, high-level decisions were made to deal with discrete situations rather than in accord with some specifically envisioned preference for the general conduct of the war. Direction came from letters of instruction and war councils among Davis, the secretary of war, and various prominent generals. The policy was, however, aggressive whenever circumstances permitted.[34]

Clearly, a great deal depended on the quality of the top-level field commanders. Davis put much credence in professional military experience and schooling; he always preferred West Point graduates for high appointments. His proclivity proved wise in some instances: certainly R. E. Lee was a fortuitous choice as a Confederate full general, and possibly, so was Albert Sidney Johnston, though Davis was overly enthusiastic about Johnston's yet unproven capacity. Naive overenthusiasm led Davis to give his old West Point classmate and friend, Leonidas Polk, a commission as major general, and to sustain him, despite his quickly manifested incompetency. Though Davis frequently protested that he was not unduly biased in his appointments, in truth he typically "showed favoritism based not on experience or performance, but upon friendship and loyalty."[35]

A houseguest marveled at Davis's presence of mind and endurance under pressure; however, it was only by iron will that Davis kept his nerves under control. Postmaster General Reagan saw two dominating characteristics in his president: with women and children (his inferiors in that patriarchal society) he could be pleasant and genial; a visiting editor thought him "brighter, more cheerful and in better health than we have seen him for many years." But with important men (peers and potential rivals), he was all duty and had no time for frivolity. He considered the facts at hand, formed his own opinions, often without consulting with his cabinet, and then closed his mind to further discussion.[36] Two days after the firing on Fort Sumter, Davis received yet another letter containing unsolicited advice, and he lost control. "I wish people would not write me advice," he exclaimed. He tore the letter in half, then, as if that had not made the point, he ripped it further into small shreds.[37]

Some observers in Montgomery had the impression that Davis worked closely and well with the cabinet, occupying himself mainly with the great issues. That, however, was the case only with postal, judicial, and financial matters; the first two of these issues were not that important, and the third was one that he did not understand. But he closely involved himself in other affairs, often to an unseen degree, especially with the War Department.[38]

On the international scene, Henry John Temple, Lord Palmerston, prime minister of England, read the news of Southern secession with unguarded pleasure. The prospect of a Confederacy of cotton-producing states, a new nation dedicated to free trade with Europe, and a weakened United States delighted him. But with secession came the unsettling realization that the provinces of Canada lay open, virtually undefended, should the North decide to invade in retaliation for any British aid to the Confederacy. Thus on May 13, 1861, Britain issued a proclamation of neutrality that granted the status of belligerent to the South and opened its ports to Rebel commerce. France followed suit with a similar declaration in June. The French, ruled by Napoleon III, expressed much interest in a joint intervention with Britain in the American war. The United States, however, had wise and able men in its State Department and diplomatic service, and they took pains to prevent any such development.

The British textile mills had grown dependent on Southern cotton; when that cotton stopped coming, the mills would begin closing. Perhaps South Carolina senator James H. Hammond's 1858 prediction (or was it a threat?) was correct:

> Would any nation make war on cotton? Without firing a gun, without drawing a sword, when they make war on us we can bring the whole world to our feet. . . . What would happen if no cotton was furnished for three years? I will not stop to depict what every one can imagine, but this is certain: old England would topple headlong and carry the whole civilized world with her. No, sir, you dare not make war on cotton. No power on earth dares make war upon it. Cotton is king.[39]

Fearing that the Union blockade might produce the result that Hammond had predicted, Britain's minister to Washington, Lord Richard B. P. Lyons, using all his powers of diplomatic persuasion, complained loudly to the Union Secretary of State, William H. Seward. After several encounters, Lyons went away with the distinct impression that the United States would recant and lift the blockade.

In spring 1861, British regulars augmented the Canadian militia; about forty-three hundred British soldiers garrisoned Canada and Nova Scotia, Lieutenanant General Sir W. Fenwick Williams commanding. Born in Nova Scotia, the sixty-one-year-old Williams had acquired a hero's reputation in the Crimean War. And on the seas, the British navy ruled absolutely. More than merely outnumbering the U.S. Navy, Her Majesty's fleet easily outclassed that of the Yankees. The American navy then consisted of 40 steam vessels and 50 sizable but quite obsolete sailing ships. In contrast, the British listed 856 war vessels, including 700 steamers and 2 nearly completed iron ships. Eighty English vessels were of such armament and size to rate classification as battleships. Meanwhile, throughout the summer the diplomatic situation continued to deteriorate further.

The women of the South, from all social classes, were among the most ardent advocates of secession. After hostilities erupted, mothers, wives, sisters, and sweethearts with scant exception rallied to the cause. The most well known, and perhaps the most romantic of these, were the many women who served as spies, some only locally but others throughout the Confederacy. The most celebrated Confederate female spies were Belle Boyd and Mrs. Rose O'Neal Greenhow, and much is known about their exploits. But many others, their names now lost, served the cause on a smaller scale.[40] Some Southern women, however, served as Union spies; like some of the men, their sympathies lay on the enemy side, and many of them acted on their feelings at grave risk.

Southern women were often adversely affected by the war when their men went off to fight. They always tried to put on the bravest front possible when loved ones departed for duty. As troops left home for the war zones, usually traveling by rail, throngs of young females turned out at every station and town to cheer them and to treat them to food and drink.[41]

Lincoln's call for troops inspired an Alabama mother to go out into the fields to find her two sons and urge them to enlist for the conflict's duration.[42] According to legend at least, virtually all young Southern women demonstrated their disapproval of any slackers. In Selma, Alabama, the girls put on a "pout and sulk" campaign in an attempt to encourage more young men to volunteer. One popular belle announced that she would not care to keep company with any military-aged male civilian. Another said that she would prefer spinsterhood to being a slacker's wife. Yet another broke her engagement because the lad was slow to enlist, sending him a skirt and petticoat with the message, "Wear these or volunteer."[43] That they were thus sending thousands of young men inevitably to violent death seemed not to occur to them, but in two or three years many were weeping in widow's weeds or begging the same young men to desert.

Their patriotic enthusiasm reached such dimensions that some women sought to take up arms themselves. Mrs. Susan Lear of Virginia wrote to Governor John Letcher in April 1861: "I for one feel able to protect a goodly number if I only had the means of defense. . . . Send me a *good* Musket, Rifle, or double barrel Shot Gun. I think I would prefer the latter as I am acquainted with its use. I believe, Sir, if a Regiment of Yankees were to come we [women] would drive them away or quell a servile insurrection." In Georgia a group of young women formed a unit for local defense: "The name of our company is the Bascom Home Guards," one of them reported enthusiastically; "we are all delighted with the idea of learning how to shoot."[44] Immediately after learning the news of Lincoln's election, some Alabama women, the "Gainesville

Unconquerables," sent word to that state's governor that they were ready to fight and that "we can leave the Old Women and children in charge of the *gallant* gentlemen."[45]

In a number of instances, women disguised themselves as men and went into military service. The Union nurse Mary Livermore wrote that the total number on both sides was about four hundred, but she had no way of knowing that; even so, many historians have taken that number as plausible. Lauren Cook Burgess has made a meticulous search for documentation and has found about one hundred fifty specific cases of women who served in the Confederate army and never were found out. Of course, if a woman was discovered, she was discharged and sent home immediately, officially labeled as being insane. Sometimes women accompanied their husbands, as was the case with Mrs. L. M. Blalock, who enlisted as Samuel Blalock, and a Mrs. Amy Clarke. But many times these warriors were just gutsy women who wanted to fight—like Sarah Rosetta Wakeman, about whom we know a great deal because of the letters she wrote home and that her descendants saved.[46] Madame Loreta Janeta Velasquez saw much service as Lieutenant Henry T. Buford, and Mrs. Laura J. Williams of Arkansas "raised and commanded a company of Texans and fought at Shiloh and elsewhere in the West."[47]

Female patriots also assisted the South's war effort in numerous other ways. Many of them ran firearms, medicines, and other vital items across the lines under their clothing or hidden in their baggage. And Southern women frequently performed as nurses, caring for the sick and wounded. After all the great battles, casualties would be carried to crowded public facilities such as railway stations, schools, hotels, and churches, where women from the vicinity would provide nourishment, blankets, bandages, loving care, and anything they could do to help render the wounded more comfortable.[48]

E. Merton Coulter describes the intense feelings of these patriotic Confederate women:

> There were unnamed women throughout the Confederacy who were as belligerently inclined as if they had worn the uniform, but probably none as ferocious as to "wear rings and ornaments made of our soldiers' bones" as was charged in the North. Yet there were Louisiana women who, after reading Butler's "Woman Order," could write such sentiments as these: "Oh! how I hate the Yankees! I could trample on their dead bodies and spit on them," and "come to my bosom, O my discarded carving-knife, laid aside under the impression that these men were gentlemen. We will become close friends once more. And if you must have a sheath, perhaps I may find one for you in the heart of the first man who attempts to Butlerize me." A Richmond editor admitted that the

enmity of the Confederate women was "more deadly than all the engines of war ever invented by man," and a Federal soldier remarked that if the Southern girls could love as they hate, "it would be well worth one's trying to get one of them."[49]

Relatively few women served as full-time nurses or administrators in the many Confederate hospitals eventually established, for there was a strong prevailing view that such positions properly belonged to men only. Kate Cumming reported such misgivings in her journal but believed that "as soon as surgeons discover that ladies are really of service, that prejudice will cease to exist. The patients are delighted to have us, and say that we can cause them to think of the dearest of all places to them now—home."[50] But even Cumming had problems being accepted by narrow-minded surgeons. When she and her assistant arrived at one hospital, the post surgeon told them bluntly that he did not approve of women in hospitals.[51] In the long run, women such as Cumming were essential, and they served long and well. The Army of Tennessee used many women as nurses and in other capacities. In November 1862 women were formally accepted into the hospital, two assistant matrons in charge of laundry and cooking; two ward matrons in each ward to see to the distribution of medicine, bedding, and food; and two chief matrons to oversee "the entire domestic economy of the hospital." They prepared food, washed dirty and infected bodies, fed patients unable to feed themselves, wrote letters for soldiers, and even joined them in prayer. Kate Cumming, working in Chattanooga, often worked from 4:00 A.M. to midnight, a routine that made many matrons and nurses so ill that they required care themselves.[52]

The ailing Rebels appreciated the works of various orders of Roman Catholic nuns, such as the Sisters of Charity, the Sisters of Mercy, and other orders, who were the only women already trained as nurses when the war began. The Sisters of Charity were most notable, but there were fewer than two hundred of them. They kept their hospitals in such good order that, together with their dignity and devotion, they were very effective.[53]

Assuredly the most notable of the women nurses on the Southern side was Sally L. Tomkins. She served as the chief administrator of a Richmond hospital, which she had founded, and did so exceptional a job that President Davis was induced to commission her a captain of Confederate cavalry.[54]

Countless numbers of other women helped the cause by making clothing for the soldiers. Early in the war, groups of women, aided by slave seamstresses when available, frequently received cloth issued by the government and fashioned it into uniforms. Sometimes a single group might outfit an entire company of troops. Later in the war, providing clothing became more and more the enterprise of an individual family.[55]

Quite early, and ever increasingly, many women—especially those who lived in urban areas—secured employment in industry or government. They worked variously in ordnance plants, where they made minié balls, paper cartridges, percussion caps, fuses, and shells; in textile mills and garment factories; and in the post offices and the Treasury. As the war went on, and more and more husbands and fathers were killed or disabled, such jobs became a form of welfare, providing a bare living to many women who would otherwise have been without support. The Treasury Note Bureau in Columbia, South Carolina, for example, provided many such jobs.[56]

In the predominantly rural South, with so large a mass of the able-bodied white male population fighting or otherwise actively supporting the war, the agricultural sector came under the day-to-day supervision of women. Only a small minority had black labor to help them, inasmuch as only one-quarter of Southern white families were slave owners. Many white women, some with and many without the help of children, had to plow, plant, weed, reap, and harvest. They killed the hogs and cured the meat, cut the firewood, and carried out all the other tasks necessary to farming. In both rural and urban areas, women had to sew and spin, as celebrated in a popular wartime song, "The Homespun Dress":

> Oh, yes, I am a Southern girl,
>   And glory in the name,
> And boast it with far greater pride
>   Than glittering wealth or fame.
> We envy not the Northern girl,
>   Her robes of beauty rare,
> Though diamonds grace her snowy neck,
>   And pearls bedeck her hair.
>
> Hurrah! Hurrah!
>   For the sunny South so dear;
> Three cheers for the homespun dress
>   The Southern ladies wear!
>
> Now Northern looks are out of date;
>   And since old Abe's blockade,
> We Southern girls can be content
>   With goods that's Southern made.
> We send our sweethearts to the war;
>   But, dear girls, never mind—
> Your soldier-love will ne'er forget
>   The girl he left behind.

The Southerners always had been a singing people, and seemingly many of them felt they could write songs, either words or music and frequently both. Said one Richmond newspaper editor, "If all the music manufactured in the South found a market, we should certainly be a very musical people." But a Macon, Georgia, publisher declared that much of it was trash. There were songs of all kinds, written in various tempi: polkas, waltzes, schottisches, and marches. There were dreamy love songs, songs that were sentimental, warlike, humorous, many often about mother or home. Some of the most frequently sung early ones were about Beauregard, the South's first great military hero: "Gen'l Beauregard's Grande Polka Militaire," or "Beauregard's Manassas Quickstep."[57]

Virginia had seceded on April 17; ten days later the state convention offered Richmond as the national capital. On May 7 Virginia officially joined the Confederacy, and on May 20, the Provisional Confederate Congress voted to accept its invitation and to move the capital to Richmond. This was motivated mainly by a desire to ensure the support of Virginia for the Confederate war effort but also in part because Montgomery proved to be a rather inadequate city for a national government. There were scant transportation linkages and woefully inadequate physical facilities, and the streets seemed to have been laid out over cow paths. The last of the government trains left at 8:00 A.M. on the morning of May 30 in ninety-four-degree heat.[58]

Richmond by 1860 had become the twenty-fifth largest city in the United States, with a population of nearly forty thousand. A little more than one-third of the city's inhabitants were black, four-fifths of them slaves and one-fifth free. Only New Orleans rivaled Richmond as a major Southern city. Industry had grown in Richmond, and it ranked thirteenth among all cities in the old Union as a producer. The new capital had the largest flour mill in the world; the Tredegar Ironworks there was the second-largest foundry in the world. The only really unfortunate fact about Richmond was its proximity to the Confederate frontier and its nearness to Washington, D.C., making the scant one hundred miles between the two capitals "the most priceless real estate in the Confederacy."[59]

Davis arrived in Richmond on May 29. The governor led a large crowd of military and civilian dignitaries to greet him. The president had suffered from illness on the trip, but he had responded at stops along the way to the crowds that thronged to see him and to shout out hurrahs for "Jeff Davis, The Old Hero!" But not everyone felt so enthusiastic or confident. Within Davis's official family, Robert Toombs groused to his friend Vice President Stephens that

"Davis works slowly, too slowly for the crisis." Toombs perceived that Davis was actually running the War Department, reducing War Secretary Walker to little more than a clerk, and thus did Toombs hold Davis personally responsible for Confederate failure to be more prepared militarily by this time. "Davis has not [the] capacity for the crisis," he complained, "& I see great troubles ahead." When Toombs arrived in Richmond, he deemed "Virginia so inadequately defended, that he believed the only reason the Yankees had not taken it yet was that they had not tried."[60]

Eventually there would be the "Confederate White House," but that was not its name during the Civil War. It was painted gray during the war and often was called the "Gray House." It previously had belonged to the Brockenbrough family, and the Brockenbrough Mansion was the most commonly used designation. Located at Twelfth and Clay Streets, the house was more imposing than the presidential residence in Montgomery, but it was not as homey. It was a rather severe Federal-style formal mansion, with a porch quite far off the ground: the first-level entrances were underneath this porch, and there was a flight of steps that led down to a garden.

Davis's home office was situated between the children's nursery and the Davises' bedroom. A cubbyhole at the stair's end served as the office for Burton Harrison, Davis's secretary, a New Orleans native and a Yale graduate. In March 1862 he took up residence in the mansion, so that when Davis was ill, and that was often, the country's business could be carried on from the president's home.

Even before the government had been moved from Montgomery, Davis had brought into his official family an aide, Louis T. Wigfall. The responsibility of the office of Confederate president seemed to be increasing exponentially, and an aide like Wigfall was a useful addition. Wigfall had been a leading fire-eater and was considerably popular with some of the elements in Congress who were beginning to grumble about the Davis administration. Reporters in Richmond noted that "the President and members of the cabinet are much fagged by their heavy duties" and appeared "somewhat faded." Still, Davis often outlasted his cabinet; during long meetings the members slipped away, one by one, until sometimes he was left to discuss affairs of state with "one weak, weary man, who has no vim to contend." Davis, one of his critics observed, "overworks himself and all the rest of mankind."[61]

At first the Davises entertained informally almost every night. Soon the president found this to be too much and thereafter he received alone, usually once a week. Often when Varina held levees, Davis elected not to attend, or to do so only briefly. He did enjoy company, but he tended to withdraw from frivolity at home. Bad news seemed to interrupt nearly every party, upsetting both him and the guests. Still, he worked the entirety of each day, either at home or in his office. Callers were surprised to find him unprotected by any guards; he was utterly accessible. A servant would meet all callers at the door and show them at once to the president. And he became ever more harried.[62]

Christopher Memminger and his Treasury Department occupied the first floor of the old U.S. custom house, just below Davis's office and the Department of State. Female clerks soon made up by far the largest part of the force working there, busily signing, clipping, and numbering Treasury notes. Many of them were society belles, happy to accept a meager salary of five hundred dollars per year, finding much patriotic satisfaction in their labors. They turned out reams of paper notes, for "the Confederate Treasury soon came to be the greatest money factory in the world."[63]

The Confederacy's first credit was a loan of $500,000, extended by Alabama just four days after the Montgomery Convention had convened, but the first cash was $389,267, acquired from the New Orleans mint, and another $147,519 from the New Orleans custom house, both seized by the state of Louisiana and then turned over to the Confederate government. Small amounts of federal funds and specie subsequently were seized from the assay office in Charlotte, North Carolina, the Dahlonega, Georgia, mint, and federal custom houses and depositories in Wilmington, North Carolina, Savannah, Georgia, Fernandina, Florida, and other locations. A total of $718,250 was obtained by confiscating funds from U.S. custom houses, depositories, and mints.[64]

The Confederate citizenry had in its private possession an estimated $20 million worth of U.S. coins. These tended to be hoarded and only in rare instances were they spent. The Congress hoped to induce the people to use them as a freely circulating medium and therefore made U.S. coins legal tender in the Confederacy, up to $10, and gave full monetary standing with fixed, stipulated values to English sovereigns, French napoleons, and Spanish and Mexican doubloons.

Once impending war seemed quite evident, the Treasury offered the remaining $10 million of the bonds that had been authorized on February 28, 1861, but this time the response was cool. The banks had paid out a lot of specie for the original loan, and citizens were reluctant to invest theirs. But the accession of the Upper South made up the difference in helping to absorb the bond issue. Richmond alone subscribed $50,000 and various wealthy individuals throughout the Confederacy also subscribed. At first the Treasury paid the interest on these bonds in specie, which rendered them more desirable as long as that continued—indeed, they commanded a higher market price than any other of the later Confederate bonds.[65]

The nearest attempt at a nationwide bond drive was the Produce Loan authorized by Congress on May 16, 1861. Each congressman became a bond agent in order to sell a portion of the $50 million issue of these bonds in his state. Other official agents also were appointed, including James D. B. DeBow, a noted economist and the editor of *DeBow's Review,* as their head. Many congressmen went out on the hustings to try to explain the law, and they successfully persuaded quite a few planters to pledge proceeds from the future sales of commodities, generally cotton.

Some of the resulting successes were impressive. Vice President Stephens, enthusiastic for once, made a speech in Washington, Georgia, the home of Robert Toombs, after which 2,000 bales of cotton were pledged, including 100 bales by Toombs himself. Word had reached Toombs that the Union general Winfield Scott had said the Confederates ought to quit because otherwise the blockade would soon starve them out. In response, as proof that he and his compatriots would have plenty to eat, Toombs sent the old general an ear of fresh corn in a box, with a card simply from "R. Toombs." The Rebel leaders exuded an air of conviviality at this point, and a British observer indicated that he found Toombs to be "unquestionably one of the most original, quaint, and earnest of the Southern leaders."[66]

But in truth Toombs was not quite so sanguine as he seemed to some. He lacked confidence in the other measures that Treasury Secretary Memminger pushed forward, and as W. C. Davis has observed, Toombs "frankly asserted that if the Produce Loan failed to finance them successfully—as indeed it did—they would have no option but to impose a high and rigid direct tax based on wealth or income, something Southerners had opposed in principle for generations."[67]

In Columbus, Georgia, throngs of subscribers set their names down for 1,510 bales, 3,000 bushels of corn, and slightly over $3,000 in specie. E. Merton Coulter notes that "a farmer near Atlanta subscribed 200 bushels of corn and 125 bushels of wheat." By the end of July Davis claimed that the value of cotton subscribed was likely to exceed $50 million, and he praised the volunteer solicitors.[68] By January 1862, subscriptions included 400,000 bales of cotton, 1,000 hogsheads of tobacco, another 1,000 of sugar and molasses, 5,000 bushels of wheat, and 270,000 of rice, all in addition to $1 million in other produce and another $1 million in currency and bank notes.[69]

On August 19, 1861, with Congress back in session following its summer recess, the Produce Loan Act of May 16 was amended to increase that bond issue to $100 million to bear 8 percent. These bonds could be paid for either in military supplies, proceeds from the sale of agricultural or manufactured products, or in specie. Senator Benjamin H. Hill of Georgia boasted that he had devised this scheme, asserting it to be unique in the world, and that it would so adequately provide the government with the sinews of war that no further taxes would be required.[70]

It did not work out so well, however, and the Treasury tried often in vain to collect these pledges throughout the entire war. The Treasury's final report revealed that the people had pledged proceeds of farm products totaling $34,476,000, but more than $11 million of the amount could not be collected either because the products had been destroyed through the exigencies of war or because people had simply refused to make good on their pledges.[71]

Additional resources were to be supplied by the so-called War Tax of August 8, 1861, which levied one-half of 1 percent on the taxable wealth of the entire Confederacy, including "real estate of all kinds, slaves, merchandize, bank stocks, railroad and other corporations stocks, money at interest," and even personal possessions like "gold watches, gold and silver plate, pianos, and pleasure carriages," excepting only Confederate bonds.[72] Memminger believed that the total value of property in the Confederacy was probably a little in excess of $5 billion; presumably that property would bring about $26 million into the treasury. He tried to shift the burden of collection to the states by offering a 10 percent reduction for states that would calculate the tax owed by their citizens and pay it by April 1, 1862. All the states did so except Mississippi and Texas.[73]

This would have been the first Confederate tax felt directly by the people, but only South Carolina, Texas, and Mississippi collected it; other states borrowed from their citizens instead of taxing them and sent the borrowed funds to the Confederate Treasury. In South Carolina the state paid and then collected from taxpayers. In Mississippi the governor and legislature disagreed over how to collect the tax, and "Texas did nothing, on the assumption that without state aid the tax was uncollectible." In the end the Confederate government collected the tax in Mississippi and Texas directly, but as in the other states, it did not secure the full amount due. The result was that less tax revenue was raised than had been anticipated, and the state and Confederate governments competed with one another in the bond market.

Furthermore, assessments were not completed according to schedule, and there was great difficulty with uniform assessment, especially of slaves. By midsummer 1862 only six states had made any returns, but $10.5 million had been paid to the Treasury. The last report of the War Tax Bureau, issued November 1863, indicated proceeds of $17.5 million as of July 1, 1863, but only one-quarter of the so-called taxes were garnered by the taxing process; the remaining proceeds were actually loans. This experience indicated both the reluctance of the states to tax their citizens and a Confederate policy of fighting now and paying later. Satisfied with what they had done in 1861, Confederates engaged in what the economic historian Douglas Ball calls "drift and self-delusion . . . disastrous inertia," until they finally passed a comprehensive tax law in 1863.[74]

Many Confederates simply rebelled against the notion of paying high taxes, at least until 1863. One planter complained that he had plenty of cotton but no money and condemned the Congress, saying, "This Government belongs to the people, and not to a little self-assuming Congress, who had no more right to levy such a tax than you and I have." But a rather more patriotic citizen said, "It may be burdensome to our people to pay it, but it will be paid most cheerfully."[75]

Most people expected that the first major land battle of the Civil War would take place somewhere in Virginia. This indeed proved to be the case, near the town of Manassas, some twenty-nine miles southwest of Washington, D.C., where a twenty-thousand-man corps was based under the fifth-ranking full general of the Confederate army, P. G. T. Beauregard. Confederates displayed a preference for naming battles after the nearest town or physical feature; hence to Southerners this battle is "Manassas." Federals preferred to name battles after the nearest stream or body of water, so to the Northerners (and generally in most common usage), it is "Bull Run," after a stream that empties nearby into the Potomac River.

In summer 1861 neither side was ready for any big engagement, but President Lincoln was hopeful that an early victory might somehow be achieved and that this would prevent the Rebel legislature from convening in Richmond. There was strong political and public pressure for precipitous action. Northern newspapers repeatedly printed the slogan, "Forward to Richmond!" Furthermore, huge numbers of the initial volunteers had been allowed to enlist for a mere three months, and the time for their terms to expire was fast approaching. It clearly was a matter of having some action right away or enduring a long and unwelcome delay that might indicate to foreign governments that the Union would make no serious attempt to enforce reunion, thus providing a pretext for recognition of an independent Confederacy. Indeed, on the very morning of the battle, July 21, 1861, Federal troops moving forward passed an infantry regiment and an artillery battery whose enlistments had expired. The men were returning to Washington expecting to muster out.

Four forces, initially separated, became involved. The first was Beauregard's, the main target for a Union army that thrust south from Washington, D.C. This force numbered thirty thousand men and was under the command of Brigadier General Irvin McDowell, a career officer, recently elevated from the rank of major, who had endeared himself to Lincoln and snared command by having been early on the scene with the right kind of supporters in high places. Two other opposing forces were located initially across the mountains, in the Shenandoah Valley, and cautiously faced each other. These included a fourteen-thousand-man army in the lower (i.e., northern, because the Shenandoah River flows northeast) sector of the valley, under the superannuated Brevet Major General Robert Patterson, and an eleven-thousand-man force in the upper valley under Confederate general Joseph E. Johnston.

McDowell began a march toward Richmond, planning to cross Bull Run and attack Beauregard's left flank. But the Federal army was poorly organized and ill-trained, and the green soldiers took two and one-half days to march about twenty miles. Beauregard, meanwhile, intended to be first to attack. He was quite aware that the Federals were on the way, thanks to word passed by the Rebel spy and prominent figure in Washington society, Rose O'Neal Greenhow, to eager young volunteer females, such as one Bettie DuVall, who enthusiastically rode horseback across the countryside with the news. (Beauregard also read the same information in readily available Northern newspapers.)

For several days the impetuous and impatient Beauregard had clamored for the Confederate officials to order Johnston to join him at Manassas, but Davis and his advisers were wisely biding their time. Johnston tricked Patterson into thinking that an attack in the valley was imminent; then at the last feasible moment, he disengaged and moved about six thousand of his men to unite with Beauregard's corps, by way of the Manassas Gap Railroad. The Confederate cavalry under Colonel J. E. B. Stuart screened Johnston's movement so well that another two full days passed before Patterson realized what had happened.

This strategic use of railroads was a spectacular harbinger of things to come in modern warfare: it had become possible to redeploy masses of troops rapidly and effectively over long distances. They could arrive unexpectedly, fresh and ready for battle. Roadbeds and rolling stock thenceforth became vital possessions. Rail junctions soon became as significant, and sometimes even more so, than road junctions. In this instance the redeployment was achieved by a mere hair's breadth: most of Johnston's men did not arrive until the actual day of the battle, and one brigade approached even after the fighting had begun.

Much depended on which side moved first, or more precisely, which side made any significant forward progress after having crossed Bull Run. On the Confederate right, some of the Rebel brigades crossed the stream, but they failed to push forward, waiting for adjacent elements to come on line while others remained in place and in confusion, awaiting further orders that they understood were to come. Meanwhile, the Union main force successfully crossed Bull Run near Sudley Church. Southern observers perched on a high hill behind the Confederate lines noted this enemy movement and sent a warning message by "wigwag" signaling (a recently devised method of communicating across distant points by waving flags according to a predetermined code).

Hot and heavy fighting soon erupted, and for some hours the contest seemed relatively close. At last, however, a Union breakthrough seemed imminent: one portion of the Confederate line was smashed when Yankee colonel William Tecumseh Sherman managed to maneuver his brigade so that it could assault a Rebel element from its flank rather than frontally, thus delivering a deadly and withering enfilade fire. But the Rebels rallied; Sherman's advance was blunted and then contained. At a precarious moment, Confederate Brigadier General Thomas J. Jackson brought up a fresh brigade of five Virginia regiments to a critical area and made the stand that gave him his famous nickname. Brigadier General Barnard Bee, trying to rally his South Carolinians, cried out to them, "Rally, men, for God's sake rally. . . . Look! There is Jackson standing like a *Stonewall*." Bee then received a fatal wound, but he had bequeathed an immortal legacy: "Stonewall Jackson" became the Confederacy's second folk hero (after Beauregard) and ultimately, perhaps, its most beloved, at least until his untimely death in spring 1863.

Following Jackson's tenacious stand, charges and countercharges swirled back and forth. Ill-trained soldiers fought as best they could, some of them showing great bravery; but in directing their movements, commanders made egregious mistakes. A critical moment came when two Union artillery batteries pushed too far forward because they confused a blue-clad Confederate regiment for one of their own, and they were ravaged by a point-blank volley, all their guns being captured by the Southerners, who then put the weapons to their own use. Indeed, the greatest confusion of the battle was caused by the lack of standard uniforms, which greatly compounded the numbers of casualties.

During the midafternoon a desperate struggle surged back and forth on Henry House Hill. The Confederate commanders continually poured reinforcements into the action, and about 4:00 P.M. McDowell's right flank was enveloped. Panic began to sweep through some quarters of the Federal ranks when anxious men heard that the Rebels were about to unleash the Black Horse Cavalry. Why black horses should have invoked any more terror than those of any other color can best be understood only by realizing that these men were inexperienced, untrained, and thoroughly fatigued and their nerves had been stretched to the limit. Here too came the first memorable instance of Confederates charging, with the dread, high-pitched shout that was to become famous as the Rebel yell. The exhausted Federals began at first a slow retrograde, but when a Confederate artillery shell hit a wagon on Cub Run Bridge, blocking the road to Centreville, the main avenue of retreat, some of the troops began to panic. The retrograde turned into a rout, further jammed by numerous civilian spectators in and near Centreville who had ridden out from Washington, almost in a picnic mood, expecting to enjoy the sights of war but who now became part of the wreckage.

The English journalist William Howard Russell was present. "I talked with those on all sides of me," he wrote. "Some uttered prodigious nonsense, describing batteries tier over tier, and ambuscades, and blood running knee deep." For these and for many other sarcastic comments about this battle, Russell became known in the United States as "Bull Run Russell," and he soon was quite resented by Northerners, leading to his virtual expulsion from the country in spring 1862.

A poem, later much beloved by rabid pro-Southerners, commemorated the episode:

> Yankee Doodle, near Bull Run
>   Met his adversary,
> First he thought the fight he'd won,
>   Fact proved quite contrary.
> Panic-struck he fled, with speed
>   Of lightning glib with unction,
> Of slippery grease, in full stampede
>   From famed Manassas Junction.

One Ohio congressman, who had gone to Bull Run for the expected festivities, described the spectacle as unique "for causeless, sheer, absolute, absurd cowardice, or rather panic, on this miserable earth. . . . Off they went, . . . anywhere, everywhere, to escape. . . . The further they ran the more frightened they grew. . . . To enable them better to run, they threw away their blankets, knapsacks, canteens, and finally muskets, cartridge-boxes, and everything else. . . . A cruel, crazy, mad, hopeless panic possessed them." But this particular observer saw only a small portion of the total Federal army, which on the whole behaved much better than did the civilians. The bulk of the army withdrew in fairly commendable order. If the Rebels had tried to advance on Washington—they were in far too much disarray themselves to have made such an attempt even thinkable—the Federals would have offered a potent defense. And so the battle ended.

The historian James A. Rawley has included First Bull Run among the seven major occurrences that he featured in *Turning Points of the Civil War.*[76]

Rawley has suggested that it was an extremely close call, that Bull Run might have been a Union victory but for a cluster of realities: if there had been by this early date a more seasoned U.S. president, as there would be later; if the Union general in chief, Winfield Scott, had been a younger and more sprightly man (he was seventy-five and physically incapacitated); if the Northern force had been commanded by a faster-moving general than McDowell, or if the Southern forces had been endowed with a less steadfast general than Jackson; and, last, if the Confederates had worn a different color of uniforms.

But Rawley has rightly concluded that Bull Run was a significant turning point because the battle struck public opinion, not only at home but also abroad, with compelling force on both sides. It framed new patterns of thought and subsequently led to far-reaching changes in how warfare would be conducted. It engendered a renewed wave of Confederate enthusiasm (the first having been in the aftermath of the Fort Sumter affair): volunteering accelerated, many of the ninety-day men reenlisted, and states began to rush into service a plenitude of fresh regiments. Perhaps Bull Run was also a turning point because a Union victory might have meant a quick capture of Richmond, a collapse of the Confederacy, and the end of the dis-Union crisis, leaving the slavery issue unsettled and vexing to succeeding generations.

Bull Run certainly jolted the thinking of a good many persons on both sides. Contrasted to what followed in the Civil War, the losses were modest, but at the time they seemed enormous. The battle cost Southerners 387 killed, 1,582 wounded, and 13 missing, for a total of 1,982 out of some 32,000 men engaged. The Federals had managed to engage only some 18,500 of their 35,000 men available, and they lost 2,896—460 killed, 1,124 wounded, and 1,312 missing.

A standard interpretation among students of the Civil War has been that the outcome of Bull Run was damaging to the South's chances in the long term because the elation of winning was quickly dulled by disappointment that there was no momentous follow-up—perhaps the effort should have been made to take Washington after all—and because the Rebel victory falsely reinforced the myth of Southern military superiority, inhibiting Southern efforts at preparedness while inducing Northerners to be more serious in subsequent mobilizations. Michael C. C. Adams, on the other hand, has suggested that in the eastern theater especially, Northerners developed a mind-set that was psychologically inhibiting: that Southerners were their military superiors. And he asserts that Bull Run "spooked" many Yankees while giving the Rebels a valid upper hand.[77]

The U.S. Congress convened the day following the battle, with a new willingness to support Lincoln's war efforts. It authorized the muster of .5 million men to serve for three years or for the war's duration. Perhaps, however, the greatest result was the passage of the Confiscation Act of August 1861, called by Rawley "the thin entering wedge of emancipation by legislation." Introduced by Senator Lyman Trumbull of Illinois, the bill provided that "if *any person* held to service or labor [read "slave"] is *employed in aid of this rebellion,* in *digging* ditches or entrenchment, or in any other way, or if used for *carrying guns,* or if used to destroy this Government by the consent of his master, his master shall forfeit all right to him and he shall be forever discharged." And from the day of the first battle to the end of the conflict, Lincoln took a firmer grip on the war's management. He started with little or no military competency, but as a strategist and commander in chief he grew a great deal during the ensuing four years.

As for Davis, he had already shown his eagerness to be personally involved in the military actions. He arrived at the battle area long before the fighting was over, and as he later recalled, "On reaching the railroad junction, I found a large number of men, bearing the usual evidence of those who leave the field of battle under a panic. They crowded around the train with fearful stories of a defeat of our army."[78] Davis was told by the young Captain John F. Lay that "he was much farther forward than he should be," that the enemy was "not entirely broken." "I am in no danger," Davis said, as he was surrounded by "gallant hearts," and he called for an artillery piece. As the battle progressed, he continued to ride over the fields, giving Colonel Jubal Early military advice and even acting as a courier for him, but chiefly tending to numerous hungry and wounded troops he encountered.[79] He felt at home on the battlefield, and this active-negative president became, for the moment at least, active-positive. He later wrote, with some poignancy, "As we approached toward the left of our line, the signs of an utter rout of the enemy were unmistakable, and justified the conclusion that the watchword of 'On to Richmond!' had been changed to 'Off for Washington!' "[80]

Davis met with Beauregard and Johnston late that night, sometime after 11 P.M., and asked about the plans for pursuit. There was silence. No such plans had been made. He asked that the freshest brigade be ordered out. He sat down and began writing an order to pursue the routed enemy, but then he was told that the officer who had reported the rout had been known in the old army as "Crazy Hill." So Davis decided not to order pursuit, and both Beauregard and Johnston concurred in that decision.[81]

Any opportunity that had existed disappeared in the night, for before daybreak, a violent and prolonged downpour rendered the roads impassable bogs of mud. The only thing to do was to send a small force to scour the country and to send the wounded back to the rear. Davis resigned himself to the reality: "Enough was done for glory, and the measure of duty was full," he said to

Beauregard and then gave him an on-the-spot promotion to full general.[82] Davis later ruminated that "the victory at Manassas was certainly extraordinary, not only on account of the disparity of numbers and the inferiority of our arms, but also because of many other disadvantages under which we labored."[83]

Despite Davis's decision, quite a quarrel ensued over whether the Confederate army could or could not have captured Washington. Some of the Richmond newspapers criticized Davis for his decision, and Beauregard blamed him because, he suggested, the president had failed to provide adequate food and transportation. Commissary General Northrop answered this charge saying that "there was plenty of provision for a march on Washington." Johnston defended the decision, admitting that the Confederate army simply had been too disorganized for meaningful pursuit, and he also cited Washington's formidable fortifications. Davis tried to soothe Beauregard by writing, "I think you are unjust to yourself in putting your failure to pursue the enemy to Washington to the account of short supplies of subsistence and transportation," suggesting instead that the leaders at the time had had inadequate knowledge of the extent of the enemy's rout.[84] Davis later wrote:

> Undue elation over our victory at Manassas was followed by dissatisfaction at what was termed the failure to reap the fruits of victory; and rumors, for which there could be no better excuse than partisan zeal, were circulated that the heroes of the hour were prevented from reaping the fruits of the victory by the interference of the President. . . . Though these unjust criticisms weakened the power of the Government to meet its present and provide for its future necessities, I bore them in silence, lest to vindicate myself should injure the public service by turning the public censure to the generals on whom the hopes of the country rested.[85]

The Rebel victory at Manassas Junction augmented the patriotic spirit that so permeated the South during 1861. By August it was possible for the *Richmond Enquirer* to report that not less than 210,000 soldiers had answered the South's call.[86] But there was much public impatience at the government's failure to take advantage of the supposed enemy disarray and to follow up the victory with tangible action.[87] As the first year of the struggle began to draw to a close, the initial public reaction to the hostilities changed. When the South failed to achieve the expected early victory to end the war and casualty lists brought home grim realities, many Southerners began to quail. Many of the early volunteers took advantage of their short enlistment terms to retire (even if in some cases temporarily) from the military.

By the time the third session of the Provisional Congress convened, July 20, 1861—the day before the Battle of Manassas—it was already apparent that the burden of the fighting would have to be borne by volunteers, not militia, and certainly not by regulars. Although most Confederates, including the congressmen, naturally derived a sense of satisfaction from the result of the battle, and some still clung to hopes that this single engagement might settle their independence, many were prudently resigned to ensure their future by continuing the military buildup. Davis was authorized to grant commissions to officers who would raise regiments in the states of Kentucky, Missouri, Maryland, and Delaware and to establish recruiting offices for individual volunteers from those states; and more important, in a bill signed into law on the same day, he was empowered to use the militia and to call for four hundred thousand volunteers to serve between one and three years.[88] While early legislation had called for one-year volunteers, in August the Congress recognized that troops might have to serve longer. Important lessons were being learned that gave the Confederacy a distinct advantage over the Union, which had only begun to resort to longer enlistments. Furthermore, Davis could accept additional volunteers to serve shorter periods of time in threatened localities. And to stretch the manpower that was already in service, Congress provided that the government could hire cooks and nurses for hospital service so that enlisted men doing such duty would be available for service in the field.[89]

Confederates rightly congratulated themselves on these accomplishments, and it soon seemed that congressional foresight was bearing fruit. In his opening message to the fifth session of the Provisional Congress, Davis enumerated recent "glorious victories at Bethel, Bull Run, Manassas, Springfield, Lexington, Leesburg, and Belmont," which he claimed had "checked the wicked invasion which greed of gain and the unhallowed lust of power brought upon our soil," proving "that numbers cease to avail when directed against a people fighting for the sacred right of self-government and the privileges of freemen." The rhetoric was shrill, but he was correct in noting that Union forces had not only been unable to extend control over much Confederate territory but also had been forced on the defensive at several points.[90] That Bethel, Leesburg, Springfield, and Belmont were cited as great victories, however, reflected naivete that was characteristic of both Northern and Southern thought. As in any war, moreover, there was a never-ending cry for more men. Woefully overestimating the numbers in Federal service at 1 million, early in 1862 Davis asked for additional troops, and the Congress responded.[91]

During the First Battle of Manassas, the Stars and Bars had not proved a desirable standard to follow in battle; it looked too much like the Union flag and sometimes could not be distinguished from it. Several Southern generals asked their friends in Congress to design a new flag. But Congressman William Porcher Miles wrote to General Beauregard that people were unflinchingly and sentimentally wed to the idea of retaining a flag that resembled the old Union banner.

On hearing this news, General Joseph E. Johnston sent out a circular request to his subordinates asking for suggestions for a battle flag design, which could be used in addition to the national ensign. From the many that were submitted, one drawn by Beauregard was selected. His design was for a red field, divided diagonally by a blue St. Andrew's cross edged in white, on which were placed thirteen white stars, one for each state claimed by the Confederacy (the original seven, the four from the second secession, plus Kentucky and Missouri, which both sides claimed). General Johnston modified the design by making the shape square instead of Beauregard's oblong and prescribed different sizes: for infantry four by four feet; artillery, three by three feet, and cavalry two and one-half by two and one-half feet.

The War Department approved the design on October 1, 1861. This battle flag of the Confederacy has mistakenly since become generally known as "the Confederate flag" and is often referred to incorrectly as "the Stars and Bars." The Confederate Congress never adopted this banner. (The design was incorporated, however, into a part of both subsequent national banners.) Two sisters and a cousin, Jennie, Hattie, and Constance Cary were visiting Beauregard's winter headquarters in Centreville, Virginia, when the approval for the design arrived. From their various undergarments, they fashioned the first three editions of the Confederate battle flag (thus they were a bit more of a boudoir pink than a martial red). Each girl sewed one flag, and each is known by the particular seamstress. These three original flags were for the troops under Johnston, Beauregard, and Earl Van Dorn. They were formally presented to the assembled soldiers in a ceremony on November 19, 1861.

Beauregard's battle flag, made by Jennie Cary, was used years later to drape the coffins of Jefferson Davis and of Beauregard himself. This flag, in all its pinkness, is on display at the Washington Artillery Museum in New Orleans. Another of the original battle flags is at the Confederate Museum, also in New Orleans. The whereabouts of the other original is unknown. There probably are, however, more copies of the Confederate battle flag in various displays and in possession of countless individuals today than there were soldiers in the whole Confederate army.

6

IN THE AFTERMATH OF
FIRST MANASSAS

Jefferson Davis began encountering difficulties with certain ultra state-rights leaders almost from the war's outset, and none was more blatantly recalcitrant than Georgia's Governor Joseph Brown. He was keenly jealous of his gubernatorial prerogatives, and he clearly regarded the requirements of his own state to be more important than those of the new country. He delayed allowing the transfer of former Federal arsenals and forts to the Confederacy; he removed the best weapons there into his own armory. He tried to forbid Georgia regiments to join the Confederate army, and when they did do so, he insisted that their state-owned arms must remain in Georgia. He called for more troops to defend Georgia's seacoast, although there was no immediate threat. He fought in every way he could sending any military units from Georgia to Virginia. Davis and War Secretary Leroy Walker both tried to placate Brown as best they could and even sometimes did give in to his demands, simply for the sake of harmony. Although Davis refrained from publicly upbraiding or denouncing Brown at this time, he did not dispute the words of the governor's political enemy, Howell Cobb—now the colonel of the Sixteenth Georgia Infantry—who described Brown as "the miserable demagogue who now disgraces the executive chair of Ga."[1]

Early on, Davis did prove himself to be "an active, involved commander in chief." The Rebel president had many decisions to make, and they were not easy. He had no illusions about how difficult the future was going to be. In a conversation with one of his friends, he asserted that the Confederates would do "all that can be done by pluck and muscle, endurance and dogged courage—dash and red-hot patriotism." Still, Mary Chesnut suggested that a "sad refrain" ran through the president's remarks. Davis did indeed expect that the war would be a long one and that the Confederates "would have many a bitter experience," for "only fools" could doubt the courage or the determination of the North.[2]

No more major action occurred in Virginia until the next year. First Manassas had been fought by the Union forces to try to nip the rebellion in the bud and to try to prevent the Rebel legislature from convening again. It achieved neither. Both sides now discerned that the conflict would not be a one-battle war. Possibly victory ill-served Southerners by taking some of the edge off their sense of urgency, but if it did so it was not a matter of major dimension.

As summer faded into fall and fall into winter, the troops on both sides settled down into permanent camps for training and waiting. A popular song that season in the South (and in the North as well) was "All Quiet Along the Potomac Tonight."

> All quiet along the Potomac to-night!
>   Except here and there a stray picket
> Is shot, as he walks on his beat, to and fro,
>   By a rifleman hid in the thicket.
>
> 'Tis nothing! a private or two now and then
>   Will not count in the news of a battle;
> Not an officer lost! only one of the men
>   Moaning out, all alone, the death-rattle.
>
> All quiet along the Potomac to-night!
>   No sound save the rush of the river;
> While soft falls the dew on the face of the dead
>   And the picket's off duty forever!

During these months the relationship between Davis and some politicians and generals began to deteriorate. Part of it was coincidental, but part resulted from Davis's poor judgment and their clashing personalities. Some of Beauregard's staff officers, for example, began referring to Davis as a "stupid fool." Davis meanwhile made fun of Beauregard's self-important array of underlings. "Whoever is too fine," Davis had said in June, "so fine that we do not know what to do with him—we send him to Beauregard's staff." Davis's friend James Chesnut heard the remark and repeated it to Beauregard. Davis, knowing about Beauregard's touchy temper, would have been better advised not to have made such a remark at all.[3]

As an active-negative president, Davis was compulsive and had difficulty handling his aggressive feelings. As he himself knew, he had a hard time deal-ing with criticism, whether it was just or not. Consequently, the criticism, which began early and grew throughout the war, steadily increased his intol-erance toward dissenting ideas and his impatience with people who disagreed with him. "The man and the hour" may "have met" in January 1861, but as far as increasing numbers of influential Confederates were concerned, that hour had been brief.

Perhaps Davis was a scapegoat for the failures of the Southern people, who were too individualistic to think that anyone else could be as smart as they were, but there is more to it than that. If Davis was difficult to get along with, and to be sure he was, it was partly because of the behavior and vituperation exhibited by so many of his adversaries. As early as February 15, 1861, T. R. R. Cobb, then a member of the Confederate Congress, wrote his wife that "the best friends of the Confederacy here [Montgomery] are troubled at these continued rumors of *President Davis* being a reconstructionist. Many are regretting already his election."[4] Almost two weeks later, when a pet bill of his had been vetoed by Davis, he told his wife that he would try to have it passed over the veto and that "it would do my very soul good to *rebuke* him at the outset of his *vetoing*."[5]

On February 28 the observant Mary Chesnut complained in her diary that "men are willing to risk an injury to our cause if they may in so doing hurt Jeff Davis."[6] Years later Robert Barnwell Rhett stated that within six weeks of Davis's election Congress had concluded that it was a mistake.[7] "Our excel-lent president Davis is not quite up to the mark," wrote one of Howell Cobb's correspondents,[8] and by the end of June 1861 Lawrence Keitt of the South Carolina delegation told Mary Chesnut that Davis's failure was a "foregone conclusion."[9] In August the wife of Congressman Louis T. Wigfall told her that a coalition against Davis had been formed, including important people in and out of Congress.[10] One of Alexander H. Stephens's friends wrote that "Mr. Davis and the peculiar people he trusts have given sufficient cause to every gentleman in the army to mutiny."[11] "Only Mr. Barnwell stands by Jeff Davis," Mary Chesnut wrote, with some exaggeration, on November 28, 1861.[12]

Sometime during summer and fall 1861 Davis had grown cold toward Vice President Stephens. Although they had consorted frequently earlier, Davis increasingly ignored Stephens. W. C. Davis observes that by his "own unco-operative attitude in Montgomery, Stephens had largely brought it on himself, but in [any] event Davis was the least collegial of men, never disposed to share even his confidences, let alone his authority."[13]

For months Davis and Stephens had no direct contact, though finally in November 1861 Davis solicited his vice president's advice concerning the choice of an officer to oversee the coastal defenses of Georgia and South Carolina. When Stephens suggested either Beauregard or Joseph E. Johnston, he was stung to learn of Davis's antipathy toward those two men. Embarrassed, Stephens realized just how much this underscored the reality of his isolation. It was the last conference between Davis and Stephens for more than a year.[14]

So disenchanted was Stephens with being an impotent vice president that he seemed not to desire to retain his office in the November general election; nonetheless, the favorable vote he received was nearly unanimous. Within a few weeks, his letters to his brother Linton began to reflect so much disenchantment with and disaffection toward Davis and the administration that "Linton for the first time began to burn them lest they fall into the wrong hands."[15]

Stephens found it disgusting that in order to find out what was going on he had to poke around newspaper and telegraph offices, "like any ordinary citizen," instead of being treated like the exalted officer he wished to be. He was after all truly "intensely interested in public affairs, and despite the growing coolness between him and Davis, he tried to temper his friends' harsh criticism of the president. What was needed, he told [his longtime friend Thomas W.] Thomas, was 'heroic patience.' But a man of his pride, not to mention conspicuous lack of patience, could take only so much."[16]

Meanwhile, Stephens was stricken with a dramatic downturn in his health, which rendered him semibedridden until February 1862. Thus did he miss much of the lengthy last session of the Provisional Congress that ran from November 18 to February 17. Even when he could take part in the proceedings, his participation was remarkably limited, and he was rarely in his seat for most of December and the latter half of January.[17]

Ill feeling toward Davis outside Congress could also be quite bitter. Stephens was just one of several important men the president had alienated in one way or another. The former governor of Mississippi, James Lusk Alcorn, a Whig who had served in the U.S. Senate, cursed Davis: "Oh let me live to see him damned! and sunk into lowest hell."[18] Such feelings were often communicated to congressmen. Early in 1862, James H. Hammond of South Carolina, also a former governor and senator, wrote Congressman W. W. Boyce that Davis ought to be impeached and that a dictatorship should be established. "West Point is death to us & sick Presidents & Generals are equally fatal."[19] Writing only a day earlier, T. R. R. Cobb, smarting because of another Davis veto, said that the House of Representatives would have deposed Davis if it had any confidence in Vice President Stephens.[20]

There was no plot to depose Davis, but there was considerable grumbling, especially whenever Confederate fortunes seemed bleak. W. W. Boyce thought Davis "no military genius," opposed his blatant favoritism of West Pointers, and feared that the South soon would be, as he quaintly put it, "Davis-ized."[21] Others were less outspoken but equally skeptical of Davis's abilities. Lewis Ayer, a congressman from South Carolina in both the First and Second Confederate Congresses, was also opposed to Davis but supported him because he felt that more criticism would only serve to hurt the cause, in which he did truly believe.[22] William L. Yancey was so anti-Davis that rather than yield "constitutional safeguards to the stealthy progress of legislative and executive usurpation," he would choose to "be vanquished in open combat with the invader."[23] The gentleman got his wish. It was more than strong, even despotic, powers of government that caused so much extreme commentary, for few people in the era of modern warfare have lived under a government as free as the Confederacy. Vice President Stephens admitted as much. In a letter to Herschel Johnson he pictured Davis as, among other things, "petulant, peevish [and] obstinate." The voluble and fiery Senator Wigfall agreed, complaining to General Joseph E. Johnston of Davis's "big-headedness and perverseness."[24]

Varina Davis provided an insight into her husband's personality when she wrote years later that he was "abnormally sensitive to disapprobation: even a child's disapproval decomposed him. He felt how much he was misunderstood, and the sense of mortification and injustice gave him a repellant manner." He was easily hurt, a dyspeptic individual, who let problems "gnaw at his vitals in silence."[25] But not wholly in silence—Davis's resentments could not be prevented from rising to the surface on occasion. He jealously guarded what he thought were the prerogatives of his office and was ever willing to write a tart letter, for example, to those who disagreed with his appointments.[26]

Robert G. H. Kean, head of the Bureau of War, noted in his diary a quarrel between the president and Congressman Edward Sparrow of Louisiana, one of Davis's staunchest supporters. Davis, Kean remarked, "seems to possess a most unenviable facility for converting friends into enemies."[27] The president himself seems to have agreed. "To me who have [sic] no political wish beyond the success of our cause, no personal desire but to be relieved from further connection with office, opposition in any form can only disturb me in so much as it may endanger the public welfare. . . . I wish I could learn just to let people alone who snap at me; in forbearance and charity to turn away as well from the cats as the snakes."[28]

On the other hand, Warren Akin, a congressman from Georgia, found Davis to be quite agreeable. "I had a long conversation with the President yesterday," he wrote his wife in January 1865. "He has been greatly wronged. . . . The President is not that stern puffed up man he is represented to be. He was [as] polite, attentive, and communicative to me as I could wish." Even so, Akin reported public rejoicing at rumors of Davis's death.[29]

Davis had shortcomings that angered other self-righteous men. He took as personal challenges affronts that larger-minded men would have ignored, and he spent long hours in argument and vindication that could better have been devoted to other purposes. Long letters to Senator Yancey over a commission for Yancey's son and bickering with Generals Joseph E. Johnston and P. G. T. Beauregard over past events are major cases in point. Less than three weeks before the fall of Richmond, Davis wrote to a disappointed officer to argue against the officer's accusation that his failure to be promoted was due to malice, and only three days before he fled Richmond, Davis took precious time to write Mrs. Howell Cobb to vindicate himself over a recent serious quarrel with Congress.[30] Davis had his enemies, that is true, but his own quirky and prickly personality was just as malignant an enemy. Although not fully apparent in the summer of First Manassas, by 1862 his behavior had become a critical problem that seriously affected his usefulness and accentuated the negative aspects of his active-negative leadership style.

The crying need for more war materials, especially in the far-flung regions, was never out of Davis's mind during summer 1861. He had received word that the pro-Confederate volunteers in Missouri had scant arms beyond squirrel rifles and shotguns.[31] On August 6 Davis persuaded the Congress to appropriate $1 million for support of the war effort there. It was not in time, for only four days later, the Battle of Wilson's Creek was fought in southwestern Missouri. It was a rather big and costly battle, and although a Confederate victory, in the aftermath the Rebels failed to secure the state, where a significant Union military presence remained, and Missouri was bitterly divided as much irregular conflict ensued.

Then on August 27, on the wind-whipped beaches of the Outer Banks of North Carolina at Cape Hatteras, an attack by a joint Federal naval and army expedition began on two sand and wood fortifications designed to protect Hatteras inlet. Eight ships and nine hundred men easily took Fort Clark. The next day the Federal naval vessels opened fire on Fort Hatteras, and after suffering severe damage, the fort surrendered. The fall of these forts sealed off an important blockade-running route, and invasion of North Carolina proved to be a valuable boost to Northern morale as well as having a negative impact on Southern spirits. It also encouraged class antagonism and the reemergence of openly Unionist sentiment in North Carolina.[32]

A third blow against the fortunes of the Confederacy—indeed one that may have been decisive in the fortunes of the fledgling nation—occurred when Confederate troops under Davis's friend, the ill-guided Major General

Leonidas Polk, entered self-proclaimed neutral Kentucky on September 3, 1861. This was in conflict with policy that had been expressed previously by both Davis and Tennessee's governor Isham Harris. To be sure, neither Davis nor Harris opposed entering Kentucky eventually, but they had elected to await political developments.

Davis's reaction to the violation of Kentucky's neutrality by General Polk illustrates his active-negative style, marked by passive-negative indecision when dealing with old friends. The very idea of a state's neutrality in a civil war may seem bizarre. Kentucky had declared neutrality at the war's outset and made it known that if either side violated it, the state would then join the other side. Kentucky was a vital state, rich in population and resources.[33] It was important for Davis to keep Confederate troops out of the state, in the hope that the Union would violate its neutrality. But Davis and the Confederacy were compromised by Polk's audacity. And Polk was Davis's longtime friend. Polk had resigned from the army only five months after his graduation from West Point in 1827 to study for the Episcopal priesthood. He had become the missionary bishop of Louisiana by the war's outset, and as Grady McWhiney observes, he "probably had been a bishop too long to be a successful subordinate general." Indeed, Braxton Bragg, to whom Polk would later be assigned as a subordinate, informed Davis that "with all his ability, energy and zeal, General Polk, by education and habit, is unfitted for executing the orders of others. He will convince himself his own views are better, and will follow them without reflecting on the consequences." Indeed, McWhiney also asserts that "Polk had resigned from the United States Army soon after graduation from West Point in 1827 [and] . . . there is no indication that Polk ever read a book on military science after he left West Point." Further, "The strategy Polk outlined [for operations in the later part of 1862] revealed how quickly he forgot what actually happened as well as some of his shortcomings as a general."[34] But Davis had unhesitatingly named Polk a major general.

Polk was in command of Department No. 2, which roughly included western and southern Tennessee and its adjacent areas.[35] As such, he was in a position to keep a close eye on events in Kentucky. He might also draw recruits from there, and in fact some Kentucky volunteers had already tried to join his army.[36] Meanwhile, Governor Beriah Magoffin of Kentucky, who was himself pro-Confederate, complained to Davis that Union authorities had "enlisted and quartered" a force within Kentucky, and he had urged their withdrawal in order to preserve his state's neutrality. Confederate troops just south of the Tennessee-Kentucky boundary also made the citizens of his state quite uneasy, he said, and he urged Davis to issue "an authoritative assurance that the Government of the Confederate States will continue to respect and observe the position indicated as assumed by Kentucky."[37]

Davis lost little time in giving those assurances, and he claimed that the "assemblage of troops in Tennessee . . . had no other object than to repel the lawless invasion of that State by the forces of the United States."[38] Davis's policy was clear to Polk, but the general had plans of his own. By the end of July 1861 he had landed at New Madrid, Missouri, worried about a possible Union move south along the Mississippi River, worried too about rumors that Union troops were soon to move into Kentucky, and eager to be there first if that proved true. Polk clearly was anticipating entering Kentucky in force for quite some time before he finally did so.[39]

In September some of Polk's troops ventured into Kentucky in order to avoid Union artillery emplacements in Missouri, across the Mississippi River from Columbus, Kentucky. Polk did not bother to inform Davis before this was done. On September 4, Governor Harris of Tennessee protested. Polk's reply was disingenuous: Davis had "delegated" him "plenary powers," and he refused to withdraw, making the bland statement, technically true, perhaps, that he "had never received *official* information that the President and yourself had determined upon any particular course in reference to the State of Kentucky."[40]

Polk had clearly violated Davis's orders. At the president's bidding, Secretary of War Walker promptly told Polk to withdraw his troops, but he simply informed Davis of his actions and justified his behavior by the "plenary power" supposedly delegated to him. "It is my intention now," he informed the president, "to continue to occupy and keep this position."[41] The necessity of Polk's action was doubtful, but it created an opportunity for Davis to correct his original blunder in appointing Polk in the first place. He could have followed up Walker's order by relieving Polk, thereby demonstrating to Kentuckians that the invasion had been unauthorized. Instead, Davis wavered.

He let his old friend off the hook, in what was surely one of the most inept decisions of the war. "The necessity must justify the action," Davis meekly telegraphed Polk.[42] The Kentucky Senate passed a resolution asking Polk to withdraw, but he refused, contending that the state was not behaving in a spirit of neutrality. Despite Davis's assurances to Magoffin, he ipso facto had approved of Polk's violation. Nor did Davis reprove Polk. He simply wrote him that "it is true that the solution of the problem requires the consideration of other than the military elements involved in it; but we cannot permit the indeterminate quantities, the political elements, to control our action in cases of military necessity. Such I regarded your occupation of Columbus to be."[43]

It was a rather weak performance. Polk had manipulated his commander in chief into approving his unauthorized invasion, which produced disastrous results (Kentucky did declare for the Union). And Polk had refused to withdraw in the face of direct orders from the secretary of war. Kentucky protested. Tennessee protested. The secretary of war protested. Davis, who had final say, even protested—for a time. But in the end, he wavered and approved of Polk's action. Friendship led to blind trust; that trust had led to Davis's uncritical acceptance of Polk's abuse of it. Davis merely warned Polk that his occupation of Columbus had to be necessary and would "of course be limited by the existence of such necessity."[44] But military necessity knew no limits; it seldom does. Polk remained, and Kentucky was lost to the South. The historian Stephen E. Woodworth believes, and we are inclined to agree, that Davis's blunder here "may have cost the Confederacy Kentucky and its best chance of final victory."[45]

On September 6 Federal troops captured Paducah. Davis, however, continued to stand behind Polk and thereafter steadfastly supported a policy of occupying as much of Kentucky as was possible. This was a clear illustration of Davis's strategic style: he relied too much on the judgment of commanders in the field, and he supported any of their decisions for offensive operation.[46]

There were other forebodings as well. Voicing a discontent within the Confederacy, a Virginia Presbyterian minister, Thomas V. Moore, expressed regret over continuing manifestations of jealousy, animosity, and rivalry among the states, especially between the "border, and cotton, and gulf, and western States," while—with just a tinge of hypocrisy—he also defended his own state against the calumny of the fire-eaters from the Deep South. And worse, some Southerners were already greedily beginning to extort handsome profits from the suffering of both middle-class citizens and the poor.[47]

Unionism was not dead. Pockets of pro-Union sentiment and sometimes outright resistance to Confederate authorities were rife by the end of 1861. In East Tennessee Union guerrillas burned several bridges, and in Arkansas an ardent Peace Society was so vexatious that Governor Henry M. Rector ordered the arrest of its members. Some Washington County, North Carolina, Unionists won elections as militia officers. Near Hillsboro, North Carolina, a candidate in an election for constable brashly announced his Unionist sympathies; his followers cast ballots marked with the American eagle. "Local militia refused to muster under the Confederate flag," George Rable has noted, also observing that the situation in North Carolina was especially murky. Rable points to the obvious conclusion: "The trouble was that loyalty to the Confederacy did not necessarily translate into support for the government (or even the abandonment of partisan goals)."[48]

Meanwhile, other sea islands off the Atlantic coast were captured by the Federals during fall and winter. These proved to be valuable coaling stations for the ever-increasing Federal blockading fleet as well as potential jumping-off points for possible raids or invasions of Southern soil.

Nevertheless, it was possible for the Confederate high command to feel upbeat as 1861 began to draw to a close. There were threats and fears, of course, but the only really bad news, as far as the strategists could perceive, came from the mountainous western portion of Virginia. There the people were strongly pro-Union, and two-thirds of the region had to be abandoned by late autumn. On November 18 Davis boasted in his annual message to Congress that instead of the enemy's "threatened march of unchecked conquest, they have been driven at more than one point to assume the defensive" and that "the Confederate States are relatively much stronger now than when the struggle commenced."[49]

On November 6, 1861, the voters of the Confederate States of America went to the polls to elect the president and congressmen of their first permanent government. The procedures for selecting candidates and presenting them, despite revealing the degree of chaos wrought by wartime conditions, reflected a return to the poorly organized informal procedures of the early Republic, a clear goal of the Confederate Constitution writers. As Rable observes, "The number of uncontested races raised hopes for national unity and the avoidance of partisan political bickering."[50] Davis himself was chosen without opposition for a six-year term. Some but not by any means all of the congressmen were not reelected.

Shortly after the election a sharp controversy erupted. Ominously, it concerned constitutional issues that supposedly had been settled. The Framers clearly had meant for the Confederate chief executive to be stronger than he had been in the Union. But Robert Ridgeway, for one, of the *Richmond Whig* expressed fear that too much power rested in executive hands. That there was any uncertainty concerning the constitutional intent and the desirability of its degree of innovation suggested the existence of ideological muddle and the probability of severe political alienation in the future.[51] All across the political spectrum, from elderly conservatives to brash young fire-eaters, there was fear that the Confederacy had established too much democracy in its new republic. David Donald has noted that the Confederacy was "astonishingly libertarian," as "disloyal elements throughout the South had almost unrestricted freedom. The real weakness of the Confederacy was that the Southern people insisted upon retaining their democratic liberties in wartime." Still, despite rare though occasionally outspoken public expression of discontent, many Confederate citizens firmly believed that their new republic was the best hope "for the survival of liberty with order."[52]

The two greatest flaws in the Confederate administrative system lay in poor relations between the central government and certain of the state governments and in Davis's propensity to enmesh himself in mountains of minutiae. Concerning the first, little that was constructive could be done because of the inherent nature of "divided sovereignty." The second was simply Davis's fault: instead of reforming administrative inefficiency, he encouraged it because he liked it. Varina sometimes heard him when he worked in his office at home, "actually singing while attending to his papers."[53]

His administrative difficulties were obvious to close observers. Running a huge army of hundreds of thousands of men was not quite the same thing as serving as secretary of war for the small U.S. Army of the 1850s. Stephen R. Mallory, Davis's secretary of the navy, considered that the president was "dilatory" in both work and decisions. Davis labored over minute details while leaving more important affairs unattended, often displaying passive-negative traits when it came to his paperwork.

He was indecisive (it was easier to answer unimportant letters than to establish future policy). Mallory described long cabinet meetings, marked by Davis's digressions, that accomplished little. Understanding the consequences of decisions made without adequate time for consideration, Davis often avoided decisions, proceeding slowly and without seeking adequate advice, some of which he most likely disagreed with anyway.[54]

New and inconsistent information made decisions even more difficult for Davis. John A. Campbell, former associate justice of the U.S. Supreme Court, assistant secretary of war, and one of Davis's key advisers, complained that the president merely drifted, that he had no grand plan for the war. The head of the Bureau of War, Robert G. H. Kean, agreed. Davis was "not a comprehensive man," Kean wrote in his diary; "he has no broad policy."[55]

Nor was Davis's administration well organized. John Beauchamp Jones, a clerk in the War Department, noted the apparent cross-purposes under which the department operated. "I watch the daily orders of Adjutant and Inspector-Gen. Cooper," he wrote. "These, when 'by command of the Secretary of War,' are intelligible to any one, but not many are by his command. When simply 'by order,' they are promulgated by order of the President, without even consulting the Secretary; and they often annul the Secretary's orders."[56]

Robert Kean, one of Jones's superiors, made a similar assessment: "I have observed recently," he wrote in August 1863, "that the Adjutant General in connection with the President acts *independently* of the Secretary of War. He refers papers for appointments directly to the President when the Secretary has never seen them."[57] Kean was at his wit's end as he observed Davis's lack of organization. "Certainly the style of business with which his time is now consumed is in our present circumstances almost a scandal—little trash which ought to be dispatched by clerks in the adjutant general's office." Davis was absorbed in "trifles," thought Kean, because he wanted "to be personally conversant about everything" and because he had weak advisers. Men like former Secretary of War Leroy P. Walker, Walker's successor, Judah P. Benjamin, and Adjutant and Inspector General Samuel Cooper, Kean thought, could not act independently and always required instruction from Davis. Another secretary of war, George W. Randolph, Keen perceived to have been frustrated by "the endless tediousness of consultations which yield no results. Hence a total absence of vigor." There was no policy, Kean asserted, "no line of action tending to foreseen results."[58]

To be sure, Davis did have a policy, but it was not systematically outlined in specific detail so that subordinates could study it, as modern military doctrine is. Davis was not much more systematic than most nineteenth-century Americans, Lincoln included. Policy was usually a general idea that military and civil leaders either ignored or simply took for granted. Nevertheless, it would have been helpful to Confederate functionaries if they had been able to study the details for some formally promulgated policy. As the historian Richard M. McMurry observes, "What the Confederacy needed was some overall military plan, some central direction, for its war effort. Only the president could have formulated, won support for, and implemented such a plan. Except for his often ineffective scheme for temporary interdepartmental movements of troops for specific purposes, Davis failed utterly to provide such leadership."[59]

Perhaps Davis failed at this point because he always had to keep in mind that there was a second locus of power with which he was often in competition, even though he recognized the vital need for cooperation. It is important to remember that the founders of the Confederacy believed that sovereignty is indivisible; they also believed that the individual states that constituted the Confederacy retained their independence and sovereignty. But instead of establishing a political arrangement whereby the Richmond-based central government was made clearly and operationally subordinate to the states in terms of power relationships, or vice versa, the South created a two-tiered jurisdiction. Confederate Southerners quite simply bore an allegiance to two distinct levels of governance.

Paradoxically, to be sure, just as in the United States (in a de facto sense), there was a division of powers between the central government and the "sovereign" states. And since this division, though real, was not clearly delineated, a twilight zone existed. As time elapsed, this zone was increasingly filled by the central government. Although no supreme court was ever created, the judiciary that did exist generally gave support to these increases in centralism. Thus the stage was naturally set for clashes between the central and the state governments, especially when any state had a strong-willed and independently minded governor.

Southern agriculture had the potential to support a prolonged war effort. The slave states produced almost all the sugar, rice, sweet potatoes, beans, and peas in the Union and more corn than the free states. An abundant wheat crop was raised annually. There were large amounts of food and numerous draft animals.[60] It was possible to convert cotton-growing land to production of even more food. The mass of the beef cattle, however, was located west of the Mississippi River, mostly in Texas.[61] And the Confederacy faced a major problem with respect to highly perishable foodstuffs and distribution because of a poorly coordinated railroad system.[62]

The upper seven slave states, Delaware, Maryland, Virginia, Kentucky, Missouri, Tennessee, and North Carolina, were major producers of grain and meat. The South did succeed in drawing considerable supplies from Kentucky and Missouri. One-third of the Union's wheat crop came from this area, as well as large amounts of oats, rye, buckwheat, barley, and corn. Beef cattle and hogs flourished here, too, and these were located close to transportation lines.[63] Numerous contracts were let for the hiring of steamboats to haul both supplies and men on inland waterways.

When the Confederacy began impressing foodstuffs, however, the practice proved unpopular. Commissary General Lucius Northrop's personality did not help, and gradually he became the single most disliked official in the South. Many people considered him to be a pet of President Davis—and to some degree this was true, though Davis truly believed in Northrop's capabilities. Northrop insightfully disputed the idea that the Confederate food supply was abundant and that the problems of distribution sprang solely from the inefficiency of the railroads: "The idea that there is plenty for all in the country is absurd. The efforts of the enemy have been too successful. . . . People have killed whole flocks of sheep, breeding stock of cattle and young cattle."[64] On August 21, 1861, he wrote to Davis, bleakly describing the Confederacy as a besieged fortress. The seceded states found themselves enclosed on two sides by water, and in the West the great desert formed an additional barrier to the outside world. The enemy to the North, previously serving as the traditional source of sustenance, threatened to invade and thus "consume the bacon of the country."[65]

Salt, essential for food preservation in a prerefrigeration era, early proved to be in inadequate supply. Northrop's department tried to obtain this valuable necessity by establishing stations that evaporated ocean water, leaving the salt residues, but Union coastal raids created an ongoing dilemma. The Confederacy attempted to increase salt production in inland deposits, such as Saltville, Virginia, and in remote locations like Avery Island, Louisiana. Sometimes poorly salted meat would rot in transport at depots.[66] Too many times armies went unfed or were inadequately fed. Overstating the case but targeting the problem, Lieutenant Colonel Frank Ruffin of the Subsistence Bureau declared in fall 1862 that the Confederacy was "completely exhausted of supplies."[67]

From the war's outset Northrop delegated responsibility to agents in the various states. These functionaries purchased or impressed goods at inflated prices from farmers and food speculators. People always complained about any impressment and also about the prices they received. Inflation increasingly vexed the Rebel South. And while farmers constantly carped about what they regarded as unlawful seizures on the one hand, on the other, commanders in the field complained about inadequate distribution of rations. Everyone seemed to be a special critic of the Confederate Commissary Department.

Many Commissary officers initially failed to build proper storage facilities, so that good food often rotted before the soldiers could eat it, especially in rainy periods. The railroad supervisors hardly knew what to do with supplies, either. In September 1861 an administrator of the Virginia Central Railroad complained that its depot in Richmond was full of flour and that no more could be stored. Only two freight cars were available to move it because the army had kept the others, evidently for storage in some cases but also from simply neglecting to unload and return the cars for additional shipments in other instances.

Joseph E. Johnston complained to Davis about his supply situation in northern Virginia in 1861, claiming that he knew where sufficient stores of bacon could be obtained. Yet he did not bother to share this information with Northrop, a strange and even glaring omission for an officer who had been quartermaster general of the U.S. Army just the year before. Thus the situation was aggravated by a problem in proper understanding of the chain of command. Davis explained that "the chief commissary with an army represents the Commissary Genl.; [he] should concur in general principles of policy but of course never let want ensue, even if the generals neglect their communications and prevent the objects aimed at by his dept from being accomplished."[68]

But the dissension was present from the beginning. Even in 1861 the commissary general was in competition with informal commissaries. Some generals appointed their own and ignored Northrop, except to send him bills for goods he had not ordered but was expected to pay for. Governors also established their own commissaries, who reported to commanders of units from their states. State commissaries and those appointed by local commanders scoured the same areas for supplies where Northrop's officers were searching, and each paid higher prices than necessary because of the competition.[69]

The Confederate supply agencies eventually did establish and operate their own factories and shops, in addition to contracting for goods. The Ordnance, Quartermaster, and Medical Bureaus also were authorized to set up a variety of establishments, such as clothing factories, wagon-making shops, medical laboratories, small arms and ammunition arsenals, and harness and shoe manufactories. These were managed by military officers assigned to the various bureaus and employing both military and civilian personnel to do the work. Congress regularly appropriated monies for these operations. Slaves also were used as laborers in building fortifications and railroads and for mining and agricultural production.

Another major difficulty arose because state governments were expected to play an active role in handling the war's logistics, but typically, or all too often, they placed narrow self-interest and local defense above the Confederate military cause.[70] Georgia's governor Joseph E. Brown believed that the conscription law, passed in 1862, was unconstitutional and suspended the draft in his state until the state supreme court could rule on it. Although the court upheld the law, Brown frequently did his best to hamper its implementation and operation. Governor Zebulon Vance of North Carolina often quarreled with the central government about attempts to regulate blockade running: the government in Richmond wanted from one-third to one-half of the cargo space reserved for military purposes. Vance threatened to burn the ships before complying with the regulation. He also refused to allow the distillation of grain into whiskey, which the medical department needed, because to do so was a violation of the laws of North Carolina.[71]

This was not the case in other states, however, and there was always a troublesomely abundant supply of alcohol for the troops. Officers often wished to issue orders banning the sale of intoxicants to their men, and within their camps they could and did do this; the problem was when the soldiers were allowed to go beyond the camp's boundaries. This in turn led early to the proclaiming of martial law, mainly for the purpose of controlling alcohol sales. Sometimes the Confederacy's drunken soldiery posed such a problem for the local citizens that they might themselves ask that martial law be imposed. Indeed, even some of the people who detested martial law could bring themselves to admit that it brought desirable results with regard to alcohol control. Mark Neely suggests that there was a deep and widespread "yearning for order in the Confederate States of America." The citizenry asked for, and received, whatever governmental force it took to achieve this end. Only at times, though, was this done by martial law; more often it was done through state legislation.[72]

When an army impressed the property of its own citizens, and sometimes even that of enemy civilians, proper payment was expected. The problem was that payment, though usually received, was not the same as adequate compensation, as far as most farmers were concerned. The impressment system eventually became tantamount to confiscation. To farmers, adequate compensation meant payment at market prices, but this concept was more vague than it seemed on the surface.

Public complaint soon required the regularization of impressment procedures, and in late 1861 Quartermaster General Abraham Myers issued a brief circular setting these down for his department. All impressing agents had to show written authority and had to give their victims certificates indicating the value of impressed goods. Impressment could be carried out only "when absolutely demanded by the public necessities, and their burden must be [equally] apportioned among the community." If slaves or teams were taken, they were to be paid for "at the usual rates of hire," and if goods were to be impressed the owner could elect to sell them to the army at "the fair appraised value" instead of having them impressed and returned; property worn out by service was to be paid for instead of being returned.[73]

Whether goods were obtained by impressment or ordinary bid and contract, the Confederate transportation system was essential, for if supplies could not be delivered to the point of need they were useless. But Confederate transportation was in fact quite inadequate. It relied on the powerful product of the industrial revolution—steam—for railroads and for steamboats. But steamboats could go only where the rivers went, and periods of high or low water could be disastrous for the timely movement of supplies. More important was the railroad, but the Southern rail network was too small. With only nine thousand miles of line, and much of that vulnerable to Union operations, compared to twenty-two thousand miles in the North, Confederates found that they could not move supplies and men as quickly as they needed and often not at all.[74] Southern rail lines were primarily designed as supplements for the road and river system, carrying produce from the farms to major markets or port cities. They did not form a network, as Northern railroads did. And Confederates were hindered by a lack of facilities to maintain their rails and rolling stock. As Emory Thomas has pointed out, "A bountiful harvest counted for little if local railroad tracks were destroyed by foes or cannibalized by friends, if the road to town were a quagmire, or if wagons and mules were impressed to serve the army."[75] Indeed, crops often were bountiful, but the peas, beans, corn, and the like often did not, could not, get to those who needed them most, whether soldier or civilian.

One way to deal with the railroad problem was to impress the rails, locomotives, and cars of one road to keep more important lines in operation, and this was frequently done. Another was to build new lines, a solution often proposed but seldom carried out. A premodern society, or one just emerging into the modern age, may be slow at innovation, and this was certainly true when it came to building railroads in the South.[76] Richard D. Brown is especially perceptive on this matter, positing that "the growing tension between the eager modernization of the North and the incomplete, reluctant modernization of the South was influential both in bringing on the war and in determining its outcome."[77]

As Jerrold Northrop Moore has noted, at this early period of the war— when problems were far more simple than they later became—"Nobody in Richmond or at Manassas seemed able to construct warehouses or make anybody else do it. . . . And the railroad cars continued to be held as storehouses at distant points."[78] Sometimes vitally needed railcars were loaded with baggage, and other times they could not be moved because of a lack of sidings. Single-track lines were blocked with cars standing idle, thereby preventing movement along an entire line.[79]

The shortage of both cars and engines was so great that Secretary of War Judah P. Benjamin, who replaced Walker in that job on November 21, 1861, sought to impress the equipment of Georgia's Western and Atlantic Railroad. Discovering that the road was owned by that state, he revoked his orders but appealed to Governor Brown for assistance in return for "any reasonable recompense that Georgia demands."[80] Brown replied that the Western and Atlantic needed all the equipment it had but graciously suggested three privately owned lines that he thought might provide the required engines and cars.[81]

The key lines of the Confederacy included one from Memphis to Charleston and Richmond and a second from Vicksburg to Charleston and then north toward Richmond through Wilmington.[82] Unfortunately for the South, the road east from Memphis was cut by Union forces early in the war, and both the alternative route and the Vicksburg route had short but significant gaps. The logical step was to fill in those gaps, but that was finally accomplished only with great difficulty.

It was not simply a question of the shortage of railroad iron; it was also a question of attitude. When President Davis recommended to Congress in November 1861 that the Confederate government should build the forty miles of line between Greensboro, North Carolina, and Danville, Virginia, in order to create an additional east-west route, some congressmen objected. Ten of them wrote an indignant protest and had it spread on the pages of the Journal of the Congress. Davis's modest proposal was attacked for invading the rights of the states and sapping "the foundation of the Constitution and public liberty;" more important, it was not considered a military necessity "because armies and munitions and military supplies have been, are now, and probably always will be mainly transported by other means." The protestors concluded that "it is not necessary to connect distant portions of the country by railroad communication, such connection being already fully and amply made."[83]

The Richmond-Danville connection was finally completed, but it took two years. With such traditional attitudes hampering the distribution of vital supplies, it is not surprising that areas of famine could not always be relieved by shipment from areas of plenty, and impressment often became an absolute necessity to feed both soldier and civilian. Areas close to frequent battlefields, such as in Northern Virginia and Middle Tennessee, were stripped frequently by the impressment officers.

The issue of fair market value was key to the impressment procedure, but it also came up in connection with the War Tax of 1861. One of its collectors complained to Senator Edward Sparrow of Louisiana: "Marketable value means the current prices which property commanded *regardless of terms*, (providing the paper with which it was purchased draws interest) when we were enjoying peace." And he added, "for if the note must be taxed at its face value certainly the property which it purchased should pay as much tax as the note." In some confusion, he asked Sparrow for a definition of market value.[84]

By fall 1861, there were widespread complaints about extortionists, meaning individuals who bought up goods and foodstuffs with a view to withholding them from the stream of commerce and selling them later at higher prices, or who were alleged to have done so. The label was applied to ordinary merchants and farmers as well as to actual speculators, however, and that created a good deal of class antagonism.

Governors complained of the problem. Alabama's governor A. B. Moore, for example, attacked those who purchased "articles indispensable to the support of the Army and of our poor people for the purpose and with the intent of extorting extravagant prices from those who might be compelled to purchase these articles," and he prohibited state agents from dealing with such individuals. He congratulated his state on harboring only a few extortionists but recommended to the legislature that it pass appropriate measures. He believed that all the Confederate states had this problem,[85] and he was no doubt correct. In Virginia, Governor John Letcher called upon the state convention "to put down the growing evil of extortion almost universally prevalent throughout the State." He complained that "the question is no longer one of fair profit, but it has become a question of how much can be extorted for a necessary article from the people." He feared extortion would create great suffering and pointed out that the family of a soldier earning eleven dollars a month could not afford salt at twenty dollars a sack.[86]

Another problem involved actual payment. The quartermasters and commissaries were expected to pay for what they took, but getting the necessary funds often proved difficult. Even before inflation became a serious problem, Treasury Secretary Memminger sometimes refused to allow funds already appropriated by Congress to be used for purchase of supplies, hoping to hold down costs and thus prevent inflation. Instead, he suggested that the bureaus use government bonds for payment, but Northrop "found farmers and suppliers everywhere reluctant to sell for bonds which would delay their actual payment for months or longer."[87] In August 1861 Northrop reported the commissary in Atlanta could no longer make purchases because the secretary could no longer provide him cash with which to pay. Another agent in Nashville "writes that only bankable funds are received for provisions, and that he has lost coffee already agreed upon because he could not use bonds, which are not bankable." An agent in New Orleans complained that "he has been required by persons who have sold supplies to return in kind what remains unused as part payment of their bills."[88] (Secretary of War Walker forwarded this letter to Northrop, who supposed that the problem was created by "some difficulty in the engraving" of Treasury notes.)

Fearing the worst from the very start, especially regarding a shortage of pork and other salt meats, Northrop had immediately purchased supplies at cheap prices from beyond the Confederate border, including Kentucky, which, still in its period of neutrality, was not enemy-controlled territory.[89] Major Frank Ruffin, one of Northrop's subordinates, estimated that 1.2 million head of hogs were packed in the North and sent South before active hostilities had broken out, more than one-third of the hog production of the United States. Even granting some exaggeration, it was an important accomplishment, and as late as January 1862 only about one-quarter of that meat had been consumed. The rest was available for future needs.[90]

Contracting for flour was more difficult. Due to a lack of funds, the commissary in 1861 was unable to purchase flour when it was low in price and had to wait until monies were received, when prices were higher. A compromise with necessity was made, and purchases were made at future market prices, whatever they might be. For this purpose Ruffin defined market price as "the application of the universally accepted commercial law that the price of any article not at a ruling market must be the price of that market less cost and charges." This resulted in an effective price for flour of one dollar per bushel for starters, although much difficulty was created by speculators.[91]

Postmaster General John Reagan's first problem in producing postage stamps was to find engravers who could provide adequate plates. Initially he sought contracts for stamps and plates in the North, but hostilities erupted before they could be completed. He then found a firm in Richmond, Hower and Ludwig, which could make crude stamps by the lithographing process. The first Confederate stamp, a five-cent denomination done in green, appeared on October 16, 1861.

Hower and Ludwig were limited both by scant equipment and experience. The scarcity of printing stones forced them, after completing an order, to remove the stamp transfers and to use the stone for other purposes, chiefly for the printing of paper money. This necessitated the making of new transfers, which invariably differed slightly, whenever another order for stamps came in. An endless variety of shades resulted from the lack of sufficient pigment to avoid hand-mixing colors and from an apparent utter disregard for uniformity by the printers. The inks were produced with mortar and pestle, muller and ink slab, laboriously manipulated by hand.

Meanwhile, on the international scene, whenever a Northern warship called at a British port, the crew found a cold reception. In England, the three Confederate ministers met unofficially with the British foreign secretary, Lord John Russell, an episode that infuriated the Lincoln cabinet. The Americans also grew irritated at British investors who financed the business of blockade running.

U.S. Secretary of State Seward countered with bold talk that upset the British cabinet. "We do not desire . . . foreign interference," he advised a London correspondent, but if it came, the United States would "not hesitate, in case of necessity, to resist it to the uttermost." He also called upon free-willed men of Canada, Mexico, and Central America to foment a "spirit of independence on this continent." As to any British recognition of the Confederacy, Seward issued something of a threat: if "this act . . . is distinctly performed, we from that hour shall cease to be friends, and become once more . . . enemies of Great Britain."[92]

In August 1861, yet another diplomatic flap occurred when U.S. Secret Service agents discovered that the British consul in Charleston, South Carolina, had been involved in direct talks with the Confederate government. At the same time, Prime Minister Palmerston requested reinforcements for Canada, citing the Union's recent defeat at Manassas and suggesting that the Federals might accept the departure of the Confederacy and grab Canada as compensation.

By autumn an uneasy calm had settled. Then came the unexpected: on November 8, 1861, personnel aboard the USS *San Jacinto,* which was cruising in the Old Bahamas Channel, spied the British mail packet *Trent,* which was bound for Britain with two Confederate foreign agents aboard, James M. Mason of Virginia and John Slidell of Louisiana, the commissioners to Britain and France. They had slipped through the blockade on October 12. The captain of the *San Jacinto,* Charles Wilkes, a cantankerous and troublemaking man, had called at Havana, Cuba, and found the commissioners there awaiting passage. The *San Jacinto* watched for the *Trent*'s departure from Cuba, began trailing the vessel, and then hailed it with a threat of force, firing two shots across the bow. A spirited argument and some hot words ensued. Then, as the irate and outspoken British captain and other officers and crew watched, Mason and Slidell, with their secretaries, were taken under guard aboard the *San Jacinto.* That some sort of trouble would occur seemed likely, and it was instigated by Federal authorities. On October 15, the Union secretary of the navy, Gideon Welles, had written Flag Officer Samuel Francis Dupont that Mason and Slidell had run the blockade on the steamer *Nashville* and asked whether a fast steamer could not be found to intercept it.[93] Mason and Slidell were considered big prizes, and it was not surprising for any enterprising captain to seek them out, even after they had transferred to a British vessel.

The *Trent* continued its voyage and delivered news of the outrage to the British, while Mason and Slidell were taken to Boston and imprisoned at Fort Warren. Wilkes's action was unprecedented and a clear violation of international law.[94] Yet public opinion in the North rendered him a hero and his actions just. Hudson Strode has asserted that "the North was cock-a-hoop jubilant." Captain Wilkes received adulation and expressions of thanks. The House of Representatives commended him; he was celebrated in New York City with a parade and feted in Boston. And Jefferson Davis, reading about the North's vociferous demonstrations, mused that "the outrage was the more marked, because the United States had been foremost in resisting the right of 'visit and search' and had made it the cause of the War of 1812 with Britain." Did Davis ponder what England might do if the United States did not back down? Surely, he thought and hoped, this would tip the scales and induce the British to come to the Confederacy's aid. For the rest of November and well into December, the affair dominated his thinking, and there was little else talked about in the South.[95]

News of the incident reached Great Britain on November 27. On hearing the story, Lord Palmerston allegedly threw down his hat and shouted, "I don't know

whether you are going to stand this, but I'll be damned if I do!" The British public uniformly supported Prime Minister Palmerston's demand for a formal apol-
ogy from the government in Washington and the immediate release of the
prisoners. Responding to the crisis, Britain began to prepare for war; soon thousands of troops were sent to Canada, and Britain's Atlantic fleet was enlarged.

By December 4, Her Majesty's government had moved to prohibit the
export of arms, ammunition, and military supplies to the Union and had issued
a veiled ultimatum to the Lincoln administration: release the commissioners
and apologize to Britain or face the consequence. At the outset of any hostilities, it was thought, British troops would attack the partially completed Fort
Montgomery at Rouses's Point, New York, on Lake Champlain, which controlled access to the Richelieu River. That three-acre stone-walled fortifica-
tion had been under construction sporadically for twenty-five years and was
defended only by the carpenters and masons who worked there. The British
felt certain that the Americans would mount some sort of offensive in that
vicinity by spring.

Furthermore, Britain intended to invade Maine. In doing so, the British
hoped first to thwart any attempted Union move into Canada; second, they
needed the Grand Trunk rail line that ran from Portland to Montreal and
beyond. The minimum plan called for employing 7,640 regulars, constituting
eight battalions of infantry, three batteries of field artillery, two batteries of
garrison artillery, and two engineer companies. A more ambitious plan envisioned augmenting this invasion force with 40,000 militia.

The British troop movement to North America began on December 18, as
1,800 Grenadier Guards and Scots Fusilier Guards filed aboard two ships in
Southampton. At the same time, the Canadians mobilized. "War, war; we hear
nothing but war," wrote one Canadian woman as she watched the frantic
efforts. The *Toronto Globe* reported that "at the corner of every street, you
hear the excited discussions as to the Mason and Slidell outrage, the next news
from England, the erection of forts, and the probabilities of a fight with the
Americans." Students, hunting clubs, and workmen formed military companies. The first transports from England arrived on December 26.

The British never entertained the idea of totally conquering the North; they
knew it was too big and too powerful for that. Losses in the Great Lakes
region would have been a bitter price to pay for the portions of territory seized,
but who knew what the future might bring, when losses might be recouped?
The post–Civil War United States certainly might be less potent, for surely at
least some portion of the Confederacy might survive.

The crisis over the *Trent* affair, however, was resolved. The ailing prince
consort, Albert, left his sickbed to read and urge revision of the ultimatum that

had been prepared for the Lincoln government. The toned-down message was accepted by the U.S. officials, the prisoners were released, and an explanation was tendered. A gloomy pall fell over the South, for as J. B. Jones wrote in his diary, "Now we must depend upon our own strong arms and stout hearts for defense." Davis gloomily noted that "it was little to be expected, after such explicit commendation of the act, that the United States government would accede to the demands."[96] Mason and Slidell made their ways to England and France. They did not, however, manage to obtain official recognition of the Confederacy.

President Davis appointed Albert Pike, a Maine-born Arkansan, who later gained much more fame as a poet and a Mason than his Civil War involvements garnered him, to negotiate with various Indian tribes on behalf of the Confederacy. Many of the Indians in the "five civilized tribes" in what is now Oklahoma were slaveholders. The superintendent of Indian Affairs, who was headquartered at Fort Smith, was pro-South, as were his agents, who were dispersed among the tribes. On July 10, 1861, a treaty arranged by Pike was agreed to between the Confederate government and the Creek Indians—the first of nine that Pike eventually was able to fashion. And on July 12 he signed treaties for the Confederacy with the Choctaw and Chickasaw Indian nations.

During the subsequent months of August and October, Pike made treaties with the Seminole, Comanche, Osage, Seneca, Shawnee, and Quapaw and finished his task with an agreement with the Cherokee on October 7. The terms of these treaties varied from tribe to tribe, depending on the circumstances of each. Ties with the five civilized tribes were stronger than those with other tribes. The Creek, Choctaw, Chickasaw, and Cherokee agreed to "perpetual peace and friendship, and an alliance offensive and defensive" with the Confederacy, and the Seminole were asked only to agree to "perpetual peace and friendship," no alliance. These five tribes were to acknowledge "the protection of the Confederate States of America, and of no other power or sovereign whatever." Other tribes, the Comanche, Osage, Seneca, Shawnee, and Quapaw, only "place[d] themselves under the laws and protection" of the Confederacy "in peace and war forever."[97] Eventually the Choctaw, Cherokee, Creek, and Seminole nations had nonvoting delegates in the Confederate House of Representatives.

From the beginning, the Confederacy claimed large portions of the West, including Indian Territory and what is now Arizona and New Mexico. On November 22, 1861, the Confederacy officially designated the Indian Territory as a department within the would-be nation, and Albert Pike, by then a brigadier general, was named its superintendent. The Indians provided the Confederacy with troops, whose chief activities were confined to the Indian Territory, from which they made raiding forays into Kansas. As a general rule Indians of mixed blood tended to be pro-Confederate; the others stood with the Union.

There were remnants of two Indian tribes within the Confederacy that had never migrated to the West: the Seminoles in the Florida Everglades and the Cherokees in the Great Smoky Mountains of western North Carolina and northern Georgia. The Seminoles played no part in the Civil War, but the Cherokees, who were much more numerous, provided several hundred enlistees who proved militarily useful for their scouting abilities, especially in East Tennessee.

Leroy Walker had not done too badly as secretary of war, considering the pressures and his blundering conjecture at first that there would be no war. But it was a crucial post, and Davis believed that Judah P. Benjamin could do better; thus the change was made on November 21, 1861. Walker had many critics, and much of what they alleged was true. Thomas Bragg, brother of General Braxton Bragg, succeeded Benjamin as attorney general. Also on this date, Brigadier General Lloyd Tilghman was named to command Forts Henry and Donelson, on the Tennessee and the Cumberland Rivers, just south of the Kentucky-Tennessee line.

Their locations were not well chosen, and they soon proved untenable, but the Confederacy had shunned building them where they should have been, near the mouths of the rivers, in deference to Kentucky's earlier desire for neutrality. The two rivers were inviting routes for Federal invasions, equally as important as the Mississippi River. After an engagement at Belmont, Missouri, the Confederates called for ten thousand volunteers from Mississippi to protect the post they had established at Columbus, Kentucky. The year ended on an ominous note.

Yet the Davis family had reason for joy: on December 6, they welcomed the birth of a new baby, William Howell Davis, named for Varina's father. His mother was proving herself, in the eyes of many, to be a complex person. According to William Cooper,

> Clever, strong-minded, willing to express her opinion, including even her continued "unaltered feelings" for her Northern friends, she drew other women to

her. In Mary Chesnut's words, she could exert "great force." At the same time, her sharp wit and biting comments could repel. . . . She displayed two sides of a forceful personality. Secretary Mallory found her "a truthful, generous good woman," whose "perception of the ridiculous is perfectly riotous in its manifestations." Yet he commented that she "lack[ed] precisely what she plumes herself upon,—refinement & judgement; and her attempts at mimicry though they sometimes amuse, are not only usually failures, but they present her in a light at once undignified and unamiable."[98]

7

FORGING THE RESOURCES OF WAR

Jefferson Davis "recognized that a 'national character' had not predated the formation of the new country, that one would have to be developed while fighting the war." He clearly perceived that he needed to think about more than defense, according to William Cooper. He "was eager for his enemy to feel the pain and horrors brought by the conflict. He agreed with the many Confederates who pressed him to take the fight into the North. He informed his brother Joseph he would much rather have the Confederate armies on the Susquehanna River than the Potomac." Yet "Davis could not do so. Reality constrained him."[1]

He was peppered with criticism for not being more boldly aggressive, and painfully to him, "Even in the face of criticism, he did not think he could explain his reasoning. 'I have borne reproach in silence, because to reply by an exact statement of facts would have exposed our weakness to the enemy.' Thus, he could only 'pine for the day when our soil should be free from invasion and our banners float over the fields of the Enemy.' "[2]

Davis had harsh words for his country's foes: "In his judgment, the war waged against the Confederacy had become 'barbarous.' The Union had 'bombarded undefended villages' and participated in 'arson and rapine, the destruction of private houses and property, and injuries of the most wanton character even upon non-combatants, especially along the Confederate border.' " He hoped to keep his people's spirits and determination sufficiently buoyed, for as he proclaimed, "Liberty is always won where there exists the unconquerable will to be free."[3] Soon, however, events proved ominous and discouraging.

On February 8, 1862, the Confederacy suffered disaster of considerable proportion at Roanoke Island, North Carolina. Some ten thousand Federals in another combined army and navy expedition attacked about twenty-five hundred defending Rebels. The place was taken and some thirty guns and fifteen hundred troops were captured. It was a scandal; the Confederate commander, the former Virginia governor Henry A. Wise, whose own son, Captain O.

Jennings Wise, was among the twenty-three Confederates killed, demanded investigation as to why the defenses had been so weak. With good reason he was eager to place the blame for the defeat and the loss of his son on someone else's shoulders.[4]

In the Confederate capital, the seriousness of the defeat was deeply felt; a back door to Richmond had been opened and a vital Southern state was seriously threatened with further incursion. The Confederate government, Rebel newspapers, and the citizenry generally saw the disaster at Roanoke Island in a much truer light than historians have tended to appreciate.

The episode also cost War Secretary Judah Benjamin his job. The government elected to let him take the heat rather than to admit to its own people or to the Yankees that the real reason for Roanoke's weakness was not the secretary's ineptitude or lack of care but that sufficient resources simply had not been available. George W. Randolph of Virginia became Secretary of War. As for Benjamin and the Confederacy's cabinet, however, the new arrangement worked for the best: Benjamin was subsequently named secretary of state, and he served the Confederacy much better in that capacity.

The Union navy was always vastly superior in every measurable way to the Confederate navy. Combined operations involving both naval and ground forces are a Civil War–era hallmark of evolving modernity in warfare; in the western theater, these began in the Henry/Donelson campaign. These battles foreshadowed the Confederate problems of inadequate resources and certain incompetent generals, especially those who held positions mainly for political considerations. Under the oversight of Albert Sidney Johnston, the Confederacy had established strongholds on the key rivers: on the Mississippi at Columbus, Kentucky; on the Tennessee at Fort Henry; and on the Cumberland at Fort Donelson. Their purpose was to prevent the Union forces from using these major arteries of commerce as routes of invasion into Tennessee and farther south. The Confederates also deployed a substantial force north of Nashville to block a Union advance southward along the Louisville and Nashville Railroad.

Throughout the war armies on both sides were usually dependent on supplies transported by river, canal boats, or railroads. Transportation by horse or by mule-drawn wagons on the unpaved Southern roads was hopelessly inefficient. Spring mud made things even worse. On long hauls the draft animals would eat the weight of their wagon's load in oats and hay, making it essential that the animals be fed from fodder secured along the route.

Thus, armies typically oriented their operations along the efficient water and rail routes. These were needed not just for transporting ammunition and war materiel but also for food for the troops and sometimes even for fodder for the horses and mules. In this respect, Civil War armies differed from those in Western Europe, the very ones with which many of the armies' regular officers were familiar. The intensively cultivated European countryside had readily supplied the large armies characteristic of the preceding two centuries, but the big armies the North and South so promptly created often could not find enough, either for man or beast, in the much less intensively farmed American South. Aggravating this supply deficiency was the cultivation in some areas of the inedible crops, cotton and tobacco.[5]

Thus Civil War armies could not usually disperse and live off the country, as armies in Western Europe had long been doing. When the war put European-sized armies into a region of extensive agriculture, conditions did somewhat come to resemble the twentieth-century style of campaigning, with the armies depending on supply from remote bases in their rear. Therefore, the opening campaigns in the western theater revolved around a struggle for control of the critical arteries of transportation.

Both Union and Confederate forces west of the Appalachians had a conventional command structure, the Confederates having a single commander, Albert Sidney Johnston, over all Southern forces from the Appalachian Mountains westward to include Arkansas, Louisiana, and the Mississippi River. Unlike the Confederate unified command, the Union forces in eastern Kentucky and Tennessee were under Major General Don Carlos Buell, and those in western Kentucky were under Major General Henry W. Halleck, who also had command in Missouri. Having mostly overcome Rebel sympathizers in Missouri, Halleck then concentrated his forces, employing river steamers to move men and supplies, and obtained effective assistance from the U.S. Navy. The navy plied the rivers with gunboats, some of which had mounted on them quite powerful guns, and some of the vessels were fitted with iron armor. Halleck aimed to take control of the Tennessee River, then move south along it until his advance had turned the Rebel stronghold at Columbus, Kentucky; and thus he would open the Mississippi.

To do this Halleck needed to take Fort Henry, which blocked the Tennessee, and then to take Fort Donelson, so he could send a force up the Cumberland River and menace the important city of Nashville. He could thus threaten to turn the Confederate force in southern Kentucky, which offered opposition to Buell and his men. Both antagonists depended on the railroad linking their positions, their bases being in Louisville and Nashville.

With Brigadier General Ulysses S. Grant taking charge of the offensive land forces and the equally capable flag officer A. H. Foote commanding the naval flotilla, Halleck had a perfect team to carry out his conceived offensive.

On February 6, 1862, Federal troops under Grant, aided by a fleet of four iron-clads and three wooden gunboats, easily captured Fort Henry. Confederate Brigadier General Lloyd Tilghman decided to save the major part of his garrison by sending all but some artillerists and those who were on a hospital boat ten miles overland to the stronger Fort Donelson on the Cumberland River.

The Federals attacked on February 13, the gunboats augmented the assault the next day, and the battle raged its hottest on the third day. Almost completely sealed off, the Confederate officers decided to surrender on February 16. There was a musical-chairs routine as Generals John B. Floyd and Gideon Pillow each abdicated the command and made their somewhat ignominious getaways in a boat that took them over the Cumberland. General Simon B. Buckner, left holding the bag, asked Grant for terms. Grant replied, "No terms except unconditional and immediate surrender can be accepted. I propose to move immediately upon your works." His reply generated his enduring nickname: "Unconditional Surrender" Grant. It was the beginning of the Union penetration of the Confederate West.

More immediately important, it opened the Cumberland to the waterborne Union advance, which resulted in the evacuation of Nashville and its occupation by Union forces on February 25. Nashville was crucial because of the factories located there. With their position thus turned, the Confederates withdrew all their forces along the railroad between Louisville and Nashville.

Sketchy news of these disasters in the West was slow to reach Davis. He wrote to his brother Joseph on February 21, indicating both his utter commitment to the cause and his confusion about the situation in Tennessee:

> All I have, except my wife and children, I am ready to sacrifice for my country. We have very imperfect intelligence of the disaster at Fort Donelson. I cannot believe that our army surrendered without an effort to cut the investing lines and retreat to the main body of the army. . . . [But] in the meantime I am making every effort to assemble a sufficient force to beat the enemy in Tennessee, and retrieving our waning fortunes in the West.[6]

After all the dreary details finally reached him, Davis was dispirited. Not only was Donelson the Confederacy's greatest loss thus far, but even worse was the fact that Kentucky seemed irretrievably lost and the way to Nashville was open. Davis soon was receiving tragic telegrams from all sorts of people pleading for him to help them.[7]

The twin disasters, as well as the vexing but insistent urging coming from General P. G. T. Beauregard, were the catalysts to induce Davis and his top governmental officials to dispatch additional troops to the western theater. Braxton Bragg left Pensacola with ten thousand men, and another five thousand were sent from New Orleans to join Beauregard's force. By late March these forces were concentrated in Corinth, Mississippi, under the command of General Albert Sidney Johnston, with Beauregard second in command.

The most learned study of the Confederate Congresses is Thomas B. Alexander and Richard E. Beringer's *Anatomy of the Confederate Congress: A Study of the Influence of Member Characteristics on Legislative Voting Behavior, 1861–1865,*[8] which seeks "to describe the relationship between a congressman's legislative performance and some of the known considerations that could have influenced him."[9]

Alexander and Beringer essentially have found close division in the great majority of roll-call votes. Moreover, Confederate congressmen often showed erratic tendencies, being swayed by personal whim or myriad mutually interacting motivations; wealth and slaveholding by a member or his constituency made no difference. Former party affiliation mattered considerably, and an individual's stand on secession was even more significant; but most important was exterior versus interior status (i.e., whether the member's home district was occupied or threatened by Federal forces). Sectionalism permeated the Confederacy, heralding possibly a stark division between the Upper South and the Lower South. Delegates from exterior areas were much more cohesive, much more prone to sacrifice, and much more committed to the Confederacy's continued existence.

Alexander and Beringer conclude "that knowing a member's Exterior or Interior status, his secession stand, and when he served in Congress is almost all that is needed to place the great majority in at least the proper half of a spectrum from strong to weak dedication to Confederate survival."[10] Their book affirms the opinions earlier propounded by scholars such as David Potter, David Donald, and Eric McKitrick, all of whom emphasize a lack of adequate leadership in the Confederate government, and most important, the problems of function (or lack of it) that resulted from the lack of political party organization. These scholars have asserted that a democratic governmental body cannot function well without party discipline because opposition elements are consistently incapable of "establishing effective alternatives to whatever executive policies they might oppose."[11]

The Congress erred in opting to conduct many of its sessions in private, arousing public suspicion and distrust. To be sure, there was need to keep sensitive military and political information secure, but the North's Congress held open sessions. The South, in contrast, violated an important principle of representative government, making the Confederate claims of superior political virtue seem hypocritical.[12] Certainly by the time of Davis's inauguration as permanent president in February 1862, political strife was already well under way in the Confederacy. And in satisfying the demands of the people for government jobs, Davis ran afoul of the concept of loyalty to former party affiliation. By March newspapers attacked him for ignoring former Whigs in the appointment of officials.[13]

In his Inaugural Address, Davis felt compelled to mention recent "serious disasters," the almost simultaneous losses at Forts Henry and Donelson and at Roanoke Island. On the occasion of this speech, there were no spring flowers blooming, as had been the case when he was first inaugurated in Montgomery, only a wintry mixture of snow and rain; inadvertently, he stepped out from under a protective canopy, and someone held an umbrella over him. He declared that all hope of "a returning sense of justice" in the North was "dispelled." Against "the tyranny of an unbridled majority . . . we are in arms to renew such sacrifices as our fathers made to the holy cause of constitutional liberty." He thought perhaps of the Battle of Buena Vista, fifteen years earlier to the very day, and he warned that the war would cost both "money and blood," but "nothing could be so bad as failure." Reverses should only stimulate resistance, as with "the patriots of the Revolution." The struggle thus far had awakened "the highest emotions and qualities of the human soul. . . . Instances of self-sacrifice and of generous devotion to the noble cause . . . are rife throughout the land."[14]

Varina had found him that morning in his room "on his knees in earnest prayer 'for the support I need so sorely.'" At the end of his speech, Davis confessed "unaffected diffidence" (just as had George Washington), and his "humble gratitude and adoration" for the protection of Providence. Then, he raised his eyes and hands upward and concluded: "To Thee, O God, I trustingly commit myself, and prayerfully invoke Thy blessing on my country and its cause." "Thus," wrote Varina, "Mr. Davis entered on his martyrdom."[15]

Davis rarely wrote out any specifics of strategy. He relied heavily on the judgment of top generals in the field because he realized he himself always would be deficient in knowledge of the local geography and the timeliness of troop dispositions, particularly in the more distant western regions. Thus he indicated to Joseph E. Johnston that he would limit himself to proposing "general purposes and views" for the guidance of commanders.[16]

On the other hand, Davis took every opportunity to go personally into the field to confer with his generals. After Norfolk was abandoned, and Johnston withdrew his army to the north side of the Chickahominy River, Davis and

R. E. Lee rode out to Johnston's headquarters. A long conversation ensued, late into the night, which induced Davis and Lee to stay until the next morning. Davis and Lee chatted on the way back to Richmond, and although both were a bit uncertain about Johnston's intentions, they agreed that apparently he would work "to improve his position as far as practicable, and wait for the enemy to leave his gunboats, so that an opportunity might be offered to meet him on the land."[17]

Davis consistently expected his top generals to undertake offensive campaigns whenever circumstances permitted. He himself, save only for a time of brief hesitation during winter 1861–1862, believed that the only way the Confederacy could win the war was to seize and press the military initiative. "The advantage of selecting the time and place of attack was too apparent to have been overlooked," he wrote to an acquaintance on March 15, 1862.[18]

To Johnston, on that same date, Davis wrote with some concern about having heard of a retrograde by the army, and—worse—one that involved the abandonment and destruction of a lot of equipment. "I have had many and alarming reports of great destruction of ammunition, camp equipage and provisions, indicating precipitate retreat; but having heard of no cause for such a sudden movement I was at a loss to believe it."[19]

Later in 1862 he proclaimed that if the enemy were allowed to penetrate too deeply into the interior, the "resources of our country will rapidly decline to insufficiency for the support of an army."[20] And to keep it from penetrating "too deeply" would require the implementation of offensive strategy. Davis wanted his vision of offensive strategy to be applied in three distinct but related ways. First, enemy invasions must be aggressively foiled. Second, the only way the Confederacy could claim those areas such as the nonseceded slave states and the western territories, which it considered rightfully its own, was by thrusting offensively into them. Third, within the essence of Davis's philosophical concept of warfare rightly conducted was an idea known popularly as "carrying the war into Africa"—that is, harking back to the Punic Wars, it is effective when one can make an enemy feel pain and threat at home because it can sap his will.

By the end of 1861, many Confederate leaders looked to the future with concern. If Federals had not extended their control significantly a year after secession began, neither had Confederates managed to make good their bid for independence. Indeed, there were already signs of stress within the South, and not only because a significant minority of the population of some slave states had preferred to remain in the Union. There seemed to be a budding antagonism between Upper and Lower South, recognized by Davis himself and by members of his cabinet. Attorney General Thomas Bragg reported in February 1862 that Davis was concerned about a possible split of that sort. "No doubt there is such a party line," wrote Bragg, "which will be headed by disappointed men."[21] This was only one aspect of an apparent attitude of depression manifested both by Davis and Judah P. Benjamin. Bragg concluded that Confederates had been "luke warm and not fully alive to our danger."[22]

The attorney general tactfully approached Governor John Letcher of Virginia about the problem of martial law being declared. "It is a delicate power to be exercised by the President," wrote Bragg, who relayed a cabinet suggestion that Letcher instead declare martial law, if he had the power to do so.[23] In reply, Letcher simply threw the issue back to Davis. The Virginia attorney general had contended that neither the governor nor the general assembly had the power to declare martial law, "as it involves the subordination of the civil to the military power . . . and the suspension of the writ of Habeas Corpus." But he believed that the Confederate Congress had the right of suspension under the war powers clause of the Constitution.[24] Davis therefore had no choice but to turn to Congress, which quickly passed a law permitting suspension of the writ. Davis approved it on February 27, 1862; it was only the second law passed under the permanent Constitution.

The text of the law was brief and gave no indication of the trouble it was to cause: "*The Congress of the Confederate States of America do enact,* That during the present invasion of the Confederate States, the President shall have power to suspend the privilege of the writ of *habeas corpus* in such cities, towns and military districts as shall, in his judgment, be in such danger of attack by the enemy as to require the declaration of martial law for their effective defence."[25] Thus a fatal confusion between martial law and the suspension of the writ of habeas corpus was introduced into the discussion of maintaining civil order and enforcing loyalty, for the two are not synonymous; martial law is military law applied to a civilian populace.

During the Civil War, martial law was often declared in and near the zone of military occupation, but suspension of the writ of habeas corpus ensured that questionable characters who had been detained would continue to be, as long as the arresting authority desired. It was appropriate when persons had been detained because there was fear of their activity if they were released and further fear that some judges would release them. This situation was often but not necessarily near an area of military operations, potential or actual. However, Southerners considered fundamental the constitutional guarantees of law and liberty and thus were extremely sensitive to any perceived threats of arbitrary arrests. Davis clearly framed his program of Confederate nationalism while consciously considering these traditions.[26]

The first suspension occurred on the peninsula below Richmond. On the very day the law permitting it was passed, Davis suspended the writ in the Norfolk and Portsmouth regions, "and all civil jurisdiction and the privilege of the writ of *habeas corpus* are hereby declared to be suspended with the limits aforesaid."[27] Orders a few days later to General Benjamin Huger at Norfolk provided detailed instructions as to his duties under the suspension, including orders to take arms from citizens, enroll able-bodied men for military service, and, most ominously, "imprison all persons against whom there is well-grounded suspicion of disloyalty."[28] Three days later Davis suspended habeas corpus and proclaimed martial law in Richmond and the area ten miles around, in order to prevent "distribution of spirituous liquors" and to seize privately held arms.[29] On March 8 a proclamation prohibiting distillation and sale of spirits was applied to Petersburg[30] and on March 14 a similar proclamation applied to five counties on the peninsula below Richmond.[31] At the end of March yet another proclamation suspending the writ and establishing martial law was applied to extreme western Virginia,[32] in early April the writ was suspended in East Tennessee,[33] on May 1 in a large section of the South Carolina coast north and south of Charleston,[34] and finally on May 3 in additional counties in western Virginia.[35] With that, Davis was done for the time being, except for one last proclamation calling on the people to go to their places of worship and beg God's protection, which they surely needed by them.[36]

The original suspension law had granted Davis more authority than some congressmen wished him to have. Within two months of its passage, Congress repented of its haste and modified the sweeping authority given the president by providing that the law would continue in force only until "thirty days after the next meeting of Congress, and no longer."[37] Davis, too, modified his application of the law. The first suspension, at Norfolk and Portsmouth, was quite sweeping, but subsequent suspensions were usually limited to restricting the manufacture and distribution of alcohol. Later suspensions also indicated that civil courts could stay open for such purposes as probating wills, entering decrees regarding property, and levying taxes. But this provision was an open admission that the courts were not only open but were also able to carry on normal civil processes after all, that in short, it was only criminal activities that would come under the jurisdiction of a military court.

In all cases persons accused of violating the provisions of the suspension proclamation were to be tried by a military court and to suffer sentences of no more than a month at hard labor if found guilty. What did it mean that military courts were to have jurisdiction over civilians where civil courts were still able to function? Simply that military courts were trusted to guard the public safety more than civil courts were. Davis was indeed seizing power. He was becoming the democratic usurper that some Confederates feared; and mindful of the future, opposition to suspension acts grew. No further acts were passed that did not have an expiration date.

No doubt some Confederates thought to beg God's protection from Jefferson Davis, not from the Yankees, for this rapid-fire series of proclamations was more than some congressmen expected when they passed the original suspension law. The populace howled. A growing feeling strongly opposing martial law was prompted by the actions of overzealous Confederate military officers, resulting in protests being lodged in Richmond. Major General Earl Van Dorn's proclamation of martial law, for example, caused Louisiana governor Thomas O. Moore to complain to Davis in righteous indignation that "no free people can or ought to submit to the arbitrary and illegal usurpation of authority." The governor did, however, assure Davis that he intended neither an attack upon him nor upon his direction of the war effort: it was the principle that concerned Moore.

The issue was aggravated by the action of local commanders who sometimes declared martial law on their own whim. The actions of the president and of some eager generals seemed to be all of one piece. More or less legitimate presidential suspensions were rendered suspicious by the unauthorized actions of some generals, especially since the generals could have asked Davis for a suspension in their areas. This was a tender point with Davis, who labored tirelessly trying to keep a balance between the Confederate and state governments. He was opposed to proposals to suspend habeas corpus throughout the Confederacy because he wished to preserve both liberty and law in the country. The debates that ensued on the matter clearly revealed that the opposition to suspension of habeas corpus arose from concerns to maintain civil authority and from a desire to keep the military subordinate to civilian government.[38] (Later, suspension was also intimately related to the pressing need to hold the army together against the zealous opposition of some state judges and governors, but this was not yet apparent in spring 1862.)

Meanwhile, manpower was becoming a problem. As early as December 1861, some congressmen had begun glancing at the calendar and noting that the one-year volunteers would begin to come to the end of their enlistments in spring 1862. Therefore, legislators encouraged such soldiers to reenlist; the reward would be a fifty-dollar bounty and a furlough of sixty days, with free transportation for those who agreed to extend their enlistments to three years, and the right to reorganize into new companies and elect new officers. New troops volunteering for three years would also receive the bounty.[39] In addition, Congress authorized the secretary of war to recruit men to fill vacancies in companies that had been "reduced by death and discharges."[40] Here Southerners showed more wisdom than their Northern counterparts, for they established a policy—not always adhered to—of recruiting replacements.

Confederate manpower policy was strengthened in January 1862, when new legislation spelled out procedures for recruitment of single individuals as opposed to fully recruited units. Vacancies in three-year companies could be filled by volunteers until they reached a strength of 125 "rank and file," and the recruits would receive the fifty-dollar bounty that was now policy.[41] Indicating a measure of desperation as volunteering faltered, Congress also authorized Davis to call upon the states for three-year men, adjusting the call to take into account the number of men each state had already provided;[42] and then it promptly passed additional legislation to recruit three-year men from among the one-year volunteers already serving, the enlistees being permitted to organize new units and elect new officers.[43] Other laws included the militia in the three-year calls by ensuring that militiamen "drafted into service by the several States, and furnished by said States to the President, for service for three years or during the war," would not be limited to six months of service as provided by previous legislation regulating the militia.[44] The bounty and furlough incentives offered to one-year volunteers were extended to the few three-month volunteers.[45]

Thus matters stood as the Provisional Congress ended its existence on February 17, 1862. The permanent government went into effect the next day, and on February 22 Jefferson Davis delivered his Inaugural Address. Its generally congratulatory tone was contradicted just three days later by the somber note struck in Davis's first message to Congress. He confessed that "events have demonstrated that the Government had attempted more than it had power successfully to achieve," referring to the humiliating surrender at Roanoke Island and to hopes that the fall of Forts Henry and Donelson might turn out to be less costly than thus far reported. With justification he blamed the disasters in part on the short terms of enlistment and complained that as a result he could not even "furnish . . . an accurate statement of the Army." He claimed that "our high-spirited and gallant soldiers" were reenlisting, but often had to go home first to attend to personal affairs in preparation for a more prolonged absence. He estimated that the army numbered about four hundred infantry regiments, with an appropriate number of cavalry and artillery regiments, which, if true, would have meant the Confederate army must have numbered about five hundred thousand men.[46]

Davis was exaggerating somewhat, for the total strength of the army in February 1862 was three hundred forty thousand, including Virginia militia, but the imbalance between those who were enlisted for a single year and those serving for the duration was striking. Only ninety-three thousand men were obligated for the war, while two hundred forty thousand (72 percent) were getting ready to pack their bags.[47] However, the cannons of war always require ever more fodder, and those of the Confederacy were no exception; but the number of men who took advantage of the offers of a bounty, furlough, and reorganization to reenlist was disappointing. Davis soon asked Congress to raise an additional three hundred thousand men, and in March 1862 he took the dreaded step of requesting legislators to enact conscription.[48]

It was obvious that some strenuous adjustments were necessary in order to enable the South to continue what might be a long struggle. Against military necessity were pitted the ideals that had prompted secession. On the one hand, the rebellious states hoped to retain authority; on the other hand, the war had begun to require compromising these principles. Davis circumvented the issue. He complained that the manpower laws had been so revised and amended as to become too complicated to administer properly, even to the extent of making it "often quite difficult to determine what the law really is," which was true, and that there was "embarrassment from conflict between State and Confederate legislation." He gilded the lily somewhat, claiming that the threat of Federal conquest had kindled the spirit of resistance to the point "that it requires rather to be regulated than stimulated," and suggested that the burden of defense "should not fall exclusively on the most ardent and patriotic." Proposing that youths under eighteen and men "of matured experience . . . constitute the proper reserve for home defense," he asked the Congress to declare men between the ages of eighteen and thirty-five subject to military service. His message did not use the dreaded word conscription, but that is what it was.[49] Despite Davis's evasiveness, it was clear to most people that volunteering was no longer sufficient to meet the demands of war.

This was a major turning point, not only in the Civil War but in American ideals of citizens' responsibility. Historians have noted this sort of development in Europe during the same era. "People were taught to serve the nation," Peter Paret has written, "a concept that until then had barely, if at all entered their awareness—the lessons being administered through a mixture of moral exhortation and police compulsion."[50] Underlining the difficulties that Confederates (and Federals too, for that matter) would experience, he has observed that many citizens were doubtful about these lessons. The result was widespread desertion and extensive misgivings, even among those who did serve. Although desertion and doubt were recognized in the Confederacy, there were also those who "were the apolitical, passive elements of the population, made up of men and women who merely wanted to be left alone."[51]

The presence of such people "called into question the validity of nationalism, of the nation itself,"[52] a problem that increasingly pressed upon the flimsy Confederate nationalism and eventually helped to destroy it. For one thing, many Southerners were more attached to their localities than they were to either the Confederacy or the Union. The frequency with which Confederate men were willing to volunteer for local defense not only hid a desire to avoid military service and to care for their families, but it also betrayed the fact "that volunteering to defend one's home may not be the most persuasive test of patriotism." And the poor unfortunate being hauled off to the faraway army might and apparently often did understand loyalty as involving only his home area.[53] It was all a question of perspective. As one back-country South Carolinian put it, "I go first for Greenville, then for Greenville District, then the up-country, then for South Carolina, then for the South, then for the United States, and after that I don't go for anything."[54] A Georgia soldier even objected to fighting alongside men from other states. "I expected to fight through this war as a Georgian not as a Mississippian Louisianan Tennessean nor any other state, and if I cannot fight in the name of my own state I don't want to fight at all."[55] This localism made many Southern men unwilling to fight in other states in the Confederate army while quite eager to fight in the militias of and in their own states. In Arkansas and Missouri, for example, there was fear that if state troops were ordered east, they would simply desert.[56]

Congressmen generally held the wider view of loyalty and patriotism and promptly responded to Davis's request for a conscription law—not without some argument, however, for there were those who claimed throughout the war and in years to follow that it had been a mistake because it undermined the enthusiasm of Confederate soldiers and would-be volunteers. There were constitutional arguments as well. Senator Williamson S. Oldham of Texas claimed that conscription violated state rights and that it was illegal unless the states gave their consent. "This was not circumlocution," Oldham claimed; "it was the theory of our government."[57] Senator Louis T. Wigfall, the other senator from Texas, disagreed with his colleague and claimed, as did Davis, that conscription was implied by the war power, which included the power to raise armies, and hence was perfectly legal.[58]

Postmaster General John Reagan had yearned from the beginning to provide more artistic stamps, although one might question why that was so important during a war for national survival. In fall 1861 he had arranged with Major Benjamin F. Ficklin, a Confederate agent in England, to purchase all manner of supplies for various government departments. In addition to his search for Blakely cannon, sabers, Enfield rifles, pistols, gunpowder and percussion caps, tea, coffee, drugs, shoes, boots, leather and dry goods, Ficklin agreed to try to secure paper, envelopes, and suitably engraved plates for postage stamps, plus the printing of a supply that would meet requirements until local printings could be made from the imported plates. Ficklin succeeded in his venture, although the first shipment was lost. Two later shipments successfully evaded capture, landed at Wilmington, North Carolina, and arrived safely in Richmond.

Ultimately, the Confederate government issued a total of fourteen different stamps. The likeness of Jefferson Davis appeared on eight of them; other great Southern Americans beloved by Confederate citizens, Andrew Jackson and Thomas Jefferson, appeared on two each, and George Washington and John C. Calhoun each on one. Selection of the subjects to be illustrated was a relatively easy matter. The government used Davis's picture as a conscious propaganda measure to help popularize the president. The South claimed Washington, Jefferson, and Jackson as its sons, equally or possibly even more strenuously than did the North. Actually, Washington had been scheduled to be pictured on the first Confederate stamp, but the use was deferred because the United States had Washington on its most commonly used stamp. Interestingly, Jackson was a popular figure with both sides during the war; the South emphasized his Southern heritage, and the North revered him for his Unionist sentiments and his fights against nullification of federal laws and state rights. The last subject to be depicted, Calhoun, appeared on a one-cent stamp for which there seemed no use by the time it became available, and it was never distributed.

Two stories attest to the quality of Davis's engraved likeness on the later issues. Mary Chesnut recorded an incident that occurred on October 11, 1864, at her home in Columbia, South Carolina: "Immediately after breakfast, General Chesnut drove off with the President's aides, and Mr. Davis sat out on our piazza. . . . Some little boys, strolling by, called out: 'Come here and look! There is a man in Mrs. Chesnut's porch who looks just like Jeff Davis on a postage stamp.' People began to gather on the street, and Mr. Davis then went in." Davis himself related a similar incident that took place shortly after one of the improved ten-cent stamps with his picture appeared: "I was walking across the park . . . on my way to my office, when I met a tall North Carolina soldier, who accosted me: 'Is your name Davis?' Yes. 'President Davis?' Yes. 'I thought so; you look so—much like a postage stamp.' "[59]

Like Reagan with the postage stamps, Treasury Secretary Christopher Memminger had difficulties in getting money printed. This was due both to the scarcity of sufficiently skilled engravers and the shortage of suitable paper. The American Bank Note Company in the North contracted to supply paper currency, but most of what it printed was seized by Federal officials. One printer in New Orleans offered so crude a product that his work was rejected, so the Richmond lithographers Hoyer and Ludwig began producing currency as well as postage stamps. There was one advantage to the poor quality of Confederate currency: counterfeiters improved on the originals, and thus fake money was relatively easy to detect.[60]

Though anti-Semitism was less characteristic of the South than it was of the North, Jewish peddlers often were accused of spreading counterfeit money throughout the country. Indeed, the Confederate Congress passed legislation to punish counterfeiting. Anyone who made counterfeit Treasury notes or plates, or knowingly passed counterfeits, was guilty of a felony. The punishment was imprisonment at hard labor for three to ten years, plus a five thousand dollar fine. Counterfeiting stocks, bonds, or coupons was also made a felony, with the same penalties. A few months later potential sentences were increased. A counterfeiter of Treasury notes, "being thereof convicted by the due course of law, shall suffer death." The counterfeiter of bonds or coupons looked forward to imprisonment at hard labor for five to ten years and a fine of five thousand dollars.[61] One counterfeiter indeed was hanged, and many others were arrested. Clever Yankees in the North began to counterfeit Confederate currency and sold it at very low prices to Northern soldiers. They brazenly advertised in the Northern press, and the fake currency became so widespread that it was commonplace for any dead Federal soldier to have a lot of it in his pockets. In 1862 the Congress passed a law threatening death by hanging for anyone caught having these types of counterfeits with intent to pass them.[62]

The populace grew quite concerned as their country's money became ever more worthless. Confederates referred to the Treasury notes as "rags" or "fodder" and equated them with the French assignats and the old American Revolutionary–era "Continental." Something had to be done soon, warned one newspaper, or the notes' value would sink so low "that at last no butcher's boy" would accept it "for an ounce of cat meat."[63] Some Confederates proposed to equate the currency in value based on cotton and tobacco, and cotton was used to support some bond issues, particularly those that were marketed in Europe. But the people reverted to custom and used gold as a measure of value, and so in effect that was indeed the standard.

The government accumulated gold, or its equivalent in sterling exchange, whenever it could, for that was essential in consummating foreign purchases. In September 1861 Memminger purchased twenty thousand pounds sterling for one hundred thousand dollars in Confederate currency, and the next year he bought about thirteen thousand pounds sterling for about one hundred six-teen thousand dollars. The later purchase indicated that Confederate notes had lost almost half their value on the international market.[64]

Meanwhile, on the international scene, the U.S. number-two diplomat in Britain, Thomas Haines Dudley, on taking up his post in Liverpool, found that Britain's main port city seemed to have become a Confederate stronghold. Confederate agents already had succeeded in arranging for the construction of warships for the South in British shipyards. On May 10, 1862, Dudley wrote to U.S. Secretary of State William Seward: "The people of this place if not the entire Kingdom seem to be becoming every day more and more enlisted" in the service of the Confederacy.[65] Dudley immediately set to work to establish an intelligence network to ferret out information about any actions being taken on behalf of the Confederacy.

Dudley, however, soon found himself engaged in an espionage duel with James Dunwoody Bulloch, a brilliant Confederate administrator who was in charge of the South's Secret Service in the British Isles.[66] Bulloch was as dedi-cated and determined to continue Confederate shipbuilding as Dudley was to stop it. The Confederate successfully promoted an ongoing effort to arrange that British shipyards provide the Confederacy with the most advanced vessels of their type then in the world.

Dudley learned of the ongoing construction of the steam-powered gunboat *Oreto* at a Liverpool shipyard. A complex legal and diplomatic struggle ensued. The customs collector in Liverpool was empowered to make final decisions on whether or not violations of Britain's Foreign Enlistment Act had occurred, but he turned out to be a Confederate agent. The *Oreto* was allowed out of port. It went out unarmed, manned by a British captain and crew; but as soon as it entered the open sea it was armed, loaded with munitions, and renamed the CSS *Florida*. It then set out at once on a long and successful cruise during which it destroyed many unarmed Northern merchant ships.

Soon after the *Oreto* departed, Dudley's spy ring discovered another ship being built for the South. Still another long and complicated diplomatic duel with Bulloch ensued. This ship's departure was delayed, too, for a time, but ultimately it also set out to sea: it was destined to become the most famous of the Confederate war vessels, the CSS *Alabama*.

The Confederate administrative agency that faced the greatest increase in responsibilities early in 1862 was the Quartermaster's Department. Congress had passed an act making that bureau responsible for providing clothing for all the troops, whereas previously individual soldiers had furnished their own clothing and were remunerated for that. Commutation was still to be paid for any soldier who did procure his own clothing, but otherwise the secretary of war was required "to provide, as far as possible, clothing for the entire forces of the Confederate States upon the requisition of the [regimental] commander."[67] This obligation was complicated by the need to supply troops from states under Union control, and for this purpose contracts were made with textile and shoe manufacturers. The problem was aggravated by the fact that some manufacturers preferred to sell in the civilian market because prices were higher than Quartermaster General Abraham Myers was willing to pay.[68]

In addition to uniforms, the quartermaster had other nonfood items to worry about. Such elemental equipment as tents, for example, required that he scrape together sufficient duck to manufacture adequate numbers to house the entire army. Fearing that he would be unable to find enough clothing, shoes, and blankets, Myers attempted to purchase not only from Southern factories but also from local markets and from abroad. His efforts met with some success, and by spring 1862 his depots were filled with marginally sufficient supplies, thanks to the contributions of the states and the inadequacy of the Union blockade.[69]

Subsistence was an obvious supply problem, although it could be better dealt with from the Confederate domestic market than could Quartermaster needs. Nevertheless, as demand grew, the commissary general ran into problems of "financial derangement, and transportation inefficiencies." Some of the difficulties were met by purchase in advance of need, to create a reserve in the hope that prices could be held to reasonable levels, but this was a forlorn hope.[70]

One of the major problems faced by the commissary of subsistence was simply lack of funding, but the department did its best to work around that difficulty. Major Frank G. Ruffin appealed to Lucius Northrop to revise the funding procedures, and in April he referred Ruffin's ideas to Secretary of War George W. Randolph. A novel practice of payment for requisitions half in cash and half in bonds created much difficulty, and more was anticipated in the

future when proposed Treasury regulations requiring an even greater proportion of payment in bonds became effective. Randolph suggested to Davis that
either more Treasury notes be issued or else the Treasury Department sell its
own bonds and turn over the resulting cash to the commissariat. Randolph
pointed out to the president that Treasury policy effectively transformed commissary agents and contractors into bond agents, and he feared that if change
were not initiated the army would be left "without sufficient subsistence."[71]
Bonds could be sold only at a discount, and Northrop complained a few days
later that additional purchases of flour in Richmond could be made only with
Treasury notes.

Furthermore, with the fall of New Orleans and the fear that the Mississippi
itself might soon be entirely controlled by the Union, notes were essential for
immediate purchase of cattle from Texas and Louisiana.[72] The city had fallen
after Union troops seized forts near the mouth of the Mississippi after midnight, April 24, 1862, and entered New Orleans April 29. This loss stunned
the capital and tore at President Davis. A niece of his visiting at the Gray
House reported that the shock "like to have set us all crazy here." She
described Richmond as "depressed," anxious that "the cause of the Confederacy seems drooping and sinking." Varina Davis declared the tidings of the
New Orleans tragedy a "terrible disaster." When Davis was informed, he
reportedly "buried his face in his hands."[73]

Soon Confederates were pushed to the extreme of trading behind enemy
lines to secure some vital supplies, Northrop using greenbacks and gold for
the purpose. Davis was indecisive when these problems were brought to his
attention,[74] but Northrop had "secured all that private persons have failed to
grasp" on the Confederate side of the lines and decided to "look to Kentucky."
As he had earlier explained to Secretary of War Benjamin, "it has become necessary to draw from beyond our lines, where our currency will not answer"
because prices would be cheaper. This plan required that he purchase gold,
which violated army regulations.[75] The meat supply was in fairly good shape
in early 1862, however; large reserves were beginning to accumulate at points
in Tennessee and Virginia, and there was little trouble with railroad delays.
The meatpacking was done in the vicinity of the armies; indeed, the Confederate armies were themselves their own meatpackers.[76]

Events in spring 1862 provided an illustration of the difficulties of supply.
Joseph E. Johnston withdrew from Centreville on March 9 and destroyed his
accumulated quartermaster and subsistence stores to keep them out of Northern hands. This affected the Confederate army in Northern Virginia for the
rest of the war and meant that supplies had to be gathered from the Deep
South through Richmond by way of the inadequate rail system.[77]

Johnston complained that he had inadequate cars and engines for moving supplies from Centreville, and Davis asked Colonel Myers if he could provide more.[78] But there was a limit; Myers replied that he had the maximum equipment on the railroad and concluded that perhaps "too many trains [were] now on that road—they are not able to pass each other in the turnout. Some engines have been thirty-six hours in making the trip from Manassas to Gordonsville."[79] Davis preferred a simpler way to overcome this supply bottleneck. Frustrated, he expressed hope in June 1862 that if the Confederacy could defeat George McClellan on the peninsula, then it might be possible "to feed our army on his territory."[80]

Similar events occurred in the West. After the retreat from Forts Henry and Donelson and from Bowling Green, Kentucky (essentially at the same time), Nashville was rendered vulnerable, and eventually the stores there were lost also. General Albert Sidney Johnston had failed to give notice of his movements so that supplies could be saved.[81]

Furthermore, the unstable supply of the components of gunpowder almost brought an end to the war by default by mid-1862 had it not been for the wise actions taken by the government. Chief of Ordnance Josiah Gorgas suggested that a special corps be created for extracting niter and for the development of metal resources. On April 11, Congress passed "An Act for the Organization of a Corps of Officers for the Working . . . of Nitre Caves and Establishing Nitre beds," which organized Gorgas's operation and outlined its duties. These included working and inspecting niter caves, purchasing niter from private parties, and estimating the amount the Confederacy would be able to produce from both public and private sources. The most important provision was that the army would get into the niter business itself, establishing niter beds and "stimulat[ing] enterprise in the production of an article essential to the successful prosecution of the war."[82]

A few days later Congress passed "An Act to Encourage the Manufacture of Saltpetre and of Small Arms," which laid down the terms under which private contractors could go into the munitions business with generous government assistance. Anyone establishing a factory to make either niter or small arms could get an interest-free advance of 50 percent of projected costs in order to construct buildings and procure machinery after the entrepreneur had put in 25 percent of his own money, the advance to be repaid from sale of his product to the government at a price agreed upon when the advance was made.[83] Gorgas's assistant, Major Isaac St. John, was named head of a special corps, the Nitre and Mining Bureau, to be run under the direction of the chief of ordnance.

At the same time, Congress loosened its purse strings and modernized its thinking, embarking on a full-fledged program of state development of the munitions and associated industries. Two days after Congress specified the details of the Nitre and Mining Bureau, it passed a short law of a single paragraph that had far-reaching consequences. This law extended the provisions of the law encouraging production of niter and small arms to other enterprises deemed to be essential, including coal mines, iron mines, and iron works.[84] Other examples of this sort of energy included an appropriation of $1 million to buy iron and $.5 million to pay contractors to cast it into "cannon shot and shells." Another $1 million was advanced to the Navy Department for the procurement of its needed iron (for ship armament) and still another $2 million was allocated for manufacturing small arms.[85]

The Nitre and Mining Bureau eventually bought up mineral rights, explored caves, negotiated mining contracts, conducted patriotic scrap drives, and encouraged civilians to make artificial niter beds. A military depot, including a powder mill, niter works, an arsenal, iron works, and a foundry for making shot and shell, was established at Selma, Alabama. In charge of the niter works was a Selma resident, Jonathan Haralson, a lawyer and later an Alabama Supreme Court justice. He ran this notice in the *Selma Sentinel* on October 1, 1862: "The ladies of Selma are respectfully requested to preserve their chamber lye (urine), collected about the premises, for the purpose of making nitre. Wagons with barrels will be sent around by the subscriber."

Thomas B. Wetmore, another Selma lawyer, then acting as provost marshal of the city, responsed to Haralson's request:

> John Haralson, John Haralson, you are a funny creature;
> You've given to this cruel war a new and curious feature;
> You'd have us think while every man is bound to be a fighter,
> The women (bless the pretty dears) should save their pee for nitre.

> John Haralson, John Haralson, where did you get the notion,
> To send your barrels around the town to gather up the lotion?
> We thought the girls had work enough in making skirts and kissing,
> But now you'll put the pretty dears to patriotic pissing.

The poem received wide circulation throughout the South and was enormously popular.

Another grave supply problem had to do with maintenance. The railroad companies were expected to pay for their own repairs, even for war damages inflicted by the enemy.[86] But as inflation grew more serious and the supplies available for railroad repair became ever more meager, the companies were too hard-pressed to make ends meet. An example with respect to the Virginia Central Railroad illustrates this problem: iron castings and wrought iron that cost four cents in 1860 cost one dollar in 1864; oil and tallow in 1860 cost ninety cents per gallon, but in 1864 that cost had skyrocketed to fifty dollars, an increase of 5,555 percent.[87]

By autumn 1862 the domestic market prices within the Confederacy had become greatly inflated. Thus were Confederate supply officials induced to resort to another manner of procurement—impressment. Speculators had made small fortunes by exploiting the quartermaster general and the commissary, so these officials responded by persuading the secretary of war to confer general impressment powers upon them and through them to the bureau purchasers. A circular went out in November from Myers to all quartermasters, giving them the official authority to impress, although only if "absolutely demanded by the public necessities."[88]

There was no escape from the difficulty resulting from inflation, especially as it related to impressment. In the first place, impressment officers would take what they needed even if they had no funds with which to pay, offering instead certificates that were to be sent to the Treasury for payment. But as the currency began to inflate rapidly in 1862, by the time the Confederate bureaucracy received a payment certificate issued to a local farmer, processed the certificate, sent payment, and the payment was received, months might have gone by. The Confederate dollars received by the farmer were inflated dollars, usually worth much less than the value of the peas or corn the army had taken months before. Many farmers felt cheated, as if they were bearing an unfair share of the financial burden of the war. They were eager to avoid impressment and by the middle of the war often would hide their crops or refuse to bring them to town to market, fearing impressment by quartermasters who waited for them along the roadways. This in turn caused food shortages in the towns and sometimes in the army as well.

The system was necessary but unsatisfactory. In Virginia, for example, by 1862 citizens were complaining to the secretary of war "about the lack of regulations for impressment, which left civilians at the mercy of military officers who wanted goods."[89] One annoyed citizen complained to the Confederate attorney general that "the 'Press masters' will go to their houses, and drag off their property to Just Such an extent as they choose; until it has not only created great excitement and distress; but bids fair to produce wide spread ruin." The special object of his ire was the impressment of slaves, many of whom died or were afflicted with disease before they were returned.[90]

Impressment was fraught with opportunities for abuse, even outright fraud. Not all soldiers who claimed to be commissaries or quartermasters actually were. Some difficulties occurred as early as August 1861, for a bill was then introduced in Congress specifically "authorizing the impressment of property of citizens of the Confederate States, or of the United States, in certain cases, for the public service."[91] Within a month a congressional committee was investigating the Commissary, Quartermaster, and Medical Bureaus.[92] This was only a hint of more stringent measures to come.

Impressment aside, it is important to remember that a great many citizens voluntarily sent supplies to the soldiers. Although precise data are not available, it well may be that voluntary contributions made the difference between actual want and minimum comfort for the Rebel troops. J. B. Jones noted such events in his diary many times, once asserting that "never was there such a patriotic *people* as ours. Their blood and their wealth are laid upon the altar of their country with enthusiasm."[93]

Although Gorgas and Myers were popular in the public's eyes, Commissary General Northrop early became a villain. Press attacks were frequent. The *Daily Richmond Examiner* in essence pursued a vendetta against him with such comments as "have we a commissariat, or have we only a stupid piece of official machinery called Commissary General, whose only claims to distinction or usefulness are that he was the college chum of President JEFFERSON DAVIS!"[94]

But one can read too much into the effect of major antiadministration newspapers like the *Richmond Examiner* and the *Charleston Mercury.* Indeed, George Rable asserts that students of the Civil War have spent too much time scanning these and too little reading the rest, and this has led many of them to exaggerate the extent of newspaper opposition to the Davis administration. In the first place, of the eight hundred newspapers published in the Confederacy, at least half of them had gone out of business by early 1862, owing to lack of paper or ink, and most important, paying subscribers. Rable points out that "although hardly exempt from provincialism and selfishness, the Southern press generally sustained the president and worked to build a national consciousness."[95]

The Davis admnistration, however, was without the presence of the vice president in the capital city from early April until mid-August 1862. The chronically ill Stephens deemed the climate in Richmond bad for him, and he was also disgusted with his status. It is unclear why he even stayed as long as he did after his reelection in November 1861, for he both perceived and deplored a measure of factionalism developing around him. According to Thomas Schott, "He greatly feared a 'break-down of the war spirit on our part. . . . We have a fiery ordeal to go through yet. It is that patience under wrong and suffering to which our people are so little accustomed.' The test, he knew, still had to be endured, and it would be 'the severest to which human nature can be subjected.' "[96]

Stephens had never been shy about expressing his opinion, and he was constantly asked to do so, but

It embarrassed him . . . to differ with the administration. [Stephens] preferred not to be put in such a position. But when he was, he always tried to answer frankly, without the least appearance of "asperity." Apparently Stephens never considered remaining silent, but then no one in the administration valued his opinion anyway. . . . What could he have said, his state of mind being what it was? The fall of Forts Henry and Donelson had plunged him into one of his most despairing moods. "The Confederacy is lost," he had told Martin Crawford [one of his many friends in the Georgia political arena] one night as they were leaving Congress. "We may not meet again." . . . At this, Crawford said, "he laid his head upon my shoulder and wept, and said that he did not care to survive the liberties of his country." . . . As bad as things were, he expected them to get worse. He had said so from the beginning.[97]

In late February Davis delivered a brief message to the initial session of the First Congress. He publicly acknowledged the "serious disasters" that had befallen the country. He admitted that he believed their genesis was in the government's attempt to defend all of its territory while lacking "the means for the prosecution of the war on so gigantic a scale." Still, he remained undaunted about the cause: "I cannot doubt that the bitter disappointments we have borne, by nerving the people to still greater exertions, will speedily secure results more accordant with our just expectation, and as favorable to our cause as those which marked the earlier periods of the war."[98]

The message, however, had the opposite effect that Davis had intended. As Cooper observes, "The president's message . . . salved neither popular dismay nor congressional unrest." Indeed, it had grievous impact: "Critics lashed out, cursing the president and even wishing for his capture by Union forces."[99] How much worse could the situation become?

8

NORTHERN POWER EMERGES

The dismal outcomes that marked Confederate military and naval fortunes during the first two months of 1862 continued unabated into March. On March 6 began the Battle of Pea Ridge, or Elkhorn Tavern, in Arkansas. Its conclusion on March 8 negated Confederate hopes of remaining in control of that state. On March 9 occurred the naval battle between the *Monitor* and *Merrimac*. Federal forces captured New Madrid, Missouri, and New Bern, North Carolina, on March 14.

The naval battles are an essential part of the Civil War's narrative. President Abraham Lincoln rightly suggested that much credit for the Northern victory should go to "Uncle Sam's webbed feet." Yet the spectacular naval innovations, the battles that involved warships, and the Northern blockade of the Rebel coast are not truly turning points of the Civil War. They were, rather, almost turning points, and they are important to ponder because they offer such crucial "might have beens." They were turning points, however, in the evolution of warfare.

Perhaps the most famous naval episode of the Civil War was the first battle in the world between two ironclad vessels of war, best described in William C. Davis's *Duel Between the First Ironclads*. It occurred on March 9, 1862, in Hampton Roads, a channel about eight miles long, formed by the James, Nansemond, and Elizabeth Rivers as they flow together into the Chesapeake Bay.

Both sides had been working feverishly to develop a usable ironclad war vessel, and it was sheer coincidence that they both achieved viable results at the same time—the USS *Monitor* and the CSS *Virginia* (often, both during and after the war, mistakenly called the *Merrimac* because it was built on the hull of an abandoned U.S. vessel of that name, which the Confederates had managed to recover). Both vessels employed much of the technological innovation envisioned by the Swede, John Ericsson, who had perfected the screw propeller. His other ideas were not new: iron armor; a gun turret, which could swivel through three hundred sixty degrees, making possible a revolution in naval maneuvers; steam power; and ventilation systems. But Ericsson incorporated these features into one superbly conceived vessel for the first time and it justly entitled him to fame.

Both vessels represented early examples of a class of ship that was long to be employed in coastal defense. By sacrificing speed and seaworthiness, relatively small ships could incorporate heavy armor and powerful guns. The Union eventually built sixty more "monitors." The original *Monitor* sank late in 1862 in a storm off Cape Hatteras. The *Virginia* was much more cumbersome and also hopelessly underpowered; thus it remained permanently in its first port until May 11, when the Rebels destroyed it to prevent its capture. Nevertheless, the Confederacy also entered into an ambitious ironclad-building program and began or planned fifty more warships using the *Virginia* casement design and actually commissioned twenty-two.

The *Monitor* outmaneuvered the *Virginia,* but neither vessel could do serious damage to the other. Shot after shot ricocheted away. As the ships closed, one of the *Monitor*'s officers believed they actually touched at least five times. The battle at last waned, when the Federals withdrew to resupply the turret with ammunition, but it was renewed a half hour later. At one point the *Virginia* ran aground but managed to pull free at the last moment before the *Monitor* was able to place a shot into a vulnerable spot.

The *Virginia* eventually concentrated its fire on the *Monitor*'s pilothouse and about noon managed to strike the sight hole, blinding the Union commanding officer and compelling the vessel to disengage. (The blinded captain eventually regained sight in one eye.) Thus the battle ended, a stalemate. Both sides claimed they had won, but that mattered little. Each contestant possessed a form of the new iron ship, and neither had gained the possibly overwhelming advantage that even temporary singular possession might have conferred.

However important the *Monitor* and the *Virginia* might have been in the history of the Civil War, they are not as important in military history as Americans commonly assume. Although they were the first to engage in a battle, other ironclads saw combat on the rivers in the western theater of war. More important, the two vessels were not the most technologically advanced ships in the world, although Ericsson's designs (especially the turret) were important. By the time of their 1862 engagement, the British navy already had ordered, constructed, and commissioned a far more powerful vessel: the *HMS*

Warrior. Ordered in 1859 and commissioned in 1861, the *Warrior* saw service until 1883. The French had also worked on ironclads and began building the *Gloire* in 1858.

Public criticism of Jefferson Davis was sparked to unprecedented degree of harshness in reaction to the scuttling of the *Virginia*. The newspapers blamed him for what they called a "panicky" act. He himself, meanwhile, hoped that Southerners could be deluded into believing that the *Virginia* as a ship was not really outclassed.[1]

Davis was concerned about what the *Monitor* might do next, and he no doubt read with interest a letter from S. Thomas, written on May 14, 1862, suggesting "a deed of heroism that would electrify the country": to board the *Monitor* at night and cut anchor ropes and chains so it would drift ashore, or stop up the smokestack, or wedge the turret so it would not revolve; sharpshooters along riverbanks could stop rescue by other boats.[2]

After the fall of Forts Henry and Donelson, and Major General Don Carlos Buell's occupation of Nashville, General Henry Halleck sent U.S. Grant, now a major general, south on the Tennessee River to replace the little holding force at Pittsburg Landing. President Lincoln meanwhile had extended Halleck's area of command to include Buell's force, and Halleck ordered Buell to march his substantial army from Nashville to reinforce Grant.[3]

As one would expect of officers trained at West Point, familiar with the Napoleonic tradition in military operations, and of veterans of Winfield Scott's army, the Confederate command appraised the situation in quite the same way as Halleck did. Thus it would seem superfluous for President Davis to have advised General Albert Sidney Johnston to exploit the enemy's dispersion by concentrating and assailing Buell's force before it completed its march to join Grant. But Johnston was not prepared to act, being in the extreme eastern part of his department, trying to better organize his huge command and only just moving troops westward.

At this time, the Confederate situation changed in the western part of the department, with the arrival of General P. G. T. Beauregard. Finding him redundant and troublesome in the small Virginia theater, Davis had sent him west to be Johnston's second in command. Though competent, Beauregard was overconfident and bumptious to boot. When he arrived, he immediately proclaimed himself to be in command in the western part of Johnston's department. Promptly concentrating for an offensive, Beauregard ordered troops from Arkansas to cross into Mississippi and instructed the troops who were still on the Mississippi to move south and to join him. Further, he called on the Gulf

Coast troops for reinforcements, thus helping to expedite the movement ordered by President Davis for troops there to move north to help resist Grant and Buell.

This order resulted in substantial numbers arriving from New Orleans and Pensacola. When Johnston and his men joined Beauregard and the force he was gathering, the Confederates decided to try to strike and destroy Grant's force before Buell could arrive. The nicely concentrated Confederate force advanced from a base of operations in Corinth, Mississippi, northeast toward Pittsburg Landing. But when near Grant's encampment, they deployed in a cumbersome array that Beauregard unwisely had devised. The Rebels were ready to attack at dawn, and despite their having done much that could have warned Grant, the Federals were surprised. Moreover, the Federals had not entrenched, as Halleck had ordered. The initial assaulting troops encountered an unready enemy, many of its men busy preparing breakfast. Grant was away, and few in the Union army had seriously expected to be attacked.

Thus on April 6 and 7, 1862, a huge battle occurred near Shiloh Church and Pittsburg Landing, Tennessee. The South prevailed on the first day of the fighting but failed to crush Grant's force. In midafternoon, General Albert Sidney Johnston took a fatal wound in the leg, his femoral artery severed. William Preston, his aide, wired President Davis that Johnston had died "gaining a brilliant victory." Later, during the night, Beauregard, who had succeeded Johnston in command, also wired Richmond, saying, "Thanks be to the Almighty, [we have] gained a complete victory."

The next day, however, the Federals regained all the ground they had lost. The battle proved to have been essentially a huge and costly draw. Two shocked nations were aghast at the casualties, which outnumbered those at the Battle of Waterloo. And the South had lost Albert Sidney Johnston, from whom much had been expected in the way of military successes.

Beauregard soon was swamped by criticism for the muddled order of march and for conduct of the battle, particularly for having halted the fighting on Sunday without first personally surveying the front or consulting his generals, but also for his failure to organize the men adequately so that they could have coped better with the renewed fighting the next morning. Such criticism, however, ignores the reality that the halt had been prudent, indeed probably necessary, given the exhausted state of the men and the extreme difficulty of crossing the terrain necessary to reach Grant's final defensive perimeter. Johnston's death compounded the difficulty of parsing through the details concerning true responsibility for the order of march and conduct of the battle. Davis, ever true to his friend, asserted that the only mistake Johnston made at Shiloh was "in not personally making the order of march from Corinth to Pittsburg Landing," instead entrusting the duty to Beauregard.[4]

It is difficult to calculate the depth of impact that the loss of Johnston had on Davis. He told those around him that "the cause could have spared a whole State better than that great soldier."[5] He told Congress that although he dared not trust himself to express it, "it may safely be asserted that our loss is irreparable." He wrote to General Earl Van Dorn: "The report that Genl. A. S. Johnston was killed sadly depresses me." William Preston Johnston, the general's son and one of Davis's aides, wrote that Davis said "not once, but many times: 'When Sidney Johnston fell, it was the turning-point of our fate; for we had no other hand to take up his work in the West.'" "How much his loss must have pierced your heart," Commissary General Lucius Northrop wrote Davis after the war; "it was a terrible trial to your fortitude." Generals Richard Taylor, Braxton Bragg, and others later looked back on this loss and agreed with Davis's assessment at the time.[6]

As for Beauregard's being in command, Davis entertained scant hopes for any successes he might attain. He believed that in halting the attack on the first day, Beauregard had given up what Johnston had nearly achieved: a great victory. Indeed, Davis clung to this belief for the rest of his life.[7] Joseph Davis apparently shared that belief, writing to his brother on April 20, 1862: "The loss of Genl. Johnston at Shiloh was felt in the disorders that followed his fall. Beauregard may possess courage & as an Engineer skill but he wants character to command respect."[8]

Johnston's body was taken by aides to New Orleans, where it lay in state, and then was buried in St. Louis Cemetery. Eighteen days later, that quintessentially valuable city fell to the Union navy and was thereafter occupied by a military force under Major General Benjamin F. Butler. (Johnston's body, years later, was moved to Austin, Texas.)

On the same day that the Battle of Shiloh concluded, Island No.10, in the Mississippi River, fell to the Federals. This opened the way to the easy capture of Memphis and set up the subsequent campaigns to take Vicksburg. Spring 1862 unfolded with one disaster after another befalling the Confederacy.

On February 21, 1861, a Confederate force had lost the Battle of Val Verde in New Mexico. Later, as a result of the engagement on March 28 at Glorieta Pass and Pigeon's Ranch, the Rebels were completely driven out of the New Mexico Territory. On February 25, 1862, a Union force occupied Nashville, Tennessee, a severe loss because of the industrial machine works thus lost by the South. On March 6, action began at Pea Ridge, Arkansas; Confederates there were badly defeated in fighting over the next two days. Eight days later, on March 14, separate Federal expeditions captured both New Madrid, Missouri, and New Berne, North Carolina.

April was no better. On April 11, Fort Pulaski in Georgia, just below Savannah, fell to the Federals, and a week later, on April 18, the U.S. Navy began a bombardment of two forts below New Orleans. They fell on April 24, and the next day the Federal fleet arrived at New Orleans. The city was immediately surrendered—a loss of tremendous importance. But it is an exaggeration, as one historian has claimed, that it had been "the night the war was lost." As one teenaged New Orleans girl wrote in her diary: "We are conquered but not subdued." Much of the Confederate populace, however, felt desperate. Some even entertained wild fantasies: "Two Confederate senators proposed a night attack on McClellan employing exotic tactics—5,000 [men] *stripped naked* to storm the camps of the enemy with the bayonet only & Kill everybody with clothes on."[9]

It is not off the mark to say that by late May the Confederacy had nearly lost the war. A quiet desperation settled over Richmond, and the Confederate government (in the dark of night, to avoid creating panic) loaded its archives onto railroad cars to be ready for instant evacuation if necessary. Publicly, Davis admitted, as he had in his 1862 Inaugural Address as president under the permanent government, that "the tide is for the moment against us," for Confederates "have had our trials and difficulties." But he claimed, "the final result in our favor is not doubtful."[10] He confessed that "events have demonstrated that the Government had attempted more than it had power successfully to achieve" and made the difficult admission that "enough is known of the surrender at Roanoke Island to make us feel that it was deeply humiliating, however imperfect may have been the preparations for defence." Yet "hope is still entertained that our reported losses at Fort Donelson have been greatly exaggerated."[11]

Privately he was honest. To General Joseph E. Johnston he confessed that "recent disasters have depressed the weak and are depriving us of the aid of the wavering" and urged that "the military paradox that impossibilities must be rendered possible had never better occasion for its application."[12]

Portraying him as "miserable," his niece confided to her mother, "I fear he cannot live long if he does not get some rest and quiet." The constant reverses "distress him so much." Varina later wrote about an evening during this period when he spoke of "the weight of responsibility distress[ing] him so he felt he would give all his limbs to have someone with whom he could share it."[13]

In these dark moments Davis began to think about God in more personal terms than he ever had before. He had often attended religious services, usually Episcopal—that being Varina's faith and also Joseph's. It is clear that he long had thought of himself as being a Christian, and in 1857 he had purchased a pew in the Church of the Epiphany in Washington. Many of his public messages referred to the Divine, and often both in public and private did he ask for blessings on the Confederate cause. Still, however, he had not actually joined any church, and he could not even recall whether he had been baptized.[14]

During this wintertime of early 1862 he made up his mind. He and Varina both began talking seriously about his joining the Episcopal Church. The Reverend Charles Minnigerode, rector of St. Paul's Episcopal Church in Richmond, on May 6 came to the Gray House and conditionally baptized Davis (i.e., if he had not been baptized already). Later Bishop John Johns presided over a special service at St. Paul's, in which Davis and two other persons received the Sacrament of Holy Confirmation. Minnigerode wrote that Davis showed his "resolute character" by leading the way to the altar rail. Varina recorded that "the joy of being received into the Church seemed to pervade his soul."[15]

In a letter to William M. Brooks, Davis again admitted "the error of my attempt to defend all of the frontier, sea board and inland; but will say in justification that, if we had received the arms and munitions which we had good reason to expect, the attempt would have been successful and the battlefields would have been on the enemy's soil." He claimed a desire to undertake the offensive, "but the means have been wanting." Brooks had informed Davis that the president had "scarcely a friend and not a defender in Congress or in the Army," but Davis hoped this was not so; no situation was ever so desperate that he abandoned hope.[16] He held frequent consultations with Joseph E. Johnston, looking for ways to reverse what he quite aptly called "the drooping cause of our country."[17] The tide of events was, however, on the verge of change.

Meanwhile, the Confederates managed to delay McClellan's advance considerably. Davis wrote to General Joseph E. Johnston, in command on the peninsula, that "I have been much relieved by the successes which you have gained, and I hope for you the brilliant result which the drooping cause of our country now so imperatively claims."[18] But Johnston was not telling Davis what his intentions were; indeed, after a February conference in Richmond, the general had resolved never to tell Davis his plans again.

Davis did his best to intervene, and immediately after writing his February letter to Johnston he left Richmond to visit the general's headquarters. He found the army on the south bank of the Rappahannock River, where there seemed to be great natural advantages. Davis asked Johnston if the south bank offered such advantages farther down, as far as Fredericksburg. Johnston admitted he did not know, not having visited that area for many years. Davis and Johnston then together rode toward Fredericksburg, and their reconnaissance did indeed confirm the Confederate force probably was inadequate to defend the town, given the terrain. Davis returned to Richmond to await news of what the enemy might do.[19]

McClellan and his men marched inexorably onward, and Richmond almost did fall. Word that Johnston was in full retreat reached the capital on Sunday, May 4; the news reached Davis in his church pew at St. Paul's.[20] Davis might have found a new measure of peace, but it provided no tranquillity as far as the safety of his family was concerned, as McClellan continued his advance up the peninsula. Davis's niece Helen Keary noted on May 4 that "Uncle Jeff. is miserable. . . . He knows that he ought to send his wife and children away, and yet he cannot bear to part with them, and we all dread to leave him too. Varina and I had a hard cry about it to-day."[21] Apparently on May 5 the family members reached a consensus that they probably should leave Richmond; thus the private baptism service, so Varina could be present. Davis wanted her to go to Marietta, Georgia, where the wife of his aide, William M. Browne, could help the family to find a sufficiently inexpensive place to stay, but Varina insisted that she wanted to be closer. They finally settled on Raleigh, North Carolina, only one day's distance by train.[22]

On May 13, Davis wrote to Varina:

Yesterday afternoon I went to the Hd. Qrs. of Genl. Johnston's Army about twenty two or three miles from here. He was out when we reached there and the distance was so great that after conversation it was decided to remain, and I rode in this morning. The army is reported in fine spirits and condition. If the withdrawal from the Peninsula and Norfolk had been with due preparation and the desirable deliberation I should be more sanguine of a successful defence of this city. Various causes have delayed the obstruction and the armament of the covering fort, whilst the hasty evacuation of the defenses below and the destruction of the Virginia [the ironclad] hastens the coming of the Enemy's Gun Boats. I know not what to expect.[23]

Many of Davis's constituents were uneasy also. Edmund Ruffin wrote in his diary, "To the morbid tenderness of conscience of a 'seeker of religion,' & a new convert, I ascribe much of the imbecility of President Davis, in failing to punish military & political criminals—deserters, spies & traitors."[24] But Davis always believed that a general in the field was in a better position to judge what to do than he was (unless, of course, Davis could get to the field himself), so he patiently accepted Johnston's retreat.[25]

On May 16, Davis wrote to Varina:

I returned this evening from a long ride through rain & mud, having gone down the James River to see the works and obstructions on which we rely to stop the gun boats. The attack of yesterday has given an impulse to the public. [As the Confederates had feared, soon after the Virginia was scuttled the Monitor and four other   gunboats headed up the James. Their attack at Drewry's Bluff on May 15, however, was repulsed.] The panic here has subsided and with increasing confidence there has arisen a desire to see the city destroyed rather than surrendered. . . .

As the clouds grow darker and when one after another those who were trusted are detected in secret hostility, I feel like mustering claws were in me, and that cramping fetters had fallen from my limbs. The great temporal object is to secure our independence and they who engage in strife for personal or party aggrandizement deserve contemptuous forgetfulness. To me who have no political wish beyond the success of our cause, no personal desire but to be relieved from further connection with office, opposition in any form can only disturb me in so much as it may endanger the public welfare.[26]

Various newspapers in both North and South printed accounts of Davis's remarks to the soldiers in Richmond, aimed at quelling any qualms they may have had about rumors of probable surrender. Addressing a crowd in Capital Square, Davis had told them

that they would fight and hold Richmond, or die there. If they were thoroughly whipped they would burn the city, as everything was in readiness, and only needed a match to be applied. They were fighting for their homes and firesides, and he for one was willing to lose his life and all he had—he would never sacrifice his honor. He incited the soldiers to fight on by telling them of outrages perpetrated by the Lincolnites and other vandals. Virginia, he said, must never be given up, and they would fight until the last.[27]

On May 17, Davis sent Johnston a hand-carried letter, again stressing the popular "determination that the ancient and honored Capitol of Va. now the Seat of the Confederate Govt. shall not fall into the hands of the Enemy." He delineated several options that Johnston might elect to follow, depending on what the enemy did next. But he concluded, "As on all former occasions my design is to suggest not to direct, recognizing the impossibility of any one to decide in advance and reposing confidently as well on your ability as your zeal it is my wish to leave you with the fullest powers to exercise your judgement."[28] Davis was, however, unaware that at that time Johnston already had crossed the Chickahominy River and retreated to within five miles of Richmond; and the Yankees could see the church steeples and hear the bells pealing.

On May 30, by then having heard of the bleak situation so near Richmond, Davis wrote to Varina:

I packed some valuable books and the sword I wore for many years, together with the pistols used at Monterrey and Buena Vista, and my old dressing-case. These articles will have a value to the boys in aftertime, and to you now. . . .

Thank you for congratulations on success of Jackson. Had the movement been made when I first proposed it, the effect would have been more important. [Davis was referring to Stonewall Jackson's victories at Front Royal on May 23 and at Winchester on May 25, marking the middle of his successful Shenandoah Valley campaign, which lasted from early May to mid-June.] . . . . You will have seen a notice of the destruction of our home. [Davis was referring to a report that had appeared in the May 30, 1862, *Richmond Examiner* paraphrasing the *Vicksburg Citizen* of May 23: "We learn that the vandals have come off their boats and battered down and utterly destroyed the residence of Jeff. Davis, and also that of Joe. Davis. Their acts of destruction and vandalism in that neighborhood were complete, leaving nothing but a bleak and desolated track behind them."]

If our cause succeeds we shall not mourn over any personal deprivation; if it should not, why "the deluge." I hope I shall be able to provide for the comfort of the old negroes.[29]

On May 31, Johnston finally struck back, in the Battle of Fair Oaks, or Seven Pines. Varina quite naturally had surmised that Davis would go to the battlefield. She wrote him on May 30: "I tremble for you in a battle—for my sake take care of yourself, and don't expose yourself—you may do much for the cause living, it is lost I fear if you fell a sacrifice."[30] And indeed Varina's fears were well founded: as soon as the sounds of firing commenced Johnston had ridden toward the front, with Lee and Davis following.[31]

The most significant result of Seven Pines was the wounding of Johnston. Seeing him being carried from the field, Davis dismounted and offered the general his hand and asked if he could do anything for him. Johnston shook his head and said that he did not know how seriously he had been hurt. Obviously moved, Davis wrote Varina that "the poor fellow bore his suffering most heroically." The wound proved to be serious, causing a prolonged disability and Johnston's replacement in command by Robert E. Lee.

Davis, meanwhile, had been riding around the battle area with Lee and met Postmaster General John Reagan, who, like Davis, was there to see the fighting. Davis should not have been on the field at all, though as commander in chief he had that right. Why the postmaster general would be involved in a military field operation is a question never answered.

Davis later told Varina about "unaccountable delays in bringing some of our troops into action," which prevented "a decisive victory," and that "heavy skirmishing" had brought "no important result. . . . The opportunity being lost we must try to find another. . . . God will I trust give us wisdom to see and valor to execute, the measures necessary to vindicate the just cause."[32]

Still later he wrote to Varina that "the Yankees had been eight or ten days fortifying the position in which we attacked them on saturday and the first intimation I had of their having slept on this side of the Chickahomana [*sic*] was after I had ridden into an encampment from which they were driven. . . . The ignorance of their works caused much of the loss we suffered."[33]

The change of command, transferring Robert E. Lee from his staff job in Richmond to an active field command, proved to be both a blessing and a curse for the Confederate military establishment. Lee brought his whole staff from Richmond into the field with him. Neither he nor the staff was ever replaced—a grave mistake. But Lee proved to be a popular and able, eventually beloved, army commander. Undoubtedly his successes in subsequent battles lengthened the life of the Confederacy. Davis and Lee had a close rapport and a mutual trust.

The historian Joseph Harsh, in his appraisal of Lee, has observed that the general had a great strength of character, combined with "an aura of aloofness that protected him from intrigue and jealousy." He pragmatically accepted every "hand dealt him by fate." "On an extraordinary number of occasions," he "found a way to impress his will on confusion around him." He displayed an "inherent, sanguine confidence to confront the most serious problems with a positive attitude." He had "a sharp eye for strategic opportunities." His new assignment "came at exactly the right moment," allowing him "to capitalize on the Confederacy's new commitment to mobilization and concentration, and, secondly, [to make the most of] the unique working relationship [he had] developed with Davis."[34]

According to William C. Davis, "Lee proved to be a far more astute judge of character than most of the South's leading generals, and better than Davis." He understood that one had scrupulously to follow a few simple rules to get along well with Jefferson Davis: "Do not question him unless he invited criticism. Do not challenge him. Keep him fully informed at all times. Do not assail his friends or cronies. Have nothing to do with the press, and eschew public controversy. Avoid politicians, especially those in the growing anti-Davis camp. Most of all remain loyal." These requirements suited Lee well, for they fit his own "notions of the proper deportment of a general to his commander in chief." Perhaps the finest line in W. C. Davis's book is the remark that "Lee was a better politician and statesman than Davis."[35]

The day after Lee was appointed to the field command, Davis was too ill to ride out to visit the army, but he wrote to Lee, "Please keep me advised as frequently as your engagements will permit of what is passing before and around you." Lee was just the man for that, and for the rest of the war he wrote to Davis "both frequently and fully." Davis loved it.[36] Lee held firmly that "Richmond *must not* fall." To add to the defensive strength, he had the men dig formidable entrenchments. Davis applauded that, saying every great general since Julius Caesar had made good use of the shovel.[37] But the ultimate purpose was not merely to defend; rather, it was to attack.

Lee and Davis had compatible ideas for Confederate grand strategy. William Cooper suggests that Davis "saw Lee in his own image—a man totally dedicated to the Confederacy."[38] Harsh writes that "Lee's strategy did not contravene Davis's concepts; it transcended them." Lee perceived that certain axioms had been well established by June 1862. The North's overwhelming statistical superiority made it quite improbable that the South could conquer it. Further, the European antipathy toward slavery made it unlikely that any foreign help would be obtained. Actually, Lee had a keen apprehension of the unlikelihood that the South could win the war in any event, but he did not allow himself to succumb to hopelessness until shortly before Appomattox. He envisioned the key to resolving the Confederate dilemma to be in seizing the initiative and in aggressive operations, in hopes of inflicting discouragement in the North to a degree that the Northern people would no longer have the will to continue the war.[39]

Lee most likely had these ideas in mind on June 25, 1862, when he commenced the Seven Days campaign, a series of offensive thrusts against the Yankees. From the start, Lee sought ways to flush the Federals into the open, where he hoped his army might destroy them while at the same time avoiding unacceptable Confederate losses. He would try to achieve a turning movement rather than bloody flank attacks. A victory would have little long-term significance if the Army of the Potomac remained a viable threat.[40]

With such a large enemy force so close to Richmond, Lee envisioned a far stronger riposte than Johnston's. Implicitly, or possibly explicitly, he chose as his model Napoleon's Jena and Auerstadt campaign against the Prussians in 1806. In this action, Napoleon had faced the enemy with his main force while sending Marshal Louis Davout, his ablest subordinate, in a turning movement into the Prussian rear. Davout with twenty-seven thousand men succeeded in blocking the retreat of sixty-three thousand Prussians. Meanwhile, defeated in their frontal battle against Napoleon, the Prussians, having lost fifty thousand casualties (one-half of those as prisoners), fled. The French pursued relentlessly, until Berlin fell. Then the French continued their advance until they reached the Baltic Sea, having occupied half of Prussia's territory.

As Lee faced McClellan's army east of Richmond, he ordered his ablest subordinate, Stonewall Jackson, to move from the Shenandoah Valley to the vicinity of Richmond. Jackson moved partly by railroad, expecting to arrive north of the Union army, where he might march into the Yankees' rear. The execution of this turning movement would have blocked McClellan's supply line, the Richmond and York River Railroad, which ran east to connect with the Chesapeake Bay.

That Jackson arrived a day later than expected was only one of the several factors that kept Lee's inexperienced army from duplicating the feat of the French veterans commanded by Napoleon and Davout. The Confederate offensive began without Jackson and continued for seven days. Although most of the assaults were meant to strike the Union troops on their flanks or rear, the maneuverability of their well-drilled adversary resulted in the Confederates failing, because they assailed the hastily entrenched enemy in front. Nevertheless, the eventual arrival of Jackson on the Union north flank, together with further Rebel attacks, concerned McClellan enough that he retreated south to the James River, which he then used for a supply line.

Lee gained a victory by pushing the enemy army away from Richmond, but the Rebels had achieved nothing compared with what Lee had been trying to replicate: the disaster that the French had inflicted on the Prussians. But Lee overlooked how limited his achievement was and pursued the Yankees with great vigor, facing them in several costly frontal clashes, the last one at Malvern Hill on July 1, which was particularly disastrous for the Confederates. Lee's army suffered 20,614 casualties compared to 15,849 for the Union forces.

Although the Confederates were badly mauled at Malvern Hill, the end result of the Seven Days campaign was McClellan's retreat from the immediate vicinity of Richmond to a new base some twenty-five miles away. Everyone on both sides saw the result as a Northern defeat. The withdrawal of McClellan's army thus constituted at least a strategic victory. But it did not satisfy Lee, who let his Napoleonic aspirations show when he said that had the campaign gone according to plan, "the Federal army should have been destroyed." Lee, Jackson, and President Davis assessed the cost of the victory, and they sought tactical lessons from the fighting. Most Confederate attacks necessarily had become frontal because the well-drilled Federals could maneuver well enough to thwart attacks aimed at their flank or rear. Moreover, Lee had erroneously thought that he was pursuing a beaten foe, when actually two-thirds of the Union army were fresh troops.

The result showed Lee, Jackson, and Davis that the Napoleonic victory Lee had envisioned was beyond the capacity of the Confederate army and that the cost of so ambitious an objective was likely to be prohibitive. In a letter to Jackson, Lee summarized the tactical consensus, saying that Jackson was "right in not attacking them in their strong and chosen positions. They ought always to be turned as you propose, and thus force them on more favorable ground." On the other hand, the campaign had vindicated their strategy by "concentrating our forces to protect important points and baffle the principal efforts of the enemy."

Davis thought that the last engagement of the Seven Days, on June 30, the Battle of Frayser's Farm, or White Oak Swamp, was of historic significance.

> This battle was in many respects one of the most remarkable of the war. Here occurred on several occasions the capture of batteries by the impetuous charge of our infantry, defying the canister and grape which plowed through their ranks, and many hand-to-hand conflicts, where bayonet-wounds were freely given and received, and men fought with clubbed muskets in the life-and-death encounter.
>
> The estimated strength of the enemy was double our own, and he had the advantage of being in position. From both causes it necessarily resulted that our loss was very heavy. . . .
>
> During the night those who fought us at Frazier's Farm fell back to the stronger position of Malvern Hill, and by a night-march the force which had detained Jackson at White-Oak Swamp effected a junction with the other portion of the enemy.[41]

Why, in light of Lee's strong preference to avoid frontal assaults, had he attacked frontally, and thus at such cost, at Malvern Hill? Despite Lee's greatness, there was a crucial flaw in his makeup: when his blood was up he could bring himself to risk too much.

As for Davis, in his typical fashion, throughout the campaign he had kept close to the fighting. "At the sound of the guns," wrote Burton Harrison, "Mr. Davis was in the saddle and off, in a moment," on his powerful and well-bred bay Kentucky—perhaps reflecting his dream to secure that state—and leading his staff a merry chase.[42] General Daniel Harvey Hill recalled that at the first of the battles, Davis was "going 'to the sound of the firing' " and the next day giving an order along with Lee at Gaines's Mill. Varina says that Davis was exposed to enemy fire "on the field every day during the seven days' fight, and slept upon the field every night and was exposed to fire all day." At Frayser's Farm Davis came under "a shower of metal and [tree] limbs" from a gunboat shell as he was trying to rally some fleeing troops. When it was all over he told Varina, "Had all the orders been well and promptly executed," Lee would have dispersed McClellan's army, and it "would never have fought us again."[43] When she had first heard the news of the withdrawal of the Federals, she had teased: "McClellan is like Gen Johnston, great in retreat."[44] Davis later described his reaction to the campaign:

Under ordinary circumstances the army of the enemy should have been destroyed. Its escape was due to. . . . the want of correct and timely information. . . . We had, however, effected our main purpose. The siege of Richmond was raised, and the object of a campaign which had been prosecuted after months of preparation, at an enormous expenditure of men and money, was completely frustrated.

More than ten thousand prisoners, including officers of rank, fifty-two pieces of artillery, and upward of thirty-five thousand stand of small-arms were captured.[45]

"My office work fell behind while I was in the field," Davis wrote Lee on July 5.[46] It was obvious, however, that the field was where he preferred to be. William C. Davis suggests that it was only when "on his horse and in the presence of an army" that Davis truly relaxed.[47] As late as 1864 he still spoke of his "repugnance to the office of chief, and his desire for the field." The next best thing, he found, was to visit the camps and the Richmond defenses on his evening rides around the town. At times an aide accompanied him, but he preferred to go alone. Dr. Minnigerode was "convinced" that Davis often used "those lonely rides" as a chance for prayer. Of course it was dangerous, and once he was indeed shot at by a sniper.[48] Certainly the chief of state had no business getting within firing range of the enemy. Yet given his proclivity for the excitement of battle, apparently such excursions were part of the attempt of an active-negative president to exercise a more active-positive leadership style.

Following the Seven Days, Davis thanked the troops for "the series of brilliant victories." Only an eyewitness could appreciate their "gallantry," as their attacks had driven the enemy "more than 35 miles," compelling "him to seek safety under cover of his gunboats." They had "done enough for glory," but they must not relax: "Your one great object [is] to drive the invader from your soil and carry your standards beyond . . . the Confederacy, to wring from an unscrupulous foe the recognition of your birthright, community independence."[49]

Davis constantly had to wrestle with the whole of the war effort. If things looked better in Virginia, there were many other worries. Beauregard had given up Corinth, Mississippi, and withdrawn the principal western army to Tupelo, Mississippi. Davis was "shocked" by news of this and sternly pressed Beauregard to explain his retrograde. Beauregard, however, pleaded that urgent business precluded his sending any early explanation. Davis wrote to Varina, "There are those who can only walk a log when it is near to the ground, and I fear he has been placed too high for his mental strength, as he does not exhibit the ability manifested on smaller fields." Davis dispatched an officer from his personal staff to obtain answers to a list of written questions that the president gave him for Beauregard. Davis also began contemplating at this time whether he ought soon to reassign him. Not one to hide his feelings, and they were bitter, Davis sarcastically remarked to Varina that "the sedentary life at Corinth must have been hard to bear."[50]

Beauregard then appalled Davis by going on a self-authorized sick leave. At that point, Davis gave up on him: since Beauregard believed the army could do without him at this time, Davis was in concurrence. Beauregard in turn was furious and believed that he had been removed solely by presidential vendetta. He described Davis as "that living specimen of gall and hatred." He called on his political allies to act to restore his position, and if they did not, he asserted, "I shall think but poorly of them & of human nature."[51]

Braxton Bragg was given command of the army. Davis liked him: early in the war Bragg had trained new volunteers rather well and then cheerfully and willingly agreed to let some other commander have them as he trained more raw recruits. Davis at this time regarded Bragg as the best commander of volunteer troops in the entire Confederate army. And even more important, Cooper observes, "Davis perceived Bragg as the opposite of Beauregard, a general who placed the cause before self." Bragg, Davis believed, "seemed to have that most valuable combination, ability and commitment."[52]

When Beauregard returned to duty he finally agreed to accept command of the Department of South Carolina, Georgia, and Florida, but he never forgave Davis for having taken the army away from him. Meanwhile the Trans-Mississippi remained quiescent. But on the Gulf Coast, the Federals in New Orleans always threatened Mobile, and they succeeded in causing Pensacola to be evacuated. Davis meanwhile was ailing off and on through June. Preston Johnston thought he knew why: "He sits up late and smokes too much."[53]

In his "terse, chaste, vigorous, classic, Anglo-Saxon English," Davis reasoned with governors and other politicians, pleading for patriotism and for putting the general good ahead of particular state interest; sometimes he threatened, sometimes he cajoled.[54] "Precise and zealous," a man of "great labor, of great learning," Davis had to consider myriad details, from finances abroad, to crops at home, to the "torpedo service" (i.e., land and marine mines).[55] He consulted his cabinet as well as all sorts of experts frequently, allowing "the utmost latitude of opinion and expression." He gave every question deep and scholarly scrutiny before making up his mind, but once it was made up, he had a rock-hard stubbornness, unless he could see good reason to change: "unchangeable," writes Stephen Mallory, "when convinced of being right." Critics called this his obstinacy; admirers saw it as his strength.[56] We would be on the mark to call it active-negative leadership.

On the other hand, even Davis's enemies admitted he worked hard for the Confederacy, that he was dedicated to the cause: According to W. C. Davis,

"When the situation demanded courage and determination, he was at his best." And one lieutenant, after observing the president in church, wrote, "He bears the marks of greatness about him beyond all persons I have ever seen."[57]

That affairs were getting desperate was illustrated by the passage of an ill-considered law authorizing the arming of newly organized troops with pikes. There was, however, a dire shortage of men as well as of arms.[58] Thus, the states became involved. Suspicious of Davis, of the proposed conscription legislation, and indeed of projected central government decisions on other issues as well, Governor Francis Pickens of South Carolina suggested to other Confederate governors that they take the initiative in supporting the war effort.

A month before Congress enacted the first conscription law, Pickens had suggested a "common plan" among the states "by which the whole male white population . . . from sixteen to fifty should be enumerated, properly classified, and held ready, under an equal plan of conscription, to be enrolled into active service whenever required." Complaining that queries to the Confederate government about coordinated plans had been ignored, Pickens proposed that the governors meet and exchange views "upon some great and leading measures by which our different States could be brought to act in concert," preferably before April, 20, 1862.[59] Clearly, Pickens had two concerns—not only to increase military power but also to provide an alternate, state-oriented source of leadership for a Confederacy that at the moment seemed to be in deep difficulty.

Thus with conscription did Davis bring into the open the infelicitous conflict of state rights versus Southern nationalism. Doubtlessly he anticipated the adverse reaction his action precipitated, but he believed in the imperative of holding short-term enlistments within the ranks and in the need for military uniformity, which the independent states severally and separately could not accomplish. Davis also argued that the draft would distribute the burden of the war more equally throughout the Confederacy. Despite powerful opposition from Governor Joseph E. Brown of Georgia and Vice President Alexander H. Stephens, the conscription law that Davis requested was passed by Congress on April 16, 1862; he approved it the same day.[60]

This first true conscription legislation in American national history subjected all white men residing in the Confederacy between the inclusive ages of eighteen and thirty-five to service for three years or the duration of the war. This included men already in the army, whose three years of service would be dated from the time of their enlistment. Men outside the draft age would be allowed to leave the army, but only after ninety days. Again, there was wisdom behind the act, for newly enrolled men were to be assigned to fill vacancies in existing companies instead of forming new units. The excess of enrolled men, those surplus to the needs of filling vacancies in existing units, were to constitute a reserve to provide replacements and to form new units, as the president determined the need. Reflecting the shortage of arms, the law also encouraged new troops to bring their own weapons; a man with his own "musket, shot-gun, rifle, or carbine, accepted as an efficient weapon," might sell it to the army or else receive an extra dollar a month pay for its use. Men held in the army who had not previously received a reenlistment bounty or furlough of sixty days would receive one. In order to avoid the stigma of conscription, any eligible male not in the army would be free to volunteer if he had not yet been enrolled.[61]

Two portions of the law created future difficulties. One continuing bone of contention was the stipulation that the law applied to men "who are not legally exempted from military service," and another provided "that persons not liable for duty may be received as substitutes for those who are, under such regulations as may be prescribed by the Secretary of War."[62] Both provisions created widespread discontent, as those risking death in the army and their families pointed accusing fingers at those in exempt occupations or who had found substitutes. But the potential difficulties of these sections were understood only by a few Confederate leaders when the conscription law was passed.

Five days later, on the last day of its first session as Permanent Congress, members passed additional manpower legislation. One law reflected concerns about soldiers' stomachs as well as the number of men available for duty by authorizing each company to enlist four cooks, who "may be white or black, free or slave persons."[63] A second law organized battalions of sharpshooters,[64] and a third provided for promotion from the ranks for a soldier "who shall have been distinguished in the service by the exhibition of extraordinary valor and skill."[65] The most significant and far-reaching law, however, was that which provided for exemptions to the conscription law.

The first exemption law was not particularly controversial, however, for it did not exempt as many categories of manpower as later laws, and it was not yet apparent that exemptions would be widely abused—or at least would be so perceived. Those who were unfit for service were exempt, of course, and perhaps Congress was negligent in not including this exemption in the body of the conscription law. Other exemptions also were quite logical, including those for employees of the Confederate government and the civil officers and legislators of both the state and central governments.

But some blanket exemptions seemed questionable. Anyone carrying the mail, including "ferrymen on post routes," was excused from service. So too were "pilots and persons engaged in the marine service and in actual service on river and railroad routes of transportation." Telegraph operators and clergymen were exempt, along with laborers in the iron industry. Newspaper printers, college professors, and teachers "having as many as twenty scholars" escaped the net, as did superintendents, nurses, and attendants in public hospitals and "lunatic asylums." Teachers of the "deaf and dumb, and blind" joined apothecaries and workers in textile factories as among those who would not be taken.[66]

Spurred by conscription, which threatened them with service, but shown a way out by the exemption law itself, thousands of able-bodied young men rounded up "twenty scholars" by offering low or even free tuition, started carrying the mail, established drug stores, or got religion and claimed they were clergymen. Some even proclaimed their allegiance to a foreign country. Lawyers richly supplemented their incomes by obtaining exemptions for clients. Counterfeit papers and furloughs made their way into the hands of the unscrupulous. Various state governors who to one degree or another opposed conscription tried to exempt many eligible men by naming them state employees.

In August 1862, Texas congressman Caleb C. Herbert expressed his indignation with conscription and declared that it "would not do to press the conscription law too far upon the people. If it became necessary to violate the Constitution . . . he would be for raising in his State the 'lone star' flag that had twice been raised before."[67] And Reuben Davis of Mississippi (no relation to Jefferson Davis) declared he would rather be a slave "than a victim of the Conscription Law."[68]

Taken as a whole, however, the manpower legislation of the first session of the First Congress was really quite exceptional. Although lax by twentieth-century standards, it was remarkable for the nineteenth century. Conscription had never been adopted in America before, although it had been discussed with some seriousness during the dark days of the War of 1812. Years later the American military thinker, Emory Upton, claimed that the draft legislation explained "for all time, the meaning and extent of the power to raise and support armies." He praised the Confederate Congress, "appalled, but not unmanned," for rising to the occasion and treating state sovereignty as a "dead letter." "The temerity of this legislation," Upton wrote, "finds no parallel in the history of the world." This was rather surprising praise, coming as it did from one who fought against the armies raised by the Confederate Congress.[69]

9

ESCALATING DEGREES OF WARFARE

"During the late winter and into the summer of 1862 [Jefferson] Davis's spirit would be sorely tested by circumstances all along his far-flung battle lines," according to William Cooper.[1] Davis kept a close personal eye on unfolding events in the East and was himself keenly involved. When on March 13, General Joseph E. Johnston had informed the president that he largely had completed his redeployment to behind the Rappahannock, Davis was surprised, responding, "I was as much in the dark as to your purposes, conditions, and necessities, as at the time of our conversation on the subject about a month since." Then Johnston reported the massive quantity of supplies he had had to destroy, deeply distressing Davis, who knew how difficult it was going to be to replace those materials.[2] Early 1862 was progressing dismally for the Confederacy.

Some irregular combat predated the Civil War's outset, especially along the Kansas-Missouri border, prompting some historians, including Dudley Taylor Cornish, to argue that the war actually began a number of years before 1861. Conditions in Missouri certainly became quite appalling. The fanatic Indianan Jim Lane recruited a brigade of Kansas troops and led them into western Missouri to burn houses, shoot citizens, and loot generally. This foray was followed by his September 22, 1861, raiding, looting, and burning of the town of Osceola, a hotbed of Southern sympathizers on the Osage River. The fighting in Missouri was cruel and irrational, and almost nobody knew just where his neighbor stood.

By spring 1862 a guerrilla war of frightful dimensions had broken out, with marauding, hangings, and slayings. The murderous pro-Confederate William C. Quantrill organized a band to combat the Kansas guerrillas. In March 1862 the Union general Henry W. Halleck, department commander in the West, issued his General Order no. 2, declaring that any man who enlisted in an irregular band would, if captured, be hanged as a robber and murderer. This only fanned the flames, and fighters on both sides gave no quarter. The struggle increased with so rapid a ferocity that by midsummer the richest and most populous counties of Missouri were ablaze in warfare.

Irregular warfare was by no means confined to Missouri. Indeed, from the Great Smokies to the Nueces River, groups of Confederate deserters, usually hiding in swamps or woods and preying on the countryside, wreaked havoc on the surrounding regions. Estimates put their numbers above ten thousand each for Arkansas and Mississippi, where companies of volunteer "rangers" took to the field to try to hunt down the lawless renegades.

In April 1862 the Confederate Congress passed the Partisan Ranger Act, authorizing organization of partisan bands that would be used to make inroads into enemy territory. These rangers would be actual soldiers, regularly received into the Confederate military service, and would wear uniforms at least similar to those of the army's. They would receive pay from the government for all arms and munitions they captured. Bands of partisan rangers sprang up rapidly. In the eastern theater they fought with somewhat more restraint than did the guerrillas in the West, where acts of warfare blurred into criminality. Eastern rangers who attracted much attention included J. H. McNeill, Harry Gilmor, Elijah V. White, and the most notorious, John Singleton Mosby. President Jefferson Davis was so favorably impressed with Mosby's accomplishments in Northern Virginia that toward the end of the war he envisioned continuing the struggle by carrying out Mosby's tactic on a grand scale.[3]

One Union officer who distinguished himself with his degree of savagery was Ivan Turchin, a Russian who had come to the United States after serving in the Crimean War. He had begun service in the Civil War as colonel of the Nineteenth Illinois Regiment, but in February 1862 he was placed in command of a brigade in Ormsby M. Mitchel's division, with which he captured the town of Huntsville, Alabama, in April. And he insisted that war should be ruthless. During the next month in Athens, Alabama—in retaliation for the townspeople's having, he believed, stoned and fired on his leading regiment— he allegedly told his men: "I close my eyes for two hours." His troops then looted stores, indiscriminately burned dwellings, and destroyed civilian property. For this action, and for allowing his wife to accompany him, Turchin was relieved from command, court-martialed, and recommended for dismissal. His wife, however, successfully petitioned President Lincoln, inducing him not only to set the verdict aside but also to promote her husband to brigadier general of volunteers.[4]

Guerrilla, partisan, and ranger actions continued to punctuate the Civil War for the remainder of its duration. As the conflict dragged on, more and more people became involved in violence, to degrees that most of them could not have imagined at the outset. This was true in operations by regular troops, too; the Civil War became gradually and unmitigatedly more violent. As Charles Royster has observed, "Americans surprised themselves with the extent of violence they could attain, and the surprise consisted, in part, of getting what they had asked for."[5]

The War Office had initially enforced conscription through the Adjutant and Inspector General's Office, but this proved inadequate; thus in December 1862 Congress established a Conscription Bureau, eventually headed capably by Colonel John S. Preston. The fifty-four-year-old Preston had attended Hampden-Sidney College and the University of Virginia before studying law at Harvard. A Virginia native, he had lived in South Carolina and Louisiana, where he made a fortune with his sugar plantation, the Houmas. He had been an aide to Beauregard at Fort Sumter and First Manassas. In August 1861 he was named assistant adjutant general of the Second Brigade of Kentucky troops. In January 1862 he assumed command of the Confederate prison camp at Columbia, South Carolina, and was in that job until he was named to head the Conscription Bureau on July 30, 1863.

Preston, who was promoted to brigadier general on June 10, 1864, managed his bureau quite ably, considering the circumstances, though not without widespread criticism. State officials, medical examiners, and other agents were designated to handle the huge task of enrolling conscripts or approving exemptions. By early 1864 this bureaucracy had grown to 2,813 officials. The bureaucracy functioned relatively inefficiently, however, especially after significant areas of territory fell under Union control. Congress abolished the bureau in March 1865, and conscription was turned over to the generals commanding the reserves in each state.[6]

The long intersession of Congress, from the adjournment of the first session on April 21, 1862, to the convening of the second session on August 18, 1862, had seen the Confederate army enjoying considerable success on many battlefields. The repulse of McClellan at Richmond and the movement of R. E. Lee's army north to fight the Second Battle of Bull Run heightened Confederate morale. But all was not well; for, in the West, Halleck advanced into northern Mississippi, and other Union forces had taken Memphis and Fort Pillow. This mixture of success and failure underlined the need for more men.

In his message to the second session of Congress, Davis noted complaints about the operation of conscription and vaguely referred to the antagonism between the states and the central government that it had engendered. He asked for better execution of the law, and most important, for a further increase in the army by extending conscription to men aged thirty-six to forty-five. As if to justify Union policy curtailing prisoner exchanges, which came in the war's later years, Davis also noted the exchange of prisoners and their return to the ranks of the army.[7]

Congress replied about six weeks later with a veritable flood of manpower-related legislation. On September 27, as Davis had requested, the draft age was extended.[8] In early October Congress moved to systematize military training by establishing "camps of instruction";[9] to catch runaway draftees by authorizing their enrollment wherever they were, even if not in their home states;[10] to establish rendezvous points in every county for medical examinations of enrollers;[11] and to encourage a flow of recruits from occupied territory by continuing volunteer legislation for states where conscription could not be enforced because of Union occupation.[12]

The most important manpower legislation, however, was a revision of the exemption law of the previous session. Like that law, it seemed entirely too broad and, as one congressman put it, it seemed to legislate men out of the army, not into it.[13] The law of October 11, 1862, was even more detailed than the exemption law of the previous April, which it replaced, and exempted more categories of men without bringing more strength to the armies. Although the act's proponents rightly pointed out that many skilled men were of less use to the Confederacy with guns in their hands than they were by raising food crops, making essential manufactured goods, and keeping the transportation system running, nevertheless, the law was clearly as much the product of log rolling as it was of serious legislative consideration. The exemptions of the previous act were incorporated into the new, and many were added, including

> the president, superintendents, conductors, treasurer, chief clerk, engineers, managers, station agents, section masters, two expert track hands to each section of eight miles, and mechanics in the active service and employment of railroad companies . . . all physicians who now are, and for the last five years have been, in the actual practice of their professions; all shoemakers, tanners, blacksmiths, wagon-makers, millers and their engineers, millwrights, skilled and actually employed as their regular vocation in the said trades, habitually engaged in working for the public, and whilst so actually employed, [provided that they sold their products within certain price guidelines].

The exemptions even included "one male citizen for every five hundred head of cattle, for every two hundred and fifty head of horses or mules, and one shepherd for every five hundred head of sheep." The seeds of class antagonism were thus sown, especially by the provision that to secure the proper police of the country, one person, either as agent, owner or overseer on each plantation . . . is required to be kept by the laws or ordinances of any State, and on which there is no white male adult not liable to do military service, and in States having no such law, one person as agent, owner or overseer, on each plantation of twenty negroes, and on which there is no white male adult not liable to military service.[14]

This, the "twenty-Negro law," antagonized small slaveholders and non-slaveholders alike; coupled with the substitution provisions of the original conscript law, it created opportunities for rich men and their sons to avoid military service that poor men could not have. As much as any other measure, these two provisions refueled the acrimonious charge that it was "a rich man's war and a poor man's fight." Though overblown, such charges had enough substance to harm the Confederacy by seriously undermining morale.

A second source of damage to morale lay in the entire exemption system, which created numerous loopholes for able-bodied men to avoid service. And the problem was exacerbated when many men did precisely that, though quite often for good reasons. By February 1865, functioning under the same basic exemption law, the Confederacy had excused sixty-seven thousand men from service.[15] Many of these men were in essential civilian occupations, and many others sought exempt positions so that they could take care of their families when famine and disorder were stalking the land. But it would be naive to assume that this was always, or even nearly always, the case. Many persons simply did not wish to serve, for whatever reasons, which no doubt included fear, but also in many cases because they did not believe in the Confederacy.[16]

Given this situation, it would have made more sense to allocate manpower in a more systematic fashion. But the South—and the North as well, for that matter—was still in transition between traditional and modern social structure, and rational managerial methods were not yet in common use.[17] Thus when Jefferson Davis finally asked Congress to curtail exemptions and instead to grant him detail power, whereby all fit men would be drafted into the army, and those actually required on the home front would be detailed back to their civil occupations, he was largely ignored. And one of the reasons why Congress objected to Davis's proposal was that it placed more power in the hands of the executive than the legislators could agree was desirable.

Other manpower-related legislation also emerged from the second session of the First Congress. Elaborate procedures were drawn up to enable the army to expel incompetent officers,[18] and the important needs of local defense were met by a law authorizing the formation of volunteer companies composed of men who were over the age of forty-five or otherwise not subject to the draft.[19] Both pieces of legislation were vital, and the local defense companies often proved essential, for they ensured that whenever the Confederate armies had to be moved, there would be a reserve force to augment their strength.

At this point the manpower issue became intricately involved with the habeas corpus issue, which at first seemed to have no relation to manpower at all. The February 1862 law permitting suspensions of the writ had been amended to expire thirty days after the next Congress convened,[20] and in summer 1862 Congress wasted no time before debating the issue so as to settle the question before the thirty-day limit was reached. The issue became even more involved because it became entangled with the problem of provost marshal regulations that affected the movement of Confederate citizens, regardless of whether habeas corpus had been suspended in their areas. Under these regulations, which Davis had not asked Congress to authorize, military authorities had been requiring citizens to get passes before they could travel on public facilities.

This was not the freedom that Confederates had in mind when they seceded, and a number of congressmen were quick to vent their fury. In August 1862, Senator Williamson S. Oldham of Texas introduced a resolution asking by what authority provost marshals were appointed and complained that "when he voted in the Senate for the act authorizing the President to suspend the writ of habeas corpus . . . he had no idea of granting him power to suspend all civil government." If things went on as they were, asserted Oldham, "the nations of the world will soon wonder what we are fighting for. Liberty will have gone from us."[21] Senator John B. Clark of Missouri agreed that it was an annoyance, but provost marshals were needed "to keep the soldiers in their places."[22] The skeptic might note that there were not many marshals in Missouri to bother his constituents, but there were a number in Texas, where Oldham's constituents might be much more bothered.

Some Confederate generals had gone even further. Senator Thomas J. Semmes of Louisiana called attention to an extraordinary proclamation issued by Major General Earl Van Dorn, ordering the death penalty for anyone convicted of trading with the enemy; Congress had considered that question also and had legislated a lesser penalty of fine or imprisonment. Van Dorn had also ordered that Confederate Treasury notes circulate at par and that newspaper editors who criticized a military officer in Van Dorn's district be fined and imprisoned.[23]

Senator Oldham complained of General Paul O. Hebert's similar behavior in Texas, "where a Yankee had not set foot since the war." In Richmond, habeas corpus had been suspended, but it rankled Oldham that "he, as a free citizen, was not allowed to go from here to North Carolina without going to the Provost Marshall's office and getting a pass like a free negro."[24]

The debates on the floor of Congress reflected concerns expressed in the

House Judiciary Committee, which had been studying the implications of martial law for personal liberty since March. On September 11, 1862, the day before the committee presented its report, General Order no. 66 seemed to relieve the difficulty. It ordered that "all proclamations of martial law by general officers and others, assuming a power vested only in the President, are hereby annulled." The committee's report praised President Davis for having exercised the authority granted him with "exemplary moderation" but expressed fear that the military possessed too much unchecked power. The committee reviewed the history of martial law and tried to distinguish between what the military could legitimately do because of wartime necessity— destruction of property, for example—and a "power in a commander, or in the President, or in Congress to declare martial law, and then, by virtue of martial law, to exercise arbitrary, absolute, and unlimited power."[25] The committee pointed out that to suspend the writ of habeas corpus "is not to establish martial law with its summary proceedings and absolute power" and concluded that "either martial law is properly styled law or it is not; if it is, it can only be established or authorized by Congress; if it is not, it is lawless power and cannot exist in a Government such as ours."[26] In the debate that followed, Congressman George W. Jones of Tennessee denied that Congress could declare martial law but agreed that it could authorize the president to suspend the writ. Most congressmen seemed to agree reluctantly with Congressman Franklin Sexton of Texas that "there are cases in these times when . . . [the writ] should be suspended," but by the president and no one else.[27]

Thus in October Congress reenacted the suspension law without reference to martial law and provided that it too would expire thirty days after the start of the next session of Congress.[28] By then the conscript law was having an impact, and many men sought to evade service by one means or another. Those already in service had fewer options; some of them viewed conscription as arbitrary detention and looked to the writ of habeas corpus to get them back into civil life. By 1863, therefore, a measure to suspend the writ would be a manpower issue because it would block one of the ways in which the army was drained of its strength.[29] Congressmen who opposed conscription therefore resorted to attacking the periodic suspension of the writ of habeas corpus, and the debates on repassage were heated.

A railroad authority was set up within the Quartermaster Bureau to maintain liaison with the various rail systems. When the government's transportation needs became urgent, military officials stepped in and took control of the operations, much to the chagrin of the civilian managers and owners.

The Confederate government secured virtually every category of war supplies successfully, from time to time, from territory that was under the control of the Union. This trade through military lines continued throughout the war on a large scale. Indeed, as the blockade gradually became more and more effective, supplies from Union territories became the Confederacy's main source of external procurement.

Nevertheless, violations of the property rights of individuals continued to occur throughout 1862, and in August Samuel Cooper attempted to remind the army of the purpose of impressment. He warned commanders that "necessity alone can warrant the impressment of private property" and ought never to be used if "supplies can be obtained by the consent of the owners at fair rates, and without hazardous delay."[30]

But it was difficult to determine the degree of necessity or delay that might justify impressment, which led to numerous rumblings of discontent. In April 1862 Congressman James Lyons of Virginia had secured passage of a resolution requiring the House Committee on Military Affairs to draw up a bill to regulate impressments.[31] Then in August John R. Chambliss of Virginia requested a bill to provide for the impressment of slaves.[32] In October Senator B. H. Hill sponsored a successful resolution asking the president to explain "by what authority of law military officers along the several railroad lines are seizing produce and provisions, the property of private individuals."[33]

Davis transmitted an answer written by Secretary of War George Randolph,[34] the text of which does not appear in the record. Quite possibly it was similar in tone to Randolph's letter on the subject to Robert E. Lee two days earlier, regarding the use of Treasury notes. Randolph instructed Lee that the notes could not be made legal tender "between individuals" but that "supplies may be impressed and paid for in Treasury Notes, and if individuals within the theater of your operations discredit the Government money they may be considered as hostile to the Confederacy, and may be arrested and removed from the vicinity of the army."[35]

The longest ongoing, and most dramatic, aspect of Civil War naval history was the gradually tightening Union blockade of the Confederate coast. Though vexing, the blockade was not completely effective; nor was it at all decisive in determining the war's outcome. The blockade grew more efficient with each passing year, but huge amounts of material were obtained by Confederate agents in Europe, and although much of it was captured by blockading vessels, untold quantities were run through safely. Even near war's end, Confederates could with fair safety take passage from Wilmington, North Carolina, probably the most difficult port to seal off.

But the best the Confederacy could do about the blockade was to take chances on losses and try to evade it, for the would-be nation was never able to obtain sufficient naval power to disrupt the blockaders. Much hope had been placed in having the advantage of an unmatched ironclad that could demolish wooden vessels. When the appearance of the *Monitor* dashed that hope, the Confederate's naval response was mainly to try to compete on inland waterways.

In this the South did rather well, as both sides made much progress in developing rams—ships armed with massively built prows. Early in 1862 the Confederate War Department purchased fourteen riverboats, and seven of these were converted to cotton-clad rams. They saw much action on the western rivers. On the Union side, Colonel Charles Ellet pioneered the conversion of river steamers into rams. Both sides continued to build and to make ever bigger and more powerful rams throughout the war. The most dramatic, and decisive, inland waterway battle was in Mobile Bay, on August 5, 1864, when the Union's rear admiral David G. Farragut gained immortal fame with his shout, "Damn the torpedoes, full speed ahead," and the Confederate defenses were subsequently demolished.

The torpedoes referred to by Admiral Farragut actually were what today are called mines. These explosive devices were frequently used, especially by the Confederacy; as the weaker side, it acted typically as the self-perceived underdog: it innovated. Confederates were more willing than Federals to rely on new devices that might provide some scale-tipping advantage. Mines, various new types of attack craft, and all the other innovative devices are described by Milton Perry in *Infernal Machines*.[36] Many land mines were used, but underwater mines were also deployed in virtually all the South's inland and coastal waterways. The Federals in turn were induced to devise defensive mechanisms, the world's first mine sweepers. Such a device was first used on April 30, 1862. Essentially a huge rake, this one was sixty-five feet long, to which were affixed large numbers of grappling hooks that were pushed ahead of a lead vessel.

Meanwhile, on the high seas, the South relied heavily on fast-moving commerce raiders. In its six-month career, the CSS *Sumter* made eighteen captures, and the famous CSS *Alabama,* which cruised for approximately twenty-one months over nearly seventy-five thousand miles, took sixty-four prizes worth more than $6.4 million.

And across the high seas, the American consul in Britain, Thomas H. Dudley, in July 1862 uncovered all the ruses that the Confederate agent, James

Bulloch, used to get warships for the South out of Britain. In that same month Bulloch signed a contract with the Laird shipyard in Liverpool for the construction of two ironclad steam-powered warships, to be armored and fitted with more firepower than any Federal naval ship then afloat. They also were equipped with formidable underwater rams. These vessels were capable of sinking nearly any wooden-hulled warship. Dudley kept a close watch on their construction, as well as on work on another screw steamer being built in Scotland, the *Alexandria*. He obtained and sent their exact dimensions to his superior, Charles Francis Adams, and to U.S. Secretary of State William Seward.

Throughout the rest of summer and fall 1862, the Confederacy's program of naval construction was pushed forward, and meanwhile both England and France continued pondering whether they should recognize the South and actively intervene in the Civil War. Cotton was running in short supply, and the textile mills were hurting. Prime Minister Palmerston on November 11 introduced a French proposal for recognition of the Confederacy to his cabinet. It proved, however, to be impossible to capture a majority of the cabinet on the issue, and it was put aside.

By summer 1862, Lincoln was beginning to consider a "hard war" policy. Before, he had hoped for a quick peace and an easy reconciliation, but now he was prepared to approve an escalation of violence. Mark Grimsley traces the evolution of Lincoln's policy from conciliation during the first fourteen months of the war, to pragmatism from July 1862 to early 1864, and to hard war for the last fifteen or so months.[37] One of the first signs of the new policy, in the East at least, was the assignment of Major General John Pope to command the Army of the Potomac (quite temporarily, as it turned out). "I have come to you from the West," Pope proclaimed to his newly formed force, the Federal Army of Virginia, "where we have always seen the backs of our enemies." Between July 18 and 25, 1862, he issued four general orders that spelled out the federal government's new approach: his army would "subsist upon the country," and Rebels would feel the pinch of deprivation. Further, Rebel civilians would be "held responsible" if Union supply or communication lines were hampered or if unconventional attacks were made on army personnel. Southern civilians within areas under Union control would be compelled to swear an oath of allegiance to the United States or else they would be forced to evacuate their homes and sent within Rebel lines.[38]

On July 13, Captain Charles Minor Blackford saw Jefferson Davis talking with Generals Lee and Jackson on the steps of the Confederate Gray House,

Lee "elegantly dressed in full uniform . . . by far the most magnificent man I ever saw"; Jackson "poorly dressed," shoulders "stooped," one "lower than the other," his cap "pulled down over one eye, much stained by weather and without insignia. . . . Davis looks like a statesman. His face is pale and thin but very intellectual and he had a graceful manner and easy bearing. He was dressed in a black suit and left a pleasing impression on anyone looking at him." Blackford was sure from the way the three shook hands in parting and the way Jackson "got on his old sorrel horse" and galloped away "in a deep brown and abstracted study" that he "had been ordered to move."[39] What they had decided to do was to gamble that McClellan would not attack Richmond from his James River base and thus to send most of the army against Pope.

The goal was to "avoid a general engagement" and to drive Pope northward, while Lee's army enjoyed the logistical benefit of being about to "consume provisions and forage now being used in supporting the enemy." Again Lee used the Jena and Auerstadt campaign as a model: he confronted Pope with James Longstreet's corps while wending Jackson's corps to turn the Union troops. Yet there was a fundamental difference between this use of the Jena and Auerstadt model and its use in the Seven Days, for Lee wished to avoid battle if he could and to drive Pope away by "maneuvering."

Jackson did turn Pope, reached his rear, and destroyed his supply depot. Then he withdrew to the west, giving Pope a clear route to withdraw from his strategic predicament by marching back to Washington. But Pope was more thoroughly duped than Lee had imagined and launched an assault against Jackson, unaware that Lee's and Longstreet's corps had come up. When at 3:30 P.M. on August 30 Pope launched his main assault, a Rebel artillery battalion under Colonel S. D. Lee hurled effective enfilade fire into the hapless Union ranks. Longstreet then unleashed a counterassault and thrust forward for more than a mile and a half, inflicting severe casualties.

Nightfall found Pope well situated near Centreville, and the pursuit ended. At 10:00 P.M. Lee sent Davis a telegram: "This Army achieved today on the plains of Manassas a signal victory over combined forces of Generals McClellan and Pope." Indeed, "through all of his marching and fighting, Lee [had] kept Davis fully informed, writing almost daily. [And] the president never doubted. With every confidence in this general, he worried only about Lee's personal safety."[40]

An elated Jefferson Davis wrote to R. E. Lee on August 30:

I have just recd your telegram of yesterday evening and rejoice at the good news it brings, though like all the lessons of life it is mingled with regret. I trust

the wounded Generals whom you mention may speedily recover and be preserved for other fields of usefulness [Richard S. Ewell, William B. Taliaferro,
and Isaac R. Trimble had been wounded. Taliaferro managed to return to action
by late 1862, but Ewell and Trimble were out until mid-1863.]. . . .

I conversed fully with Genl [William N.] Pendleton before he left here and
aske[d] him to proceed directly to your Head Qr[s] to confer with you and give
you suc[h] information as would enable you t[o] show me with the necessary
precision how I could best promote the success of your operations and generally
secure that cointelligence between us which is desirable to both. . . . .

May God preserve and direct you. Very Truly Your friend.[41]

Three days later Davis sent a message to Congress claiming "that God has
again extended his shield over our patriotic Army" and calling Second Manassas "a second signal victory on the field already memorable by the gallant
achievement of our troops." He praised Lee and "our toil-worn troops" for their
having achieved a victory over superior numbers.[42] And on September 4 he
issued a proclamation asserting that the enemy who had "laid waste our fields,
polluted our altars, and violated the sanctity of our homes" had been quashed
at Manassas; the Confederate forces had "been blessed by the Lord of Hosts
with a triumph" of "retributive justice." He also expressed his delight over a
"brilliant" victory in the West (Richmond, Kentucky, also on August 30) and
proclaimed September 18 as a day of national prayer and thanksgiving.[43]

On the very morning of the day of his tremendous victory at Second
Manassas, Lee had mentioned in a message to Davis the possibility that "we
shall be able to relieve other portions of the country." Then, according to
Joseph Harsh, with suddenness, "the possibility had now become likelihood.[44]

Abraham Lincoln had relieved Pope and restored McClellan to command,
entrusting Little Mac with the task of coping with General Robert E. Lee.
Thrusting his army into Maryland was Lee's main strategic intent; asking for
Davis's approval, he said this was "the propitious time" to "afford her an
opportunity of throwing off the oppression to which she is now subject," and
he hoped to gather supplies, particularly "clothing, shoes, and medical
stores."[45] This strategy was precisely in tune with Davis's desires. Just on the
eve of the anniversary of First Manassas, he had disparaged any doubt "as to
the advantage of invading over being invaded." As he wrote to a critic, "My
early declared purpose and continued hope was to feed upon the enemy and
teach them the blessings of peace by making them feel in its most tangible
form the evils of war." He insisted that "the time and place for invasion has
been a question not of will but of power."[46]

Davis even envisioned the possibility of going beyond Maryland, into
Pennsylvania and Ohio. He prepared a proclamation to be issued to the

Northerners declaring that the "sacred right of self-defence demands that if such a war is to continue its consequences shall fall on those who persist in their refusal to make peace." He also indicated a desire to influence state governments in the Union and implied a hope of swaying the 1862 elections. Davis enthusiastically thought that Marylanders would rise to support the Confederate army. He sent Lee the outline of this proclamation, which asked advancement of "the design of subjugating a people over whom no right of dominion has been ever conferred either by God or man" and asking them to make a separate peace. Davis left the name of the state blank in his proclamation, so that Generals Braxton Bragg and Edmund Kirby Smith could use it, too. They were invading Kentucky at the same time that Lee made his thrust into Maryland.[47]

Fording the Potomac River on September 4, Lee's ragged Rebel soldiers, many of them barefooted, marched with high hopes, their regimental bands playing "Maryland! My Maryland!"

> The despot's heel is on thy shore,
>   Maryland!
> His torch is at the temple door,
>   Maryland!
> Avenge the patriotic gore
> That flecked the streets of Baltimore,
> And be the battle-queen of yore,
>   Maryland, my Maryland!

According to Cooper, never during the ensuing campaign into Maryland, or thereafter, "did Davis express any reservation about the propriety of Lee's decision." And "not only did Davis approve, he attempted to join Lee." Davis left Richmond on the morning of September 7, but when he reached Warrenton, he realized that Lee and the army were already too far away, and he returned to Richmond, much to Lee's relief.[48]

In his aborted attempt to join Lee, Davis was accompanied by Enoch L. Lowe, a former governor of Maryland, now a pro-Confederate, voluntary exile in Richmond. Although Lowe had no formal position, both Davis and Lee hoped that he might be able to help the Confederate army by influencing civilian affairs in Maryland. Lowe continued from Warrenton after Davis elected to go back to Richmond and did meet with Lee in Maryland. Unfolding military events, however, nullified Lowe's mission.[49]

Lee did not find in the Marylanders' response to his presence what he had hoped for. Though he found "sympathy" in the state, he was soon forced to say, "I do not anticipate any general rising." And one did not come. But Lee told Davis, thus revealing his intentions, that if successful here, he would go on to Pennsylvania, "unless you should deem it unadvisable."[50]

This Confederate incursion into enemy territory, however, was intended to be a raid, not an invasion, for Lee expected to have to return to Virginia at least by winter. He wished to feed on the enemy's country while also protecting the harvest in Virginia. Further, if a battle were fought, though in truth Lee did not wish to precipitate any major engagement, a Rebel victory on Northern soil might well bring European diplomatic recognition of the Confederacy. It just might force the North to accept terms.

In Frederick, Maryland, Lee formulated his plans. (There, the elderly Barbara Frietchie denounced Stonewall Jackson's Rebels in a probably apocryphal confrontation later immortalized in a John Greenleaf Whittier poem: "Shoot, if you must, this old gray head, but spare your country's flag, she said.") Lee needed at least a rudimentary line of communications to bring him ammunition and other basic supplies. For this he intended to use a wagon route from Winchester, Virginia, through Harpers Ferry into Maryland; but a significantly large Federal garrison held Harpers Ferry. Jackson's corps would be diverted to take it, thus dividing the Confederate army and leaving it precariously vulnerable to defeat.

Moreover, a copy of Special Order no. 191, detailing the separate movements, fell into Union hands. For some never-explained reason, it was wrapped around three cigars and then lost. The precious bundle was spotted lying in a clump of grass by Private Barton W. Mitchell of the Twenty-seventh Indiana, part of McClellan's advanced skirmishers, while he lay resting. Barton showed the document to Sergeant John M. Bloss. "As I read," Bloss reported in one of the war's great understatements, "each line became more interesting." Within forty-five minutes of the initial find, the paper swept through the hands of the men in the chain of command up to McClellan, who "gave vent to demonstrations of joy." Orderlies and staff officers went "flying in all directions." But McClellan did not act with celerity, and precious time was wasted.

On September 15, most fortuitously for the Confederates, Harpers Ferry fell. Jackson's corps snatched quite a prize: seventy-three pieces of artillery, thirteen thousand small arms, 200 wagons, and 12,500 prisoners. This was the largest single surrender of U.S. troops during the entire war. Jackson achieved this success not a moment too soon; for, following their success at the South Mountain gaps, the Federals were diverting more units to oppose the attackers at Harpers Ferry. Jackson thus began hurrying as many of his troops as practicable up the road toward Lee and the main Rebel army at Sharpsburg.

As the daylong Battle of Antietam ensued, the Federals launched five successive but poorly coordinated assaults, serially from north to south, and then stalemate ended the struggle. Nightfall at last brought the end of the single bloodiest day of the Civil War, and, indeed, the single bloodiest day of the American military experience. The South lost 13,724 to McClellan's 12,469; but another 12,500 Federals had been taken at Harpers Ferry. Photographers reached the Antietam battlefield before the dead were buried, and the horrifying pictures, widely distributed, shocked the public. Both armies had hurt each other tremendously, but neither had gained the critical advantage, and no further fighting seemed to offer rational promise. The battle dictated that the campaign must end. Lee's army could no longer be supplied, and it was impossible for it to disperse and forage. There was nothing for the Southerners to do but to disengage and return to Virginia.

The aftermath brought an end to McClellan's military career. Lincoln could neither understand nor tolerate that no effective pursuit was made and that no further destruction of Lee's army was attempted. Early in November, seven weeks after the battle, McClellan was relieved of his command. When R. E. Lee was informed that the Young Napoleon had been removed, he remarked to James Longstreet, "I fear they may continue to make these changes till they find someone whom I don't understand." Although the president was extremely disappointed, he nevertheless regarded the outcome of the battle to be a sufficient example of victory to justify, without his action seeming to reflect any tinge of desperation, a preliminary proclamation of emancipation. The Union war aim was now refined and made more complex. Originally it had been simply the goal of restoring the Union by force; now it was gradually, though inexorably, to destroy by force the institution of human slavery in the United States.

Antietam thus became a singularly major turning point in the war; had it turned out otherwise, the battle might have become to the Confederate States of America what Saratoga was to the American states in 1778. But autumn 1862 marked the moment when two major Southern thrusts onto non-Confederate soil were blunted and turned back: the advance by Braxton Bragg into Kentucky had also been stymied. Furthermore, freedom, not just Union, became a Northern goal.

President Davis was not upset over the outcome of the Sharpsburg campaign and said little about it publicly. The operation had never been intended to be an invasion, wherein the Confederacy would try to seize and hold Union territory; Lee's army simply had been propelled home sooner than expected and hoped. It is likely that Davis was gratified over having been able to take some of the war to the enemy on his own ground.[51]

Supply problems had hampered the Manassas and Maryland campaigns equally. Principally this was caused by the inability of extant trackage to carry the necessary tonnage. The Virginia Central Railroad ran north from Richmond for 20 miles, then branched west to Gordonsville. There it joined the Alexandria line, north 60 miles to Manassas Junction. The total distance from Richmond is 123 miles. Virginia Central had sufficient cars and locomotives to maintain five trains specifically for R. E. Lee's army. Confederate trains averaged ten cars each, and each car had a maximum capacity of seven and one-half tons.[52] Allowing an average of five cars per train for carrying ammunition, grain for horses, and other necessary materials, five cars could be allotted to rations. By having two trains loading at the Richmond depot, two trains unloading at Manassas, and one train moving, a workable schedule of supply could be established. At an average speed of 25 miles per hour, the one-way trip of 123 miles could be accomplished in about five hours. By scheduling a minimum of two arrivals at Manassas daily, ten carloads of rations would be made available to Lee's army each day. At seven and one-half tons per car, this comes to seventy-two and one-half tons, exceeding the required fifty-five tons, six hundred eighty pounds the army actually needed. If the schedule had been maintained, a considerable surplus could have been accumulated. In one week of operation, the schedule could provide 131 percent of actual needs.

But the physical capacity of the railroad to supply Lee's army during this stretch of time was not the deciding factor. Elements such as passenger trains running on the same track, breakdowns, inefficient supply officers and railroad officials, graft, lack of timely loading and unloading, and shortage in availability of certain necessary items interacted. Unfortunately for the Confederacy, the fighting ability of its main army suffered from inefficient logistical support, not only when it first became starkly evident during the Manassas-Maryland campaigns but also through the rest of the conflict. Genuine efforts were begun late in 1862 and were accelerated by 1863 in order to get better control over the supply process. But it was almost 1864 before the proper focus was brought to bear and viable solutions were implemented.

Beginning in late 1862, Price Control Boards were established, aiming at the regulation of specific items of need. These boards periodically published price schedules. But the government-set prices generally were so low as to preclude any profit making by the producers; indeed, in many instances, the prices were below the costs of production.

The great shortages of food and forage, to a considerable extent, determined the tactics that various combat commanders felt able to employ. Collection parties ranged as far as seventy miles away from the main body of troops, but they could carry only light loads because of the poor condition of

wagons and horses. The impressment of goods from civilians proved controversial, and many protests were lodged in Richmond. The negative impact on
morale among the populace was tremendous.

The Maryland campaign occurred in simultaneous conjunction with an ambitious Confederate thrust into Kentucky. General Braxton Bragg had been told
by the Confederate War Department that he could adapt whatever strategy he
thought best. When he did decide to act, as Cooper points out, "like Lee,
Bragg did not ask for Davis's specific permission to implement his strategy,
but he too kept the president informed. Davis was delighted with the possibility that the Confederates could retake Tennessee and possibly move into
Kentucky."[53] Bragg successfully bypassed Don Carlos Buell's Federal Army
of the Ohio in Nashville and entered the Blue Grass state. From September
15 through 17, Bragg's army besieged Munfordville, Kentucky. The Federal
garrison, numbering slightly more than four thousand men, surrendered the
town on the same day as the Battle of Antietam.

An elated Jefferson Davis wrote to General Bragg on October 17: "I have
followed your progress with pride and anxiety. The brilliant achievements of
your army claim the thanks of the country and as the Chief Magistrate of the
Confederacy it gives me pleasure to acknowledge the value and heroism of
the services rendered in Kentucky."[54]

But the rest of the Kentucky campaign unraveled unfavorably for the Confederates. The Battle of Perryville, on October 8, Kentucky's major engagement of the war, obliged Bragg's withdrawal into East Tennessee. Combined
with Lee's recent return to Virginia from Maryland, this setback concluded a
major phase of the Confederacy's ill-fated grand strategy. Just as they had
hoped in vain to find recruits in Maryland, the Confederates initially harbored
expectations of finding willing numbers of them in Kentucky. "We found
indeed 32 men who were willing to be Colonels, 32 willing to serve as Lieut
Cols and Majors, any quantity ready to tack on their collars the bars of a Captain or Lieut, but few, very few willing to serve in the ranks," commented one
Confederate captain; *"Kentucky is subjugated."*

The actual situation in Kentucky was slow to be communicated to Davis.
On October 19 Gustavus A. Henry wrote him that although he believed it was
clear that Bragg was retreating from Kentucky, nonetheless Henry thought
the Battle of Perryville "was a brilliant affair." He commented that his friend
Benjamin F. Cheatham had shown particular gallantry, his division having
lost twenty-two hundred in killed and wounded while the enemy losses were

supposedly five thousand. He also expressed an opinion concurred in by Samuel Jones, that "the army is dissatisfied with Genl Bragg, not at his rigid discipline, but on account of his retreat."[55]

The hope in Kentucky that sympathetic young men would join the army if the army would come to them was not fulfilled.[56] Bragg proclaimed liberation to the Kentuckians and thought for a time that men were "flocking" to the cause.[57] He attempted to enforce the Confederate conscription law, which only threw "the whole country into a feverish state" and encouraged thousands of men to flee northward or to the mountains. Kirby Smith found few takers for the arms he had brought hoping to issue, and he concluded that "their hearts are evidently with us, but their blue-grass and fat grass are against us." Bragg thought that "the love of ease and fear of pecuniary loss are the fruitful sources of this evil."[58] Davis confessed at the end of October that "the results in Ky. have been to me a bitter disappointment."[59]

Although these two fall offensives had failed, their aftermaths were quite different. Lee had elicited a measure of love from the men in his command and the staunch allegiance of both officers and men. The Army of Tennessee was a different story. Braxton Bragg was in no way beloved by his men, and possibly worse, for "he did not have the trust of all his officers, particularly those most senior." Edmund Kirby Smith dispatched a private messenger to Richmond to convey his opinion of Bragg's ineptitude. Leonidas Polk, who "had done much to hurt and little to help his commanding general," tried to entice other generals to join him in calling for Bragg's removal. Polk had made various negative and even some untruthful statements about Bragg, even going "so far as to say Bragg had lost his mind." Davis liked these generals, especially Bragg and particularly Polk; what should he do? He ordered the three of them to travel to Richmond for individual conferences.[60]

Davis made "a calamitous decision. He continued Bragg in command of the Army of Tennessee; he left Polk in that army and promoted him to lieutenant general; he retained Smith as commander of his department, also promoted him to lieutenant general, and told him to cooperate with Bragg. In sum, he made no changes at all." Davis's response owed much to his personal biases and unwise loyalty to men who did not truly measure up to his estimate of them. "The president permitted his perception of commitment to influence his judgement about effectiveness." Just before the Kentucky campaign, he had denied Bragg's request to reorganize his officer corps; now at its conclusion, and with stark evidence that it needed to be done, Davis refused to do it himself. "For emotional and practical reasons Jefferson Davis stood fast. The cancer he did not even attempt to excise was left to grow more virulent."[61]

One final huge battle took place in the east in 1862, at Fredericksburg, Virginia. Major General Ambrose E. Burnside had replaced McClellan. From mid-October into November, Union troops gradually shifted southeastward. Lee had located in defensive array at Fredericksburg, Longstreet's corps in the strongest position, on the left, Jackson's strung out toward the right. The Federals crossed the Rappahannock River using pontoons on December 12. The dominating terrain feature in Longstreet's sector was an elongated steep elevation known as Marye's Heights. Near the base of the hill ran an old sunken road, and in front of that stretched an old stone wall, behind which the most advanced of the defenders could enjoy formidable cover.

Almost all day, hapless Union troops were hurled forward in futile assaults. Longstreet remarked that "the Federals had fallen like the steady dripping of rain from the eaves of a house." When General Joe Johnston, far away in the western theater, read of this episode, he remarked, "What luck some people have. . . . Nobody will come to attack me in such a place." And the battle occasioned Lee's classic remark to Longstreet: "It is well that war is so terrible—we should grow too fond of it." Of his impatient critics who later asserted that Lee should have counterattacked and that he missed a golden opportunity to do so here, Lee remarked privately to J. E. B. Stuart, "No one knows how brittle an army is." He really meant that no one adequately apprehended the strength of the defense. On exulting over the outcome of this battle, President Davis, in a rare attempt at public humor, announced that a few of the Yankees who had earlier clamored "on to Richmond" had finally gotten there: as prisoners.[62]

As 1862 waned, Davis enjoyed a tenuous but rather widespread degree of support. With the notable exceptions of Joe Brown and Zebulon Vance, the state governors supported the draft or kept their reservations to themselves. In early December William L. Yancey spoke to the Alabama General Assembly, strongly supporting the congressional authority to put every available man in the army. It was a rousing display of national harmony.

Davis was not without his critics, and harsh ones at that. Perhaps most notable was his former friend Louis T. Wigfall, now in the Senate (the Davises and the Wigfalls had had a bitter falling out). Besides his potent influence in the Senate, Wigfall also had important friends in the principal western and eastern armies. By late 1862 he had decided that Davis was a great fool, "trying to be both president and general in chief," a task that even Napoleon would have found daunting.[63]

The reality at year's end was that although it appeared to be strong, "much of the president's support was tenuously conditional, ebbing and flowing with each change in the economic and military situation."[64] Despite the appearance of solidity, the truth was that within Davis's official family things were not harmonious: there were rumors that he and Vice President Stephens had had a falling out, there was a cabinet crisis, and there was always grumbling about military appointments. These added up to serious internal divisions in the Confederate government.[65]

The rumor about rancor between Davis and Stephens was essentially true. Whether or not they exchanged bitter words is moot; they were estranged. The two men did not have a conference for more than a year after their meeting in November 1861. When Stephens returned to the capital in August 1862, after a long sojourn in Georgia, neither Davis nor any member of the cabinet felt they had any time to see him until after a number of days had passed. Stephens felt he had been snubbed, and he was right. The two never got along well after that, even though Stephens always denied harboring any personal antipathy toward Davis—it was simple disagreement. Apparently, a frosty relationship between Davis and Stephens was a mutual choice.[66]

The cabinet crisis had to do with War Secretary George W. Randolph. It is possible that Davis felt threatened by Randolph's social position in Virginia: he was Thomas Jefferson's grandson. In fall 1862, Randolph and Davis had differences over the recapture of New Orleans and provisioning the army by trading with the Union through that city, selling cotton for supplies. The trade would bring needed supplies and would also serve to make contacts in the city that would presumably assist in a future uprising. Davis approved at first, but when the required troops were needed elsewhere, the plan was put on hold. When events permitted, Randolph attempted to resume executing the plan, but Davis did not respond.[67] About the same time, the two men had differences over command authority. Randolph authorized General Theophilus Holmes, located in Arkansas, to move across the Mississippi River to assist General John C. Pemberton. Davis's objection was not to the idea of moving Holmes; indeed, he had approved Randolph's warning to Holmes that such a move might be necessary. When Randolph issued the order, however, Davis rebuked him for exceeding his authority and directed that the order be revoked.[68] Randolph took umbrage, there was an exchange of nasty notes, and on November 13 he resigned. Davis then made what proved to be an excellent choice for his replacement, James A. Seddon—another Virginian, which Davis specifically wanted.[69] But in his method of deciding, he exacerbated his relationship with Wigfall, who wanted either Joseph E. Johnston or Major General Gustavus W. Smith for the post. Davis pretended to be open to Wigfall's advice, but when they talked about it the president already had made up his mind. Wigfall learned of the done deal when newspapers announced the Seddon appointment prematurely, and he was furious. It was the last straw for him, and his bitter criticisms of Davis's policies were hurtful.[70]

With Seddon settled in at the War Department and Joseph E. Johnston going to Chattanooga, Davis decided that he needed to make a western trip. He prepared

> for a lengthy, but in his mind, essential journey. . . . Davis was no imperial traveler. An observer noted that "his dress was plain and unassuming and his baggage was limited to a single leather valise, with the initials 'J.D.' marked upon the side." This eyewitness described "a man rather above the middle stature; of slight but well proportioned figure," with handsome features. A sprinkling of gray in his hair along with gray whiskers and "graceful manners" added dignity. An "expression of good humor" dominated his countenance as he spoke in a "voice soft and persuasive, yet distinct and full toned."[71]

On December 9, with two aides and a servant accompanying him, Davis left Richmond by train and reached Chattanooga two days later. The next day, with a band playing the "Bonnie Blue Flag" and colors flying, the party departed early and reached Murfreesboro, Bragg's headquarters, early in the evening. On December 13, accompanied by Bragg and Johnston, Davis reviewed the troops and briefly addressed them. He expressed "his complete confidence in their devotion and ability." He also visited with many of the officers at his quarters. One recalled the occasion: "He was quite agreeable and gentlemanly in manner, and on the whole I was rather favorably impressed by him." Davis felt that he had found the army "in fine spirits and well supplied." He felt confident that this force could halt any Federal advance, but he deemed that it was not strong enough to retake Nashville.[72]

Davis's party, accompanied by General Johnston, left Murfreesboro early on the next day, bound for Chattanooga and subsequently for Mississippi. It was while in East Tennessee that the welcome news of Lee's great triumph at Fredericksburg reached him. The party then passed through Atlanta and Montgomery, where Davis spent a day, and continued to Jackson, where they arrived without fanfare on December 19. Next Davis boarded a train for Vicksburg to examine the defensive works there and to review the troops. Then he returned to Jackson and traveled to North Mississippi to confer with General Pemberton. There he conjointly celebrated the great Confederate success that had occurred at Holly Springs on December 20, which destroyed U.S. Grant's supply base and thus stymied an intended Union overland thrust toward Vicksburg.

Again Davis reviewed the troops and then returned to Jackson for Christmas dinner with a niece.[73]

On the day after Christmas, Davis addressed the Mississippi state legislature in a ninety minute speech in which he admitted for the first time that recognition of the Confederacy by foreign powers was unlikely: " 'Put not your trust in princes,' and rest not your hopes on foreign nations. This war is ours; we must fight it out ourselves, and I feel some pride in knowing that so far we have done it without the good will of anybody."[74] The speech was also self-revelatory. Defending his administration, he made it clear that he had not been ignoring the barbs hurled at it by critics; indeed, the president had heard every word they said and would not forget.[75]

But fight on the fledgling nation must. Yankees and Southerners could never again live in any kind of harmony because the enemy had revealed himself to be the progeny of Oliver Cromwell and his Roundheads, bred in "the bogs and fens of the North of Ireland and of England" and inclined to vile and evil ways.[76] Confederates, on the other hand, descendants of the bold and chivalrous cavaliers, were a different sort. It was all myth, of course, and one that Davis had never previously suggested that he believed.

Davis then declared that from the beginning his policy had been that the Confederacy should try to fight its battles on the enemy's soil. The power possessed by the foe had alone prevented that. But, he asserted, considering the overwhelming odds and the resources arrayed against them, "The wonder is not that we have done little, but that we have done so much." Trying to allay the growing suspicion that the conflict was a rich man's war and a poor man's fight, Davis acknowledged that "the poor do, indeed, fight the battles of the country. It is the poor who save nations and make revolutions." But the rich were fighting, too, he maintained, and he tried to show how important the recent "twenty-Negro Act" had been, in case of an insurrection, "to keep our negroes in control."[77]

It was a remarkable speech. Davis tried to put the best face on the Confederate experience thus far, saying, "we have always whipped them in spite of disparity of numbers." It was not true, of course. Further, trying to give heart to the thousands who he knew would read his speech in the newspapers, Davis declared that "in all respects, moral as well as physical, we are better prepared than we were a year ago."[78] Clearly, he was trying hard to be the ardent leader who might stir the people's passions.[79] The active-negative president was attempting to reach out to Southerners as he had never done before—as he had never really had to do before—and his words indicated that he welcomed the chance at vindication. Was he beginning to develop a sense of what the twentieth-century politicos call PR, public relations? It almost does seem so.

Whether the effort would be effective, and whether he would follow up this public initiative remained to be seen.

After the speech, Davis and Johnston returned to Vicksburg, where they stayed for two days. On December 28 Davis left for Jackson and departed for Mobile the next day. That same day, General Pemberton's command, directed on the field by Brigadier General Stephen D. Lee, repulsed a river-based assault on Vicksburg led by General William T. Sherman. The year thus ended on a happy note for the Confederacy. After inspecting Forts Gaines and Morgan, which guarded the entrance to Mobile Bay, on the last day of 1862, Davis began the final leg of his trip. He spoke briefly in Atlanta on the evening of New Year's Day. On January 3, 1863, his train passed through Augusta and Charlotte and then on to Raleigh, where he gave an optimistic twenty-minute speech.

Declaring that his every act was aimed at victory, he proclaimed that "the cause, . . . is above all personal or political considerations, and the man who at a time like this, cannot sink such considerations, is unworthy of power." In Petersburg, Virginia, on January 4, Davis assured some one thousand to fifteen hundred well-wishers who greeted his train that "as certain as the earth now revolves upon its axis, so surely will peace and independence be established." Later that day, he returned to Richmond and home. He had been traveling for twenty-seven days, traversed approximately three thousand miles, made numerous public appearances and speeches, and always engaged in what he called "promoting the noble cause."[80]

The Great Seal of the Confederacy. The image of the equestrian statue of George Washington from the front of the Virginia capitol on the Great Seal of the Permanent Confederate Government indicates the continuity the Confederate leadership felt from the old government to the new. It was engraved in England and brought in through the blockade in late 1864 but was never used by the Confederate government. (Courtesy The Museum of the Confederacy, Richmond, Virginia. Photography by Katherine Wetzel.)

"Submarine Boat *H. L. Hunley,*" by Conrad Wise Chapman. The *Hunley* was the first submarine to engage in a successful combat operation, although it was lost in its first engagement after sinking the USS *Housatonic* in the harbor at Charleston. (Courtesy Valentine Museum/Richmond History Center, Richmond, Virginia.)

A Confederate bond. This one-thousand-dollar Confederate bond was issued in March 1863 under provisions of the loan of February 20, 1863. The last coupon would have been paid and the bond would have matured on July 1, 1868. Some of the coupons were redeemed before the fall of the Confederacy, although, as the note indicates, at least in this instance one coupon was used as currency. (Negative X3 53042, File SC 2134, Courtesy State Historical Society of Wisconsin.)

Confederate Treasury Note. Treasury notes, such as this one hundred dollar note, promised payment to the bearer after a treaty of peace with the United States. This note was issued under the Funding Act of February 17, 1864. (Courtesy The Museum of the Confederacy, Richmond, Virginia. Copy photography by Katherine Wetzel.)

Private fractional currency. For lack of coins with which to make change, many private companies found it necessary to issue their own fractional currency. Despite the official look of the design, this fifty-cent note is actually nothing more than a private IOU. (From the U.S. Civil War Center exhibit, "Beyond Face Value," courtesy Jules d'Hemecourt, Louisiana State University Library Special Collections.)

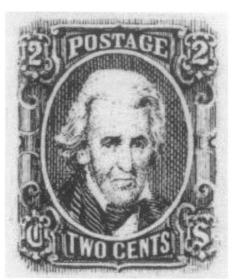

Confederate postage stamps. The poor pictorial quality of Confederate postage stamps reflected the lack of modern printing facilities in the Confederacy, as a result of which some stamps were printed in England. They also reflect the pantheon of Confederate heroes, as this five-cent portrait of Jefferson Davis, the ten-cent Thomas Jefferson, the two-cent Andrew Jackson, and the twenty-cent George Washington illustrate. (Illustration courtesy John L. Kimbrough, M.D.)

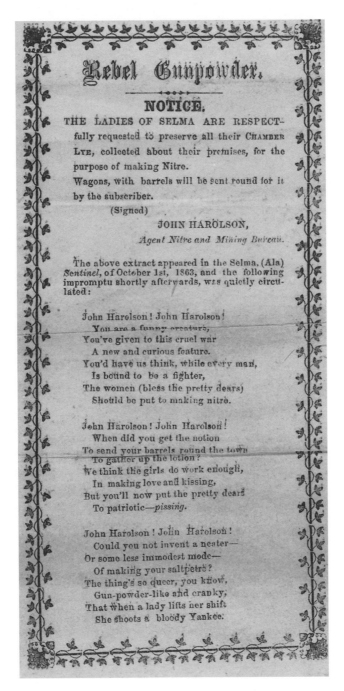

Rebel Gunpowder.

NOTICE.

THE LADIES OF SELMA ARE RESPECT-fully requested to preserve all their CHAMBER LYE, collected about their premises, for the purpose of making Nitre.

Wagons, with barrels will be sent round for it by the subscriber.

(Signed)

JOHN HAROLSON,

Agent Nitre and Mining Bureau.

The above extract appeared in the Selma, (Ala) *Sentinel,* of October 1st, 1863, and the following impromptu shortly afterwards, was quietly circulated:

John Harolson! John Harolson!
  You are a funny creature;
You've given to this cruel war
  A new and curious feature.
You'd have us think, while every man,
  Is bound to be a fighter,
The women (bless the pretty dears)
  Should be put to making nitre.

John Harolson! John Harolson!
  When did you get the notion
To send your barrels round the town
  To gather up the lotion?
We think the girls do work enough,
  In making love and kissing,
But you'll now put the pretty dears
  To patriotic—*pissing.*

John Harolson! John Harolson!
  Could you not invent a neater—
Or some less immodest mode—
  Of making your saltpetre?
The thing's so queer, you know,
  Gun-powder-like and cranky,
That when a lady lifts her shift
  She shoots a bloody Yankee.

"REBEL GUNPOWDER"—Notice to the ladies of Selma. This doggerel verse of questionable taste illustrates the lengths to which Confederates were forced to go in order to manufacture sufficient munitions (Broadsides, Wars, Civil War [ready prints]. 1863, ink on paper, ICH: 22104, AHD, 384, courtesy Chicago Historical Society.)

10

THE THREAT OF EMANCIPATION

There was no New Year's Day reception at the Confederate Gray House in 1863 since Jefferson Davis was not yet back from his western tour. He did make a public appearance on the night of January 5, before several hundred serenaders outside the executive mansion. Standing on the portico, Davis's aide introduced him as "the President of the United States" but quickly corrected himself.

Addressing the crowd, whom he called "Friends and Fellow Citizens," Davis made the most of the slip: "Of the title as corrected, I am proud—the other I would scorn to hold." He was enthusiastically applauded. As he had from the beginning, he identified the Confederacy as "the last hope, as I believe, for the perpetuation of that system of government which our forefathers founded—the asylum of the oppressed and the home of true representative liberty." He said that the "ancestors" of this audience had declared "the great principles of human government," which the Confederates embraced as their own. He assured his countrymen, "You have shown yourselves in no respect to be degenerate sons of your fathers. You have fought mighty battles, and your deeds of valor will live among the richest spoils of Time's ample page."[1]

Davis expressed pleasure that the enemy had been halted in Virginia, Tennessee, and Mississippi. Indeed, as William Cooper observes, he suggested, "The Confederacy was growing proportionately stronger than the Union. 'Now deep resolve is seen in every eye, an unconquerable spirit nerves every arm.'" He proclaimed that determination existed both on the home front and in the ranks. "With such noble women at home, and such heroic soldiers in the field, we are invincible." And then he closed with an appeal to the Almighty: "May God prosper our cause and may we live to give to our children untarnished the rich inheritance which our Fathers gave to us."[2]

On January 1, 1863, as he had promised one hundred days previously, Abraham Lincoln signed and issued the Emancipation Proclamation. The ending of slavery was added as a fundamental Union war aim. The Proclamation was as much a military measure, perhaps even more, than it was a humanitarian gesture. In the words of James McPherson, "Lincoln had embraced emancipation both as a way to weaken the Confederacy by depriving it of slave labor and as a sweeping expansion of Union war aims. No longer would the North fight merely for restoration of the Old Union—a union where slavery flouted American ideals of liberty. Now the North would fight to give that Union 'a new birth of liberty,' as Lincoln put it almost a year later at Gettysburg."[3] As McPherson has further stated, "Organization of black regiments marked the transformation of a war to preserve the Union into a revolution to overthrow the old order."[4]

Making the war a fight to end slavery also seriously diminished any chance of European intervention. Britain's leaders, especially, had strong expectations that the South might ultimately prevail, and indeed for the sake of a weaker United States, they hoped so; but the populace was sufficiently antislavery that Britain simply could not intervene with that issue so plainly on the table. Other powers however, did take some advantage of the ongoing American Civil War: Spain reannexed Santo Domingo, and France intervened in Mexico, establishing a "protectorate." But as long as England stayed out of the Civil War, they followed its lead.

"For Davis," Cooper observes, "the Emancipation Proclamation represented the culmination of the savage war waged upon his country." In his eyes, this Proclamation was nothing more than "the barbarism of the enemy," which he "excoriated." Now, because of this pseudomilitary necessity, the Yankees revealed themselves to be "worse than hyenas."[5] Davis saw Lincoln's Proclamation as confirmation of what he and others had long believed: the ulterior purpose of the Republican Party from the beginning had been forced abolition. Quite simply, Davis felt, the war itself was proof of the lengths to which those people would go in order to free the slaves. The result, he proclaimed in a heated message to Congress, was a measure by which "contented laborers . . . of an inferior race," were to be "doomed to extermination, while at the same time they are encouraged to a general assassination of their masters by the insidious recommendation 'to abstain from violence unless in necessary self-defense.'" Lincoln had struck at the vitals of the Southern social system, and reaction was accordingly extreme, if not irrational. Thus, from the world's history of evils, Davis chose Lincoln's Proclamation as "the most execrable measure recorded in the history of guilty man."[6]

Davis cited a great many admissions by Lincoln "that he was utterly without constitutional power" to issue this Proclamation. His whole Republican Party had concealed their purpose by the "perfidious use" of just such "solemn and repeated pledges," Davis said. This was "the complete and crowning proof" of the uses to which the Republicans "intended from the beginning to apply their power." The "despotism" from which the South had escaped was "now apparent to the most skeptical." But happily, "This proclamation is also an authentic statement by the Government of the United States of its inability to subjugate the South by force of arms," showing other nations "our just claims to formal recognition." One effect was sure: "A restoration of the Union has been rendered forever impossible."[7]

It was Davis's intention to ask that all Union officers who fell captive should be turned over to civil authorities and charged and tried under extant laws concerning incitement of servile insurrection. Enlisted men, on the other hand, should be treated simply as prisoners of war because they were only following their orders. A number of congressmen were in fundamental agreement with Davis, especially as to the question of emancipation, which immediately became involved with the issue of Federal use of black troops. Because two Union generals, David Hunter and John W. Phelps, had raised a few black soldiers in spring 1862, in August of that year the Confederate War Department had issued general orders declaring that these officers were outlaws, rather than enemies, that all white officers with regiments of former slaves were also outlaws, and that if captured these individuals were "not to be regarded as a prisoner of war, but held in close confinement for execution as a felon."[8]

Some congressmen began to call for war without quarter, "under the black flag." Gustavus Adolphus Henry, the senator from Tennessee, asserted that Confederates should "neither ask nor receive quarter from this day henceforward." By declaring a war of extermination, Henry claimed, "we would not be troubled with invasion hereafter."[9] Mississippi senator James Phelan strongly agreed: "I am now and ever have been in favor of fighting this contest under the black flag."[10] In keeping with this sentiment, a resolution proposed by Congressman James Lyons of Virginia urged Confederate citizens to "kill and destroy" all Union military personnel unless they be "a regular prisoner of war," and that after January 1, 1863, "no officer of the Lincolnite Army or Navy ought to be captured alive, and if so captured, he ought to be immediately hung."[11] Congressman Ethelbert Barksdale of Mississippi offered a less drastic resolution but nonetheless supported Davis's proposed policy.[12]

In the next session the debate heated up again. Congressman Lyons once more declared that all captured Federal officers should be hanged without trials because he feared "the uncertainties of trial by jury."[13] After considerable debate, the Congress passed a "joint resolution on the subject of retaliation" in May 1863, which pronounced that Union officers leading black troops "shall be deemed as inciting servile insurrection, and shall, if captured, be put to death, or otherwise punished at the discretion of the court." However, the president could commute their punishment, and captured black soldiers would be turned over to the "State or States in which they shall be captured, to be dealt with according to the present or future laws of such State or States."[14]

The U.S. government could not stand idly by while such threats were made, and in General Order no. 100, April 24, 1863, which was drawn up by Francis Lieber, an expert on international law, the Union declared its policy that all men in Federal uniform, including former slaves, were entitled to all the rights of a prisoner of war and threatened due retaliation for any deviation from that practice. Since the United States had no legal power to enslave, its only retaliatory option would be a sentence of death.[15] But it was always difficult to tell if an unfortunate soldier, of any race or rank on either side, had been killed after capture, or killed while attempting escape, or simply not allowed to surrender. The treatment of black soldiers as prisoners was a problem, to be sure, and it was among the issues that led to the breakdown of the cartel for prisoner exchanges in 1863. The black flag, fortunately, was not officially raised by either side. It is true, however, that racially motivated atrocities were perpetrated at Milliken's Bend, Louisiana, and at Fort Pillow, Tennessee, by Confederates, and at Poison Springs and Marks' Mills, Arkansas, by Union soldiers.[16]

Eighteen sixty-three began badly for Davis. At first it was believed that Braxton Bragg had won a great victory at Murfreesboro, but then came the news of egregious failure on the second day of fighting. By February the temperature in Richmond was ten below zero, and the James River froze over. The anniversary of Davis's inauguration, Washington's birthday, was "the ugliest day I ever saw," war clerk J. B. Jones wrote in his diary. "With a northwest wind howling furiously," snow fell night and day until it was "nearly a foot deep, and the weather very cold." None of this boded well for Davis's chronic neuralgia and respiratory troubles. Indeed, he told Clement Clay on March 10 that "ill health has prevented" an earlier reply to a letter.

These circumstances may have been the catalyst for a proclamation Davis issued on February 27 naming March 27 a day of fasting and prayer, proper to "a people who acknowledge the supremacy of the living God." It urged Confederates "to prostrate yourselves in humble supplication to Him," with "devout thankfulness for signal victories," and with "prayer to Almighty God that he will . . . scatter our enemies [and] set at naught their evil designs." When the day came, Colonel Josiah Gorgas exempted his armorers, saying *"laborare est orare"* (to work is to pray), but Davis went to St. Paul's Episcopal Church for the special service.[17]

Critics continued to evaluate his presidency. "Mr. Davis seems to have learned but one rule of government," the novelist Augusta Jane Evans complained to Beauregard on March 17, 1863, "that laid down by Machiavelli in the celebrated sophistical dictum, 'the dissensions of great men contribute to the welfare of the state.'" Davis of course had profited from the "dissensions of great men," because his opposition was fragmented and unorganized.[18]

Still, the president remained a potent symbol of Confederate nationalism, at least as it was defined by the elite citizenry. George Rable observes that despite Robert E. Lee's having eclipsed Davis in popularity by early 1863, both among the soldiery and the populace, still "it was the president who had helped create the political culture of national unity whose basic features had now appeared." That is, the Confederacy's core beliefs and values had emerged "in speeches, textbooks, sermons, and family conversations, in public ceremonies, school-rooms, churches, homes, and army camps."[19]

The general mood was growing more optimistic in early 1863, making the occasional bitter attacks on Davis seem especially self-serving and petty. One of the most scathing was generated by the wealthy Mississippi Whig, James Lusk Alcorn, who was still filled with bitterness because he had been passed over for several military appointments he had coveted. In the privacy of letters to his wife, Alcorn denounced Davis as a "miserable, stupid, one-eyed dyspeptic, arrogant tyrant who now occupies his cushioned seat at Richmond, draws his twenty-five thousand a year, and boasts of the future grandeur of the country which he has ruined, the soil which he has made wet with the tears of widows and orphans and the land which he has bathed in the blood of a people once free, but now enslaved. Oh, let me see him damned and sunk into the lowest hell."[20] Alcorn was not alone; his ideas were shared by many former Unionists, half-hearted secessionists, and Whigs who had not been particularly enthusiastic about leaving the Union in the first place. Many became strong Confederates, of course, but others supported the cause while at the same time wishing that it had never come to exist. Such men were among the first to weaken and among the first to blame Davis when events did not go well. There was always a reservoir of disgruntled, rejected men like Alcorn, and they proved to be one of the Confederacy's weakest links.

On April 2, 1863, a bread riot broke out in Richmond, and Davis's "resonant voice" played an unusual role in helping to quell it. Standing on a horseless dray, he addressed a mob of women and boys: "You say you are hungry and have no money. Here is all I have; it is not much, but take it." He turned out his pockets and then said, "We do not desire to injure anyone, but this lawlessness must stop." The mob had begun its work by grabbing food, but soon it was looting jewelry and clothing stores. The mayor had "read the Riot Act, and as this had no effect he threatened to fire on the crowd," just as Davis had appeared. At first the boys hissed at him, "but after he had spoken some little time with great kindness and sympathy, the women quietly moved on, taking their food with them." They continued to mill around, were given food that day and the next, and finally were disbursed by the City Battalion.[21]

Varina, who was away at the time, returned to find that her husband had no voice left. J. B. Jones reported on April 22 that Davis was "dangerously ill—with inflammation of the throat." This "recent attack" had "commenced with diurnal fever and was followed by bronchitis," Davis told his brother Joseph on May 7. It was rumored that Davis was in danger of losing the sight of his other eye: "Total blindness would incapacitate him for the executive office. A fearful thing to contemplate!" Jones wrote. But the war clerk was quite relieved when on May 6 Davis sent over, from his Gray House office, fifty-five letters that he had read, with several endorsed "in his own hand . . . so he has not lost his sight." Davis told Joseph that he had not missed any "official duties," except that since he could not talk, "personal interviews" had been impossible. Now, happily, he reported that "the cough only remains," and "the present debility is no doubt much due to confinement and anxiety." He required several more weeks, however, to recover, and the chronic anxiety remained.[22]

There was much to aggravate Davis's anxiety. In the midst of his illness, on May 3, Federal general George F. Stoneman's cavalry swept within three miles of Richmond. Mary Chesnut, who had spent the night with the Davises, the next morning observed that Davis looked "feeble and pale." She watched while her husband and Custis Lee loaded Davis's pistols for him and they rode off, Davis in his physician's open carriage. The president "exhibited the finest spirits," said J. B. Jones, and enjoyed the "zeal of the old men and boys" marching out with muskets. No fight occurred for the home guard, though Stoneman had a skirmish with regulars at the South Anna Bridge. A month later the Richmond citizens were formed into a brigade, under Custis Lee; his father needed every one of the regular soldiers.[23]

Money was needed as well as soliders. The government sought to wage war on a "fight now, pay later," plan and ultimately refused to enact any realistic program of taxation. At first, loans were a major source of government income, followed by unbacked paper money, the Treasury notes. The first major loan was that of May 16, 1861, the Produce Loan,[24] by which produce could be solicited as well as money, its proceeds being pledged to the loan. This $50 million loan was hardly sufficient, and on August 19 Congress passed an act raising the amount to $100 million.[25] This loan would presumably soak up excess Treasury notes in circulation, to ensure that the money supply did not become too large and thus be inflated, but these and other attempts to stabilize the currency failed.[26] These loans were expanded in December 1861[27] and further extended to $250 million by legislation passed at the end of the first session of the First Congress, April 19, 1862. That legislation also provided that agricultural products could be accepted as "in-kind" payment.[28] In addition, bonds were authorized, many of which also circulated as a medium of exchange. By the end of 1862, over $.5 billion dollars in unbacked Treasury paper was in circulation,[29] opening the doors to runaway inflation that proved devastating.

Even congressmen complained, for their increasingly inadequate salaries soon forced many of them to cut personal costs by sharing accommodations. Soldiers and their families grumbled about military pay being too low, and in 1863 the bread riots in Richmond and several other cities were the direct result. Gold was hoarded. In May 1861 a gold dollar was worth $1.10 in Treasury notes, but by fall the price had risen to $1.15, and during 1862 the gold dollar steadily rose in value from $1.25 to $3.00.[30]

A fundamental problem lay in the reality that as the government continued to print more and more money and bonds, taxes receded to where they did not even meet the interest on the public debt. Money became cheaper and cheaper and prices always inched up. By early 1863 a widespread public outcry for more tax legislation erupted, surely an unusual spectacle: people begging to be taxed. But as one Richmondite put it: "We shall soon have to pay $27,000 for a barrel of flour. It is now $30 and beef 85 cts a pound." One Georgia editor wrote that "the error in the beginning was in not taxing heavily and severely enough to have kept prices down to a specie standard." Another editor, this one in Virginia, suggested that the people might be willing to support the war by taxes alone; Georgia senator Herschel V. Johnson warned that without more taxation, "universal ruin would be the consequence"; Robert Toombs asserted that the government simply had to cease printing more money; and a disgusted Vice President Alexander Stephens expressed a belief that $120 million in taxes could be raised annually. Even Christopher Memminger declared that he believed the people were "fully prepared for the payment of a high tax" and that he favored one on general property and income.[31]

Davis responded by calling on the Congress to levy more taxes, but there were several problems, one of the most important being a flaw in the Constitution. That document made it impossible to levy any direct tax unless it was apportioned according to population, which meant that a census first had to be taken. (The War Tax, itself a direct tax, had been constitutional because it was passed under the provisional constitution, which, unlike the permanent

Constitution, had no limitation on levying a direct tax.) According to the Constitution, a census was to take place not later than within three years, but war prevented it. A direct tax would have been essential to raise significantly large sums of money because two-thirds of the wealth of the Confederacy was in land and slaves. Memminger rightly conceived that the government could levy the required taxes only in the unoccupied districts.

There had been grumbling in Congress, indeed enough that consensus was slowly being created. One tax bill that might have met Confederate needs, at least for a time, was proposed on March 11, 1862, by Congressman Muscoe R. H. Garnett of Virginia. He offered a resolution requesting the House Committee on Ways and Means to study a proposal to raise "a revenue by excise and export duties," but it languished in committee.[32] On March 19 Congressman Franklin B. Sexton of Texas attempted to influence tax legislation by introducing a tentative resolution urging that any revenue bill that might be passed should avoid the taxation of credits (i.e., promissory notes or other interest-bearing evidences of debt), but that if such taxes were necessary, they be levied on such instruments only to the extent that they were in excess of the potential taxpayer's liabilities. Instead, Congress made the problem worse by authorizing another issue of Treasury notes.[33]

Paying close attention to all of this, Davis was somewhat more alert to fiscal problems during 1862 than he had been previously, but he said nothing about new taxation in his message of August 18 to open the second session of the First Congress. Then Congressman John B. Chambliss of Virginia, owner of forty-eight slaves in 1860, urged a tax on the "peculiar property" that was so plentiful in the Confederacy: a tax on slaves. Not altogether unself-serving, he also urged that owners should be compensated for slaves lost in the course of the war.[34] Most notable, however, was the apathy of both houses of Congress on the tax issue. A few solitary souls here and there urged that new taxes were essential, but most discussion concerned only details of the 1861 War Tax and how it was turning out to be less effective than originally expected.

By September, however, pressure for fresh tax legislation was once again manifest. A tax bill came out of committee on September 11 and was printed and circulated. Nothing, though, was done. It surfaced again on September 22 but never was incorporated into resolution, and it sat on the calendar until October 2, when it officially was postponed.[35] On September 23, one of the main proponents of new tax legislation, Duncan F. Kenner, a Congressman from Louisiana, acknowledged that it was difficult to advocate heavy taxes but also remarked "that we had not come here to lighten the burdens of the people, but to devise measures for the support of Government." Except for the War Tax, he noted, "we had placed our financial system alone upon the credit of the Government, based upon the future resources of the country." He pointed out that there was an inevitable limit to credit on such a basis.[36] "The true basis of credit, public or private," he noted, "was revenue or property," and printing Treasury notes was not a creation of revenue. Therefore, he concluded, it was obviously necessary to resort to taxing property.[37]

On October 3, Congressman Francis S. Lyon of Alabama sided with Kenner and called upon the Congress "to save our Government." Denying that one could simply "prevent the paper currency from depreciating," he likened such a notion to "the law of perpetual motion." William W. Boyce of South Carolina expressed a willingness to go even further and urged "a system of comprehensive taxation." Desultory discussion then followed in the Committee of the Whole over the next several days but was hampered by an ominous inability to raise a quorum. Then on October 6 the bill was tabled. A motion was then passed asking the Ways and Means Committee to report a bill simply raising sufficient revenue to meet interest payments that would be due on the debt up to January 1, 1863.[38]

A tax bill was reported out on October 9, and at the same time another bill was proposed to cut interest rates to 6 percent, an action that indicated the utter naivete of the congressmen toward the value of money. Meanwhile, President Davis asked Congress for legislation providing for payment of loans by raising sufficient taxes to cover their payment.[39] But again Congress drifted. A House resolution was offered that called for the raising of "revenue by taxation" and urged that the body stay in session as long as it took to do it, but it was voted down. On October 10 the House postponed the tax bill, and it simply died on the floor. No comprehensive tax legislation was passed in the second session of the First Congress, a body which came to its apathetic end on October 13, 1862.

Davis's leadership on the tax issue thus was utterly lacking in 1862, despite his obvious awareness of the problem: it even grew weaker as the year progressed. Perhaps he was too pressured by concern over the failed Antietam and Perryville campaigns. He was warned on October 6 by Secretary of the Treasury Memminger that $460 million in Treasury notes would be in circulation by May 1, 1863, and that this would lead to serious depreciation of the currency "and finally disaster, unless sufficient remedies are provided." Memminger wanted loans from Confederate citizens in proportion to their income (which would necessarily have to be forced loans) and also a yearly levy of the War Tax as well as a reduction of interest on Confederate bonds. At the least this was a war tax program of substance, more in keeping with the realities of the seriousness of the Confederate financial position than other measures proposed by individuals either within or without the higher levels of government.[40] If Davis paid much attention to his treasury secretary's proposals, he did not act on them at all.

The press and the general public condemned Congress for its inaction. Pressure was building to a point that Davis hardly could continue to ignore it. On January 10, 1863, he received a report from Memminger that almost $.5 billion in Treasury notes were outstanding and a recommendation that Davis should at once order this amount to be reduced to $150 million by the issuance of bonds, taxes being used to pay the interest and the principal on them.[41]

Thus, Davis at last moved to deal with the critical issue of finances. When the third session of the First Congress convened on January 12, he called attention to the "increasing public debt, the great augmentation in the volume of the currency, with its necessary concomitant of extravagant prices for all articles of consumption, the want of revenue from a taxation adequate to support the public credit," and he urged legislative action. If only some action to curb the redundancy of the currency was taken, Davis said, he believed "there is little doubt we shall see our finances restored to a sound and satisfactory condition."[42]

Memminger then recommended avoidance of cumbersome stamp duties, license taxes, and the like, suggesting instead a reliance on a 1 percent property tax and a 10 percent tax on earned income (both of which he thought could be collected more easily). Three weeks later, the House began serious consideration of a bill to provide these, and within a month it did pass a measure very much like the one Memminger wanted. In the Senate, however, strong feeling was expressed that a property tax was unconstitutional. The Senate changed the House bill drastically, and a conference committee subsequently struggled for weeks to come up with compromise proposals that might satisfy both houses.[43]

On April 24, the first comprehensive tax law was passed. Trying to levy an effective tax within constitutional bounds, Congress had come up with an ingenious approach: avoid taxing land and slaves and instead squeeze revenue from every other conceivable source. A one-time ad valorem 8 percent tax was levied on all farm and forest products and a 1 percent tax on all money held as of July 1, 1863. There was also an exhaustive series of occupational and license taxes, such as five hundred dollars for bankers and forty dollars for bowling alleys. On sales of commodities, an additional tax was levied, for example 10 percent of gross sales by retail liquor dealers and 1 percent of gross for butchers and bakers. Hotels were classified by value into five categories and required to pay from thirty to five hundred dollars. And an income tax was instituted, varying with the amount and source of the income. Salaries would henceforth be taxed at the rate of 1 percent between one thousand and fifteen hundred dollars and 2 percent on all above fifteen hundred dollars, except that men in the army and navy would be exempt. Other kinds of income, up to five hundred dollars, would be exempt, but everything over that would be taxed from 5 percent to 15 percent, the higher rate to apply to incomes of ten thousand dollars or more. A flat 10 percent tax was levied on profits derived from the sale of farm products, clothing, or other objects commonly dealt in by speculators, unless earned in the course of regular retailing. This was intended to inhibit speculation.[44] Earnings and profits from lands, however, were exempt, Congress devising instead a special agricultural tax, one-tenth of farm produce, collected in kind—hence the tax in kind. Subject "articles were carefully enumerated: wheat, corn, oats, rye, 'buckwheat or rice,' sweet and Irish potatoes, hay and fodder, sugar, molasses, cotton, wool, tobacco, peas, beans, and ground peas." To ensure that any given farmer might still feed his family, he might exempt "50 bushels each of sweet potatoes, Irish potatoes, and wheat, 100 bushels of corn and 20 bushels of either peas or beans. Also, each farmer must give 3/50 of all pork, in the form of cured bacon. On all cattle, horses, and mules not used in cultivation and on all asses, he must pay a tax of one percent." The farmer would deliver all products in sacks or other containers furnished by the government to depots, if not more than eight miles away.[45] (The tax was variously amended later.)

To administer the tax in kind, the secretary of war and the secretary of the treasury would function cojointly. E. Merton Coulter suggests that had it been adopted earlier, it might indeed have had an adequate impact in averting the redundancy of Confederate currency. But the tax was exceedingly difficult to administer: preventing widespread cheating was a challenge, and the tax was unpopular, particularly among small farmers who never before had been obliged to pay any tax of any kind. Isolated districts often were ignored by collectors while easily accessible regions were forced to make most of the contributions. Unfortunately, also, there was much waste due to inefficiency: a great deal of produce rotted at depots and much else was stolen.[46]

The comprehensive tax bill of April 24, 1863, a practical failure in the long run, did produce some notable success during its first year or so. The Confederacy raised $82 million in internal revenue during its first year, levying taxes in 338 districts in ten states, and raised another estimated $40 million from the tax in kind. This compares quite favorably, as economic historian Richard Franklin Bensel notes, with the $39 million raised by similar Union legislation a year earlier. Furthermore, these Confederate receipts were even more impressive in comparison with those of the Union when one considers that they were raised from a "much smaller stream of commerce . . . and, everything considered, probably constituted a significantly greater burden on the population."[47]

Nevertheless, the Confederacy had delayed this crucial legislation by at least a year after its need had become clearly manifest. This "seriously undermined the value of Confederate currency and made many civilian monetary transactions with the government unwelcome."[48] The reason for the delay, other than that it obviously was a painful step to have to take, is unclear. One could surmise that the Confederate legislators were ignorant of economic realities, but given their intellect, their financial standings, and their backgrounds that seems absurd. Perhaps the military success achieved against General McClellan on the peninsula instilled a sense of overconfidence. Perhaps there was lingering surmise that the war would not last so long after all. Antietam and Perryville, however, surely rendered this line of reasoning invalid.

Douglas Ball's conclusion seems close to the mark: although much of the legislative thinking is unknown, because of secret sessions, "it is clear that the Congressmen, like their successors today, were far more interested in protecting the special interests of their constituents than in developing a well-articulated tax program." As proof, Ball points out that Memminger's "simple two-part tax scheme" became an amalgamation of income tax, tax in kind, and excises.[49]

Ironically, the most effective part of the law was not the income tax but the 10 percent tax in kind, which Memminger supported only in a last-minute message sent to Congress in April 1863, as part of an effort to provide provisions and to mitigate the odious impressment system. Presumably speculators would be shut out of the loop, and the government would have less need to issue more Treasury notes.[50] Yet the tax in kind had serious disadvantages in addition to the obvious problems created by theft or spoilage; it stimulated inflation, because there were fewer commodities offered for sale, without a compensating reduction in the supply of money. Indeed, use of the printing press continued, and that increased the amount of money in circulation, which led to still more inflation.[51]

Ball points to class issues, concluding that "the inability to levy direct taxes worked a gross inequity because the slave-holders were enabled to evade contributing to a new nation established for their special benefit." A Congress composed largely of slaveholders could not even bring itself to "devise a slave-holders 'license fee' or similar enactment." These men, Ball concludes, rightly we think, "had no intention of contributing their appropriate share to the Confederacy."[52]

Because there were periodic debates on repassage of laws authorizing suspension of habeas corpus, it was inevitable that there would be some controversy between national and state authority, especially in states where the legality of conscription was challenged. In Tennessee in 1863, General Simon Bolivar Buckner took one Abe Tipton prisoner, but Tipton had gotten a writ of habeas corpus, and Buckner was required to produce Tipton. Buckner refused on the ground that "Tipton is held as an open and avowed enemy of the Confederate Government. He is held by the Military Authorities, under the laws of the Confederacy. I do not recognize the right of a State Court to interpose between me and my duties as a Confederate Officer." Confessing that "it is difficult to ascertain, under our system of Government, legally and Philosophically, the right of a Military Commander to exercise such power," Attorney General Thomas Watts nevertheless ruled that Buckner's refusal was insufficient. "He should have stated the facts, and not his conclusions from the facts. He should have shown under what specific charge Abe Tipton was held, and who he was, and by what authority specially he held him in custody." And Buckner had to maintain the rights of the prisoner by taking him before the judge, a conclusion reached in part by relying on the decision of Roger Taney in *Booth v. U.S.,* which involved the infamous Wisconsin defiance of the authority of federal courts in the 1850s. But once a Confederate officer showed a state court that he operated under Confederate authority, Watts thought, there was nothing that the state judge could do. With this action, Watts had upheld the authority of both conscription and the right of the president to suspend the writ, and, as he thought, had provided a "rule for determining the boundaries of Jurisdiction between the State and Confederate Authorities."[53]

Although state courts in Alabama and some other states agreed, some courts in Georgia and North Carolina did not.[54] By no coincidence whatever, these were the two states in which officials most disputed the constitutionality of conscription. The issue of state versus Confederate authority was a touchy one, especially in the absence of a deciding body such as a Confederate supreme court, and it is no surprise that this is the only significant opinion on the subject that was issued by the Confederate attorney general. It was a question best left alone.

The third session of the First Congress enacted significant manpower laws. Engineer troops were organized,[55] both a volunteer and a provisional navy were established,[56] and seamen aged eighteen to forty-five were continued in service for three years from their enlistment, by a law paralleling one applied to the army a year earlier.[57] Most important, Congress acted on the exemption issue at the behest of President Davis. In his message in January 1863 to the First Congress at the opening of the third session, he requested revision of the exemption law passed the previous October. He remarked that numerous complaints had been received "of the inequality of its operation" and expressed hope that "some means will be devised for leaving at home a sufficient local police without making discriminations, always to be deprecated, between different classes of our citizens."[58] This somewhat ambiguous statement was actually a plea to deal with increasing class tensions created by the twenty-Negro law, by which able-bodied whites supervising the labor of twenty or more slaves on plantations where there was no one else fit for the task could be exempt. They were deemed necessary to police the slaves and to ensure that slave manpower was efficiently used for the production of foodstuffs and other goods of war. Many a planter's son was thus exempted under this law while many a yeoman's son went off to war.

On May 1, a new exemption law went into effect. It was an ineffectual effort to meet the objections of those persons who claimed that the twenty-Negro law smacked of favoritism. The overseer provision of the previous law was repealed, and a new overseer exemption was enacted, which looked to the average Confederate to be very much the same as the previous one. Plantations with twenty or more slaves and no able white male to superintend them could get an overseer, provided that the man selected was indeed an overseer by occupation before the passage of the draft law, that the law would not apply where slaves "have been placed by division from any other farm or plantation," and that the owners of the slaves would pay a five hundred dollar yearly exemption fee. Moreover, Davis won a limited measure of the detail authority he craved, for the law also provided that "such other persons shall be exempted as the President shall be satisfied ought to be exempted in districts of [the] country deprived of white or slave labor indispensable to the production of grain or provisions."[59] These two enactments indicated clearly that the exemption problem was caused not only by resentment from the body of nonslaveholders and small holders but also by the prospect of widespread food shortages. Indeed, shortly before the passage of this act, the Congress had requested Davis to urge the agricultural interests to plant food crops during the coming year rather than cotton and tobacco,[60] and he had promptly responded with an address to the Confederate citizenry warning that previous success should not mislead them into the belief that the war would be over soon. It was essential to plant subsistence crops, because food stocks were down as a result of drought and low yields the year before, especially in the areas from which the army drew its supplies. Even where crops had been bountiful, transportation difficulties had made it problematic to move them to where they were needed.[61] Those Confederates who claimed that the widely condemned twenty-Negro law was essential to the production of food, for both the army and the citizens, had strong arguments in their favor. A slave population did have to be closely watched, and more important, it had to be effectively directed to food production or the war effort would be seriously compromised, as Davis indicated in his address.

Another exemption measure in this session spotlighted the rigidity of the Confederate system. The October 1862 exemption law had curtailed postal exemptions, but on March 18, 1863, Davis informed Congress that unless they were restored, it would be impossible to provide mail service to large portions of the Confederacy. He estimated that only fifteen hundred men would be lost to the service,[62] but that was about fifteen companies of troops. Congress responded, however, and exempted mail contractors and drivers.[63]

The strain on military recruitment caused by postal exemptions was nothing compared to that caused by the exemption of state militia. Officers subject to militia duty by the declaration of a state were exempt under the law of October 11, 1862,[64] and state governors were often quite liberal in their militia exemptions. This was especially true of Governor Joseph E. Brown of Georgia, with the result that many men who by all right should have been contributing to Confederate defense were not. Congress did nothing to remedy the situation, and by the end of the war North Carolina had fifty-six hundred men exempt as state officers, and Georgia had eighty-two hundred, amounting altogether to fourteen regiments of combat troops.[65]

Added to this controversy was the habeas corpus issue. Although there was some sentiment to renew the existing law when it expired in February 1863, elections were approaching the following fall and most congressmen were willing to allow the law to die quietly. Efforts by Mississippi congressman Ethelbert Barksdale, long a friend of Jefferson Davis, to renew suspension, failed, much to the relief of many of his colleagues and Confederate citizens in general.

However, the spring session of 1863 revealed that a desperate manpower situation was rapidly developing. So many soldiers and officers were absent without leave that it was thought necessary to pass a law denying them pay for any period of unauthorized absence.[66] The problem increased the following summer, and in July Davis exercised his authority under the conscription law to call out all white men aged eighteen to forty-five who were not exempt or not already in service.[67]

Impressment was still another controversial issue Congress faced. The spirit of the impressment officers' orders was often ignored and eventually rather severe legislation had to be passed to regulate them. But internal antagonism over this did not become so great as to force legislation until Congress finally passed a comprehensive law on the subject early in 1863.[68] The necessity for this legislation may be inferred from the provision that "property necessary for the support of the owner and his family, and to carry on his ordinary agricultural and mechanical business . . . shall not be taken or impressed for the public use." That incidents of this sort frequently occurred, however, was indicated by the proviso that when an owner complained about such property being taken, the matter would be referred to arbitration.[69] Generally, the property assessed was agricultural, though sometimes it might be manufactured items or raw materials.

Sometimes, however, slaves were impressed, for of course they too were property. Shortages of labor had occurred as early as 1861, and some localities experienced insufficient labor for the army even before conscription was begun in 1862. In areas close to hostilities or permanent encampments, this manpower drain created a problem when the army found it necessary to construct fortifications or other military structures. As early as fall 1861, officials in Virginia were unable to hire workers to put up winter quarters.[70]

The need for impressment of labor became ever more apparent, and legislation and regulations were promulgated to provide slave labor. The impressment of slaves was regulated by the laws of the state in which the impressment occurred, or in the absence of such laws, by regulations of the War Department. A number of states accepted the invitation to pass their own laws regulating slave labor, among them Louisiana, Mississippi, and Virginia.[71] The Confederate legislation of March 1863 specified that in no case were slaves to be impressed if their labor could be hired with the voluntary consent of the owner.[72] By early 1863 slave labor was already frequently impressed, and the procedures were prescribed in the same legislation that provided for the impressment of food and material. The impressment would be carried out under state law if such existed, and only if slaves could not be hired from their owners. No slaves were to be taken from plantations engaged in raising provisions "except in case of urgent necessity."[73]

Commodities, especially foodstuffs, were usually the objective of the impressment officers. The basic problem was that in an inflating economy, impressment officers were continually amazed by the high prices farmers demanded for their crops, and farmers felt victimized by the low prices the military expected to pay. Under the circumstances farmers were tempted to withhold their crops from markets in anticipation of higher prices, which further disturbed the government and impressment officers. Farmers were accused of speculation, feeding on the need of the army and the misery of the people in order to fill their pockets. Though some farmers did so, others simply did not see why they should bear an unfair burden by paying what amounted to a subsidy to the government. It was a problem to which there was no satisfactory solution.

Furthermore, this was a burden that was not spread evenly. The need to impress a farmer's crops would naturally be greatest near the scene of military operations. Some farmers in remote areas were seldom faced by the exactions of the impressment system, but those who were located along the line of march or in an area in which several armies might be concentrating for an offensive movement could count on their crops being levied time and again. A major army might have as many men as the population of a congressional district, thereby doubling food needs in a relatively small area.[74] The rations that these hungry men consumed, though meager by the standards of the modern American army, nevertheless called for considerable local sacrifice. In 1862, a soldier's daily ration included three-fourths pound of pork or one and one-fourth pounds of fresh beef; eighteen ounces of flour; peas, beans, or rice; and coffee, sugar, vinegar, salt, and soap, with more when on the march. Whiskey was permitted when the troops were fatigued, and substitutions were allowed, such as tea for coffee or desiccated vegetables for fresh beans or rice.[75] Even a small army of ten thousand men might consume twelve thousand five hundred pounds of beef and twenty-five bushels of beans a day.[76] Many a locality had a hard time coming up with provisions in such quantity without causing shortages among the civilian population, especially if the army was going to be around for a while.

Moreover, inflation as well as transportation played an important role in exacerbating the impressment problem. In Virginia in spring 1863, horseshoes that had cost $.25 in 1859 had risen to $1.00, and a pair of coarse shoes for slaves had gone up from $1.50 to $15.00. Yet when farmers raised their prices to keep up, they were vilified by charges of extortion.[77]

Devalued Confederate Treasury notes caused farmers to be reluctant to accept them, but if the army could not buy, it had to take. Impressment therefore intensified as inflation increasingly gripped the country. The campaigns of summer 1863 set off a new round of inflation that ensured impressment would only get worse.[78] By that time, the difference between what impressment agents paid and what farmers could get on the open market had become a shocking scandal.[79] As Douglas Ball notes, "In July 1863, the impressment price for corn was merely 70 percent of the market price." A year later it was only 20 percent, a drop of 50 percent, which translated into a tremendous drop in purchasing power. In the meantime gold had increased from nine dollars in Treasury notes to twenty dollars to twenty-three dollars, a decline of over 50 percent in the gold value of the dollar. "Quite obviously," Ball remarks, "this price differential constituted a highly discriminatory tax"; he concludes that it accounted for about 16 percent of the revenue of the Confederate government.[80]

In the face of this discriminatory tax, some farmers actually cut production. Impressment was thus tied to the taxation system. As inflation caused prices to climb, Confederates were more motivated to have a rational government taxation system rather than being taxed by the inflationary spiral. The rate of inflation, in a de facto sense, sometimes approached 10 percent a month,[81] and it played an important role in undermining home-front morale, which led in turn to demands that Congress act. Ball concludes that "impressments, together with the ubiquitous currency inflation, were the government's only effective method of taxation."[82] This was true even after the long-awaited passage of comprehensive tax legislation in 1863.

Under the circumstances, the hapless Confederate commissary general, Lucius B. Northrop, frequently received more than his share of the blame, both for the need for impressment and for the way it was carried out. Most historians are agreed that Northrop was a shining example of cronyism, and generally speaking, a failure on whom must rest much of the blame for the ultimate Confederate defeat. However, Lynda L. Crist has observed that "Northrop's efforts were more often than not stymied by the lean, complex Treasury Department and the non-cooperation and deficiencies of Southern railroads."[83]

Local commissaries often were quite attentive to the pleas of governors and local commanders and therefore ignored the commissary general except to make complaints. This conflict between the commissary general and local commanders was never settled. In the western theater, General John C. Pemberton "received permission to exclude from his district all commissary and food-producing agents not of his army." Northrop's complaint to Davis about this was to no avail, and indeed Pemberton set off a long trail of what proved to be mischief. Vicksburg, which Pemberton had been assigned to defend, was part of the Mobile, Alabama, foodshed, and when Pemberton prohibited movement of foodstuffs from his area, the civil population around Mobile was threatened with famine. This forced General Simon Bolivar Buckner to allow public access to his commissariat, thereby creating a shortage of subsistence in his army. In the end, much of what Pemberton gathered spoiled from exposure at Port Hudson.[84]

Northrop's biographer, Jerrold Northrop Moore, has carefully explained the difficulties of supply and impressment, at least so far as the commissary is concerned. And the same problems were at work for the quartermaster and medical supply functions. Northrop was obliged to deal with field commanders who had little understanding of supply problems and thought that they could simply demand, or scour the countryside, and lo, subsistence would appear.

Davis himself apparently had a reasonable grasp of the reality of his supply problem but very little insight into what to do about it. There was distress every time the army camped near an urban area, and no doubt at Davis's prompting Adjutant and Inspector General Samuel Cooper issued a general order prescribing behavior in such encampments, including prohibition against taking private property "except when indispensable for the public service, and then only by orders of competent authority, and in the manner pointed out in the Army Regulations and orders of the Quartermaster and Commissary Departments."[85] On January 15, 1863, the Congress, increasingly interested in impressment, requested Davis "to communicate to this House all general orders of impressment, together with the instructions and regulations under the same recently issued by the War Department, or any bureau thereof."[86]

In reply, Davis sent the House a copy of impressment rules approved shortly before by Secretary of War James A. Seddon. These authorized the quartermaster general to "impress army supplies, labor and transportation (except that belonging to railroad companies and government contractors), when he shall think it necessary to the public service." These supplies were to be paid for "at reasonable price not exceeding in any case, rates ordered from time to time by the Secretary of War." Enough was to be left with the owner for the use of his family or plantation, and if possible impressment was to be made from speculators rather than from producers. This order also applied to the Commissary Department.[87]

The result, for example, was that wheat was plentiful in parts of Virginia but could not be purchased for less than $3.00 a bushel. "If this state of things is permitted to continue," warned Frank G. Ruffin and James R. Crenshaw, "the army cannot be fed."[88] They proposed a corrective policy to set prices based on average prices in the five years prior to the war, adjusted by an assumed 50 percent depreciation of the currency, a "moderate profit," and some transportation costs. Other commodities, such as items produced in limited areas or brought through the blockade, would be priced higher. Under this proposal, prime white wheat would be priced at $3.50 per bushel of sixty pounds, the price determined by the average price of the five years prior to the war ($1.60) plus 118.75 percent.

Davis was by then determined to handle the issue more firmly than he had in the past. In his message of January 12, 1863, to open the third session of the First Congress, he vaguely mentioned the need for comprehensive legislation on the subject of taxation, which was closely related to issues of impressment and supply.[89] Many Confederates were more aware of the inadequacies of the supply system, especially impressment, than Davis was willing to admit publicly, although he received sufficient negative feedback to pressure him to revise the impressment system. Governor Vance of North Carolina, for example, complained of "speculation and extortion [that] seems to have seized upon nearly all sorts and conditions of men," causing want among the poor. A notable abuse in North Carolina, as elsewhere, was the presence of speculators from other states who "swarm in the land," falsely claiming to be Confederate impressment agents.[90]

It was clear changes had to be made. A few days after Davis's message was read to the Congress, Senator William E. Simms of Kentucky offered a resolution pointing to the "inherent and inviolable right" of Confederate citizens to hold property. It urged that

> the right to defend the same and his domicile from unlawful invasion, seizure, or conversion shall not be impaired or questioned, and that all such seizures or impressments or any such property, by any officer or agent of this Government, are in violation of the plainest provisions of the Constitution, are destructive of the most sacred rights of the citizen, and an unwarranted breach of the plighted faith of the government to the citizens thereof, and are therefore void.[91]

Simms's resolution never passed, but it was a clear indication that the system demanded reform. Early in the session, Congressman John Goode of Virginia complained of "injustice and outrage by the impressing officers [that] were already frequent and would become universal, unless some early and adequate reform was effected." He particularly objected to inadequate appraisals,[92] and offered a resolution in the House calling on the Committee on the Judiciary to consider a bill "to secure to the owners of private property taken for the use of the Government a fair and just compensation."[93] M. R. H. Garnett, also of Virginia, criticized the invasion of people's homes by agents, "some of whom, despite the best guards of the [War] department in making these appointments, must be dishonest."[94] Other Virginians also voiced concerns about impressment, and for good reason. Virginia was one of the great sources of supply for soldiers and animals and was the most convenient place to forage for Robert E. Lee's Army of Northern Virginia. A Tennessee congressman, Landon C. Haynes, touched the heart of the issue in a resolution demanding that goods be impressed at market value.[95] In February 1863 both Senator Simms and Senator Louis T. Wigfall had introduced impressment legislation; others followed.

To Wigfall, inflation was one of the most serious issues, but to pay at market prices was impractical since that would incur a huge postwar debt. Currently, prices were "exorbitant," he thought, making it difficult to supply the needs of the soldiers at prices "to enable the soldiers after the war to return to their own vine and fig trees, without being harassed by grinding taxation."[96] Wigfall feared that the price of flour would go up to thirty dollars if market prices had to be paid,[97] but they went higher than that before it was all over.

Class issues were also involved. Senator Allen Taylor Caperton pointed to the injustice of paying a farmer only half the thirty dollar value of his flour, thereby forcing the farmer "to contribute out of his own pocket fifteen dollars towards the support of the government." This was dangerous because other farmers grew tobacco and cotton, which the government did not need to impress, and these farmers would contribute nothing from their pockets.[98] Senator Gustavus Henry of Tennessee contributed a telling bit of humor to the debate, pointing out the meaning of market price when he referred to "Richard III when down in the dust and blood of Bosworth field, offered his 'kingdom for a horse.' "[99] Impressment was a hot issue by this time, for the supply situation had become so critical that many farmers were losing their crops to the army at prices they could not bear because they were being paid considerably less than market prices.

Impressment of slaves was also an issue, for many Confederates agreed with Congressman Garnett that unless slave impressments were restricted, farmers would be unable to supply the needs of the country. He claimed that this was the case in some Virginia counties, which "were already so drained of their slaves as scarcely to have labor enough left to raise a mere subsistence."[100] Quartermasters and commissaries finally received official authorization to follow a formal impressment procedure, as continual bickering over the supply system became so great that the need for Congress to pass a comprehensive law was obvious to all. Argument over details, including the rights of private property, delayed passage of the legislation until March 26.[101]

Just a few days before, the Adjutant General's Office had issued general orders that would have dampened much criticism of the way impressment was carried out had they been issued a year earlier and strongly enforced. Attempting to clarify some public "misconceptions" and to stop impressment officers from violating war department rules, on March 19 Samuel Cooper ordered "that no officer of the government shall, under any circumstances whatever, impress the supplies which a party has for his own consumption, or that of his family, employees, or slaves," and that except "in a case of exigency" no officer was to "impress supplies which are on their way to market for sale on arrival."[102]

Even these orders did not meet the most troubling feature of impressment, which was the right of the citizen to receive "just compensation," as prescribed by the Confederate Constitution. What that meant and how it was to be determined was as difficult a question in early 1863 as it had been in summer 1861, when it came up with regard to the War Tax. The issue was simplified somewhat in February 1863 when Attorney General Thomas Watts issued an opinion concerning the seizure of railroad iron, stating "that the measure of damages in such cases [of seizure], is the *fair market value of the property converted at the time and place of seizure,* with interest on that value from the time of conversion."[103] Lacking a supreme court, the Confederacy often relied on the Attorney General's Office when legal questions had to be settled, so Watts's opinion carried considerable weight.

The March 1863 legislation legalized the practice of impressment and tried to hedge it with safeguards. When necessary, the army could impress what it needed, but when the owner and the impressing officer disagreed over the value of the property being impressed, the value was to be determined by two "disinterested citizens" of the locality, one to be chosen by the officer and one by the owner. If they disagreed, "these two shall choose an umpire of like qualifications, whose decision shall be final."[104] The impressment officer would then pay the owner the compensation agreed upon and give him a certificate identifying himself, describing the property taken, and certifying that the action was essential and the required property could not be secured in any other way. If the impressing officer was unable to pay, the hapless owner could get payment from "the proper disbursing officer."[105] Sometimes this complicated procedure would be impractical, in which case the law provided that the army could take the property and its value would be assessed later by the same procedure. If necessary, the secretary of war himself could issue a general order taking private property if he felt purchase was impractical, with the value being determined by disinterested citizens.[106]

To administer these cumbersome procedures, the president was to appoint a commissioner from each state, the governor was to choose a second, and the two were to act as a board for that state, "whose duty it shall be to fix upon the prices to be paid by the government, for all property impressed . . . so as to afford just compensation to the owners thereof." Once again, if the arbitrators did not agree, they would select a third person to act as umpire. These prices would be published in a schedule at least every two months and distributed for general information.[107]

If the impressing officer believed that the price or quality judged by the panel was incorrect, he could pay what he judged to be a proper price and then send his decision to the state authority, which would make the final judgment.[108] Despite the painstaking efforts of the Congress to ensure just payment to the victims of the impressment law, however, there was much public opposition and the Georgia Supreme Court pronounced the Confederate law unconstitutional because "just compensation" was not guaranteed.[109]

These rules created problems by their complexity and by the failure to deal adequately with the issue of compensation. A string of orders came from Richmond dealing with prices and procedures. For example, in May 1863, General Cooper issued a schedule of prices to be paid for impressed goods in Virginia and Georgia. Good flour, super fine, could be taken for $35.00 per

196-pound bushel along the lines of some Georgia railroads, but for $40.00 per 196-pound bushel along the lines of other roads. Prime shelled corn was seized for $2.25 for a 56-pound bushel in some places, and for $1.50 elsewhere. Sweet potatoes were either $2.60 or $1.50 per 60-pound bushel, depending on where in Georgia it was impressed. Dried apples were $4.00 a bushel, and a pound from a good side of ham was $.85, in Georgia at least. That 56-pound bushel of corn went for $4.00 in Virginia, and the sweet potatoes for $5.00 as well. The hire of labor, teams, wagons, and drivers was also specified, and the owner of a six-horse team, with wagon and driver, got $16.00 per day if he paid for the rations himself but only $8.00 per day if the government paid.[110] Food, forage, tallow, alcohol, iron, and leather goods were all included. In South Carolina the following September, dried apples were worth $3.00, shelled corn $2.00, and the Irish potatoes $2.00.[111] Over the course of the war these schedules were periodically revised upward, due to inflation.

As a result of the depredations wreaked by the CSS *Florida* and the CSS *Alabama,* and the looming threat of the Laird rams, the U.S. Congress authorized President Lincoln to issue letters of marque. On March 3, 1863, Lincoln signed the new legislation permitting Union privateers, an act that was a direct threat to British shipping. A few weeks later several members of Lincoln's cabinet organized a covert mission to Britain to further enhance Thomas Dudley's espionage operations. This was known as the Forbes-Aspinwall mission, headed by John Murry Forbes and William Aspinwall. They were funded with $10 million worth of new government bonds, to be used to attempt to buy any warship that might be being built in Britain for the South.

But the scheme was made public by a leak to the *Times* (London), which in a detailed article revealed the real purpose of the Forbes-Aspinwall mission. Despite the sympathies for the South harbored by many of the British political leaders, the laboring masses hated slavery and keenly supported free labor in the North. Thus, public pressure put a quietus on the possibility of more British aid for the Confederacy.

Following the infamous Mud March—a failed maneuver in late January 1863—the Army of the Potomac got still another commander: Joe Hooker replaced Ambrose Burnside. During late winter and early spring 1863, R. E. Lee was genuinely mystified as to Hooker's intentions. On one count, though, Lee guessed correctly: Northern public opinion and political realities would induce the eastern army to take the offensive again.

On March 17, 1863, the relatively small Battle of Kelly's Ford, near Culpeper, Virginia, was fought. Federal cavalry under William Woods Averrel crossed the Rappahannock at Kelly's Ford and were strongly engaged by Confederate troops, who rushed to halt the Union advance. In brush-covered country and on the Wheatley Farm, the hard-fought contest raged until late afternoon. Casualties were 78 for the Union and 133 for the Confederates, and these included "the gallant John Pelham," who had become a hero in the Battle of Fredericksburg and was earmarked as a rising young officer. R. E. Lee, in reporting the affair to Davis two days later, was gratified that George Stoneman's "whole force was driven back by Fitz Lee's small brigade." He spoke of a profound sense of mourning for the loss of Pelham and expressed hope that he might be promoted posthumously.[112] It was said that at least three girls put on mourning costumes, each thinking herself to have been his fiancee.

> Just as the spring came laughing through the strife
>   With all its gorgeous cheer;
> In the bright April of historic life
>   Fell the great cannoneer.
> The wondrous lulling of a hero's breath
>   His bleeding country weeps—
> Hushed in the alabaster arms of death,
>   Our young Marcellus sleeps.

Hooker mapped out a plan to meet the demand as he now perceived it. The main maneuver element would consist of three corps, swinging northwest of Fredericksburg, along the Rappahannock, and then crossing that river and subsequently the Rapidan. Two corps would stay in front of Fredericksburg, holding the Confederates in their defensive positions. The two remaining corps would be held in reserve and used to exploit any advance. To enhance his chances of success, Hooker sought to divert Lee's attention by sending the Federal cavalry on a raid to try to disrupt Lee's communications. The infantry got under way on April 27. This was a propitious time because Longstreet was away with much of his corps on a foraging expedition around Suffolk; Lee stood in position with only sixty thousand men.

The ensuing battle proved to be Lee's most brilliant achievement in the field. J. E. B. Stuart brought Lee a report that the Federal right flank extended westward from the Wilderness Church along the turnpike, and though refused slightly (that is, angled near the endpoint so as to present a protective defense sidewise against any flank attack), it was not resting on any natural obstacle.

In a flash Lee realized that he was presented with a precious opportunity. He determined to make that the main point of an attack, using the twenty-six thousand men of Stonewall Jackson's corps. Jubal Early's division would remain in place before Fredericksburg.

Lee's plan was risky because it meant further dividing his already out-numbered army. On the night of May 1, in a council of war, Lee and Jackson reached a final decision. (This meeting was the last between Lee and Jackson, for the latter was fatally wounded the next day. It became the subject of the most famous, and most beloved in the South, of the postwar paintings depicting episodes of the conflict: *The Last Meeting,* by E. B. D. Fabrina Julio.)

The assault on May 2 brought spectacular results. The Federal force was stung badly and sent scurrying in disarray. The Union loss stood at 17,287; the Confederate casualty list numbered 12,821. But the most immediate and obviously crushing Rebel loss was General Jackson, who was seriously wounded, by accident, by elements of his own command. Taken from the field hospital by wagon to a farm twenty-five miles away, he was expected to recuperate. "Give [Jackson] my affectionate regards," Lee told one of Jackson's chaplains who visited his headquarters on May 7, "and tell him to make haste and get well, and come back to me as soon as he can. He has lost his left arm, but I have lost my right." On that very day, however, Jackson's physician diagnosed that pneumonia had set in. Nothing could be done. Jackson died at 3:20 P.M. on May 10, 1863. His last two outcries, in delirium, were for his logistics chieftain and for his most reliable combat subordinate, A. P. Hill. Then Jackson died with the words on his lips that became a Southern euphemism for death for at least two generations: "Let us cross over the river and rest under the shade of the trees."

> What are the thoughts that are stirring his breast?
>   What is the mystical vision he sees?
> "Let us pass over the river, and rest
>   Under the shade of the trees."
> Has he grown sick of his toils and tasks?
>   Sighs the worn spirit for respite or ease?
> Is it a moment's cool halt that he asks,
>   "Under the shade of the trees."

Davis, despite his illness, had done what he had been able to do to reinforce Lee, but otherwise he was generally a passive observer as the events unfolded. It lifted his spirits when the news arrived on May 3 that Hooker was being beaten decisively and Lee was thanking "Almighty God for a great victory." On May 4 Davis wrote a special commendatory message to R. E. Lee:

> I have received your despatch and reverently unite with you in giving praise to God for the success with which He has crowned our arms. In the name of the people I offer my cordial thanks to yourself and the troops under your command for this addition to the unprecedented series of great victories which your army has achieved. The universal rejoicing produced by this happy result will be mingled with a general regret for the good and the brave who are numbered among the killed and the wounded.[113]

And on May 7 Davis wrote his brother Joseph:

> The battle recently fought on the Rappahannock was certainly a great victory, in view of the thorough preparation of the Enemy and his superiority of numbers, not less than two to one. . . . If the forces ordered up join Genl. Lee in this present condition of the two armies I hope we will destroy Hooker's army and then perform the same operation on the army sent to sustain him.[114]

But the news of Jackson's wounding deeply concerned Davis. He kept a servant constantly at the telegraph office and sent servants to meet each incoming train in case there was any news. When the outlook turned grim, on May 9, Davis sat silently at home keeping vigil until midnight or later. Jefferson and Varina prayed throughout the night that Jackson died. The body was sent down by train on May 11, the coffin "wrapped in a handsome flag Mr. Davis had sent for the purpose."

This was, of course, the Stainless Banner, the new national flag that had just been adopted. For Davis, Cooper observes, Jackson's death did not match that of Albert Sidney Johnston as a personal blow. But he "recognized Stonewall's special place, stating that 'a great national calamity has befallen us.' "[115] Davis was able, with difficulty, to go with Varina to the governor's mansion "to take a last look at the patriot saint," but the next day he had to ride in a carriage "looking thin and frail" as the cortege of honor bore Jackson's body through the streets. That afternoon, some twenty thousand persons passed through the capitol to view "the hero's face," whose "expression of shining calm shed a species of ghostly radiance over the countenance." Davis was suffering from more than his illness, and a tear fell from his eye onto Jackson's corpse. Someone next to him tried to broach some subject of business, and Davis said, "You must excuse me. I am still staggering from a dreadful blow."[116] To a visitor at the Gray House after the funeral, Davis remarked, "I am still staggering from a dreadful blow. I cannot think."[117]

It was a devastating loss for the South, for Jackson was a much beloved folk hero. Even more serious, however, was the loss of numerous other important or promising officers; Southern command resources were beginning to diminish. Douglas Southall Freeman has pointed out, always before this there had been available suitable replacements for lost officers, but no longer was that so. Indeed, Lee previously had concluded that an infantry corps with thirty thousand men or more was too large for a commander to handle, especially in wooded situations. He had, however, refrained from restructuring so long as he had the two extraordinarily capable men, Longstreet and Jackson. Now he felt forced to divide the Army of Northern Virginia into three infantry corps with three divisions each. Richard S. Ewell was promoted to the rank of lieutenant general and replaced Jackson, and Ambrose P. Hill, also raised to lieutenant general, was made commander of the new Third Corps.

The staggering blow of Jackson's death came just as Davis was reeling from another bit of devastating news: a Union army was ravaging Mississippi. Enough boats had run past Vicksburg's batteries one moonless night to supply General U. S. Grant below the city and to ferry him across the river.

The Confederate government finally yielded to the urge to design a new national flag and adopted it on May 1, 1863. This banner used Beauregard's battle flag as the union—a square two-thirds the width of the whole—with a field of white. Nicknamed the Stainless Banner, it became widely known as the Stonewall Jackson flag, because the first time that many people saw it was when it was used to drape his coffin while he lay in state at Richmond.

Just as had been the fate of the Stars and Bars, however, the Stainless Banner was not destined to be much of a success. Its unusual length, twice the hoist, gave it a rather misshapen appearance. And when it was hanging limp it was difficult to tell the Stars and Bars from the Stars and Stripes; moreover, a limply hanging Stainless Banner was easily mistaken for a flag of truce or surrender. Thus the battle flag continued to play the most significant role in combat operations.

The Confederate navy had been using the Stars and Bars, there being no other official Rebel navy flag. But on May 24, 1863, Secretary of the Navy Stephen Mallory authorized three new banners: a new ensign, jack, and pennant. The new ensign was simply the Stainless Banner with its proportions reduced to one and one-half to one. The naval jack was the square battle flag in a rectangular rather than square shape. (Today, most so-called Confederate flags are actually the naval jack.) The naval pennant was a streamer one foot wide at its head and seventy-two feet long, tapering to a point.

By 1863 some semblance of Confederate civil religion had begun to emerge. Normally it would be fathers who would instill into their children basic political and cultural values, but with so many men involved in the war effort, during—and even continuing immediately after—the Civil War, this function fell mainly to women.

Wartime schools faced a challenge in instilling nationalism, as teachers tried to redefine national allegiance and to introduce new patriotic symbols to children who were more often than not quite distracted. As George Rable puts it, "The flag and songs of a new nation had to replace the old ones; American history became an Old Testament prelude to the New Testament story of a Southern Confederacy developing under providential protection."[118]

While it was a delicate and possibly also tricky business, establishing Confederate schools became essential to developing Southern character. Teachers' conventions passed resolutions promising to use only Southern texts, and several publishers tried to rise to the challenge by producing good Confederate textbooks—although in truth the differences were mainly cosmetic. Their most distinctive feature was a brazen defense of slavery, augmented with the appropriate passages of Scripture. Otherwise, the books exalted Southern superiority primarily by bad-mouthing Northerners. George Rable calls this "negative nationalism" and suggests that it had no chance of building a strong sense of cultural identity.[119]

Teaching the broader civil religion was carried out for adult Confederates mainly by preachers, who for the most part readily admitted their role as nationalistic propagandists. With an enthusiasm that denied reality, W. T. D. Dalzell thanked God for the "unanimity which has characterized men of all shades of opinion previous to this struggle; and the total obliteration of party feelings and party names, uniting to sustain the administration."[120]

There was thus a tinge of Confederate civil religion, but it was thin and not potent enough to meld itself into the hearts and minds of the citizenry. In spring 1863 it is fair to say that public support for Jefferson Davis's policies continued, but that support lacked strong foundations.[121] Victory still seemed possible, and if it came, then there would be time enough for further nurture of patriotism. But if victory did not come, then the civil religion, such as it was, would prove to be a weak and ineffectual force, although it did have a role to play in the postwar era.

11

UNION POWER AFFIRMED

The Confederate Military Department system in the long run was more of a hindrance than a help in conducting the war efficiently. Nevertheless, certain aspects of the system proved to be wise choices. In autumn 1862 Jefferson Davis created the Department of the West to coordinate efforts in East Louisiana, Alabama, Mississippi, and Tennessee. For the command of this department, the president had available a general whose credentials suggested that he was fully equal to such a large responsibility: Joseph E. Johnston. By then Johnston was sufficiently recovered from the wounds he had suffered at Seven Pines. Though he would have preferred the direct command of an army, he readily accepted the assignment, understanding that he was to operate in Napoleon's manner, that is, by concentrating forces within his huge department.

He chose to make his headquarters in Chattanooga, Tennessee, arriving there on December 4, 1862. The department had two principal forces and subareas of responsibility: Middle Tennessee, defended by Braxton Bragg's army, with its headquarters in Tullahoma, where he had taken his army after his dramatic Kentucky campaign. The other subdepartment was that of Mississippi and East Louisiana, with forces there commanded by John C. Pemberton. Johnston was anxious to inspect his department, as was Davis, who arrived in Chattanooga on December 10. The two men were together for more than a week and had ample time to discuss how the department would function.

Davis and Johnston visited Bragg at his nearby headquarters and then journeyed together to Mississippi to make an estimate of Pemberton's situation and plans. While at Bragg's headquarters, Davis ordered Carter L. Stevenson's large division sent from Tullahoma to supplement the forces defending Vicksburg. Two important strategic judgments emerged from this journey. First, Bragg's spectacular railroad movement from northern Mississippi through Mobile to Middle Tennessee to initiate his Kentucky raid evidenced how steamboats and the railroad allowed armies a new kind of rapid strategic mobility over large areas. Davis did not hesitate to use the railroad when he ordered Stevenson's division to move from Tullahoma to Vicksburg by way of Mobile. The direct route by road was shorter but much slower.

The second strategy was the pipeline concept. Davis suggested stationing Stevenson's division at Meridian or Selma (between Vicksburg and Mobile) because he and Johnston both understood the potential of the railroad to enable the Confederate forces to be concentrated in space over so large an area. Placing Stevenson's division on the railroad between Mississippi and Tennessee used the troops as if they were in a pipeline: when additional troops were introduced at one end, a comparable number would emerge from the other.

Later, when Pemberton alerted Johnston that Grant was reinforcing William Rosecrans, immediately men began moving from Vicksburg toward Mobile, and men from Mobile were promptly en route toward Tullahoma. Before the movement was halted, however, it became clear that Grant was not reinforcing Rosecrans. Nevertheless, the first units of the Mobile garrison had reached Tullahoma about the same time that men from Vicksburg had approached Mobile, proving the concept's efficiency. (This pipeline concept proved useful later in the war, along the Atlantic seaboard.)

D avis delivered a long speech on December 26, 1862, in Jackson, Mississippi, praising the people of Vicksburg for enduring their tribulations and for their determination:

> The sacrifices which have already been made, have perhaps, fallen heavily upon a *portion* of the people, especially upon the noble little city of Vicksburg. After Memphis and New Orleans had fallen, . . . Vicksburg became the object of attack , . . . [and] Vicksburg received the shock of both fleets. . . . Nobly did the little city receive the assault, and even the women said, "Rather than surrender let us give them the soil, but with the ashes of our dwellings upon it." [This] was the heroic devotion of a people who deserve to be free.[1]

There had been occasional grumbling during 1862 that Davis and his administrators did not send adequate military forces to the western theater; perhaps that had been true but most assuredly not because the president had no concern for the West, particularly for his home state. He had promoted Major General John C. Pemberton to lieutenant general on October 10, 1862, highly recommended by both Robert E. Lee and Samuel Cooper, to take charge of overseeing the defense of Mississippi. Further, Davis recently had taken pains to push R. E. Lee to name some colonel in the Army of Northern Virginia to be promoted to brigadier general and sent to Vicksburg for on-the-spot supervision of the city's defense. Stephen D. Lee was the man selected. In his speech Davis both warmly identified with and praised "his people" and sang the praises of Pemberton, the Philadelphian who had chosen the Southern side, and S. D. Lee, the twenty-nine-year-old West Pointer:

> This was the land of my affections. Here were spirited the little of worldly goods I possessed. I selected a general [Pemberton] who, in my view, was capable of defending my State and discharging the duties of this important service. . . . I find that, during his administration here everything has been done that could be accomplished with the means at his command. I recommended him to your confidence as you may have confidence in me, who selected him. For the defense of Vicksburg, I selected one from the army of the Potomac, of whom it is but faint praise to say he has no superior. He was sent to Virginia at the beginning of the war, with a little battery of three guns. With these he fought the Yankee gunboats, drove them off, and stripped them of their terrors. He was promoted for distinguished services on various fields. He was finally made a colonel of cavalry, and I have reason to believe that, at the last great conflict on the field of Manassas, he served to turn the tide of battle and consummate the victory.[2]

Though Davis himself continued to esteem Pemberton, in fact he ultimately proved to be a failure in his duties as lieutenant general. S. D. Lee, on the other hand, sparkled as a brigadier, succeeded in his personal command defending Vicksburg against the first major assault, and ultimately was twice again promoted. Then he too reached the level where his competence was somewhat lacking.

Control of the entire Mississippi River was a principal Union war aim from the outset. By early 1862 the Federals had seized all but a 110-mile stretch. At the endpoints of that segment lay Port Hudson, Louisiana, and Vicksburg. These two points the Confederates managed to hold tenaciously, for they were strong as well as valuable places.

In late 1862 the Federals commenced an onslaught at both ends of the segment. On November 16 a Federal fleet steamed upriver from Baton Rouge and briefly bombarded the Port Hudson batteries. The boats then withdrew, leaving that sector quiet for nearly a month, but on December 13 they returned and resumed pressure. The Yankees could not take Port Hudson, however. It held out against a siege, even after Vicksburg finally fell, after which the Confederates' continuing effort to hold it was pointless.

From the North, directing the Union effort, U. S. Grant launched the first of his six efforts against Vicksburg before the year's end. But he was unable to secure the cooperation and coordination he needed. This phase of his efforts ended with the Battle of Chickasaw Bayou on December 29.

Grant's subordinate, Major General William T. Sherman, led 33,000 men in an attack against a "reorganized brigade" of 2,700 men commanded by Brigadier General Stephen D. Lee, with another 2,700 Rebel defenders who served in and around Vicksburg. Lee was both lucky and efficient in directing his defense. The terrain provided a funnel effect, forcing many Federal soldiers to bunch up in the killing zone, and a morass of mud and water meant that many Federals had to cross a log bridge. The attackers managed to advance to within 150 yards of Lee's rifle pits, but then a withering "storm of shells, grape and canister, as well as minie-balls which swept the front like a hurricane of fire" shattered their ranks and forced the survivors to retreat. It was "a repetition of Balaklava," lamented the commander of one of the lead attack-brigades, Federal Brigadier General John Milton Thayer, recalling a famous battle from the recent Crimean War, with its "Charge of the Light Brigade," "although mine," Thayer said, "was infantry and Earl Cardigan's force was cavalry." The Federal casualties totaled 1,776; the Confederates lost only 207. On December 31 a truce was arranged for the burial of Union dead, and then Sherman reloaded onto his river transports and steamed back to Memphis. Grant, however, was not a man who would let things lie; his men would be back, and his efforts would continue.[3]

At the same time, Jefferson Davis began to assert more influence on the situation in the western theater. But according to William Cooper, there was a "fundamental command problem in the Department of the West [which] had never been solved."[4] Johnston had proclaimed that a choice between defending Mississippi and Tennessee was a political decision, one that should be made in Richmond, not by a general in the field. Davis thus coldly assigned definite priorities and decided that holding Vicksburg and the stretch of the Mississippi River between it and Port Hudson were more important than securing wider control in Middle Tennessee. He told Braxton Bragg to fight in Tennessee if possible, but he authorized a fallback to the Tennessee River near Chattanooga, thus countenancing the abandonment of hundreds of square miles in a region from which the Confederacy desperately needed supplies and manpower. Davis believed that retaining the linkages with the Trans-Mississippi was more vital.[5]

Yet at crucial moments, Davis seemed indecisive. He received and rejected a proposal from Johnston that forces under Pemberton and Theophilus Holmes (then in command of the Trans-Mississippi Department) should be ordered to cooperate. He did order Bragg to dispatch a full division of his army to Mississippi, however. Although Davis gave Bragg a direct order, he merely sent suggestions to Holmes, leaving final decisions up to that general's shaky judgment. William C. Davis suggests that Davis was allowing himself to be hamstrung by his own military department system. He could bring himself to give Bragg an order to reinforce Pemberton because the two men had been loosely combined in Albert Sidney Johnston's old Department of the West, but Holmes had not been a part of that.[6]

Certainly Davis tried to keep abreast of how things were going. He kept his aides busy scurrying around the whole Confederacy, visiting and checking on the various armies. In March 1863 he sent Preston Johnston to Tullahoma, Tennessee, and Joseph C. Ives to visit Pemberton at Vicksburg and then to Port Hudson.[7] Davis certainly never intended that Pemberton should allow himself to become bottled up: "My purpose [was] an attack on Grant when in the interior by combined forces of Johnston & Pemberton, thus alone was a complete victory expected."[8]

Though the reports concerning Johnston and his activities were less than encouraging, Davis chose to give this man, whom he disliked, a lot of slack. Indeed, it is to Davis's great credit that he was more patient with Johnston than he ever was with any man in his lifetime. But Johnston had reached a point where Davis should have replaced him. Beauregard, however, was the only available alternative, and Davis was doggedly resolute that Beauregard never again would be considered for any important command. William C. Davis suggests that this was President Davis's greatest mistake of 1863 and quite possibly his greatest of the entire war.[9]

Davis's frustration was heightened by nagging illness. Once he was heard to cry out, "If I could take one wing and Lee the other, I think we could between us wrest a victory from those people."[10] More than once Davis daydreamed of taking an active command himself, but even more so did "his pain-fogged mind" ruminate on the Confederacy's scant supply of truly capable top-level generals. No doubt he had Johnston, Beauregard, and perhaps also Bragg and Pemberton in mind when he lamented to his brother Joseph that "a *General* in the full acceptation of the word is a rare product, scarcely more than one can be expected in a generation but in this mighty war in which we are engaged there is need for half a dozen."[11] As Cooper observes, "While Richmond and Johnston frustrated each other, their supposedly common enemy acted."[12]

Demonstrating that it could be done, on February 2 the Union ram *Queen of the West* ran south past the Vicksburg batteries. Until it was lost a dozen days later, this warship wreaked havoc upon both the Mississippi and Red Rivers; and its presence was a harbinger of what followed: Federal naval power proved to be key to the ultimate success of Grant's campaign against Vicksburg. Grant immediately set into motion a series of schemes to get at the city, though the first four of them were unsuccessful.

In mid-April Grant managed to force things to a head. Several diversionary thrusts were made: first, Major General Frederick Steele's division moved by water from Young's Point to Greenville, Mississippi, and then thrust inland on a marauding expedition. Second, Colonel Benjamin H. Grierson led 1,000 cavalrymen on a raid from Grand Junction, Tennessee, to Baton Rouge. Third, Sherman's corps made an elaborate feint from the North. Then, on April 16, in the middle of the night, Rear Admiral David D. Porter's fleet ran south past the city. Even though hit often by enemy fire, all but one of the boats passed safely by. They met Grant at Hard Times, Louisiana, to which the troops had marched overland. The troops boarded and were ferried across the river.

Meanwhile, the numbers of Confederate troops in Mississippi had been bolstered by a concerned Rebel high command. Pemberton possessed an army of some 32,000 men; Johnston had another force of some 6,000. Contending against this array, Grant's field force numbered 41,000 men.

Grant moved with celerity, wanting to get between the two Confederate forces and to seize the Mississippi state capital in Jackson. On May 12 an engagement erupted at Raymond, fifteen miles from Jackson. Johnston arrived in Jackson on May 13 and telegraphed Richmond that because the Federal forces had inserted themselves between Mississippi's capital and Vicksburg, he had arrived too late. Again Johnston and the Richmond authorities bogged down in a futile and stupefying dialogue about his command authority. Davis urged action, wiring that "we cannot hope for numerical equality and time will probably increase the disparity." But even then Johnston was quarreling with the Confederate War Department over how many men he actually did have.[13]

Johnston was spending this precious time trying to fashion for himself what Cooper calls "a cocoon of security." He neither tried any serious measure somehow to join forces with Pemberton or to thrust at Grant. Johnston could envision nothing but defeat. He believed he had been given an impossible assignment, and he wanted the record to show that. He responded to his wife's expressed concern about his reputation: "Don't be uneasy on the Subject." He asserted that everyone would realize that he did not have a very powerful army, and the people would judge him as a soldier "who discharge[d] his duty manfully & responsibly [and who] will always be respected." There was no legitimate way that the administration could blame him. Showing that he possessed at least a modicum of self-awareness, he told his wife, "I cannot be a great man, Nature & the President will it otherwise." As Cooper observes, "Here Johnston was half right. He did not possess the moral strength and self-confidence for greatness as a captain, but the president wanted nothing so much as for him to prevail." Throughout May and June, the situation in Mississippi "utterly frustrated Jefferson Davis. . . . Almost daily he sent dispatches to Johnston, Pemberton, or Governor John Pettus. . . . A harrowed Davis urged Pettus to call for a levy en masse. He even wired Johnston 'if my strength permitted I would go to you.' "[14]

On May 14, outnumbered almost five to one, Johnston withdrew northward. In brief fighting that afternoon, Grant seized the state capital. Then, leaving a minimal guard to protect against any sudden return by Johnston's men, Grant turned his main force toward Vicksburg.

Pemberton's army stood between the Federals and their goal. On May 16 Pemberton attempted to hold Grant east of the Big Black River by accepting what proved to be a major battle at Champion's Hill. It was bloody, described by one Union brigade commander as among "the most obstinate and murderous conflicts of the war." Still, the Confederates were outgeneraled, out maneuvered, and finally finessed. They elected to withdraw to the Vicksburg defenses, fighting delaying actions as they went.

On May 18 the siege of Vicksburg began. On May 31 Davis wrote to R. E. Lee: "Gen'l Johnston did not, as you thought advisable, attack Grant promptly, and I fear the result is that which you anticipated." He confessed that he could not avoid entertaining reproachful thoughts; "it would be unkind to annoy you" with them. As to Pemberton, "all the accounts . . . fully sustain the good opinion heretofore entertained of him."[15] How wrong he was: Pemberton was two steps above his maximal level of competence—the characteristic that was the great bane of the Confederate command structure.

From fire belched by gunboats on the river and from the constantly shooting troops in the encircling lines, the Vicksburg citizens and the defenders suffered onslaughts against nerve and will. The gunboats lobbed into the city huge mortar shells, some making impact holes as deep as seventeen feet. On the field, the situation was vividly described by Confederate corporal Ephraim Anderson: "The enemy continued to prosecute the siege vigorously. From night to night and from day to day a series of works was presented. Secure and strong lines of fortifications appeared. Redoubts, manned by well-practiced sharpshooters, . . . parapets blazoning with artillery crowned every knoll and practicable elevation, . . . and oblique lines of entrenchments, finally running into parallels, enabled the untiring foe to work his way slowly but steadily forward."[16]

At last, on July 4, 1863, after forty-seven days of siege, Pemberton and all but two of his officers agreed that they should surrender. The Federal losses amounted to 4,910 during the siege; the Confederates had suffered casualties amounting to 1,872. The captives numbered 2,166 officers, 27,230 enlisted men, and 115 civilians employed by the army. All were paroled save for 1 officer and 708 men, who preferred to go north as prisoners. The Rebel army also yielded its entire complement of equipment: 172 cannons, large amounts of every ammunition type, and some 60,000 shoulder weapons.

The loss of equipment was to be felt far beyond the confines of Vicksburg, however, for as Davis noted on July 20, in a letter to Reuben Davis: "By capture, purchase and manufacture we had accumulated a good supply but the fall of Vicksburg & Port Hudson has brought us not only the loss of all in the hands of the troops but by some strange mishap the arms sent to be forwarded to the trans-Mississippi were to a considerable extent taken to those places and lost also."[17]

Davis blamed Johnston; the president saw Pemberton largely as an innocent victim. The chief of ordnance Josiah Gorgas commented to Davis that Vicksburg had fallen from want of food. "Yes," replied Davis, "from want of provisions inside, and a general outside who wouldn't fight."[18] On July 8 Davis sent a somewhat snide telegram to Johnston:

> Your dispatch of 5th inst. received. The mistakes it contains will be noticed by letter. Your dispatch of 7th inst to Sec of War, announcing the disastrous termination of the siege of Vicksburg received the same day.
>
> Painfully anxious as to the result I have remained without information from you as to any plans proposed or attempted to raise the siege. Equally uninformed as to your plans in relation to Port Hudson I have to request such information in relation thereto as the Government has a right to expect from one of its commanding Generals in the field.[19]

Johnston's wife noted that "he laughs at [Davis's] rebukes," adding that he had told her that "no indignity from Davis could drive him from the service." Mary Chesnut reported at that time that "the president detests Joe Johnston, for all the trouble he has given him. And General Joe returns the compliment with compound interest. His hatred of Jeff Davis amounts to a religion. With him it colors all things."[20]

Davis elaborated on his concern over Johnston and also on his remaining high hopes in his July 20 letter to Reuben Davis:

> I hoped that the popular confidence in Genl: Johnston would have given him large reinforcements by the uprising of the people. Why was it not so? Did they want that inspiration which you invoke, the exhibition of boldness in action. . . . Much has been lost but with fortitude and energy the evil may be yet greatly repaired. Let every man who can bear arms rush to the rescue. Regard the army as a nucleus, not as the force on which the country depends solely for defense.

Let no man plead exemption or ask for repose. A short tour, a vigorous onslaught by the masses fighting for their firesides and their families, is what our necessity claims.[21]

There soon followed another bitter personal loss for the president, and for that too he ultimately placed blame on Johnston. Joseph Davis had moved the family possessions, including all of Jefferson's books and papers as well as his furnishings, into what he hoped were safe places. But a slave revealed the hiding places, and for two days hundreds of Yankee soldiers rummaged and plundered, taking boxes outside and smashing them open and throwing his letters and papers to the winds. Brierfield's carpets were cut into pieces as souvenirs and saddle blankets; the draperies were hauled into soldiers' tents. The men took delight in appropriating Davis's walking sticks and especially reveled in drinking his wine. One small portrait of Davis was repeatedly stabbed with knives until it disintegrated. For months afterward, various of Davis's personal letters were published as curiosities in Northern newspapers, and stories were rife about others of them being read publicly for entertainment of Union soldiers and citizenry.[22]

Davis still clung to his belief that Pemberton had made a keen sacrifice by coming South; and, although most everyone now condemned him, Davis had said "I can imagine nothing more unjust and ungenerous" than to suspect him because of his Northern birth. At least some Confederates agreed with Davis on this point. Though Pemberton resigned his lieutenant generalcy, he nonetheless later returned to uniform and selflessly served the Confederacy as a lieutenant colonel of artillery in Virginia. Nonetheless, and especially in the weeks and months following the fall of Vicksburg, the populace vilified him as a pariah, and criticism of him quickly turned into attacks on Davis as well.[23] Pemberton's usefulness was indeed ended, but Davis, unlike the general public, perceived the real failure was among his top generals. As he wrote later, "My confidence in General Johnston's fitness for separate command was now destroyed." He informed Lee of events in the West and remarked that there were those "who, faithful but dissatisfied, find an appropriate remedy in the removal of officers who have not succeeded. They have not counted the cost of following their advice. Their remedy to be good should furnish substitutes who would be better than the officers displaced."[24]

Even as late as August 27, Davis was still railing. In a letter to James M. Howry, an acquaintance who lived in Oxford, Mississippi, he wrote:

The disasters in Mississippi were both great and unexpected to me. I had thought that the troops sent to the State, added to those already there, made a force large enough to accomplish the destruction of Grant's army. That no such result followed may have been the effect of mismanagement, or it may have been that it was unattainable. An investigation of the causes of the failure is now in progress; though, as the misfortunes have already come upon us, it would afford me but little satisfaction to know that they resulted from bad Generalship and were not inevitable.[25]

The president, however, failed to sense public attitudes, let alone how to effectively try to mold them. One War Department official suspected that Johnston had "more real popularity in the country than the President has."[26] And that assuredly made deciding what to do with Johnston next a difficult if not also a chancy matter.

The embittered people of Vicksburg did not themselves again celebrate the Fourth of July until patriotic fervor during World War II induced them to do so. But the news that Vicksburg had fallen sparked jubilation throughout the North, especially when, just a few days later, Port Hudson, too, capitulated. Taking that place had cost nearly 10,000 Union men, dead, wounded, or physically impaired from disease or exposure, compared with the Southern losses of only 871. At last, however, "The Father of Waters," as President Abraham Lincoln gratefully proclaimed, again flowed "unvexed to the sea."

The fall of Vicksburg was a major turning point in the Civil War, particularly given that the Battle of Gettysburg concluded the day before the city fell, because it dealt such a tremendous psychological blow to the Southern populace. Furthermore, there was no parallel to what Grant had achieved in taking Vicksburg: "not Lee in the Gettysburg campaign, nor [Stonewall] Jackson in the Valley campaign, nor McClellan in the Peninsula campaign." Indeed it probably was Vicksburg that set the course for U. S. Grant's later elevation to lieutenant general, when on February 29, 1864, the Union revived that rank, and his concomitant appointment as general in chief.

Joseph Hooker's sophisticated Chancellorsville campaign had differed considerably from Ambrose Burnside's inept attack at Fredericksburg. Hooker had the numbers and the strategic understanding (supplied by Montgomery Meigs) to drive Lee's army south of the Rappahannock and so deprive it of food and forage from the productive area between that river and Richmond.

This concern highlighted the need for a defensive turning movement, which could threaten Hooker significantly and cause him to withdraw from the Rappahannock, thus securing the critical logistical area south of the river. Further, a movement north would open new sources for food and forage. If Lee could push his raid even into Pennsylvania, his army could subsist on Northern goods while his quartermasters and commissaries in Virginia brought in food and forage necessary to sustain the Confederate army in the coming winter.

Lee's successful turning movement in the Second Manassas campaign had provoked a defensive battle; that campaign's extension into Maryland had led to another unentrenched defensive battle at Antietam. Lee's planned thrust therefore prompted various generals such as James Longstreet, Wade Hampton, and others to speculate about what might occur next. The most attractive model for a perfect defensive battle was Fredericksburg. There the terrain had aided the defense, and Longstreet had introduced the use of field fortifications to give the defenders better cover while shooting at exposed attackers. Since that battle, the Army of Northern Virginia had developed a passion for entrenchment. Indeed, it had fortified much of the Rappahannock upstream from Fredericksburg.

Many students of the war have misread the Confederate high command's main motive for undertaking the Gettysburg campaign because of an incorrect and unsubstantiated claim made by the Confederate postmaster general, John H. Reagan, in his 1905 memoirs. Reagan asserted that the Gettysburg campaign was meant to be a distracting counteroffensive, alleviating the dismal Confederate situation in the western theater, where Vicksburg was under siege.

In truth, General Robert E. Lee much earlier had contemplated an attempt like the Gettysburg campaign. The Confederates having scored two major victories within the past five months by summer 1863, Southern morale and optimism were high, and Lee at last felt ready. His true motives for the Gettysburg campaign were pragmatic: he wanted to stymie any Federal plan for a summer campaign in Virginia; he hoped to crush the Federal troops then occupying the lower end of the Shenandoah Valley; and, similar to the situation in September 1862, when he had entered Maryland, he wished to give the people of Virginia a respite from the fighting and a chance to produce a good crop. Above all, he wanted to spend the summer maneuvering and absorbing supplies taken from the enemy in lower Pennsylvania. This was to be a prolonged raid; it was not an invasion because he had no intention of taking and holding territory.

The Federal force, under Major General Joseph Hooker, responded soon enough: rumors abounded that the Confederates were on the move. To check them out, Hooker ordered cavalry reconnaissances that resulted in battles, at Franklin's Crossing on June 5 and at Brandy Station on June 9. The Battle of Brandy Station was of considerable symbolic importance. It was a cavalry fight of the most classic kind: bugles sounding, sabers flashing, revolvers discharging, dust and smoke and confusion everywhere, and the outcome long in doubt. Both sides fought with great determination and skill. But there was no decisive outcome, really. By late afternoon both sides had had enough, and the Federals withdrew, unmolested. An unusually large number of the wounds sustained were caused by sabers, more than in any other Civil War battle. The significance of the battle was that before Brandy Station, Federal cavalry had been commonly regarded as notoriously inferior to the Confederate horse soldiers, but their performance here matched that of the Southerners, proving that the Yankee cavalry at long last had come of age.

Meanwhile, Colonel Arthur James Fremantle of the British Coldstream Guards was on his way to visit Lee's army when he stopped in Richmond on June 17. Judah P. Benjamin, "a stout dapper little man," took him to tea at the White House. Fremantle thought the president's face "emaciated, and much wrinkled," but his features good, "especially his eye, which is very bright, and full of life and humor. . . . He looked what he evidently is, a well-bred gentleman. Nothing can exceed the charm of his manner, which is simple, easy, and most fascinating." Fremantle, who had come all the way from the Rio Grande, noted in his journal: "Many people have remarked to me that Jefferson Davis seems in a peculiar manner adapted for his office . . . a brave man and a good soldier . . . the only man who . . . was able to control the popular will. People speak of any misfortune happening to him as an irreparable evil too dreadful to contemplate." Josiah Gorgas, too, had noted on July 2, when Davis's physician was "seriously alarmed about him," that his death "would indeed be the most serious calamity that could befall us."[27]

Lee's army was on the move. Long marches each day in high heat took a toll on his men, but on June 18 a cold front brought heavy rains, cooler temperatures, and even some sleet. Along the way, some Confederate elements encountered resistance, and a few clashes occurred, but Lee moved his army easily into Pennsylvania. His men then began a lavish ingathering of all manner of goods, including some blacks who supposedly were escaped slaves (they were sent south). The northeastern public panicked at Lee's advance, and Lincoln called out one hundred thousand militia; but in truth he remained calm, reasoning correctly that Lee was making not an invasion but a raid, and further, that his army would be vulnerable so far from its base. This reality presented the Union forces, Lincoln proclaimed, with "the best opportunity we have had since the war began."

But the days of June trickled away, and by his inaction Hooker exhausted the last shreds of confidence that Lincoln and General in Chief Henry W. Halleck might have had in him. On June 24 Hooker asked for orders, saying that except in relation to his own army, "I don't know whether I am standing on my head or feet." On June 27 Hooker was relieved, and one of his corps commanders, Major General George G. Meade, was given command of the Army of the Potomac. Lee astutely rated Meade as more able than Hooker but assessed that the change of command, coming at so critical a moment, would cause difficulty in the transition.

Thus, Lee continued the campaign in a mood of blinding exhilaration. He was ill, perhaps gravely so, having recently suffered a probable minor heart attack. Moreover, he was ill-served by his principal subordinates in the battle, truly missing the services of Stonewall Jackson.

Shortly before dawn on July 1, 1863, a chance engagement took place a few miles northwest of Gettysburg, the episode that gradually escalated into the full-scale, three-day Battle of Gettysburg. By midafternoon the Confederates had swept through and captured Gettysburg. But the beginnings of a Federal occupation of Culp's Hill induced General Richard Ewell to halt; he did not advance any farther, despite Lee's orders to secure the heights below the town "if practicable."

The first day of the battle ended as an apparent Southern victory. The Federal's Eleventh Corps had lost over four thousand men captured, and many more stragglers were in considerable disarray. But Lee still did not know precisely where the enemy forces were located; the absence of J. E. B. Stuart's cavalry was sorely vexing.

Lee ordered his two corps on the field to avoid any general engagement until Longstreet could bring his corps to join the main force. During the night, the whole Confederate army united, except for one infantry division and Stuart's cavalry, and lined up in position along Seminary Ridge. The Federal army consolidated and occupied the "fishhook" formed by Culp's Hill, Cemetery Hill, Cemetery Ridge, and the Round Tops.

On the second day of the battle, Lee's inclination initially was to renew the attack on the Federal right. But Ewell and Jubal Early talked Lee out of that plan, stating flatly that they could not take Culp's Hill or Cemetery Hill either, recommending instead that Longstreet assault the Round Tops. Longstreet was opposed to attacking at all, urging instead that the Confederate army stand on the tactical defensive. But Lee had his blood up and overruled Longstreet, ordering a main effort against Meade's south flank.

When Longstreet's assault finally did begin about 4:00 P.M., there still were but few Union troops situated on Little Round Top. Major General Dan Sickles, without permission, had moved his men forward, beyond their assigned sector, into what came to be called "Sickle's Salient," comprising the Peach Orchard, the Wheat Field, and the rock-strewn morass called Devil's Den, areas of bloody fighting and at times hand-to-hand combat.

Luckily for Meade, the Federal army's chief engineer, Brigadier General Gouverneur K. Warren, seized the initiative at Little Round Top and insisted that troops be rushed to occupy that critical hill. Two Federal brigades, those of Brigadier Generals Stephen H. Weed and Strong Vincent, got enough men onto Little Round Top in time to repulse the Confederate onslaught, not, however, before some tense and precarious moments passed.

There were several more hours of desperate and vicious fighting, especially in the Devil's Den and even more so in the Wheat Field, with Sickles's Third Corps being driven rearward, though fresh divisions from the Fifth, Sixth, First, and Twelfth Corps rushed in to plug the gaps. As night fell, the Confederate attacks fizzled. The Federals were quite secure, with numerical superiority and their left flank well covered.

During the night, despite Longstreet's vehement objections, Lee decided to assail the Federal center the next day. What could have made Lee feel that it was propitious for an assault wave to cross a little more than a mile of artillery-swept open ground, slightly uphill? How could this eighteen-to-twenty-minute rapid walk directly into fierce enemy fire be made and the attackers arrive with enough cohesion and vigor to break a line of determined defenders? Lee had tried both ends of the enemy position and found them too strong; perhaps they were weakest in the center. Further, Lee erroneously concluded, the Yankees were probably demoralized. And the plan was not without recent precedent. Only four years earlier, Napoleon III at Solferino had smashed the Austrian center, commencing with a heavy artillery bombardment and following it with a vigorous frontal assault.

The charge would be co-led by one of Longstreet's division commanders, Major General George H. Pickett, his own division making up about one-third of the assault force. Major General James J. Pettigrew would command the wounded Henry J. Heth's division and constitute the main assault force on the left. The name "Pickett's Charge," first used by the Richmond press, is a misnomer. In the bitter aftermath, Pickett himself came to wish that the attack had been named "Longstreet's Assault," for it was a dismal failure.

"Too bad . . . TOO BAD . . . OH TOO BAD," Lee cried out in anguish. "The task was too great," he told the survivors of the assault and admitted that it was his fault. And it indeed was Lee's fault: he had fought his worst battle and lost miserably. But to Lincoln's great disappointment, no concluding mop-up pursuit followed the great battle. Brigadier General John D. Imboden's Confederate cavalry covered the Army of Northern Virginia as it disengaged and limped south, crossing the Potomac River on July 14 and returning to Virginia. Ironically, in the meaningless rear-guard action at Falling Waters, West Virginia, the gallant General James Pettigrew, who had remained relatively unscathed in Pickett's charge, was mortally wounded.

It is too easy, and misleading, to think of the Civil War's final outcome as already decided by early July 1863. Which side ultimately would win was not at this point merely a matter of time. Lee's army was weakened significantly, to be sure; never again would it be able to assume the strategic offensive. And since Vicksburg fell July 4, soon leaving the Mississippi River under Federal control, the Confederacy was split geographically. Yet it still retained a remarkable degree of viable potency. It proved able to redeploy internally and scored a morale-boosting victory just a few months later at Chickamauga. The war continued.

The Battle of Gettysburg, even to those who participated in it, may not have been nearly the devastating turning point that many observers then and ever since have assumed. One of Longstreet's quartermaster officers, Edgeworth Bird, wrote to his wife: "We found the enemy posted in a terribly secure position. Now, I know, we should not have attacked him there on the high hills and mountains, but we did so." And who could be sure that Union morale and will would continue to support this bitterly hard-fought and costly war?

New foraging areas had been a major motive for the Gettysburg campaign, and ironically, logistical considerations hurried Lee's departure from Pennsylvania. To make the most of the fertile farms there, Lee had sent foragers out in all directions. But the presence of Meade's army precluded searching to the east, and the Pennsylvania citizenry and their militia made foraging difficult for the Rebels. Meade, in friendly country and with a railroad nearby, could wait as long as he pleased and had no intention of attacking Lee while he was in any strong position.

So Lee thus began his withdrawal, cautiously followed by Meade and his army. When the Rebel force reached the Potomac, Lee took up a position with the river at his back. If a battle of annihilation were possible, Lee was risking it. But it was not possible, and both Lee as well as Meade perceived that. And here, unlike his defenses at Antietam, Lee saw to it that his position was thoroughly entrenched. Meade declined to accommodate Lee, who had dared hope he could lure the Federals into an impossibly costly attack.

Keeping in mind his motives in making the advance into Pennsylvania, and its outcome, Lee evaluated the campaign as a "general success." He was satisfied to have been able to feed his army at enemy expense while the Virginia crops were brought in, free of molestation.[28]

Davis had been seriously ill during the final days of the Gettysburg campaign. He was unable even to go to his office, and his physician expressed grave concern. There were rumors in the War Department of his impending death. While the causes of his difficulties are unknown, William C. Davis suggests that they may have been induced by anxiety. In the face of impending disaster in Mississippi, and given that he believed in a success in Pennsylvania, Davis at last was ready to sack Joseph E. Johnston. But on July 9 arrived

Lee's bitter message that after three bloody days, he had been forced to retire.[29] Recognizing the significance and ultimate impact of the Battle of Gettysburg, Cooper observes, "would have to await time and perspective. . . . But from the moment he heard about the fall of Vicksburg, Davis understood full well its meaning."[30]

Summer 1863 proved to be an unhappy time for the Confederacy. Not only was it reeling from devastating defeats at Gettysburg and Vicksburg, but the people were also increasingly feeling the pangs of hunger and war-enforced hardship. Prices were spiraling, there were serious transportation problems, hoarding caused further shortages at marketplaces, wages were not keeping up with inflation, and there were inadequate relief programs in operation. A severe crisis in morale swept through many parts of the South. Quite naturally, many people cursed their central government.

"If we had won Gettysburg," Davis told an interviewer in 1881, "the moral effect of that victory would have brought peace." Although he appears to have had little input into Lee's plans for the Gettysburg campaign, Davis never publicly questioned his general's decisions. Davis explained in an 1877 letter that "a victory over the Army of Meade would have ensured peace on the only basis we were willing to accept it, Independence. To have maneuvered Meade into the defenses of Washington City would not have concluded the War, and there he would have been unassailable." He believed that "though not defeated at Gettysburg, we had suffered a check." Varina remembered that during the campaign Davis "was a prey to the acutest anxiety" and privately longed to be with Lee and the army.[31]

Following the disaster at Gettysburg, R. E. Lee offered to resign, but Davis regarded even himself as more expendable than Lee. Indeed, Davis wrote, "If a victim would secure the success of our cause, I would freely offer myself." This idea was an echo from the Book of Common Prayer's Communion Service, which offers the "full, perfect, and sufficient sacrifice" of Christ. Davis felt sure that "many of those most assailed" would be willing victims, too, "if their sacrifice could bring such reward." During the next winter Lee, in a discussion about the Gettysburg campaign with Henry Heth, confessed "as stupid a man as I am can see after a battle is over the mistakes that have been made."[32]

Yet the spirit of Lee's army was neither broken nor greatly crushed by the campaign. "No one in the army has had his confidence in Gen. Lee in the slightest degree impaired by the last month's campaign," wrote a correspondent on July 8. One veteran stated that "the Army would have risen in revolt if it had been called upon to give up General Lee." "Demoralized they never were," observed another correspondent, "only a little depressed by the toil and privation of the recent raid into Pennsylvania." These hardships, however, did cause a rise in the desertion rate.[33]

The Gettysburg campaign in no way diminished Davis's confidence in Lee. But Vicksburg did continue to enrage him as far as Johnston was concerned. Louis T. Wigfall noted in a letter to C. C. Clay on August 13, 1863, that Wigfall had been told the president "was almost frantic with rage if the s[l]ightest doubt was expressed as to [Lee's] capacity & conduct. He was at the same time denouncing Johnston in the most violent . . . manner & attributing the fall of Vicksburg to him & to him alone, regretting that he had been sent to the West & accusing himself of weakness in yielding to outside pressure."[34]

"The clouds are truly dark over us," Davis wrote to Theophilus Holmes on July 15. The twin disasters of Vicksburg and Gettysburg had pushed the Confederacy to the brink, and if there were any hope at all of retrieving its fortunes, the fledgling nation quite simply would have to resort to a stark escalation of the horrors of the war. The use of land and sea mines must be unleashed in full, even though many people regarded them as offensive, immoral, and unchivalrous weaponry. Other schemes were suggested for possible clandestine operations. Still, the president drew a line at some proposals even though he himself frequently claimed that the Union had abandoned any pretense of following the ordinary usages of warfare. He refused to countenance arson or indiscriminate destruction of civilian property, at least until 1865. And he refused to encourage several proposals that suggested either attempting the capture or the assassination of Lincoln and his cabinet, referring them to Secretary of War James Seddon without comment.[35]

12

THE MEANING OF THE WAR

In the immediate aftermath of Vicksburg and Gettysburg, Jefferson Davis had received a gift that lifted his spiritual feelings. To Eliza Cannon Cannon he wrote a letter on July 18, 1863, thanking her for a gift copy of the Holy Bible, which contained the books of the Apocrypha. This was, he said, "a portion of the scripture with which I had no previous acquaintance and I am truly obliged to you for the introduction."[1] This strange omission indicates inattention to the daily offices and the laxness of Dr. Charles Minnigerode's pre-Confirmation instruction of Davis, for the Apocrypha is prominently included in the Episcopal lectionary. Perhaps the new readings gave the president some measure of peace as he coped with myriad crises.

There were rebuffs on the diplomatic front. Repeated attempts to persuade Britain to reconsider its policy on intervention or recognition failed. This, combined with the painful reverses in Pennsylvania and Mississippi, made for a barren summer in the South. Davis finally concluded that maintaining a diplomatic mission in England was not only futile but embarrassing. In early August he ordered James Mason to leave London and thus ended efforts by the Confederacy to establish official relations with Britain.

Even before the catastrophes at Vicksburg and Gettysburg, in early June Vice President Alexander Stephens had written from his home in Crawfordville, Georgia, to Davis, suggesting that the time might be right for peace overtures to Lincoln's government. Stephens proposed that he be appointed to go to Washington on a mission to discuss prisoner policy, with the "hope that *indirectly* I could now turn attention to a general adjustment upon such basis as might ultimately be acceptable to both parties" and end the war. Stephens did make clear to Davis, however, that he "entertain[ed] but one idea of the basis of final settlement or adjustment; that is, the recognition of the sovereignty of the States and the right of each in its sovereign capacity to determine its own destiny." As William Cooper points out, "At this point Stephens was not scheming to undo Jefferson Davis's great cause."[2]

Davis immediately responded by wiring Stephens, asking him to come to Richmond. The vice president obeyed, and the two had several conferences late in June. Davis proposed that Stephens should go to Washington under a flag of truce. Stephens departed on board a steamer on July 3, unaware of what was happening that very day at Gettysburg. He got as far as Newport News, Virginia, where on the next day he did indeed under a flag of truce make his mission known. After waiting for two days, he got word from Washington that the Federals would not enter into any negotiations with him, and that in effect closed the matter. He could do nothing else save go back to Richmond. But along the way he made a few speeches, appealing to the people that they not lose heart in the face of the recent disasters. He also told his audiences that reconstruction was impossible and that "such an idea must not be tolerated for an instant."[3]

Throughout the ensuing torturous months President Davis faced growingly bitter political opposition. "Shrill invective continued to spew from his bitterest personal enemies." Always at the forefront, Robert Barnwell Rhett called the president "silly and disastrous." His fellow South Carolinian, James H. Hammond, concluded that Davis was "a Marplot always." Equally adept at scathing language, Robert Toombs damned Davis as a "stupid, malignant wretch."[4] Vice President Stephens shared his friend's vision but probably not "his vehemence or intemperance." Still, "even if he could not quite share in Toombs's radicalism, . . . Stephens heard similar sentiments from other close sources, including [his brother] Linton, who hinted in October that Davis might have to be removed by assassination if more democratic means failed."[5] Although hostility to conscription lay at the heart of antiadministration sentiment, it was not alone. Other issues, such as impressment and disappointment with the length of the war, were surely as important during this period; and martial law, suspension of the writ of habeas corpus, and the mounting specter of inflation were also responsible for widespread criticism of Jefferson Davis. Nevertheless, as Cooper observes, "This band of viciously hostile critics remained small." Indeed, "Across the Confederacy, Davis's dominant image was that of a patriot striving to secure the great goal—independence."[6]

Indicative of the crisis in manpower procurement and retention was Davis's proclamation of August 1, 1863, calling upon deserters to return to their units promptly and offering "general pardon and amnesty to all officers and men . . . now absent without leave who shall with the least possible delay return to their proper posts of duty" within twenty days. Davis included several reasons why men might have gone absent without leave, but he excluded any wish "to escape from the sacrifices required by patriotism." Indeed, instead, he praised the "courage and fortitude" that Confederate citizens had demonstrated during more than two years of frightful combat. As Davis iterated, the terrible war had become even more monstrous because of the enemy's "design to incite servile insurrection and light the fires of incendiarism wherever they can reach your homes." The Federals, he believed, had taken that barbarous route because "of their inability to prevail by legitimate warfare. . . . Fellow-citizens, no alternative is left you but victory or subjugation, slavery, and the utter ruin of yourselves, your families, and your country. . . . The victory is within your reach," he promised. All that was needed was for those "called to the field by every motive that can move the human heart" to join their comrades facing the foe.[7]

Though it bore the marks of mercy, the proclamation was actually a plea to recruit for the army and a telling admission that there were so many deserters that they formed an important part of the manpower pool from which the army would have to draw in order to maintain its strength.[8]

The situation was so unstable and uncertain in the western theater that Davis felt inclined to urge his best general, Robert E. Lee, to go there and take command. Lee, however, gave several reasons why he wished not to do so, and Davis demurred. Lee wanted to launch yet another offensive against the Army of the Potomac, but when Knoxville, Tennessee, fell early in September, the western situation was deemed so desperate that Lee agreed to send Longstreet's corps there. Again, Davis wanted Lee himself, but the general said no and Davis acquiesced.[9]

Increasing rumblings of discontent among the western generals had begun to reach Davis during the summer. Braxton Bragg's health was poor, inducing both Leonidas Polk and William J. Hardee to believe that he would not be in condition to command the army, should a battle come. Polk even went so far as to question Davis's judgment, despite their long and close friendship. "I am somewhat afraid of Davis," he had written in August. "I do not find myself willing to risk his judgment. . . . He is proud, self-reliant, and I fear stubborn." If only Davis would "lean a little less upon his own understanding" and a little more on "minds in the land from whom he might obtain counsel worth having," Polk complained. Of course, the vain bishop-general referred here to himself, although he truly was more a part of the problem than he was of the solution.[10]

Chickamauga proved to be the greatest victory achieved by the Confederate Army of Tennessee in the entire war, but according to Cooper, "it did nothing to change the personality of the army's high command." Indeed, "Instead of congratulating each other on a hard-fought victory, the generals blamed each other for not winning more stupendously, for not destroying the enemy." Bragg relieved Leonidas Polk, his senior subordinate and most bitter critic, along with another lieutenant general, for not obeying orders. Polk and

Longstreet entered into a rancorous letter-writing campaign. Following Polk's dismissal, the long-lived anti-Bragg faction of corps and division commanders drew up a petition to send to President Davis demanding Bragg's removal. Twelve general officers signed it.[11]

Davis left Richmond on October 6 to visit the war fronts in the western theater, hoping "to be serviceable in harmonizing some of the difficulties in Bragg's command."[12] Bragg simply did not comprehend the breadth or depth of his generals' opposition. As Davis traveled, "at each little town people clamored for the president, who spoke and shook hands to 'ovations.'" He arrived in Atlanta on October 8, taking time both there and then in Marietta publicly to praise Georgia's war effort, and his hearers greeted him with warm cheers. When Davis detrained at his destination, "hundreds of soldiers greeted him with cries for a speech. After mounting his horse, he raised his hat and shouted: 'Man never spoke as you did on the field of Chickamauga, and in your presence I dare not speak. Yours is the voice that will win independence of your country and strike terror to the heart of a ruthless foe.' Amid shouts, he waved and rode to Bragg's headquarters on Missionary Ridge, where he spent the night."[13]

After touring Chickamauga and conferring with Bragg and his principal subordinates, Davis authorized him to relieve Lieutenant General D. H. Hill, who had long been at odds with Bragg. Davis delivered a message to the Army of Tennessee on October 14, saying "though you have done much, very much yet remains to be done. Behind you is a people providing for your support and depending on you for protection. Before you is a country devastated by your ruthless invader."[14]

After three days of discussions, Davis made "an incredible decision." He kept Bragg in command of the army, even though he acknowledged "the painful fact" that "the harmony and subordination" essential for success were absent. Davis applied a bandaid of sorts by replacing Polk with Lieutenant General William J. Hardee. And, as Cooper points out, "Emphasizing how his perception of commitment could destroy reality, he even hoped to find a place in the army for Pemberton, at that moment perhaps the most discredited Confederate general." Because Davis possessed an absolute conviction that the Confederacy demanded commitment to cause over personal relationships, in this instance Cooper suggests it became "a mantra." He was clinging "to his creed despite a year of futility in pacifying the venomous relations menacing the Army of Tennessee." Cooper concludes that "the decision to retain Bragg as commanding general of the Army of Tennessee was disastrous."[15]

Davis then traveled west through Selma, Alabama, but not long afterward he sent Howell Cobb to visit the army for several days in order to report on the situation. It did not look promising. On October 24, U. S. Grant, who had arrived from Cairo, Illinois, to take command of the forces in Tennessee and north Georgia, succeeded in opening a supply line, the "cracker line," at Brown's Ferry on the Tennessee River, greatly relieving the Northern troops in "besieged" Chattanooga. Cobb wrote to Davis on November 6 with discouraging news: "I have just returned from Genl Braggs—headquarters—after spending several days with the army," and avowed that "my opinion about the state of things there, is not worth much." He explained, "It is very unfortunate that there does not exist more cordiality & confidence between Genl Bragg & Genl Longstreet." He also observed that "between Genl Bragg & Genl Buckner the feeling is bad," and "it would be well to yield to the application of Genl Buckner to be relieved—I venture to say the same in reference to Genl Cheatham." On the hopeful side, he indicated, "I left the army with the conviction that Bragg—had the confidence of his army—and that there was as much unity & good feeling & confidence as could be hoped for—or indeed expected—in an army like ours—composed of such a variety of dispositions." He concluded, "Genl Bragg—has a heavy job on his hand & needs every aid he can get."[16]

Meanwhile, in Virginia, on October 9 the Bristoe campaign began, lasting until October 22. Though it was a mild success for Lee's army in the aftermath of Gettysburg, it proved to be the last offensive operation that the Army of Northern Virginia could foment.

The situation in Tennessee did not bode well, and soon it turned tragic, with twin disasters: on November 24, the Battle of Lookout Mountain (or the Battle Above the Clouds), and on November 25, the Battle of Missionary Ridge. The war thus entered its end-game phases. What was well understood by myriad people, even if Davis continued to waver, was that Bragg had to go. The governor-elect of Alabama, Thomas H. Watts, wrote to Davis on November 27 to assure his continuing support and friendship but also to report "unpleasant as well as pleasant truths"; Bragg "is unfit to command . . . he has not the confidence of the Country—He has not the confidence of his Generals, nor the subordinate officers and the rank and file." Indeed, what happened at and after Chickamauga was egregious: "The golden opportunity was lost—criminally lost. . . . [Bragg] has not one particle of *common sense* and he has less *heart* than any man I ever knew." Watts concluded by asserting to Davis that "your own character for wisdom, prudence and patriotism has been impugned, because you still retain him in command."[17]

Soon, however, Davis was spared the agony of having to relieve Bragg: the defeat at Chattanooga at long last prompted Bragg to submit his resignation from field command. On November 30 General Samuel Cooper wired Bragg at Dalton, Georgia: "Your request to be relieved has been submitted to the President, who, upon your representation, directs me to notify you that you are relieved from command, which you will transfer to Lieutenant-General Hardee."[18] But Hardee's command was meant to be only an interim one; Davis was not inclined to elevate him to a full generalcy. Indeed, on December 7 Davis strongly considered sending R. E. Lee to Dalton to help reorganize the tarnished Army of Tennessee. But Lee did not wish to do that and so indicated during a visit that Davis asked for on December 8. After much soul-searching, for he did not wish to do so, Davis on December 16 decided to give the army command to his much-distrusted general, Joseph E. Johnston. There was hardly any other choice open to Davis at this time.

After its adjournment on May 1, 1863, Congress did not meet again until December, after the fall congressional elections. Those elections reflected rather disconcerting reality: "Rather than a simple contest between supporters and opponents of Jefferson Davis, the elections of 1863 became a crazy quilt of idiosyncratic, almost apolitical contests conducted before a largely apathetic though sometimes angry electorate."[19] Many voters just stayed home, but in some areas they turned out in droves to vote against incumbents and any challengers who supported unpopular war policies. In other parts of the Confederacy, voters showed a firm support for the cause. The Confederate elite was becoming increasingly fragmented among ultranationalists such as Louis Wigfall, Davis supporters, libertarians, various moderates, and political trimmers. A search was emerging for a political middle ground, and it soon became a dominant theme. But the rise of so many lesser-known political activists "only boded greater political instability."[20]

The instability was promoted by a rather jolting change of congressional membership, which reflected voters' unhappiness with Gettysburg, Vicksburg, and Chattanooga as well as their displeasure with the conduct of the civil government on conscription, habeas corpus, taxation, and impressment. Some of the former Secession Democrats of 1860–1861 found themselves rejected in favor of former Unionist Whigs. The extreme example was in North Carolina, where the delegation to the Confederate House of Representatives that had been three-fifths Democrat was suddenly changed to nine Unionist Whigs and only one Secession Democrat. About half the Unionist Whigs in the first House returned to serve in the second, and the same proportion applied to Secession Democrats. The new faces, however, were men who had been predominantly conservative in the secession crisis; two-thirds of them had been Unionist and three-fifths had been Whigs. The first House contained twice as many Secessionists and Democrats than Unionists and Whigs, but the balance in the second House was about even.

Leaving occupied areas out of consideration, in fifteen districts Unionists had replaced Secessionists, and Unionists remained in another sixteen. Most of these thirty-one districts were located in a chain in the Appalachian and Piedmont regions. Somewhat similar results occurred in races for governor-ships and state legislatures. For example, Whigs won the governor's chair for the first time in Alabama and Mississippi.[21] This does not mean that a peace movement had taken over the Congress, although a few of the new members did hope for a quick peace, even if on the basis of reconstruction of the Union. Basically it was a sign that many loyal Confederates now looked for future leadership to come from men who had been less rash in their behavior two and three years earlier. It also probably was an early sign of the development of primitive political parties beginning to emerge. One Alabama newspaper reported a "revival of party," with a "regular party organization" functioning in some counties in the central part of the state.[22] Meanwhile, a Conservative Party entered the lists in North Carolina, with some peace groups apparently performing party functions such as making nominations and calculated appeals to the public.[23]

The lame-duck fourth session of the First Congress had to meet the prob-lems made apparent by military disasters that occurred in summer and fall 1863. The stresses of the preceding months told heavily on the government, on public morale, and on Jefferson Davis. His December 7 message to the open-ing of Congress recited a long series of woes. But he claimed that at least the enemy "has been checked," and the army was "in all respects in better condition than at any previous period of the war." Nevertheless, he called for even more troops. He desired to strengthen the Confederacy, he said, "by restoring to the Army all who are improperly absent, putting an end to substitution, modifying the exemption law, restricting details, and placing in the ranks such of the able-bodied men now employed as wagoncrs, nurses, cooks, and other employees as are doing service for which the negroes may be found competent."[24]

Substitutes had long been thought to be more likely to desert than other soldiers. A year before Davis's message, a commander of a camp of instruc-tion in Virginia complained of the desertion of conscripts and paid special attention to the tendency of substitutes to do so. Four-fifths of the troops in his camp were substitutes who deserted within twenty-four hours of their arrival. He urged that "either an example should be made of them or the principal be in some manner held responsible."[25] Such desertions had become so frequent that "dissatisfaction has been excited among those who have been unable or unwilling to avail themselves of the opportunity thus afforded of avoiding the military service of their country."[26] Advertisements appeared in prominent newspapers, and dishonest substitute brokers charged exorbitant fees for their services. Many of the stand-ins came from the dregs of Southern society and soon deserted. Some commanders refused to accept substitutes into their ranks because morale problems seemed always to accompany the surrogate soldiers. Senator Allen T. Caperton of Virginia reported that the price for a substitute ranged between a mere five hundred dollars to a truly dear sum of three thousand.[27] Those who agreed to serve as substitutes were frequently older men, who were often not up to the physical challenge of active campaigning.

Some persons argued, as many congressmen did, that to take into the army those who had furnished substitutes would be a violation of a contract. Senator James L. Orr of South Carolina argued that it would be an ex post facto law, and "the government had accepted the substitutes without condition. If a substitute deserted the remedy of the Government was against the substitute," not the person who had procured him. The deserting substitute might be caught and shot. If he were returned to the army, and the principal had in the meanwhile been drafted, the army would have an extra man.[28] Senator Edward Sparrow claimed he had evidence "that substitutes as a rule would and did desert," which was "a fraud upon the Government."[29] Men like Sparrow agreed with Davis that it was reasonable enough that if a man's substitute deserted, he was again liable for service himself.

As for exemptions, Davis sought to make the system more equitable and efficient by enrolling all eligible men into the army and detailing essential workers back to their civilian jobs. Indeed, many of these jobs could be done by workers over forty-five; Davis even desired to raise the conscript age limit in order to mobilize the manpower of the older middle-aged men more efficiently. Guards, units searching for deserters, and soldiers working in the various bureaus could be older men, and many white cooks, teamsters, and laborers could be replaced by blacks, a proposal Davis urged Congress to legislate.[30]

In conclusion, Davis suggested the creation of an Invalid Corps, to be composed of men no longer fit for field duty but fully capable of desk jobs or other sedentary duty.[31] Congress responded. In the closing days of 1863, substitution was ended,[32] and a week later those who provided substitutes were made eligible for enrollment.[33] An Invalid Corps was established in February 1864.[34]

As for Davis himself, in the waning months and weeks of 1863 he seems to have turned more and more to his religion for comfort. He went often to church. The tender, typically hidden, side of his nature was more manifest. He pardoned criminals and commuted death sentences. Ever more under widespread public censure because of the hardships suffered by the populace, Davis exuded mercy even as he himself ever more needed it. It was a cold, cheerless Christmas in Richmond. " 'The Ham the Lamb the Jelly & the Jam' are now of the past," a friend told Davis. "It is now 'Small Hominy sometimes called Grits.' " The people were tiring and beginning to lose heart.[35]

Confederate strategy need not have failed. America's Vietnam experience should dispel premature conclusions about the invincibility of overwhelming numbers and resources; the weaker side can attain victory. It is a matter of utilization and execution. The Confederacy almost succeeded. Jefferson Davis gradually improved as generalissimo, but he peaked late in 1863, and thereafter his competency deteriorated. The key to victory lay in a national application of ideas developed by Napoleon Bonaparte and Frederick the Great, ideas studied in America albeit through a filter of imperfect perceptiveness, by Pierre G. T. Beauregard. It was he who could have been the architect of success had not circumstances destroyed his opportunity. Yet, Grady McWhiney has pointed out, Beauregard and Davis had come to hate each other.

Davis needed coordination and a staff with a capable chief. Instead, he labored in a haze of snarled or inadequate networks. He never escaped tension and discord, standing squarely in the middle between his powerful and trusted adviser on the one hand, Robert E. Lee, and the "western concentration bloc" on the other. Lee made valuable but provincial and costly contributions to the Confederate war effort; indeed, it is not a distortion to equate him with Frederick the Great, but "unfortunately for the Confederacy, he was only a Virginia Frederick."[36]

The western concentration bloc was composed of four groups: the Abingdon-Columbia, the anti-Bragg, the Kentucky, and the Beauregard. For whatever varied reasons, they sagaciously desired to use the troops dispersed throughout the western theater to launch a series of concentrations along interior lines so as to allow effective operations against the most vulnerable Union armed forces, as was partially accomplished in late summer 1863 at the Battle of Chickamauga. The ideas of the western concentration bloc did prevail, but they were belatedly adopted, ill-executed, and never unreservedly pursued. This shortcoming, coupled with neglect of logistics, failure to devise a method of rapid identification and use of the most capable combat leaders, and removal and reassignment of officers who had risen beyond their level of competence, brought about the war's final results.

As early as the fall of Fort Sumter, many Southern blacks volunteered to serve in the Union army. President Abraham Lincoln long resisted this and in March 1862 even overturned an order issued by Major General David Hunter that would have freed all the slaves in Georgia, South Carolina, and Florida. At first, the Union's official policy was to cooperate in the return of escaped slaves to their owners, but Major General Benjamin F. Butler refused to do this, instead giving them shelter within his lines. When asked if he were harboring escaped slaves, he replied, "No indeed—what I am holding is *contraband of war.*" Forever after, liberated slaves were referred to as contraband.

The first official black unit organized by the Federal government was the First South Carolina Volunteers (later renamed the Thirty-third U.S. Colored Infantry), composed of liberated slaves and commanded by Colonel Thomas Wentworth Higginson, who later wrote *Army Life in a Black Regiment.* The Union promised automatic and permanent freedom from slavery to all blacks who enlisted in the Northern army and to their families. A series of significant engagements in mid-1863 brought black combatants considerable public notice and recognition for their toughness and dedication: an assault on May 27 against Port Hudson, Louisiana; a battle at Milliken's Bend, Louisiana, on June 7, which proved one of the most hard-fought engagements of the entire war, resulting in 30 percent of the blacks being killed or wounded; and on July 18 a grand assault on Battery Wagner, on Morris Island in Charleston Harbor.

Davis was disgusted and outraged over the North's option to use blacks as soldiers. The previous November 26 he had sent identical letters to each of the Confederate governors, in which he suggested that the federal government was trying "thus to inflict on the noncombatant population the horrors of a servile war."[37] Now it was a matter of facing reality: blue-clad black troops were on the move.

That the Federals had managed to foment a significant threat against Charleston so soon after the loss of Vicksburg and the disaster in Pennsylvania was unexpected bad news for Davis, and his nerves were quite visibly frayed. It seemed that Beauregard had been caught napping, and Davis had Seddon send him a stiff reprimand. But Davis was quickly able to compose himself again, and he received the spy Rose O'Neal Greenhow and dispatched her on a secret mission to Europe. When Battery Wagner did not immediately fall, the war clerk J. B. Jones noted in his diary that "the President is quite amiable now. The newspaper editors can find easy access and he welcomes them with a smile."[38]

The assault on Battery Wagner became one of the Civil War's most famous episodes. It was commemorated in the movie *Glory* and is described in Peter Burchard's *One Gallant Rush* and Luis F. Emilio's *A Brave Black Regiment* (the 1990 edition is more helpful). No black regiment attracted as much public interest as did the Fifty-fourth Massachusetts. Its young commander, Colonel Robert Gould Shaw, came from a prominent family, one quite politically active and also deeply involved in the antislavery crusade. The ranks of the regiment were made up of volunteers, both free blacks and runaway slaves. Also serving in it were two sons of the most eminent black American of the era, Frederick Douglass.

In their desperate and unsuccessful attempt to capture Battery Wagner, which never was taken (the Confederates elected to abandon it on September 6, 1863), the Fifty-fourth Massachusetts paid a fearful price. The spy known as Rebel Rose, Rose O'Neal Greenhow, was in the St. Michael's Church tower, with General Beauregard's permission, and could see the assault. In a letter to Jefferson Davis written on July 19, 1863, she said that the fire from Fort Sumter was deadly and accurate, "the slaughter of the Yankees was terrific," with losses estimated at fifteen hundred; the Rebels lost about one hundred. "The storming party put the negro regiment in front and they have fought with desperate valor."[39]

The task of taking Battery Wagner was nearly an impossible one. The battery was a huge and powerful earth fort built across the narrow neck of Morris Island at the harbor's mouth. No flanking approach was possible: ground troops had no avenue of assault but a frontal one. Unobstructed fields of fire were buttressed by massive emplantations of land mines.

The Confederate inventor, General Gabriel Rains, had been sent to Battery Wagner to give special attention to the defenses and to direct the deployment of torpedoes (as exploding mines were called during the Civil War) equipped with his new and quite potent Rains fuse. Sand offered perfect camouflage, completely obscuring the shallow emplacement of deadly devices detonated as if by a hair trigger.

Though some of the attackers carried the regimental colors up to the parapets, they could not penetrate, nor could they stay. The survivors were forced to retreat. The Fifty-fourth Massachusetts lost over 40 percent of their number, including their popular young colonel. Shaw was buried in a mass grave with the black troops who fell with him. Union forces sent under a flag of truce a request that Shaw's body be returned, for a military funeral. Some Confederate general reportedly replied to the emissary, "We have buried him with his niggers." Many Northerners resented this remark, but Shaw's father considered it an honor for his son to be in a mass grave with the brave black soldiers and asked that it remain untouched. Shaw and his men are honored by a magnificent memorial on the edge of the Boston Common (although the injustice of omitting the names of the black soldiers from the memorial was corrected only in recent years), and a number of poems have been inspired by the fate of the Fifty-fourth.

> They buried him with his niggers!
> A wide grave should it be.
> They buried more in that shallow trench
> Than human eye could see.
> Ay, all the shames and sorrows
> Of more than a hundred years
> Lie under the weight of that Southern soil
> Despite those cruel sneers.

The Fifty-fourth Massachusetts demolished all the doubts and uncertainties about whether blacks could be good soldiers. Beyond question, they had proved their worth as combatants, and a tremendous increase of their numbers in service followed. Blacks eventually took part in 449 Civil War engagements, 39 of them major ones.

Blacks were hugely supportive of the Union war effort. More than 34,000 Northern blacks served in the army, over 15 percent of the 1860 free black population. The precise total of all black troops cannot be ascertained; an officially recorded number is 178,892. If this is correct, some 80 percent of the black troops were former slaves. Some 7,000 blacks became noncommissioned officers. Black troops eventually made up one hundred twenty infantry regiments, twelve heavy-artillery regiments, ten batteries of light artillery, and seven cavalry regiments, constituting by the end of the war slightly more than 12 percent of the Union's land forces. Quite significantly, the number of black troops in the Union army toward the end of the war equaled approximately the total number of Confederate soldiers still present for duty, a ratio that had profound psychological impact on Southerners.[40]

The South, in its outrage over the North's use of black troops, at first promised that those who might be captured would not be accorded any rights as prisoners of war. Quite understandably, men from black units had a morbid fear of falling captive; and, vice versa, Southern soldiers especially feared becoming prisoners of blacks. On May 1, 1863, the Confederate Congress passed a resolution declaring that all white officers captured while serving with black troops were summarily to be put to death or otherwise punished at the discretion of a court-martial for inciting insurrection, and the black soldiers themselves were to be turned over to the states in which they were captured, to be punished according to state law.[41] Both sides threatened retaliation in kind against any atrocity inflicted on a prisoner. In bitter frustration the South eventually backed down from making good its threats against black prisoners or their white officers. A trump card was added in the person of Confederate Brigadier General W. H. Fitzhugh Lee (R. E. Lee's second son), who was captured while recuperating from a wound he had suffered at Brandy Station on June 9, 1863. He was not exchanged until March 1864.

The issue of race aside, to be a prisoner of war was, as it always is, a fearsome experience. Even though the people of both sides thought that the other side tortured and otherwise mistreated prisoners, neither side actually had any systematic policy of maltreatment. The problems sprang primarily from exposure, overcrowding, and disease, though sometimes—in those days of primitive medicine—they sprang also from poor medical care and malnutrition. At one time or another the United States captured 462,634 men, the Confederacy 211,411. The Union paroled on the field 247,769, and 25,976 died in its prisons; the Confederacy issued 16,668 field paroles, and 30,218 died in its prisons. The mortality rate was slightly more than 12 percent in the Northern prisons, and it was 15.5 percent in Southern prisons.

Although the South's prisons became the more infamous in history, it was the North at the outset that inclined toward denial of prisoner-of-war rights. Because the Lincoln administration insisted that the Union was inviolable, it therefore refused to agree that captives it might take were anything other than traitors. First Manassas changed that. There the Confederates captured about 50 Union officers and approximately 1,000 enlisted men. Neither side could afford callously to mistreat prisoners without the other side's taking reprisal. The main problem, which continued to recur throughout the war, was the unforeseen taking of large numbers for whom there were inadequate prison facilities. The January–February 1862 Burnside expedition against Roanoke Island resulted in the capture of 2,500 prisoners, and when, on February 16, 1862, Grant seized Fort Donelson he took 15,000 prisoners. Nothing more than minuscule preparations had been made to receive and properly incarcerate such large numbers of men.

Life often was rough in the prisons of both sides. The South, with its extreme heat, and much the poorer materially—particularly so with the passing of time—in many instances was unable to maintain healthful conditions. The most notorious of the Civil War prisons was located at Andersonville, Georgia, a huge outdoor stockade occupied between February 27 and September 5, 1864, by an ever-increasing number of unfortunate Federal inmates.

There are 12,912 known graves there, but some estimates place the total number of deaths at this prison much higher.[42] The North, too, sometimes had
heinous problems in prisons, mainly due to overcrowding. (It has been said
that the Pulitzer Prize–winning novelist MacKinley Kantor, who wrote *Andersonville,* might just as ably have written an anti-Northern study, *Elmira.*) Many
people believed that Southerners deliberately mistreated the prisoners they
held, a belief that virtually induced a war psychosis in the North. Popular
clamor demanded tougher treatment of the captive Southerners, and often-
times officials acquiesced, especially in punitive reduction of food rations.

Informal arrangements were sometimes made between particular generals to exchange or parole prisoners. In July 1862 Confederate Major General
Daniel Harvey Hill and Union Major General John A. Dix completed negotiations for an exchange cartel. Never completely satisfactory in its operation, since disputes occurred, the cartel nevertheless did result in many
thousands of officers and men being paroled and exchanged. On December
17, 1863, owing especially to dissatisfaction with respect to exchanges of
black troops and their officers, the North in essence repudiated the Dix-Hill
cartel and appointed Major General Benjamin F. Butler as a special agent of
exchange to oversee such matters in the future. But Confederates refused, as
a rule, to deal with Butler, ostensibly because of his infamous "woman order,"
issued when he commanded Union occupation forces in New Orleans. Nevertheless, special exchanges continued to be carried out, from time to time by
local commanders, until April 1864, when General U. S. Grant ordered the
cessation of further exchanges, realizing that the North with its much larger
manpower resources could stand allowing ever larger numbers of captives to
languish in prison much more readily than could the South. It was still
another way that the North wore the South down. But it resulted in conditions within the prisons becoming even more overcrowded and unhealthful
for those unfortunates who simply had to wait out the war while languishing
in captivity.[43]

Beginning in a significant degree by mid-1863, U.S. greenback paper dollars permeated the Confederacy, brought in by invading Federals and by prisoners of war, and they began to compete with the Confederate money. Both
were a fiat currency—backed only by the promise of a government; but the
greenbacks early began to circulate at a premium. In the period after the Battle of Gettysburg, the rate went up, and it took four Confederate dollars to buy
one greenback dollar. As the situation worsened, finally in 1864 the Confederate Congress made it illegal for people to "buy, sell, take, circulate or in any

manner trade in any paper currency of the United States" unless they lived behind Federal lines. Ironically, however, because the Federal money could be used in shady transactions on the frontier, the Confederate government Treasury eagerly seized eventually whatever greenbacks it could get.[44]

Inflation had a major impact on Southerners, of course, but the conflict affected domestic life in many ways. Like all wars, the Civil War hurried up marriages. A Richmond newspaper editor, commenting on the fact that marriages in that city had increased 90 percent during the war, observed that the people were "evidently preparing for a long war, and taking wise precautions against any serious decrease of population."[45] Social life went on much as usual. Children in Rebel families were told that Santa Claus, a true Confederate, "had slipped across the icebound blockade of the Potomac" or that he had "run the gauntlet of the Wilmington blockaders in his gossamer ship."[46]

Holidays were observed. Particularly popular in the Confederacy were the Fourth of July, Halloween, and Washington's Birthday. Valentine cards, however, were sacrificed because the times were "too stern, the mails too uncertain, and gilt-edged, and flowered and embossed stationery too expensive in these blockade days, to admit of such indulgences."[47] Social and cultural activities continued. The theater was popular. Reading was widely indulged in— Victor Hugo's *Les Miserables* became a best-seller in the South. There were musicales; minstrel shows; and tableaux vivants, often thrown as fund-raisers; and there were innumerable private parties and dances. President Davis and his wife often held their own social affairs and official receptions. Later in the war, parties were often leaner occasions, with few or no refreshments, sometimes called "starvation parties." Excursions in boats down the James River were very popular. Occasionally military units even put on tournaments, mainly to entertain ladies who visited the troops.[48]

Smoking tobacco was enormously popular. Some people indulged in cigars, but nearly all smokers used pipes. (Cigarettes were universally regarded as effeminate until World War I.) For men, hunting and boxing were widespread favorite sports. And in the words of Ellis Merton Coulter: "War breeds both heroism and decadence. Gambling, drunkenness, thieving, demagogism, faultfinding, carping criticism, and general moral disintegration suggest the darker side."[49]

Drinking alcohol was as widespread among the populace as it was among the soldiers. Saloons were everywhere. At times there was a whiskey shortage, but generally it remained available. In 1864 the Confederate government made it illegal to sell liquor by the drink, but clever saloon keepers resorted to half-pint bottles that made drinking easy for anyone who wished to do so.

It was once facetiously asserted that men were "cutting off their mustachios to keep from losing a tenth part of every drink by capillary attraction."[50]

The Civil War soldier, on both sides really, was typically a young man away from home for the first time—and except when wounded, suffering hardship, or in battle—having one hell of a grand time.[51] Many of them were lusty, whoring, drinking, gambling, cussing, tobacco-chewing fellows. And they sang songs, some joyful some bitter sweet, in the camps.

> We're tenting tonight on the old camp ground,
>   Give us a song to cheer our weary hearts,
> A song of home,
>   And friends we love so dear,
> We've been tenting tonight on the old camp ground
>   Thinking of days gone by.
> Of the loved ones at home that give us the hand,
>   And the tear that said "good-by."
> We are tired of war on the old camp ground,
>   Many are dead and gone,
> Of the brave and true we've left their homes,
>   Others been wounded long.

During the second half of the war, when things looked increasingly bleaker, many of the Rebels chose to desert. By the war's end there were well over one hundred thousand deserters roaming about in various locations throughout the South. Even Mark Twain admitted to voluntary resignation. For less than a month he had been a second lieutenant in the Marion Rangers, a company of Missouri Confederate militia. His adventures found their way into a short story, "The Private History of a Campaign That Failed." His company shot at a man, whether enemy or not they never knew. Twain fired his gun along with the others, and the man was killed; Twain feared it might have been his bullet that did the job. The enthusiasm of the company for fighting then quickly dissipated, and Twain decided that he had had enough. He learned very little about soldiering except what a retreat was like, and of retreats he learned quite a lot. He wrote years later, "I know more about retreating than the man that invented retreating." His story illustrates the confusion on both sides during the early weeks of the conflict, and as he learned much later, it turned out that the Union troops from whom he was retreating were led by Ulysses S. Grant.[52]

Confederate venereal disease records are quite incomplete—the Confederacy stopped keeping them after 1862—but Bell I. Wiley has found various evidence that suggests the rate was comparable to that of the North. Eighty-two of every one thousand white men in the Federal army were affected with syphilis, gonorrhea, or orchitis. The rate for black troops was somewhat less: seventy-seven per one thousand.[53]

The most popular pastime in every city, North as well as South, was to spend time with women. One New Hampshire soldier wrote home from Virginia: "We cannot get any thing here but f____ king and that is plenty." The *Memphis Bulletin* reported on April 30, 1863, that "our city is a perfect beehive of women of ill fame. The public conveyances have become theirs by right of conquest. . . . Memphis is the great rendezvous for prostitutes and 'pimps.' When a woman could ply her vocation no longer in St. Louis, Chicago, or Cincinnati, she was fitted up in her best attire and shipped to Memphis, and in more cases than one to prevent the 'package' from being miscarried, was accompanied by gentlemen with the insignia of rank."[54]

Prostitution became such a vexing problem in Nashville that 150 girls were rounded up and loaded onto a military transport and sent to Louisville and Cincinnati, but in both of those cities when officials found out what had happened, the girls were shipped back to Nashville.[55] Controlled prostitution did not exist in the United States before the Civil War, but by 1863 both Nashville and Memphis required prostitutes to register with the local health departments, submit to medical examinations, and carry to show on demand dated and signed documents attesting to their current condition.[56]

One Confederate soldier visiting Danville, Virginia, went "over the River one night" to the red light district. "The Reynolds Gals are going it at 25 cents per round & *dog throwed in*." God only knows and one shudders to imagine what the dog did, but the soldier added, "That is a promising prospect, isn't it? There is a good chance for a man to get *vaccinated* if he has anything to do with them."

Racy pictures were as commonly available during the Civil War as they are today. It should not be greatly surprising that photographers took nude and partially nude pictures: artists for centuries had been painting the unclad female form. The Chattanooga *Daily* advertised:

Photographs—Rich, Rare, and Racy

A very beautiful picture of the handsomest women in the world; a peculiar rich-colored photograph in oil, taken from life; beautiful to behold. This is really a magnificent picture, a perfect gem. She is a bewitching beauty. Price 50 cents. Sent free by mail in a sealed circular envelope.

The sex researcher Alfred Kinsey and his team of collaborators collected a number of Civil War–era sexually oriented pictures, which remain today at Indiana University.

Of course not all, indeed far from all, the boy-girl relations during the Civil War were of a sordid nature. The soldiers loved the company of women, whenever they could get it. Older ladies universally had a mother image among the soldiers and often were called by that title. Any favor or attention from younger women was always prized. "Lorena" was an extremely popular love song:

> The years creep slowly by, Lorena,
>   The snow is on the grass again;
> The sun's low down the sky, Lorena,
>   The frost gleams where the flowers have been,
> But the heart throbs on as warmly now,
>   As when the summer days were nigh;
> Oh! the sun can never dip so low,
>   Adorn affection's cloudless sky.
>
> A hundred months have passed, Lorena,
>   Since last I held thy hand in mine;
> And felt the pulse beat fast, Lorena—
>   Though mine beat faster far than thine;
> A hundred months—'twas flowery May,
>   when up the hilly slope we climbed,
> To watch the dying of the day,
>   And hear the distant church bells chime.[57]

The next most popular amusement after sex was drinking alcohol. It was such a problem that it drew the attention of the Confederate Congress. Recognizing that total control of alcoholic consumption was probably impossible, the Congress aimed at urging the officers to set good examples. All officers found guilty of drunkenness were to be cashiered or suspended from service or publicly reprimanded, depending on the seriousness of the incident.[58] "Mollie, tell your paw that if I had his brandy out here, I could with ease sell it for 40 dollars per gallon," one Confederate soldier wrote to his wife from camp. "Some men will give the last dollar for a drink of liquor." Almost any major event, especially a battle or a review, was the occasion for a big drinking spree. The easiest way to obtain alcohol was from the medical personnel, who always had an ample supply of it. Alcoholism was highest among this group.

Military life was not all vice. There were great religious revivals on various occasions. Bible societies distributed thousands of religious books and tracts; many of the men's diaries reveal that they meditated on God and both hoped and prayed that He was on their side—or perhaps, rather, that they were on His.[59]

But few indeed were those Rebels who never gambled. It has been said that if the crucifixion of Jesus Christ had taken place in Richmond in 1863, some Johnny Reb, like the Roman soldiers at the foot of the Holy Cross, would have been the first to roll dice for the seamless robe. The forms of gaming ranged widely. Even lice, the most common camp pets as well as the most common body tormentors of Civil War soldiers, were raced against each other. One man who had become well known for having the fastest louse was eventually found out: he used a china plate for the races, which he heated in advance of the contest. Gambling was unquestionably the favorite pastime in the field—unless, of course, female companionship could be had.[60]

Women of all classes experienced great personal and physical hardship during the war. The poor, of course, bore the brunt of it. The impoverished residents of towns and cities suffered the most. States, counties, municipalities, churches, and philanthropic societies provided some relief, but it was never enough.[61]

As a general rule women who lived in invaded areas suffered greater hardship than those who lived in the interior. Part of this hardship was due to the great dislike and fear that Southern women had for Union soldiers. Rape was rare during the Civil War but it did occur. Surprisingly, more black slave women than whites were raped, and one modern scholar has speculated that this was an act of domination—to use the Southern white's human property in wantonly degrading sexual activities.

The women who stayed at home, when obliged to confront the invaders, did so in various ways. Some women greeted the Yankees with cordiality, either because they did espouse some genuine Unionist sympathies or because they hoped by doing so to obtain various favors. Most Rebel women, however, truly hated the Yankees and could not bring themselves even to pretend friendliness. Nannie Haskins, a Clarksville, Tennessee, teenager, wrote in her diary early in 1863: "I never see [a Yankee] but what I roll my eyes, grit my teeth, and almost shake my fist at him, and then bite my lip . . . and then turn away in disgust." Another young woman in Fredericksburg, Virginia, wrote to a friend in May 1863, after the Federals had retreated through the town following the Battle of Chancellorsville, "My only amusement was watching them bury their dead."[62]

In New Orleans and other Southern cities occupied by Federal forces, women cursed the Yankees, cheered for Jeff Davis, pretended to be nauseated whenever they encountered Union soldiers on the streets, and stepped off sidewalks to avoid being close either to them or to the Union flag. Some women doused the Federals with dishwater or with the contents of their chamber pots, poured from their rooms above streets when the men passed.[63]

The verbal clashing between Southern women and Yankee soldiers is amusingly illustrated by an occurrence in West Tennessee in July 1862. Private William H. Parkinson of Illinois wrote to his family:

> As we came out . . . from Jackson, we met quite a nice young lade, with a young Gent riding by her side. Nevins [the Colonel] spoke to her very polite & she Hurrahed for Jeff Davis. He paid no attention to it. As she passed on the boys spoke very polite to her, raising their hats, but she answered in the same way. As she was passing a sergeant in the rear of the Reg. he was just in the act of raising his hat to her, when *she belched out* "Hurrah for Jeff Davis." He did not raise his hat, but said, "By G____d Madam, *your cunt* is all that saves your life."[64]

Many women all over the South organized into groups to raise money. Special projects to outfit gunboats were popular. Many valued personal possessions were raffled off, including jewelry, china, silverware, watches, vases, almost anything that could be spared. In Charleston a doll called "Daughter of the Confederacy" was sold. Such efforts paid off: the Georgia women paid for the CSS *Georgia,* the South Carolina women paid for the construction of the *Palmetto,* and the CSS *Virginia,* also financed by women, was launched in June 1863.[65]

The president faced some tough challenges from various state governors. The gravest trouble spots were North Carolina and Georgia, where the governors were staunch opponents of many of Davis's policies. The ironic reality was that Davis, the great prewar champion of sectional and local rights, now found himself compelled to act as perhaps the leading nationalist in the Confederacy. He tried to court good relations with Governor Zebulon Vance of North Carolina, but he achieved only mixed results. Vance would quarrel with him over appointments and commissions, both within and outside the state. The real fight festered over suspension of habeas corpus. Joseph E. Brown of Georgia was the meanest of Davis's gubernatorial opponents. Seemingly a humorless controversialist, savoring argument for its own sake and enjoying goading the president into what he called an "exhibition of temper," Brown was just the kind of man to clash with someone like Jefferson Davis.[66]

But state rights had another aspect. It was indeed a problem that tended to rip the Confederacy apart, as the governors' clashes with Davis and the central government illustrate. The obverse of these problems, however, was that the states served as alternate centers of power and often provided important supplements to the work of the Confederate government. In Alabama, for example, Governor John Gill Shorter did his best to help the Confederate government with the ticklish problem of slave impressment. He impressed labor to work on fortifications, trying to placate planters while meeting the needs of Confederate defense in his state. He often arranged state payment for the slaves' owners and claimed to have impressed ten thousand slaves by August 1863. His work was so unpopular that many Alabama impressment agents quit their jobs; and after the Confederacy passed the impressment law of March 26, 1863, Shorter was tempted to give up his efforts and let the Confederate government take the heat. According to Malcolm C. McMillan, however, "He was so involved by that time that he apparently felt it was a matter of honor and patriotism to continue." Shorter himself attributed his defeat for reelection to his strong efforts to support the Confederate government by impressment of black labor. In Shorter's personal opinion, it was "the strongest element which carried the state so largely against me." He also worked hard to help supply Alabama troops in the field, established one Alabama hospital in Richmond and another in Mississippi, and persuaded the state legislature to use the credit of the state to underwrite Confederate credit by passing a resolution to guarantee the Confederate debt.[67] As George Rable has observed, with some exaggeration perhaps, the Confederate government eventually began "to show a certain maturity and, if not more efficient, had grown more centralized and powerful," which certainly did not endear it to many Southern localists. Nevertheless, Rable concludes, as early as 1862, "a few visionaries even decided that states' rights doctrines had outlived their usefulness."[68] Other historians have suggested that "the state-rights controversy did not constitute a new loss to the Confederacy and that it was, on balance, an asset."[69]

The impressment issue became one of the defining issues for supporters of the state rights–localist argument. It placed severe strain on internal consensus because, like conscription, it touched on many aspects of daily life.

Over the course of the war schedules of impressment prices were periodically revised upward, due to inflation. In August 1863 Virginia prices were little changed from the previous months.[70] They continued the same in October, except for the addition of a few new items to the schedule,[71] although a few selective upward revisions were made in November.[72] Official prices in Virginia had begun to creep up by December, however. A pound of salt pork or lard, each worth $1.00 in October, was scheduled at $1.10 in December, and bacon went from $1.00 to $1.25 a pound, a 25 percent increase in just two months.[73]

No wonder citizens worried, especially since schedule prices always seemed lower than actual going prices in the marketplace. In Alabama the May 1863 schedule had not even set a price for Irish potatoes or wheat, which may have indicated adequate local supply, thus not requiring impressment.

However, sweet potatoes were set at $2.30, while beans and peas were set at $1.75 for a sixty-pound bushel. The value of a first-class artillery horse was set at $400 and iron boiler plate at $500 a ton. But the August schedule reveals growing anxiety. Although beans, peas, and even boiler plate remained the same, and sweet potatoes were lowered to $1.00, Irish potatoes and wheat were raised to $2.00 and $3.00, respectively, and the artillery horse had gone up to $600.[74] The January 1864 schedule raised beans and peas to $2.00, sweet potatoes to $6.00, and wheat to $5.00, in each instance for a sixty-pound bushel. Although Irish potatoes were cut to a dollar, military livestock was becoming dear and scarce; the artillery horse was now valued at $800.[75]

Commissary General Lucius Northrop had long foreseen the need for pricing legislation, and he understood the inflationary consequences of doing nothing. But he also understood the nature of the transportation issue and its obvious relation to supply. With government encouragement, a conference of railroad presidents met to deal with the issue in Augusta, Georgia, late in December 1863.

The executives could not agree on uniform procedures or on a regular schedule between Richmond and Montgomery, but they did agree that rates ought to be raised. The railroads were recalcitrant because army officers ordered cars from one road to another without arranging for their return, and impressments of cars and engines had disrupted the work routines of employees, affecting their efficiency. And of course equipment was wearing out rapidly. William L. Wadley, the Confederate government representative to the conference, earlier had reported in despair that "there is not a railroad in the country which has an efficient force today."[76] Wadley's solution was for each road to coordinate its activities by appointing its superintendents as assistants to him and to follow his orders for the shipment of government freight on their lines.[77] The next month Wadley was ordered to apply some serious pressure to the railroads. He was appointed to act with Isaac M. St. John, chief of the Nitre and Mining Bureau, and with a representative of the navy to "examine and advise on what railroads in the Confederate States the iron on their tracks can best be dispensed with [sic]."[78]

The following June Secretary of War James Seddon formally ordered the removal of iron from unimportant roads for use on other lines and for manufacture of ordnance,[79] and in January 1864 the order was extended to ore, timber, and anything else needed to produce iron.[80] But not everyone agreed which roads were unimportant. Seddon complained to Governor John Milton of Florida that the railroads were so impaired by heavy use and enemy action that "taking iron from the less valuable roads . . . is an imperious necessity" and scolded him because "honor, patriotism, and public spirit" were not sufficient to overcome "obstructive measures against an object so necessary to the public safety." He was particularly upset by injunctions issued by a circuit court in Florida that had prohibited the removal of vital rails.[81]

Robert E. Lee, also concerned about transportation, had complained early in 1863 about the lack of supply for his army, which caused him to cut the ration of salt meat. He did not know whether lack of provisions or poor management was the real culprit. In either case the result was scarcity, and he wrote Davis suggesting that more efficient management of the railroads would help.[82] Quartermaster General Abraham Myers reported to Seddon that he had read Lee's letter but complained that Assistant Adjutant General Wadley, whose special duty was to superintend rail transport, had not provided Myers with information necessary to report on the condition of the railroads.[83]

In turn Wadley wrote Seddon—based on the evidence of his recent experience—that "there is a degree of demoralization extant [among railroad managers] which induces some to make all manner of excuses rather than take hold honestly to do the work." He proposed to achieve amelioration through a law authorizing the government to take over an inefficient railroad, but with only "moderate" compensation; fear of losing their railroads with only small repayment would supposedly encourage owners to become more cooperative.[84] A high-priced buyout might be such an attractive prospect that inefficiency would be encouraged. The situation was coming to a crisis. Railroad legislation would come in its time; until then a better system of impressment would supposedly correct the supply problem.

In the regulations issued to implement the impressment law, Adjutant and Inspector General Cooper announced that the War Department "hereby recognizes impressment as a legal and operative mode of securing necessary supplies of subsistence, medical and quartermaster's stores." But he reaffirmed the provision of the law that property required by farmers and manufacturers for the consumption of their families or workers was not to be taken.[85] Nevertheless, the army's needs were pressing. In less than a year the chief of the Nitre and Mining Bureau was directed "to impress copper, coals, and such other minerals as may be needed,"[86] and General Lee later wanted to impress "supplies intended for consumption" because producers were laying in stores for a longer period than they had before impressment cut into their subsistence.[87]

There was quick general agreement that the impressment system was not functioning satisfactorily under the new legislation. A convention of commissioners of impressment from Tennessee, South Carolina, Georgia, Alabama, and Mississippi had therefore been held in Atlanta in July 1863. It reported instances of disregard of price schedules and urged a uniform schedule throughout the Confederacy.[88] Secretary of War Seddon thought that the system worked so poorly he feared for the fate of General Bragg's army, then engaged in the siege of Chattanooga, and begged the assistance of Governor Joseph E. Brown.[89] In reply, Brown complained of "outrages" by impressment authorities and "robberies upon the people" and urged purchase rather than impressment at less than market price.[90]

In South Carolina, the legislature complained of inequitable and unnecessary seizures, which often left families without sufficient food for their own needs,[91] and the North Carolina House of Commons reported impressments by unauthorized officers and soldiers.[92] From Alabama, Governor Watts declared that it was better "to pay double price than to make impressments,"[93] indicating the continuity of the market-price controversy.

In November and December 1863, in Mississippi, circumstances were reported to Davis as bleak. Jacob Thompson, a member of the state legislature, wrote to the president on December 23, "I found a great concentration of feeling with the people against the Military Authorities." This, he said, "had grown out of the reckless and illegal and oppressive manner in which the impressment laws had been executed," although he added optimistically that "very recent orders from Depart. Hd. Qrs. have in my judgment remedied this evil." What remained, however, was "another cause of exasperation," which "lies in the order for suppressing trade with the enemy and in the manner of its execution."[94] Northwestern Mississippi was destitute, owing to the proximity of so many Union troops and the devastation of the countryside from any number of marauding raids. Oxford is only seventy miles from Memphis, and "salt & bacon could not be had elsewhere." Thompson advised, "Do nothing to advise or encourage trade: but I would not punish the necessitous in their efforts to secure what all would approve [them] in obtaining if possible."[95]

For his part, Commissary General Northrop complained of the scarcity of meat and the high prices paid for it and breadstuffs by cities and private organizations. They often paid considerably more than appraised prices, thus making sellers dissatisfied with government prices.[96]

Florida had special problems as Union armies advanced along the Mississippi, curtailing supply from the Trans-Mississippi. In March 1863, even before the fall of Vicksburg, General Bragg's army had required four hundred thousand pounds of meat a month but received only one hundred ninety-one thousand pounds. Bragg's supply officers had looked to Florida for relief, for it was common knowledge, rather overstated, that huge herds of beef cattle were to be found there.[97]

Bragg had not been the only general looking to Florida for his meat supply; General Beauregard's army in South Carolina had been augmented, pending a suspected Union invasion, and his commissary was strained to the limit trying to meet the needs of the enlarged force.[98] Normal cooperation between Confederate authorities and Florida cattlemen had ceased. The contract system fell victim to the armies' needs, and smuggling had become common.[99]

As more and more provision left Florida, supply in that state grew scarce, and the abuses of the impressment system were exacerbated.[100] The situation grew worse following the fall of Vicksburg because that defeat had cut the potential of Texas to supply meat on the hoof to Confederate armies east of the Mississippi River. The Florida situation was made still more intolerable by the failure of the Confederacy to complete a railroad into Georgia (thereby slowing supply and requiring more men to move cattle), the conscription of experienced drivers, the failure to detail enough of them back to the beef trade, and the actions of speculators.[101] "In the end," writes Robert A. Taylor, "Florida beef only prolonged the conflict and did not alter its outcome."[102] In any event, there were not as many cattle in Florida as either the army or some cattlemen had estimated.[103]

Naturally, Florida's governor John Milton protested the screws being put to his state. For example, in January 1864 he criticized the impressment of milch cows, which caused troops, "indignant at the heartless treatment of the rights of citizens," to desert and join the Federal army. Such "lawless and wicked conduct" also angered Florida troops in Georgia and Virginia.[104] Milton forwarded a letter from one of his constituents, reporting families left without corn, their cows taken, and "they left to starve; their husbands slain on the battlefield at Chattanooga."[105] Milton's criticism had some effect: Samuel Cooper later ordered that milch cows and breeding stock be spared,[106] but for the time being this was one of the few categorical concessions made to the general outrage. No one seemed satisfied with the law.

As the months went by, inflation increasingly turned impressment into a forced loan because citizens were reimbursed less than the value of what was taken from them. This point was noted by the Georgia Supreme Court in November 1863 when it upheld the Confederate impressment law, "provided that . . . provision be made for prompt and just compensation," but it went on to rule that prices set by impressment commissioners did not constitute "just compensation" and were therefore illegal.[107] The Alabama Supreme Court was more reasonable, holding that "property is held subject to an inherent right in the government to appropriate it to the public use, when the public good may require it to be done."[108] Nevertheless, reimbursements often took so long that some citizens were truly subject to confiscation of property because they never were repaid. (By the end of the war, $.5 billion of unpaid impressment vouchers were still outstanding.)[109]

Thus, the 1863 legislation did not come close to correcting the problems involved in impressment. Jefferson Davis pointed to the continued difficulties in his message to the fourth session of the First Congress, on December 7, 1863. He blamed problems on "the disordered condition of the currency . . . [which] imposed upon the Government a system of supplying the wants of the Army which is so unequal in its operation, vexatious to the producer, injurious to the individual interest, and productive of such discontent among the people as only to be justified by the existence of an absolute necessity." It was not possible to purchase on the open market except at ruinous prices, declared Davis, and he claimed naively that previous impressment legislation had relieved the problem of hoarding. He did not yet understand that it was up to him to initiate corrective measures. He did not ask for a change in impressment legislation, asserting that the solution lay "in the restoration of the currency to such a basis as will enable the [War] Department to purchase necessary supplies in the open market."[110] This may have been an accurate assessment of the way things should have been, but it did not show a very good understanding of the way things actually were.

Senator Herschel V. Johnson of Georgia agreed with Davis's interpretation of the impressment problem and explained to Vice President Stephens that impressment was necessary because although soldiers had to be fed, farmers would not sell until the currency problem was remedied. He did not like the idea of a set schedule of prices for each state but preferred arbitration on the local level when there was a dispute about the just price. After all, the question was not one of adjusting prices, but of getting supplies. To Johnson, "just compensation" did not necessarily mean "market price," but there was no alternative if market prices were necessary to acquire needed supplies.[111]

As it turned out, Senator Johnson's ideas were more in line with congressional thinking than the ideas of Jefferson Davis. Opposition to Davis's apparent apathy was led by state rights–oriented congressmen, who secured a change that made the law somewhat more to their liking.[112] In February 1864 an amendment to the impressment law provided that impressed goods be paid for at the time of impressment, unless the owner appealed the price. Under this law the owner of impressed goods would receive a certificate stating that the Quartermaster's Department needed the articles listed and that the impressment officer was obligated to "pay you for the same, upon delivery, the reasonable prices set down respectively, that I deem to be a just compensation for the same," which was followed by a description of the property and the price established. The certificate would inform the owner that if he did not accept the price, compensation would be made according to the impressment law, "and you must not remove or transfer the same, unless otherwise agreed upon, and to be at your risk and expense as long as the property is in your possession." In case of disagreement between impressing agents and owners, the compensation would be turned over to the appraisers for their adjudication.[113]

Commissioners appraising the value of impressed property were to use a standard of "just compensation for the property as impressed, at the time of impressment," and their decision was to be final, although this revised system was not quite market-price compensation.[114] The War Department regulations that implemented the act contained detailed instructions about procedures that underlined the concern of the government that impressment not be considered oppressive. Once again, no supplies were to be impressed that were necessary to the consumption of the owner, "his family, employees, or slaves, or to carry on his ordinary mechanical, manufacturing, or agricultural employments."[115]

Although supplies and equipment were the main focus of the legislation that regulated the impressment of private property, labor was property, too, in the form of slaves. Not only were slaves conscripted for labor with and for the army, but they were also impressed. Much labor was needed, but naturally there existed a limit to the amount of such property that could be taken. If too many slaves were removed from the plantations, farms, and factories, the civilian economy would be impaired. It might become impossible for industry to supply the goods of war and for agriculture to feed the military and even the general population. Thus, in the regulations issued to implement the law, Adjutant and Inspector General Cooper emphasized that barring emergency, slaves were not to be impressed from plantations on which provisions were exclusively raised without the owner's consent, nor would more than 5 percent of the slaves in a county be taken at the same time. The period of impressed labor would be sixty days.[116]

Postmaster General Reagan achieved some economy by encouraging the public to use postage stamps for small change, thus increasing the department's capital assets. This practice went over quite well, for small coins had all but disappeared, and it was extremely difficult to make change for less than one dollar. In addition to postage stamps, there came into circulation a wide variety of "shinplasters"—private notes, generally in denominations under one dollar. One person, however, reported seeing a two-cent shinplaster redeemable in persimmons. Shinplasters were issued illegally by almost every kind of business, including merchants, railroads, taverns, saloons, butchers, bakers, and even by various individuals. These were actually a form of promissory note.[117]

Quite a few of the shinplasters were fraudulent, and there were so many of them in circulation that they became a serious problem. "Great God what a people," exclaimed a Mississippi editor, "two hundred and fifty different sorts of shinplasters, and not one dime in silver to be seen!" Another editor, in Georgia, said that the shinplasters "hop out upon us as thick as frogs and lice of Egypt, and are almost as great a nuisance." One Virginian avowed that "we are cursed with the most infernal currency in the world. The State is literally overrun with trash, that may be wholly worthless." The shinplasters declined so in value that they were not worth the effort to counterfeit. By mid-1863 beggars refused to take fifty-cent shinplasters, and one in Richmond rudely told one profferer that she already had plenty of "that truck" and that she would be satisfied with nothing less than a five dollar bill.[118]

In addition to persuading the public to use postage stamps as money, Reagan also economized by reducing the franking privilege, by driving sharp bargains with railroads to carry mail; and by charging ever-increasing postal rates. There actually was some collecting of Confederate postage stamps by philatelists during the war, thus giving the postal service some small additional revenue. With the effects of inflation, postal workers' actual wages dropped to almost ridiculously low levels, but Reagan usually managed to maintain full employment because the holders of jobs in the mail service remained exempt from the military draft.

Personnel shortages and discontent did ultimately develop. In 1863 the Richmond clerks went on strike for higher wages, but the government promptly broke it by drafting some of the strikers. Southern sentiment strongly disapproved of labor stoppages. Meanwhile, the Post Office counteracted some of its problems by hiring the aged, disabled, or women to run the smaller offices.

No one in the government, except the Post Office Department itself, had a franking privilege. Though an obvious economy measure, the Southern people long had disliked the franking usages under the old government. Abolitionists had sent out a lot of propaganda in that way. In the Confederacy, members of Congress, military officers, musicians, and privates could send letters without prepayment of postage, but the recipient was obliged to pay postage due. Many soldiers did use this method, though congressmen typically shunned doing so as impolitic. The military use of postage-due mail was called a "field frank." Robert E. Lee used an unusual form of the field frank, and the envelope gives the impression that perhaps they did move through the mails without payment of postage. Such, however, was not the case. Lee signed letters with his signature in place of a stamp, just as he had in the old U.S. Army, and sometimes the letters reached their destinations without having any stamp or other markings attached. Most of the Lee covers that remain today are in the Library of Congress. Postage on them actually was paid by the recipients.

One old folklore joke has a former Rebel colonel offering an opinion, between mint juleps, that "we could have beaten the Yankees with cornstalks, suh! But they would not fight with cornstalks." The historian Emory Thomas asserts that the speedy level of industrialization, ex nihilo really, is "the most striking thing about the Confederate economy."[119]

To be sure, the wartime South did not resemble an industrial giant, nor, actually, did it come even close to industrial equity with the North. But it is significant that the nearly totally agrarian region, which it had been, managed to gear up and produce enough to sustain it through four years of truly modern warfare.

Although there had been a number of successful industrial enterprises in the prewar South, there had been no socioeconomic class of industrial capitalists. During the conflict, the government—especially the War Department—assumed the roles that such a class would have played and directed an impressive program. The government either did the manufacturing itself, establishing goodly numbers of arsenals and factories scattered throughout the South, or it manipulated and controlled and nurtured private manufacturing. It did so by means of draft exemptions for those involved in needed fabrication, enforcing priorities on transportation and raw materials, and passing laws prescribing maximum profit margins. One historian has assessed that "no country, since the Inca Empire down to Soviet Russia, had ever possessed a similar government-owned (or controlled) kind of economy."[120]

The Confederates slowly and only rather grudgingly came to perceive that cotton was not the potent king that they had hoped. "To Southerners' chagrin, 'King Cotton' proved to be a puppet monarch whose strings the Confederacy did not control."[121] The major European powers clearly needed cotton, but it did not necessarily have to be Confederate cotton, and they were able successfully to increase their imports of Egyptian cotton. Both Britain and France would have liked the Confederacy to prevail, not only to ease that strain (which was not totally alleviated by Egypt) but also to realize other benefits that might accrue from a permanently disunited States.

Throughout 1862 the European mills could buy only a fraction of their needs, and they had to pay premium prices for what they did get. Sometimes they had to reduce operating time, and they occasionally were obliged to shut down entirely. Certainly the working classes in both England and France suffered. Nevertheless, inasmuch that the Union had made the obliteration of slavery a major war aim, there was little chance that England or France would grant recognition, unless the South achieved unmistakable and major victories in the field. This, of course, they did not do.

But if the Confederacy could not get formal recognition, they could and did manage to do a lot of sub rosa business abroad. The main architect of Confederate commerce abroad was James Dunwoody Bulloch. His greatest success had been in securing the *Alabama,* the Confederacy's most potent and effective commerce raider. But there erupted an ominous and foreboding flap over the *Alexandria*. In April 1863 the British seized the newly built ship and held it, pending an investigation of its intended use. It was later released, but the incident revealed there was going to be severe future limitation on how much material could be secured in Britain. In fall 1863 Bulloch suffered his worst frustration when the British government seized two rams. His future attempts to buy and outfit cruisers were curtailed and much less successful.

One of the most notable of the Confederate successes in foreign business negotiation resulted in the Erlanger Loan. Erlanger and Company of Paris was an extension of a family-banking concern centered in Frankfurt. The Erlanger Loan was basically a high-risk cotton-bond issue. One British economic historian described it as "perhaps the most audaciously successful loan of the century."[122] Because of the blockade, only a small amount of cotton was ever collected by bondholders, with the result that the Confederacy netted about $8.5 million dollars. The Confederate envoy to France, John Slidell, had been introduced to Emile Erlanger in late September 1862. He was extremely sympathetic to the Southern cause (indeed his son eventually married Slidell's daughter).

Within a month an agreement had been reached (pending approval in Richmond) on an issue of £5 million (£1 then equaled $4.85 in gold). Judah Benjamin, by then secretary of state, found the terms "so onerous that we could not assent to them" and negotiated a new deal with the Erlanger agents for a £3 million loan, with the Confederacy entitled to a larger percentage of the profit. The bonds were made available beginning in March 1863, and despite the decline in their value after the military reverses that ensued, as well as the amount the Confederates spent on attempted market manipulation, the Confederacy did raise a considerable sum. Most of that was used in Europe to buy ships and arms.[123]

The Erlanger Loan provided a significant boost in morale to the Confederates. According to Thomas, it encouraged many of them to believe that "European money was a stronger endorsement of the Southern nation than diplomatic recognition, and that financial interests might rekindle political interest."[124]

As 1863 drew to a close, the political fragmentation and division extended not only throughout the army but also throughout the civil administration. On his trip to Bragg's headquarters in October, Davis had "traveled through a divided nation filled with increasingly fearful and disheartened people." According to George Rable, "Yet for all his faults, the president (along with Lee) remained the personification of the Confederate nation."[125]

Davis's trip to visit the Army of Tennessee was the initial segment of a month-long journey through the heartland of his country. From Missionary Ridge he returned to Atlanta and on October 14 started west. In Montgomery, he boarded a steamboat for an overnight run down the Alabama River to Selma. There he gave a speech and visited the Confederate naval foundry. Then he boarded a train for Demopolis, where he spoke, lunched with a member of Congress, and met with Generals Johnston and Hardee. The generals joined him on a trip to Meridian, Mississippi. On the morning of October 18 Davis took a brief twenty-mile train ride to Lauderdale Springs to visit his brother Joseph and his mortally ill sister-in-law Elize, who died six days later. He continued to Jackson and to Enterprise, Alabama, where he reviewed troops, and then returned to Jackson. In a speech in the capitol he appealed to Mississippians to rise up and throw off the invader. Then he went to Brandon, Mississippi, and again to Meridian before heading east. He spent two days in Mobile, reviewing troops in the area and gave a brief speech asserting that the Confederate cause was stronger than it had been a year earlier. He went to Montgomery, to Atlanta, and then departed for Savannah, making brief remarks along the way. Cooper observes, "At Macon a 'hurrahing' crowd greeted him and 'carried him off in triumph' to a hotel, where he addressed a large gathering." After dinner a special train transported him to Savannah, and from there he went by boat to examine the coastal fortifications.[126]

Throughout the journey, "The politician Davis was in action. According to an eyewitness, he gave many hands a hearty shake, meeting 'every one as if he had met an old friend.' "[127] Davis was determined to sustain public morale in these dark times because he felt that "the only alternative to a continued war for independence was a 'slavish submission to despotic usurpation.' " The president made brief upbeat speeches aimed at boosting public confidence and support for his administration at train stops along his route. From Savannah Davis went to Charleston, speaking twice en route. Then he inspected troops and visited the islands guarding the harbor. From Charleston, his train took him to Wilmington, North Carolina, where he spoke on November 5 and toured nearby fortifications, telling defenders "they were fighting for their liberty, their homes, and their sweethearts." His final remarks he delivered in Goldsboro, North Carolina, and on November 7 he arrived in Richmond. He had been on the road for thirty-two days. "Everywhere, from war-ravaged Mississippi to the protected Atlantic coast, he had been enthusiastically received. His reception gave credence to one editor's claim that the president enjoyed 'the heart and confidence of the people.' "[128] He tried as best he could to show his own selfless devotion to the cause, and he hoped, though largely in vain, that he could elicit such devotion in others.[129] But given his negative personality, his efforts were limited; this was as close as he ever came to waging a modern public relations campaign. Such appeals to the public might well have had a strong positive effect on Confederate morale and will, but it is unreasonable to suggest that a nineteenth-century president should have acted in ways adopted by twentieth-century American presidents.

On December 24 James Mason wrote to Davis that "it is very certain that the British Ministry remain obdurately determined against recognition, but I am equally satisfied that three fourths, if not a larger number of the English people would applaud and sustain the Ministry in an opposite course, were it adopted, and in this number I include nearly every man in the higher and the educated classes." He further reported, on a hopeful note, that there was "an Association in process of being formed in England, for the avowed purpose of bringing recognition about." And, Mason continued, "I have never entertained a doubt that our recognition by England would bring the war to an end and have always impressed this upon our friends in that country."[130] Even if Mason's remarks were delusional in their degree of optimism, they undoubtedly gave the anguished Davis at year-end some encouragement.

Davis was as upbeat as he could bring himself to be. On the same day that Mason wrote the president, Davis wrote a long letter to Joseph E. Johnston: "The reports concerning the battle at Missionary Ridge show that our loss in killed and wounded was not great, and that the reverse sustained is not attributable to any general demoralization or reluctance to encounter the opposing Army. The brilliant stand made by the rear guard at Ringgold sustains this belief."[131] The exact figures of killed, wounded, and missing at Missionary Ridge are obscure, but it is probable that Bragg lost some 15 percent of his 46,200 men and Grant about 10 percent of his 56,400. The rearguard stand made by Patrick R. Cleburne's division at Ringgold, where the Confederates were outnumbered four to one, was one of Cleburne's "finest hours," and in February 1864 the Confederate Congress voted him a resolution of thanks.[132]

Davis continued, "The chief of ordnance reported that notwithstanding the abandonment of a considerable number of guns during the battle, there were still on hand, owing to previous large captures by our troops, as many batteries as were proportionate to the strength of the Army, well supplied with horses and equipment."[133] There were, according to Bragg's report, thirty-eight pieces of Confederate field artillery captured by the enemy at Missionary Ridge, and two siege guns were disabled and abandoned.[134]

It was true, however, that in the waning weeks of 1863 the Army of Tennessee did show measurable signs of revival; between December 3 and 20 its number of effectives increased from 30,127 to 35,079. And official records at the year's end placed its total strength at 98,127 present and absent. Thus, at this point Davis felt inclined toward optimism regarding his new western army commander, Joe Johnston, telling him that the existing intelligence "induces me to hope that you will soon be able to commence active operations against the enemy."[135]

Investing by inches. These burrows were used by Union soldiers for protection as they slowly tightened the lines around Vicksburg in June and July 1863. (From Francis Trevelyan Miller, editor in chief, *The Photographic History of the Civil War in Ten Volumes* [New York: The Review of Reviews, 1911–1912], vol. 2, *Two Years of Grim War*, 1911, 201).

Atlanta, Georgia. Confederate palisades and chevaux-de-frise near Potter House. Chevaux-de-frise were timbers or tree trunks into which sharpened wooden spikes were placed. These nineteenth-century equivalents of barbed wire were part of Joseph E. Johnston's extensive defenses. (Courtesy Library of Congress, Prints and Photographs Division, LC-B8171-3643 DLC.)

Opposite:
Richmond, Virginia. General view of burned district. In April 1865, retreating Confederates set fire to supplies and factories to keep them out of Federal hands. The fires spread, with the result that Richmond was one of the few urban centers to suffer extensive war damage. (Courtesy Library of Congress, Prints and Photographs Division, LC-B8171-7110 DLC.)

Petersburg, Virginia. Confederate fortifications with chevaux-de-frise beyond. Traverses against cross fire. The zigzag pattern of these traverses around Petersburg was designed to limit losses from cross fire or successful enemy penetration of the trench system. Note the chevaux-de-frise in the background. (Courtesy Library of Congress, Prints and Photographs Division, LC-B8171-3302 DLC.)

13

WAR LEADERSHIP IN SUPREME TEST

Balloting for the Second Congress had begun in May 1863 and spilled over into 1864, for there was no specific national election day. Furthermore, as William Cooper asserts, "Almost everywhere the soldier vote was consequential, and the army was a stronghold for the president." Discontent did affect a substantial percentage of the ballots cast by the general populace. "Yet the elections did not turn into a referendum on either the Davis administration or the president personally. . . . Opponents of one or both disagreed with themselves as often as they agreed." Differences were so widespread and various that no organized or unified opposition materialized. "Davis took no part in the elections," writes Cooper. "He did not back any slate of candidates, nor did he urge voters to return those who championed his policies and throw out those who did not. His stance illustrated his view of Confederate politics." Indeed, "The cause had become his politics, and he wanted to believe that all Confederates were as committed to it as he. He was a Confederate, meaning, in his mind, that ideology and politics had merged."[1]

The outcome was a qualified endorsement of former Unionists and Whigs, but it was not a repudiation of Davis, according to Cooper: "Each election was almost idiosyncratic." Yet "the most helpful suggestion for understanding the basic division in Confederate politics posits two groups: those who pursued 'the politics of national unity' and those who advocated 'the politics of liberty.' The former supported almost any measure and the growth of executive power in the name of Confederate independence, while the latter depicted acts like conscription and suspension of habeas corpus, as well as a powerful executive, as dangerous threats to fundamental rights and liberties."[2] Cooper further observes that these

definitions associated with national unity and liberty may be [useful] in comprehending Confederate politics, [but] they do not fully explain Jefferson

Davis, . . . [who] had his way with Congress. . . . The frustrated minority that disliked the measures as well as the man flailed away, often with personal diatribes against the president. Henry Foote denounced Davis as "vain, selfish, overbearing, ambitious, intriguing, and a slave to his prejudices and partialities." He shouted for "the people to rise, sword in hand, to put down the domestic tyrant who thus sought to invade their rights." But vicious verbal barrages could not derail Davis's legislative success.

The president could be considerate and gracious, though he stiffened when he spotted any deviation from his definition of commitment to the cause. Following a visit to the president, one congressman depicted him as "out of temper." His upbraiding could ruffle feelings, and he did make enemies. But until the end he never lost the good will [perhaps acquiescence is a better word] of a congressional majority or the upper hand in legislative matters.[3]

Eighteen sixty-four arrived with President Davis expressing confidence. He and his wife hosted an afternoon reception on January 1. Aides were "in full fig, swords and sashes." The many guests included both civilian and military as well as members of Congress. "The large numbers in attendance left their mark on the president and first lady. Davis's right arm became 'stiff with the New Year's shaking' and Varina's 'hand tender to the touch.' "[4]

Despite the festivities on New Year's Day, the Davises felt the financial pinch, just as did most of the other Confederates. In January 1864 the president sold two slaves to raise $1,612, and two months later he let three of his horses go in order to glean another $7,330. Varina sold her carriage and team for $12,000, though well-wishers then raised the monies to repurchase and return those to her. Their meals were ever more austere. Davis might be late to dinner, and frequently he did not go to bed until sunrise or just before; he grew more indifferent to food, sometimes forgetting to eat.[5] Worry weighed on his shoulders as he sought ways to rescue his faltering cause.

He had not been encouraged by the letter of January 2, which General Joseph Johnston had sent in reply to Davis's December 23 missive. Although Johnston admitted that he had "not yet been able [personally] to observe the condition of the army," nonetheless he judged, "from the language of the general officers, that it has not entirely recovered its confidence." Serious, too, if not worse, the artillery "is deficient in discipline & instruction—Especially in firing. The horses are not in good condition." Johnston agreed with Davis concerning "the importance of recovering the territory we have lost," but he believed that "difficulties appear to me in the way." The two most obvious choices for offensive operation seemed forbiddingly difficult. "We have neither subsistence nor field transportation enough for either march." Johnston concluded, "I can see no other mode of taking the offensive here, than to beat the enemy when he advances, & then move forward," and he advised, "to make victory probable the army must be strengthened."[6]

Although Johnston was pleased once again to be in an army command, he did not change his attitude toward Davis. "During the fall of 1863 and on into 1864," Cooper observes, "he whined incessantly about anyone's believing he bore any responsibility for Vicksburg. He viewed his new command as vindication and a triumph over the president, but he still mistrusted Davis. With one colleague he shared his conviction that 'Mr. Davis will not place me in any position where there is any chance or possibility of success.' "[7]

"At the outset Johnston and Davis disagreed fundamentally over military operations," Cooper points out. "Davis urged Johnston to go on the offensive, or at least to plan for such a move. He even sent a personal emissary, Brigadier General William N. Pendleton, formerly Johnston's chief of artillery, to confer with Johnston and convey the presidential view." But "responding to the president, Johnston expressed serious misgivings about undertaking any such operation." Johnston's subsequent communications to Davis, telegrams of January 12 and 13 and a letter on January 15, did not reflect much change for the better: "Not only can we not hope soon to assume the offensive from this position, but . . . we are in danger of being forced back from it—by the want of food & forage—Especially the latter." He concluded by asserting dissatisfaction with his principal subordinates: "I beg leave again to express the hope that your excellence will strengthen this army by appointing to it Lieut. Generals," for the very value of having corps organizations at all "seems to me to depend upon having competent Lieut. Generals to command them."[8]

The situation continued to look bleak for the rest of January and for most of February. But Davis's

thoughts never strayed far from his fighting men. On February 10 he penned a public letter to "Soldiers of the Armies of the Confederate States" that was issued as a general order and carried in newspapers. He began by congratulating them for their "many noble triumphs" achieved in the "long and bloody war" gripping the nation. Special gratitude went to those who could have left the service upon expiration of their enlistments, but who instead "heeded the call only of your suffering country." Although as president he could not share "your dangers, your sufferings, and your privations in the field," he assured them, "with pride and affection my heart has accompanied you in every march; with solitude it has sought to minister to your every want; with exultation it has marked your every heroic achievement."[9]

But as Davis began to turn his mind toward the anticipated spring campaigns, he had to face the reality that conditions in North Carolina were very poor, with much of the populace indignant and incensed over the state of the war effort and its effect on the home front. On February 19 William L. Maury returned to Richmond with a letter from James M. Mason, reporting that both Mason and John Slidell despairingly had concluded "the final and total failure to get out any [more] ships for our Government either from England or France."[10]

Recognizing that the overall situation was quite bleak, Davis hit upon the notion of bringing Braxton Bragg to Richmond. Perhaps some adjustment at the highest level of the command apparatus could produce some beneficial results. On February 24 he ordered Bragg to take office as commanding general "charged with the conduct of military operations in the armies of the Confederacy." But instead of bolstering the level of confidence, there was widespread outrage; the Richmond press vilified Davis. "When a man fails in an inferior position," the *Richmond Whig* editorialized, "it is natural and charitable to conclude that the failure is due to the inadequacy of the task to his capabilities, and wise to give him a larger sphere for the proper exertion of his abilities."[11]

Stripped of its sarcasm, the editor's assessment did make some sense. Certain people indeed are capable of higher tasks, despite failure in lower positions, and Davis knew that Bragg had good organizational abilities. Though Bragg's health, temperament, and reputation had rendered him useless in high-level field command, he still could be a good staff officer. He could take some of the administrative load off Davis's shoulders, if Davis would let him, and he could facilitate the logistical support of the Confederate armies. Davis did not propose a role for Bragg far from that played by War Secretary James Seddon and Adjutant General Samuel Cooper, both of whom, but especially the latter, were really only high-level clerks. Bragg simply would relieve each of them of some of their duties, all three serving more usefully and effectively. But the critics did not see the move in that light.

Davis misjudged the utter unpopularity of the appointment, and he erred in making it while Congress was out of session. The anger the appointment aroused haunted him for the rest of the war. This burden, along with his continuingly declining health, rendered him even more negative—irritable, ill-tempered, and less able to deal effectively with the enormous problems of the war effort, now nearly in shambles.[12]

Davis admitted to Congress in February that "discontent, disaffection and disloyalty" prevailed among those who had "enjoyed quiet and safety at home" even as others had sacrificed virtually everything for the Confederate cause. Peace meetings and outright Unionism gave heart to the Yankees, comforted traitors, reconfirmed the fears of the fainthearted, and discouraged patriotism.[13]

Yet George Rable reminds us, "It is easy to exaggerate the extent of opposition to the administration and forget that Davis retained considerable public trust." He had his numerous apologists, and some of them hurled rejoinders equally as vitriolic as those criticisms thrown by detractors such as Edward A. Pollard of the *Richmond Examiner.* The real question was whether most white Southerners would remain true, not to Davis but to the Confederate cause. Governor Zebulon Vance, for his part, still believed that "the great mass . . . continue hopeful and earnest," hopeful of preserving their independence and property from negation and destruction, determined to preserve their liberties from the scourge of "vassalage." Even Vice President Alexander Stephens agreed that loss of territory would be relatively unimportant if only Confederates remained inspired by their revolutionary ancestors and "remembered that a liberty-loving people *would* ultimately triumph."[14]

Davis's dark mood was further exacerbated on March 1. Bragg arrived in Richmond just when a cavalry assault against the city under Colonel Ulrich Dahlgren was stymied. Dahlgren, whom Varina recalled as being a "fair-haired boy" in "black velvet suit and Vandyke collar," was killed.[15] Those in the column who were not killed were taken captive.

On Dahlgren's body were found orders to burn the city and to release the Northern prisoners held there. General Fitz Lee brought these papers into Davis's private office while he was conferring with Secretary of State Judah Benjamin. Davis read the orders, "making no comment" until "he came to the sentence, 'Jeff. Davis and *Cabinet* must be killed on the spot.'" He laughingly said, "That means you, Mr. Benjamin." Perhaps this banter reflects how close Davis and Benjamin had become. Some persons called him "Mr. Davis's pet Jew." He called himself "a personal friend." Both Davis and Varina took delight in the witty and cultivated Benjamin. Still, Benjamin was a favorite butt of Davis's enemies.[16]

As for Dahlgren's captured followers, a majority of the cabinet and Bragg insisted that Davis live up to his frequent threats "for violation of the usages of war" and execute one-tenth of them (Bragg argued for all). Public support for this was "unanimous." Benjamin recalled "heated" discussion when "Davis alone" argued that these men "had been received to mercy . . . as prisoners of war, and as such were sacred; and that we should be dishonored if harm should overtake them." Only Davis's "unshaken firmness" saved them. According to Postmaster General John Reagan, Davis said, "If we had known [their plans] and could have shot them with arms in their hands, it would have been all right," but "in an emphatic manner [he] said that he would not permit an unarmed prisoner to be shot; and so the matter ended."[17] Davis immediately released the captured papers to the press, to illustrate what a rabble of plunderers and assassins were serving in Lincoln's armies.[18]

Davis had Dahlgren's special orders photographed and sent to General George Meade, "with an inquiry as to whether such practices were authorized by his Government; and also to say that if any question was raised as to the copies, the original paper would be submitted."[19] The Unionists did not reply.

The populace had continued to clamor for more and better tax legislation. "The truth is," one Alabama editor had observed late in 1863, "we need more courage in Congress now, than we do in the field." Thus, on February 17, 1864, the last day of the First Congress, several vital pieces of legislation were enacted, including three long-debated, crucially significant financial measures. The first was a new Tax Act, which boldly ignored the constitutional prohibition of a direct tax before a census was taken. Treasury Secretary Christopher Memminger long had been concerned by the lack of adequate taxation. He believed that there was "a general power to levy taxes" and that under the circumstances of war, the constitutional requirement for a census "must be considered as in suspense." This was quite a long jump for him, a state rights man, but necessity knew no law.[20]

Since land and slaves were two properties the Confederacy possessed in abundance, Memminger believed they were fair game for taxation. He suspected that the taxable property in the fledgling nation was worth about $3 billion and proposed a 5 percent tax on all of it, which would thus yield about $120 million. Of course $120 million is far less than 5 percent of $3 billion, but the difference is a telling sign of those times: Memminger's calculations included $30 million that the government would not receive because of tax evasion, bureaucratic inefficiency, and administrative costs.[21] This tax, plus another $300 million in loans, would meet (presumably) all Confederate requirements for 1864. Half of this income would be used for expenses and the other half to pay interest on a new loan that would be designed to pay for additional supplies and to soak up some excess currency in circulation. This law, the economic historian Douglas Ball writes, would be the Confederacy's "last clear chance."[22]

In his December 7, 1863, message to open the fourth session of the First Congress, Davis went through the usual litany: explaining how bad things were but how promising prospects nonetheless existed. He observed that "about two-thirds of the entire taxable property in the Confederate States consists of land and slaves" and pointed to the embarrassing requirement for a census before any direct taxes could be levied. He acknowledged that the 1863 tax law had pressed upon everything but land and slaves, thus creating an unfair burden on the owners of the remaining one-third of taxable property. The new tax law, said Davis, would take an extended time to bring in significant income, thus requiring additional issues of the nefarious Treasury notes. Davis agreed with Memminger that, everything considered, a direct tax was both constitutional and immediately required.[23]

The finances were indeed in a state of wreckage, or certainly close to it. The April 1863 tax legislation had brought in only $27 million by February 1, 1864, and that was not enough to meet needs.[24] Surely, it now seemed clear, some kind of effective taxation of land and slaves would be the key to putting the Confederacy's fiscal house in order.

The Congress started the session apparently determined to deal with the tax issue. Early tax proposals, some along the lines that Memminger and Davis had requested, others not, were referred to committee for study. By January 1864 some bills were out of committee and being debated. The debates were largely in secret session, so it is impossible to know just what the issues were, except that there were numerous log-rolling efforts to ensure that some items would be taxed while others would not. There was, for example, an attempt by Congressman Muscoe R. H. Garnett of Virginia to distinguish between land purchased since January 1, 1863, for speculation and land purchased for cultivation by the owner.[25] After a series of amendments and attempted amendments, the proposal was included in legislation to be acted upon the morning of January 22, 1864. Although it passed, it was reconsidered and voted down that evening.[26] The House bill finally was repassed, that same evening, and three days later was sent to the Senate.[27] It was, as historian Wilfred Buck Yearns has written, "the usual combination of boldness and timidity."[28]

The main issues were what should be taxed and at what rate. The Senate version levied about half the tax of the House version. The bill passed the Senate on a voice vote on February 13. The House disagreed on the changes, and the Senate called for a conference committee.[29] By then the session was almost over, and the need for heavier taxes was more obvious than ever before. Under pressure of the moment and aware of the need, the Senate gave in and agreed, thus the Tax Act of February 17, 1864. Davis signed it the same day.[30]

This tax legislation included the new property tax of 5 percent that Memminger wanted (adjusted downward for agriculturalists paying the tax in kind), but it did not tax slaves. Gold, silver, and jewelry were taxed at 10 percent. The assessed valuation of property would be determined by the local 1860 market value, unless it had been purchased since January 1, 1862, in which case the assessment was the actual amount paid. This would hit speculators (a popular idea), but it would also hurt refugees (not so good). Shares in joint stock companies would be taxed at 5 percent, assessed according to current local market value. Likewise, a 5 percent tax was levied on gold and silver coin and bullion, money held in foreign countries, bank notes, and interest-bearing Treasury notes. Profits from dealing in gold, silver, foreign exchange, liquor, grain, meat, leather, shoes, cloth, wagons, coal, iron, and other commodities were taxed an additional 10 percent above previous levies, if derived from trade between January 1, 1863, and January 1, 1865—again hitting speculators but also some legitimate businessmen. Joint stock companies would pay for inflation, at the rate of a one-quarter portion of the profits over 25 percent. Exemptions ranging from one hundred to one thousand dollars were allowed for heads of families, minor children, sons killed in the war, war widows, and disabled soldiers. The tax was reduced on property damaged by enemy action.[31]

There were, naturally, complaints. There were too many exemptions. Sums due on one tax could be deducted from sums due on others, making accurate computation of taxes owed quite difficult. Produce kept on farms was not taxed, which proved a boon for hoarders. Accusations were made that stock companies paid too much, that landed interests paid too little, and that the tax on government bonds violated a contract. But it was a comprehensive law and desperately needed.[32]

These new taxes were in addition to those levied the previous April, during the third session of the First Congress. These were now amended by the second important piece of financial legislation, also passed on February 17. The amendment to the tax law of April 24, 1863, levied the same sort of occupational taxes as the earlier law. Bankers were required to pay a five hundred dollar occupational license tax, auctioneers paid fifty dollars plus 2.5 percent on sales, wholesale liquor dealers had to cough up two hundred dollars plus 5 percent on gross, with similar provisions applying to pawnbrokers, distillers (but distillers of fruit for ninety days or less got a cut rate), brewers, lawyers, tobacconists, jugglers, pool hall owners, butchers, bakers (no mention of candlestick makers), peddlers, doctors, and circuses. If income was derived from rents on houses, lands, factories, mines, mills, machines, and the like, up to 10 percent of rental income could be dedicated for maintenance. There was an income tax of 1 percent on annual salaries between one thousand and fifteen hundred dollars, and 2 percent on incomes above fifteen hundred dollars (military personnel excepted). Total incomes were subject to a 5 percent tax if over five hundred dollars, rising to 15 percent on incomes over ten thousand dollars. Agriculturalists owed a 10 percent tax in kind on commodities (military widows, wounded soldiers worth less than one thousand dollars, and farmers worth less than five hundred dollars were exempt). The law went into tortuous detail, covering levies on naval stores, credits held outside the Confederacy, bowling alleys, and on and on, with great detail regarding procedures for the tax in kind.[33] It was the part of law that nowadays makes accountants and tax lawyers dream of prosperity.

On the same day that Congress passed the revised tax laws, it enacted the third essential piece of financial legislation of the session. This was a highly complicated law passed in a desperate attempt to reduce the amount of surplus currency in general circulation. Well over $1 billion worth of notes had been authorized from time to time, and some authorizations had been without limit. Some note issues could be exchanged for bonds bearing what was thought to be an attractive rate of return, 6 to 8 percent, but fixed income investment did not appeal to many people when inflation sometimes ran as high as 10 percent per month.[34]

One solution was to make Treasury notes legal tender, just as the Union had done with its greenbacks. Several such proposals were made by congressmen and by private citizens, but to no avail. There was social pressure to accept the notes, as indicated by the Richmond newspaper editor who depicted anyone who refused: "His avarice is superior to his patriotism. He is an Esau who would sell his birthright for a mess of pottage. . . . He is a Judas who would betray his Lord."[35] During 1862 the inflated notes had passed well enough in general circulation, and now Secretary Memminger feared that if a legal tender law were enacted, the public would wonder why and might conclude that Congress expected that soon the notes would not pass.[36] The same Richmond editor divided those who refused a Treasury note into two classes: "good people," who refused "from a distrust of its stability and solvency," and "scoundrels," and he agreed with Memminger that "the legal tender remedy would only make people suspicious."[37]

In any event, a rapidly inflating currency will pass easily in general circulation; each holder desires to get it out of his hands before it loses any more value. Indeed, debtors love inflation, for it enables them to "get rid of just debts" by repaying in a currency that is worth less than the debt incurred. The effect, some people in the Confederacy complained, was that inflated money "has ruined many an honest creditor by putting him in the power of a fraudulent debtor."[38] Although Congress never passed a legal tender law, some states did make Treasury notes receivable for their own taxes, and Virginia provided that if a bank refused Treasury notes, its own notes would no longer be accepted in payment of taxes.[39] Legal tender or not, therefore, Treasury notes passed with remarkable ease throughout the war.

Meanwhile, the excessive issue of notes, the failure of taxes and bonds to absorb the excess, and an increasing shortage of consumer goods caused inflation to increase rapidly. At the time of the April 1863 tax law, a gold dollar in Richmond was worth $5.50 in Treasury notes, but by early 1864 it was worth $20.00 to $25.00—a fourfold decrease.[40] In an effort to halt this disastrous slide, Memminger proposed that the states guarantee the Confederate debt, but that plan failed when some states refused to cooperate while others imposed conditions.[41] The real solution was for the Confederate government to use its taxing power, which it had begun to do in April 1863, but tax laws are slow to take effect.

In absence of effective tax laws, Confederates could resort to forced funding, "the last step," as Douglas Ball puts it. Funding by bond issues had been incorporated in every currency act through March 23, 1863. Confederates did buy those bonds—over $224 million in 7 and 8 percent bonds between October 1862 and August 1863. But many Treasury notes thus retired were reissued and new note issues exceeded the dollar value of the notes that were destroyed. Thus the currency in circulation actually increased rather than decreased.[42] The difference was that funding had been voluntary, in the hope that citizens would be persuaded by patriotism or by favorable interest rates to buy bonds so that the Treasury notes could be retired. Forced funding was another breed of cat—it was repudiation (or the next thing to it), a word that caused many Confederates to shiver and to begin hoarding gold or U.S. currency if they had the opportunity.

For this reason the Congress passed an act to prohibit dealing in the paper currency of the enemy, on February 11, 1864.[43] In December 1862 U.S. greenbacks had circulated in Richmond at a premium to Confederate Treasury notes, $4.70 in Treasury notes being required to obtain $1.00 in greenbacks. By December 1863 the premium was fourteen or fifteen to one, according to Tennessee Congressman Henry S. Foote. In addition to complicating the currency problem, the greenback premium was highly embarrassing. But a premium was logical: presumably the U.S. government would be willing to redeem its paper notes sometime in the future whether it won the war or not; if the Confederacy lost, then its paper would be worthless.[44]

Even so, there was considerable public support for forced funding. The editor of the *Richmond Dispatch* demanded replacement of the current "paper medium with another that will approximate more nearly the standard of gold." His plan was to defer payments on the current debt until after the war, to issue new and limited debt at low rates of interest, and to establish a new currency. In Alabama the general assembly called for reduction of the amount of circulating paper, resolving that "the people of Alabama will cheerfully submit to any tax which the Congress may impose for the purpose of reducing the volume of currency and appreciating its value; *Provided* the tax be not too oppressive in amount, or unequal in its operation." An Alabama editor was more explicit. He called on Congress to reduce the paper currency by heavy taxes, more bond issues, forced funding, and no new issues of notes. Even the Tallapoosa County Grand Jury added its support, claiming that if the currency problem worsened, "our army must melt away, and our country will be overwhelmed."[45]

To relieve the situation, Memminger proposed a forced loan of $1 billion in 6 percent, twenty-year bonds. Notes not funded before a six-month time limit expired would become valueless. Noteholders would be forced to choose between buying bonds (at a none-too-favorable rate in an inflationary economy) or suffering repudiation. The loan would be covered by a new 5 percent tax on property and credits. Old issue notes would no longer be accepted by the government after April 1, 1864 (July 1 in the Trans-Mississippi), though private parties could still accept them at face value if they so opted. That is, according to Richard Todd, "The currency was to be forcibly reduced by compelling note holders to withdraw their notes from circulation and fund them in bonds or face a tax of 5% along with eventual repudiation." Memminger admitted again that his proposal would violate the contract between the Confederate government and citizens with Treasury notes stuffed in their pockets, but the alternative would be disaster. Davis agreed.[46]

In his message to Congress, Davis asked for immediate attention to financial issues and reminded congressmen "that a prompt and efficacious remedy for the present condition of the currency is necessary for the successful performance of the functions of government." The $600 million in currency already in circulation was three times the amount needed, Davis asserted, and it had led to a "corrupting influence" on public morals and a "spirit of speculation." Voluntary funding would no longer work; "the evil," observed Davis, "has now reached such a magnitude as to permit no other remedy than the compulsory reduction of the currency to the amount required by the business of the country." It was no longer possible, he said, to calculate "future values" while "all fixed wages, salaries, and incomes" had been rendered "inadequate to bare subsistence." He supported Memminger's call for conversion of notes to bonds, accompanied by taxation to ensure payment of the bonds.[47]

Congress did not get off to a promising start. Although the issue was introduced on the first day of the fourth session of the First Congress, there was argument over whether it should be considered in the Committee of the Whole, or referred to the Committee on Finance, or to the Committee on Ways and Means, or to a special joint committee. This debate took the better part of three days; it finally ended with the issue being sent to a special committee of the House.[48] This special committee reported "a bill to tax, fund, and limit the currency" on December 31, after three weeks' consideration, a remarkably speedy job even by the standards of the twenty-first century.[49]

Once again the arguments are uncertain, secret sessions having created a wall that separates us from knowing what they were. The committee bill, somewhat like Memminger's proposal, provided that all noninterest-bearing notes above five dollars in denomination would be fundable by 6 percent bonds until March 1, 1864, and by 4 percent bonds thereafter. Notes would be accepted for funding at face value until May 1, 1864, and thereafter at a declining percentage of face value until August 1, 1864, when they would become worthless. A new issue of $200 million in Treasury notes receivable for taxes was also authorized.[50]

W. W. Boyce of South Carolina, an antagonist of Jefferson Davis, proposed instead that future taxes be paid in specie or in the specie value of the inflated Treasury notes and that the government issue of tax-free 6 percent bonds be redeemed by a dedicated tax.[51] Tennessee congressman William G. Swan proposed a thirty-year .83 percent tax on real estate. Property owners paying this tax by July 1, 1864, would receive 6 percent thirty-year bonds; a sinking fund would be established to pay off the bonds.[52] Other proposed amendments would have altered deadlines and interest rates or even referred the whole subject back to committee. There was yet another proposal to make Treasury notes legal tender. After a confusing mass of amendments, on January 16, 1864, the House passed the bill by a narrow thirty-eight to thirty-two margin and sent it off to the Senate.[53]

The Senate had to await the House bill before it could engage in serious consideration of the funding issue. As the body prepared to deal with funding and other tax questions, the senators requested an accounting of the size of the national debt. Secretary Memminger reported that the Confederate debt was on the order of $1.1 billion, including $300 million in bonds and stock, $90 million in call certificates, $720 million in noninterest-bearing Treasury notes, $100 million in interest-bearing Treasury notes; and these figures did not include any of the unpaid impressment certificates.[54] Apparently the Senate was so stunned by these figures that later the same day it indefinitely postponed a bill for another issue of Treasury notes and (in secret session) turned its attention to a bill to redeem the outstanding notes and "restore the public credit."[55]

The House bill met the same sort of fate in the Senate as it had in the House. In fact, the committee report on January 27, 1864, was laden with so many amendments as to create virtually a new bill.[56] These amendments were then struck out and a substitute inserted. Additional amending did not seem to improve the bill very much, so the Senate defeated it on its third reading by a narrow ten to eleven tally and returned it to a select committee. On February 4 the committee reported a refined bill, which would have lowered the interest rate on the bonds used to fund Treasury notes to 4 percent and authorized the issue of $200 million of new notes, to be called "exchequer notes."[57] The Senate passed the bill and returned it to the House, which thoroughly chopped up the Senate amendments, even to the extent of inserting a new tax bill,[58] whereupon the whole mess was returned to the Senate. A conference committee was appointed that redrew the bill, and both houses finally agreed on February 16, 1864.[59] The president approved it the next day. "At last," wrote one editor, "Congress has acted boldly," and he proclaimed that "taxation or repudiation is the inevitable outcome."[60]

Under the funding law of February 17, holders of noninterest-bearing Treasury notes denominated at over five dollars were given until April 1 (July 1 in the Trans-Mississippi), to exchange their notes for 4 percent, twenty-year bonds or for a new note issue at two-thirds face value. Notes of one hundred dollars denomination not exchanged for bonds before the deadlines would no longer be acceptable for payment of monies due the government and would be taxed at one-third of their value plus 10 percent per month until received by the government. Five dollar notes were fundable under much the same terms, except holders had an extended deadline, July 1 (October 1 in the Trans-Mississippi). However, notes could be funded at that reduced value (two dollars in new notes for three dollars in old notes) until January 1, 1865—one hundred dollar notes being excluded from the privilege—after which they would be worthless.

To provide the new notes, the secretary of the treasury would issue new notes payable two years after a treaty of peace had been ratified. States holding notes could fund at face value in 6 percent, twenty-year bonds until January 1, 1865, after which they could fund at two-thirds of face value. By these provisions, all old notes would eventually become worthless and would be replaced by a new (and smaller) issue. To keep the government going and to circulate the new notes, the Treasury was to issue $500 million in tax-free, 6 percent, thirty-year bonds.[61]

Presumably this legislation would reduce the circulating currency to less than two-thirds of the amount then in use, since the noninterest-bearing one hundred dollar bills would become worthless if not exchanged for bonds. Congress expected many smaller bills would also be exchanged for bonds, to avoid reduction in value if converted to the reissue of currency.[62]

The amount of currency outstanding before funding began is uncertain. E. Merton Coulter gives the figure of $973 million, but Richard C. Todd estimates $800 million—quite enough by any calculation. By April 1, 1864, $250 million was funded into the requisite 4 percent, twenty-year bonds, with more to come in the Trans-Mississippi.[63] The one hundred dollar notes were now valueless, but the other notes still in circulation could be exchanged at two-thirds face value for 4 percent bonds or the new issue of notes. Actual amounts are quite uncertain. Some bills were lost, destroyed, or mislaid, to the extent that the actual amount in circulation may have been less than $300 million. But the records are confused.[64]

The Confederate humorist, Charles H. Smith, writing under the name "Bill Arp," summed up the situation as well as anyone. "It is whispered around in select circles (and that is how I came to hear it)," he wrote, "that this bill would not have passed, but Mr. Memminger lost his account-book when they had the last big scare in Richmond, and he informed Congress that there was no way to tell how much money was out, without calling it all in again. He was asked to say about how much he thought was in circulation; and he said he hadn't charged his memory particularly, but according to his recollection there was *six hundred millions* or *six thousand millions*—he was not certain which."[65]

The basic effect of the law was intended "to reduce the currency by compelling note holders to (1) fund their notes in 20-year 4% registered bonds or (2) exchange them at the rate of $3 in old for $2 in new notes," which is reasonably close in principle, if not in detail, to what Memminger had suggested.[66] In any case, it smacked of repudiation, which it would have been save that many citizens ignored the law.

The funding system worked temporarily, despite some evidence of a financial panic, as in short order some Richmond merchants raised their prices sharply.[67] By the end of April 1864, almost $1 billion in Treasury notes was outstanding, with additional notes being issued under the February 17 law. Many notes of the old issues had been withdrawn from circulation, and the premium on gold declined. When the law was passed, gold was at twenty-three dollars in Treasury notes, but it dropped to seventeen during spring 1864. By September, however, it was back at twenty-three dollars. It ranged between thirty-four and forty-nine dollars at the end of 1864, and in March 1865 it reached as high as seventy dollars. By then, though, the question no longer was very important. Since the effect of the law was only temporary, it further undermined public confidence in the Treasury Department and led to Secretary Memminger's resignation in July 1864. He was replaced by George A. Trenholm, a rich international cotton merchant and banker.[68]

By October 1864 almost $300 million in new notes had been issued, but only $29 million of those notes had been issued in the three-for-two exchange mandated by the February 1864 legislation. Trenholm admitted the failure of funding when he supported the legislation of December 19, 1864, which extended the funding deadline to July 1, 1865. In the meantime, the old and new note issues circulated side by side, even though the old was "nominally repudiated."[69]

Davis expressed the optimistic assessment that some $300 million in old currency would be exchanged for the new, but nonetheless he still feared that this would leave a redundant currency. He might cling to some shred of hope, but Vice President Stephens long since had given up any. In April 1864 he privately declared to Secretary of War Seddon, "Our finances are now a wreck. Past all hope, in my judgment." He was far from alone: about the same time South Carolina Congressman William W. Boyce concluded that the Confederacy's credit was beyond restoration.[70]

The old money that the Treasury received was to be mutilated and burned, but occasionally bills were saved from the fire and passed again. The design of the new issue of notes was similar to the old one, and the caustic editor of the *Richmond Examiner* ridiculed it. He thought that to see the faces on the notes "with that unchanging expression of ineffable melancholy which the engraver has given to all of them, (for on the best specimens of the Confederate currency Davis is doleful, and Stephens saturnine, Hunter is heavy, and Clay clouded with care, Memminger is mournful, and even Benjamin the buoyant is *bien triste*), and to have constantly in sight the evidence of the country's trav[a]il and impecuniosity, were enough to drive even a well-regulated mind to lunacy." Only chivalry restrained him from commenting on the features of Mrs. Francis W. Pickens of South Carolina (wife of the governor), whose face was on the one hundred dollar notes.[71]

None of the three new finance laws passed on February 17 worked out very well; they displeased fully as many people as had the previous legislation. Stephens thought them "neither proper, wise or just," and Memminger predicted that their "flagrant injustice would provoke severe criticism, if we were in quiet times." But another Georgian pointed to the worst, and inevitable, result: "Thousands will be utterly ruined by this taxation. . . . Thousands will be reduced to beggary and starvation. . . . But I will not comment farther upon the spawn of Congress whose members generally have merited the curses and contempt of every one."[72]

Congress faced more problems than financing the war. They also had to deal with conscription and exemption laws. Some index of the problem of desertion was indicated by the content of a law that was passed to punish those who might encourage desertion,[73] but Davis was frustrated with the slow course of legislative action, and just a few days before the end of the third session of the First Congress he appealed again for conscription extension and enrollment of troops for local defense. Such troops would have a dual role, for they would be essential in maintaining agricultural production and acting as a reserve for use in local emergencies. "If the spirit which rendered the volunteering so general among all classes of citizens at the beginning of the war were still prevalent," complained Davis, "there would be no necessity for the proposed legislation. . . . But as this is not that case, it is necessary that conscription for local defense should replace volunteering."[74]

Congress reacted quickly this time. In truth, it had been working on the conscription and exemption issues since the start of the session, but as was so frequently the case, not much major legislation was passed until near the end of the session. On the last day of the First Congress, February 17, Davis signed into law bills establishing an Invalid Corps,[75] extending the draft ages from eighteen to seventeen and forty-six to fifty, revising the exemption laws, and authorizing details.[76] Men aged eighteen to forty-five had their term of service extended once again, just as it had been in the original conscription law of April 1862, and those aged seventeen and forty-six to fifty "shall constitute a reserve for State defense and detail duty, and shall not be required to perform service out of the State in which they reside."[77] Henceforth, clerks, guards, laborers in the military bureaus, and the like, were to be between eighteen and forty-five who were no longer fit for field duty, but the president was to have wide authority to detail "artisans, mechanics, or persons of special skill" to special duty.[78] The cumulative effect of these laws might almost seem to be equivalent to a levy en masse, except for the somewhat tightened but still generous list of exemptions. There was widespread opposition to such a sweeping recruitment of the army, and one of the Richmond newspapers (whose editor enjoyed an occupational exemption himself) called it a confession of weakness that was not justified by the military situation.[79]

Modified exemption provisions granted excuses to clergy, "superintendents and physicians of asylums for the deaf, dumb and blind and of the insane," editors, public printers and essential journeymen printers, physicians over thirty years old and in actual practice (but not including dentists), presidents and teachers in educational institutions with at least twenty students, and overseers of fifteen or more fit slaves where no other white adult male was available, provided that they delivered a specified amount of foodstuffs to the army and sold their produce to the government or to soldiers' families at prices equal to the prices paid for impressments. The president or secretary of war could also "exempt or detail such other persons as he may be satisfied ought to be exempted on account of public necessity, and to insure the production of grain and provisions for the army and the families of soldiers."

Exemptions for men engaged in public transportation were curtailed somewhat, but exemptions for essential workers in the postal service were not.[80]

There was serious internal opposition from civilians and from congressional delegations, and further appeal by Jefferson Davis. On February 3, the president sent an anxious, even hysterical, message to Congress. He noted that "the zeal with which the people sprang to arms at the beginning of the contest has . . . been impaired by the long continuance and magnitude of the struggle," and he complained that

> discontent, disaffection, and disloyalty are manifested among those who, through the sacrifices of others, have enjoyed quiet and safety at home. Public meetings have been held, in some of which a treasonable design is masked by a pretense of devotion to State sovereignty, and in others is openly avowed. Conventions are advocated with the pretended object of redressing grievances, which, if they existed, could as well be remedied by ordinary legislative action, but with the real design of accomplishing treason under the form of law. To this end a strong suspicion is entertained that secret leagues and associations are being formed. . . . And yet must they, through too strict regard to the technicalities of the law, be permitted to go at large till they have perfected their treason by the commission of an overt act?

Spies, thought Davis, were coming and going, even in the midst of Richmond, and indeed, he was not far wrong on this point, at least. He further spiced up his chilling warnings with word that there were "secret movements among the negroes fomented by base white men" and that "[Benjamin] Butler is perfecting some deep-laid scheme" to bring about a slave rebellion. In some areas "civil process" had been used to decimate the army, and generals were called away to answer writs on the eve of campaigns. Davis feared that the increasing use of the writ of habeas corpus to get men out of the army would encourage "desertion, already a frightful evil [which] will become the order of the day." And, he asked, "Must these evils be endured?"[81]

Davis's answer was, of course, no. Although he clearly had exaggerated the evils, his concern was quite understandable, for they did exist. The problem was that the miscreants, whoever they were, were frequently released on a writ of habeas corpus if they were arrested. Indeed, the Georgia legislature specifically encouraged the practice. In December 1863 that state legislature ordered that "any judge of the Superior, or Justice of the Inferior Courts, whose duty it is to grant such writs," who refused to grant habeas corpus when requested, would "forfeit to the party aggrieved, the sum of twenty-five hundred dollars."[82] Davis's solution to such problems fulfilled the prophecy of

Congressman William Waters Boyce: indeed, the president did seek more power, the power to suspend the writ of habeas corpus again.[83] This was not the sort of outcome that Confederates had seceded and gone to war to achieve, but Davis saw no other choice, and he consoled himself with the hope that "loyal citizens will not feel danger, and the disloyal must be made to fear it." He also hoped that "the very existence of extraordinary powers often renders their exercise unnecessary," but this was the sort of threatening attitude that bothered some Confederates.[84]

Senator E. G. Reade of North Carolina, for example, was upset by such statements, for North Carolina was a suspect state by now, including both its leadership in Congress and at home, and a vocal opposition objected to severe measures such as suspension of the writ. "I am really alarmed for the consequences," he wrote. "Right now, when the soldiers are tendering their blood & the people are pouring in their treasures in tithes and other taxes is this a time to exhibit distrust towards them?" Reade trembled at the thought of Davis's power if the writ were suspended.[85] Some Virginia congressmen agreed with Reade because of the provisions of their state constitution, and Georgia senator Herschel V. Johnson as well as Vice President Stephens used Davis's proposal to continue their generally friendly but vehement argument over the constitutional behavior of their president. But the crisis was pressing.

Because of this conflict, "Stephens now broke publicly with the administration," as Cooper observes. The vice president became "an articulate ally," of Davis's bitterest political foe: Governor Joseph E. Brown of Georgia.

> "A long letter to Davis detailed [Stephens's] views of how the Confederacy should fight the war. In the epistle, he took exception to the president's position, which he termed 'execrable.' He wanted no conscription, no impressment, no suspension of the writ of habeas corpus. . . . In a lengthy address before the Georgia legislature in mid-March, Stephens denounced the Davis administration as the embodiment of tyranny; the escape from oppression in 1861 had ended up in the dungeon of despotism."[86]

As Thomas Schott has observed: "Defense of the Confederate cause to him did not mean blind loyalty to its government."[87]

The vice president had other close collaborators, his younger brother Linton and his friend Robert Toombs, who "lived in their own world." However, as Cooper points out, "These raging Georgians howled, but they accomplished little. Davis and his definition of the Confederate cause had stalwart supporters in the state, such as Howell Cobb and Confederate senators Benjamin Hill and Herschel Johnson. Like Senator Johnson, a friend of Stephens's who worried about increased executive authority, many Georgians refused to follow the dissidents' lead, . . . maintaining trust in Davis."[88]

Schott has observed, however, that in losing the support of his vice president "[Davis] blundered seriously in casting aside the man himself. The vice-president was a political force to be reckoned with. Had Davis been half the politician his masterful counterpart in Washington was—Lincoln had forged an effective administration out of such disparate elements as Chase, Seward, Welles, and Stanton—he might have recognized the foolishness of treating Stephens like a cipher."[89]

Congress reacted to Davis's request for renewed suspension of habeas corpus with great hesitation; many Confederates were seriously concerned that conscription and especially the suspension of the writ of habeas corpus robbed them of the very sort of rights they were fighting to maintain. Congressional response was, therefore, a tightly written measure. After a preamble that carefully justified the action, the legislation declared the writ suspended, but only in cases "of persons arrested or detained by order of the President, Secretary of War, or the general officer commanding the Trans-Mississippi Department." It then designated thirteen precisely defined circumstances, including such offenses as treason, conspiracy to overthrow the government, assisting the enemy, spying, encouraging slave insurrection, and the like. The provision that addressed the heart of the manpower question, however, suspended the writ in cases "of desertion or encouraging desertions, of harboring deserters, and of attempts to avoid military service: *Provided,* That in cases of palpable wrong and oppression by any subordinate officer, upon any party who does not legally owe military service, his superior officers shall grant prompt relief, to the oppressed party, and the subordinate shall be dismissed from office."[90]

No officer would be compelled to answer any writ or to release anyone held in custody under the order of the president, secretary of war, or the commander of the Trans-Mississippi Department. Congress hedged its bets, however, for the law would be effective only until "ninety days after the next meeting of Congress, and no longer."[91] The refusal to give the president more sweeping authority indicated increasing resentment over the powers exercised by the president. As Congressman Boyce noted, it was evidence of a growing organization among those who opposed conscription. Open opposition to conscription was not quite respectable in many quarters. Thus many congressmen, governors, and ordinary citizens who opposed it could and did oppose suspension of the writ of habeas corpus, firm in the knowledge that the community was more likely to support them than if they opposed conscription outright.

This was especially true in Georgia, where a cohort of politicians, including Governor Brown, Vice President Stephens, Linton Stephens, and assorted newspaper editors, led a movement in the state legislature to oppose suspension. Frank Owsley has cited this reaction as a major example of the weakening of the Confederate government because of an excessive devotion to state rights.[92] But not everyone opposed suspension of the writ. Brown and the Stephens brothers sought to include Senator B. H. Hill, but he would have none of it.[93] The legislature met, Brown attacked the suspension as similar to "letters *de cachet* by royal prerogative,"[94] and Linton Stephens listed his objections, followed by the vice president.[95] The resolutions passed by the Georgia legislature asserted that "under the Constitution of the Confederate States there is no power to suspend the privilege of the writ of habeas corpus," except as limited by the due process clause and "the right of the people to be secure in their persons, houses, papers, and effects . . . and no warrants shall issue but upon probable cause." The only legal warrants, thought Linton Stephens, were those that came from "a judicial source."[96]

Senator Herschel V. Johnson joined his colleague, B. H. Hill, in his opposition to the divisive actions of the Georgia legislature. Writing to Alexander Stephens, he denied that Davis's suspension of the writ had struck any blow at personal liberty; Stephens replied that Johnson "would not believe though one were to rise from the dead." Denying that he had any antipathy or hostility toward Davis, Stephens said that his feelings were "much more akin to suspicion and jealousy than of animosity or hate." Davis was "a man of good intentions, weak and vacillating, timid, petulant, peevish, obstinate, but not firm. And now I am beginning to doubt his good intentions. . . . His whole policy on the organization and discipline of the Army is perfectly consistent with the hypothesis that he is aiming at absolute power. . . . My hostility and wrath (and I have enough of it to burst ten thousand bottles)," he claimed, "is not against him, or any man or men, but against the thing—the measure and the policy which I see is leading us to despotism." With surprise that anyone could possibly think him antagonistic toward Davis, the vice president told Johnson that "you surely have heard me in conversation speak of his weakness and imbecility, but certainly with no bitterness of feeling, and . . . more in sorrow than anger."[97]

The most ominous piece of manpower legislation was passed on the last day of the congressional session. Compliant with Davis's request made early the previous December to amend the law of April 21, 1862, which authorized the army to hire cooks, teamsters, and laborers, whether white or black (thus freeing more whites for field duty), Congress responded with the appropriate legislation to hire blacks only. Free black males aged eighteen to fifty were held liable to duty with the army working on fortifications, in government factories, or in military hospitals. While engaged in such duty, they would receive eleven dollars a month, clothing, and rations, and those whose labor was more valuable elsewhere could be exempted by the secretary of war. Slaves could also be put to work with the army, the wages being negotiated with the owners and paid to them. If the army were unable to get enough slaves by the voluntary action of owners, then those that were needed could be impressed.[98]

The legislation had frightening implications, for these black men were in truth conscripts. And if they were not uniformed soldiers in the army, they were with the army: they received clothing and rations, and the free blacks received the same pay as army privates. In practice, then, blacks were doing everything that whites did, except fight. And already there were persons who were proposing, just as there were others who were fearing, that blacks soon would be committed to doing that, too.

The first session of the Second Congress opened on May 2, 1864, and ended just six weeks later. Although manpower questions were discussed, enough congressmen found previous legislation either satisfactory or entirely too extreme; no further legislation was passed for the time being. The successful defense of Richmond by General R. E. Lee led to some complacency among Confederate leaders, many of whom doubted that Union determination would withstand the heavy casualties being inflicted on the Federal army. Under these conditions, the need for manpower did not seem as pressing as it had previously.

Once again habeas corpus was a subject of intense debate, although no new law was passed. The issue was rather to repeal the old law, which still had ninety days to run after the first session of the Second Congress convened, and which was about twice as long as the session lasted. The emotional recoil against the previous draconian legislation continued, even though the longer the congressmen debated, the less time the existing law would continue on the books. The Virginia congressman William C. Rives, an old Jacksonian who had been in Paris and seen the bloodshed of the French revolution of 1830, defended the suspension:

> Engaged in an exterminating war of the most tremendous magnitude, waged by a ruthless foe, governed by no rules of humanity, obeying no laws of war, occupying a large part of our territory . . . our capital in a state of standing siege for three years, we may say; the enemy's cannon sounding in our ears from day to day, yet we are assured by gentlemen that Congress made a dangerous inroad upon the liberty of person and speech, and exercised an unwonted stretch of power in passing the act suspending the writ of *habeas corpus*.[99]

Rives stood in the minority this time, however, and even Davis's own state of Mississippi had doubts about suspending habeas corpus again. The legislature went so far as to instruct the two senators to vote to suspend the current act, although Mississippi senator Albert Gallatin Brown had made it clear that he disagreed with the actions of the legislature, concluding, "Let us first establish that we have States before we quarrel about the 'rights of the States.' "[100] The highly opinionated congressman Henry S. Foote of Tennessee countered the notion of disloyalty that Davis had cited, calling it "a phantom, a myth, a vapor; the mirage arising from a diseased eye."[101] This was a cruel stab at Davis, who by then was blind in one eye. The two men had long detested each other with an enthusiasm that had increased when Foote had defeated Davis for the governorship of Mississippi by only 999 votes in the 1851 election.[102] Now in the Confederate Congress, Foote took every opportunity to censure the Davis administration. But other congressmen agreed with Foote, albeit for more legitimate reasons. John P. Murray, from Tennessee, attacked the notion "that in order to get liberty you must first lose it."[103]

Yet by this time, the war was once again getting close to the capital in Richmond, and the self-confidence that so marked the Southern forces two years before, when McClellan was pushed away from the vicinity, was seriously diminished. The repeal bill was defeated, and in a House resolution passed on May 13, Davis was asked if the reasons justifying his previous request for suspension still existed and if there were any new reasons to suspend the writ.[104] Davis replied as shrilly a few days later as he had before. The law had been "salutary" in its operation and "enabled our gallant armies, under the providence of God, to beat back the vast invading forces which still threaten us." Ending suspension "would be perilous, if not calamitous." Its very existence had been so effective that it had rarely been used, and the law had effectively checked the use of the writ by those who desired to avoid conscription. Davis underlined his conclusion with the ominous remark "that if those who have expressed dissatisfaction with the new law had been in possession of the information which it was my duty to communicate to you, and which may not yet be revealed without injury to the public interest, they would fully have approved the exercise of the power of suspending the writ."[105] Although he surely desired another suspension law, he knew which way the wind was blowing and did not ask for one. The previous law therefore died as scheduled, in early August 1864. Although debate continued in that session, there was no further significant legislative action on the matter.

The last session of the First Congress made additional provisions for the systematic use of black labor, including hiring slaves from their masters and obligating free black males to labor for wages. If these did not prove sufficient, the secretary of war was empowered to impress up to twenty thousand slaves under the provisions of the previous law.[106] Since the need for labor was more pressing, the regulations stipulated that the maximum period of service would be twelve months, if necessary, rather than sixty days.[107]

The question of paying for impressed labor was just as difficult as the question of paying for impressed crops or manufactured goods and was aggravated by the propensity of impressed slaves to run away—a form of spoilage, as an impressment officer might have put it. In Virginia in January 1864, $.5 million was required to pay owners whose slaves had escaped or died while working on the defenses of Richmond.

Using the Virginia figures as a basis, one Confederate officer informed the secretary of war that the government owed owners approximately $3.1 million.[108] Quite often even the availability of slave labor was an issue, sometimes because owners simply did not want to lose control of their slaves. But in some areas slaves and free blacks were already at work in the fields and fortifications under state law or local police, and a Confederate call only disrupted essential work in one area in an attempt to put the labor force to work on equally essential work in another area. This was not an efficient way to proceed, as former congressman John B. Baldwin pointed out.[109]

Congressmen and citizens alike continued to be upset with impressment, both of goods and slaves, but when the Second Congress met for its first session in May, Davis did not mention the impressment problem. In January 1864, salt pork and bacon prices had remained stable on the Virginia impressment schedules, though lard had gone up to $1.25.[110] By April, bacon in Mississippi ranged from $1.15 to $1.75, depending on quality and location; lard cost $1.50 to $1.75.[111] By April salt pork in Virginia had gone up to $2.60 a pound, bacon to $3.00 a pound, and lard to $3.00 a pound. However, most commodity prices remained about what they had been the previous January.[112]

This modicum of stability was due in part to the legislation of February 17, which funded the prior existing currency with a new issue; it was also a sign that producers were being squeezed even harder. As the value of Treasury notes inflated (as measured by the price of gold), impressment prices went up slowly. By comparison, in Richmond $1.00 in gold had cost a purchaser $1.10 in Confederate Treasury notes in summer 1861. During summer 1862 the price rose to $1.50 in Treasury notes, and during summer 1863 gold rose from $7.00 to $13.00. By January 1864 $1.00 in gold set back a purchaser $20.00 in Treasury notes, and a year later the price had risen to between $45.00 and $60.00.[113] The situation was similar for impressment victims in the Trans-Mississippi West; in January 1862 $1.00 in gold had equaled $1.50 in Treasury notes, but by January 1865 it would be up to $18.00 to $26.00.[114] No wonder producers clamored for market-price impressment.

There were over one hundred items in the Virginia schedule of prices, and most remained the same from April to early May 1864. Among the exceptions were peas, beans, Irish potatoes, and sweet potatoes, which jumped from $4.00, $4.00, $4.00, and $5.00 per bushel to $12.00, $12,00, $5.00, and $8.00; most notable were huge increases in iron, which more than doubled.[115] Not only was pricing unsatisfactory, but there was also some confusion as to what the law meant. At least in parts of Virginia, farmers and quartermasters differed over exactly what was to be assessed. Some quartermasters thought that the "gross crop of corn" was to be assessed for the tax in kind, but some farmers disagreed. They thought that only the corn that was left over after fattening hogs ought to be assessed; to tax the gross crop one-tenth, then tax the pork one-tenth, would, they argued, be like taxing some of the corn twice.[116]

Even as Davis wavered, not really knowing what to do, some congressmen attempted to pass additional impressment legislation. On May 28, Senator William A. Graham reported a "bill to provide supplies for the army and to prescribe the mode of making impressments,"[117] which, among other things, would have taken impressment out of the hands of quartermasters and commissaries and confined impressment duty to officers carrying out the collection of the tax in kind.[118]

The problem, according to Senator James L. Orr of South Carolina, was that impressment often took away a family's necessary subsistence.[119] Many citizens and legislators were strongly opposed to the impressment law, at least as it functioned. There was no excuse for withholding surpluses from the army, but the *Montgomery Weekly Advertiser* reflected citizen frustration with the system in an angry editorial that labeled impressment "one of the most dangerous prerogatives of power," because "force becomes the rule, and purchase the exception." The editor demanded that the army adhere to General Cooper's standing order on the subject, which had prohibited impressment of supplies that a farmer needed "for his own consumption, or that of his family, employees, and slaves," or of supplies that were on the way to market.[120] Senator Williamson S. Oldham of Texas claimed that quartermaster officers "only looked to the grant of power and proceeded to exercise it according to their own notions." Never one to mince words, Oldham conjectured that "the country would be benefitted if about seven hundred quartermasters, who violated the law, were hung."[121] The bill passed the Senate on June 1 by the close vote of ten to seven,[122] but the question was lost when the House of Representatives tabled the bill by a one-vote majority.[123] Thus, the Congress failed in this session to resolve any of the impressment problems. The system simply continued, providing some necessary supplies to the Confederate war effort but at the same time creating and exacerbating bedeviling difficulties.

Major General William T. Sherman viewed the railroads around Meridian, where the Mobile and Ohio and the Southern Railroad of Mississippi crossed, as an inviting target for destruction. Huge stores of military supplies were stockpiled there, and the railroad junction made it a key spot. Sherman's attitude toward the South was hardening. In 1862 he had written to his brother, Senator John Sherman of Ohio, "It is about time the North understood the truth, that the entire South, man, woman, and child is against us." And in that year he had indicated to Ulysses S. Grant that "we cannot change the hearts of the people of the South but we can make war so terrible that they will realize [its folly], however brave and gallant and devoted to their country" they may be. In 1863, to a Southern woman who complained about his soldiers' stealing, he answered, "Madam, . . . War is cruelty. There is no use trying to reform it; the crueler it is, the sooner it will be over."[124]

The Meridian campaign was one of the most significant raids of the 1863–1864 winter, one that combined almost all the elements in Grant's intended new strategy. It was both a test of the concept and a dress rehearsal for the subsequent 1864 campaigns in the West. Mark Grimsley has pointed out that "Grant had approved the Meridian expedition, and it formed a good example of the sort of war he expected to conduct against the South." The operation had three objectives: to cripple Confederate rail support, to destroy an area supplying Southern troops with staples, and to reduce the possibility of further Rebel operations in the region in order to scale down the number of Union troops needed to protect Federal navigation on the Mississippi River.

Lieutenant General Leonidas Polk had command of the Department of Mississippi, Alabama, and East Louisiana. He had two divisions of infantry and two of cavalry, with his headquarters in Meridian. One of Polk's infantry divisions, that of Major General William W. "Old Blizzards" Loring, was at Canton; the other, under Major General Samuel G. French, was encamped at Brandon. Major General Stephen D. Lee had charge of the cavalry. A series of telegraphic messages had flashed back and forth between the Confederate leaders and the high command in Richmond. Polk strongly suspected that the ultimate Federal objective was Mobile, Alabama.

What could S. D. Lee and his meager cavalry do to deal with the situation before them? Almost as soon as the Yankees left Jackson, Southern cavalrymen poured back into the city; but the only Confederate force between the Yankees and Brandon was a 40-man detachment, which was easily pushed aside.

The Yankees thrust on through Brandon on the afternoon of February 7. Reflecting on the result of their passage, one Union soldier wrote in his diary: "Brandon . . . was none the better nor richer for our occupation, foraging and fire doing fearful work, and as usual attacking the loveliest and costliest first." Another wrote, "There was considerable foraging done today, in the line of hay, corn, meat, hogs, chickens, and turkeys." On February 8 the Federals moved from Brandon to Morton, elements of the Fourth Mississippi Cavalry resisting, but they were forced rearward.

Polk then tentatively decided that some major attempt must be made to turn back the marauding columns. During the night of February 7 Confederate troops streamed into Morton, and all available locomotives and railroad cars were rushed to Meridian to evacuate the stores. Brigadier General Francis M. Cockrell's brigade traveled by rail from Mobile, reaching Morton a few hours before daylight. Confederate strength now stood at 20,933.

When the Yankees arrived in Hillsborough, at 9:00 A.M. on February 10, shots were fired at them from several of the houses. In retaliation, the Federals set fire to nearly every house in the town. The Yankee infantry then moved out, but a Rebel patrol dashed to the bridge across Beaver Dam Creek, set it afire, and delayed the Yankee wagon train in its crossing. Later in the day, the Federals encamped on Tallabogue Creek, three and one-half miles east of Hillsborough.

The Yankee column reached Tuscalameta Creek, near Hillsborough, on February 11, only to discover that the bridge across it had been burned. This was the first of four creeks that had to be crossed that day. Nevertheless, the troops covered thirteen miles, but it was one of the hardest and most tiring marches of the expedition. The Yankees had pushed into harsh and difficult country. The weather was cold and nasty, the swamp almost impenetrable. There was mud everywhere and tangled underbrush. Wagon after wagon bogged down. During the night, small bands of Rebels constantly harassed Yankee pickets.

As February 12 dawned cold and clear, the Federals again moved out. S. D. Lee was at Decatur with the two Rebel cavalry brigades. The Yankees trudged out of the Tuscalameta swamp and entered the rolling, sparsely settled pine country that stretched to the east. Meanwhile, as the Federals continued pushing forward, Confederate cavalrymen again harassed them. Trees were felled to block the roads, bridges were burned, and snipers were liable to fire at any moment. By late in the evening, however, cavalry in the lead of the Yankee column were within fourteen miles of Meridian.

Davis at this point assumed a direct role in directing the resistance. On February 13 the president telegraphed General Joseph Johnston, asking what he could do to strike at the enemy "before he establishes a new base." Johnston was apparently puzzled at any suggestion of releasing some of his force, so he did nothing. Then Davis sent him a preemptive order to detach William J. Hardee's infantry corps to proceed with all possible speed and to unite with Polk's force. But Davis and Johnston both had delayed too long.[125]

During the night, S. D. Lee received orders from Polk to move into Meridian to cover the infantry, which would retreat toward Demopolis, Alabama: "If there is any road by which your command may turn to the left and strike the Meridian and Decatur Road west of Meridian, so as to get in between the enemy and Meridian," then they were to do so. Only one of Lee's two brigades was able to get to Meridian; the other was compelled to detour southward. Most of the Confederate supplies and materiel were already out of Meridian, the rest being moved as fast as possible, under the trying circumstances.

Beginning February 14, as Sherman put it, "For five days 10,000 men worked hard and with a will in that work of destruction. . . . Meridian, with its depots, store-houses, arsenals, hospitals, offices, hotels, cantonments no longer exists." The Federals also destroyed about one hundred fifteen miles of railroad, sixty-one bridges, and twenty locomotives. At the recently established Confederate armory where small arms had been manufactured, a number of shotguns, rifles, carbines, and three pieces of artillery were captured.

In the houses and outbuildings the Yankees ransacked barrels of molasses, corn meal, and flour. Foraging parties came back laden with hams, pork shoulders, and bacon. At a lumberyard they found choice pine lumber, which one soldier recalled was "confiscated and taken to camp, and before night nearly every soldier in the 17th Army Corps had a comfortable but rudely constructed shanty, with a floor in it and was prepared for a good night rest secure from rain."

The destruction was thorough and methodical. The men had lived off the country as they moved, saving their own supplies, consuming food and fodder meant for Confederate sustenance, destroying what lay in their path, and leaving behind burning buildings and desolation. S. D. Lee spoke of "the Sherman torch" and contended vehemently for the rest of his life that Sherman had acted in a wantonly vindictive manner. "Was this the civilized warfare of the nineteenth century?" Lee asked, asserting that more than three-fourths of what Sherman destroyed was private property. Though this was true enough, most of it was critical to the Southern war effort, as Sherman reasoned. And much of it was to be used in a manner beneficial to the Northern war effort. According to Mark Grimsley, Sherman's destructiveness generally was premeditated, controlled, and limited; it was not unmitigated, all-out war by the Federal military against a hapless civilian populace.

Although some Federal elements encountered costly resistance on their return trek, for the most part, the main force successfully crossed the Pearl River and marched unmolested back to Vicksburg. They had been on the march for thirty days, having traversed some three hundred sixty miles not only along roads but also through swamps, creeks, mud, briars, and undergrowth.

One of the most significant results was the number of black refugees that accompanied the returning Union column. Estimates of the exact number vary, but one was posited by R. L. Howard, a Union soldier-diarist: "Over 5,000 came in with us," he wrote, "of every age, quality and condition." Some Confederate estimates were lower. The *Chattanooga Daily Rebel* reported that Sherman's raid had cost Mississippi three thousand slaves, and asserted that the Yankees claimed four thousand. These slaves, wrote the editor of the *Rebel*, were worth at least $5 million and could have been saved if their owners had withdrawn them. But owners had not taken their slaves out of Sherman's path; therefore they were lost, and with them went all the labor they might have performed for the Confederacy. This was a vital lesson for the future. And so the Meridian campaign ended.

Yet very little went well for this group of hapless blacks, freed from enslavement but not succored by their deliverers. The Federals persisted in retreating much faster than the blacks could go and left no provisions for them; the blacks were simply abandoned. Several letters reached President Davis describing the pitiable condition of these people, many of them mothers with hungry and fretting children in tow. Davis felt a deep sense of distress and indignation over the situation. As for Sherman's Meridian campaign, Davis blamed the Federals' ultimate success on Johnston's failure to act. Indeed, the president even intimated that Sherman's force might have been so mangled that his future in the Federal plans perhaps would have been considerably lessened in significance.[126]

The Confederates could take some small comfort in having forced the termination of a raid. But the Federals had successfully tested the concept of army-sized raids, which played a major role in the Union's end-game grand strategy, and somewhat less successfully, the concept of concerted advance. Given the significance of this harbinger of the final Union strategy, it is surprising that the Meridian campaign has been somewhat neglected by most historians of the Civil War. Nor was it mentioned by Jefferson Davis in *Rise and Fall* or by Varina in *A Memoir.*

There is yet another quite interesting might-have-been story of significance in Civil War naval history: it centers on the Confederacy's split second of success in developing an operational submarine. Had the Confederacy been a bit more efficient, had it managed to build more than one viable submarine, and had the one it built been able to survive its first combat cruise, the outcome of the war might have been different.[127]

The first meaningful success occurred in New Orleans. There, at the Leeds Foundry, several models were fabricated. One of the financial backers, Horace L. Hunley, a well-to-do sugar broker, took an intense interest in the project and himself became unquestionably the greatest expert of his time on submarine design, construction, and operation. After New Orleans fell in April 1862, Hunley and the other submariners moved to Mobile, Alabama, and subsequently to Charleston, South Carolina.

All the Confederate submarines were screw-driven, powered by cranks turned by men inside, which never gave as much motive power as was desired. Experiments were conducted using primitive electric motors, but ultimately the best the Southerners could do was to devise a way to increase the number of crank operators. The final model of the Confederate submarine set an endurance record of an astounding two hours and thirty-five minutes below the surface before coming up safely.

In August 1863 the submariners transferred their equipment from Mobile to Charleston, hauling the sub on two railroad flatcars. At Charleston, after a few practice dives, a fatal accident occurred on August 29, 1863. The sub was fished from the bottom, refitted, and Hunley himself decided to be its pilot. He truly was a good submariner, but he too perished in a freak accident on October 15. Again the sub was raised; still dedicated to the enterprise, the other builders supervised its cleaning and repair. They renamed it the CSS *Hunley,* in honor of its late skipper.

With a carefully trained crew, the *Hunley* made several successful practice dives and thereafter commenced regular cruising. The plan was to hit and methodically destroy the blockading squadron. For the sub to attack, however, many conditions had to be just right: an ebb tide was needed to set out and a flood tide to return, the wind must be scant, and the moon must be dark.

Finally, there came a night when conditions seemed promising, and at dusk on February 14, 1864, the *Hunley* cast off on its last but history-making voyage. Its prey, the USS *Housatonic*, lay at anchor a few miles south of the entrance to Charleston Harbor. A warning sounded at the last minute, but it was too late: the torpedo exploded and the *Housatonic* sank. Most of its crew were picked up by nearby boats, but five Yankee sailors were never found. What, however, of the *Hunley?* The Federals assumed it escaped, and the Confederates fervently hoped that it had. But the submarine did not come back. Its loss marked the end of Confederate submarining. Yet it was the beginning of a revolution in warfare.

The vessel lay on the bottom of Charleston Harbor until it was discovered in the late 1990s, and in 2001 the *Hunley* was raised and found to be in an impressive state of wholeness. It eventually will be cleaned and put on display, probably in Charleston. The remains of the crew were found; and even a gold piece that had been struck by a bullet at the Battle of Shiloh, saving the life of that particular crewman, was removed from the submarine. The human remains were slated for burial with full honors.

Not mine, O Lord, but thine; not mine, O Lord, but thine." Over and over Davis prayed this as he walked the room, back and forth, back and forth, "the livelong night." Mary Chesnut heard the steps in the drawing room below, where she kept vigil. There was no sound but the heavy "tramp of Mr. Davis's step as he walked up and down the room above." The Gray House was "as silent as death."

Indeed, death had once again visited the Davis family: on April 30, 1864, Joe had fallen from the porch and was fatally injured. His skull was cracked, and both legs were broken. No one saw him fall. A passing army officer ran over to the child and began rubbing him with camphor and brandy. Davis arrived, and his face had "such a look of petrified . . . anguish [as] I never saw." Davis watched the boy die, the president's "pale, thin, intellectual face, already oppressed by a thousand national troubles transfixed into a stony rigidity . . . speechless, tearless." Someone came with a message, and Davis tried to write a reply but suddenly cried out, "I must have this day with my little child."

Burton Harrison, who himself had become almost like a son to the Davises, took charge of the funeral arrangements. Mary Chesnut saw the five-year-old laid out, "white and beautiful as an angel—covered with flowers," and "Catherine, his nurse, lying flat on the floor by his side, weeping and wailing as only an Irish woman can. . . . Cheap—that. Where was she, when it all happened?" But the Davises never blamed Catherine. Thousands of children brought flowers to Joe's grave in Hollywood Cemetery the next day. "The dominant figure" that haunted Mary Chesnut was "that poor old gray-haired man. Standing bareheaded, straight as an arrow, clear against the sky." Varina, seven months pregnant, was also stricken. Harrison spoke of her "passionate grief" and of Davis's "terrible self-control." The next day Davis was back at work in his office.

A year to the day after little Joe's death, Mary Chesnut noted that "the Confederacy has double-quicked downhill since then."[128] For Davis, downhill had begun the previous December, when he felt impelled to appoint Joseph E.

Johnston to command the Army of Tennessee. At least Johnston was popular, and the appointment contrasted sharply to the widely criticized appointment of the unpopular Braxton Bragg as Davis's military adviser. Josiah Gorgas observed that army officers believed that Bragg with his "quick decided spirit" would *"assist"* Davis in "military matters," which Gorgas thought was needed. "The President is not endowed with military genius, but who would have done better?"[129]

Davis was hampered by any number of related factors. The shortage of food, for example, affected military strategy. In January 1864, General Howell Cobb had written Davis from Dalton, Georgia, that Johnston's army had to retake the Middle Tennessee farmland or it would starve. Davis, who had already urged that this be done, wanted the move to start at once, to catch the enemy off guard. He discussed plans offered by Hardee, Beauregard, Longstreet, Polk, and the Kentucky generals-in-exile. These suggestions were finally distilled into one plan, which Bragg sent to Johnston on March 12.[130]

The country above Chattanooga, through which Johnston was supposed to slash his way, was mountainous, and his transport was questionable. Johnston was not at all inclined to try it, but he misled the authorities in Richmond by pretending to agree. An exasperated Davis finally sent General William Pendleton to prod Johnston, who then proposed a plan "without the hazard of ruin involved in the other," by keeping the battle "this side of the Tennessee" River. Then he added the old dream: "Press [the enemy] back to the Ohio." Bragg, Davis, and Pendleton agreed that this plan was "now perhaps the best that can be done." "Now" was April 21. Johnston never did attack. He had decided that the right approach—his own all along—was to wait for the enemy to attack him and then to counterattack.[131]

Cooper observes that "Johnston thought only in defensive terms. . . . For him in the spring of 1864, as in 1863 and 1862, no offensive movements could be undertaken unless everything was just right. Of course, that condition never obtained, and Johnston would never risk his army or his reputation. On a letter to Bragg in which Johnston stated firmly he would have to await the enemy's initiative, the president noted: 'read with disappointment.' "[132]

For three years the North had battered the South but had been unable to crush it. The Union army's direction, however, was about to change: on March 12, 1864, U. S. Grant was elevated to lieutenant general and made general in chief of the U.S. Army. His plan called for numerous simultaneous advances; indeed, he intended five of them to assail the South from different directions, canceling out all enjoyment of interior lines.

So it was more than ordinary business that lured Davis back to his office the day after his son's funeral. Varina said that the Confederacy was "encompassed so perfectly that we could only hope by a miracle to overcome our foes."[133] Within the next week, the first of Grant's synchronized attacks erupted. Despite Davis's postwar study of Jomini, the president never understood that Grant was a great strategist. Clinging to the "Grant is a butcher" myth, Davis asserted later:

> General Grant's theory of war was, "to hammer continuously against the armed force of the enemy, until by mere attrition, there should be nothing left."
>
> Military genius, the arts of war, the skilful handling of troops, superior strategy, the devotion of an army, the noble self-denial of commanders, all must give way before the natural forces of "continuous hammering" by an army with unlimited reinforcements, and an inexhaustible treasury, and well-filled commissariat, and all directed by an unanimous people.[134]

General John C. Breckinridge was able to stop General Franz Siegel halfway up the Shenandoah Valley, and joined by cadets from the Virginia Military Institute, trounced him at New Market on May 15. Benjamin Butler led an expedition toward one of Richmond's vital lifelines, which ran through the Department of North Carolina and Southern Virginia, where Beauregard had just recently assumed command. Butler's movement gave him his chance to get back into the field. Davis seized the opportunity, too, going out to Drewy's Bluff to view the fighting.[135]

In the ensuing days Davis was personally involved in seeing to the security of Richmond. He named General Custis Lee to head the civilian brigade, and Robert Ransom Jr. was to be in charge of the regulars stationed within the city. Pemberton was tapped to take over the city's artillery, and Bragg was warned to be ready to take some command himself. But Davis felt the ultimate responsibility was his. He was "constantly on the field." On May 11, he telegraphed General R. E. Lee: "Sorely pressed by enemy on south side . . . now threatened by the cavalry . . . I go to look after defence. . . . May God have you in His holy keeping."[136]

A bitter blow fell on May 11, at the Battle of Yellow Tavern, where the gallant J. E. B. Stuart was mortally wounded. The Federal cavalry under Major General Philip Sheridan had been sent to cut R. E. Lee off from Richmond and to "thrash hell out of" Stuart. Shot through the abdomen, Stuart was taken to Richmond. Davis went to him immediately: "He was so calm, and physically so strong, that I could not believe that he was dying, until the surgeon, after I had left his bedside, told me he was bleeding inwardly, and that the end was near." "Mr. Davis came home," said Varina, "and knelt with me," praying "that this 'precious life might be spared to our needy country.' " Again, the answer to prayer was no.[137]

On June 1, Lee attacked Grant, between Old and New Cold Harbor. Sheridan and his dismounted men, back with the main force, beat off two assaults "solely and entirely," said E. Porter Alexander, "because he had magazine guns." Repeating carbines were a major technological advantage; almost the whole of Lawrence Keitt's South Carolina regiment of "near a thousand men" was cut down, including Keitt. The next day Lee entrenched, and though Grant had no repeating weapons, when he attacked, the casualty rate reversed. On June 3, Grant rashly committed the biggest mistake of his career: he attacked en masse at Cold Harbor, and in just one hour he lost thirteen thousand men. If Grant's country continued to support his policy, argued Henry Kyd Douglas, "the science of war [is] reduced to a sum in mathematics . . . [and] the outlook for the Confederacy . . . hopeless."[138]

In the ensuing days and weeks, even as R. E. Lee's reports grew darker, the more cheerful Davis became, having, as Varina said, "a childlike faith in the providential care of the Just Cause by Almighty God." But Davis had been quite concerned by reports of the general trying to lead his men personally into battle. He wrote Lee, first thanking him for the recent "glorious deeds," but then declaring, "I have been pained to hear of your exposure of your person. . . . The country could not bear the loss of you, and, my dear friend, though you are prone to forget yourself, you will not, I trust, again forget the public interest dependent on our life." Lee obeyed. The cry from his men, "Lee to the rear!" was heard no more.[139] As for Davis, whenever he could he rode out to visit the army. His spirits rose or fell, depending on what he learned at headquarters.[140] It had long been noted by his close associates that Davis was always happier in the field, away from administrative duties and the papers, files, and desks that accompanied them. It was but one more example of his active-negative presidency, as was the fact that when most knowledgeable Confederates began to understand what the outcome of the war must be, Davis became even more optimistic. While some observers thought the situation hopeless, such a word was not in Davis's vocabulary. "If hope had not lighted the thorny path of duty," he said later, "conscience required that path should be followed wherever the same might lead." Without hope, said Varina, he could not have spoken, as he always did, "words of hope to the soldiers—he was too sincere." E. Porter Alexander thought that historians "will doubtless write that . . . the time had now fully arrived for President Davis to open negotiations for peace." And he was condemned for not doing so by some. But Lincoln offered only reconstruction, and this Davis called "degradation."[141]

He did put some hope, but only a faint degree, in the Northern peace movement. His dogged hope was for an ultimate military victory. He told Governor Zebulon Vance, who was fighting a move by W. W. Holden for a separate peace in North Carolina, that "to propose peace, is to invite insult and contumely." The enemy Congress forbade any terms "except absolute, unconditional subjugation or extermination," and Lincoln's "repeated rejections of all conference with us," seemed to "shut out all hope that he would ever treat with us, on any terms." The South would simply have to whip the enemy "out of his vain confidence in our subjugation. Then and not till then will it be possible to treat of peace."[142]

Nevertheless, to show that he was for peace if the South's independence was not in question, Davis told his trio of agents in Canada to explore the possibility of talks. Horace Greeley gladly put out the feeler for them. Lincoln, in reply, spoke of "the whole union" and "the abandonment of slavery" and referred to the Confederacy as merely "the armies now at war against the United States," confirming Davis's analysis. No meeting took place. And Grant pressed doggedly on.[143]

In summer 1864 Davis said of the war, "I saw it coming, and for twelve years I worked night and day to prevent it, but I could not. The North was mad and blind." The point is that even then, Davis deeply believed and wished to illustrate that the South bore no responsibility for the bloodshed. But Northerners felt the same way. The U.S. Secretary of State William H. Seward rejected the idea that the Rebels were fighting fundamentally to defend and preserve slavery; rather, the rebellion sprang from and was sustained by "the pride & passion & self-commitment of the enemy."

For some Southerners, the very activity of fighting seemed to arouse new and stronger emotions. Simply because the war had begun was reason enough that it must go on; the outrages that occurred after the firing on Fort Sumter were in themselves even stronger incentives to fight on than had been the reasons to go to war in the first place. The bizarre reality that Davis was as committed to prosecuting the war as the disillusioned Stephens was to opposing its continuance combined with another reality: both men were fatalists. Davis kept predicting an ultimate Southern victory, and he continued to do so until at last he was captured in the field.

14

THE GREAT HOPE:
THAT LINCOLN BE DENIED
REELECTION

President Jefferson Davis had one general in command of an army with whom he was fully pleased, according to William Cooper:

> While regular messages continued to pass between Davis and Lee, the proximity of the Army of Northern Virginia to Richmond permitted the two men to meet more often. The general came to the capital, but the president, accompanied by various companions, also rode out to army headquarters. These rides could cover more than twenty miles, and the visits could last far into the night. Sometimes Davis did not leave Lee until the moon was up. Such excursions could also place him in danger. On at least two occasions, despite the presence of guides, the presidential party rode beyond Confederate positions. But in each instance cries from men in gray brought an unharmed president back to within friendly lines. Once, visiting a battery on the James, Davis came under fire from Federal units only a few hundred yards away. Seemingly unperturbed, he finally yielded to the pleas of officers, "smiled, turned," and withdrew.[1]

On June 27, 1864, Varina gave birth to Varina Anne, their last child. Later known as "The Daughter of the Confederacy," (a title bestowed on her by General John B. Gordon, the first commander in chief of the United Confederate Veterans) she gave her parents much joy and helped to assuage their grief over the recent death of her brother. Nevertheless, in the Davis's mansion was a small room that Varina decorated with the carved wooden chains and statues sent to her by Confederate soldiers held in Yankee prisons, rendering it a somber if not a sardonic chamber.

Davis himself seemed to grow more and more mellow. He showed many small kindnesses, and he began to be softhearted on the subject of executions. "The broadcast, inevitable interposition of his prerogative of pardon," complained Beauregard's close friend, General Thomas Jordan, "made it plain to the men of the army that there was the fullest immunity for desertion." The opposition press harangued him, and he actually did relent and allow some sentences to be carried out. Still, he maintained his position so often that Attorney General George Davis complained that "it was the most difficult thing in the world to keep Mr. Davis up to the measure of justice. He wanted to pardon everybody."[2]

During this time span,

> the president's moods ranged from grim to light. After he spoke to the former prisoners, some women friends asked if the men would like going back to the army. Davis answered, "it may seem hard." Then he pointed to some twelve- to fourteen-year-old boys playing nearby and said they too "will have their trial," possibly with rats as their rations. On other occasions his spirits were buoyant and he would indulge his fondness for telling stories. One companion heard incidents involving two of his heroes, Andrew Jackson and Zachary Taylor. Visitors to the presidential office were invariably impressed by his charm and graciousness.[3]

Although he made bold and sometimes sanguinary public statements condemning Yankee atrocities, Davis could not bring himself to allow or to order ruthless retaliation. Partisan warfare had become ugly in the Trans-Mississippi, especially in Missouri, where Union officers sometimes ordered the summary hanging of captured Rebel guerrillas. Members of Davis's cabinet urged him to execute Federal prisoners held in Richmond's Libby Prison in retaliation for every Rebel who was hanged. Davis demurred. If the Confederacy captured any Union officer responsible for such an atrocity, he said, "I would hang him high as Haman. . . . But I have not the heart to take these innocent soldiers taken as prisoners in honorable warfare, and hang them like convicted criminals."[4]

Davis continued to drive himself even when ill, and he was ill more and more often. He continued to involve himself in minutiae, even in August 1864 trying to cope with a shortage of soap for the soldiers. Everything was in short supply. Even stationery for the Executive Department ran out, and Davis was compelled to use Treasury Department letterheads. But increasing tensions took their toll, and he exhibited more frequent erratic swings of temper. Sometimes he lashed out even at his friends, including the fair-haired Lucius Northrop.[5]

By early fall it had long since been apparent that the placement of Braxton Bragg in the position of general in chief was not working. He was thought to be an outrageous flatterer, bad tempered and jealous, who spied on his peers and took credit for their ideas. "Bragg gets worse and worse, more and more mischievous," War Clerk Robert G. H. Kean declared on September 25. "He resembles a chimpanzee as much in character as he does in appearance." In effect, the president reduced Bragg to command of the newly designated Department of North Carolina, and the general left Richmond on October 17. "Prying, indirection, vindictiveness, and insincerity are the repulsive traits which mark Bragg's character, and of which together or separately I see evidence of almost daily," remarked Kean in his secret diary.[6]

By late summer and fall 1864, the Confederate military had nearly reached the end of its rope: Union success in Georgia and in the Shenandoah Valley and the bloody stalemate that had resulted at Petersburg made the situation seem ultimately hopeless, and there were renewed outcries for peace. Some secret societies actively tried to undermine the Davis administration; but the peace movement was no more effective than it had ever been—and that was not very much. Members of the peace movement could not agree on acceptable terms; moreover, the lack of organized opposition and the absence of political parties, along with the general hostility to politicians harbored by so many Southerners, added up to a more potent weakening of Davis's opponents than of the president's administration.[7] Nevertheless, the opposition was strong enough and sufficiently threatening to Confederate strength as Davis perceived it that he was considerably upset. It soon became even more threatening.

By September 1864, William Waters Boyce of South Carolina was a deeply troubled man. A member of the Congress, Boyce had been watching the deterioration of Confederate fortunes for some time. Most likely influenced by the recent, shocking capture of Atlanta, Boyce wrote a public letter to President Davis to explain the problems of the South as he saw them. He underlined some of the difficulties with Davis's administration that worried him and, he asserted, many other loyal Confederates.

Boyce made it clear that he did not seek peace at any price, nor was he about to throw in the towel. He did make it clear that Davis was not playing the role that many Confederates expected of him. Policies had been established that he and many of his fellows opposed. Boyce and others were unhappy about the recent extension of conscription, the constant and huge issues of almost worthless paper money, ineffective efforts to reduce the amount of that money in circulation, the tax in kind, government seizure of control over the railroads, the building of new railroads by the government, impressment, government regulation of exports and imports, and, among other things, suspension of the writ of habeas corpus.

Boyce's list of objections was like a catalog of the most controversial and, as Davis would have said, the most necessary policies. Boyce wanted these policies reversed:

> We have been at war not quite four years, and what is the result? Is not our Federal Government in the exercise of every possible power of a national central military despotism? Suppose there were no States, only provinces, and unlimited power was conferred upon you and Congress, what greater power would you exercise than you now do? . . . Indeed if you were appointed Military Dictator, what greater powers could you exercise than you do now?[8]

Boyce apparently thought that a successful war could be fought with a minimum of sacrifice, but from the modern point of view, he seems to have been extraordinarily naive. No doubt Davis thought as much when he read Boyce's diatribe. But the congressman and the president represented the polar opposites of a major controversy within the Confederacy, and the logic of argument was not solely on the side of Davis and power. By mid-1864, the pressure of impending defeat required Confederates to come up with definitive answers to some basic questions. Just how powerful should the Confederate government be? Just how much power should Davis himself exercise? At what point would centralized power compromise and even destroy the Southern version of liberty that Confederates (Davis included) always maintained they had gone to war to preserve? Halfhearted measures would not hold off the enemy much longer; lines had to be drawn and prices calculated.

Davis and Boyce were in agreement, after all, that the Confederacy and their notion of liberty must be preserved. But they disagreed over the measures that were necessary and the presidential powers requisite to achieve them. Davis always argued from necessity, and that disturbed Boyce. If the powers are necessary, he wrote, "that is precisely my argument. My argument assumes and requires that necessity. It is plain that our government exercises the powers of a central despotism." Boyce was not just a complainer. Granted that strong, centralized authority was needed to wage a modern war, nevertheless he had a good point. What more power, indeed, could Davis have exercised if he had been a dictator? Almost every important measure that Davis asked Congress to grant him he received, except more rigid control of manpower and extended suspension of the writ of habeas corpus. Operating in a system that was essentially democratic—for white men—Davis, in a democratic way, nevertheless acquired powers far beyond the expectations that nineteenth-century Americans in either North or South ever supposed their governments would exercise. This, of course, was Lincoln's experience, too. And Boyce was correct in noting that in some respects the Union government had out-stripped the Confederacy in the centralization and seizure of power.

It is not surprising that there were those in both sections who agreed with Boyce in fearing that the demands of war would undermine liberty rather than preserve it. In February 1865, when it was already too late, Governor Joseph E. Brown of Georgia expressed the same sort of fears as Boyce, albeit in a less temperate voice. "Our constitution has been violated and trampled under foot," he claimed, "and the rights and sovereignty of the States . . . have been prostrated and almost destroyed by Confederate congressional encroachment and executive usurpation." The previous May, Congressman John P. Murray of Tennessee looked to the North and called Lincoln a usurper; in the South, he claimed, "we have bad men, traitorous men in our midst, but we have good strong laws, and good hempen rope for them." There were sanctions if men overstepped the proper bounds; and he for one was willing to use them, for he was mystified and disturbed by the notion "that in order to get liberty you must first lose it." Brown agreed and complained that "we are fighting for anything but independence," noting that Confederates had possessed that in "the old government." Independence, "without the recognition of our rights and liberties by our rules, is not worth the blood of the humblest citizen. We must gain more than this in the struggles," he concluded, "or we have made a most unfortunate exchange."[9]

Boyce's letter preempted Davis's argument, for Boyce supposed that he would be told that the "necessity is limited to the war, and when peace returns we will go back to our old state of liberty."[10] As it turned out, American government did return to its "old state of liberty" after the war (although some Southerners may have disagreed during the Reconstruction years), and the reunited government never exercised such strong powers again until the twentieth century. But in 1864 the historical tradition within which Americans of both sections matured drew heavily from the English Civil War and the French Revolution, both of which provided excellent examples of military necessity paving the way for an extended diminution of civil liberties.

Within American traditions of 1864, therefore, Boyce was right. The point is that Davis was a usurper of sorts, as Boyce implied. Davis was not a despot, and he was not mindlessly arbitrary or capricious. But with the aid of an often compliant Congress, and under the pressure that a disastrous and bloody war placed on both the legislative and executive branches of the Confederate government, Davis achieved unequaled powers. If Boyce (or Governor Brown or Representative Murray) thought of this president as a usurper, he had good reason to do so. But Davis had help in achieving his power; he had received it in a constitutional manner and process. To be sure, he interpreted the Confederate Constitution differently from some of his critics, but he performed no coup d'etat, he tore up no part of the Constitution, he dissolved no Congress, he sent no legislators packing, he placed no military officers in civilian positions (except on a temporary basis), he suppressed no newspapers, he closed no courts; he was indeed a democratic usurper, at least as far as many other state-rights or libertarian Confederates were concerned.

Some historians deny this, contending with Paul Escott that Davis was not so much despotic as nationalistic. One of the few true Confederate nationalists, Davis was so swayed by his vision of an independent Confederacy that he more or less assumed that others were equally enthusiastic. But Davis was mistaken. Thus, he could not understand when others seemed less willing than he to alter their thinking and adjust to profound needs. Davis was willing to give up slavery, for example, in order to achieve his vision of an independent Southern republic—but most other Confederates were not. And because Davis seemed unable, or perhaps did not understand the need, to strengthen citizen morale and to educate his fellow Southerners about their true goal as he saw it, many of them naturally did not understand what he was about, what he was doing, and hence could see him, as Boyce did, only as a despot.[11]

Clearly Davis was a wartime American president operating not so much in the tradition of past presidential behavior but within the experience of future wartime presidential powers. He, and Lincoln as well, were forerunners of the crisis presidents of the twentieth century. Davis must be judged, then, not so much in light of what had gone before him but as a precursor of a modern American president confronting the most extreme crisis. Davis was an American president, after all, and he was faced with the knowledge that failure might not only mean but would definitely ensure the extinction of his country. It was a heavy burden, and if Davis aggravated men like Boyce, Brown, Murray, and others, he may be forgiven. Indeed, given the danger that the Confederacy faced, some twenty-first-century readers may possibly conclude that Davis's great failure lay not in grasping so much power but in grasping so little and that the president's failure must be shared by a Congress that either could not understand the Confederacy's problems or was insufficiently dedicated to its independence to provide the power the executive required. The times demanded more.

By fall 1864 Davis began to realize this and launched a speaking tour to justify his actions and to counter the arguments of Boyce and others throughout large areas of the South. Indeed, many people agreed with Boyce, even before the publication of his letter, which was widely reprinted throughout the Confederacy. It seemed to throw Davis into a flurry of activity and perhaps even panic. Finding little comfort in the apparent disarray of his opposition, he was quite worried about its spreading, and he left Richmond to try to bolster public morale. On September 22, he spoke to a hastily assembled crowd in Macon, Georgia. He assured his audience that Sherman's line of communications was so precariously stretched that it had to be dangerously thin and that the Federal army could not possibly remain long in Georgia and would be forced to withdraw just as Napoleon had been obliged to pull out of Russia. But then he turned viciously on his critics, like Joe Brown. The governor, despite his bitter opposition to Davis's policies, was popular with his constituency, primarily because they saw him as looking after their best interests. Then, in a statement that no doubt shocked his audience, Davis admitted that some two-thirds of all Confederate soldiers were absent without leave.[12]

Davis traveled on to Montgomery, where he gave a stunningly different speech. Optimistically, he suggested that the recent setbacks should lead only to redoubled efforts and tenacity.[13] Later he spoke in Augusta, Georgia, and offered a historical analysis of the Confederate predicament, recalling the conservative foundations of Confederate nationalism: "Ours is not a revolution," he told his audience. "We are a free and independent people, in States that had the right to make a better government when they saw fit. . . . We are not engaged in a Quixotic fight for the rights of man; our struggle is for inherited rights." As George Rable has described it: "The cause remained grounded in the local and the particular as opposed to the universal and the ideological. . . . The president was unfortunately delivering several different messages to several different audiences, and his analysis of the conflict had become as fragmented as Confederate politics itself."[14] Few actions reveal Davis's narrow view more than his comment about "Quixotic fight for the rights of man." The Confederacy was not engaged in such a fight, but the belief that men are is what persuades them to fight on, even to surrender their own lives. He was undermining his own cause.

Desperation gave Davis's words a dangerously unrealistic quality. He downplayed the general hardship and ignored the chronic food shortages, once more calling up the example of the Revolution of 1776. Despair and exhaustion had taken their toll on Davis, too, just as they had on a huge segment of the populace he was trying to enhearten and bestir. In Columbia, South Carolina, he seemed "alternately resigned and exasperated." Rable suggests that "careful listeners must have been shaken by the speech's dissonant elements."[15]

Despite any dissonance, Davis still "remained a respected if not exactly a beloved leader." Even his harsh critic Robert Toombs considered him "impregnable on the peace issue." The opposition remained weak because it was disunited. And sometimes bitter critics, like Louis T. Wigfall, temporarily muzzled their rumblings. He himself made a swing through eastern and southern Texas, defending conscription, impressment, and the new tax measures. Davis might hear the occasional barb hurled at him; for example, a disheartened North Carolinian complained to Vice President Stephens that Davis's "life was a burden to the Confederacy and a curse to our people." But such remarks were an index of the degree to which rational argument and civility had declined. The economic, political, and social fabric of the nascent nation was unraveling—and this condition "both appalled and fascinated Confederates."[16] Davis's speaking tour was a mixed success, surely. His message was not always the same, but a clear thread of desperation ran through each speech. It was time to count the cost and to make good the promises that Confederates had made to one another when they started down the road to independence. More significantly, perhaps, Davis finally recalled the importance of going to the people to stir their enthusiasm and to lift their morale. He was at last beginning to act like a modern crisis president.

The terms of the currency reduction law that Congress passed on February 17, 1864, proved to be so confusing that most people were simply indifferent, not caring whether their money was old or new. Old money actually continued to circulate until the war's end. After all, neither old or new was truly sound; everything was based on blind trust. To add to the financial confusion, the various states also issued large amounts of their own currency.

Treasury Secretary Christopher Memminger was not wholly to blame, but public clamor forced him to resign on June 21, 1864. He defended himself by saying that he had been compelled "to administer plans which I neither originated nor approve. You know how anxiously I endeavored to provide means to prevent a Redundant Currency. I have always disliked the supporting of the Government by Treasury Notes. But Congress would give nothing but Notes & Bonds—and when we failed to pay specie for Interest the Bonds lost their availableness."[17]

To replace Memminger, Davis named George A. Trenholm, a successful and well-known South Carolina banker and businessman. Trenholm had established a European branch of his trading firm in Liverpool—Fraser, Trenholm and Company—that served as a European financial agent for the Confederacy. He had made a fortune in blockade running, controlling as many as fifty blockade runners for shipping cotton, and probably was the richest man in the Confederacy. His appointment was enthusiastically and favorably received.[18] According to E. Merton Coulter, "If there was a financial wizard in the Confederacy, it was Trenholm." When he became secretary of the treasury, congressmen and citizens alike hoped that he would restore the public credit. He resolutely asserted that no more currency would be issued, and he tried to increase government income by increasing both bond sales and taxes. He exported more government-owned cotton to secure foreign credit (and the government owned a great deal of that commodity: throughout the war it bought at least 474,471 bales). He planned to sell foreign credits for currency and to use the latter to pay the soldiers their back pay and to cover numerous other unpaid obligations. Trenholm was more like Davis than most in his commitment to the Confederacy. He could not understand "why the people could never see and think of the Confederacy as part of themselves—not something far away—and why they as one great family did not come to the rescue."[19]

The War Department supply bureaus meanwhile were busy buying up cotton, tobacco, and other agricultural staples for shipment to depots where the goods could be secured by civilians who had been specially authorized to make trips through the lines into enemy territory. The Confederate Congress had made it illegal for residents to hold U.S. currency; it provided instead for the redemption of U.S. monies into Confederate currency to facilitate the government's accumulation of U.S. monies in order to sustain the trade across the lines. Moreover, gold, when and if the Treasury possessed enough of it, was also used for across-the-lines trade. These military supply policies had evolved over time, in trial and error, as had the South's war administration in general.

Labor, like supplies, fell short of Confederate needs. By fall 1864 free black labor was stretched as far as it would go. Many laborers deserted; in Virginia, there simply were not enough qualified "light duty" men to guard them.[20] It therefore became necessary to impress five thousand black laborers for service with the Army of Northern Virginia, each county being assigned its quota.[21] This time the need was so great that the Bureau of Conscription impressed the labor, despite some soul-searching as to whether a commanding general had the power to impress this sort of private property without going through state officers. Secretary of War James A. Seddon acknowledged that Virginia law provided that the governor could impress slaves for public use and that accordingly the War Department previously had sent a requisition to the governor. But he excused the variation on the ground that "the existing circumstances did not admit of the delay necessarily involved."[22]

The Bureau of Conscription was used again in December 1864.[23] In Florida the legislature was so upset by the proceedings in Virginia that it passed a law demanding all impressments of slave or free blacks to be made in accordance with Florida law and nullified any impressments made in violation of state law.[24]

By December the Virginia schedule of impressment prices reflected the unreality of official Confederate pricing. Peas and beans had declined, and potatoes had remained stable, which meant there was now even more pressure on producers to evade the law because of inflation. Flour had jumped from $22.00 per barrel to $33.00, and some other commodities had risen in proportion.[25] The price schedules were not so high elsewhere, reflecting less intensity in carrying out impressment in those states. In Georgia, for example, in October 1864 bacon was $1.50 a pound, beans $3.00 a bushel, Irish potatoes $4.00 a bushel, pig iron $110.00 a ton, and boilerplate $625.00 a ton.[26] The population was suffering severely because of inflation. Privates in the army earned $11.00 to $14.00 a month. Even congressmen had found it hard to live on a salary of $2,760.00 per year, especially if their wealth was in real estate and their slaves were located behind Union lines.[27] Many resorted to sharing accommodations and communal messes to cut expenses.

In 1863 Texas congressman Peter W. Gray had written a colleague in exasperation, "The currency—Lord have mercy!— Don't speak of it. I am barely living now."[28] Early in the next year Congressman Caspar Bell of Missouri had expressed fears for his living if he were not reelected.[29] In August 1864 a woman in Richmond paid $5.00 for a paper of pins, $25.00 for a pound of butter, $6.00 for a dozen eggs, and $4.00 for a quart of milk.[30]

Inflation drove impressment, and impressment drove inflation. An untutored preacher wrote North Carolina's governor Zebulon Vance to appeal for his help against "speculations & extortioners, who will not let them [the people of North Carolina] have the Leather for less than from $250 to $300 per lb and cotton yarn, at $6.00 and anything else in proportion, Have you not the power to stop this . . . unless this speculating is stopped the poor must pearich [sic] and the army starved."[31] Everyone in authority knew something had to be done to alleviate the difficulties. If Davis appeared to be uncertain about what to do, others were becoming more aware that this was an issue that demanded legislative attention. The system was in disarray. Senator James L. Orr informed Secretary of War Seddon of the strange case of a woman who twice offered to sell her molasses to the army but was turned down for lack of transportation. She then transported it to another city herself, where it was impressed.[32]

By July 1864 protest was widespread. Virginia congressman John Goode Jr. wrote to Seddon that the current schedule of impressment prices was "unthinkable." Public opinion, Goode reported, held that the government could get all the grain it needed at $10.00 per bushel, but the schedule set the price at $30.00 per bushel. Goode feared that repudiation was ahead. Furthermore, counties also had to impress grain to supply the needs of soldiers' families. He explained:

They cannot impress at a lower rate than the Government, and how can they pay the enormous debt which will be incurred by paying $30 per bushel for wheat, $24 for corn, and $25 for corn-meal? How are the non-producers of the country to live when the inevitable effect of this action must be to double the prices of the necessaries of life in the markets? The seller will say at once that if the Government is giving $30 for wheat the market price will be $60, and many of them will hoard with the expectation of realizing that price.[33]

Congressman Goode had his prices wrong, but his reasoning was clear enough.

Soldiers were also upset with the high prices, which inevitably affected their families. One wounded soldier complained that the price commissioners had raised wheat to over $5.00. If "this great crime" were not reversed and wheat cut to $5.00, "thousands of good soldiers will quit the ranks for home or Yankee-land."[34] Three days later Seddon received another complaint about the new schedule. The anonymous writer claimed that farmers would supply grain at the previous schedule and pointed to the problem of a 6 percent rise in the schedule when the value of the currency had depreciated by one-third. He voiced an increasingly familiar concern: "Does it mean repudiation of Currency— starvation of the poor and general bankruptcy? . . . For god sake put a stop to this abomination—else our only hope is in the lord."[35] When the Southern poor first entered military service, they had been assured that their families would be cared for, but the promise had not been fulfilled.[36]

Many farm families suffered not only from inflation and shortages of essentials but also from depredations committed by troops and deserters from both armies. "The whole country is full of men on horseback," an anonymous citizen reported to Jefferson Davis, "claiming to belong to the Cavalry, going through the land destroying what is left by the Soldiers for their wives & little ones & often without remuneration. . . . Can't you protect the families?"[37] The impressment officers (or those who pretended to be but actually were not) were so harsh that Governor Milton of Florida thought it possible that some of the Florida troops would desert to protect their families; and indeed, some of them did.[38] When forced to choose between the Confederacy and their families, thousands of soldiers gave the latter first claim on their loyalty. One soldier reminded Governor Pettus of Mississippi that "*our families first and then our country . . . we are forced to this or starve.*"[39]

Such soldiers were not cowards; the decision to desert was often a brave one, for it meant risk of death if they were caught. One soldier wrote President Davis, requesting

the Hartfull (*sic*) Priverlidge of wee Poore Retched meserable creatures to return to our companyes and Bee Good Soldiers for the remainder of the Civil

War we are men That is away from our companyes That come to se our Poore
Suffering familyes and want To go Back but are a fraid of The punishment wee
ask forgiveness.[40]

A woman, probably a wife or a mother of a soldier, wrote Davis that she knew
of many deserters who would go back to the army if they would not be punished, for "they are ashamed and afraid to go back."[41] Appeals like these had
motivated Davis to issue his August 1863 amnesty proclamation to deserters
who returned to the ranks within twenty days of its publication in their states.[42]

Indeed, many soldiers then did return, if they could do so with safety and if
they could see to it that their families were satisfactorily taken care of. Describing his childhood experiences during the conflict, Joel Chandler Harris
explained the situation by quoting some of the soldiers he had encountered:

"What do you call those here fellers . . . what jines inter the army an' then
comes home arter awhile without lief or license?"

"Deserters," replied Joe, simply.

"So fur, so good," said Mr. Pruitt. "Now then, what do you call the fellers
what jines inter the army arter the'er been told that their families'll be took keer
of an' provided fer by the rich folks at home; an' then, arter they'er been in a
right smart whet, they gits word that their wives an' children is a lookin' starvation in the face, an' stedder gittin better it gets wuss, an' bimeby they breaks
loose an' comes home. . . . They hain't got nothin' but a little piece er lan'. They
goes off expectin' their wives'll be took keer of, an' they comes home an' fines
'em in the last stages. What sorter fellers do you call them?"[43]

And so, as one Virginian reported, "a good many deserters are passing the
various roads daily," patting their rifles and remarking "this is my furlough"
to anyone who might challenge them. A citizen who informed on such men,
or "even says anything disapprobating desertions from the Army, the next
thing his house is burned, and he [is] waylaid and murdered, or beaten nearly
to death."[44]

By mid-1863, there was much public discussion of this issue. The elites
were aware of the suffering of the poor, and from a combination of sympathy
and the need to quell internal tensions, they advocated assistance. In September an Alabama newspaper editor pointed to the problems of inflation and its
effect on workers and those on fixed salaries. He laid the blame on greedy
merchants and predicted that "unless some movement can be made to work a
change, there is great danger that the Confederacy itself may go up."[45] In
December 1863 the Alabama legislature passed a law to restrict the distillation of grain in order to made it available for bread.[46] In early 1864 the editor

of the *Chattanooga Daily Rebel* noted the increase in cost of living in just the past month and denied that the high prices were imposed by Jews, as many Southerners claimed. He laid the blame instead on "Southern Shylocks" (a poor alternative, since Shylock was a Jewish caricature). "There are," he continued, "deep mutterings here among the suffering poor, and if there is not a tumble of prices, before long, there will be a tumble of pricers."[47]

Soldiers and civilian workers as well expressed their needs, often writing Davis himself. In September 1864 some wounded soldiers reported their discouragement over the number of able-bodied men in safe places "speculating and extorting on our families until twelve months wages will not more than buy our wives a pair of cotton cards and one bushel of salt." They warned that they were "tired fighting for this negro aristocracy" and asserted that "it is about as easy for a camel to pass through the eye of a needle as for a rich man to enter the ranks of our army."[48]

On August 25, 1864, an anonymous worker in the Engineering Department wrote Secretary of the Treasury Trenholm that his department had not been paid in three months. With three sons in the army he was "now utterly destitute and know not today how I shall procure food for my family tomorrow."[49]

One particularly pitiful appeal came in November 1864 from the superintendent of a county poorhouse. He wanted to buy provisions from bonded farmers to support the thirty-five to forty women and children under his care, reporting that their "condition is helpless and deplorable in the extreme." They had grown their own potatoes but could not buy corn or pork because those commodities were "mortgaged to the Government," and farmers with a surplus were prevented from selling because of their government contracts. Indeed, "even the few barrels of corn made at the Poor Houses are subject to the tax in kind." Seddon's endorsement, however, simply noted that he could do nothing because sales were legally restricted to the government and to soldiers' families.[50] A little creative administration was called for; a clever secretary of war or a less negative president could have found a way around this law. Is it any wonder that the poor were sometimes as resentful of their own government as they were of the Union army?

The Alabama leadership, among others, was fully aware of such problems. Governor John Gill Shorter, in his "Circular Letter to the Planters of Alabama" of March 16, 1863, called on planters to plant even less cotton than the already restrictive cotton planting law allowed because many of the Alabama poor were barely subsisting; failure to raise more provisions could bring disaster.[51] In October the governor's brother, Eli Shorter, a former U.S. congressman, proposed that one hundred rich planters each contribute one hundred dollars and five hundred bushels of corn to help feed the soldiers' families.[52] Also in

October a public meeting was held in Montgomery on the issue, and a resolution was passed urging that after the tax in kind was paid, the surplus grain of the county should be used to supply "the wants of indigent families."[53] An anonymous Alabama citizen called for more aid to soldiers' families, demanding that "if need be the whole productive power of the state should go to the support of our army, indigent soldiers' families, and home consumption. Not a dollar should be hoarded as surplus accumulation."[54] In November the Alabama legislature passed a joint resolution calling upon the Confederate Congress to pass a law exempting the families of nonslaveholding soldiers from payment of the tax in kind[55] and another resolution requesting that Congress exempt producers in those parts of the state "overrun by the public enemy" from paying it.[56] Other states took similar measures.

In August 1863 Quartermaster General A. R. Lawton complained to the secretary of war that requisitions from his department were not being answered. He referred to Treasury figures that showed $35 million in War Department requisitions remained unsigned in the Treasury, and $34.5 million of these were to meet expenses of the Quartermaster General's Department. Another $13 million in requisitions still remained in the War Department, which left poor Lawton's bureau with almost $48 million in unpaid requisitions. As Lawton gently but firmly put it, "If this state of things is to continue it is apparent that the effect must be to render the operations of my branch of the public service inefficient, if it does not paralyze it altogether."[57]

Lawton wanted action, and he was justified in his desire. In June 1864 the Virginia legislature appropriated $1 million for the relief of soldiers' families located behind Union lines.[58] The economic situation at home so angered one soldier that he declared, "Our poor tender-hearted men will not stand it to read there [sic] letters that come from home sawing [sic] that me and your poor little children are nearly staavrd [sic] and I have knowed it many cases [sic]."[59] Jefferson Davis was aware of such attitudes but hoped that state legislatures would "[relieve] the sufferings of the poor and [quieten] the anxiety of the soldiers in regard to the condition of their families."[60] He did not understand that it was up to him to initiate corrective measures.

But payment was often difficult to make. In June 1864, Secretary of the Treasury Memminger asked Secretary of War Seddon to stop paying impressment claims because he would run out of money, especially if the then-current bill to fund and issue new currency were passed by Congress. He urged that certificates of indebtedness be used instead.[61] Seddon replied that Memminger's idea was impractical because such certificates were not accepted by the people. Seddon hoped Memminger would raise the necessary funds by hypothecated bonds or loans.[62]

One proposed remedy for abuses of impressment became law in June 1864. Congress passed a bill to hire agents to hear claims for payment for supplies "taken or informally impressed." If the agent and the Treasury agreed, payment was to be authorized.[63] According to Wilfred Buck Yearns, "This was tacit admission that the government could not effectively protect its citizens from damage, and a further indication that congress would sanction any kind of property seizure."[64] Secretary Seddon, however, was worried that the agents would be too weak to resist pleasing their neighbors; they "should possess sufficient firmness to resist their sympathies and deal equitably with both the individual and the Government."[65]

Some of the commissioners empowered with the prerogative of setting prices had their own ideas. Those officers from Alabama, Mississippi, and Georgia suggested in August 1864 that the commissary general and the quartermaster general simply require producers to make "the whole of the surplus production of wheat, corn, oats, rye, fodder, bacon, beef, lard, &c . . . subject to the order of the Confederate Government, to be paid for at commissioners' rates." This measure would presumably eliminate speculators, and it would meet the market price by eliminating the market. It was a hopeless plan, born of desperation.

Commissary General Northrop remarked in his endorsement, "When the Secretary of War is invested with despotic power he may issue the appropriate orders to effect this plan. When he can punish inflexibly and vindictively every violation of the rules he may hope to have it observed."[66] Other petty officials were also proposing even more draconian measures. Market pricing would have been a better solution, but one of the great objections that citizens raised to the impressment system was that prices were not uniform. Set, as they were, by commissioners in each state, farmers along the border of one state or part of a state might discover with dismay that they received less for their grain or meat than other farmers who were neighbors but actually lived in another state or even elsewhere in the same state. Conferences were called in August to seek a possible remedy.[67]

In the face of difficulties with producers who evaded impressment by switching crops to tobacco or cotton, which the government did not need, or concealing their produce, the Confederate government was forced to take extreme steps. Still refusing to adopt the popular solution of market pricing, the government applied pressure on farmers with conscription exemptions. This move created a class of exempts known as "bonded agriculturists." They were to sell any surplus to the army or to soldiers' families at the prices set by the state impressment commissioners or else themselves go into the army.[68] Apparently about fifty-six hundred potential soldiers were exempt in this manner, east of the Mississippi River alone.[69] Commissary General Northrop looked at such men with a skeptical eye and ordered his commissaries to report to the secretary of war any bonded agriculturists they discovered who violated the law by bartering their surplus or selling it on the open market to any comer. Such an exempt would find himself in the army after all.[70]

In mid-September 1864 Secretary Seddon urged the commanders of reserves in Georgia, Virginia, South Carolina, North Carolina, Alabama, and Mississippi to use force if necessary to obtain supplies from farmers who hid their produce.[71] Seddon claimed that "extraordinary efforts are now specially necessary to maintain even scant supplies for the [two main] armies." He begged the two Georgia senators, Benjamin H. Hill and Herschel V. Johnson, to go to southwest Georgia, which had been a key area for obtaining subsistence, and plead with the people to send supplies.[72] It was essential for the Confederacy to tap the hinterlands because plantations close to rail lines had been exhausted and farmers were less willing to sell to the government at the rates set in the schedules.[73] This sort of pressure often encouraged officers with poor judgment to make impressments they should not have made. Sanctions provided to punish such agents seldom made their way through the bureaucratic thicket.

One officer in the Nitre and Mining Bureau reported an instance where an iron furnace had been forced to shut down because an impressment officer had seized the supplies of the contractors and furnaces, "thereby causing the actual starvation of some of the furnace mules." The officer's relief was ordered, but apparently that action was never carried out.[74] Despite problems of this nature, Davis had only hinted at impressment in his messages to the first and second sessions of the Second Congress in May and November 1864.

The strong objection to the impressment system was voiced by Senator Albert Gallatin Brown, who introduced a bill on November 17 "to prevent illegal impressments and to punish lawlessness" by impressment officers.[75] Brown proposed that whenever impressment took place the officer be required to provide the victim with "a statement in writing, specifically reciting the law under which such impressment is made," and if any impressment took place in violation of the law, the officer involved would be dropped from the rolls of the army and immediately drafted and returned to the army as a private."[76] As Brown put it, in the Department of Mississippi, "Impressment had become another name for robbery. Such things were done under the name of impressment as would make the blood curdle."[77] Members of the Florida legislature were among those who agreed with Brown, and they petitioned Congress to compensate persons who had suffered from illegal impressment.[78]

As 1864 dragged to an end and 1865 began, the flawed impressment system functioned erratically, providing the armed forces with essentials to be sure, but doing so in such a way as to create much additional hardship. The result was myriad numbers of disheartening letters from the home front to the soldiers. Many a trooper reached his breaking point when reading such letters and deserted.

Like the impressment system, the Confederate military structure was far from perfect. Just after the Battle of Chickamauga both James Longstreet and Braxton Bragg had recommended the promotion of John Bell Hood, and President Davis on October 29, 1863, noted that he would promote him to lieutenant general.[79] There was brief consideration of giving Hood a departmental command, perhaps that of the Trans-Mississippi, but it seemed most appropriate that he fill a corps command in the Army of Tennessee. There was no open slot for another lieutenant general, but Davis resolved that problem by withdrawing Daniel H. Hill's name for that rank (Davis had appointed Hill, but the Senate had not confirmed him, so the president substituted Hood's name). The only known official inquiry into Hood's fitness for the field came with casual questioning, to which Hood replied that he needed only a small carriage and all his former staff officers, who knew his manner and approach. The Senate confirmed the promotion on February 4, 1864, with date of rank to be September 20, 1863—the day he had sustained his wound at Chickamauga.[80] Cooper has observed that "military historians have often condemned Hood for destroying the fine army he had inherited from Johnston, but some have been impressed by his effort. . . . On the battlefield he tried to emulate Lee. But he was no Lee."[81]

John Bell Hood was born in Owingsville, Kentucky, on June 1, 1831, and graduated from West Point in 1853, forty-fifth in his class of fifty-two and not a serious student. He had 196 demerits, just 4 short of expulsion. He served first in California and then Texas, becoming a Texan by affectation. He resigned his commission on April 17, 1861, and on April 20 was commissioned first lieutenant of cavalry in the Confederate States Army. On May 31 John B. Magruder put Hood "in charge of all the cavalry on the York River," and he was elevated to the rank of major.

On July 11 Hood rode out of camp with about eighty troopers, trying to find some of the "thieving Yankees" who occasionally left their base at Newport News to pillage nearby farms. A group of Federals tried to ambush Hood's column, and he led his mounted troopers in a charge, resulting in a complete rout. Magruder praised Hood in a report to Lee, calling the skirmish "a brilliant little affair." A delighted Lee forwarded Magruder's report to President Davis. Richard McMurry asserts that "Hood had demonstrated skill as a small unit leader" and that "it is probable that the praise he won for the July skirmish influenced his selection later that year for a new assignment to a more important command." This was Hood's October 1, 1861, elevation to the rank of colonel and to the command of the Fourth Texas Infantry Regiment.

On October 22, Hood's regiment was combined with the other Texas units in Virginia to form a brigade; Colonel Louis T. Wigfall was promoted to brigadier general and assigned to its command. But on February 20, 1862, Wigfall resigned from the army to take office in the Confederate Senate. Hood was promoted to brigadier general and replaced Wigfall. His promotion was, in McMurry's words, "the major mystery of his career," for truly he as yet had done nothing to distinguish himself. But he was a West Point graduate (and Davis always preferred academy men for high-level military appointments). Hood's promotion to brigadier general set the stage for his emergence as a major figure in the Confederacy. Within six months he was a central figure in the war.

The first known meeting between Hood and Jefferson Davis occurred on May 22, 1862. Davis had ridden out to observe Major General Gustavus W. Smith's wing of the Army of Northern Virginia carry out an expected attack. Davis sought out someone to give him a summation of events, and found Hood. "He told me he did not know anything more than that they had been halted," Davis wrote Varina. To Davis's inquiry as to Smith's whereabouts, Hood "said he believed he had gone to a farm-house in the rear, adding that he thought he was ill." McMurry suggests that Davis rode off, perhaps concluding that General Joseph E. Johnston had bungled the planned attack, and Davis's distrust of him loomed large in Hood's future. William C. Davis suggests that at this meeting "perhaps the sad-eyed young general's calm impressed the president."[82]

When in October 1862 James Longstreet and Stonewall Jackson were elevated to lieutenant generals, George Pickett and Hood were promoted to fill the vacated major generalships. Hood was to rank from October 10, 1862, and was assigned a division command under Longstreet. The next July, at Gettysburg, Hood was severely wounded in the left arm, thereafter losing all use of the limb. But until then his performance in the battle had been spectacular.

Details on Hood's life for the ensuing few weeks are skimpy, but by early September he was in Richmond. There was never much doubt that he would return to duty. On September 18, he joined his division in the woods along Chickamauga Creek, just in time to lead them in battle. Again, typically, he performed boldly and well, until he was struck in the right leg by a bullet. He fell from his horse into the arms of an aide and refused to leave the field until he was sure his men were driving the enemy. Once in the care of surgeons, his damaged leg was amputated at the thigh.

By October 8 Hood was asking when he might return to duty. He could sit up and hoped soon to be ambulatory, and he wanted to be kept informed on army politics. By late October he felt able to travel. He went first to Atlanta, later to Wilmington, and finally to Richmond, where he spent three months during winter 1863–1864. By early January, he was able to ride a horse, and President Davis frequently invited him to go on excursions about the city. Gossip centered on the obvious friendship between the two, and one must suspect that it influenced Davis's future decision making.

Numerous historians have concluded that during winter 1863–1864, Hood nurtured a close friendship not only with Davis but also with Braxton Bragg, who was brought to Richmond early in 1864 as the president's military adviser. This in turn leads to the assertion that Hood later was a spy for the administration in Johnston's army. McMurry, however, has insisted that "there is little real evidence to substantiate these charges," and his conclusion seems sound.

An administration spy? Well, perhaps, as events unfolded. Davis did treasure having detailed information about what was going on in the Confederacy's armies. Robert E. Lee knew this and fulfilled Davis's yearnings; Joseph Johnston preferred keeping his cards, if he had any, close to his chest. However, given Davis's undoubted commitment to the Confederacy, the very idea of his involvement in some scheme to risk the well-being of a major army and possibly the very survival of the Confederacy itself in order to undermine Joseph Johnston is absurd.

But it is a harder call to delineate the precise nature of the Davis-Hood relationship. Beyond doubt they were close: Davis took Hood on numerous rides about the capital; they often got together at social events; Hood once escorted Mrs. Davis, and they sat at a small table talking for more than an hour after the others had left the room; at least once Hood borrowed Davis's carriage; and at least once Hood sat in the president's pew at church, Davis helping the unsteady amputee down the steps afterward. The historian Richard Dyer suspects that perhaps Davis was using the popular Hood to enhance his own public image. Almost certainly Davis and Hood discussed various strategic possibilities and what might be done militarily. Hood praised Davis in just the right ways, once urging that he take personal field command: "I would follow you to the death!" he asserted. The two agreed that the South needed somehow to seize the initiative.

Hood garnered the adulation and admiration of a wide array of people. He even received as a gift from General Beauregard in spring 1864 a cane carved from a Fort Sumter flagstaff that had been shot down during the siege there. Hood's doctor went to Europe to secure the finest artificial leg available for the general. But was Hood trying to apple polish? Mary Chesnut saw a lot of

"Sam" Hood—as she said his friends had called him ever since West Point, and no one remembered why—and she liked him a lot, noting in her diary that "General Hood's an awful flatterer." Hood certainly told Davis what he liked to hear. But was Hood fawning over Davis with his own advancement in mind? McMurry observes that it is impossible to know for certain, but "Hood was a naive and romantic man"; as much as anyone else in the Confederacy he might simply have been sincere in his praise of Davis. In 1866, when the president was imprisoned—thus quite without power either to reward or to punish—Hood wrote to Stephen D. Lee that Davis was "the greatest man of America—the martyr of modern times."

Aside from his physical limitations, Hood, among the major generals, clearly was the most qualified, by experience, to be selected for corps command. He had been in major combat, often boldly leading his troops and often turning the tide of battle. Most significantly, he had been a major general for sixteen months by the time of his promotion. Moreover, counting the time he had served as a temporary commander, he actually had been in charge of a division for nineteen months. At Chickamauga he had successfully led a conglomerate command that amounted to a corps. Thus, by all logic, assuming one can accept his physical limitations, Hood was the best possible choice from the available pool. Steven Woodworth does not agree, however, asserting that "while Davis could undoubtedly have done worse than Hood in his selection of a corps commander for the Army of Tennessee, he probably could have done better too." Woodworth points out that Hood at thirty-three simply had not "demonstrated a mental and emotional stability beyond his years that might have justified vesting him with such heavy responsibility."

Hood wrote his first letter from the field to Davis on March 7, 1864. In it he expressed hope that the Army of Tennessee might be strengthened, thus enabling it to attack the enemy rear. Other letters followed over the course of the next two months. The army, he assured Davis, was in fine condition, but it needed more manpower. If it were adequately built up, it "should be sufficient to defeat and destroy all the Federals on this side of the Ohio River." Hood wrote similar letters to Bragg and to Secretary of War Seddon; but his optimism was a contrast to Johnston's gloomy assessments. McMurry asserts that "it is impossible to know Hood's motive in writing these letters." It is certainly probable that Davis had asked Hood to write, but whatever the motivation, Hood's letters precipitated a tense and testy debate between Johnston and the Richmond authorities. Both Davis and Hood should have had the judgment to avoid a correspondence that short-circuited others in the direct chain of command.

By early April Hood's letters began to contain stringent criticism of Johnston for his sluggishness. James Eckenrode and Brian Conrad suggest that this marks the beginning of "what was, in effect, an intrigue looking to the removal of Johnston from the command of the army." It was Hood's lifelong habit to correspond unofficially without going through channels, and indeed, this was a common practice in the Confederacy. Hood was not the only general then writing critically of Johnston: William Hardee, J. E. B. Stuart, and Joe Wheeler did so, too. Henry P. Brewster had been with the army since it left Dalton, and as he prepared to depart for a visit to Richmond on May 21, Hood gave him a letter to give to the president, urging that Davis have a conversation with Brewster about the army, its proximity to the enemy, and its various activities. Ellsworth Eliot Jr. suggests that the letter was written without Johnston's knowledge and that this was "certainly unethical."

After the Army of Tennessee had retreated to Cassville, Georgia, Johnston perceived an opportunity to demolish Sherman's army. Sherman was trying another of his typical wide turning movements, and Johnston wanted to slam against one isolated enemy wing, destroy it, and then go after the other. Hood's division was part of the assault force. But Hood discovered that leading a corps was much more complicated than heading up a brigade or a division. Typically careless about details, he neglected to order an adequate reconnaissance, and suddenly a Union force of undetermined origin and size appeared on his flank and rear. Although these enemy troops actually were but a small portion of Sherman's army that had taken a wrong turn, Hood misapprehended and panicked. He hurriedly pulled his troops back from the planned jumping-off point for the intended attack and set them furiously to digging entrenchments to fend off this "vicious and nefarious" assault force. Johnston was shocked at first by Hood's report, but soon Johnston was wallowing in doubt, ultimately concluding that Hood had perhaps been prudent.

During the actions near Cassville on May 19, 1864, and New Hope Church on May 28, Johnston began to perceive inklings that Hood would not or could not perform at top efficiency. Possibly, too, Hood, seeing Johnston retreat, had grown more openly scornful of and abrasive toward his commander. Their rift soon widened. Louis Wigfall, a friend of both Johnston and Hood, visited army headquarters and confided to Johnston that there were rumors in the capital that Davis was planning to replace him with Hood. Not long after, Hood had grown confident enough or angry enough to discuss his disagreements with Johnston publicly.

As the Atlanta campaign unfolded, Davis grew increasingly dissatisfied with Johnston's defense. On July 2, 1864, Johnston began abandoning Kennesaw Mountain for positions he had prepared in his rear. Soon his back was to the Chattahoochee River and Sherman was in sight of Atlanta. This made Davis "more apprehensive," but "at this distance I cannot judge . . . the best method of averting calamity." He had stripped other commanders of men until there were no more to send: "[We] are dependent on your success." And Davis had much more on his mind too; other crises cried for attention. He had to order reserves to Mobile; wire James Chesnut, now a general heading South Carolina's reserves, that "Charleston is in great danger"; and alert Robert E. Lee that "the expedition is spoken of on the streets. Shall it *proceed*[?] . . . If not *stop it as* you deem best." He refered to a joint sea and land action to release the prisoners at Point Lookout, Maryland, that was indeed aborted: a good thing, since the prisoners already had been moved.[83] Cavalry operations added to Davis's anxiety. John Hunt Morgan, the "Thunderbolt of the Confederacy," raised Southern spirits by raiding in Kentucky, but then he was forced to retire to the Tennessee-Virginia mountains in defeat. Sherman ordered out from Memphis a special force to hunt for Nathan Bedford Forrest, who was about to attack the Union railroad from Nashville. Forrest, outnumbered and out-equipped as usual, had scored the greatest victory of his career on June 10 at the Battle of Brice's Crossroads in northern Mississippi.

On July 10 Senator B. H. Hill reached Richmond from Georgia on a mission from Johnston, Governor Brown, and Wigfall. Davis by then had been besieged with "delegations, petitions, and letters" urging him to replace Johnston. He treated this "clamor" as he had that against Sidney Johnston and R. E. Lee, by ignoring it. He had given in to that sort of pressure once only, in appointing J. E. Johnston to army command for a second time, and now he much regretted that. Judah Benjamin witnessed Davis bearing abuse from people "ignorant of the facts" and thought "it . . . a spectacle really sublime to observe the utter abnegations of self."[84]

Davis had just sent Bragg to gather facts in Georgia, but Hill could provide them since he had come straight from the Kennesaw line at Marietta. Davis "took up the facts one by one," said Hill. Davis read to Hill the urgent cries for help from Dabney Maury in Mobile and from S. D. Lee in Mississippi. The latter wired that "A. J. Smith had left Memphis with fifteen thousand men . . . to punish Forrest and the people." As Hill later reported, S. D. Lee "had only seven thousand men including the commands of Forrest and Roddy . . . but anyhow, with or without [reinforcements] . . . [Lee] should meet Smith and whip him too. 'Ah! there is a man for you' said Mr. Davis." But then the president showed Hill a dispatch from Johnston announcing that he had crossed or was crossing the Chattahoochee River.[85]

Davis knew that high command changes "usually work evil, if done in the presence of the enemy." Thus he told Hill, "The idea of having to remove Gen. Johnston now was a terrible one." Still, he had to consider replacements. "He thought Hardee the best man probably but he would not accept the command."

Hill recalled that "Mr. Davis, with an earnestness and feeling I think I never saw him manifest on any other occasion, said, 'Oh! I would rather risk Joe Johnston than any of them. There is not a better fighter in the army if he will only fight." For his part, Hill wired Johnston on July 14: "You must do the work with your present force. For God's sake, do it."[86]

Davis finally lost patience on July 17, and ordered Johnston to relinquish his command to Hood. This decision has been one of the most vociferously debated by participants in the war and students of it ever since. Richard McMurry's analysis is a good one: he breaks the matter down into separate questions. Should Johnston have been replaced? Yes, that was justified. Was Hood the best and most logical choice? Given the critical situation and the proximity of the army to enemy contact, the new commander had to be someone who was with the army already; thus there were no realistic possibilities other than Hardee or Hood. Davis had been pondering the possibilities for a while, and until July 15, he seemed to have been leaning toward Hardee. On that date, Bragg telegraphed Davis, and then wrote him a long letter, indicating that Hood was popular with the men and, given his known penchant for aggressiveness, his appointment would have a good effect.[87]

Larry Nelson points out that replacing Johnston with Hood had political and diplomatic dimensions.[88] Senator B. H. Hill had reminded Johnston of the military importance of Sherman's campaign and that if Sherman occupied Atlanta, "not only Atlanta, but Richmond must fall; not only Georgia, but all of the States would be overrun." After that "Lincoln's power at the North would be absolute, his reelection certain, and the war for independence must be prolonged for years." But if Sherman could be defeated, "Lincoln's power will be broken, his reelection defeated by a straight out peace candidate, and we shall speedily end the war on our own terms." Hill also maintained that foreign recognition would be more likely, a point that Johnston understood very well.[89] In his memoirs Johnston expressed the view that the importance of Atlanta had been so exaggerated in the North that the populace there were persuaded "that its capture would terminate the war." To defeat Sherman, therefore, would have had a profoundly negative impact on Union morale, "so much, perhaps, as to have enabled [the Union peace movement] to carry the presidential election, which would have brought the war to an immediate close."[90] As pressure for Johnston's removal mounted, Hill stressed the effect that military victory in Georgia would have on the forthcoming Union election. "Undoubtedly," Nelson observes, "the Federal election was among the welter of considerations that led to the removal of Johnston and the appointment of John Bell Hood to command the army."[91]

Davis's fundamental dilemma was that the Confederacy's manpower pool for top-level commanders was too scanty. No one other than R. E. Lee had demonstrated the ability to lead an army successfully against a larger force. Davis took a gamble in elevating a man whose "most conspicuous qualities were those of the post-1830 antebellum South; physical bravery; aggressiveness; superb combat leadership; intuitiveness; emotionalism; impatience; lack of attention to obstacles, planning, and detail. These characteristics made Hood and others of his generation fine regimental, brigade, and division commanders."

Thus, at the age of thirty-three, "Hood became the last and youngest of the eight full generals of the Confederacy." (The promotion was not confirmed as permanent, however, and after his final failures he reverted to Lieutenant General.) He already had risen above the level of his competence, "above the level where courage and combat leadership sufficed," and now he was one step above that: he truly had reached a level of incompetence.[92] Could events subsequently have unfolded differently? Of course: Hood was not utterly inept; both history and historians have been less than kind or fair in assessing him. As McMurry writes, "One division commander summed up the situation well when he wrote on July 18: 'Hood has "gone up like a rocket." It is to be hoped . . . that he will not come down like the stick. He is brave, whether he has the capacity to Command armies (for it requires a high order of talent) time will develop. I will express no opinion.' "[93]

Early in August Hardee asked to be transferred. A flurry of telegrams was exchanged among Hardee, Bragg, and Davis, prompting Davis finally to say that he was sorry Hardee found his situation in the Army of Tennessee so unpleasant. Hardee pressed further, saying that his service under Hood was "personally humiliating" and added that Hood had approved his request. Davis then communicated to Hood that "General Hardee's minute knowledge of the country, and his extensive acquaintance with the officers and men of the command, must render his large professional knowledge and experience peculiarly valuable in such a campaign as I hope is before you." Hardee then let the matter drop, for the time being, but his resentment toward Hood continued unabated; McMurry has asserted that "his attitude hampered Hood's effort to defend Atlanta." Albert Castel, on the other hand, in *Decision in the West: The Atlanta Campaign of 1864,* credits Hood with having but scant if any real chance of successfully defending Atlanta.

Davis was rightly anxious to keep Hardee with the army because of the vexing shortage of officers competent to command a corps. Carter L. Stevenson now headed Hood's old corps, but Hood did not deem him suitable for the job, even temporarily. After conferring with Hardee and Alexander P. Stewart, Hood put Benjamin F. Cheatham, Hardee's senior division commander, in temporary command of the corps. He then asked the War Department to send him Mansfield Lovell, Wade Hampton, or Stephen D. Lee—in that order of preference. Lee got the job.

Lee was an able officer and could have been a magnificent division commander—ironically, one of the few command positions he did not fill during his remarkable career, rising through every rank from captain to lieutenant general. But Lee was younger than Hood by one year; both of them were too young either for corps or army command, and Lee had even less experience leading large bodies of troops than Hood had had the previous winter when he had been given a corps. McMurry and Woodworth agree that Patrick R. Cleburne might have been a better choice, but Cleburne was ensnared in the army's vicious in-fighting and politics.[94] Lee's arrival did not end Hood's problem with command assignments for long: Stewart was wounded on July 20 in the Battle of Ezra Church, incapacitated for two weeks, and thus Cheatham was once again pressed into corps command. This shift, in conjunction with other calamities—Major General W. H. T. Walker was killed on July 22 and Major General William W. Loring, one of Stewart's division commanders, was seriously wounded at Ezra Church—necessitated further changes. Indeed, Hood was obliged constantly to seek able leaders to head his divisions, brigades, and regiments. Perhaps Davis might have had keener insight into this problem, but even if he had, he could have done little to facilitate the process.

The fall of Atlanta followed immediately. Hood unleashed a short series of aggressive attacks, was defeated, and had no choice but to abandon the doomed city. On September 2 the Federal troops marched in. The news dealt "a stunning blow" to Davis and his advisers. "No hope," Mary Chesnut wrote. "We will try to have no fear." Davis, according to Cooper, "recognized the danger to his army and even more to his cause. Preserving Atlanta had been the psychological as well as military goal of the campaign."[95] Its loss proved to be a major factor in ensuring the reelection of Abraham Lincoln early in November. Other factors included a victory scored by Philip Sheridan in the Shenandoah Valley and the failure of raiding troops who were within five miles of Washington, D.C., to get any closer.

Thus, "for the third time in less than two years, [Davis] decided that a western trip was essential." The president departed from Richmond by rail on September 20, bound for Georgia. "At stops along the way crowds, including many women, gathered at depots to see him. Observers commented on his worn, burdened look; one reflected, 'poor man he pays for *his* honors.' Yet Davis still spoke in a firm and vigorous voice. His brief remarks always emphasized his continuing confidence in the Confederate cause."[96]

He reached the army's vicinity on a rainy Sunday, September 25. He hoped to boost morale; "he was eager to show his unflagging belief in the soldiers, and at the same time he wanted to stand publicly by his young commander." But when he reviewed the troops there was a sour note: "This time Davis received salutes but heard no cheers. . . . The reception given Davis provided a telling commentary on the condition of the army. And he was affected."[97]

Davis discussed strategy with Hood, who proposed that he move his army into North Georgia, suspecting that Sherman would follow, thus luring the Federal force away from Atlanta. If, on the other hand, Sherman headed south, then Hood would be close on his heels. Davis authorized his general to proceed with these plans, with one exception: should Sherman try to force Hood away from his communications, then Davis warned him that he must fall back westward on Gadsden, Alabama, where he would have secure supply lines coming from the southwest. He would also then be closer to Lieutenant General Richard Taylor, commander of the Department of Alabama and Mississippi.[98]

"Command structure," Cooper points out, "as well as strategy received Davis's attention." Hardee finally got his way and was allowed to leave the Army of Tennessee; Davis put him in command of the South Carolina–Georgia–Florida Department. At the same time Davis brought in Beauregard to head the Military Division of the West, the theater embracing troops under both Hood and Taylor. This was one more attempt at an idea ahead of its time, one now beyond the country's capacity as well. At least Beauregard, with his Napoleonic flair and zest, was suited to the command more than Johnston had been. Cooper terms the creation of the new department and the selection of Beauregard to command it "a master stroke."[99]

Still, the loss of Atlanta, coupled with Lincoln's reelection, meant that the Confederacy's chances of survival were slim; yet Davis remained cool. Answering a recent cry for reinforcements, he replied that "no other resource remains," but he also said that it seemed never to have entered his mind that the end was inevitable. After his western tour, the president headed back to Virginia, with stops in Augusta and Columbia. On October 3 he delivered a major speech to a crowd of cheering citizens in Augusta: "Brave men have done well before against greater odds than ours, and when were men ever braver? . . . We are fighting for existence; and by fighting alone can independence be gained. . . . But do I expect it? Yes, I do." Charles Francis Adams, the Northern diplomat, said that Davis made "no fatal mistakes. . . . [He] did the best possible with the means. . . . Merely the opposing forces were too many and too strong for him."[100]

On October 6, after more than two weeks on the road, Davis returned home. In addition to a number of short talks, he had given four major addresses. Newspapers carried them, and thus did his words reach far beyond his immediate audiences. The president concentrated on four major topics:

first, "our cause is not lost." Cooper observes, "He prophesied that the invading Federal host would meet the same fate that befell the French in Russia a half century earlier." Second, there were too many men away from their armies. Third, he addressed women; they had already done much,

> but now, Davis proclaimed, "you must do more." He said Confederate women "must use your influence to send all to the front, and form a public opinion that shall make the skulker a marked man, and leave him no house wherein he can shelter." Davis even incorporated romance. "And with all sincerity, I say to my young friends here, if you want the right man for a husband, take him whose armless sleeve and noble heart betoken the duties he has rendered to his country, rather than he who has never shared the toils, or borne the danger of the field." He attempted to convince women that their ultimate safety depended upon the defeat of the enemy.

Davis's fourth point was that "only battlefield victory would guarantee Confederate success."[101]

Davis proclaimed that independence was the only Confederate hope. "We are fighting for existence," he asserted, and as Cooper writes, "and that struggle, [Davis] averred, demanded war measures. Even though he could not predict 'how many sacrifices it may take,' he again expressed no doubt about the final outcome. In his mind, all Confederates comprehended the enormity of the stakes." Moreover, Davis said, "I believe that a just God looks upon our cause as holy, and that of our enemy as iniquitous."[102]

The final crisis over manpower arose after the fall of Atlanta and peaked after the fall of Savannah at Christmastide 1864. The handwriting was on the wall, and everyone who had access to reasonably accurate information and whose thinking was not swayed by blinding psychological commitment knew what the outcome would be. Many of these individuals desired to fight on, however, for honor, possibly to attain better surrender terms, or because they were afraid to voice their convictions.

Shortly after Atlanta fell, North Carolina's governor Zebulon Vance wrote to Governor William Smith of Virginia, decrying "the great evil of desertion," calling for food for the poor, worrying about the peoples' despondency, and urging that "beyond all else *Men must be sent to the armies of Gens. Lee and Hood.*" Given his location in Richmond, Smith already had perceived this without Vance's help, but where could men be found? Vance thought of two sources: "Large numbers, no doubt, are in the various departments of the Confederate Government," but he confessed that "there are also numbers engaged in the various State Departments who might be spared," including many who were administering those governments. And Vance admitted there were a number at home because "the principle of State Sovereignty rendered it improper to allow the Confederate Government to conscript them." He thought that the latter group was "numerous in all the states," and he hoped that they could be put into the army without significantly damaging state administration or unduly compromising state rights. He proposed a meeting of the governors east of the Mississippi River to ensure uniform action on this and other pressing issues, to be held in October, just before the next meeting of the Congress.[103] Smith thought Vance's idea could "give rise to much misinterpretation," but he nevertheless agreed to the meeting.[104]

The moments of decision came when manpower issues were considered in the last session of the Confederate Congress, which began on November 7, 1864. Lee's army was held in the trenches around Petersburg, and Sherman was on his way to Savannah. The noose grew ever tighter in Virginia, and Union troops were marching across Georgia, South Carolina, and North Carolina. "We can make this march and make Georgia howl," Sherman had said as he struck out, and he was successful—even quite beyond Georgia.

At the start of the session, Davis congratulated the Confederacy on recent military victories, noted that poor Sherman "has been unable to secure any ultimate advantage" from the capture of Atlanta, and contended that "there are no vital points on the preservation of which the continued existence of the Confederacy depends."[105] The great issue was to put more men into the ranks. Davis suggested two remedies and hinted at a third. He wanted a revision of conscription with fewer exemptions and a general militia law; he suggested that slave soldiers might be needed. Pointing to occupational exemptions, he called them "unwise" and indicated his belief that they were indefensible, even in theory. He looked upon "defense of home, family, and country" as "universally recognized as the paramount political duty of every member of society. . . . Nothing can be more invidious than an unequal distribution of duties and obligations."[106] He pointed out the obvious: not every member of an entire occupational class was equally necessary at home, and he mentioned the entire list: telegraphers, miners, teachers, editors, shoemakers, and the like. The solution was to replace blanket exemptions with a system of details, concentrating even more power in the executive by making him a manpower czar.[107] This was the sort of proposal that so upset W. W. Boyce, Alexander H. Stephens, and Joseph E. Brown.

Davis also emphasized the manpower situation by requesting that Congress pass a general militia law, a request he had made before. Pointing out that militia laws varied from state to state, he justified his present request by the power possessed in the Congress to raise armies. His goal was a law that would permit the executive, rather than the governors, to call militia to active service.[108] He also demanded changes in the cavalry, to end the requirement that men furnish their own horses, and he indicated a desire for legislation to provide for the consolidation of understrength regiments and companies. Absence of the latter often forced a commander into illegal reorganizations or else impaired the efficiency of a command.[109]

At this point, Davis at last touched on the South's "uneasy ghost," as a newspaper correspondent later called it. There had been some proposals for the use of slaves as soldiers ever since the beginning of the war, but such ideas never had been widespread until the last year or so. Davis was caught in a dilemma. He had no doubt of the potential usefulness of slave soldiers, but he knew that many other leading Confederates did harbor such doubts. Some few Confederates did come to the idea of slave soldiers quite early in the war. Indeed, in December 1861 Mary Chesnut reported in her diary that one of the local overseers—by her own admission quite an unusual man of that class— had declared that "our only chance is to be ahead of [the Yankees]—free our negroes and put them in the army. . . . [Slavery] is a thing too unjust, too unfair to last. Let us take the bull by the horns. Set 'em free, let 'em help us fight, to pay for their freedom."[110] Gradually more and more Confederates, many of them in influential positions, came to realize that they must play the slave card.

In January 1864, General Patrick Cleburne had proposed a plan to use slave soldiers, a plan that illustrated that "the experience of soldiering had made him a Confederate." Cleburne was born in Ireland in 1828 and had served in the British army before immigrating to the United States in 1849, settling in Arkansas in 1850. His commitment to the cause of Southern independence was total; but at the same time, his revolutionary proposal demonstrated that although he had lived more than a decade in a slave society, "he never fully grasped the complicated role of slavery in Southern society." As Craig Symonds notes, "It proved to be a fatal error."[111]

Cleburne understood the numbers game. He knew that conscription had nearly reached its limit, that desertion had increased, and that only thirty-five thousand men were present for duty in the Army of Tennessee. More men were needed desperately. Where else could they be found except in the slave population? Cleburne was not impetuous, and he was not the first to make such a proposal. Thomas C. Hindman, for example, a fellow general in the Army of Tennessee and one of Cleburne's former political associates, published a letter in a prominent newspaper calling on the Confederacy to arm some of its slaves and to free them as a reward for their service. By December 1863 Cleburne was talking about the idea with some of his staff and friends on an informal basis. The reaction was skeptical, and his chief of staff "was positively appalled." Undaunted, Cleburne polished his proposal and presented it to his commanders. They proved more supportive, although, as Symonds assumes, some of them no doubt agreed more out of respect for their superior officer than out of agreement with his ideas. He then requested a meeting of the general officers of all the army, and presented his proposal to them.[112]

Cleburne painted a tragic picture. "We have now been fighting for nearly three years," he said, "have spilled much of our best blood, and lost, consumed, or thrown to the flames an amount of property equal in value to the specie currency of the world," leaving the Confederacy "nothing but long lists of dead and mangled. Instead of standing defiantly on the borders of our territory or harassing those of the enemy, we are hemmed in today into less than two-thirds of it. . . . Our soldiers can see no end" and "are sinking into a fatal apathy." The inevitable consequences would be subjugation: "the loss of all we now hold most sacred—slaves and all other personal property, lands, homesteads, liberty, justice, safety, pride, manhood." The Confederacy was thus reduced, Cleburne thought, because "slavery, from being one of our chief sources of strength at the commencement of the war, has now become, in a military point of view, one of our chief sources of weakness." He feared that Davis's solution, ending substitution, revising the exemption law, and using black men for some noncombat duties, would be insufficient. He proposed to "retain in service for the war all troops now in service" (which was done in February 1864), "and that we immediately commence training a large reserve of the most courageous of our slaves, and further that we guarantee freedom within a reasonable time to every slave in the South who shall remain true to the Confederacy in this war."[113]

General Cleburne asserted that his plan would have advantages quite beyond providing for more manpower. Aid would come from abroad, the North would be denied the moral advantage of its antislavery position, blacks in the Union army would have no further motive to fight (and many presumably would desert to the South), and Northern citizens would "have leisure to look at home and to see the gulf of despotism into which they themselves are rushing." No black recruits would await oncoming Northern troops, white fear of insurrection would disappear, and "it would remove forever all selfish taint from our cause and place independence above every question of property." The statement was signed by Cleburne himself as well as by thirteen of his officers, ranging in rank from a solitary captain to three brigadier generals.[114] Cleburne's analysis was precise and logical, but it showed little understanding of the psychology of his countrymen: "The more Cleburne talked and the more he pressed his case, the more he challenged the fundamental assumptions and values of his audience." Hindman offered partial support, but so far as is known, none of the other officers did.[115]

Although General Joseph E. Johnston ordered that the memorandum not be sent to Richmond, or even discussed further within his own command, General W. H. T. Walker took it upon himself to send it to Jefferson Davis.[116] Davis at once ordered that all discussion of the matter be suppressed.[117] But Cleburne was not the only person in the Confederacy who was thinking along these lines, and the idea recurred with increasing frequency over the next few months. By the end of the year Cleburne had been killed, but his idea was far from dead. By now the issue had engaged the minds of many thoughtful Confederates. Mary Chesnut reported in her diary later that month that "the Army of the West desire the negroes freed and put in the ranks. They wonder why it has never been done before," and she implied that she had heard this news from John C. Breckenridge.[118] Even as some Southern editors and politicians began to speak out on the idea publicly in fall 1864, the question had already entered Davis's mind.[119]

In his November 1864 message to Congress, Davis skirted the issue. He referred to the legislation of the previous February 17, which authorized the military use of black men as cooks, teamsters, and workers, and complained that the law was insufficient. He had recourse to a legalism that undermined the theory of slavery. Pointing to the difference between impressing the labor of a slave and impressing the slave himself, he asserted that the slave bore "another relation to the State—that of a person." The special and often dangerous services performed by slaves demanded that the Confederacy "acquire for the public service the entire property in the labor of the slave," and he asked Congress for forty thousand slaves for useful duties. Davis even proposed freedom as a proper reward "for a zealous discharge of duty after service faithfully rendered," implying that emancipation might be a result of the war after all, at least for some slaves.[120] For the time being, Davis drew the line, however, dissenting "from those who advise a general levy and arming of the slaves for the duty of soldiers." Yet he issued his warning, a clear signal of his real thinking: "But should the alternative ever be presented of subjugation or of the employment of the slave as a solider, there seems no reason to doubt what should then be our decision."[121]

This was clearly a trial balloon. Davis knew that many Confederates did not think the situation serious enough to warrant calling black soldiers to their defense and that other Confederates would prefer to lose the war rather than resort to blacks entering the ranks, whether slave or free. Others thought that blacks would not fight, but Davis thought from his own experience that slave soldiers would fight. In his years as a planter he had on one occasion armed his own slaves and led them against a band of armed whites who had tres-passed on his land.[122] As he later explained to the governor of Virginia, his idea was to prevent more black men from fleeing north to join the Union army, and he thought enlisting them in the Confederate army first would be the most effective way to achieve that end.[123]

Davis was forcing the issue that he had suppressed earlier in 1864, when Cleburne had pointed out the obvious. He thought the general's idea was pre-mature then, but there can be no doubt that he too had often turned the mat-ter over in his mind. He had considered the possibility of slave soldiers when in early 1864 he had proposed the enlistment of black auxiliaries as laborers and teamsters with the army.[124] The Cleburne proposal, he knew, was more than many of the Southerners could then accept. But by fall 1864, he had come to realize that the situation was graver than most of his contemporaries seemed to perceive, and so he inspired one of his few public relations campaigns of the war. Although some cabinet members denied that the government was con-sidering such a revolutionary step,[125] Secretary of State Judah P. Benjamin soon began writing letters to drum up support.[126] As 1864 elided into 1865, the idea was being staunchly promoted, both in public and in private. And much to Davis's gratification, early in the new year it received positive response, not only from Congress and the army but also from an encouragingly sizable seg-ment of the general public—but its size was deceptive.

The Confederate high command and the civil leadership, if not yet ready to admit that they could not win the war by decisive military accomplishment, at least began to entertain thoughts of an alternative: placing hope in sapping Northern will and morale. Some individuals believed that if Lincoln was somehow denied reelection in November, then events would unfold that would result in a permanent Confederate independence. Many historians, too, have subsequently continued to cling to such a belief.

The efforts exerted by the Confederate leadership to influence such an out-come focused on four areas. First, some victories in the field were needed: the South had to turn back Sherman's invasion of Georgia and save Atlanta, and they had to repulse Grant's drive toward Richmond. Second, they needed to provide strong encouragement to the Northern peace party, particularly the war-weary Peace Democrats, or Copperheads. Third, they had to provide assistance to the active Southern sympathizers in the North. Fourth, and most daring, they needed directly to subvert the presidential election and stir dis-affection, even panic, among Northerners. They had to employ acts of espi-onage, subversion, and destabilization to achieve these ends.[127]

Davis, for his part, established an unofficial diplomatic mission to Canada. Once again, his poor judgment in men doomed the mission to failure. He appointed Jacob Thompson, a Mississippian and probably corrupt Democratic Party hack, and Clement C. Clay of Alabama, a servile flatterer whose primary avenue for favor in the government was that he could never say no to Davis. The two commissioners and their assistants quickly quarreled over the management of Confederate funds, and Clay soon relocated his office away from Thompson's headquarters in Toronto. This split ruined any chances of their effectively cooperating.[128]

They did make one notable effort toward producing a desired result, however. They fomented an attempt to destabilize Union finance by buying up gold in New York and sending it to Canada, believing that a severe shortage of hard money in the North would result and then bring on an economic panic. The attempt failed because of inadequate funding. Thompson and Clay subsequently tried numerous other harebrained schemes to foment terrorism in the North, but none came to any fruition whatsoever.[129]

Davis consulted with a Confederate agent operating behind Union lines and learned of a "secret political organization existing throughout the North with a membership of 490,000 men," doubtless the Knights of the Golden Circle, the Sons of Liberty, or the Knights of America.[130] He talked with Captain Thomas Hines about getting Confederate prisoners back.[131] But whatever Davis planned, he did so with the view of influencing the Union election of 1864. He did not expect total success, but he hoped at least that the failure of Confederate attempts to secure a negotiated peace with a new federal administration would steel the Confederate will by making it clear that battlefield victory was the only way to independence.[132]

In July 1864 two unofficial Northern emissaries, James R. Gilmore and Colonel James Jaquess, arrived in Richmond with Lincoln's permission but "were not authorized to transmit proposals or to speak for" Lincoln. They asked Davis his peace terms and apparently were naive enough to believe that he might be persuaded to agree to something less than independence. Davis soon sent them packing, however, having demonstrated to the Confederate citizenry that there was no alternative to independence and that was to be achieved by success on the battlefield. Some Confederates thought that the incident was proof that Lincoln was under pressure from a Northern peace movement.[133] Indeed, optimism fed on itself and convinced many Southerners that Lincoln would lose the election and that peace and independence soon would follow, which is not as unreasonable as it may now seem, since even Lincoln had doubts about his probable reelection.[134]

Ultimately then, it was as William C. Davis asserts: things might have turned out differently—"*If* Jubal Early had captured Washington and held it for some appreciable time. *If* Sterling Price had wrested Missouri from the Union and been able to hold it. *If* the forts at Mobile had been able to repulse Farragut and his fleet. *If* Lee had been able to take some action against Grant, however small, to embarrass him in the trenches at Petersburg. And most important of all, *if* Joseph E. Johnston or John Bell Hood had been able to turn Sherman decisively, not just away from Atlanta, but back on his base at Chattanooga."[135]

Lincoln himself earlier had suspected that he could not win reelection in November, but two factors turned the tide in his favor: the Democratic Party essentially shot itself in the foot by incorporating a peace plank in its platform, and military victories buoyed up public morale. Admiral David Farragut took Mobile Bay on August 5. General Sherman captured the city of Atlanta on September 7. General Philip Sheridan soundly defeated Jubal Early's army at the Battle of Cedar Creek on October 19. Sterling Price lost the Battle of Westport on October 23, and his force was ground to pieces in the rearguard engagements on October 25 at the Marais des Cygnes River and Mine Creek, Kansas. The CSS *Albemarle* was sunk on October 27 near Plymouth, North Carolina. Petersburg was under siege, and most everyone on both sides perceived that it was only a matter of time until the city fell. Lincoln easily and decisively won reelection. His victory ensured that the Northern war effort would continue until its successful conclusion; and Davis could do nothing about that.

What then of the "Great Hope"? If McClellan had been elected, would that necessarily have meant Northern defeat? William C. Davis asserts that "he was an egomaniac. He still fancied himself the greatest general of the age. Now he would have been commander in chief. . . . Are we really to suppose that this man, of all men, . . . would have chosen to snatch defeat from the jaws of victory, recall his armies, evacuate Richmond and New Orleans and Nashville and Chattanooga and Mobile and Pensacola, free Confederate prisoners, hand back tens of thousands of square miles of conquered territory, and send Jefferson Davis a basket of roses and a note saying, 'You win'?"[136]

No. The only logical way that a McClellan victory could lead to peace negotiations was for the war to go on long enough and for Jefferson Davis to no longer be Confederate president.[137] His nonreelectable term would have expired in 1868. He lived until 1889, so he probably would not have died in office from natural causes. He might of course have been assassinated—but he was not. Given the events that did in fact ensue, could the war have been continued until 1868? Certainly not in any conventional sense.

15

THE WINTER OF GREAT DISCONTENT

As Emory Thomas observes in his general history of the Confederacy:

> By the fall of 1864 the major campaigns had gone against the Confederacy. Atlanta had fallen, and the Army of Tennessee wandered back over the familiar ground of its former campaigns a much weaker force. Richmond survived and would survive longer, but the Army of Northern Virginia was no longer capable of maneuvering against the enemy except, in the end, to flee.
>
> Significantly in 1864 while the attention of most of the world focused upon the major military themes—the campaigns for Richmond and Atlanta—the Confederate's war developed a disturbing major theme. The war became base and desperate, and the baseness and desperation produced a kind of counterpoint, a sad, minor theme to accompany the major chords. To be sure, the war had never been the grand parade which Southerners had expected in 1861.
>
> Even before 1864, men such as Quantrill had embraced the aspect of premeditated brutality even as President Davis bewailed atrocities committed by the North. However in 1864 the meanness mounted and threatened to become a major theme.[1]

Quantrill and his four hundred fifty-odd Bushwhackers had burned and murdered during the sacking of Lawrence, Kansas, on August 21, 1863, in retaliation for the earlier Jayhawker raid on Osceola, Missouri. About one hundred fifty men and boys died and $1.5 million in property was destroyed. Only women and smaller children were spared, although a few men did manage to escape. One eyewitness said, "The town is in a complete ruin. The whole of the business part, and all good private residences are burned down. Everything of value was taken along by the fiends. . . . I cannot describe the horrors."[2] The sacking of Lawrence was a stark illustration of the long, drawn-out bitter and vicious struggle. It may not be quite accurate that William T. Sherman said "War is hell," but the description fits these aspects of the Civil War.

The guerrilla activities had a rather small effect in determining the war's outcome, however. In the East, particularly, they never occurred on nearly a large enough scale to produce decisive results. And especially in the West, the Confederate government was never really able to control the guerrillas. They were simply carrying on criminal activities, not effectively augmenting the general military effort.

After Lincoln's successful reelection, General U.S. Grant could avoid the risk he might otherwise have felt compelled to take in operations against Lee's force at Petersburg. Grant now wanted a multiplicity of new offensives against the Confederacy, and "chief among them," Brooks D. Simpson observes, "was Sherman's drive through Georgia, to be followed by operations along the North Carolina coast."[3]

Despite the high measure of discontent that pervaded the Confederacy during this unhappy winter, as George C. Rable asserts, "At the beginning of 1865, many Confederates both inside and outside the army still believed their fledgling nation could win its independence. . . . Unswerving patriots found grounds for hope during the war's gloomiest days. Thus morale did not collapse [at the outset of] 1865, as has been commonly asserted." Indeed, Rable—perhaps the most widely read scholar of Confederate newspapers—tells us that "newspapers across the Confederacy echoed and amplified" positive "sentiments. Despite setbacks, the Lord would still bless the Southern people, a Richmond editor maintained." As Rable points out, "Civilian determination remained the key to victory."[4]

Indeed, on Christmas Eve, 1864, Southern troops managed to stymie a Federal assault on Fort Fisher near Wilmington, North Carolina, and the Federal fleet was scattered. "Many Rebels rejoiced as if a great battle had been won. . . . The scattering of the Federal fleet was interpreted as yet another sign of divine favor. The Almighty had sent a gale to defeat the enemy's 'great Armada,' North Carolinian Edmondson maintained; 'God's hand had been apparent' through the whole operation."[5]

After such rejoicing in many parts of the Confederacy, "the fall of Fort Fisher on January 15 [1865] seemed a particularly devastating blow to public confidence," Rable observes. Still, he continues, "even such a military catastrophe, however, did not radically change the thinking of fervent patriots who quickly recovered their psychological equilibrium." The crux of the matter now was "Sherman's devastation of Georgia and the beginning of his march into the Carolinas, [which] posed a much larger challenge for Confederates trying to look on the bright side of things." And at the heart of it was the certainty that "whichever the case might be, even the optimists agreed that some-how Sherman must be stopped."[6]

Hope that the South might still gain the wherewithal to do what was nec-essary continued into the beginning of 1865 in the expectations that foreign recognition might at last be obtained. Indeed, Rable points out, "In January 1865 newspaper reports again claimed the British and French were on the verge of intervention." Was it possible? Even if the British were not part of the equation, "many [Confederates] still thought the French would inter-vene . . . to protect their Mexican interests." (The French had taken advantage of the Union's troubles and violated the Monroe Doctrine by establishing a puppet regime in Mexico.) Rable describes one Southerner's perspective:

> On January 30, 1865, in an hour-long speech, Congressman Daniel DeJarnette of Virginia put a clever twist on all this speculation. He proposed an alliance with the United States to uphold the Monroe Doctrine and drive the French from Mexico. In turn, the Federals would recognize Confederate independence. This idea rested on the belief that the Yankees' wily secretary of state, William H. Seward, was scrambling to find an ally against the European powers.[7]

The Confederate government provided the best postal service it could, and within the safely held territory it was impressive, except for the vexing slow-ness. "Ten *days* from Lynchburg" to Richmond, grumbled one impatient patron; "an ox cart could do better." In 1864 an irate Georgia newspaper edi-tor complained that in "point of facility and dispatch" mail service had "ret-rograded at least two centuries since the war began." The Congress eventually took note of the slowness of the mails and provided for a fast service to apply only to letters and government dispatches that bore an increased rate of one dollar per half-ounce. For ordinary mail, the service became increasingly worse, although it did continue.[8]

Citizens resorted more and more to private express companies for trans-porting mail, especially across the lines, to the armies, or to and from the Trans-Mississippi. For quite some time these companies did considerable busi-ness at moderate rates, but their activities eventually ground or were forced to a halt. After that, daring adventurers usually could be found who would carry letters across borders, for prices that ranged from one to three dollars each. One enterprising private mail carrier used a kite to get mail across the lower Potomac into Maryland. One small boatload of mail ran the blockade into Vicksburg while the siege was going on. Absalom Grimes, the most famous of the Confederate mail runners, transported thousands, perhaps even millions, of pieces of mail across the Mississippi River at innumerable points, aided by an extensive network of assistants—mostly young women—who relished being involved in these "secret and valued duties."[9]

Most of the delays in mail delivery were beyond the postmaster general's control. Parts of the postal establishment began to crumble when border areas of the Confederacy were invaded at the outbreak of war, and wherever the Union armies marched they did more damage to it. Union soldiers seemed greatly to relish demolishing Southern post offices and taking or destroying postal equipment. No doubt the Rebel government made a psychological blunder when it insisted on a postal system that paid its own expenses, for this necessitated rates that were almost twice what the people were accustomed to. Yet they became quite willing to pay even higher prices if only they could get service.[10]

Until the end, the mails kept moving. The post office incurred no debts. It stimulated Southern businesses and helped to operate new ones. It provided employment and later a convenient arrangement whereby civilians could perform necessary tasks, thus freeing more able-bodied men for service in the army. Perhaps most important, it provided an uplifting and cheering element, keeping the soldiers in contact with home and friends with one another. No Confederate governmental activity outside of raising the armies touched the Southern people so closely as the mail system.

The historian Charles Fair, in his *From the Jaws of Victory,* has observed that poor generals characteristically denounce subordinates for their defeats. John Bell Hood was no exception; he began to allocate blame in September 1864, after the fall of Atlanta. Hood wrote Davis, blaming William Hardee and again requesting that Richard Taylor be sent to relieve him. When Davis did not immediately respond, Hood wrote another letter thoroughly lambasting Hardee, placing full onus upon him for the recent losses and indicating that it was "of the utmost importance that Hardee should be relieved at once."[11]

Another serious problem Hood had with generals was in regard to the departure from the army in mid-September of Brigadier General Francis A. Shoup. At his own request, Shoup, the army's chief of staff, was relieved. But Hood appointed no new chief of staff, most of Shoup's former duties devolving upon Major Arthur Pendleton Mason.[12] Administration in the Army of Tennessee had never been exemplary, but now and afterward it virtually fell apart. According to June I. Gow, Hood "was [n]either interested in administrative problems, [n]or indeed even aware of them," and poor administration played a major role in the tragic events that ensued. Again, Davis, as an active-negative president and caring as he did about administration, should have been watching closely enough to have intervened.[13]

Hood then tried to bolster morale by seeing that the men were paid. Davis did become involved in this matter, telegraphing Hood on September 17 that a special requisition was being made to pay the army.[14] Hood next addressed the problems of supply, informing Davis that the army was in great need of shoes and clothing. Hood also tried to secure flour and shoes, finally issuing a circular urging that moccasins be made from beef hides for the barefooted men. Perhaps at least equally pressing was the problem of ensuring an adequate supply of munitions, more artillery pieces, and horses, saddles, and related equipment. Still, Hood reassured Davis that he intended to be active: "I shall continue to interrupt as much as possible the communications of the enemy."[15]

These were important matters; Hood seemed to be justifying the confidence Davis had placed in him. Davis liked Hood's plan to make Sherman's communications his objective, and Richard McMurry concludes that it "was as sound as anything the Confederates could have devised."[16] Davis indeed decided to visit the army. Reaching Hood's headquarters at Palmetto, Georgia, on September 25, he spent two days reviewing the troops and listening to complaints from the various generals. There were many derogatory evaluations of Hood, especially from Hardee. But Davis did as much soothing as he could, and as he later described it, he and Hood discussed "the operations which might retrieve what we had lost from the time the army left Dalton."[17] Davis also at this time created the Military Division of the West, with P. G. T. Beauregard in command.[18]

The president apparently achieved success in his main goal: to raise the army's morale; but he let his elation loosen his tongue a bit too much. In a speech in Columbia, South Carolina, he proclaimed: "[Hood's] eye is now fixed upon a point far beyond that where he was assailed by the enemy." Sherman read the speech in a newspaper a few days later and remarked that "the taking of Atlanta broke upon Jeff. Davis so suddenly as to disturb the equilibrium of his usually well-balanced temper, so that . . . he let out some thoughts which otherwise he would have kept to himself." Sherman heeded Davis's warning and turned to meet the expected threat to his communications.[19]

Hood, however, had a plan different from the one he and Davis had agreed upon: he would leave Georgia to the Federals and move into Alabama, then to Tennessee. According to some scholars, Hood acted without first consulting Davis, the War Department, or Beauregard or even informing them of what he was doing. His plan, as McMurry says, was but "a wild dream." Steven Woodworth asserts that "the plan skirted about the far edges of reality," but then he paraphrases Herman Hattaway, who had written, "but under the circumstances it might have been as good as anything else he could have done— provided he moved very fast and made no mistakes."[20]

Events soon unfolded badly for the Confederates and ended in disaster. Much blame for Hood's action fell upon Davis and his alleged full approval of the Tennessee campaign. Davis's most sympathetic biographer, Felicity Allen, observes that the "evidence is inferential," and she builds a plausible argument that Davis had not approved it. And as William Cooper observes: "The strategy decided on by Hood and Davis at Palmetto and agreed to by Beauregard at Augusta permitted an offensive campaign *only* so long as Sherman dutifully followed. Should he turn back to Atlanta and strike for the sea, then Hood was to become the hunter." It seems likely that a possible campaign into Tennessee was among the many items discussed during Davis's visit to the army; but what Davis wanted, and approved of at the time, was a harassment of Sherman's line of communications, in the hope of precipitating a battle under conditions favorable to the Confederacy and a subsequent defeat of Union forces in detail.[21]

At least two important lower-echelon generals agreed that Davis should be exonerated in regard to Hood's thrust into Tennessee. Stephen D. Lee wrote to W. T. Walthall on July 20, 1878, that he "never believed that Davis inaugurated Hood's Tennessee campaign."[22] And William Nelson Pendleton asserted in his memoirs, "The President was, I learn, as much amazed as everybody else at that strange manoeuvre of Hood's, and shocked to find he had left all Georgia at Sherman's mercy."[23] It would seem that the best that can be said on this is that Davis, in his active-negative persona, left too much to be decided by his subordinates until it was too late to take significant action to change the decision, whether the president thought it wise and worth the risk or not.

According to Cooper, "Hood conveyed his intentions to Beauregard at Gadsden, Alabama, on October 20. Initially Beauregard exhibited little enthusiasm, but after two days of discussion he altered his opinion, even indicating some excitement about the plan. He authorized Hood to go forward into Tennessee." Although Beauregard raised many objections, and the relationship between him and Hood eventually became abrasive, he did a great deal to facilitate matters and to arrange for the army's needs: he "urged on his subordinate the absolute necessity for speed. Hood had to get into middle Tennessee before the Federals were ready for him." On Beauregard's insistence, Hood reopened full communication with the War Department, and no major objections were lodged against his intentions. He wrote to Davis, saying that "should [Sherman] move . . . south from Atlanta, I think it would be the best thing that could happen for our general good," and he gleefully added, "Beauregard *agrees with me* as to my plan of operation."[24] Although Braxton Bragg advised against it, Davis, with some reservations, approved the movement. He too was perhaps deluded by Hood's dream. Woodworth's final conclusion is that "it can be said in defense of Davis that the situation may have been desperate enough to justify the desperate campaign Hood proposed and Davis allowed."[25] On September 26, Mary Chesnut recorded that her husband had told her Custis Lee was urging Davis to replace Hood with Beauregard, but Davis remained undecided. She subsequently wrote that in October Davis was again defending Hood's conduct.[26]

Thomas L. Connelly and Archer Jones suggest that Davis was elated over the launching of a western offensive; indeed, "it is not, perhaps, too much of an exaggeration to say that a western offensive had become even more of an *idée fixe* for Davis than it had been [long before] for Beauregard and that Davis, the convert, was more devout than Beauregard, the prophet."[27] Cooper observes that "after the war, Jefferson Davis tried to exempt himself from complicity in Hood's project. Calling the invasion 'ill-advised,' he claimed in his memoirs he had no knowledge until after the fact that Hood had decided not to follow Sherman. He even denied Hood's fatherhood of the plan and insisted that Beauregard forced it on Hood." This is merely Davis's post facto bitterness toward Beauregard. "The contemporary documents leave no doubt that Davis knew from the beginning what Hood was about. . . . Approving Hood's offensive, he gambled again, just as when he appointed Hood army commander. This time the stakes were even higher."[28]

Nevertheless, as it transpired, both Beauregard and Davis botched their proper functions. Beauregard "did not understand the limits of his authority" and therefore "manifested an almost total lack of initiative and exerted little of his vague authority in dealing with Hood's Tennessee campaign." Davis, dominated as he was by his active-negative character, possessed so intense and ultimately so warped a concern with strategy, that it "seems to have involved a neglect of logistics."[29]

The president exhorted Hood to defeat the Federals before their army could be reunited or reinforced. "You may first beat him in detail," Davis wrote, "and subsequently without serious obstruction or danger to the country in your rear advance to the Ohio River." As the campaigns progressed, Davis gave Hood tactical advice only occasionally. William C. Davis believes that the president probably censured himself privately after the disastrous Battle of Franklin. Earlier in the war, Davis would not have allowed any general, even R. E. Lee, to launch such a campaign unilaterally. As the weeks passed, Davis increasingly doubted Hood's generalship: the president tallied the total casualties Hood suffered in his first ten weeks in command and compared them, unfavorably, with those of Johnston's last ten. William C. Davis concludes, "that Davis allowed Hood to proceed shows just how distracted and exhausted he was by now."[30]

But Cooper points out, "Hood failed to heed Beauregard's admonition to make haste and get into Tennessee as quickly as possible; indeed Hood stayed for three weeks in Tuscumbia. The dashing, even impetuous Hood sat down. Not until November 21 did he advance into Tennessee. The reasons for this delay have never been convincingly explained." McMurry asserts that there is no apparent justification to conclude that Hood's physical impairments altered his thinking or his conduct; but McMurry's subsequent study, *The Road past Kennesaw: The Atlanta Campaign of 1864,* indicates that he may have been taking a derivative of laudanum as a painkiller, and this assuredly could have clouded his judgment. Bruce Catton, in *Never Call Retreat,* Thomas L. Connelly, in *Autumn of Glory,* and McMurry assert that Hood had no plan when he moved north from the Tennessee River except possibly to take Nashville by getting there ahead of John M. Schofield; he was not trying to cut him off.[31]

Cooper then comments on Davis's message to Congress:

> While Hood marched in place at Tuscumbia and Davis in Richmond waited on Hood to move, the Second Confederate Congress convened for its second session on November 7. On that day the president submitted his message, which contained much of the same spirit that characterized its predecessors. To the world, Davis still expressed optimism about Confederate prospects, though he did concede that the lawmakers were gathered during "a time of such public exigency."
>
> Moving away from geographic reporting, Davis asserted that ultimate Confederate triumph did not depend upon holding any specific area or place, even Richmond. In his view, "the indomitable valor of its troops" and "the unquenchable spirit of its people" controlled the outcome of the war, in which the Confederacy would surely prevail. "There is no military success of the enemy which can accomplish its destruction," he declared. In this sense, Davis reified the Confederacy; it became more idea than physical space, or even a government.[32]

And in this high-stakes gamble, at Spring Hill Hood almost pulled it off—almost did cut off General Schofield's 28,000 men from General George H. Thomas's main army. But lacking proper supervision, the Confederates allowed Schofield to move unmolested to Franklin.

The Confederates then fought the costly Battle of Franklin on November 30, sustaining severe losses totaling 6,252 men, including 5 generals. Hood was totally routed on December 15 and 16 in the Battle of Nashville. After disengaging, he at first hoped to be able to remain in Tennessee, on the line of the Duck River, but when he reached Columbia he had enough information on the army's battered condition to convince him that they must go back into northern Mississippi.

When the disastrous Franklin and Nashville campaigns were finally over and the army had limped into winter quarters, Hood resigned his command. He made his way to Richmond, where he took a room in the Spotswood Hotel and worked on reports of his campaigns, even as far back as the operations around Atlanta, including some material quite critical of Johnston's conduct before Hood had relieved him. When Hood had first arrived in Richmond, criticism of Davis for having relieved Johnston was rife, and there is some credible evidence that Davis used Hood ("perhaps unknowingly," McMurry points out) to bolster his own defense against his detractors.[33]

After Hood submitted his reports, he was sent to the Trans-Mississippi on a fact-finding mission, possibly to probe the feasibility of moving troops across the river. Before departing, Hood wrote a touching letter to Davis: "Please never allow anyone to cause you to think for one moment, that I did not know that you were ever more than ready to assume all responsibility naturally belonging to you. I know sir you were in no way responsible for my operations whilst Commanding the Army of Tenn. Believe me Sir ever your sincere friend, And I pray God, may ever bless & protect you." McMurry observes that "Hood's willingness to accept responsibility for the Nashville Campaign is a theme that he espoused for the rest of his life and one that indicates the sincerity of his admiration for Davis."[34]

Davis in *Rise and Fall* quoted from a letter sent him by Tennessee governor Isham G. Harris, written on December 25, 1864: "I have been with General Hood from the beginning of this campaign, and beg to say, disastrous as it has ended, I am not able to see anything that General Hood has done that he should not, or neglected any thing that he should, have done." Davis wrote, "To this I will only add that General Hood was relieved at his reiterated request, . . . and that it was in no wise due to a want of confidence in him on my part."[35]

General William T. Sherman occupied Savannah, Georgia, on December 21, just in time to present it to President Abraham Lincoln as "a Christmas present." There was assuredly little Christmas joy in the Confederacy. As Cooper observes:

> Worry and growing concern reached into the Executive Mansion, where Varina shared with a close friend the emotional toll these desperate times were taking on her and her husband. Just after Jefferson's return from his western trip, she informed Mary Chesnut in South Carolina, "We are in a sad and anxious state here." Repeating herself with emphasis in the same letter, she confided, "Strictly between us, *things look* very anxious *here*." Varina said she could not read and spoke of being "so constantly depressed" that she dreaded writing. She reported her husband "extremely well—for him—but very anxious." Fully understanding the crucial nature of Hood's campaign, she wrote on November

20, "Affairs west are looking so critical now that before you receive this you and I will be in the depths or else triumphant." There was no triumph, only ever-deepening depths.[36]

Yet despite the wretchedness of the situation,

> Varina Davis strove to bring enchantment into her house. Despite immense difficulties, she orchestrated with the help of friends a pageant of joy in which for a brief moment reality was suspended. Upon learning that the orphans in the Episcopal Home had been promised a Christmas tree, she included them in her plans. . . . During the night, the president had cake sent out to the White House guards. The holiday spirit reigned. . . . The next day reality returned . . . [and] the year ended on a blacker note than anyone had thought possible. . . . No glittering social events marked New Years Day 1865 in Richmond. . . . Throughout the Confederacy, despondency and even despair greeted the turn of the year.[37]

Davis certainly had acerbic enemies. None more "relentlessly blasted Davis and blamed him for each defeat," points out George Rable, than his "old nemeses such as Vice-President Alexander H. Stephens and Governor Joseph E. Brown of Georgia." Perhaps it is tragically true that the president had lost the loyalty of some of the fighting men, too: "in early January a Georgia regiment reportedly cheered the false rumor that the president had died."[38]

Yet Rable has pointed out that

> disenchantment with the administration appeared to be confined mainly to elite circles. One editor dismissed Davis's critics as "malcontents, traducers, friends of the North in disguise; and a host of sickly, timid, apprehensive men who have become their dupes and instruments." The president appeared to be much more unpopular with certain politicians and generals than with the public at large. Admirers still compared him to George Washington. . . . Indeed, many newspapers remained loyal to the administration and sanguine about Confederate prospects right up to the end.[39]

R. E. Lee was elevated to general in chief by congressional demand in January 1865. This command rearrangement, Bragg's discomfiture with his position, Virginia's withdrawal of two militia regiments from Confederate command, and above all, the necessary recall of J. E. Johnston to army command were seen by the populace as humiliations of Jefferson Davis. " 'Tray, Blance, and Sweetheart, bark at him,' " wrote J. B. Jones. Yet through it all he moved with aplomb. Lee, on the other hand, was sanguine, for as Rable observes, "Lee had a higher opinion of Johnston than he would ever dare confide to Jefferson Davis. [And too] James Longstreet, Wade Hampton, and Howell Cobb all believed that bringing back Johnston would restore public confidence and boost morale among the troops assigned to stop Sherman."[40]

By February 1865, Secretary of War Judah Benjamin broke official silence by speaking publicly on the matter of employing blacks as Rebel soldiers, urging that slaves who volunteered should be accepted and sent to the army immediately. He asked R. E. Lee for an expression of opinion from the army to counter opponents who claimed that the presence of slave soldiers would cause white soldiers to desert.[41]

In the previous fall Davis had suggested to the Congress that it might want to consider manumission for "zealous discharge of duty" and for "faithful service." But Davis was then not quite ready to propose using slaves as actual soldiers. That should wait "until the white population proved insufficient to man the armies."[42]

Nevertheless, early in 1865 Davis was urging the idea privately, and he received with gratification the information that it was being well received in many quarters. A citizen in Cuthbert, Georgia, for example, spoke out enthusiastically for the idea. New recruits could come only from the black population of the South, and he called on his fellow Confederates to "away with pride of opinion, away with false pride." "Some say," he noted, that arming black soldiers would be "giving up the question, What, giving up the question to grip it the tighter?" If the government could take fathers, brothers, and sons, it could take property, and "he who values his property higher than his life and independence is a poor sordid wretch . . . a slave in spirit." As many black men should be put into the field as Davis and Lee thought necessary.[43] Yet another citizen pointed to the Union army and concluded that "escaped slaves fight and fight bravely for our enemies; therefore a freed slave will fight." He also believed that if the Confederacy granted amnesty to all slaves who had joined the Federals, they would soon desert and come back South. Accordingly, he called for the prompt abolition of slavery.[44]

The issue was clearly a heated one; many congressmen fought the notion to the very end. As one of them put it, "The country was beginning to learn that all abolitionists were not in the North."[45] Another complained that slave soldiers "would make a San Domingo of our land."[46] And a citizen in North Carolina urged that every soldier who enlisted in the Confederate army should receive a slave and fifty acres of land at the end of the war, plus all the Union's black soldiers they would capture.[47]

The idea gained imminence when circumstances grew even bleaker on the battle lines. On January 15, 1865, Fort Fisher fell, closing the ocean access that Wilmington, North Carolina, had enjoyed. This meant the loss of the last open port that blockade runners could penetrate with any ease. The news, Cooper observes,

> had a "stunning effect" in Richmond. A distraught President Davis called the loss "unexpected" and immediately wired the Confederate commander to find out whether the fortress could be retaken. . . . Within a week Sherman began his invasion of South Carolina. . . . President Davis fully understood the grave conditions confronting his country and his presidency. [Yet] he still blamed "malcontents." They had seized upon the situation and "created a feeling hostile to the execution of the rigorous laws which were necessary to raise and feed our armies, then magnifying every reverse and prophesying ruin they have produced public depression and have sown the seeds of disintegration."
>
> As always, Davis had difficulty coping with the abundant evidence that not all Confederates shared his utter commitment to the Confederate cause. He could not contemplate failure. Varina certainly spoke his mind in saying that "everything also even to extermination we expect to bear unless the liberty for which we began it is grant[ed] to us." "The foundations of our political life," she continued, "are laid deep in the blood of our nearest and dearest. I am sure it has not been shed in vain."[48]

Some congressmen were in full support of the notion of using black troops. John T. Lamkin confessed to his wife that "slavery is played out whether we win or lose," and emancipation would come regardless of the outcome of the war. By January 1865, this slaveholder admitted that he no longer cared about slavery. His slaves had helped his wife in her home-front tasks, and he intended "to place all my faithful servants in such a condition that they shall profit by their faithfulness to us."[49] Others in authority were also wrestling with this problem and its implications. By this time, however, the most authoritative voice in the Confederacy was no longer that of Jefferson Davis; it was Robert E. Lee's.

When Andrew Hunter, a member of the Virginia state senate, wrote Lee requesting the general's opinion on the question, he acknowledged that the public was divided and that "a mountain of prejudices growing out of our ancient modes of regarding the institution of Southern slavery will have to be met and overcome before we can attain to anything like that degree of unanimity so extremely desirable in this and all else connected with our great struggle."[50] Hunter made it plain to Lee that the general's opinion would become public, and with that in mind Lee responded a few days later. He preferred to rely on the white population for soldiers; but since the Union was increasing its strength with black soldiers, who would destroy slavery in any case, "whatever may be the effect of our employing negro troops, it cannot be as mischievous as this," wrote Lee. And he further underlined the basic issue: "whether slavery shall be extinguished by our enemies and the slaves be used against us, or use them ourselves at the risk of the effects which may be produced upon our social institution." He thus recommended not only that black troops be used but that they also be emancipated upon enlistment, in order to ensure efficient service. He also urged "that whatever measures are to be adopted should be adopted at once."[51]

Citing the need to fill the ranks of the armies, Davis also recommended important legislation involving basic reconsideration of conscription and the accompanying issue of exemption. Slave soldiers might or might not be accepted by Congress; but there was considerable support pressuring the legislators to accept Davis's recommendation to modify the exemption system. The blanket exemption still offered was, Davis scolded, "unwise, nor is it believed to be defensible in theory." Defense was a duty that devolved on all citizens in a country "where each citizen enjoys an equality of rights and privileges." Although some individuals in certain lines of work might be more useful at home than in uniform, "it is manifest that this cannot be the case with entire classes," and he asked that Congress grant more discretion in this matter to the military authorities. Davis also asked for a general militia law to overcome the embarrassment created by a lack of uniform legislation from state to state.[52] But this important legislation was a long time coming, reflecting the obstinacy of some congressmen and the discouragement of others. The delay also reflected much of the turmoil of Confederate politics in 1865. While some members were indeed surrendering to the inevitable, others engaged in unnecessarily extended argument over important issues, such as creation of a chief adviser's position to be filled by Robert E. Lee, shuffling of generals, suspension of habeas corpus, and of course the entire manpower question, including use of slave soldiers.

If Virginians thought that Davis was failing to reassure the country, others thought that he and his supporters were too vigorous in his insinuations against those who disagreed with him. His unwavering commitment to the cause ironically made him seem out of touch with the suffering, depressed, and disheartened populace. Rable observes that "the war brought out both the best and the worst in Jefferson Davis, magnifying both his strengths and weaknesses." The paradox kept him from being able to elicit from very many others the kind of pure dedication to the cause that he himself harbored. He "lost the capacity to learn from experience. Instead of mellowing with age, he ossified; rather than becoming wiser, he became the brittle symbol of a collapsing revolution."[53] But the same might be said of many historical figures who found themselves at the head of a losing cause.

Early in 1864, for example, North Carolina senator E. G. Reade had felt it necessary to reassure the president about his state's attitude toward the war, but he nevertheless feared that Richmond authorities "are so prejudiced against N[orth] C[arolina] that extreme measures will be resorted to against her citizens." As for Davis, Reade thought him "as bitter as gall, & I shall feel much alarm if he shall be clothed with unlimited power [to suspend the writ of habeas corpus]."[54] Such mistrust of Davis continued throughout the war.

As Reade's remarks indicate, habeas corpus was still a major issue in the last congressional session and the last few weeks of the war. In this session, three bills to authorize further suspension passed either the House or the Senate, but none passed both. Failure of passage was not due to lack of Davis's efforts. He had asked for a suspension bill on November 9, 1864, claiming that when the previous law expired, "serious embarrassment" resulted in Mobile, Wilmington, and Richmond when the military was unable

> to arrest and hold suspected persons against whom the testimony was sufficient to give full assurance that they were spies or holding treasonable communication with the enemy, though legal proof could not be adduced to secure their commitment and conviction by the courts, either because of the character of the evidence or the necessity for concealing the sources of information which were not infrequently within the enemy's lines.[55]

He asked for suspension once again, virtually on the eve of the evacuation of Richmond, claiming that such a law was "not simply advisable and expedient, but almost indispensable to the successful conduct of the war."[56] By a narrow margin the House finally passed a bill similar to that of 1864, but the Senate amended it to allow state courts to issue the writ when the conscription question was involved. This measure violated the very purpose of the law, and the House never bothered to pass the Senate amendment. In the end, the opponents of suspension of the writ triumphed; the two houses of Congress failed to agree, and the final bill died in March 1865 when a last effort in the House also failed in the Senate. The war ended soon afterward.[57] Habeas corpus was intact; the Confederacy was not. The greatest support for suspension in the Second Congress had come from those men who had been elected by regions already overrun by the enemy, whose constituents and families would never feel the effect of the law. Opposition, on the other hand, centered in the newly selected delegates from Georgia and North Carolina.[58]

The issue of suspending habeas corpus was one of the most perplexing problems that the Davis-led government faced. As a constitutionalist, Davis tended to seek a constitutional solution. He reasoned that the authority to suspend the writ had to come from Congress, and on three occasions he had asked for and received passage of acts authorizing suspensions. But though the Congress failed to grant him all that he needed and desired in this regard, that failure probably did not alter the final course of the war, and it certainly was not the result of any firm adherence by the congressmen to the doctrine of state rights. It was always an agonizing matter of trying to retain the writ as a safeguard against potentially despotic government.

That the Confederacy did suspend the writ as much as it did is the truly significant point. This was a meaningful step toward ensuring the government's authority to direct the war as it in fact existed at those moments and at the same time to preserve the security of the would-be nation. The war effort was thus much more centralized, and Southerners were brought more potently under the jurisdiction of the central government. As John Brawner Robbins asserts:

> The issue forced a choice between liberty and law and military necessity. Some, expressing a sincere concern for the preservation of personal liberty in a time of vastly increasing military establishment, questioned the wisdom of suspending the writ of habeas corpus. Others strongly defended the constitutional right of the government to suspend the writ in war time; still others accepted suspension as a necessity to achieve the higher goal of Confederate independence. . . . Those who defended the doctrine of state rights, for the most part, merely played on the lowering morale of a war weary people facing defeat and the end of their dreams in order to advance personal political ambitions.[59]

Others used the issue as a proxy for opposition to any sort of conscription, and all the opponents—and proponents—were facing not only defeat but also the end of their cherished hopes and dreams.

Much of the manpower legislation that Davis had requested in his November 1864 message falls under the heading of patchwork. Most of these requests were enacted without great difficulty. Early in the last session of Congress, an act of the previous February, holding the seventeen-year-olds and those aged forty-six to fifty solely to duty in their own states and prohibiting their use elsewhere, was repealed for sixty days, a clear sign that manpower was growing short somewhere, primarily in Georgia.[60] In January 1865 it was suspended indefinitely.[61]

If further evidence of a frightening shortage of soldiers was needed, it was provided by the January 1865 extension of the law creating the Invalid Corps.[62] In the cavalry, quartermasters were to put the horses of enlisted men on their property lists and pay them according to the appraised value of the horse. The law also provided that any cavalryman who left his command or "commits any wanton insult or injury to the person or property of any loyal citizen of the Confederate States" was to be transferred out of the cavalry. This was a telling statement, as was the law's last proviso (this just two months before the end of the war), which required that a book of tactics should be provided to each cavalry officer.[63]

In addition, a law was passed to provide for the creation of new units to be composed of the consolidated remnants of units from the same state; supernumerary officers would be allowed to form new organizations of their own, or they would be dropped from the rolls—but in the event of the latter, they would then be conscripted. Similar provisions applied to staff officers of depleted units and to returned prisoners of war.[64] The artillery was also subject to reorganization, primarily to ensure an appropriate number of officers and that artillery horses received proper care.[65] An obvious and long-needed measure was the conscription of men of the usual ages who resided permanently in areas occupied by Federal forces, who might now be conscripted into the reserves of whatever state in which they were now found.[66]

One of the vital pieces of legislation was the new conscription law. Coming only after interminable debate, it was passed March 7, 1865, far too late to have much impact on the fighting. It abolished the Conscript Bureau, provided that commanders of state reserves would enforce the conscription and exemption laws, and declared that "all applications for exemption and detail, except as hereinafter provided," would be decided by these officers.[67] Even this was not sufficient, and a week later Davis complained about the rather generous provisions of further legislation still under consideration in Congress. Skilled workers in government employ were to be exempt from all military service, although Davis pointed out that such workers constituted a major portion of the local defense forces.[68] A second proposal would eliminate "all details and exemptions heretofore granted by the President and Secretary of War" and would prohibit any such details or exemptions in the future. Davis pointed to the folly of putting essential and experienced workers into the ranks and begged that these two provisions be eliminated from forthcoming legislation.[69]

Even as he urged Congress to refine legislation still under consideration, he objected to the conscription bill he had just received a week before. Exemptions under that law would have to be certified by physicians, and Davis pointed out that the number of physicians required (three for each congressional district, two of them from the army) would pull one hundred fifty physicians from active military duty and that the grounds for exemption were exceedingly vague, allowing the continued exemption of men who might be fit for limited duty.[70]

Meanwhile, Congress, having given up hope for all practical purposes, was preparing to adjourn. Senator Williamson S. Oldham, arriving a month late from Texas for the session, noted,

The people [were] greatly dispirited and disheartened; [their] confidence was gone and hope was almost extinguished. There existed [in Congress] a listless apathy in regard to the most important measures of legislation demanded by the crisis. Many of them were vindictive, vituperative, and violent in their denunciations of President Davis and his cabinet, and were open in ascribing all the misfortunes of the country and its then imperilled condition to their incompetency. Others were open in the acknowledgement that they had lost all hope, and were busy in sowing the seeds of despondency and despair amongst the people. . . . Some of them seemed to be preparing for anticipated events, and to place themselves in a position which would attract the favorable consideration of their masters when the Confederate cause should fail. Very many members, patriotic, true, and faithful, appeared to be stunned, almost paralyzed by the condition of things.[71]

Many legislators had already left for their homes, anticipating the final collapse and hoping to get out of Richmond and back to their families while they still could. Others, their escape routes already cut or homes now occupied by Union forces, remained in Richmond but seldom bothered to attend the daily meetings of Congress. Attendance at the beginning of the session was usually about eighty or ninety Congressman, but by January it was usually in the seventies. In March it had fallen to less than sixty present on some roll calls.[72] On March 9, Davis asked the Congress to postpone its adjournment and warned of an important message to come. Four days later, he sent that message, an anguished appeal that Congress cancel its forthcoming adjournment sine die and to continue consideration of major questions.

Among the several vital issues that Davis wanted settled were the use of black soldiers, a general militia law, and "a law of a few lines repealing all class exemptions."[73] The sluggish Congress finally responded with another law to diminish exemptions and details, which ended the overseer exemption for men under the age of forty-five and allowed the president and secretary of war to grant limited exemptions to men unfit for the field, or over age forty, or to laborers possessing special skills and employed by the Confederate or state governments. All other details were terminated.[74] A final modification of exemptions for railroad and canal employees passed two days later and was the last legislation on the subject.[75]

The last major issue was a proposal to supplement military strength with black labor and soldiers. Congress acceded to Davis's suggestion that more black labor was needed by providing that all free black and enslaved males between the ages of eighteen and fifty "shall be held liable to perform any labor or discharge any duties with the army," including work on fortifications, manufacture of munitions, hospital duty, road work, or the like. These auxiliaries would be paid; the owners would receive the pay of the slaves. The secretary of war and the commander of the Trans-Mississippi could hire as many such laborers as desired; if more were needed, they could be impressed, though this power was limited in order to ensure that each state contributed its proper share of black labor.[76] However, legislation passed a few days later removed the limitation.[77]

That these laws, if properly and promptly enforced, could have provided an important addition to the strength of the army was clear, but even though some white soldiers would thereby be released for field duty, there was still need for additional troops. This need could be met only by black soldiers, causing many Confederates to scratch their heads in bewilderment at what the war was about in the first place. Georgia's governor Joseph E. Brown told his state legislature that the slaves were needed at home for their labor and reasoned that "if we are right, and Providence designed [the slaves] for slavery, He did not intend that they should be a military people. Whenever we establish the fact that they are a military race, we destroy our whole theory that they are unfit to be free."[78] Major General Howell Cobb, also from Georgia, seldom agreed with Brown, but he agreed in this. "If slaves will make good soldiers," Cobb told Secretary of War Seddon, "our whole idea of slavery is wrong."[79]

Nevertheless, the law for slave soldiers that Davis had so urgently requested weeks before, when it might have done some good, was finally passed—when it was too late. Davis was authorized to ask for as many slave soldiers as he desired, "to perform military service in whatever capacity he may direct." These troops were to be paid on the same basis as white troops. If not enough men could be raised otherwise, Davis could call on each state for its proportional quota of three hundred thousand troops, black or not, "to prosecute the war successfully and maintain the sovereignty of the States and the independence of the Confederate States." A key provision of the law was found in the final section, which prohibited "a change in the relation which the said slaves shall bear toward their owners, except by consent of the owners and of the States in which they reside."[80] But this provision, clearly designed to discourage emancipation, was finessed by the Confederate War Department. When regulations were issued to implement the legislation, they stated specifically that slave soldiers would be accepted only if emancipated by their owners.[81] Thus emancipation became the sine qua non, but it was too late to object. A few black soldiers were recruited, suited up, and drilled on the streets of Richmond, but the city fell and the war ended before nearly any of them saw any service in the field.[82]

Although controversial and frustrating, the Confederate conscription system had a tremendously favorable impact. Coming more than a full year before the Union also resorted to conscription, it gave the Confederacy renewed vigor on the fields of battle until midwar. The statistical picture looks rather impressive. Even if the large figure of 87,863 is accepted as the number of men just east of the Mississippi who were exempted, very few of those who were excluded from service for some specific reason escaped eventual military service of some kind. Though not proving it, Thomas L. Livermore, in *Numbers and Losses in the Civil War,* has estimated that the total Confederate strength finally amounted to 1,082,119 men (and women disguised as men); thus the South may have mobilized a force that large from a total white population of fewer than 9,000,000, a remarkable feat. It is a reasonable assumption that the draft supplied about one-third of the total who served. But this ignores the draft's most important aspect: inducing men to volunteer rather than be conscripted. General John S. Preston's records indicate that there were 81,993 conscripts and another 76,206 who volunteered to avoid the draft.

By early 1865 the manner of impressment was not nearly so important as the problem of getting supplies by any means at all. Commissary General Lucius Northrop was in despair. Noting that General Beauregard could order impressments and enforce the order because "he has the good will of the people generally to aid him," Northrop pointed out the fate of General Lee in Virginia. That state was the scene of turmoil, destruction, and heavy enemy occupation, an area drained of supply where "the officers of this bureau can no longer impress, because they have no power to enforce it, and the people will not surrender their stores."[83]

The problem of payment was still a major difficulty. Secretary of the Treasury George A. Trenholm wrote Davis in January that defeat had "affected the confidence of the public in government securities, and it is impossible at this time to render them available for the supply of means. There is no demand, either for the non-taxable bonds, or the Certificates of indebtedness." How to pay for goods, whether impressed or obtained by contract? Trenholm concluded that "taxation is at present the only resource in the power of the government." Even though taxes took time to collect and the Confederacy did not have time, Trenholm begged for more taxes, hoping to use specie from the banks in the meantime to purchase currency.[84]

This was too little, too late. Not long after, General Lee complained to the secretary of war that his men were without meat for three days because his chief commissary had none, his rations were low, his clothing supply inadequate, and his army was facing "battle, cold, hail, & sleet." He feared for the fate of the Confederacy if the Commissary Department were not reorganized. The physical strength of the men would fail, and lacking forage, some divisions were scattered, due to lack of supplies. "Taking these facts in connection with the paucity of our numbers," Lee wrote, "you must not be surprised if calamity befalls us."[85]

Davis knew the situation well and endorsed it revealingly: "This is too sad to be patiently considered and cannot have occurred without criminal neglect or gross incapacity."[86] That same day he told Seddon to buy food for Lee's army from the public if none was available in the commissary and demanded that commissary officers act at once. "The meat should be put in the cars and sent off before they sleep," he said. He also urged Seddon to send whiskey, although there were many contemporaries who argued that the army already had too much of that. "The distress of our brave defenders" Davis told Seddon, "renders me uncontrollably anxious."[87] And well he might have been uncontrollably anxious: by the end of February, so critical had the food situation become that prominent citizens of the Richmond area were asking the public to donate food to the Army of Northern Virginia.[88]

On March 10 Alexander R. Lawton, who had become quartermaster general in February 1864, summed up the situation for the new secretary of war, John C. Breckinridge, who replaced Seddon on February 6, 1865. There was enough forage in North Carolina, plus a little in Virginia, to support the armies in those areas for three months, but there was a problem with transportation and protection of the area in which it was located. He suggested that this supply be kept for horses and not transferred to the commissary, as had been done previously, asserting that this way it would last longer. In South Carolina and Georgia there was enough forage, but lack of money precluded its purchase. The railroads were doing remarkably well, considering the poor shape they were in, and would probably be adequate if used only to move supplies. Animals were lacking for field transportation, and once again lack of funds precluded purchase of those that were available. Sufficient ambulances and wagons were being fashioned, but horses were urgently needed. Clothing was in short supply, due to the blockade and the destruction of factories. The troops were supposedly better clothed than formerly and were well supplied with shoes. But there was a lack of money to pay for items already received.[89]

Despite these tales of woe and countless others like them, Congress was slow in acting during its last session. The Bureau of Conscription continued to impress slave labor as needed, and in a circular issued December 12, 1864, apportioned twenty thousand slaves by state, with Virginia, both of the Carolinas, Alabama, and Georgia to supply twenty-five hundred; Mississippi and East Louisiana fifteen hundred; and Florida and Tennessee five hundred.[90]

South Carolina, however, and subsequently other states as well, sought to evade the levy of slave labor by passing legislation that limited the use of South Carolina slaves to within the state, and even then only on the coast and fortifications. If slaves were drafted for the Confederacy, owners would get credit for that draft, thereby ensuring that the total number of slaves impressed within the state by either government was limited to the number set by the state.[91] John S. Preston, superintendent of the Bureau of Conscription, was alarmed by this sabotage of the manpower system, justifiably fearing that other states soon would follow South Carolina's policy. As he put it, with special and heated reference, not only the "designing knaves" in the South Carolina legislature but also Governors Brown of Georgia and Vance of North Carolina "have saved the Confederacy the shame of an idiotic suicide."[92]

Why was South Carolina in such a recalcitrant mood? One of Preston's subordinates offered an explanation: There had been too many calls for slaves, slaves had often been treated poorly, and the burden of slave impressment had been distributed unequally, "so that the well affected [owners] are very reluctant to respond to any call, whilst the factious and unpatriotic, the lukewarm and the disaffected, now so numerous, are ready to interpose every possible hindrance to the execution of such impressment." He added, "The slaves themselves are very averse to this labor and their owners sympathize with them, feel for them, and are disposed to screen them"[93] A conscription officer in South Carolina flatly informed Preston that no slaves could be obtained in that state except by ignoring its laws, which he did not advise.[94]

General Preston thought that to meet the desperate situation Confederate legislation should be passed authorizing the War Department to negotiate with each state for slave impressment, and he concluded that "a regiment of cavalry with bloodhounds in every county in the Confederacy would not obtain the slaves unless by the intervention and use of State laws and State authorities."[95]

Additional legislation for the impressment of slaves was passed in February, this time without limitation as to the number that might be impressed or the period of their service.[96] Moreover, strict control was finally established over railroads, water transportation, and telegraph lines by legislation that amounted to their impressment, too.[97] But the supply problem remained, causing an impatient Davis to issue his appeal of March 13, calling for urgent action and begging Congress not to adjourn as scheduled but to remain in session and continue to attend to important business.

It was too late to do anything to change the outcome of the war, however, and Davis was one of the few Confederates left who did not understand this. In addition to other needed laws, he asked for still more new impressment legislation. With the passage of the February 1864 law that required market-price payments, Davis now contended that it had become "impossible to supply the Army, although ample stores may exist in the country, whenever the owners refuse to give credit to the public officers. [Therefore] it is necessary that this restriction on the power of impressment be removed." The problem was that market-price impressment was too expensive and that "the limit fixed for the issue of Treasury Notes has been nearly reached," so that, as in the earlier stages of the war, the Treasury could not always provide the required funds. An additional problem was that the recent tax laws had not yet had time to generate revenue.[98]

Davis claimed that he did not like the idea of tampering with the market-price provisions of the impressment law, but he also claimed it was absolutely necessary to do so. "There is really no market price in many cases, and the valuation is made arbitrarily and in depreciated currency. . . . None believe that the Government can ever redeem in coin the obligation to pay $50 a bushel for corn, or $700 a barrel for flour." He proposed that values be estimated in coin and the government be obligated to pay that price plus interest, or that the government turn to the desperate expedient of in-kind transactions, just as it had done in the 1863 tax in kind on agricultural products. He even proposed that if necessary the Confederate government repay in kind and to "make the obligations thus issued receivable for all payments due in coin to the Government." Whether or not Congress approved his proposal, he begged that the law be changed in some way to meet the army's necessities.[99]

Thus, the impressment issue was still tied up with the problems of the Treasury, even as the Confederacy wound down to its last days. Taking their cue from the president, the Congress did pass a new impressment act, which became law on March 18, 1865. Schedules of prices were no longer to be used for impressments, but the most important provision was the flat statement that in the future "just compensation . . . was to mean the usual market price of such property at the time and place of impressment."[100] The proponents of market-price impressment had finally won.

By the provisions of another act approved the same day, Congress revised impressment still further, stipulating that "it shall not be necessary to pay the price at the time of impressment, when the parties from whom such property is impressed shall refuse to receive therefor certificates of indebtedness issued under authority of the act."[101]

Whatever good these laws might have done if passed at an earlier time, it was too late now. The Congress would permit the army to take whatever its impressment officers wanted under the plea of necessity, but it no longer made much difference. Congress adjourned later the same day, and the government evacuated Richmond two weeks later.

Price schedules were still issued, and on March 27, Virginia wheat supposedly was worth twenty-five dollars a bushel; peas and beans thirty dollars a bushel; and Irish and sweet potatoes twenty dollars a bushel, reflecting 500 and 600 percent increases over December 1864. Unaccountably, other items rose but little in the same four months, most likely because there was so little available at any price. Lard, bacon, and salt pork each rose only about one dollar a pound, and iron just marginally.[102] But in truth, there was no iron to be had, and precious little meat. The market existed only in theory, and any payments—whether in Treasury notes or certificates—would be worthless when, if, and anywhere the producer tried to pass them.

Despite the true bleakness of the situation as 1864 waned and 1865 began, and even into early February, a considerable degree of determination and high morale did still persist. Rable observes, "To say that morale plummeted for the rest of the war would oversimplify a complex reality." Actually, in early 1865 "a great patriotic revival began." And indeed "Confederate leaders made one final attempt to rally their people against the Federal onslaught. Several governors issued firebreathing proclamations." But as Rable observes, matters were becoming increasingly tenuous: "A belief that somehow independence could yet be won persisted but now depended much more on abstract assertions than faith in any tangible means of deliverance."[103]

16

THE BATTLEFIELD REALITIES IN 1865

Snow blanketed the ground in Richmond on New Year's Day 1865. It was a Sunday and Davis went to church. He was feeling rather better physically than in recent times, but his mind was troubled. "The malcontents," as he called them, were complaining about the length of the war and were publicly urging that men not comply with conscription or subsistence procurement procedures. "Magnifying every reverse and prophesying ruin, they have produced public depression, and sown the seeds of disintegration. Men of the old federal school are they who now invoke the laws of state rights to sustain a policy which, in proportion to the extent of its adoption, must tend to destroy the existence of the States of our Confederacy, and have them conquered provinces."[1]

Davis, the old champion of localism, seemed to be standing almost alone as the ultra-Confederate nationalist. Disloyal men recently had declared the Free State of Southwest Virginia and installed a governor, a commanding general, and a militia. Perhaps worse, by this time, every state except South Carolina had seen some of its sons form regiments of volunteers and go off to serve in the Union army.[2]

At a January wedding party in Richmond, one observer thought the fifty-six-year-old president "thin and careworn. Naturally refined in his appearance, his hair and beard were bleaching rapidly; and his bloodless cheeks and slender nose . . . gave him almost the appearance of emaciation."[3]

Despite physical debility, Davis remained defiant, firm, and resolute. In his November 1864 message to the Confederate Congress, he had declared, "Not the fall of Richmond, nor Wilmington, nor Charleston, nor Savannah, nor Mobile, nor of all combined, can save the enemy from the constant and exhaustive drain of blood and treasure which must continue until he shall discover that no peace is attainable unless based on the recognition of our indefeasible rights."[4]

But during the first three months of 1865, Davis had to grapple with several crises, which, according to the historian and archivist Michael Ballard,

"threatened the credibility of his bold words."⁵ Davis's most pressing problem was that he simply did not have an adequate force to stop Sherman from
his marauding raids. To get such a force he needed better cooperation from
state officials, and that was nearly impossible.

On January 24, 1865, the Confederate Congress again offered the Federals
a prisoner of war exchange. This time General U. S. Grant accepted. He had
previously refused exchange so as to cut down on Southern manpower; now
apparently he could see the end, and Northern victory was in sight. Moreover,
humane consideration of the severe sufferings of Northern captives, so keenly
revealed by the thousands of prisoners that were freed by Sherman's raiding
forces, induced the Union to change its policy.

Davis had always been enraged over the prisoner of war problems. As
Varina later wrote:

> The cause of all the sufferings of the men of the South who starved and froze
> on Johnson's Island and at Point Lookout, and those of the North who suc-
> cumbed to the heat and exposure at Andersonville, and died for lack of proper
> medicines (made contraband by their own Government), was the violation of
> the cartel for the exchange of prisoners by the civil and military authorities of
> the United States.
>
> The reasons for this violation are obvious. The South, hemmed in on the land
> by a cordon of bayonets, and on the sea-coast by the enemy's fleet, had only
> the male population within its borders from which to recruit its armies; while
> the North, with the ports of the world open to her, could replace the immense
> losses incurred in battle and by capture, and find ample "food for powder" in
> every country and among all peoples; so their armies were easily augmented
> by large enlistments of foreigners and negro slaves captured in the South.
>
> With this bountiful supply of material it seemed to matter little to her if a
> few thousands of such rank and file were, in violation of the cartel, detained in
> Southern "prison pens." The majority of these mercenaries had not even a com-
> mon language in which to communicate their woes to the people for whom they
> were paid to fight or die.⁶

Davis had from the beginning hoped that prisoners would be treated
humanely and quickly exchanged. After the schooner *Savannah* had been captured on July 6, 1861, Davis wrote Lincoln:

> It is the desire of the Government so to conduct the war now existing as to mit-
> igate its horrors as far as may be possible; and, with this intent, its treatment of
> the prisoners captured by its forces has been marked by the greatest humanity

and leniency consistent with public obligations; some have been permitted to return home on parole, others remained at large under similar conditions within this Confederacy, and all have been furnished with rations for their subsistence, such as are allowed to our own troops. It is only since the news has been received of the treatment of the prisoners taken on the *Savannah* that I have been compelled to withdraw these indulgences and to hold the prisoners taken by us in strict confinement.[7]

Some considerable measure of quid pro quo did ensue, both sides being induced to treat prisoners reasonably well and to exchange or parole them; each side having prisoners forced the other to refrain from inhumanities. But after Grant ordered exchanges to be stopped, Davis was especially vexed. As Varina wrote in her memoir, "Finding that exchanges could not be made, we offered their sick and wounded without any equivalents. Although the offer was made in the summer, the transportation did not arrive until November, and the most emaciated of the poor prisoners were then photographed and exhibited 'to fire the Northern heart.' "[8]

At the war's conclusion the only man to be tried and hanged for war crimes was the former commander at Andersonville, Captain Henry Wirz. Though Wirz's commanding officer, General John H. Winder, escaped the same ultimate punishment by dying in February 1865, he was widely denounced. Davis never abandoned his belief that there had been no war crimes committed, and shortly before his death he wrote a full account of the story of Andersonville, "the condition of affairs therein, and the causes of the mortality." It was published in January and February 1890 in *Belford's Magazine* and later in pamphlet form. Varina believed that "it should be a complete vindication of the Confederate authorities before all fair-minded men."[9] As for Winder, Davis wrote of him in *Rise and Fall* as being "a man too brave to be cruel to anything within his power, too well bred and well born to be influenced by low and sordid motives." Davis asserted that there were many facts "illustrative of his kindness to the prisoners after he went to Georgia, and they were in keeping with his conduct toward the prisoners at Richmond." Indeed, Davis stated, it was "this later fact, together with his sterling integrity and soldierly character, [that] had caused his selection for the chief control of Confederate prisons."[10]

Davis was partly correct in his assessment of Winder. Winder's biographer, Arch Fredric Blakey, contends that he was "a humane jailor, far more so than his Union counterpart," until 1863. After the Emancipation Proclamation and the end of the exchange cartel, however, he "betrayed few signs of a humanitarian nature." He "became hardened to the suffering of all his captives, Confederate and Union alike," and "he authorized brutal punishment." But the Northern charge that he was "a murderous beast" was untrue, and he "was an early and earnest advocate of exchange." Indeed, he sometimes paroled prisoners on "his own responsibility" when it became apparent that he could not properly supply their needs. From Andersonville he received numerous communications regarding the disaster that was taking place among the Union soldiers under his nominal control, and he sincerely desired to alleviate conditions. He attempted to disperse the prisoners and build more prisons, but he was frustrated by inadequate guards, an unreliable commissary, and a disintegrating Confederacy. He became commissary general of prisons in November 1864 and managed to improve conditions somewhat, but he soon recommended that the Federal prisoners be sent home, whether exchanged or not.[11]

Actually, a great deal of the blame for the prisoners' plight may be laid on Davis himself. The Federals suspended exchange, in part because he refused to repatriate black prisoners, a point on which the Union could hardly compromise. In any event, both Wirz and Winder had made efforts to alleviate the horrible conditions in the Confederate prisons that were, at bottom, caused by the uncompromising policies of both governments.[12]

William T. Sherman issued orders on January 19 for his men to thrust into the Carolinas, and the destruction was even harsher than it had been in Georgia. On February 17 much of Columbia, South Carolina, was burned. Although the fires were largely accidental, and made more intense because of the huge numbers of bales of cotton stored in the city, the burning of Columbia also ignited a bitter controversy. The Confederates, and many Southerners ever since, considered it a prime example of Sherman's inhumane way of making war. Actually, a good many of the Union troops helped in trying to fight the flames. Jefferson Davis, however, believed what the majority of his countrymen believed.[13]

As he wrote in *Rise and Fall:*

Hypocrisy is the tribute which vice pays to virtue; therefore General Sherman has endeavored to escape the reproaches for the burning of Columbia by attributing it to General Hampton's order to burn the cotton in the city, that it might not fall into the hands of the enemy.

General Hampton has proved circumstantially that General Sherman's statement is untrue, and, though in any controversy to which General Hampton may be a party, no corroborative evidence is necessary to substantiate his assertion of a fact coming within his personal observation, hundreds of unimpeachable witnesses have testified that the burning of Columbia was the deliberate act of the Federal soldiery, and that it was certainly permitted, if not ordered, by the commanding general. . . .

Were this the only instance of such barbarity perpetrated by General Sherman's army, his effort to escape the responsibility might be more successful, because more plausible; but when the eulogists of his exploits note exultingly that "widespreading columns of smoke rose wherever the army went," when it is incontrovertibly true that the line of his march could be traced by the burning dwelling-houses and by the wail of women and children pitilessly left to die from starvation and exposure in the depth of winter, his plea of "not guilty" in the case of the city of Columbia can not free him from the reprobation which outraged humanity must attach to an act of cruelty which only finds a parallel in the barbarous excesses of Wallenstein's army in the Thirty Years' War, and which, even at that period of the world's civilization, sullied the fame of that otherwise great soldier.[14]

The fact was, though, that the Confederacy lost Columbia and soon thereafter Charleston as well.

That Davis was simply not up to the enormity of his task was now a common sentiment among his friends. Reuben Davis assessed him as qualified for "rulership in a settled and powerful government." Davis, he observed, would have succeeded where "a firm, strong hand to guide, and a polished intellect" were needed. But "a revolution calls for different qualities," including flexibility. "Gifted with some of the highest attributes of a statesman," he asserted, Jefferson Davis "lacked the pliancy which enables a man to adapt his measures to the crisis." The war clerk J. B. Jones echoed such sentiments: "He has not the broad intellect requisite for the gigantic measures needed in such a crisis." Worse, perhaps, Davis's personality would not permit him to court people like William L. Yancey and Governor Joe Brown, men whose help he needed.[15]

There were calls for Davis to reorganize his government. Although there was almost no organized effort to force a coup, there was a great deal of pressure placed on the president by the Congress, the press, and the general public. Some officials were targeted because of their inefficiency or their bad luck in having difficult jobs to do; extremely vocal politicians and editors, though lacking any organized effort, howled for their heads. Other opposition took the form of pressure to change the cabinet.

One way to force such change was by means of legislation. On December 10, 1863, Senator Robert Ward Johnson of Arkansas had introduced a bill "to limit and define the term of office of the Secretary or principal officer of each of the Executive Departments," which was immediately given first and second reading and printed.[16] A week later the proposal was referred to the Committee on the Judiciary, and a month later it was reported back with amendments and a recommendation for passage.[17] The bill provided for set terms for cabinet officers, which would expire at the end of each Congress. The reason then given for passage of this bill was that if a secretary held office until removed by the president, he might thus hold office for life, if each new president decided to retain him.[18] This, of course, was a most unlikely contingency, but that was not what then concerned the lawmakers. It was clear that as the First Congress drew to a close that a group of dissatisfied congressmen eagerly looked forward to changes in leadership when a new Congress convened. The bill itself, however, was never passed; action on it was postponed from time to time, and it died in the last days of the First Congress. But the incident revealed the pressure that congressmen applied to the president, and it tended to hold the cabinet members' feet to the fire.

If congressmen could not change the law, they clearly could exert other pressures. Thus Davis found himself under fire on several fronts. The Virginia congressmen were trying to restore national confidence and stem a congressional declaration of nonconfidence in Davis's cabinet (or so they claimed; some observers thought that they were actually trying to promote such a declaration). The delegates' solution was to ask Davis to form a new cabinet.[19] Speaker of the House Thomas S. Bocock tried to warn Davis that passage of such a resolution was quite likely and urged "that something must be done, and that promptly, to restore confidence," a statement Davis chose to take as "a warning, if not a threat."[20] Secretary of War James Seddon construed it as a threat but one directed at him, not at Davis, because it called for resignation of all cabinet officers; and moreover, it came from his own state's delegation. Insulted and discouraged, Seddon resigned and was replaced by John C. Breckenridge on February 6, 1865.[21]

Other heads rolled. Brigadier General John S. Preston, the head of the Bureau of Conscription, was removed simply by eliminating his bureau. Colonel Lucius B. Northrop suffered the most abuse, and although Davis clung to him far longer than he should have, at last Northrop relieved his friend of further embarrassment by resigning in February 1865. He was replaced by Isaac M. St. John, who was promoted to brigadier general. Thirty-seven years old, St. John had graduated from Yale in 1845. He had been a civil engineer on the staff of the Baltimore and Ohio Railroad and in 1855 had returned to his native Georgia to take charge of construction of the Blue Ridge Railroad. When the Civil War began he volunteered for army service and was made a private in the Engineering Corps. In February 1862 he was elevated to captain of engineers, and in April of that year he was sent to Richmond to head the Nitre and Mining Bureau. As commissary general St. John devised a system of collecting supplies directly from the people and rendering them immediately available for use by placing them in staging areas, where they could be picked up and sent directly to troops in the field. It helped, but it came too late to delay the collapse of the forces.

In an effort to ensure that better military advice and leadership be found and heeded, Congress passed legislation calling for the appointment of a general in chief, and it was commonly assumed that Davis would name Robert E. Lee. On February 6 the president did so. The legislation spelled out no specific powers for the general in chief, and Davis still had any power he wished in the way of staff appointments. The president's full authority over the military remained in effect.

By early March congressmen were worn out and dispirited, and they engaged in little productive work.[22] "I hope the badgering of congress does not annoy you," Joseph Davis wrote Jefferson the day after it adjourned. "Much of it I am convinced is from personal resentment." The attacks on the president did indeed gnaw at and annoy him. As William C. Davis notes, "He raged inside as always when questioned or challenged." "Faction has done much to cloud our prospects," the president told Howell Cobb's wife on March 30, "and [to] impair my power to serve the country." He added, "Whether truth can overtake falsehood has always been doubtful."[23] But this critically late date in the war was assuredly not the time for Davis to be writing letters of vindication.

The myriad men who railed against him never coalesced into an effective, unified opposition; thus, they seldom offered any meaningful alternatives. But it also meant that the best Davis could do was to appease his detractors individually, because as a group they seldom presented any organized opposition.[24]

The truth was that Davis had indeed wielded great power. He succeeded in getting virtually all his desired legislation enacted. In the entire four years of his presidency the only veto that Congress overrode was a minor bill that allowed newspapers to send their issues to soldiers free of postage.[25]

Thus when Congressman William W. Boyce had rebuked Davis as a usurper in September 1864, he was correct. The power of impressment, to be sure normally exercised by governments at war, had been used so ruthlessly that it played a major role in turning many ordinary Confederates against their government. Many a nominal Confederate had become a calculating Unionist when he saw what was happening to his subsistence under the pressure of impressment. Confederate officials truthfully contended that what the law did was necessary, but that was precisely what bothered Boyce. Necessity, he thought, had created a despotism, and that is not what the Confederates had gone to war to try to create. Minor functionaries came in contact with masses of citizens, forcing them to surrender a portion of their living and generally paying them less than its true value in an open market. Theirs was an oppressive government, many Confederates thought, and their attitudes created resistance to the same government they had fought and sacrificed to help establish. Like many others, Boyce had begun to think that the consequences of the war effort, in this case the abuses of the impressment system, rendered the war quite bluntly a mistaken adventure.

Jefferson Davis played his usual active-negative role in the impressment issue by allowing others to exercise the power characteristic of that sort of leadership.[26] As Congressman Boyce pointed out, the impressment power had been necessary, and Davis seized it, though without much enthusiasm for his task. Indeed there had been times—during the first session of the Second Congress and in the early weeks of its second session—when Davis seemed not to have realized the enormity of the subsistence problem and did not push as hard as he should have to make impressment more effective. Davis appears then to have fit the passive-negative mold, for he let the issue, vital as it was, simply drift.

Or perhaps Davis did not understand supply well enough to assert himself meaningfully, for he could be, and typically was, quite assertive on other military issues. On questions of strategy, tactics, personnel, and day-to-day administration, he was not always the expert he thought himself to be, but he did feel confident, and his initiative proved less likely to fail than it did in the matter of impressment.

Or perhaps the supply problem, especially regarding subsistence, was so intractable that Davis did not bother to devote as much attention to it as he did to other issues because he correctly perceived it would have been a waste of time. As passive-negative presidents of the twentieth century have done with other issues, Davis possibly saw impressment as an issue that should come to him, rather than he to it.[27] His level of commitment on impressment was nowhere near as great as it was on strategy, conscription, suspension of the writ of habeas corpus, or even foreign policy, an area he really did not know much about.

Impressment was also a sign that the Confederacy was increasing its pace of modernization. Richard D. Brown suggests that the Civil War "may be understood as a crisis whose boundaries and structure were determined by the uneven process of modernization," and he points out that the war itself was a modernizing force in both the North and the South.[28] The impressment issue is perhaps the best illustration. A modern bureaucracy had to be created to carry it out, one that exercised unprecedented authority over the citizens it served. Transportation had to be controlled as never before, and railroads, still a novel method of military transportation at the beginning of the war, were absolute necessities for moving subsistence and other supplies and for strategic redeployment of troops. By the end of the war, no thinking Confederate would have attempted to stop construction of rail links on the grounds of impracticality or unconstitutionality, as some of them had done in 1862. Indeed, the modern welfare state had its predecessor in the use of impressment to supply the subsistence needs of the civilian population. And when blacks were impressed to serve as laborers for the Confederate army or to build fortifications or to work in factories and shops turning out goods for the military, the Confederacy unconsciously had begun its own emancipation program.

When the Congress legislated impressment, it worked within the framework of a democratic system. But many soldiers from nonaffluent families legitimately asked how democratic a system was that weighed more heavily on the poor than on the rich and middle classes; their answer to their own question did not satisfy them. The result was that many of them went home, abandoning the war effort, because their families were deprived of subsistence by impressment officers. With their young men conscripted, these families could not properly plant crops, tend them, or harvest them and were thus left with no means to feed themselves.

As much as conscription or the writ of habeas corpus, perhaps even more, impressment was an issue that drove a fatal wedge into the Confederate community and ultimately undermined the entire war effort. One Confederate had written in December 1863 that "the whole question now turns on food. If we can get meat enough, or our Soldiers will do on less than enough, we can weather all the other blunders of Mr. Davis & the Generals."[29] He then had hopes, but his fears were more realistic: impressment was one of the insurmountable problems that affected (and afflicted) the entire Confederacy and helped to explain the final results of the contest. In William Blair's study of Virginia's war effort, he notes that what the Confederacy needed—and failed to do—was "to restore faith in the currency, resolve transportation difficulties, and adopt adequate taxation. Instead, the Confederate Congress enacted impressment."[30]

Late in 1864 the Northern politician Francis P. Blair Sr. concocted a scheme wherein the Union and Confederate governments might band together to drive the French out of Mexico. Lincoln, hoping that the Radical Republicans' preferences for harsh peace policies might be stymied, agreed that Blair should make an unofficial visit to Richmond. On January 18, 1865, Lincoln had given Blair a letter stating that he might tell Davis "that I have constantly been, am now, and shall continue, ready to receive any agent whom he, or any other influential person now resisting the national authority, may informally send to me, with the view of securing peace to the people of our one common country." Blair failed to convince President Davis that his scheme had ultimate merit, because the difference between Lincoln's and Davis's mind-sets was irreconcilable: Lincoln saw "one common country" and Davis two separate countries. Davis, however, did see the proposal as an opportunity to silence some of the defeatist sentiment within the Confederacy and to steel the fledgling nation for another year of hard war. Despite the desperate status of the Confederate cause, he could not let it enter his mind that there was no chance left.[31]

Thus, on January 28, 1865, Davis named John A. Campbell, Robert M. T. Hunter, and Vice President Alexander H. Stephens, all vociferous critics of Davis—and leaders of whatever formal peace movement there was—to a commission authorized to cross through the lines at Petersburg and request that a peace conference be held. According to William Cooper, "Davis made politically astute as well as able choices for his commission."[32] Stephens fortuitously was in Richmond for the congressional session instead of in Georgia. They left Richmond for Petersburg and the Federal lines on January 29, hoping to be allowed to pass through and go on to Washington. But on January 30 Lincoln issued a pass to allow the three to go only to Fort Monroe.

The next day Lincoln issued instructions to Secretary of State William H. Seward to go to Fort Monroe and confer with the commissioners "on the basis of my letter to F. P. Blair, Esq., on Jan. 18, 1865." Lincoln was willing to confer on restoration of the national authority in all the states but would not budge from his position on abolition of slavery, and there could be no cessation of hostilities short of a Confederate capitulation.

Lincoln himself left Washington on February 2, bound for Hampton Roads, arriving at Fort Monroe in the evening and going aboard the *River Queen* to meet with Seward and the three Confederate commissioners. The next day they engaged in lengthy discussions, which became known as the Hampton Roads conference. Lincoln began with pleasantries and reminiscences but firmly indicated that nothing could be considered before the national authority of the United States was recognized within the rebellious states. Someone broached the subject of a joint operation in Mexico; Lincoln said this could not be considered, because it would be impossible for the United States to make any treaty with the Confederate States.

Someone suggested an armistice, but Lincoln said this was impossible until after reestablishment of the United States. The Confederates asked him about reconstruction policies; he replied that the Rebel troops must be disbanded and that the national authorities would resume their functions. Courts would decide matters of property rights. Both Lincoln and Seward gave personal assurances that they believed Congress would be liberal. But the Thirteenth Amendment, abolishing all slavery in the United States, already had been approved by Congress and was in the process of being ratified by the states.

The Confederate commissioners complained that it sounded like Lincoln was demanding nothing short of unconditional submission. Seward replied that this particular word had not been used, nor had it been implied. Lincoln said that if the matter were left in his hands he indeed would be liberal but that he could not guarantee what Congress might decide. Lincoln told a few more stories, and the mood was friendly, but nothing serious came of the negotiations. Indeed, there were no negotiations.

Lincoln returned home on February 4 and reported to the cabinet. He again communicated to General U. S. Grant, through War Secretary Edwin Stanton, that "nothing transpired, or transpiring with the three gentlemen from Richmond, is to cause any change hindrance or delay, of your military plans or operations."[33] When word of Lincoln's inclination toward an easy peace policy circulated among Republican ranks, havoc erupted.

The Confederate commissioners reported their failure to Davis, who was quick to circulate widely a full account of the Union demands. As Cooper observes, "The public reacted as Davis both desired and anticipated."[34] J. B. Jones noted that as news of the peace mission's failure hit the streets of Richmond, "now the South will soon be fired up again." He was right.[35] It did indeed provoke the resurgence of Southern patriotism and the stifling of defeatist talk for a time, thus fulfilling Davis's original goal in the matter.

As Michael Ballard puts it, "If Jefferson Davis intended to undercut the Southern peace movement, he succeeded admirably." Upon hearing the results of the conference, the Confederate public suppressed any sentiment it might have harbored for further negotiations. The commissioners' report tended to rekindle the fighting spirit of the populace: according to Cooper, "Senator Benjamin Hill informed the president that the outcome at Hampton Roads had revived the war spirit in Georgia," and he called "Davis's handling of the matter 'the most admirable master stroke.' "[36] Ballard observes, "The Hampton Roads conference . . . proved something of a political master stroke for the harried Confederate president. Some of his most vehement press critics praised him for his efforts to attain peace."[37] But it was rather inappropriate to seek public relations triumphs at this late date.

To the end of his life, Davis genuinely believed that the Union goal was subjugation.

That it was the purpose of the Government of the United States to subjugate the Southern States and the Southern people, under the pretext of a restoration of the Union, is established by the terms and conditions offered to us in all the conferences relative to a settlement of differences. All were comprehended in one word, and that was subjugation. If the purpose had been an honorable and fraternal restoration of the Union as was avowed, methods for the adjustment of difficulties would have been presented and discussed; propositions for reconciliation with concessions and modifications for grievances would have been kindly offered and treated; and a way would have been opened for a mutual and friendly intercourse. How unlike this were all the propositions offered to us, will be seen in the proceedings which took place in the conferences, and in the terms of surrender offered to our soldiers. It should be remembered that mankind compose one uniform order of beings [a strangely ambiguous statement from a slave owner and a staunch supporter of slavery] and thus the language of arbitrary power has the same signification in all ages.[38]

According to Cooper,

Davis followed up on his public relations triumph and made several speeches in which he boldly predicted victory. In Richmond on February 6 Virginia governor William Smith called a public meeting to reaffirm Confederate loyalty. Three days later an even more impressive affair took place. A band led a march from the Governor's Mansion to the African Church, a substantial structure often used by whites for large gatherings. During the afternoon and evening an estimated 10,000 people congregated in and around the building to listen to ringing speeches by Benjamin, Hunter, and others.[39]

The president delivered a particularly strong oration at this meeting. Cooper suggests that "Davis glimpsed his countrymen as he wanted to believe them, equally as determined as he not to let their cause fail. On the rostrum he became a man possessed."[40] Davis predicted bringing the Union to its knees by summer. He managed even to impress Vice President Stephens, who "termed the president's performance 'brilliant,' even though he considered Davis's predictions of victory 'the emanation of a demented brain.' "[41] Years later, Stephens ruminated on this particular speech and wondered if Davis was "relying on something I and the world generally knew nothing about." He mused that Davis might have been thinking of some Canadian schemes or perhaps somehow of fomenting an uprising among the disaffected people in the North. Stephens also speculated that perhaps Davis's apparent new confidence had something to do with a plan for "the abduction of the heads of their Government."[42]

There were indeed a number of such plans discussed, some of them seriously. Davis knew about several plans; he did occasionally send agents into the enemy capital. But to what degree he was involved in clandestine schemes we do not, and possibly cannot, know. There was, however, a Confederate Secret Service, and there was a Confederate plan to overthrow the Union by capturing Abraham Lincoln. There is some good research, though some of it has speculative underpinning, that the Confederate Secret Service carried out covert action and was involved in the schemes to capture or kill Lincoln.[43] But Secretary Benjamin made sure that most of the records of its activities were destroyed, so we do not know the whole truth.

According to Cooper,

> The existence of Confederate plots to abduct Lincoln and others cannot be doubted, but connecting them directly to President Davis is much more difficult. [He] consistently denied authorizing any kidnapping, which he said would end in killing because he claimed he did not believe Lincoln could be captured unharmed. He also turned aside other schemes he defined as criminal, such as a proposal to send ships into northern ports loaded with infected blankets, beds, and other items to introduce yellow fever and smallpox into the population. Nor did any other responsible Confederate official ever cite Davis's involvement in any such intrigues. Even so, modern historians have built a strong circumstantial case in which Davis sanctions attempts to kidnap Lincoln.[44]

Secretary of the Treasury George A. Trenholm espoused great hopes for the year 1865, however, he was also realistic enough to expect that his hopes most likely would be dashed. Primarily, the problem of redundant currency was worse than ever before. Trenholm proposed to reduce the amount of Treasury notes in circulation from $400 million to $150 million by taxation and the sale of bonds. The remaining $150 million of notes would be redeemed after the war and would then no longer be valid currency; they would be retired by continuing the tax in kind even after the war.[45]

Legislation to execute this plan was passed in March 1865. It provided that the certificates of indebtedness that had been issued under the February 17, 1864, funding legislation would be receivable for payment of taxes and duties. It was not any magic force, but it was the best that Trenholm could do. He wrote on the original copy of the law that he agreed with it, "but it will be clearly seen that the economy with which purchases may be made will greatly depend upon the amount of taxation levied."[46]

New taxes were still essential. The current Confederate debt was about $1.5 billion,[47] and in January 1865 Trenholm was induced to beg Congress to raise $750 million in taxes to fund the currency and to support the coming military campaign. In February Davis, in desperation, informed Congress that "the urgency for the passage of some revenue bill has now become so pressing as to threaten the gravest consequences. . . . Our affairs are now in a position so critical that [any] objections . . . may well be waived in favor of any scheme of finance or taxation."[48]

Additional income was so essential to keeping the army together that Davis indicated he would accept any tax law, for even an ill-advised law would be better than none at all. The Congress, for its part, failed to think of any significant new scheme and on March 11 passed a conglomeration of tax provisions that "imposed extreme rates upon the objects covered by previous tax laws."[49] This legislation called in some taxes sooner than previously scheduled and continued in effect the tax in kind and the income tax, but it repealed the right to deduct both of these taxes from the property tax. Specie and credits that were held abroad were taxed at 20 percent. Jewelry, watches, plate, and other gold and silver goods were taxed at 10 percent, money and credit at 5 percent. Profits from business transactions were to be taxed as regular income, plus another 10 percent, but business profits above 25 percent were to be taxed at 25 percent. All other property, whether owned by individuals or corporations, was taxed at 8 percent (based on 1860 values). These taxes (except the tax in kind) were then rendered subject to a surtax of 12.5 percent. Exemptions under previous law were continued, however.[50] On March 17 Congress passed, in secret, its last tax law. This provided that in case a specie loan failed, a 25 percent tax in kind would be due on April 1 and levied on coin, bullion, and foreign exchange.[51]

The Confederacy collapsed before these laws had any significant effect. As E. Merton Coulter has observed, "The Confederacy was now sinking fast, financially, militarily, and spiritually." Douglas Ball is more specific: "When Confederate leaders at last realized the validity of Marcus Cicero's remark that 'taxes are the sinews of the state,' the treasury was bankrupt, the currency debauched, and the economy, the army, civil morale, and the foreign credit of the Confederacy alike beyond redemption."[52] Tax laws that might have been useful if passed in 1861 or 1862 were not helpful now, and the comprehensive taxes of 1863 and 1864 never brought in enough.

Just how much income was raised by Confederate taxation is a difficult question to answer. Coulter has estimated that it was about 1 percent, but surely that is too small a figure to be correct.[53] A careful reading of more recent studies suggests that a larger proportion of income was derived from taxes; Richard C. Todd indicates 7 percent, and Douglas Ball 9 percent.[54] Whichever estimate one accepts, the amount is ridiculously small.

Just one month before the war's end Trenholm finally conceived of a desperate idea that he believed might bring about his hopes of adequately financing the Confederacy. His pleading at last led the Congress to pass a law permitting the Treasury to be financed by direct contributions from patriotic citizens: "donations of money, jewels, gold and silver plate, and public securities."[55] Trenholm himself donated $200,000 in currency and securities. Despite the despair and defeatism that had permeated the populace, many Confederates volunteered a "last heroic display of patriotism" and sacrifice. To give but one example, the citizens of Staunton, Virginia, "subscribed 130 barrels of flour, 7,100 pounds of bacon, and $150,000 in bonds"; Confederates elsewhere were equally generous with gifts of gold, jewelry, heirlooms, and food.[56] (Although if the inhabitants of Staunton, in well-gleaned Virginia, had this much to give in voluntary donations so near the war's end, one wonders about how much they and more isolated areas might have withheld from the cause in earlier stages of the war and what its effect might have been.)

None of this, to be sure, was sufficient to keep the Confederacy financially viable and alive. At the end, the government owed its citizens a vast debt in the form of unpaid impressment certificates, rentals, interest, and other obligations. This debt included the pittance owed to the soldiers, who had often not been paid for months. How much the amount was is uncertain. Coulter estimates it as between $400 million and $600 million, but Ball puts it at $1.9 billion on October 31, 1864.[57] Surely it was well over $2 billion by the end of the war.

Even at this point, the Congress was dealing with more than taxes. To remedy the problem of the Stainless Banner being easily mistaken for a flag of truce or surrender, on March 4, 1865, the Congress approved still another new national flag—though the point of creating a new flag at this late date is debatable at best. The Stainless Banner was altered so that it had a broad vertical stripe of red added to its outer end. The new flag's dimensions were altered, too, rendering its width two-thirds instead of one-half the length.[58] This flag was not produced in much quantity, and a great many troop units never were issued one. Consequently, when the surrenders came, the typical ensign to be furled in surrender ceremony was a Stainless Banner.

Perhaps the most popular of all poems memorializing the Confederacy was "The Conquered Banner," written by the Roman Catholic poet-priest of the Confederacy, Father Abram J. Ryan:

Furl that Banner, for 'tis weary;
Round its staff 'tis drooping dreary;
 Furl it, fold it, it is best;
For there's not a man to wave it,
And there's not a sword to save it,
And there's not one left to wave it
In the blood which heroes gave it;
And its foes now scorn and brave it;
 Furl it, hide it—let it rest!

Furl that Banner, softly, slowly!
Treat it gently—it is holy—
 For it droops above the dead,
Touch it not—unfold it never,
Let it droop there, furled forever,
 For its people's hopes are dead!

Davis clearly knew that the populace would be aghast at the idea of using blacks as soldiers, but it was crucially necessary to try to convince them to do it. They would have to be led slowly to accepting such a change. There was indeed an initial blast of outrage, but the president stood firm and gradually he was able to garner considerable support for his idea. In February 1865 he wrote to the Mobile, Alabama, editor John Forsyth: "It is now becoming daily more evident to all reflecting persons that we are now reduced to choosing whether the negroes shall fight for us or against us, and that all arguments as to the positive advantages or disadvantages of employing them are beside the question, which is, simply one of relative advantage between having their fighting element in our ranks or in those of the enemy."[59] Judah P. Benjamin, in a speech the same month, expanded upon Davis's sentiments: "Let us say to every negro who wishes to go into the ranks on condition of being made free—'Go and fight; you are free'!"[60]

Thus was Davis now openly committed to arming the slaves immediately and granting freedom as compensation. He decided to see if this new policy might produce benefits on the diplomatic front. He dispatched Louisiana congressman Duncan Kenner to Great Britain and France to let them know that the Union war aim of obliterating slavery was no longer unique, that it would occur with Confederate victory, too. Kenner also was to point out to them that their failure to intervene now and help the South to win would forever cost them their goal: a weakened and divided United States. D. P. Crook has characterized this tactic as little more than "a last-minute bid to avoid humiliation" of reunion on Northern terms. It failed, Michael Ballard observes, "largely because Britain and France had already decided the Confederacy was doomed.[61] In assessing why Kenner did not succeed, Cooper concludes that "the Confederacy was tottering, and the British knew it."[62]

As surprising as it may seem, the public attitude toward the idea of using black troops gradually began to swing toward agreement with Davis. Everyone could see that the military situation was desperate, and numerous citizens wrote Davis letters assuring him of their support. Even some of the initially hostile newspapers changed their slant. After Congress approved raising black soldiers on March 13, 1865, President Davis was then authorized to call upon owners to volunteer their slaves, and it was generally understood, though not specifically stated, that any slaves who did fight for the Confederacy would be made free by action of the states. Actually, Davis had shown some finesse in his handling of the issue. He had demonstrated his unstinted willingness to take any measures necessary for victory, and he made a favorable impact on public opinion. Despite his gains, however, strong hostility toward his administration remained throughout the early months of 1865.[63]

A few troops were raised and training began. Negro soldiers in Confederate gray became a common sight in Richmond by late in March. The measure came too late to have any impact, however. It had taken Davis too long to convince enough other leaders that the time for this step had come. Arguing with one senator before the measure had been passed, Davis declared, "If the Confederacy falls, there should be written on its tombstone, 'Died of a theory.' "[64]

Many Confederates from time to time throughout the war gave lip service to the assertion that they were fighting the conflict for reasons other than slavery and the concomitant way of life the institution allowed. Some individuals perhaps espoused this delusion; certainly Davis did. But what did most of the populace truly believe? Drew Gilpin Faust asserts that "historians have tended to understate the importance of slavery within southern consciousness during the war."[65] Vice President Alexander H. Stephens, who explicitly asserted that slavery was what the South was fighting for, is misleadingly posited as the great exception, but in truth his attitude was very nearly universal. Leaders of the secession movement all across the South had cited slavery as the most compelling reason for Southern independence.

As the conflict unfolded, the defenders of the would-be nation tried to cling to their rationalization that the war was just and that there was divine sanction underpinning the Confederacy. "Superintending inferior, helpless Africans, assisting in their 'remedial advancement,' converting them to Christianity, protecting them from the destructive notions prevalent in much of the rest of the world—these were God's purposes for the South," Faust asserts.[66] True enough, it seemed, but what happened when the war clearly went badly for the South? Perhaps the great and long-suppressed guilt over slavery, and the undeniable reality that the system was not as benevolent as most Southerners wanted to believe, required some sober reassessment of war aims and justification.[67]

One blatant example of the attempt to salve Southern consciences was manifested in motivating the myth that the slaves were contented with their lot. The "faithful servant" stories were rife in innumerable newspapers and periodicals.[68] Minstrel shows proliferated in the Civil War South, although before the war, minstrelsy had been largely, almost exclusively, a Northern fad. The point is, minstrel shows romanticized the realities of plantation life and were suggestive of the blacks' loyalty to their owners.[69]

One of the war's great paintings, completed by the Virginia artist William D. Washington in 1864, *The Burial of Latane,* depicts the alleged black-white relationships in the slave South. Washington had studied under Emanuel Leutze, and for inspiration he looked to such patriotic works as Benjamin West's *Death of Wolfe* and his teacher's *Washington Crossing the Delaware.* The *Burial of Latane* illustrates the makeshift funeral performed for the hapless Confederate, Captain William Latane, who had died among strangers. The Union forces, in control of the area, forbade the services of any clergy. An aged matron aided by a faithful slave "join together to inter the fallen hero and to sanctify his grave." Faust has discussed the underlying meanings and symbolism of the painting:

> In their portrayal of virtue, personal sacrifice, and heroism as the essences of national greatness, these works invoke Christian iconography to extend a quasi-religious dimension to their subject matter. . . . *[The Burial of Latane]* speaks specifically to the peculiar circumstances and realities of the Confederate situation, for it directly reflects prevailing notions of southern nationalism and the place of slavery within the Confederacy. The ethereal light shining from the heavens and the uplifted face of the woman serving as preacher represent the illuminating power of God's favor. The mourners assembled for this Christian rite are a surrogate family of whites and blacks. . . .
>
> But the painting not only depicts disparate unity, it also depicts hierarchy. The white women and children are shown in light, signifying God's favor; the black figures are more in shadow. And despite their mutual endeavor, the races are kept apart: the slaves are all "segregated," so to speak, on the other side of the painting. Huge numbers of viewers thronged to see the painting, and thus did it become "the focal point of a new ritual of national self-affirmation." The adoring viewers of this scene depicting sacrifice, added their own sacrifices, by dropping money into the bucket situated below the painting.[70]

The realities, in countless examples, showed that slaves were anything but consistently loyal either to the peculiar institution or to their masters. More and more white Southerners were compelled to embrace the uncomfortable reality that theirs was not a benevolent society for blacks. Was it too late to make it so? Many desperately hoped not. Slave religion had to be nurtured; slave marriages and the sanctity of slave families had to be respected. "Throughout the [Civil War] South," Faust observes, "denominational organizations at all levels, from local congregations to nationwide conventions, appointed committees and passed resolutions on these issues." At least three state governors spoke out, vociferously urging reform. Interestingly, "had the war not ended the South's national experiment, the reform movement might well have" accomplished its goals.[71]

In 1865, with the Confederacy at last abandoning the continuation of slavery as the sine qua non war aim, how much longer could the beleaguered white citizenry be expected to continue paying the bitter price essential to continuation of the struggle? Jefferson Davis was one who would, and he was deluded into believing that a great many others would, too. But he was wrong. Confederate nationalism collapsed.

Historians laud Lincoln for his achievement in presiding over the Union's ultimate victory; Davis's performance, on the other hand, has elicited much controversial commentary, sometimes quite negative. As one might expect, it is a strong temptation to make Davis look bad when he is to serve as a foil for Lincoln; this phenomenon has been described and ridiculed in an article by Ludwell Johnson. Clearly, Confederate strategy was not foredoomed to fail. What then of Davis as opposed to Lincoln as war leader? For the first eighteen months of the conflict, both men grappled with the same problem of grand strategy: trying to keep or to get the border states to adhere to their cause. Mark Neely points out that Davis's problem was the more difficult: "Davis became a salesman; Lincoln became a warden or truant officer." Neely further suggests that Lincoln more keenly "recognized the realities of power." The Northern president was able to employ coercive policies to suppress dis-Unionism; Davis was finessed into holding off on rampant disallowance of civil liberties in order to lure the peoples in the border states to the Confederate side by suggesting that they might then enjoy more freedom.[72] But after the border states were irretrievably lost, Davis never subsequently hesitated to put security of the Confederacy ahead of civil liberty.

On the issue of Davis versus Lincoln, David Potter, noting the Union's economic advantages, has asked "whether the differences between Union and

Confederate political performance [were] not as great or greater than the economic [and military] disparities—whether in fact, the discrepancy in ability between Abraham Lincoln and Jefferson Davis was not as real and as significant as the inequality in mileage between Union and Confederate railroad systems?" Not wishing to minimize the very real difficulties faced by the Confederacy, he has nevertheless suggested that the South made serious mistakes in managing public currency and revenue, dealing with the potentially valuable cotton crop, gathering subsistence by means of impressment, and mismanaging slave labor. Political leadership, writes Potter, "left much to be desired," and he concludes that "there is a great deal of evidence to justify placing a considerable share of the responsibility for the Confederacy's misfortunes directly at the door of Jefferson Davis."[73]

Potter has claimed that Davis came up short in three vital areas: his relations with both officials and citizens, his concept of the presidency, and his role as commander in chief. He was less tactful than Lincoln when dealing with the prickly personalities of some of his subordinates, and he spoke in platitudes. He had difficulty admitting when he was wrong, was too conservative to be a revolutionary leader, busied himself with military minutiae, imposed the departmental system and administered it unimaginatively, and dispersed his forces rather than concentrating them as he should have. Potter concludes, "It hardly seems unrealistic to suppose that if the Union and the Confederacy had exchanged presidents with one another, the Confederacy might have won its independence."[74]

If indeed not everything about the Confederate Military Department system was unwisely construed, most of it was. In innumerable instances, Davis failed to use the system in a satisfactory manner. This territorial system in some respects was well suited to the Confederacy's inherent parochialism and state-rights philosophy, but it became too intertwined with Davis's strategy. He placed great (though to be fair not unbending) emphasis on the need to protect all territory. The real flaw was that few (if indeed any) of the officers who served in the departmental command were fit for their jobs (largely because there was no universal and clear job description for this position). Worse, there was no officer or official to oversee and to ensure that coordination and interdepartmental cooperation be achieved. Too often either men or resources or both were ineffectively allocated. This was illustrated in sharp relief at the end of the war when fewer than one-third of the Rebels still under arms were actually facing either of the two main Yankee armies.

Archer Jones and Thomas Lawrence Connelly Jr. have showed that Davis started with superior military knowledge and experience and gradually improved as generalissimo, but he peaked late in 1863; thereafter his competence deteriorated. The lost key to Confederate victory lay in a national application of ideas best understood by Beauregard, among the Southern generals. He could have been the architect of success had not circumstances (and enmity) destroyed his opportunity.

Davis needed better input, such as could have been provided by a general staff with a capable chief. The president never escaped tension and discord, standing squarely in the middle between his powerful and trusted adviser on the one hand, Robert E. Lee, and the so-called western concentration bloc on the other. Lee made valuable contributions, but they were too provincial and too costly. The western concentration bloc desired to take advantage of dispersal in the western theater and to launch a series of concentrations exploiting interior lines, allowing effective operations against the most vulnerable Union armies. These ideas were adopted too belatedly, ill-executed, and never unreservedly pursued.

Perhaps Davis's ultimate failure as a war leader was in being unable to inspire the Southern people to feel as dedicated to the continuation of the military struggle as he was. By early 1865 he was willing to accept the obliteration of slavery, if only that might bring Confederate independence. There long had been grumbling about a "rich man's war and a poor man's fight," but to give up the true reason for waging it indeed was too much for many of the Southern people to bear.

Abraham Lincoln possessed virtually no military knowledge at the war's outset, but he was a quick learner. He became a conventional mid-nineteenth-century military strategist who fully shared the ideas of his West Point–trained generals. Both he and they analyzed military efforts in terms of lines of operations, rightly believed in the superiority of the defensive over the offensive, and saw in turning movements the best way to overcome the power of the rifle-strengthened defense. Lincoln derived these ideas primarily from his generals but also from the military realities as he perceived them in the course of the war.

Lincoln grasped by early 1862 (about the same time that he also came to regard a "hard war" policy as acceptable and appropriate) that battles were unlikely to be decisive and that the means of victory lay in occupying the enemy's territory and breaking his lines of communications. To do this, it was necessary to overcome the enemy's advantage of enjoying interior lines. Quite early Lincoln explained that his "general idea of the war" was that "we have the greater numbers, and the enemy has the greater facility of concentrating forces upon the points of collision; that we must fail unless we can find some way of making our advantage an overmatch for his; and that this can be done by menacing him with superior forces at different points, at the same time; so that we can safely attack one, or both, if he made no choice, and if he weakens one to strengthen the other, forebear to attack the strengthened one, but seize, and hold the weakened one, gaining so much." This was a rudimentary way of stating the "principle of simultaneous advance," the key to Union victory.[75]

In his memoirs, U. S. Grant implied that there were no simultaneous advances until he became commanding general and inaugurated them in Virginia and Georgia in May 1864. Yet Lincoln had ordered such a concentration in time for the first winter of the war, when he ordered all the Union armies to advance on February 22. At that time, however, the president had overlooked a virtually insuperable obstacle to winter military operations in the South. The four or more inches of monthly rainfall in the Southern states ensured that there would be deep mud both on and off the roads.

The idea of simultaneous advance continued to be refined in Lincoln's mind. There followed three attempts to make simultaneous Union advances, but they produced mixed results: Halleck and McClellan in spring 1862; Grant, Rosecrans, and Burnside in fall 1862; and Grant and Hooker in spring 1863. It was not that the strategy could not work, or that Lincoln became apprehensive. The difficulty was that he did not have anyone who could implement it adequately on a grand scale, until he at last found Grant.

The fundamental problem was that R. E. Lee's army was too strong and taking Richmond too difficult. Lincoln and Halleck, his de facto chief of staff, thus came to accept stalemate in Virginia, stressing the western theater instead. Yet the strategy for the West differed from that in the East. It aimed at territorial and logistical objectives, because the goal was not necessarily total military victory but a breaking of the Southern people's will to continue the contest.

In the meantime, until that could be achieved, Lincoln somehow had to keep Northern will sufficiently buoyant and cohesive. It was a struggle, as soul-searing battle deaths and the apparent impossibility of achieving victory soon enough nearly eroded Northern morale. Nevertheless, Lincoln and the North had the advantage, because the South, quite simply, had an insufficiently potent civil religion.

The appointment of John C. Breckinridge on February 6, 1865, as the Confederacy's fifth secretary of war marked a shift in the relationship of Davis with that office and a redefinition of the role it played in the war's concluding weeks. Davis previously had been heavily involved in helping to run the office. Breckinridge's appointment was a tacit recognition that Davis's previous iron hold on power in Richmond was waning. Among his predecessors, Breckinridge was the only one, save possibly George Randolph, "who neither feared nor stood in awe of Jefferson Davis."[76]

The Confederate War Department had its own direct telegraph lines, which was for the best because by early 1865 the incoming news was so uniformly unhappy that the government felt it wise not to release it to the general public until the right time came—then it could be framed to present a better face, if possible. Indeed, as W. C. Davis points out, "War Department censorship of news from the fronts was already an accepted fact and had been for months."[77]

On March 9, a letter arrived for War Secretary Breckinridge signed by General Robert E. Lee. W. C. Davis observes that "the letter could not have been more depressing." "The military condition of the country," wrote Lee, "is full of peril. . . . It seems almost impossible to maintain our present position. The army cannot be kept together, and our present lines must be abandoned." There was also an even more shocking comment in the letter: "I have received tonight your letter of this date requesting my opinion upon the military condition of the country," and Lee had given his succinct response "to enable you to make the use of my answer, which you desire." Breckinridge wanted to use Lee's written judgment that he expected "imminent and utter disaster for the Confederacy" to try to persuade Jefferson Davis to give up the hopeless dream of victory and to try to shape the best peace terms possible.[78]

Most thoughtful Southerners, when they could bring themselves to think about it, perceived that an inevitable end was in sight. Indeed by late 1864 there was a small but vocal group of dissidents who wanted to oust Davis from office because his policies were such that they stymied hope of peace. W. C. Davis asserts that "Stephens was convinced that the only hope lay in the assertion of the sovereign powers of the individual states to force Congress to change Davis's policy. Some thought they needed another revolution." Robert Toombs, a totally embittered critic of Davis, "favored the simple overthrow of the president, even if by violence. 'Begone Davis,' he bellowed, while [Robert Barnwel] Rhett openly called for deposing the president and installing Lee as interim dictator."[79]

Lincoln's reelection did not plunge Davis into any mood of discouragement. He "refused to be discouraged," observes W. C. Davis. "Rather, he argued, this proof that the North would never compromise or give up should only make the Confederates redouble their determination. The language of apocalypse began to echo in the executive office as occasionally he hinted that the South must have either complete independence or complete destruction. . . . Vice President Stephens, on a rare visit to the capital, suggested that the president's optimism was 'the emanation of a demented brain.' "[80]

Breckinridge had a mind-set starkly different from Davis's. As W. C. Davis observes, "Breckinridge was an instinctive moderate. . . . He confessed to friends that he had little expectation that the rebellion could succeed, and was not certain in his own mind that he thought it ought to succeed." At the war's outset, once he had committed himself to the struggle, Breckinridge proved himself a good leader of men in combat. "By January 1865, the Kentuckian was the twelfth senior-ranking major general in the army, and had seen service in more states of the Confederacy than any other general in the service, led a division or corps in three different field armies, and commanded his own small army as well. People of the Shenandoah hailed him as the new Stonewall Jackson." As secretary of war Breckinridge was determined to play a significantly stronger and more individually personal role than had his predecessors. "Every bit the diplomat that Davis was not," he wanted to use his skills to fashion a peace that would bring what was best for the populace.[81]

To be sure, Breckinridge was not working from the outset of his term as secretary to force a surrender. He was the strongest of the five men to hold that post during the war, and he worked long and hard to infuse efficiency and effectiveness into the war effort. It was he who forced Davis to dismiss Lucius B. Northrop as commissary general. Breckinridge's early actions as war secretary immediately produced a much needed boost in morale. "If we had had Breckinridge in Walker's place at the beginning," mused Mary Chesnut, "what a difference it might have made."[82]

By early February 1865 Breckinridge was convinced that the best course was to begin trying to get a good peace. "Knowing Davis's resolution," W. C. Davis points out, "the secretary decided that the best way to approach him was not by direct confrontation but rather a steady accumulation of persuasions." He asked the heads of each of the bureaus in his department to submit written assessments of their current condition and to estimate how nearly they thought they could continue operations. In two days he had the statements, and "they painted a portrait of disintegration, inadequate funds and resources, and insufficient manpower." Then, on Valentine's Day, Lee personally visited the War Department, and thereafter he and Breckinridge met frequently. By this time Lee's mood was pessimistic.[83]

"On February 25, during a cabinet meeting, [Breckinridge] brought up for the first time the subject of evacuating Richmond. Davis refused to discuss it, but at least Breckinridge got it on the table." Indeed the war secretary was well along with plans and preparations for the necessary evacuation he expected. "Finally on February 26 or 27, Davis relented enough to meet with Lee and Breckinridge to discuss evacuation if it became necessary." W. C. Davis reports an amusing anecdote:

At this same meeting yet another peace plan proposal came forth in a rather bizarre suggestion from a Union general in the army facing Lee that there should be a cease-fire during which officers and their wives would call on each other between the lines. Presumably it based its hopes on the prewar fraternity between the families of many of the opposing commanders, thinking that somehow out of their renewing acquaintances they would be less willing to continue fighting each other. Meanwhile their generals-in-chief should conduct discussions looking toward a military surrender short of defeat that might lead to a general peace. Breckinridge thought the idea at least worth an effort.[84]

Davis was not very hopeful and proved to be right in his scepticism when he allowed the generals to make the attempt. Of course it came to nothing, but it gave Davis "yet another example of Yankee recalcitrance to publicize."[85]

By early March Lee was convinced that the end was near, and he visited with Breckinridge, the two of them again expressing their hopes of opening peace negotiations. Breckinridge did what he could, soliciting a great many written statements from a variety of Confederate officials and high military men, and presented this package to Davis on March 12. Davis, ironically, "may have hoped that instead of inspiring gloom, these reports could serve to awaken Congress and the people to the new sacrifices necessary for victory," W. C. Davis observes. As it turned out, the reports were sent to Congress, but "unfortunately, in his message Davis had so irritated Congress by chiding them for laxity and failure to meet his expectations, they devoted much of the remaining few days to drafting lengthy rejoinders. . . . In the process, the message containing Breckinridge's package was tabled."[86]

Breckinridge tried one more time. He called a meeting in the Richmond hotel room of Senator Henry Burnett of Kentucky. Present were Robert M. T. Hunter and Allen Caperton of Virginia, Louis T. Wigfall of Texas, and George G. Vest and Waldo Johnson of Missouri, senators all—and since only fifteen members of the Senate remained in Richmond, these six represented a powerful bloc. Breckinridge told them frankly that he was convinced the Confederacy was doomed. "What I propose," he said, is "that the Confederacy should not be captured in fragments, that we should not disband like banditti, but that we should surrender as a government, and we will thus maintain the dignity of our cause, and secure the respect of our enemies, and the best terms for our soldiers." He then came to his powerful and poignant conclusion: "This has been a magnificent epic, . . . in God's name let it not terminate in a farce." Still, no one would act.[87]

But as the end approached, Breckinridge continued to play his hand as wisely as he could. W. C. Davis asserts that the fact that the Confederacy "fell as it did, as a nation rather than as piece-meal bands led by Davis and others,

owes much to this Kentuckian and his vision of the Confederacy in posterity."
R. E. Lee later said of Breckinridge, "He is a great man. I was acquainted with
him as Congressman and Vice-President and as one of our Generals, but I did
not *know* him till he was secretary of war, and he is a lofty, pure strong man."
According to W. C. Davis, Breckinridge's "lasting contribution to the history
of the Confederate States is not that he might have won its independence [had
he become war secretary earlier] but that he managed its defeat in a manner
that lent his stature to the cause itself."[88]

Davis himself simply refused to heed his prudent war secretary. "We are
fighting for Independence," he had said earlier, "and that, or extermination,
we *will* have." As W. C. Davis puts it, "There could never be reunion, he maintained, for hatred and bitterness between North and South were now cemented
in the soil of both by the congealed blood of hundreds of thousands of the
slain. 'Our children may forget this war,' he said, 'but *we* cannot.' Rather, 'now
it must go on till the last man of this generation falls in his tracks, and his children seize the musket and fight our battle.' "[89]

17

THE END IN VIRGINIA

Jefferson Davis was facing defeat. Yet according to William Cooper,

> Even with the awful public pressures and the lingering maladies, Davis could still impress people. His face, despite thinner and more sallow cheeks, marked a man of 'extraordinary determination,' an Irish visitor remarked. Even though he looked 'thin and careworn,' with his hair and chin whiskers 'bleaching rapidly,' his gray eyes remained 'bright & clear.' In March 1865, an eyewitness pictured 'a graceful, spirited gentleman.' Davis showed his spirit at a wedding where he gleefully claimed his 'tribute kiss' from the blushing bride.[1]

Moreover, as Varina later wrote,

> As hope died out in the breasts of the rank and file of the Confederate Army, the President's courage rose, and he was fertile in expedients to supply deficiencies, and calm in the contemplation of the destruction of his dearest hopes, and the violent death he expected to be his.
>
> As late as April 1, 1865, he wrote to General Lee from Richmond, of the difficulty of finding iron enough to keep the Tredegar works employed, and said: "There is also difficulty in getting iron even for shot and shell, but I hope this may for the present be overcome by taking some from the Navy, which under the altered circumstances may be spared. . . . The question is often asked, 'will we hold Richmond,' to which my only answer is, if we can; it is purely a question of military power. The distrust is increasing, and embarrasses in many ways."
>
> Events now rapidly culminated in the over-whelming disaster he and our brave people had striven so energetically to avert. The gloom was impenetrable.[2]

Michael Ballard suggests that during the first three months of 1865 Davis had conducted himself in a keenly shrewd manner, "perhaps more acutely than at any other time during his presidency."[3] Yet his actions had not completely stopped criticism of him, nor had he done anything efficacious to stop the Confederacy from falling apart. As that began to happen, people blamed Davis and their government, becoming ever more vocal in their criticism. As March began, diarists noted that it "came in gloomy and melancholy," that "people are almost in a state of desperation," and that "God's hand has been laid heavily upon our unhappy land." Neither Davis nor the government could offer them much comfort.[4]

As the first three months of 1865 came to an end, many—perhaps most—Southerners finally had concluded that they had lost the war. Still, many of them uttered desperate calls for Robert E. Lee or Joseph Johnston or both to wave magic wands and work miracles. Despite their grudging admission of defeat, the populace still clung to larger-than-life perceptions of their generals; but they began to turn against Davis. And they began to plead for peace negotiations, believing that something could be salvaged and that many if not most of the South's political institutions might be preserved.[5]

If the war were to be lost, however, someone or something must be to blame. The people were unwilling and unable to see that their generals had failed, so they blamed impending defeat on Davis and the government. Davis, during the last three months, had been constantly criticized, and he never responded effectively or wisely to criticism. Further, he and the Congress fought over delays in pending legislation and the looming adjournment of the session. The disarray that he found himself in made him seem weak. The words one Richmond resident had uttered earlier in the year seemed significant: "He is in a sea of trouble, and has no time or thought for anything except the safety of the country. I fear the Congress is turning madly against him. It is the old story of the sick lion whom even the jackass can kick without fear. It is a very struggle for life with him."[6]

What then, is operative in this falling apart? A war was coming to its end. Americans have never been good at confronting defeat. As Mark Grimsley and Brooks D. Simpson have pointed out, "Some years ago the political scientist Fred Ikle lamented the failure of historians to examine the termination of wars with anywhere near the zeal devoted to their causes and conduct."[7] They then observed "that [the Confederacy's] bid for independence was doomed was not obvious to all Southerners in early 1865."[8] The matter of how the Civil War did finally turn out is well worth pursuing. Indeed, "the final months of the Confederacy . . . offer fascinating opportunities—as a case study in war termination."[9]

The end of the Civil War recently has been the subject of quite a number of books, including Noah Andre Trudeau's *Out of the Storm: The End of the Civil War, April–June 1865*, and Michael Golay's *A Ruined Land: The End of the Civil War*, which "allows the voices of those touched by the Civil War to speak for themselves," thus showing "the impact of victory and defeat on the ordinary Americans who both influenced events and were caught up in them."[10] And then there is Jay Wink's *April 1865,* which, as we were going to press, was on the national best-seller list. Although not our cup of tea, the work offers a good lesson for historians like us who envy Wink's sales success. As he points out, "At the end of the Civil War, acts of revenge could have torn us further apart. That didn't happen, thanks to the wisdom of leaders in both the North and South," who "gave America a second chance."[11]

Finally "aware that Richmond would soon fall," Cooper observes, "Jefferson Davis planned accordingly."[12] On March 29, 1865, doubtlessly with pain and reluctance, he dispatched his family to Charlotte, North Carolina, where a furnished house had been rented for them. Many of their own possessions had been sold. In the hurry of the departure, however, the check received for them was never cashed; it hardly mattered, however, since the Confederate notes were virtually worthless.

Davis told Varina that "for the future his headquarters must be in the field, and that [his family's] presence would only embarrass and grieve, instead of comforting him." Varina took only her clothing from the executive residence. Accompanying her were her four children (Maggie, nine; Jefferson Jr., seven; Billy, three; and Winnie, nine months), her younger sister, and Jim Limber, a free black orphan whom the Davises had adopted. Burton N. Harrison, Davis's private secretary, was their escort and bodyguard. The entourage was completed by Treasury Secretary Trenholm's four daughters. Davis gave Varina instruction in loading and firing a small pistol just before she left. And fearing that she might be subjected to unbearable humiliation if taken captive, he told her, "if reduced to the last extremity, at least force your assailants to kill you."[13]

Davis, of course, "would not leave until the last possible moment," writes Cooper, "which came somewhat sooner than he expected."[14] When he saw Varina and her party off at the Danville Railroad, he said, "If I live you can come to me when the struggle is ended, but I do not expect to survive the destruction of constitutional liberty." Varina believed him and recalled that as she left, "it was evident he thought he was looking his last upon us."[15]

April began with Jefferson Davis's presidency still not quite over, but as Michael Ballard observes, by then "it had become more symbolic than real." Collapse of so many local governments rendered tax collection little more than a farce. Most of the military districts outside of Virginia and North Carolina were on their own. There were only occasional telegraphic contacts between Richmond and commanders in Georgia, Alabama, Mississippi, and Florida.[16]

Jefferson Davis nevertheless stubbornly maintained that somehow the Confederacy ultimately would survive and prevail. R. E. Lee had visited Richmond in March and was impressed with Davis's "remarkable faith" in the ongoing cause and his "unconquerable will power." Lee assessed his president as "pertinacious in opinion and purpose." Davis meanwhile had written a letter to his old friend Braxton Bragg that suggests Lee had misinterpreted him: "We both entered into this war at the beginning of it; we both staked everything on the issue, and have lost all which either public or private enemies could take away."

> Davis thus admitted to Bragg that the cause seemed hopeless while making clear that he would not let such thoughts dominate him. He felt he had risked all and now faced the prospect of losing all. He certainly found no enticement in peace terms that confirmed defeat by effecting reunion. He had to work to save the Confederacy, as much to justify his own beliefs and the role he had played as to preserve the cause. In his view, this was the only option available.[17]

By late March Secretary of War John C. Breckinridge was thinking about the immediate future. He advised North Carolina governor Zebulon Vance to have the track gauges of his state's railroads adjusted to match those of Virginia so that "in the event of disaster" the government could run the Virginia rolling stock south.[18]

April 1 dawned in Richmond with the populace seizing any pretext they could to inject some gaiety into their lives, now almost totally on the dreary side, by indulging in April Fool's Day jokes. Unfortunately for the Confederacy's military hopes, however, on that day Grant launched another thrust toward the Southern right, threatening Five Forks, a vital road junction to Lee's rear. Lee countered by moving nineteen thousand men, one-third of all that he had left, to oppose nearly fifty thousand Federals. When it was over, about eleven hundred Confederates had been killed or wounded and another fifty-two hundred were prisoners.

This was the coup de grâce. R. E. Lee's hopes of holding his Petersburg lines any longer crumbled. The Southside Railroad west of Petersburg was now untenable, and Richmond was reduced to possessing the single line of the Danville Railroad—and even that stood in danger of being cut by Yankee cavalry raiders. For Lee, it was a matter of hours, rather than days, as to how much longer he could stay. He asked for a meeting with Breckinridge or Davis or both, to determine his next course of action, and W. C. Davis thinks that he "probably took time for a brief visit late that night."[19]

There were almost no government officials left in Richmond by this time save for Davis and the cabinet. The news of the loss at Five Forks sent waves of shock though the populace, for everyone understood the meaning. "Breckinridge," W. C. Davis tells us, "spent most of the day at the War Department, alternately dealing with incoming telegrams, calling out the city's reserves to assume places in the defenses as Lee was forced to withdraw portions of his command to cover other threats, and himself taking a hand at packing the department's remaining archives in crates. During the evening Admiral Raphael Semmes, . . . joined him, as did a government clerk, W. H. Swallow, and together they passed the hours well into the night at their packing."[20]

After they had finished, Breckinridge and his helpers walked together to the State Department offices. There they found Secretary of State Judah P. Benjamin apparently as imperturbable and cheerful as he always was, sitting on top of a crate of records, singing a silly ballad he had composed himself, "The Exit from Shocko Hill." W. C. Davis points out that this "was, quite literally, graveyard humor, since their building on Franklin Street was in fact only a few blocks' walk from Shocko Hill, site of the city hospital and one of its older graveyards." Just then General Samuel Cooper came in and, reacting to Benjamin's poor taste, chided that "Nero fiddled while Rome was burning."[21]

On April 2, at 4:30 A.M., Grant hurled a massive onslaught against the Petersburg trenches, and the main defenses crumbled. Lee was able to extricate his remnant, but Union troops occupied Petersburg by nightfall. The Confederate government was compelled to evacuate Richmond. Thus, on April 3 Union troops occupied not only Petersburg but Richmond as well, and on April 4 President Lincoln visited the erstwhile Confederate capital, as the Appomattox campaign commenced.

R. E. Lee immediately telegraphed Davis that he could no longer hold his lines at Petersburg and thus could not further protect Richmond. It was an incredibly beautiful spring day. The Richmond streets had been crowded with churchgoers whose spirits were invigorated by the wonderful weather. In the minds of many, fears of R. E. Lee's failure were subdued. Breckinridge was at an early service at the Broad Street Methodist Church, where he received the first of a series of telegraphs Lee sent. The war secretary at once went to his office to await further news. As W. C. Davis observes, "When the telegraph wires went silent for some time to come it seemed an evil portent to all. Benjamin, as well as [War Clerk Robert G. H.] Kean, [presidential aide Francis] Lubbock, and others, joined him at times in the vigil, and [Postmaster General John] Reagan and [Assistant Secretary of War John A.] Campbell stopped in on their way to church. Then at 10:40 A.M. came the word that Lee must abandon his defenses that night, and perhaps even sooner."[22]

Cooper reports that "Postmaster General John Reagan, who had been at the

War Department when the telegram arrived, headed to the Gray House to inform the President. On the way he met Davis en route to church. After listening to Reagan, Davis continued on."[23] Cooper observes that "When Davis entered St. Paul's, one who saw him often noted his appearance: 'the cold calm eye, the sunken cheeks, the compressed lip, were all as impenetrable as an iron mask.'" Davis was in his usual place, kneeling for the antecommunion, when the sexton approached him and gave him a telegram reporting that the army would evacuate its lines, including Richmond, that night. Actually, as Ballard and Cooper point out, the traditional story, asserting that this was Davis's first inkling of the situation, is false; Davis already knew about the telegram and its contents before the church service.[24]

The congregation, packed to the walls, saw him rise, deathly pale but absolutely calm, and go out "with his usual quick military tread." Davis later wrote of the moment: "The occurrence probably attracted attention, but the people had been too long beleaguered, had known me too often to receive notice of threatened attacks, and the congregation of St. Paul's was too refined to make a scene at anticipated danger." As Cooper writes, "Although Davis had known that Lee would soon give up Petersburg, that it happened so suddenly surprised him." After Davis left the church, several more people, all connected somehow with the government, also departed, after being given messages by the sexton, who made several trips up and down the aisles.[25]

Davis walked down the hill to the executive offices, in order to roust Richard Ewell's defense force and to see about packing his official papers. He called his cabinet into session and also summoned Governor William Smith and Mayor John Mayo. On the way to this meeting, Naval Secretary Stephen R. Mallory encounted Secretary Benjamin on the street. According to W. C. Davis, "Benjamin [was] smiling as always, cigar in his mouth, twirling his gold-headed cane in his fingers as if he had not a care in the world. To himself Mallory thought the secretary of state rather like 'the last man outside the ark, who assured Noah of his belief that "it would not be such a h—ll of a shower, after all."' But it was bravado, for Mallory could see well enough that Benjamin was already shaken by the news, which had spread quickly."[26] If the populace had wavering opinions of Davis, his loyal cabinet members did not: "Their loyalty to President Davis remained firm," observes Ballard. "They would support his decisions as long as possible."[27] Breckinridge particularly, in the days ahead, "would be a key adviser to the president and would become a central figure in the retreat of the government."[28]

There was no talk, at least not in front of Davis, about this being the end of the cause. There was still hope that Lee would be able to join Johnston's force and continue the war. Although there was no talk of the leaders having to leave the country, W. C. Davis points out that "Breckinridge was already planning how to get them all away."[29] As Davis later wrote,

> The event had come before Lee had expected it, and the announcement was received by us in Richmond with sorrow and surprise; for, though it had been foreseen as a coming event which might possibly, though not probably, be averted, and such preparation as was practicable had been made to meet the contingency when it should occur, it was not believed to be so near at hand.

Ballard suggests that this explains why Davis calmly went to church, even though he already knew of the situation at Petersburg. Quite simply, "Davis still did not appreciate the severity of the crisis. It took Lee's later message delivered to him at Saint Paul's to move the president to act."[30] The staff hurriedly packed those documents they deemed significant enough to retain. They did not do as good a job as they might have, however, and some important papers addressed to Davis later turned up in private hands; a large portion of others unfortunately were burned.[31] Secretary Benjamin seems to have been almost alone in his having earlier taken the situation as seriously as he did, and he had seen to the disposition of the records of his department carefully. Tragically for historians, however, Benjamin personally burned the records of the Confederate Secret Service.[32]

As Davis walked home, women ran from their houses to ask if the city were to be given up, saying, Davis later recalled, "If the success of the cause requires you to give up Richmond, we are content." The "affection and confidence," Davis said, "of this noble people in the hour of disaster were more distressing to me than complacent and unjust censure would have been." Alabama senator Clement C. Clay dropped in for a visit with Davis and found him "hastily packing a valise, his clothing and papers scattered in little heaps about." That night Davis removed the Confederate government south to Danville, Virginia.[33]

Davis had spent his last day in the Confederate capital conducting himself remarkably well, most observers thought. There are many accounts of the day, some written soon after and others many years later. According to Ballard,

> Most agree he kept control of his emotions as he left Saint Paul's. Accounts generally support the conclusion that he conducted himself calmly and presidentially for the remainder of the day and at the depot that evening. Those who recorded their observations, . . . wanted the world to know that President Davis did not leave Richmond a beaten man, a leader in disgrace. Like the cause he would come to represent, he could be described in none but approving terms.[34]

"That evening President Davis walked back to the Executive Mansion for the final time," says Cooper. "To inquiring citizens who stopped him, he confirmed that the government would leave the city. After gathering up a few belongings he 'sat on a divan in his study, sad, but calm and dignified,' conversing with those around them. When the carriage arrived to take him to the Richmond and Danville depot, he lit a cigar and got in." When Davis got to the station he found Breckinridge busily overseeing the final preparations for loading the two waiting trains, one for the officials and one for the Treasury. W. C. Davis points out that "one thing was clear. No one in the cabinet, least of all Benjamin, was exerting any authority or taking any responsibility now, none but the secretary of war. Breckinridge told Davis that he would remain behind to direct the rest of the evacuation. That done, he would ride west with an escort and try to reach Lee and his retreating army."[35]

The train chugged out of the city at 11:00 P.M. At the last moment Davis had sent one of his aides back to the Gray House to retrieve the family spoons and forks, which the president had forgotten to pack. It was too late, however; the train could not wait, and so the presidential cutlery had to go with Breckinridge.[36] Davis left Richmond still clinging to his buoyant expectation of ultimate success for the Confederacy. "At this point," Cooper observes "Davis had no thought of surrendering the Confederacy. He did not consider the cause lost. . . . This setback did not sound the death knell for '[our] most sacred cause'; instead, it meant 'a new phase of the struggle.' " "Reality for Davis," writes Ballard, "was what he determined it to be, and he still had faith that somehow Lee would save the day."[37] Among the others, however, Benjamin alone seemed to be in good spirits. "Delving into history," W. C. Davis points out, "he reminded them of other peoples who had recovered from darker hours than this."[38]

As the train chugged on, several times crowds met it as it passed through towns. When they learned that Davis was aboard, everyone wanted to see him and to shake his hand. Congressman Horatio Bruce thought "the president kept up a bold front and spoke encouragingly to the people when he spoke at all." A soldier on the platform at Clover Hill, Lieutenant John S. Wise, said, "I saw a government on wheels, . . . It was the marvelous and incongruous debris of the wreck of the Confederate capital." Finally sometime between 4:00 and 5:00 P.M., the train pulled into the Richmond and Danville Railroad depot just across the Dan River from that town of six thousand.[39]

Robert E. Lee's sorely depleted army tried to swing around and elude the Federals, attempting to travel to Danville, where Lee vainly hoped they might be able to unite with what was left of Joseph E. Johnston's army. Lee wanted to use the still-operational Richmond and Danville Railroad, but when he reached Amelia Court House, he had to wait for twenty-four hours before trains brought him badly needed supplies. To his bitter dismay, logistics men, incorrectly thinking that ammunition would be the Rebels' first need, had sent no food. Meanwhile, Federal cavalry cut the railroad at Jetersville, forcing Lee to abandon his hopes of using the railroad and his hungry men to scurry across the rolling countryside toward Lynchburg.

On April 6 nearly one-fourth of Lee's army was entrapped and captured at Sayler's Creek, the last major engagement between the Army of Northern Virginia and the Army of the Potomac. Lee then began to lead his remaining thirty thousand men in a north-by-west arc across the Appomattox River. But Philip Sheridan's cavalry and most of two infantry corps hurried to block the way into Lynchburg and seized the Confederate supply trains at Appomattox Station. Beginning at dawn on April 9, units of the Confederate corps commanded by Major General John B. Gordon and Fitzhugh Lee's cavalry desperately probed the Union lines and made some encouraging progress for a time, but they soon found the powerful Union infantrymen to be strongly emplaced in lines that were too formidable. The Yankees began to drive forward, and at the same time other Federals attacked the Confederate rear guard.

After listening to all reports of the situation, Lee took final action and then declared to his listeners, "It would be useless and therefore cruel to provoke the further effusion of blood, and I have arranged to meet with General Grant with a view to surrender." Truce flags fluttered, and couriers arranged a meeting between Lee and Grant. Early that afternoon, in the parlor of the house belonging to Wilmer McClean, Lee surrendered.

On April 12 a notable ceremony took place at Appomattox Court House. The Federal troops formed along the principal street, and the Confederate army passed in formal surrender ceremonial parade. Major General Joshua Chamberlain described it: "On they come, with the old swinging route step and swaying battle-flags. In the van, the proud Confederate ensign. . . . Before us in proud humiliation stood the embodiment of manhood; men whom neither toils and sufferings, nor the fact of death, nor disaster, nor hopelessness could bend from their resolve; standing before us now, thin, worn, and famished, but erect, and with eyes looking level into ours, waking memories that bound us together as no other bond." The bugle blared, and the Federal lines shifted to the marching salute of carry arms. General Gordon at the head of the Rebel parade saw the salute and whirled on his horse, dropping the point of his sword to his boot toe and ordered carry arms—"honor answering honor." These actions were repeated down the line. Eric McKittrick has aptly asserted that this ritual of surrender was crucial in molding the mind-sets of the soldiers, who accepted the war's outcome rather more readily than did the civilian populace.

As George Rable observes, when word of Richmond's fall circulated about the Confederacy, the great faith that so many people had placed in R. E. Lee's capabilities made that news "all the harder to swallow." This was especially so "for women living as refugees or on isolated farms and plantations whose spirits had often soared with the most improbable rumors." But one should not be misled, Rable asserts: "The evacuation of the capital hardly dashed all hopes." Indeed, "efforts to shore up public morale surprisingly persisted."[40]

D avis's first concern was news: during seventeen hours on the train he had heard nothing. He and his staff, Trenholm, and Mallory found temporary quarters in the mansion of William T. Sutherlin, a wealthy retired major and quartermaster. Benjamin and Reagan also found quarters in the homes of other wealthy Danville citizens. Lower-level officials secured rooms in other private dwellings; the clerks were shunted off to the town's two hotels. Davis immediately sent a brief telegram to Varina to let her know that he was safely out of the capital.[41]

Danville had been chosen for several good reasons. It was between Lee and Johnston's armies, it seemed probable that it could be defended, it had a good stock of quartermaster supplies, a railroad repair shop, and even ordnance machinery. Too, it had good rail connections southward should retreat be necessary. Keeping the seat of government in Virginia was psychologically important. Davis had rebuffed the various objections to Danville that had been voiced in the many discussions about it by proclaiming "that he would not leave Virginia until Lee was whipped out of it." He repeated this assertion a number of times during the ensuing several days.[42]

Rising early the next morning, he found much to do in his new capital. He was determined to try to establish a government there that would be more or less secure, while Lee moved to make a junction with Johnston and then to interpose the combined army between Danville and Grant's force. He wrote to Varina on April 6: "We are now fixing an executive office where the current business may be transacted here and do not propose at this time definitely to fix upon a point for the seat of Govt in the future. I am unwilling to leave Virginia, and do not know where within her borders the requisite houses for the Depts and the the Congress could be found."[43]

Davis held his first cabinet meeting in Danville on the morning of April 4. The desperate atmosphere seemed to call for him to prepare and issue some kind of proclamation to the Confederate populace. Right after the meeting he went into the Sutherlin's library and wrote his message: As W. C. Davis observes, "Davis's pen revealed that he had lost none of his ability to make silk purses of sow's ears." He later claimed that he had sought in his message neither "to diminish the magnitude of our disaster nor to excite illusory expectations." Yet "viewed by the light of subsequent events," he admitted, "it may fairly be said it was over-sanguine." He began with a review of Lee's retreat and the loss of Richmond. "It would be unwise, even if it were possible," he wrote, "to conceal the great moral, as well as material injury to our cause." But then, incredibly, he began to imply that perhaps the fall of Richmond was actually a benefit. Defending the city had kept Lee tied in his trenches for months.[44]

> We have now entered upon a new phase of a struggle the memory of which is to endure for all ages, and to shed ever increasing lustre upon our country. Relieved from the necessity of guarding cities and particular points, important but not vital to our defence with our army free to move from point to point, and strike in detail the detachments and garrisons of the enemy; operating on the interior of our own country, where supplies are more accessible, and where the foe will be far removed from his own base, and cut off from all succor in case of reverse, nothing is now needed to render our triumph certain, but the exhibition of our own unquenchable resolve. Let us but will it, and we are free. . . . Relying on . . . our God, let us meet the foe with fresh defiance, with unconquered and unconquerable hearts.[45]

Was Davis actually calling for a continuing conflict characterized by partisan warfare on a grand scale? Take to the hills and doggedly snipe at the Yankees until they finally gave up? Several eminent historians believe so, most notably Emory M. Thomas, W. C. Davis, and Michael Ballard.[46] But Cooper maintains that Davis did not want a guerrilla struggle: "To him waging a guerrilla campaign was *not* an acceptable option. He believed the social price far too high. His closest aide, William [Preston] Johnston, reported him as saying 'Guerrillas become brigands, and any government is better than that.' "[47]

W. C. Davis suggests that if Davis "genuinely believed what he was saying, as he later suggested that he did, then it was little short of delusional."[48] Still, if Davis had changed his mind and wanted to wage a guerrilla struggle, it was not a new idea. "Davis *had* hinted at this in the past," W. C. Davis points out. Guerrillas had hampered Union operations in 1862 along the western end of the Memphis and Charleston Railroad, throughout most of the war in Missouri, and at various other locations. They had vexed Union commanders constantly. Thus, determined Confederate citizens, many of them journalists, had periodically called for guerrilla warfare. One such appeal came from J. D. B. DeBow, who supported such a strategy, urging that Confederates should "sacrifice . . . military punctilio" and "prepare for guerilla war." Davis seemed to be indicating that he at last was firmly in that camp, too. If forced to withdraw temporarily from any state, "again and again will we return, until the baffled and exhausted enemy shall abandon in despair his endless and impossible task of making slaves of a people resolved to be free."[49]

One of DeBow's supporters was an Alabama newspaper editor who had been compelled to publish his newspaper in Georgia because his hometown had been occupied by Union forces. He printed with approval a letter that had appeared in a Mississippi paper, in which the writer urged that "the longer we remain 'tender footed' in regard to adopting the guerrilla mode of warfare, which is not only right and proper, but *natural,* the longer we will be subjected to the hellish insults and damning outrages of the accursed race of God-denying Yankees."[50] Davis, however, was not very successful in his attempt with his latest message to rekindle public confidence. Circumstances dictated that the message reach only a scant number of people. The *Danville Register* published it on April 5, but Davis's words were meaningless by the time other Southern papers printed the message. Handbills containing the message were distributed, but the audience they reached was hardly sufficient for the words to enkindle any significant resurgence of Confederate morale.[51]

As W. C. Davis points out,

> The trouble was, in looking at history, Davis chose to learn all the wrong lessons, or rather to misuse it to support his own flawed expectations. No separatist movement in recent history had won out against heavy odds without being the client state of another power that could feed it material support or even manpower. . . . [Moreover,] the high country of southwestern Virginia and western North Carolina, northeastern Georgia, north Alabama, and eastern Tennessee, the regions where his new partisan armies would have to take refuge, were also precisely those areas most heavily infected with Unionism and anti-Confederate sentiment since the beginning of the war. He would be placing his soldiers in a position where they could obtain almost nothing from outside, among a people who would not support them from within. . . . Years later even he admitted that his expectations were "over-sanguine," which was as close to a confession of outright error as he ever came.[52]

Nevertheless, despite the lack of clarity in Davis's proclamation, his words were not intended to be a call for unrestrained partisan struggle. "In fact, Davis's correspondence and actions during the flight of the Confederate government from April 2 to May 10," observes William B. Feis, "not to mention the 'new phase' declaration itself, reveal that the Confederacy's chief executive *never* embraced the guerrilla option and instead proposed something quite different and far less extreme."[53]

What then did Davis mean? As Feis points out, "When Davis stated that should 'we' be driven from Virginia by the weight of Union numbers, 'we' would return again to the Old Dominion, he was *not* referring to guerrilla bands but to the Army of Northern Virginia that on April 4, was as far as he knew still marching toward Danville to continue the fight."[54] Davis was trying to resurrect the spirits of the people. In that effort, however, he failed.

When Davis's proclamation hit the streets, "the immediate reaction showed just how far the president was drifting from the sentiment of the people," according to W. C. Davis. Colonel Robert Withers, the commander of the small garrison defending Danville, read the proclamation and subsequently discussed it with a number of others. "I neither saw nor heard of anyone," he said, "who was much enthused by the assurance."[55]

It would have broken Davis's heart had he known of the bitterness in Richmond, even as he was trying to breathe new hope into his people. He was out of the city, but citizens there had to endure Yankee occupation and the rumor that the president had actually fled town wearing a dress, disguised as a woman.[56]

General Joseph E. Johnston understood the president's message as an appeal to continue tolerating the bloodshed of a war he now regarded as impossible to win. "It would be the greatest of human crimes for us to attempt to continue the war," he wrote in his memoirs, for "the effect of our keeping the field would be, not to harm the enemy, but to complete the devastation of our country and the ruin of its people."[57] Davis's notion would have meant that the port cities and manufacturing centers would have to be abandoned. The Rebel forces would have to try to subsist in the mountainous regions of the Confederacy, mainly Appalachia, probably the single most destitute section of the country.

Davis remained spirited and determined to the end. He simply could not envision reconciliation with the North on any terms, and he had long held that "we are fighting for Independence, and that, or extermination, we *will* have." Yet however implausible it may seem, he was talking still about conventional warfare. As W. C. Davis asserts, "He himself had long since crossed a river of no return."[58] Perhaps in some uncanny way, Davis was shifting to an active-positive leadership style. How could this be? Because, we conclude, Davis *had become delusional.*

Clement Eaton has suggested that Davis "overworked his frail physique for the cause of Confederate independence, but in the end the people did not appreciate his efforts." Eaton then quotes Josiah Gorgas's diary entry of March 2, 1865: "The President has alas! lost every vestige of the public confidence.

Had he been successful his errors and faults would have been overlooked, but adversity magnifies them." Davis had shown a magnificent devotion to the Confederate cause but lacked the necessary charisma of a true leader. Thus, "He could not inspire the Southern people with a similar selfless devotion."[59]

By April 6, in fear that the Federals might raid and then sweep past Danville's rather weak defenses and thus capture the Confederate Treasury, Davis and Trenholm decided to dispatch it by rail to Charlotte, where there was a vault. A group of naval midshipmen, who accompanied the Treasury train to Charlotte, spent some of their idle time writing letters or practicing their knots, some of them making "sailor art," like Turks' heads and ornamental hangings. "A few of them," W. C. Davis observes, "with literal gallows humor, tied hangman's knots."[60]

"We had a good time at Danville," Davis's aide Preston Johnston wrote. Mrs. Sutherlin, however, grew increasingly concerned as she watched Davis each day. He seemed uniformly "pleasant and agreeable and self-possessed," she noted, but he either would not eat or at times consumed only a little. He seemed to take comfort only in the mockingbird that sang outside his window each morning and in having afternoon conversations with Sutherlin in the family library. Davis's moods alternated rapidly between optimism and resignation. From moment to moment he might talk of his delight in farming, recall with nostalgic pleasure his Mexican War days, or describe in detail the fall of Richmond while at the same time reasserting his firm confidence in Robert E. Lee.[61]

Although Davis was kept more current on events in Virginia and North Carolina, he tried hard to keep abreast of what was going on elsewhere. He was particularly interested in Alabama and Georgia, perceiving that his further retreat might have to be in that direction. But on April 2, James Harrison Wilson's raiders had driven Nathan Bedford Forrest's cavalry from Selma and captured that important city and its valuable ordnance works.

Davis's extreme stress over such news as this was understandable, and to relieve emotional tension he took an active part in supervising the Danville defenses. He liked being in the field and around military personnel, and from doing so he derived bits of cheer, which elevated his mood. Inspecting the various fortifications, he concluded that they were inadequate and gave orders that they be improved.[62] His behavior gave every evidence of a depression severe enough to render him incapable of acting according to reality.

Major Sutherlin himself comprehended before Davis did that the president could not remain in Danville much longer. One evening as they were smoking cigars together, Sutherlin reminded Davis of the locations of Grant's and Sherman's forces. "Do not delay so in your journey," the major cautioned, "let your movements be as rapid and veiled as possible." Davis replied, "Major, I comprehend the situation exactly. It is all clear before me and I would not evade it if I could. For myself I care nothing—it is my dear people that I am thinking of—what will become of my poor people!"[63] Was he beginning to sound like a king?

No word had come from R. E. Lee, meaning that either he had met with some shattering reverse or the pursuing Yankees had come between his line of retreat and Danville. Navy Secretary Mallory could see that Davis expected no good news. "To a few, very few," he reflected, "they were days of hope; to the many they were days of despondency, if not of despair; & to all, days of intense anxiety."[64]

Then on April 8 an exhausted Lieutenant John S. Wise, dispatched from Lee's headquarters, arrived in Danville with important news. Davis's secretary Burton Harrison, newly arrived from Charlotte, interrupted a cabinet meeting in the Sutherlin dining room to inform Davis that Lee had lost one-third of his forces at Sayler's Creek, making it impossible for him to reach Danville. The president and his cabinet needed to leave soon. Quite out of touch with reality, Davis seems to have thought that young Wise was unrealistically pessimistic and that surely all was not lost. The next day, Palm Sunday, Davis went to church as usual. In the afternoon came more bad news; Davis got the message Lee had dispatched on April 6, delineating the dismal situation that his army faced. Still, Davis remained resolute.[65]

When Harrison had arrived he had brought with him a letter for Davis from Varina, which she had written just the day before. "I know that your strength when stirred up is great," she wrote, "and that you can do with a few what others have failed to do with many." The Almighty would yet deliver them and their cause, "through his own appointed agent," and she believed that agent was her husband. "Now Sutherlin's wife," observes W. C. Davis, "concluded from Davis's manner that ultimate success was only a matter of time, that 'he would fight to the end, beyond the end.' "[66]

According to Cooper, "On the tenth, even though no official news had reached him, Davis informed Joseph Johnston that 'little doubt' existed about Lee's fate."[67] Later that afternoon, word of Lee's surrender at Appomattox Court House reached the president and his cabinet. Captain W. P. Graves burst in with the unwelcome news. He gave his note to Davis, who read it and then passed it around to the others. As each man read the dreaded missive, "a great silence prevailed for a moment." Mallory wrote that the news "fell upon the ears of all like a fire-bell in the night," an allusion to Thomas Jefferson's statement forty-five years earlier about the extension of the slavery controversy into the Missouri Territory.[68]

The news made it clear that with no armed forces between Danville and Grant's army, the Confederate government by necessity must pack up and move again, perhaps even as soon as that very evening. Davis at once wired Johnston, informing him of Lee's surrender. "By now he no longer concealed his agitation," W. C. Davis points out. Governor William Smith, who was trying to reestablish Virginia's state government in Danville, came to call and heard from Davis the fearful news. General Josiah Gorgas, the chief of ordnance, thought the president "was evidently overwhelmed by this astounding misfortune."[69]

In shock, the group ate dinner, and then Davis prepared a farewell message to Danville mayor J. M. Walker:

> Permit me to return . . . my sincere thanks for your kindness shown to me when I came among you, under that pressure of adversity which is more apt to cause the loss of friends than to be occasion for making new ones.
>
> I had hoped to have been able to maintain the Confederate Government on the soil of Virginia. . . . I had hoped to have contributed somewhat to the safety of your city. The desire . . . was rendered more than a mere sense of public duty by your generous reception of myself and the Executive officers who accompanied me. The shadows of misfortune . . . have become darker, and I trust you accord to me now as then your good wishes and confidence in the zeal . . . with which I have sought to discharge the high trust . . . conferred upon me.[70]

"Gloom the densest was abroad," said one Danville citizen, "and in harmony with its horrors the sky poured out its torrents, making Danville the most miserable and muddy place I ever tried to drag my feet through." Several observers thought Davis's mood considerably agitated. With his penchant for focusing on minutiae, he "wasted part of the day consulting with railroad authorities" about possibly changing the gauge of the track or alternatively building fortifications so that equipment might be protected. But Federal cavalry was threatening, which forced the realization that any plans they agreed to could not be executed. Governor William Smith, who had fled to Lynchburg, came to Danville to confer with Davis and found him "walking to and fro in his yard, evidently in great excitement." Mallory correctly perceived that Davis had been "wholly unprepared for Lee's capitulation."[71]

The president and cabinet packed "in such a hurry," writes W. C. Davis, "that each took little more than a valise with essential toiletries and a few changes of shirts and underclothes. Everything else they would have to leave behind in the rush to get to the depot by the appointed hour." Around 9:30 P.M. Davis took a carriage to the depot to catch a train for another journey farther south. While waiting for the departure, "Reagan stood atop his trunk, while

[Attorney General] George Davis and Benjamin sat on their luggage, bags that in Benjamin's case included a cooked ham given him by his recent hosts." (Either the hosts were insensitive to Benjamin's Jewishness or, as is almost certainly the case, Benjamin was a cultural but not an observant Jew.) The group's destination was Greensboro, North Carolina, some fifty miles south of Danville.

18

THE PSEUDO-CONFEDERACY

From Danville, Jefferson Davis and his entourage traveled toward Greensboro, North Carolina. When the Treasury train, which had followed them later, had covered half the distance, however, it had to stop at the Haw River, for Union cavalry raiders had burned the bridge the night before. Indeed, the Yankees had struck not more than five minutes after Davis and the cabinet train had passed over it. When informed of this, Davis replied "A miss is as good as a mile." As W. C. Davis observes, "The old bravado was returning after his recent shocks." The president's aide, William Preston Johnston, was with him as he detrained and perceived that he seemed "as collected as ever."[1]

Confederate officials entered a different atmosphere from the one they had enjoyed at Danville. Greensboro was marked by indifference, and no crowds turned out to greet the Confederate government. Secretary Stephen Mallory saw that "there were many commodious and well-furnished residences in and about" the town, "but their doors were closed . . . against the members of a retreating government." Burton Harrison soon discovered the cool reception was due to the "fear that, if they entertained us, their houses would be burned by the enemy, when his cavalry got there." No wonder, then, that "they found very few sympathizers," as the postal clerk Charles E. L. Stuart observed. Indeed, W. C. Davis points out, "Some townspeople forthrightly and repeatedly asked the visitors, 'how long are you going to stay?' "[2]

The Confederate officials simply ignored Greensboro's inhospitality and settled in. Most of the presidential party, with two exceptions, set up headquarters in a "dilapidated leaky passenger car," where they "ate, slept, and lived." William Preston Johnston could only say of Greensboro that they "got along." He sent Varina Davis a note, trying to alleviate her concern for her husband in this situation, writing "we are a fixture for the present and are comfortable fixed." Looking back on events of the last few days, Harrison confessed that "an age seems to me to have passed." John Taylor Wood gave Davis a bed in the apartment he had rented.

Davis had been slightly ill since his departure from Danville, but he continued to function. "At Greensboro," William Cooper asserts, "President Davis's chief goal was to devise a plan to carry on the war."[3] "Davis felt the return of even more of his resolve," observes W. C. Davis, "the sort that could be sustained only by unrealistic optimism." Preston Johnston echoed his chief's optimism, saying, "The loss of an army is not the loss of the cause," and "there is a great deal of fight in us yet."[4]

The officials ate well in Greensboro, for rations were well stocked there. Mallory later described the cabinet members' demeanor: the men tried to put on a happy face, but beneath the pretense the harsh reality lurked that whatever was left of the Confederacy was crumbling away. "The times," commented Mallory, "were 'sadly out of joint' just then, and so was the Confederate Government."[5]

Davis himself displayed none of that sentiment. He began to feel better and found his fighting spirit reviving as well. When General P. G. T. Beauregard arrived on a train from Raleigh, he immediately noted that Davis certainly seemed not to be a beaten man. Of course, Davis and his officials were most eager to hear all the news that Beauregard could give them concerning the military situation in North Carolina.

After setting up his own headquarters in boxcars near the depot, Beauregard presented his analysis, and it was depressingly pessimistic. "If anything," W. C. Davis points out, his report was "shaded even darker by his own conviction that they were beaten." Further, Beauregard had bad news about the Federal cavalry's depredations in Alabama and Georgia, the work of the raiders under James Harrison Wilson. There was more bad news from General Richard Taylor, indicating that Mobile was on the verge of being captured. Other devastating military threats loomed in parts of Mississippi. But as he spoke, Beauregard sensed that Davis was apparently unshaken, believing that with proper use of its resources, the Confederacy could survive, even if forced across the Mississippi River, where it could join the forces under General Edmund Kirby Smith. When the meeting ended, and as Beauregard left, he noted that he was "amazed at this evidence of visionary hope on the part of the President."[6] "But perhaps," muses W. C. Davis, Beauregard was "not surprised, as he never placed much faith in Davis's military judgment."[7] Davis was so committed to his duty as he perceived it that he could not yet comprehend the significance of the reports he received.

Davis's surviving Greensboro correspondence gives further evidence of his continuing positive but out-of-touch attitude. In reply to a message from North Carolina's governor Zebulon Vance, Davis indicated that he had not received any official message that R. E. Lee had surrendered but that there was information from reliable scouts that left no doubt that it was so. He continued, we must redouble our efforts to meet present disasters. An army holding its position with determination to fight on, and manifest ability to maintain the struggle, will attract all the scattered soldiers and daily and rapidly gather strength. Moral influence is wanting, and I am sure you can do much to revive the spirit and hope of the people.[8]

Meanwhile, the dying continued.

Davis suggested via telegram that General Johnston, Secretary of War Breckinridge, whom Davis expected to arrive soon, and General Beauregard should confer as soon as they could. And Davis added, "The important question first to be solved is at what point shall concentration be made, in view of the present position of the two columns of the enemy, and the routes which they may adopt to engage your forces before a prompt junction with General Walker and others." There were very few troops left to concentrate by any route. Davis rather quickly dispatched two follow-up telegrams, which suggested he was quite unsure what ought to be done concerning concentration, finally saying that Johnston should come to Greensboro, "to save time and have all information."[9]

Johnston arrived by train the next morning. Instead of going directly to the president, however, he met first with Beauregard. They spent the next several hours conferring. "Besides sharing a loathing of Davis," W. C. Davis observes, "they were alike agreed in their conviction that the fighting must end and quickly, and now they consulted on how best to present a united front when they met the president." Near noon Davis summoned them. But instead of hearing their views, "Davis simply lectured generals and ministers alike. Their cause was *not* defeated, he told them."[10]

Davis held two critical cabinet meetings, one on the afternoon of April 12 and one the next morning. Johnston and Beauregard were included in both. The two generals assumed that Davis simply wanted them to brief him on the military situation, but they quickly found that Davis was ready to give rather than to obtain information. He asserted that conscripts and deserters could be gathered and the Confederacy could quickly field an army quite large enough to push on with the conflict. Both Beauregard and Johnston pointed out that if men had deserted in less desperate times, they assuredly were unlikely to come back now. Nor could any reliance be placed on the hope of raising new conscripts. Davis remained oblivious and ordered more discussion the next day, when Breckinridge would arrive, with more hopeful information.[11]

Breckinridge finally arrived in Greensboro, late in the evening of April 12, and confirmed that R. E. Lee had indeed surrendered.[12] In talks that ensued, Beauregard and Johnston "agreed in the opinion that the Southern Confederacy was overthrown." Nothing was left but for Davis to initiate negotiations with General Sherman. Mallory agreed: it was time to negotiate. But to Mallory's urging that Johnston point out this course to Davis, Johnston demurred, believing that the task properly belonged to the president's "constitutional advisers." Johnston nevertheless declared that at a scheduled meeting the next day, "you will not find me reticient."[13]

Johnston bluntly informed Breckinridge that further resistance was futile, and indeed it would only add to the sufferings of both the South's soldiers and people, with no beneficial effect on a cause that was simply dead. As W. C. Davis observes, "Johnston argued that the only power remaining in Davis's hands now was that of ending the war by giving up resistance, which he ought to do at once. Breckinridge, of course, agreed and had felt the same for weeks." Johnston's and Beauregard's words, Steven E. Woodworth asserts, were "wormwood and gall to Davis."[14]

Davis and some of his entourage apparently thought there was still a good opportunity to work out a negotiated peace if desired, "even *after* the Confederacy's military options had been exhausted."[15] Whether that was true or not, Davis would have none of it. His choice was to eschew any negotiated peace short of outright independence. As Steve Woodworth asserts, "The most striking question about the collapse of the Confederacy is not why negotiation failed but, rather, why it was never attempted in earnest, on a realistic basis, on the Confederate side."[16] Woodworth concludes that "a reasonable Confederate effort at peacemaking in early 1865 would have entailed accepting the inevitable and negotiating other valuable considerations. What Davis had to offer was an early and assured end to hostilities, saving thousands of lives and millions of dollars."[17] Davis was not inclined to do so.

The next morning, April 13, most of the cabinet, Davis, and later the two generals met in John Taylor Wood's apartment. "As he did so often," Cooper observes, "Davis began with small talk, but soon he became serious. He admitted the scale of recent disasters, but did not think them fatal."[18] As W. C. Davis puts it, "It was the old mantra yet again. Renew their spirit, bring their stragglers and deserters back into the ranks, and they could yet achieve their independence. Johnston did not speak at first, perhaps dumbfounded by Davis's optimism."[19]

Davis later wrote that at this meeting, despite "the gravity of our position. . . , I did not think we should despair." He reviewed current matters with his government officials and then called the generals in. As he conceived it, this conference with Beauregard and Johnston "was not to learn their opinion as to what might be done by negotiation with the United States government, but to derive from them information in regard to the army under their command, and what it was feasible and advisable to do as a military problem." Davis was not a man who ever wanted to hear any talk about surrendering.[20] By this time he was beyond reality.

Postmaster General John Reagan recalled this meeting as "one of the most solemnly funereal I ever attended." Still, Davis presided in his usual fashion, spoke on a number of unrelated topics, and finally came to the issue that so concerned everyone else present. "Of course we all feel the magnitude of the moment," Mallory recalled Davis saying. "Our late disasters are terrible; but I do not think we should regard them as fatal. I think we can whip the enemy yet, if our people will turn out. We must look at matters calmly, however, and see what is left for us to do. Whatever can be done must be done at once."[21]

A silent pause followed. Davis thought Johnston to be reserved and "far less than sanguine," and he was right. Neither of the two generals thought that any hope remained. They assessed Confederate strength as twenty-five thousand effectives as opposed to three hundred thousand under Grant and Sherman. Johnston stated that he believed the Southern people were hopelessly war weary and "will not fight." Indeed, he listed the disadvantages of the situation: overwhelming odds, increasing desertions, deficient supplies, and poor morale. He then declared, "It would be the greatest of human crimes for us to attempt to continue the war." It was time to initiate negotiations, he thought, and it was President Davis who should do it. Mallory sensed Johnston's bitterness and noted, "The tone and manner, almost spiteful, in which General Johnston jerked out brief decisive sentences, pausing at every period, left no doubt as to his own convictions." As W. C. Davis observes, "Johnston spoke deliberately, the expression on his face mirroring the somberness of his words, and revealing as well the utter detestation he felt for Davis. . . . It would be a crime to continue the war, Johnston concluded. The president should immediately open peace negotiations."[22]

Two or three minutes of silence followed. As Johnston had spoken, Davis sat fumbling with a piece of paper "without a change of position or expression." After a long pause, Davis asked Beauregard for his opinion. He was in full agreement with Johnston. Another silence followed. Davis then turned to the cabinet members for their reaction to what the generals had said. As W. C. Davis points out, "This was the moment Breckinridge had been working toward since he first asked Lee for his own report, and the same from his department heads, some two months earlier." Davis had no support from them; all except Benjamin agreed with the two generals. "Only Benjamin advocated war," observes Cooper. "Reagan actually brought up what no one else had been willing to mention: capitulation. For the first time, the official family had broken ranks; it no longer stood as one with the president."[23]

Davis was obviously annoyed and objected vociferously that the United States surely would not recognize his authority to negotiate. Johnston countered that perhaps the opposing commanders could serve as intermediaries. Reagan then suggested terms that Johnston might offer to Sherman, including disbanding the Confederacy's military forces, recognition by the South that the U.S. government and Constitution prevailed everywhere in the prewar nation, preservation of the currently extant state governments, assurance of individual political rights and of no prosecutions except for Davis and the cabinet, permission for all Confederate soldiers to return unmolested to their homes, and an immediate cease-fire truce while any other issues were settled. Davis then dictated a letter with these proposals; Johnston signed it and Davis authorized him to take it to Sherman.[24]

Mark Grimsley argues that "within the American tradition of civil-military relations such a stem was almost unthinkable [that is, for military leaders to balk at their commander in chief's insistence on continuing warfare in a struggle they were convinced was lost]. Yet the story of the Confederacy's final months is, in large part, the story of how its generals shifted from trying to fight a lost war to trying to end it. They, more than their civilian counterparts, found the courage to say 'enough.' "[25]

"It seems apparent," Grimsley asserts, "that by [February 22, 1865] Lee believed the Confederate cause was hopeless." And thus did he begin communicating with certain civilian officials, including Breckinridge—who was also a Major General.[26] When he eventually was forced to surrender his army, it "completely transformed the strategic situation. There was now no possibility whatever of even checking, much less defeating Grant or Sherman."[27] Beauregard and Johnston tried to convince Davis of that reality. Davis, however, wanted somehow for Johnston to disengage his army from contact with Sherman's and to move it, or at least a significant part of it, safely away to fight again another day elsewhere.[28]

It was significant that Davis's message to Sherman did not include the word *surrender:*

> The results of the recent campaign in Virginia have changed the relative military condition of the belligerents. I am therefore induced to address you in this form of inquiry, whether, in order to stop the further effusion of blood and devastation of property, you are willing to make a temporary suspension of active operations, and to communicate to Lieutenant-General Grant, commanding the Armies of the United States, the request that he will take like action in regard to other armies; the object being to permit the civil authorities to enter into the needful arrangements to terminate the existing war.[29]

Michael Ballard suggests that Davis was contradicting "his own argument that Federal officials would not recognize their Confederate counterparts. He may have intentionally done so to sabotage the negotiations and thus keep the struggle for independence alive. His performance during the conference certainly underscored his belief that the peace talks would fail." W. C. Davis agrees, observing that "an armistice in the meantime only served his purpose by allowing more time for him to inspirit his soldiers and his people. . . . In short, Davis had nothing to lose by letting Johnston have his way, because he knew that he could himself prevent anything coming of the meeting. . . . In his own obsession with independence or nothing, he simply could not grasp that for the rest—probably even Benjamin—independence had for some time ceased to be a consideration."[30]

As Davis understood things: if the armistice talks should fail, then Johnston was to follow him southwest, with all the cavalry and artillery and all the infantry that could be mounted, to join him and other Confederate troops still remaining in the Gulf states. Johnston left the meeting with more realistic expectations of the future than Davis had.

This meeting was an important indicator of the decline in Davis's status and authority as president. His cabinet always before had stood with him in his resolve to fight on; now, with the exception of Benjamin (who may have been only humoring his old friend), they were ready to yield. Davis was standing virtually alone. Whether deluded or simply pure in his faith or both, Davis ended the meeting manifesting true belief that all was not yet lost. He was still president and he was going to exercise his power (what little remained), whatever others might think. "When the generals and ministers departed," W. C. Davis notes, "Davis remained at Wood's and allowed the iron mask to fall from his face. Seeing the mood revealed on Davis's face, Wood wrote in his diary that 'depression is universal and disorganization is setting in.'"[31]

Breckinridge and Benjamin, W. C. Davis notes, "approached the president either singly or together and suggested that it was time to consider plans for his escape from the country. That presented a challenge, for Davis told them both that no matter what happened, he would not leave Confederate soil so long as there was an organized band of men anywhere willing to resist. Before they left Greensboro, Davis's attitude was common knowledge among all the cabinet." Mallory mused that "he shrank from the idea of abandoning any body of men who might still be found willing to strike for the cause, and gave little attention to the question of his personal safety."[32]

Davis's attitude was complicated by a tenuous situation in North Carolina. Governor Vance had entered into discussions concerning negotiating a return of North Carolina into the Union. A deal had been struck to permit a special train to pass through the military lines so that an appropriate conference might take place. When Archer Anderson, Johnston's assistant adjutant general, learned of this scheme, he telegraphed both Johnston and Davis. Davis's response was to order the arrest of Vance's commissioners. "No intercourse with the enemy permitted," the order stated, "except under proper military flag of truce." Vance wired an explanation to Davis, saying, "It is not my intention to do anything subversive of your prerogative or without consultation with yourself." What Vance had done, however, belied his words. Davis fired back: "I could not attribute to you such purpose as you disclaim, and your military experience and good judgment will render it unnecessary to explain why the commanding general cannot properly allow any intercourse with the enemy except under his authority and with his full knowledge and consent."[33]

The train carrying Vance's emissaries was soon recaptured by Federal cavalry, and the diplomats met with Sherman. The general expressed doubts about a truce. Vance meanwhile headed to Greensboro to see Davis personally. The governor's emissaries had made no headway with Sherman, but Johnston was in communication with him. One observer thought that the spirit of the Army of Tennessee remained "defiant, and more than ready to try conclusions with Sherman in a pitched battle." Rumors that Johnston might surrender to Sherman squelched this notion precipitately, and a rapidly increasing number of soldiers opted to desert.[34]

The collapse was continuing elsewhere in the Confederacy. James Harrison Wilson's cavalry wandered through Georgia without resistance. On April 12, Confederate forces evacuated Mobile, and only hours later Federal forces occupied it.[35]

Davis at last received the official message from R. E. Lee himself reporting the surrender. Lee's son, Robert E. Lee Jr., was standing near Davis when the telegram came at headquarters. Young Lee noted that before Davis had seen the message, he seemed at ease and confident, again reiterating his belief that the war could be continued and that success might crown further operations, west of the Mississippi. Now Davis turned away as he "silently wept bitter tears." Young Lee remembered that "he seemed quite broken . . . by this tangible evidence of the loss of his army and the misfortune of its general. All of us, respecting his great grief, silently withdrew, leaving him with Colonel Wood."[36]

This message from General Lee, in his hands at last, proved to be the catalyst that induced Davis to accept the opinion of his staff and the cabinet that the government should be moved farther south, perhaps to Charlotte. Regardless of how things might turn out between Sherman and Johnston, the Confederate high civil officials would be in harm's way if they did not move promptly.

Moreover, they needed to be close to the seacoast because if negotiations did fail, they wanted Davis to be able to leave the country. Such, generally, was the mind-set of most of the entourage that would accompany Davis as he fled further south. As W. C. Davis puts it, "The secretary of war would take control of the retreat of the government, and make Davis's escape from Yankee hands his own special mission."[37]

On April 15, the remnants of the Confederate government once again made ready to move. "Davis himself," observes W. C. Davis, "was scarcely involved in preparations for abandoning Greensboro, being often lost in a black mood. 'Everything is dark,' he wrote to Varina by courier on April 14." Secretary of the Treasury George Trenholm was incapacitated, so Davis took charge himself of the Treasury funds. He ordered that thirty-nine thousand dollars in silver be transferred to Beauregard's army train; another two hundred eighty-eight thousand in bullion and coin would be carried with Davis's entourage for the government to use as operating funds. The bulk of the Treasury, however, had been sent from Danville to Charlotte on April 9. Under the command of Colonel William Parker, the train, with the money aboard, had left Charlotte on April 13; unknown to Davis, Varina and the children were also on this train. She had grown fearful of capture because of the many movements of Federal cavalry in the vicinity.[38]

Escape from Greensboro proved difficult, for the railroad had been severed by Union raiders. A train of wagons and ambulances was hastily assembled, though Davis, Mallory, Breckinridge, Reagan, and Davis's aides left on horseback. Breckinridge and Beauregard had managed to scrape up a small cavalry escort for them, consisting of about thirteen hundred horsemen, and led by the war secretary's cousin, W. C. P. Breckinridge. There was also a small group of armed Mississippians, who Ballard surmises were refugees from R. E. Lee's army, who rode along to provide additional protection for Davis.[39] And so, stretching through the late afternoon and early evening, the Confederate government struck out on its way toward Charlotte, about eighty miles to the southwest.[40] "Even before Davis and his retinue were gone," W. C. Davis observes, "a mob formed and stormed the warehouses, looting them at will, and quite a number of returned soldiers were among their number. That alone told Mallory their plight. 'The plundering disposition thus displayed was painfully significant of the futility of all further effort in behalf of the Confederacy,' he lamented." Indeed, "It showed how even Confederates could now sink quickly to the lowest ebb of human behavior."[41]

Davis and his entourage had a hard journey that first day, horses and wheels often sinking into muddy roads. Davis and Breckinridge rode at the head of the column, and a Greensboro resident peered at them intently as they passed;

he long remembered "the graceful forms and dignified countenances of the two horsemen riding side by side." Years later he confessed that at that moment, "I wept for them and my country." W. C. Davis reports that "Davis appeared moody, visibly showing his depression. [Mallory observed that] 'this was the first day on which I had noticed in him any evidence of an abandonment of hope,' "[42] Most of the rest of the group were low in spirit, too, but not Benjamin, who puffed a cigar and recited Tennyson's poem on the death of the Duke of Wellington. They made only ten miles that first afternoon, and most of the group spent the night of April 15 encamped near Jamestown. Davis and his officials found lodging in a nearby house, but a servant did not recognize Davis—despite that he looked like a postage stamp—and put General Cooper in a private bedroom instead. Davis and "one or two others were presently provided for elsewhere," wrote Harrison, "and the rest of us bestowed ourselves to slumber on the floor, before the roaring fire."[43]

The trip resumed the next morning, with better horses; Davis even rode a sporty filly that his host had presented to him. "Davis's spirits seemed to return to him during the ride," W. C. Davis writes, "he always took cheer when out of doors on horseback." Harrison reported that "he seemed to have had a great load taken from his mind, to feel relieved of responsibilities." W. C. Davis notes that "the moodiness disappeared, and in its place, Davis was once more cheerful, unusually so. His conversation turned on literature, Lord Byron and Walter Scott, to his favorite themes of horses and dogs he had owned and loved, even horticulture and wildlife." Harrison observed that "his familiarity with, and correct taste in, the English literature of the last generation, his varied experiences in life, his habits of close observation, and his extraordinary memory, made him a charming companion when disposed to talk." W. C. Davis suggests that "Davis's spirits no doubt stemmed from his own conviction that he was leading them not to the end but only to a new beginning."[44]

They still made their way slowly and with difficulty and finally encamped about four miles from Lexington. For total lack of available housing there, Davis shared accommodations with the others at the campsite. Later in the evening Breckinridge received news of several messages for him in Lexington; one was from Johnston, asking for Breckinridge's "immediate presence" at the negotiations with Sherman. Davis dispatched Breckinridge back to Greensboro, asking Reagan to accompany him. Reagan had written up a list of terms as a basis for negotiation, which Davis was sure would be rejected. "Davis fully believed," writes W. C. Davis, "indeed hoped, that negotiations would fall down on those very terms authored by Reagan. . . . The postmaster's presence would be Davis's guarantee that no substantial variation or compromise would come. Without realizing it, Reagan was being sent as Davis's concealed weapon to kill a peace."[45]

While Sherman submitted the agreement to the Federal government for approval, Davis and his remaining caravan continued their movement south. They were very near Salisbury by the evening of April 17. Frank Vizetelly, an artist-correspondent for the *Illustrated London News,* had joined the group at Greensboro and sketched for his paper the party's precarious crossing of the Yadkin River. Tension could be sensed, as Federal cavalry were known to be roaming nearby. The travelers set up camp across the river; Davis was invited by the local Episcopal minister to be his houseguest for the night. This rendered the president rather cheery, and he stayed up late, chewing on an unlit cigar and discussing how sad the effects were of R. E. Lee's surrender.[46]

The trip continued toward Concord the next day. Some of the group, finding the going to be too unpleasant, were happy to be able to board a train that was carrying excess baggage to Charlotte. At Concord, Davis had a tent pitched, but then a local resident, Victor Barrister, invited him and his cabinet to spend the night in his home. Many of the town's citizens paid calls during the evening and the next morning, to express warm greetings to Davis.[47]

The president and his entourage arrived in Charlotte on April 19. Despite that the city and county had been strongly supportive of the war effort, attitudes had begun to sour. The town itself was beautiful, as one soldier noted: "This Charlotte is a sweet little town and Spring in all her loveliness is here, breathing freshness and fragrance through the rose bordered streets." But the governmental officials were not so enthralled with the people. As one asserted, "Of those citizens that I have seen, only a very small minority possess the air of respectability. Of the ladies the same seems to be the rule." As Cooper observes, "Fearing reprisals, some people refused to take the president into their homes. On April 16, for the first time, Davis and several cabinet secretaries camped out."[48]

Finding a suitable house for Davis proved difficult, indeed just as hard as it had been in Greensboro. Harrison had written Varina, asking her to search for the needed accommodations, but she had departed with the specie train and no one knew where she was. Secretary Mallory struck a balance in his estimation of the people's degree of welcome to the government, believing that the officials were received with "kindness and courtesy," but it was clear that the cause was hopeless. A superintendent of the Southern Express Company offered Davis quarters in his home. This proved acceptable, though some of the citizenry grumbled about Davis residing in the domicile of a Yankee. Otherwise, the residents were remarkably cooperative in providing for the government's needs, even permitting them to establish their headquarters in the Charlotte branch of the Bank of North Carolina.[49]

"Davis still hoped for some miracle," Cooper observes:

> In a brief, impromptu address to soldiers, he declared, "the cause is not yet dead." "Determination and fortitude," he claimed, could yet bring victory. [Otherwise,] "Davis tried to busy himself with the duties of chief executive. He deliberated with his cabinet about Joseph Johnston's peace negotiations. He worked to obtain artillery and cavalry for the defense of Charlotte. He also sought information on Federal movements in South Carolina and Georgia. . . . When approached by officers who had escaped capture at Lee's surrender or were not present at Johnston's, he encouraged them to head south and keep up the fight.[50]

A large crowd gathered outside the house where Davis was lodged and called for him to speak. He thanked them for this display of affection under such depressing circumstances and promised that he would see that the struggle for independence continued as long as the people desired. He admitted "having committed errors, and very grave ones," over the war's course; nevertheless, he was as dedicated as ever to "the preservation of the true principles of constitutional freedom."[51]

But even as Davis spoke, he was upstaged by the arrival of startling news: a wire arrived from Breckinridge telling of Abraham Lincoln's death. Cooper writes that "all accounts of the occasion agree that Davis voiced regret at Lincoln's death."[52] Davis remarked on the "extraordinary" nature of the message. Some of the crowd heard him and shouted requests that the wire be read aloud. It was. And then the president finished his speech, but it is doubtful that many of his listeners paid much attention, the news about Lincoln being so stunning.[53]

Many Confederates all over the South believed that Lincoln was personally to blame for the Union army's heavy destruction of their homeland. When in March 1865 John Wilkes Booth failed in his effort to capture Lincoln, some individuals, possibly even some in the Confederate high command, gave consideration to blowing up the White House at a time when a conference of senior Union officials was taking place. But the plans went awry and were abandoned, providing the catalyst that induced Booth to execute his own plan to kill Lincoln. He fired a bullet into Lincoln's head while the president was viewing a play at Ford's Theater on the evening of April 14. Lincoln died early the next day.

Davis, although certainly not shedding any tears for Lincoln, regretted that the assassination occurred. As Cooper observes, "Lincoln would have been more lenient on the South than his successor was likely to be. Davis expected no favors for himself or his fellow Confederates from Andrew Johnson."[54] Some observers later claimed Davis was cheered by the news, but Mallory, who was present, noted that Davis called the initial news "a canard." Nearly everyone who was with Davis when the news of Lincoln's death reached him later agreed that he had expressed regret.

Davis was not so fortunate, however, with the interpretations of his attitude toward Lincoln's death by a great many other people. He had a foretaste of what was to come the next day during church services. The minister, as did nearly all who offered homilies on that unhappy Easter Sunday, spoke about the assassination, calling it a "blot on American civilization" and predicting that the South was going to suffer because of it. And as he spoke, Davis later said, the minister often looked directly at him. "I think the preacher directed his remarks at me," he lamented to Preston Johnston and Harrison, "and he really seems to fancy I had something to do with the assassination."[55]

As W. C. Davis points out,

the moment Lincoln died, there were many Northerners and even Southerners who suddenly "remembered" new words in some of Davis's early war speeches in which supposedly he had boasted that Southern armies would march all the way to Philadelphia and beyond if the Yankees did not give them their independence. Now they recalled him threatening to burn and destroy Northern cities and assassinate Lincoln and the whole Washington Congress. Within a few weeks, Davis's host Bates who was not even present until after the fact, added to the fiction. [Bates] would claim in May that after reading the telegraph, the president reacted with a quotation from *Macbeth:* "If it were to be done, it were better it were well done," meaning Davis approved the act and that Johnson, Seward, and others should have been killed as well.[56]

There was little or nothing now for the remnant government to do except wait for the return of Breckinridge. According to W. C. Davis,

The government was at a virtual standstill, and what time Davis spent in his makeshift office, he passed either in monitoring the continuing deterioration of forces in the field, or on inconsequential affairs, such as trying to find saddles for some of [General Basil W.] Duke's troopers and handling a dispute over rent due from the government for warehouse space in Salisbury. If Davis felt optimistic, those around him did not share his hope. "Disintegration is setting in rapidly," [presidential aide John Taylor] Wood noted. "Everything is falling to pieces."[57]

Davis was pleased to get a letter from Varina, who reported that she was safe and had been warmly received in Abbeville, South Carolina. Their young son was ill, and she was depressed over the situation, but otherwise she assured him all was well. Relieved, Davis threw himself into routine correspondence. He tried to get information concerning Federal troop movements in South Carolina, and he notified Howell Cobb in Macon, Georgia, that he should try to gather whatever force he could and make some attempt to block James Harrison Wilson's raiding cavalry.[58]

Breckinridge and his party, grappling with many difficulties in their travel, finally got to Charlotte early in the morning on April 22 and gave Davis a full report on the peace agreement between Johnston and Sherman. They had worked out a rather attractive deal with the Union general. Indeed, they had even broached the subject of getting some financial reparation out of Washington in return for the enormous loss in capital investment in black slaves. "Lincoln had more than once proposed the idea," observes W. C. Davis, and "given the financial devastation of the South after four years of war, restitution even in pennies on the dollar could save them from a prostration that might last for decades. . . . Indeed, when the details of Sherman's terms became known to Northern friends of [Breckinridge], some, like fellow Kentuckian James Speed, Lincoln's attorney general, declared that Sherman 'had been seduced by Breckinridge.' "[59]

At a cabinet meeting that evening Davis asked each member to prepare a written assessment of what to do. They worked on the requested documents all night and the next day. Everyone, including Benjamin, agreed that the terms should be accepted. The only alternative would be partisan warfare, and as Mallory said, that "would be more disastrous to our own people than it could possibly be to the enemy." The cabinet questioned whether Davis had constitutional power to dissolve the Confederacy, but nearly all of them believed that the circumstances nullified taking that into consideration. As Attorney General George Davis said, and most agreed, the president should act "for the speedy delivery of the people from the horrors of war."[60]

Actually, the cabinet members were quite satisfied with the agreement. It did not seem dishonorable to Benjamin or to George Davis, who thought Confederates were willing to accept "far less liberal [terms] than the convention proposes." Reagan even believed that because the document contained no mention of slavery, the institution might be saved.[61]

Jefferson Davis, however, had quite a different set of opinions. Primarily, he believed that the Federal authorities would reject the agreement. According to Cooper,

> On the twenty-third [of April] President Davis attended church and heard the sermon "And Thus It Must Be." That afternoon he wrote his wife a long letter,

which he sent by messenger. Lee's surrender "destroyed the hopes I entertained when we parted," he explained. He admitted that deserters and stragglers were not now coming back into the ranks. "Panic has seized the country." "The issue," he confessed, "is one which it is very painful for me to meet." He envisioned agonizing options: "On one hand, is the long night of oppression which will follow the return of our people to the 'Union': on the other, the suffering of the women and children, and carnage among the few brave patriots who would still oppose the invader, and who, unless the people would rise en-masse to sustain them, would struggle but to die in vain. . . . I have sacrificed so much for the cause of the Confederacy that I can measure my ability to make any further sacrifice required, and am assured there is but one to which I am not equal—My wife and my children—How are they to be saved from degradation or want is now my care."[62]

He suggested to Varina that she should try to escape, going either to Texas or to some foreign country, whichever "may be more practicable." He intended to leave Charlotte quite soon, and if "a devoted band of Cavalry will cling to me," he too would try to make it to Texas, and "if nothing can be done there which it will be proper to do," he would push on to Mexico, "and have the world from which to choose a location."[63]

The president meanwhile tried to reestablish contact with North Carolina's Governor Vance. This proved successful, and Vance arrived in Charlotte late in the afternoon on April 23, to attend a meeting with Davis and the cabinet. When Vance inquired about the future, Davis suggested that he gather as many North Carolina soldiers as he could and go to the Trans-Mississippi. This was not what Vance wanted or expected to hear, and Davis's proposal was met with silence. Breckinridge broke it by insisting that more fighting would accomplish nothing and that Vance should stay and take care of his people as best he could. Davis sighed and reluctantly agreed.[64]

Davis at last yielded to the arguments posited by his cabinet members and telegraphed Johnston his approval of the Breckinridge-Sherman agreement. But he cautioned the general: "Further instructions will be given as to the details of negotiation and the methods of executing the terms of agreement when [I am] notified by you of the readiness on the part of the general commanding U.S. forces to proceed with the arrangement."[65]

After several days passed, reality at last cleared Davis's mental fog, and he abandoned whatever scant hope he might have had for any acceptable peace. The Confederate government, the scant part of it still left, once more began preparations to move, in an atmosphere of total disarray. On April 27, the cabinet assembled in Charlotte for its final meeting. Harrison had already departed, going to Abbeville to try to check on Varina and her party's safety.[66]

There was not much of substance that could be done at this meeting. The leadership resigned or simply went away.

The Subsistence Bureau managed only to continue distribution of supplies to some returning soldiers and to hospitals. The Ordnance Bureau was totally gone, although Josiah Gorgas had one final meeting with a board of examiners to consider the last cadet's qualifications for promotion to lieutenant; he passed. But the pathos of that event lingered in Gorgas's mind. He thought that among all his Confederate experiences, nothing so often entered his mind as "that twilight examination of the *last* Confederate Cadet."[67] Most of the remaining archives were left in Charlotte. The State Department records and the Great Seal of the Confederacy already had been deposited in the Mecklenburg County Courthouse.[68]

On April 26 the government officials loaded up wagons; and Davis, with five cabinet officers, his aides, and a cavalry escort, mounted horses to go to Abbeville, in western South Carolina near the Georgia border. Despite that the Breckinridge-Sherman agreement provided for "universal amnesty," Breckinridge was prescient enough to know that he and Davis quite probably would be dealt with harshly by the Northern government. Whatever Davis might be entertaining in his mind, Breckinridge was dedicated to getting himself and Davis and the rest of the party out of the country as soon as possible.[69] Lincoln himself had said months before that he would prefer that Davis and the others simply leave the country. "Breckinridge had helped to beat Sherman, so it seemed," observes W. C. Davis, "now he had to beat Davis."[70]

Furthermore, "Having seen the negotiations result favorably, and Davis apparently yielding at least to the consensus of his cabinet, the secretary of war regarded the safety of the president as now his first priority." Breckinridge had even been able to secure from Sherman a tacit agreement "that he would not interfere with any effort to get Davis out of the country, so long as it came soon." But "within hours of Breckinridge's notifying Johnston that Davis's acceptance was on the way, Johnston sent another telegram. . . . It was all for nothing. Washington rejected Sherman's agreement. . . . Once again the Yankees gave Davis what he wanted."[71] What was left of the Confederate government now left Charlotte, with the officials in quite a different mind-set from that of Davis.

As Michael Ballard observes, "Jefferson Davis did not ride out of Charlotte a dispirited man." One person who spied him thought that he looked "sad and, indeed, hopeless," but just a few days before Davis had asserted, "I *cannot* feel like a beaten man." Again, Ballard writes, "Davis never allowed his personal feelings to interfere with his convictions," or, we might add, his delusions. The enthusiasm exuded by his cavalry escort lifted his spirits. Mallory, however, was worried by the president's response and the horse soldiers' bravado about taking the fight across the Mississippi River. Davis, wrote Mallory, seemed to lose all concern for his personal well-being.[72] His emotional commitment to the Confederacy still blinded him from seeing the disintegration all around him.

Many contemporaries agreed that Davis was flying from reality. One Confederate noted with sadness, "Poor President, he is unwilling to see what all around him see. He cannot bring himself to believe that after four years of glorious struggle we are to be crushed." Charles E. L. Stuart thought that Davis's attitude went even deeper than irrational denial: "The principle he had contended for was still as dear to him as ever," but the ability "to reflect its features [*sic*] himself was irrevocably gone. He felt himself unseated but not dethroned."[73]

The entourage spent the first night out of Charlotte at Fort Mill. One of the officers suggested to Davis that the leisurely gait they maintained indicated that he was "travelling like a president and not a fugitive."[74] Trenholm, his health continuing to worsen, wrote out his resignation the next morning. He thanked Davis for his "kindness and courtesy." Davis responded: "You may have forgotten that I warned you when you were about to take office that our wants so far exceeded our means that you could not expect entire success and should anticipate censure and perhaps the loss of financial reputation."[75]

A hurried cabinet meeting was held under a big tree on the lawn of William White's home, and John Reagan was named interim secretary of the treasury. Reagan did not want the appointment and argued that he already had enough to do. But there being virtually no Treasury left, Davis countered that "there would not be much for the Secretary of the Treasury to do." So Reagan took charge of the eight hundred thousand dollars in paper and the eighty thousand in bullion.[76] This done, they sat outside and watched their host's two sons, Eli and John, play marbles in the yard. Someone suggested that the men should join the boys. "At once," W. C. Davis relates, "the president, the secretary of war, secretary of state, and the postmaster-treasurer were on their knees, marbles in hand, spending an hour at a spirited contest amid peals of laughter, while Mallory watched and saw good evidence of many hours' employment in their own boyhoods, as they revealed a sure grasp of the rules of the game."[77]

The governmental remnant continued southwest, along its intended route of just over 180 miles. They crossed the Catawba River on a pontoon used as a ferry. "What a sight to see Jeff Davis and Breckinridge and the Cabinet standing on the pontoon," wrote Tench Tilghman, a Maryland native with the party. "They reminded him of King Robert the Bruce withdrawing into the mountains of Scotland with the faithful," writes W. C. Davis, "to bide the time for their return. But Tilghman did not expect a return. 'The cause has gone up,' he concluded. 'God only knows what will be the end of all this.' "[78]

The party encamped near the Broad River on the evening of April 28. Meanwhile, Johnston had officially surrendered on April 26, and the news reached Davis and his party, further instilling gloom.[79] And "with that act," observes Mark Grimsley, "Gen. Joseph E. Johnston ordained the final fate of the Confederacy. The surrender in North Carolina transformed the hitherto orderly retreat of the Davis government into the 'flight into oblivion' of memory."[80]

Grimsley has speculated on how the campaign in North Carolina might have turned out differently. Beauregard had elected to defend both Augusta and Charleston: "Within the framework of what political scientists have styled 'war termination' scenarios," this decision was "quite sensible" from the perspective of securing the best possible situation for favorable peace negotiations, because "a Confederacy still in possession of these two important cities would appear stronger than a Confederacy that had lost them." But doing this left Sherman a relatively clear path to Columbia.[81] There were two possible ways to stymie his advance. First, since he moved in separated columns, a concentration of sufficient force could have been directed at one, thus inflicting defeat in detail. Second, since Sherman was depending on supplies gleaned from the countryside, these could have been destroyed. Yet "few Confederate soldiers could muster the ruthlessness to carry out a 'scorched earth' policy." Indeed, Grimsley asserts that "it is fair to observe that the dearth of significant Confederate resistance was a critical factor in Sherman's triumphant, desolating advance."[82]

Johnston subsequently chose to surrender, and as Grimsley observes, "Here the role played by the military commanders takes on new significance. Consider the moment when Davis's cabinet finally turned against him and insisted that he open negotiations with Sherman. The catalyst was not John C. Breckinridge, John H. Reagan, Stephen R. Mallory, or any other cabinet official. It was Joe Johnston." Indeed, "his unilateral decision to surrender rendered that government a mere gaggle of fleeing fugitives."[83]

Quickly absorbing the news of Johnston's surrender, Davis soon regained his composure and spent much time riding among the accompanying cavalrymen. According to W. C. Davis,

> Micajah H. Clark [the acting treasurer] found the president especially impressive at such a moment. "To me he appeared incomparably grander in the nobleness of his great heart and head, than when he reviewed victorious armies returning from well-won fields," he thought. . . . Clark saw him presenting an almost serene face, "beguiling the tedium of the weary miles with cheerful conversation, reminiscences, and anecdotes—as a gracious host entertaining his guests." Everyone knew that this proudest of men must be suffering within, but what he felt he kept to himself. Mallory frequently observed him at rest stops,

when Davis stretched out on a blanket, his head resting on his saddle, or sat leaning against a tree, cigar in mouth, and regaled his associates with reminiscences.
"He was always more at ease, & pleasantly talkative in the woods, than under a
roof," said Mallory, "and he decidedly preferred the bivouac to the bed room."[84]

Often along the way Davis managed to perform some act of kindness for
citizens he encountered. Children would find their way onto his lap, and they
brought him flowers while he told anecdotes. Once when the party stopped
for a drink of water, "the lady of the house asked Davis if he was the president," notes W. C. Davis, "and on his answering, she held up her infant, saying, 'He is named for you.' Davis reached into his pocket and took out a gold
piece, giving it to her to keep for the child. As they rode off again, he confided
to Reagan that it was the last coin he had."[85]

The party crossed the Broad River on April 29 and pushed on to Abbeville.
In the nearby village of Unionville, they had lunch in the home of Brigadier
General William H. Wallace, who had surrendered with R. E. Lee. They
reached Cokesbury the evening of May 1. Davis meanwhile had sent Preston
Johnston off on a locomotive south to Chester to fetch Braxton Bragg and his
wife to join the party; the president wanted his opinion of their military
prospects. Bragg told Davis that he thought it was useless to continue the
struggle, and scouting reports indicated that there were strong Federal cavalry
forces wreaking havoc seemingly everywhere. W. C. Davis suggests that "the
president must have felt crestfallen when the general said not what he wanted
to hear but that he agreed with the cabinet and felt that any further fighting
was pointless."[86]

The next day, Davis received news from Varina and from Burton Harrison.
They were trying to go toward Atlanta, by way of Washington, Georgia, and
would wait there for instructions from Davis. But on April 30, General
Richard Taylor had agreed to a truce to discuss surrendering all the Confederate forces in his Department of Alabama, Mississippi, and East Louisiana.
This would further reduce any scant chance that Davis might successfully
make his way overland to the Trans-Mississippi.[87]

As the retreating party trudged on, crowds turned out and cheered. Women
and children often lined both sides of the road and even strewed flowers.
Affected by the adulation, Davis stopped and spoke. One of those present
recalled that "great tears rolled down his haggard cheeks as he bade us be
cheerful—trusting always in the wisdom and goodness of God who doeth all
things well." In Cokesbury, Davis received "generous gifts of fruit and flowers, and the warmest expressions of sympathy and affection." During the entire
trek, Cooper observes,

Davis was cordial and sociable. He chatted pleasantly with all, including cabinet members, aides, Carolinians he encountered, and soldiers in his escort. All reported him calm and relaxed, at least outwardly. In "very bright and agreeable conversation," often with a cigar in his mouth, he talked about men, books—especially Sir Walter Scott and Lord Byron—dogs, how to build roads, and generally about earlier days. Not much business was transacted.[88]

Around 10:00 A.M. on May 2, the tired fugitives reached Abbeville. Davis stopped at the home of Armistead Burt, "an ardent supporter," Cooper says, "who had been a prewar congressman. Burt had been Varina's host until her departure two days earlier." Breckinridge spoke with the cavalry commanders and sensed trouble: morale was declining and many of the troopers had become truly convinced that the war was over. Breckinridge determined that Davis should call a council of war. Between 4:00 and 4:30 P.M. Davis, Breckinridge, Bragg, and the five cavalry commanders conferred in the Burt parlor. "On this occasion as at Greensboro and Charlotte," Cooper says, "Davis talked about continuing the war. Admitting the bleakness of the situation, he professed it no worse than the black days of the American Revolution." But Davis's opening statement also revealed the haphazard nature of his party's sojourn: "It is time that we adopt some definite plan upon which the further prosecution of our struggle shall be conducted. I have summoned you for consultation. I feel that I ought to do nothing without the advice of my military chiefs."[89]

The officers were "taken aback," Cooper says. "The cavalry commanders remonstrated while Breckinridge and Bragg kept silent. The commanders voiced a unanimous opinion: they could envision no military future." Davis listened to each officer's report on the condition of his men, and then firmly replied that the cause was not yet lost. Even if Davis could get no more soldiers than were with him now, he continued, three thousand would be a sufficient core for the people to rally around.[90]

Once again, an embarrassing silence followed. The officers finally blurted out, each of them, that continuation of the war was not possible. Still oblivious, Davis was offended and asked them why they were still in the field. "We answered," wrote Basil W. Duke, "that we were desirous of affording him an opportunity of escaping the depredation of capture. . . . We said that we would ask our men to follow us until his safety was assured, and would risk them in battle for that purpose, but would not fire another shot in an effort to continue the hostilities." Davis's face paled, his body trembled, and he left the room clinging to Breckinridge for support. Soon most of the remaining cabinet departed, and most of the military escort also left. For Davis, reality had finally broken through the cloud; he agreed "that all was indeed lost." Davis, Cooper points out, "would never again meet with military commanders as their commander in chief."[91]

Meanwhile, despite not having received expected instructions from Davis, Varina and her party again departed because there was smallpox rumored to be in the area and Winnie had never been vaccinated. They did soon find a place where the vaccination was obtained, and then they pushed on to Washington, Georgia, where Varina wrote a letter to her husband. She expressed her "intense grief at the treacherous surrender [by Johnston] of this Department" and said she wished for Davis to have a safe conduct through "this maze of enemies." She informed him that she and Harrison had decided "to go on a line between Macon and Augusta and to make towards Pensacola, and take a ship or what else I can." Harrison added his own postscript, saying that Johnston's surrender had induced him to cancel any plan of going to Atlanta since the city and its surrounding area were now in Union hands. On May 2, Varina's wagon train rolled southwest.[92]

To the east, in Abbeville, Davis gradually recovered his composure. Micajah Clark noticed the president trying to cheer up the folk he met along the route, and Francis Lubbock thought Davis "entirely calm and unaffected." "Jefferson Davis retained command of himself," asserts Cooper. "Even on that cheerless afternoon in the Burt parlor he impressed. One brigadier recorded that he had never seen the president 'show to better advantage.' According to this officer, 'the union of dignity, graceful ability, and decision, which made his manner usually so striking was very marked in his reception of us.'" One of the midshipmen, however, thought that "Davis's party reminded him of some pitiful Central American revolutionary junta on the run."[93]

Captain William H. Parker called on Davis and tried to convince him that he was in imminent danger of capture if he did not leave at once—not just Abbeville but the country. Again Davis declared he would never leave Southern soil in inglorious flight. "The mere idea that he might be looked upon as fleeing, seemed to arouse him," and that was the heart of the matter, the captain concluded. W. C. Davis asserts that "Davis's own towering pride drove him now. Contrary to what he had written Varina just a few days before, unconsciously he was willing more soldiers to fight and even die, not just to keep alive a cause that all objective men knew was dead, but to spare him the personal humiliation of defeat or flight."[94]

Basil Duke offered his own analysis:

Mr. Davis seemed overwhelmed with a sense of the national calamity; he at times exhibited some impatience and irascibility, but I never witnessed in a man a more entire abnegation of self, or selfish considerations. He seemed to cling obstinately to the hope of continuing the struggle in order to accomplish the great end of Southern independence—his whole soul was given to that thought, and an appearance of slackness upon the part of others seemed to arouse his indignation. . . . I think the very ardor of his resolution prevented him from properly estimating the resources at his command.[95]

"There in Burt's Abbeville parlor, after three months of battle with the president," observes W. C. Davis, "Breckinridge finally won by burying any further practical hope of renewing the cause." He allowed the president to rest for an hour and then

met with him again and found his resistance much reduced, though his composure had largely returned. Breckinridge pressed on him the necessity henceforth he should waste no more time dallying on the road but must leave that night with the reduced escort, collect his family at Washington or wherever they were to be found on the road, and make haste for Florida. . . . Indeed, Breckinridge may have presented the case to Davis in the form of an order, for hereafter the president made little effort to give instructions to anyone for a while, suggesting that his resistance had finally collapsed. . . . Breckinridge was sufficiently satisfied of the president's cooperation that he notified the brigade commanders that Davis had given in.[96]

"Following the council of war," Cooper writes, "the bulk of the escort was paid and dismissed from service. Toward midnight on May 2, 1865 a much smaller band left for Washington, Georgia, around fifty miles to the west." The entourage reached and crossed the Savannah River at Vienna. Davis dispatched a message to Brigadier General John C. Vaughn, commander of one of the escort cavalry brigades, to check on the possible presence of Federal cavalry in Washington.[97]

W. C. Davis observes that "the Savannah was more Rubicon than rest stop for Judah Benjamin" and suggests that "perhaps he was uncertain that the president was going to honor his promise to get out of the country. . . . Whatever the reason, *this* was as far as he was going to go with Davis." He told the president that he was going his own way, to escape by way of Florida, Cuba, or the Bahamas. Davis asked Benjamin to look after the diplomatic funds there, "with a view to arranging further credit with foreign suppliers for Kirby Smith, and then to rejoin him in the Trans-Mississippi." Benjamin masked his intent when saying final good-byes to Davis, but to Reagan, who asked where he was going, he gave a more honest answer: he was going "to the farthest place from the United States, if it takes me to the middle of China."[98] Benjamin eventually made his way to the seacoast and secured passage to England, where he subsequently had a comfortable life and successful career.[99]

It was Breckinridge's idea that Davis should strike out on his own with only a couple of guards, to try first to get to Florida and then to Cuba, but the secretary in truth was still laboring to persuade him to accept the idea of any kind of escape. Reagan joined in the conversation and the two cabinet ministers suggested that Davis should disguise himself as a common soldier; but most important, the president must leave the eastern states. Davis, however, began to feel "better and stronger, as he always did in the saddle. . . . He began wavering in his resolve. . . . Once more he started to raise objections to the idea of flight." But Breckinridge applied considerable eloquence, and Davis finally assured "him that he consented now to being spirited out of the country."[100]

Washington having been determined as safe, the Davis party headed there. Around noon, they rode into the town square, throwing the residents into "the wildest excitement." Many citizens removed their hats in respect. Here lived Davis's blustery political opponent Robert Toombs, but W. C. Davis observes, Toombs "would make no effort to see the president," at least not at first. Davis was attired in his "full suit of Confederate grey"—his pseudo uniform. It was here, that "at last, Davis got irrefutable confirmation that Johnston had actually surrendered." Bone tired, he went at once to a room in the J. J. Robertson home and immediately fell asleep. In Washington, Cooper observes, "all pretense of an organized government and official military activity was dropped."[101]

Meanwhile, at the rear of the column and still near the Savannah River, Breckinridge had troubles. Of the some twenty-five hundred cavalrymen present, only a few hundred were willing to go on. The rest wanted to go their own way, but first they wanted to be paid. "Discipline was gone," complained Quartermaster Joseph Brown with the wagon train, adding that this was "one time it was not pleasant or safe to be a quartermaster." "The cavalrymen," W. C. Davis observes, "had become 'a mob.' Breckinridge at once fell back on a weapon he had used many times before . . . his eloquence." He calmed the men down, and finally agreed that they would indeed be paid. This then was done, though with much time consumed and with great difficulty.[102]

The degree of demoralization and collapse of discipline induced Breckinridge to send word to Davis that he could count on no more than a few hundred men. "Should Davis make any change in his plans," writes W. C. Davis, "Breckinridge needed to know at once."[103] On finishing his much-needed long rest, Davis arose, only to find that Secretary Mallory was determined to resign; the president had no recourse but to accept. Davis took a moment to write a brief note of thanks to this man for his good service and loyalty over four years past, but according to W. C. Davis, "at least one man riding with Davis complained that 'Mr. Mallory deserted us,' [and this] added evidence that the hour of 'every man for himself' lay not far distant."[104]

Robert Toombs relented, W. C. Davis observes, and "even offered to extend money and his carriage to Davis, though it was surely more from concern over the Confederacy being humiliated by the capture and prosecution of its president than from any concern for Davis the man. But that was as far as he would go. . . . He adamantly refused to invite Davis into his home or even to see him."[105]

Shortly after Mallory's departure, General Arnold Elzey and other prominent men in Washington called on Davis, urging him to recognize his personal danger and to travel thereafter with more speed and less publicity. W. C. Davis writes that Davis took this admonition "to heart, but most immediately his concern was for his family." He had received word that Harrison, with Varina and the family entourage, was only twenty miles distant along the rail line out of Washington. "Having been abandoned by everyone, it seemed, hereafter the president would take only his own counsel."[106]

On the morning of May 4, Davis made some crucial decisions. There had been no word from Breckinridge since his message of the previous evening, saying that he was paying off the soldiers who demanded it in specie. By then Davis had absorbed enough information about impending danger from nearby Yankee troops that he had decided he could delay in Washington no longer. He sent a message to Breckinridge that he was going to leave.[107]

Davis then made two momentous decisions. First, he informed Micajah Clark that he was appointing him to be the acting treasurer of the Confederate states, Davis's last official act as president, as it turned out. Clark paid off the cavalrymen, sent money to Augusta to assist paroled soldiers, and transmitted funds for Braxton Bragg and Breckinridge to use in the Trans-Mississippi West. The rest of the worthless paper money was burned, with Reagan assisting. Some of the remaining specie was deposited in the local Washington bank, and eighty-six thousand dollars was given to navy officer James Semple, who was to transport it either to Charleston or Savannah. From there, it was hoped the assets could be shipped to Confederate agents in foreign ports.[108]

Second, Davis called a conference with his staff. He decided to dissolve the government, which was rapidly dissolving anyway by itself, and to continue trying to reach his wife, accompanied by only a small escort. He had intended only a temporary dissolution of the government; still out of touch with reality, he expected to reassemble it at a more opportune time. But the morning conference had "an air of finality about it," Michael Ballard suggests. More than one of the people involved did not fail to notice the irony of having dissolved the government in a town named Washington. One of them recalled, "Providence has the most inscrutable ways of exhibiting His purposes."[109]

For himself, Davis announced, he would not take the route through Florida after all. He would try to move south and then west, still in hopes of slipping through Union lines and reaching General Richard Taylor's army in Alabama. How ironic, and tragic, for even at that moment Taylor was in the act of surrendering at Citronelle, Alabama, the Department of Alabama, Mississippi, and East Louisiana. Davis, however, believed he might be able to assemble sixty thousand to eighty thousand men, almost all cavalry, and subsist them and their mounts on Texas cattle and grass. He naively believed he could resurrect an army in the Trans-Mississippi and "continue to uphold our cause." When he left the meeting, however, General Alexander R. Lawton said sadly to a bystander, "It is all over; the Confederate Government is dissolved."[110]

By 10:00 A.M. Davis was ready to leave, dressed as usual in a suit of gray. As he made his farewells, he clasped the hand of the Reverend H. A. Tupper, the town's Baptist minister, who had tried to offer spiritual comfort to Davis; and the president said, "Though He slay me, yet will I trust in Him." A number of the people present offered tearful good wishes, and Frank Vizetelly, the journalist still traveling with the disintegrating government, saw tears in Davis's eyes, too. "This, I suppose, is the end of the Confederacy," mused General Arnold Elzey's wife.[111]

At nearly 2:00 A.M. on May 3, the group at last moved out, Davis's column now less than twenty men. The group headed toward the Savannah River bridge and Georgia. Meanwhile Union authorities posted a one hundred thousand dollar reward for Davis. "At this point," observes Cooper, "what had been a retreat turned into flight."[112]

John Headley later wrote a moving account of the scene as they bade farewell:

> The tender-hearted sons and daughters of Georgia, the young and the old stood about in groups and spoke in whispers and some wiped away tears. There was for the moment the stillness of a benediction and there was a look of despair on every face. . . . But never a murmur of lost respect or of blame for the vanquished President fell from the lips of citizen or soldier. Even the mothers of buried boys and the widows whose husbands were among the slain . . . did not chide or weep alone for their own. This disconsolate hour was bitter in sorrow, in desolation and in terror, and the spirits of all were transfixed upon the cause of the common woe.[113]

On May 6 Davis finally received news of Varina, who was only a few miles ahead, near the village of Dublin. There were also reports that stragglers and deserters were stalking her column, so Davis determined he would immediately try and find his family.[114] Around midnight, while the rest of Varina's party slept, Harrison and two teamsters were serving on picket duty. As Harrison wrote later,

> We heard the soft tread of horses in the darkness approaching over the light, sandy soil of the road. The teamsters immediately ran off to arouse the camp, having no doubt the attack was about to begin. I placed myself on the road to detain the enemy as long as possible, and when the advancing horsemen came near enough to hear me, called "Halt." They drew rein instantly. I demanded "Who goes there?" The foremost of the horsemen replied "Friends," in a voice I was astonished to recognize as that of President Davis, not suspecting he was anywhere near us.[115]

It had been six weeks since they had separated, but now, most happily, the Jefferson Davis family was reunited.[116]

"Davis chose to unite the two parties," observes Cooper, "even though the combination would slow him down. On Sunday, the seventh, he rode with Varina in her ambulance. The surroundings matched the desolation of the fleeing family. . . . A member of the escort described one campsite as a 'miserable piece of woods very confined & bad water.'" All along his rearward route, Davis had been arranging for depots of supply to be established. On the one hand, if the Confederacy could maintain any meaningful resistance, then it might sue for some kind of peace terms with a remnant of dignity; on the other hand, it seems certain that Davis himself never envisioned surrendering, as long as he could keep any troops at all in the field. But as Cooper points out, "By this time no organized Confederate resistance existed east of the Mississippi, though Davis did not know it. On May 4 General Richard Taylor had surrendered all the forces in his department, and five days later General Nathan Forrest bade his men farewell. Only Edmund Kirby Smith in the Trans-Mississippi kept the Confederate flag flying. For Jefferson Davis that banner had become his rainbow in the West."[117]

On April 26, 1865, General Joseph E. Johnston had surrendered his forces to those of General William T. Sherman. One of the Confederate corps commanders, Lieutenant General Stephen D. Lee, for the second time in the conflict, was now a prisoner of war (he had been at Vicksburg when it fell). After the surrender ceremony the sad and weary soldiers started for home. Their short-lived nation was collapsing and their way of life never would be the same again.

During the uncertain years ahead, their society and their whole culture would be altered largely by the will of a people whom they considered different. Few other Americans have ever had to bear such an experience.[118] Lee's chief engineer, Major Sidney A. Jonas, rather touchingly testified to the feeling that many of the men had when he presented Lee with a Confederate bill, on which he had written "Lines on a Confederate Note":

> Representing nothing on God's earth now,
>   And naught in the waters below it,
> As the pledge of a nation that's dead and gone,
>   Keep it, dear friend, and show it.
>
> . . . .
> We knew it had hardly a value in gold,
>   Yet as gold each soldier received it;
> It gazed in our eyes with a promise to pay,
>   And each Southern patriot believed it.
> But our boys thought little of price or of pay,
>   Or of bills that were overdue;
> We knew if it brought us our bread to-day,
>   'Twas the best our poor country could do.

Davis himself was not so resigned. He had authorized Johnston to negotiate with Sherman; he did not approve of unconditional surrender. As he wrote from Washington, "This Department has been surrendered without my knowledge and consent." Johnston, however, urged the other generals still in the field to do as he had, perhaps even usurping the office of the presidency, saying, "The pacification was announced by me to the States immediately concerned." Years later, in *The Rise and Fall of the Confederate Government,* Davis wrote, "Something more than courtesy required that the Executive should have been advised if not consulted"; he had "never expected a Confederate army to surrender while it was able either to fight or to retreat." There was a difference in the circumstances that R. E. Lee had faced and those Johnston confronted: "General Lee was forced to surrender and General Johnston consented to do so."[119]

James Harrison Wilson's cavalry overran Davis's encampment at daybreak on May 10, near Irwinville, Georgia. "The last possible chance to get away was gone," Cooper observes. "Finally, it was all over. The journey that had begun in the garden at Brierfield ended in the piney woods of south Georgia. It had lasted exactly fifty-one months—February 10, 1861, to May 10, 1865."[120]

There are numerous accounts of the capture, and details are contradictory. Davis and his wife had matching dark-gray raglans, rain gear, really. In his haste, Davis grabbed his wife's. Draping the raglan over his shoulders, he stepped out of the tent and calmly began walking toward the nearby woods. Varina rushed out after him and threw her own black shawl over his head and shoulders. Then she had her children's mulatto nurse grab a bucket and run toward him so it would seem they were simply going to the creek to get water.

But Corporal George Munger nabbed him. "God's will be done," muttered Davis. Union cavalrymen surrounded Davis and Varina as they walked arm in arm back to their tent.

W. C. Davis observes, "There he struggled against the profound mental and emotional upheaval of the past few minutes in order to regain his wonted iron self-control, even as at last he was forced to come to grips with the now inevitable fact that his dreams of continuing the cause were dying before his eyes like the fading embers at his feet." When he was first interviewed by a Union officer, Lieutenant Colonel Benjamin D. Pritchard, Davis proclaimed, "It would be bad enough to be the prisoner of soldiers and gentlemen; I am still lawful game, and would rather be dead than your prisoner."[121]

Davis and his family, transported by ambulance to Macon, Georgia, arrived at the hotel where General James Harrison Wilson made his headquarters. Remarkably, according to W. C. Davis, a strong guard of Union soldiers "in what was probably an unthinking spontaneous act, . . . brought their carbines to the 'present arms' position. . . . It would be the last formal salute Davis would ever receive as president of the Confederacy, ironically given him by his enemy."[122]

Davis and Reagan were the first high officials of the Confederacy to be captured, but the tally began to grow rapidly. Vice President Stephens simply waited at his home, Liberty Hall, in Crawfordville, Georgia, for Union soldiers to come and take him into custody. Finally, all of the now-defunct Confederacy's high officials were in custody, except for Benjamin and for Breckinridge, who got safely to Cuba and eventually to England, where W. C. Davis says he "attempted to settle remaining Confederate affairs."[123]

One question preyed upon countless Southerners' minds, from the moment they heard of R. E. Lee's surrender: how could the Lord allow the wicked to triumph? As George Rable observes, "Inveterate diarists either fell silent or scribbled rambling, disjointed entries. Reality was so hard to grasp." But even the surrender of Lee and his army did not result in the immediate disappearance of what Rable calls "the chimera of independence." That came only at the end, when "even the most sanguine had to face facts. . . . After learning that Davis had been captured, Ellen Renshaw House admitted that the Confederacy was dead. 'All our sacrifices, all the blood shed has been for nothing,' she wrote in a diary that usually overflowed with determination and optimism. 'The southern people have no one but themselves to thank for it. They did not deserve their freedom or they would have gained it.' "[124]

The woman's raglan and shawl Davis was captured in subsequently became the catalyst for later tales that he was taken captive while disguised as a woman. An officer later approached Varina, demanding her shawl as "part of

Mr. Davis's disguise." She held out both the shawl and the raglan and demanded that he choose. He took both. U.S. War Secretary Edwin Stanton subsequently issued an order that "the woman's dress in which Jefferson Davis was captured" should be brought to Washington.[125]

Northerners made much of the moments of surrender as weakness, targeting Confederate soldiers in general and Davis in particular. They concluded that the manlier men had won the contest. The Northern victory, many would claim, proved that the assertions of antebellum Southern men had been a sham. The perception of Davis as a cross-dresser, a faux woman, became for many Northerners the symbolic embodiment of the entire Confederacy within one persona. Within the next few months, in magazines, in museums, and in private homes throughout the North, images of Jefferson Davis decked out in feminine attire were displayed. W. C. Davis points out that this was done specifically "to reduce his stature in the eyes of former Confederates and lessen the chance of his becoming a symbolic rallying point for future resistance." In any event, the image took on a larger-than-life measure of credibility, and "generations passed before all but the most credulous accepted that the 'hoop skirt' stories were false."[126]

Clement C. Clay and Davis were kept under close guard, and as Davis later wrote, "After some days' detention, Clay and myself were removed to Fortress Monroe, and there incarcerated in separate cells." The Davis family, though not imprisoned, were shown no favors. As Davis described it:

> Not knowing that the Government was at war with women and children, I asked that my family might be permitted to leave the ship and go to Richmond or Washington City, or to some place where they had acquaintances, but this was refused. I then requested that they might be permitted to go abroad on one of the vessels lying at the Roads. This was also denied; finally, I was informed that they must return to Savannah on the vessel by which we came. This was an old transport-ship, hardly seaworthy [and certainly lacking in creature comforts]. My last attempt was to get for them the privilege of stopping at Charleston, where they had many personal friends. This also was refused.[127]

Davis eventually was imprisoned at Fort Monroe, Virginia. For a time he was kept in irons. He suffered dreadfully from his various maladies and came dangerously near death on several occasions. But he did not want to die; indeed, he much desired a trial, to exonerate both himself and the Cause.[128] In *Rise and Fall* his described his captivity:

> Bitter tears have been shed by the gentle, and stern reproaches have been made by the magnanimous, on account of the needless torture to which I was

subjected, and the heavy fetters riveted upon me, while in a stone casemate and surrounded by a strong guard; but all these were less excruciating than the mental agony my captors were able to inflict. It was long before I was permitted to hear from my wife and children, and this, and things like this, was the power which education added to savage cruelty.[129]

A photograph of the reigning pope, Pius IX, arrived—a gift for Davis from the prelate with whom he had corresponded in 1863. It was in a large wooden frame, which was carved at the top with the papal tiara, and Davis's great niece said that to receive it was "a distinction never before conferred on any but crowned heads." In the Holy Father's hand was an inscription: *Venite ad me omnes qui laboratis, et ego reficiam vos, dicit Dominus,* which Davis knew from the "Comfortable Words" in the Anglican Communion Service: "Come unto me all ye that are heavy laden and I will refresh you."[130]

He never got his trial, but there was a trial—that of Captain Henry Wirz, the supervisor of the prison stockade at Andersonville, Georgia, for war crimes— in which Davis was implicated. The "specification" of "charge I" was changed to include the names Jefferson Davis, James A. Seddon, and other Confederate leaders of lesser rank. Allegedly, he had conspired with Wirz, "maliciously, traitorously, and in violation of the laws of war, to impair and injure the health and destroy the lives—by subjection to torture and great suffering; by confining in unhealthy and unwholesome quarters . . . and by furnishing insufficient and unwholesome food—of large numbers of Federal prisoners."[131] Twenty-five-year-old General Nelson A. Miles, who was the commander of Fort Monroe, noted that Davis "carefully preserved" all the reports of evidence in the Wirz trial. Wirz was found guilty and hanged, but it was never proved that Davis had conspired with him to harm the prisoners. In a sense, however, the guilty verdict was levied not just on Wirz but on the whole South.[132]

In truth, Davis had done all in his power to prevent the tragedy of Andersonville. To a friend in later years he wrote, "It would be impossible to frame an accusation against me, more absolutely and unqualifiedly false."[133] Davis had complained bitterly during the war that he was hampered from exchanging prisoners by Northern policy. The prisoners had "the same rations as the soldiers," though the latter seldom had enough to eat themselves.[134]

After two years of captivity, Davis was given a hearing in Richmond and he was paroled. He was only "reprieved, not free"—still a prisoner, bailed to appear at the next session of court. His release brought "great jubilee," as Judah Benjamin phrased it, to the Confederate world.[135] Davis still hoped he would come to trial. He never did. The Civil War was all over.

Confederate Commanders. With Compliments Travelers Insurance Company. *Left to right:* A. P. Hill, John Bell Hood, Jefferson Davis, J. E. B. Stuart, Stonewall Jackson, Robert E. Lee, James Longstreet, Joseph E. Johnston, Pierre G. T. Beauregard, and, in a background portrait, Albert Sidney Johnston. Lee's reputation grew even after the war, as indicated by his central position in this Gilded Age advertisement for the Traveler's Insurance Company. Much the same could be said of Davis and most of the other generals pictured, but not of Braxton Bragg, who is conspicuous by his absence. (From CIV-1, courtesy The Filson Historical Society, Louisville, Kentucky.)

The Burial of Latane. W. D. Washington's 1864 painting attempted to portray the devotion of women, slaves, and children to the Confederate cause. It became a postwar symbol of the Lost Cause, and reflected a sentimental dream of what the Confederacy might have been, especially regarding slaves. (Courtesy Judge DeHardit. Lithograph, engraved by A. O. Campbell, published by William Pate and Company, New York, 1864. The Museum of the Confederacy, Richmond, Virginia. Photography by Katherine Wetzel.)

Opposite:
"SCENE IN RICHMOND, VA. The President stands in a Corner *telling his beads,* and proclaims A THIRD FAST, . . . while . . . the sufferings endured by the people have never been paralleled in history."—*(Rebel Paper.)* A northern newspaper ridiculed Davis's May 3, 1862, proclamation of a day of prayer by quoting from an unnamed Southern newspaper. "Telling his beads" refers to Davis's baptism and confirmation at St. Paul's Episcopal Church in Richmond on May 6, 1862. (From *Harpers Weekly,* June 7, 1862, 368. Courtesy Elwyn B. Robinson Department of Special Collections, Chester Fritz Library, University of North Dakota.)

"Jeff at the Receipt of Customs; Or, Southern Taxes Being Paid in Kind." This exaggerated cartoon humorously captures the confusion created by the tax in kind. (From *Frank Leslies Illustrated Newspaper,* October 2, 1861, 352. Negative X3 53043, courtesy State Historical Society of Wisconsin.)

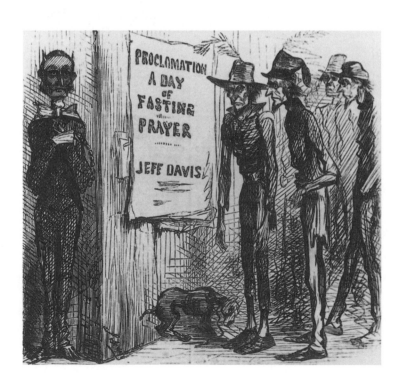

Opposite Top:

"The Finances of the Rebellion." This cartoon illustrates the very real confusion of Confederate finances in contrast to Davis's naively optimistic report in his Message to the Confederate Congress of August 18, 1862. (From *Harpers Weekly,* September 6, 1862, 576. Courtesy Elwyn B. Robinson Department of Special Collections, Chester Fritz Library, University of North Dakota.)

Opposite Bottom:

"THE REBEL FLEA. You put your Finger on him, and he isn't there." *Harper's Weekly* ridicules Union General Henry W. Halleck for his cautious advance on Corinth, Mississippi, after the Battle of Shiloh in 1862. Halleck was so slow that General Beauregard was able to evacuate his entire army before Halleck knew it. (From *Harpers Weekly,* July 12, 1862, 435. Courtesy Elwyn B. Robinson Department of Special Collections, Chester Fritz Library, University of North Dakota.)

Jeff Arming for the Final Struggle.—[Imitated from Venus Arming Mars.] Northern newspapers delighted in the story that Jefferson Davis was captured while wearing women's clothing. (From *Frank Leslies Illustrated Newspaper,* June 3, 1865, 176. Negative X3 53044, courtesy State Historical Society of Wisconsin.)

Confederate Soldier Leaving Home. Confederate Soldier Returns from War. The use of paired before-and-after pictures was a common nineteenth-century way to illustrate an individual's life course. Similar pictures from the era show the evils of alcohol or gambling or the rewards of hard work.

"Confederate Soldier Leaving Home," by Henry Mosler, Dusseldorf, 1868. (Events, Wars, Civil War, Lithographs—II, chromolithograph ICHi 13865, courtesy Chicago Historical Society.)

"Confederate Soldier Returns from War," by Henry Mosler, Dusseldorf, 1868. (Events, Wars, Civil War, Lithographs—II, chromolithograph, no ICHi number, courtesy Chicago Historical Society.)

"Jefferson Davis as an Unprotected Female!" This is one of the multitude of Northern cartoons lampooning Davis on the widely believed but false claim that he sought to avoid capture in May 1865 by wearing women's clothes. An accompanying quotation from the *New York Daily News* of May 15, 1865, reads, "He is one of those rare types of humanity born to control destiny, or to accept, without murmur, annihilation as the natural consequence of failure." (From *Harpers Weekly,* May 27, 1865. Courtesy Elwyn B. Robinson Department of Special Collections, Chester Fritz Library, University of North Dakota.)

Epilogue

———

THE POSTWAR DAVIS

———

Jefferson Davis insisted to the end of his life that he had done no treason and that he could prove it. To J. W. Jones, he proclaimed with "flashing eye . . . 'Oh, if they had only dared to give me the trial for which I begged. . . . I would have shown . . . that in making war upon us . . . the North was . . . the real 'traitor' to the Constitution.' " But he was left in suspense: "The case was continued till spring."[1] Benjamin Hill reported in 1874 that Davis "demanded a trial," being "most anxious to vindicate the innocence of his people; or, in himself, expiate their guilt by an ignominious death!"[2]

On Christmas Day, 1868, President Andrew Johnson issued a general proclamation of amnesty for former Confederates. The Rebels thenceforth could no longer be prosecuted, only disqualified for public office. Davis's lawyers had by then argued that the Fourteenth Amendment penalties overrode the charge of treason. When Judges Underwood and Chase failed to agree, Davis's case was sent to the U.S. Supreme Court, but it never ruled on it. Under Johnson's proclamation, "a *nolle prosequi* was entered and [Davis] was finally discharged." Yet as Varina observed, "The accusation of complicity in [Lincoln's] assassination was never withdrawn, and the epithet of 'traitor' was hurled at his head by every so-called orator, patriot, or petty penny-a-liner in the North."[3]

Davis lived until 1889, and both he and his wife published long, exculpatory memoirs, which did not sell well when initially published and are disappointing now for their scanty personal revelations and lack of analysis. W. C. Davis observes of Davis's that "typical of the man, it was no memoir at all, but an apologia, a defense of himself, a prosecution of his enemies—Union and Confederate—and a justification for the South in seceding and for the Confederacy in seeking independence."[4] Davis never changed his mind on the ideology that underpinned the Confederacy.

"What he did not wish to admit," asserts W. C. Davis, "he simply wrote out of his history. Inconvenient facts he ignored, and embarrassing incidents he expunged. His failures were really those of others; his only mistakes had been putting faith in subordinates who let him down."[5] The war, Davis wrote, proved only that secession was "impracticable," but he contended that "this did not prove it to be wrong." He expressed hope that "on the basis of fraternity and faithful regard for the rights of the States, there may be written on the arch of Union, *Esto perpetua*."[6] W. C. Davis points out that "in the rush to publish he did not even allow time to write all of it himself, and engaged two writers, one for each volume, . . . At the end, when he read the final text in print, he was more than once surprised to see what they had written on his behalf."[7]

Perhaps many Southerners were as deluded as Davis. "Even in defeat," George Rable writes, "many Confederates could imagine a different outcome. As one psychological study has noted, 'People can enjoy the experience of wishful thinking as long as they are willing to pay the price of painful disappointment when reality does not unfold as expected.' " Rable concludes that "to say . . . Confederate morale collapsed in the spring of 1865 is to tell at best a partial truth" because "rationalizing and making excuses had almost become like a narcotic, dangerous and addictive but also attractive." In observing the immediate postwar South, Rable has suggested that "this air of unreality would unfortunately suffuse Southern thought for the next several decades and beyond, casting a long shadow over those who experienced a crushing defeat without either acknowledging it or reckoning with its causes."[8]

To his relative, Mary Stamps, whom he called "Molly," Davis once confided a new sadness: "this tone to which I see a proud, honorable people reduced."[9] Once, after a visit to Davis's home in Memphis, the rector of St. Lazarus Episcopal Church, Dr. John Thomas Wheat, said to Robert Ransom: "If that man were a member of the Romish Church he would be canonized as a saint, and his sufferings . . . should forever enshrine him in our hearts as vicarious sacrifice."[10]

During the postwar period, and even after Davis's death, his public image underwent various transformations. W. C. Hesseltine contrasted Davis with R. E. Lee: the former looked backward at the idealized, prewar South, as he persisted in remembering it; the latter was prominent among those former Confederate leaders who looked ahead at a new and ultimately better South.[11] As Thomas L. Connelly has pointed out, in the late nineteenth century, when Lee came to be revered virtually as a Christ-like figure, then someone had to be blamed for Confederate defeat, and who better than the erstwhile failure of a president?[12] In a clever spoof of the Civil War Centennial Connelly listed a number of factors vital to "Confederatesmanship"; high among them was that one had "to *hate* Jefferson Davis."[13] Nevertheless, Davis has had many admirers in numerous quarters since the Civil War ended. Indeed, he still does to this day.

Davis said in an 1882 speech, "Our cause was so just, so sacred, that had I known all that has come to pass, had I known what was to be inflicted upon me, all that my country was to suffer, all that our posterity was to endure, I would do it all over again."[14] He retired in 1877 at Beavoir, an estate near Biloxi, Mississippi; his benefactor, Sarah Dorsey, like so many people, saw Davis as "the embodiment of our Cause."[15]

Appendix

———

BARBER'S MODEL OF PRESIDENTIAL LEADERSHIP

———

A president's style, James David Barber believes, is characterized by how he performs his political functions of "rhetoric, personal relations, and homework."[1] His "politically relevant beliefs," especially his notions of "social causality, human nature, and the central moral conflicts of the time" will dictate his behavior in office. These, in turn, are related to his sense of self-esteem (5). The key to classifying presidential performance therefore lies in determining how active a president is and whether he sees his political role as a positive or a negative experience. Thus Barber proposes four alternative leadership experiences, depending on the combination of activity and perception: active-positive, active-negative, passive-positive, and passive-negative (8–10). He uses these leadership styles to analyze American presidents since Theodore Roosevelt, but there seems to be no reason why the same structure could not be applied to analyze earlier, more activist presidents such as Andrew Jackson, Abraham Lincoln, and Jefferson Davis.

The active-positive presidents enjoy active lives and have high self-esteem; they tend to see themselves as making progress toward their personal goals, and they tend to be rational, "using the brain to move the feet." In contrast, the active-negative president is as active as his active-positive counterpart but enjoys it less. His behavior is "compulsive" and seemingly lacking in "emotional reward." He may seem power hungry and ambitious, and he has to check his "aggressive feelings." His political life is a struggle to hold power, and he is constantly pursued by a conscience that urges perfection (9).

Passive-positive presidents tend to be "compliant" and "other-directed," as they search for the affection that is their reward "for being agreeable and cooperative." Self-esteem is lacking, although such a president may present a surface optimism in order to banish doubt and secure encouragement. Political success is an unlikely outcome for such a president. Passive-negative presidents may be "dutiful," but they will also be ineffective and may withdraw "from the conflict and uncertainty of politics by emphasizing vague principles . . . and procedural arrangements" (10).

To Barber, then, the active-positive seeks "results," the active-negative desires "power," the passive-positive hopes for "love," and the passive-negative must content himself with "civic virtue." However, these are not rigid classifications; they are behavioral "tendencies" that may help us understand presidential administration, and surely other leadership conduct as well (10). Thus John F. Kennedy tended to withdraw, placing him partly in the passive-negative camp; Harry S. Truman was compulsive and hence somewhat active-negative; Franklin Roosevelt tended to be compliant and thus passive-positive. But these three, believes Barber, were predominantly active-positive. To use language Barber does not use, the categories are ideal types.[2]

Barber illustrates the use of these categories by analyzing the twentieth-century presidents from Theodore Roosevelt through George H. W. Bush. No doubt most readers will disagree with some of Barber's evaluations (certainly we do), but the utility of his analysis should become clear. Nor is character the only important facet to consider if, like Barber, one wishes to predict behavior of future presidents, or if, like us, one wishes to achieve better insight into the actions of past presidents. One must also consider the "power situation," the "climate of expectations," and the "character, worldview, and style" of the president. But to Barber, the "core of the argument . . . is that Presidential character" is most important and that this character "comes in four varieties," based on how active a president is and whether he enjoys politics (4).

For example, George Washington's "dedication to duty" fits the passive-negative type, and John Adams's "work and worry," impatience, and irascibility make him an active-negative. Thomas Jefferson tended to be active-positive. His politics were directed by reason, and he had wide interests and good humor. James Madison had something of the passive-positive in his character, for he was "compliant," irresolute, and compromising (10–11).

Active-positive presidents enjoy their use of power much more than the other types do. They are convinced of their ability to do their job, and though they pay close attention to it and learn what they must about the problems they face, they are not totally immersed. They are still objective and still able to laugh at themselves. For such leaders "the future is possible," and it may be manipulated by "imaginative experimentation." Their character learns by experience; they "abstract propositions, principles, rules of conduct, and so forth" that will guide them in analogous problems in the future. Their character adapts and grows because their minds are sufficiently free from "distorting influences to see the facts clearly and to organize them productively." Moreover, the active-positives are excited by their work, and the excitement infects their followers. Such, for example, were Franklin Roosevelt, Truman, and Kennedy (267, 363–64, 374). Even Gerald Ford fits the model, Barber thinks, for he kept his humor, grew in office, and took charge of the presidency (395–96).

Barber thinks Ford's successor was also an active-positive, for Jimmy Carter had a desire for results, albeit with a dash of active-negative compulsiveness. Carter put in long, active hours, and although he had his bad days, he generally enjoyed the presidency (431, 446–47). These active-positive presidents had several qualities in common, among them self-confidence, flexibility, desire for results, and ability to "see the strengths hidden in public confusion and to connect with those strengths" (490). These suggestions, originally appearing in the 1985 edition of *Presidential Character*, have been somewhat modified in the 1992 edition.

Carter's character, for example, was certainly active, though not quite so positive as Barber had believed a few years earlier (446–47). He had an unsuccessful presidency, Barber wrote, because he lacked "clear priorities" and the ability to negotiate—he snubbed essential leaders of both parties one after another. "He learned, but he learned late" to prioritize (434–36), and it took him two years to stop trying to work around the political leadership and instead to learn to negotiate with it. Nevertheless, Barber looks on Carter as an active-positive president, despite some discouraging setbacks (436–39, 401, 440, 446–47). These introduced a negativity into Carter's character, and although Barber places him in the active-positive category, he waffles a bit; some readers might conclude that Carter's inevitable bitterness over the Iran-hostage situation (to take only one instance) puts him more in the active-negative category than Barber wants to admit. But this merely reminds us that these categories are not fixed, that all presidents betray varying characteristics, and that we deal here with "tendencies and broad directions," not rigid behavioral types (10).

Barber's discussion of Bush is less satisfactory, for it betrays a profound bias and has all the earmarks of a rush job. More than any other problem, the defining affair of the Bush administration was surely the Gulf War, and Barber's 1992 edition was clearly published too soon after that event to use it to analyze presidential character or anything else. Nevertheless, Barber places Bush with the active-positive presidents, albeit with "a very major problem in the realm of world view, resulting in catastrophic disasters," i.e., the Gulf War (397). He saw Bush as an aristocrat—a wheeler-dealer "working for the welfare of the rich"—who had a "hunger for mission" and finally found it when Iraq invaded Kuwait.[3]

The active-negative presidents are of most interest to us, for Jefferson Davis seems to fit that model far better than he does the other three. They differ from the active-positives in that the active-positives "accumulate experience without accumulating anxiety, frustration, and guilt"; the active-negatives do not (333). Active-negative presidents are immersed in their problems and, like Woodrow Wilson, Herbert Hoover, and Lyndon Johnson, may have such "immense emotional commitment" to particular policies that it leads to their downfall when their policies are unsuccessful (295). These three meant well, but Wilson was defeated on the League, Hoover on the depression, and Johnson on Vietnam (13–47). Barber contends that such presidents "experienced severe deprivations of self-esteem in childhood" at the hands of "parents who denigrated, abandoned, or failed to provide for the child." Their resulting "anger was turned inward, against the self, [and] repressed and denied." Each then "developed an extraordinarily demanding conscience which required at once rigid self-control and superior achievement." This "deep attachment to *achievement* . . . [is] a way to wring from his environment a sense that he is worthy. . . . Whatever style brings success in domination is adopted and rigorously adhered to; but success does not produce joy" (85, 121). The active-negative president thus becomes rigid and pursues unsuccessful policies, despite evidence of failure. These policies are linked to the president's personality.

For active-negatives, policies become moral issues, on which compromise "is seen not only as mistaken but evil." In an effort to achieve success, the active-negative president works ever harder and becomes more convinced of his sacrifice for the nation. He becomes isolated, alone, and feels that he has been deserted by those who should be assisting him. More and more he calls for the loyalty of his followers and sees himself as bearing the nation's burdens virtually alone. Frustration produces anger that may be directed toward the inner circle at first but later extends to "weak and immoral people on the outside." These must be defeated; the alternative is his own defeat, which must be resisted to the utmost. For the active-negative, says Barber, "surrender is suicide, an admission of guilt and weakness" (46–47).

The active-negative is a perfectionist, who tries but cannot be equally accomplished in everything he attempts. He is inevitably afflicted by a sense of failure and by the demands of conscience as well, which impose "a felt necessity for the *denial of self-gratification*." He prides himself on his restraint in the face of provocation and is therefore much concerned with *"controlling his aggression."* Reality becomes too complex for him to handle, so he tries to neutralize conflicts "by *invoking abstract principles*" (81–82). He may channel his anger toward an enemy, "but the most pervasive feeling in the active-negative's makeup is *"I must.* He is a man under orders, required to concentrate, to produce, to follow out his destiny as he sees it." There is likely to be a never-ending conflict between virtue and power and the helpless "feeling that whatever one does, one has no choice." He appears energetic and "extraordinarily capable," but in time he becomes "extraordinarily rigid, becoming more and more closed to experience, including the advice of his ardent allies" (82). His critics will not understand the stress that the active-negative undergoes and will question his goals. However, "he rides the tiger to the end." An active-negative president will have failed "but in the failing [will have] found proofs that he had been right all along in seeing the world as he saw it and in acting as he had to act" (83). Jefferson Davis fits this profile remarkably well.

Barber believes that Richard Nixon was another such president, a variant of the active-negative type. He could be defeated on issues without "feeling personally threatened . . . [because] his investment [was] in himself." However, if an issue reached "his central concern, the concern of self management," there would be a "strong inner response" (143). The "compulsiveness of the active-negative person, which usually takes the form 'I must,' with Nixon invariably became 'I must do it my way.' " Things often did not work out his way, however, so this active-negative president took "his stance as a suffering martyr" (148, 147).

For Nixon, "The burdens outweigh[ed] the enjoyments, the responsibilities outweigh[ed] the pleasures." There might be "a grim satisfaction in endurance" but little spontaneous enjoyment.[4] Nixon had to keep himself under firm control, resisting the urge "to lash out at his enemies." He was frequently characterized as "introverted, self-contained," "cautious," "patient," "aloof," or "reserved." Nixon, the archetypal active-negative, exerted much energy in self-control. "Indeed, aggression and its control provide a central theme in Nixon's makeup"; but for the active-negatives, "political competition furnishes a ready arena for releasing anger." To Nixon, as to the other active-negatives of the twentieth century, Wilson, Hoover, and Lyndon Johnson, there is an "onward-and-upward, suffering-and-striving orientation," in which the individual is constantly "testing and checking the condition of his power and virtue." This is reflected in the "sense that crisis is life." Nixon "found in the suffering his work entailed a confirmation of his own goodness and a basis for disdaining pleasure," and a simple reading of Jefferson Davis's memoirs confirms the close if not wholly exact fit for him as well. The task was to manage the self, "particularly the control of aggression and hard resistance to the dual temptation to fight and to quit."[5]

The passive-negative presidents, such as Calvin Coolidge and Dwight Eisenhower, were not so extremely committed as the active-negatives, but "they tend to fall back on stylistic continuities, on regularly pursued systems and habits of behavior" (295). They pose a danger to the nation because of their tendency to drift. They represent a national need for reassurance, and "their elections represent a public sigh of relief after a period when the apparent aggressiveness or corruption of politics has worn down the people's political energies" (169). They appear to have entered politics with reluctance, and they tend to "withdraw from the conflict and uncertainty of politics to an emphasis on vague principles and procedural arrangements." Such an individual is in politics because of "his sense of duty, which leads him to compensate for feelings of uselessness by becoming a guardian of the right and proper way, above the sordid politicking of lesser men" (170).

For Coolidge and Eisenhower, the problems of politics were to be faced with "irritated resignation. They were performing duty under duress, not crusading after some political Holy Grail." Presidents of this sort resist intrusion and are bothered by the requirement that they perform. When there are problems, the "problems should come to them rather than they to the problems, and . . . their responsibilities were limited primarily to preserving the fundamental values by applying them to disagreements no one else in the system could resolve." Such a president actively avoids tasks he does not like and meets "the demands of conscience" by telling himself he does not enjoy doing his duty. He does not initiate action; issues are brought to him, "and there are too damned many of them" (193). The passive-negative serves because he has no satisfactory "answer to the question, if not you, who?" If unaccustomed to informal negotiation, he will drift away, in Coolidge's case to an "increasingly abstract rhetoric," in Eisenhower's case to become the "final arbiter of otherwise unresolvable conflicts" (489).

The passive-positives, William Howard Taft, Warren G. Harding, and Ronald Reagan, on the other hand, have a more flexible style than the passive-negatives, but they get in trouble when their rigid character and need for affection bump up against problems that point to the need to change their ways (295–96, 230). They have a need to "communicate love" and may thus appear extremely congenial (194). They are, says Barber, "political lovers," although their experience teaches them not to love politics (194–95). Taft and Harding each had a need "for someone to devote himself to, to help, to love" (208, 216–17). Such people are vulnerable; they seek to win that love by their personality, bargaining in a "marketplace of affection" to satisfy their needs. "What Harding and Taft feared," wrote Barber, "was the double-binding situation where the mass love which the Presidency provided could be sustained only by firm aggressive action against their close friends" (223). Reagan, too, fit the mold as "a passive-positive linked through his extraordinary rhetorical style to a public ready . . . for just such a hopeful and reassuring personality" (230). Referring to all three passive-positive presidents, Barber asserts, "The people's desire for community in an age of fragmentation [and] their need to sense themselves as members sharing in the national doings, strike a chord within the passive-positive President. . . . He came to expect that almost everyone would like him and that those who did not could be placated by considerateness and compromise. He needed that" (486).

The active-positive presidents, such as Franklin Roosevelt, Truman, Kennedy, and, to a lesser extent, Ford and Carter, are clearly Barber's favorites (but not Bush—a president may be too active or may be active in the wrong ways). At this point Barber betrays his bias, to be sure, for almost everyone will rank these leaders above Harding and Coolidge. The difference is that Barber tries to explain why these are favorites in terms of their activity in and enjoyment of political life; he makes sure that he describes his favorites as active men who generally enjoyed themselves. To some extent he achieves his bull's-eye by throwing his dart, then drawing the target around the point it hits.

On the other hand, it is apparent from careful reading of Barber's work that his model provides a useful way to look at presidential behavior—indeed, the behavior of any leader—if not taken slavishly or too seriously. According to Barber's model, Jefferson Davis was clearly an active-negative president, with perhaps an occasional hint of passive-negative.

NOTES

Prologue

1. Jefferson Davis, "Farewell Speech," in *The Papers of Jefferson Davis,* ed. Haskell M. Monroe Jr., James T. McIntosh, Lynda Lasswell Crist, and Mary Seaton Dix, 10 vols. to date (Baton Rouge: Louisiana State University Press, 1971–), 7:23 (hereinafter cited as Davis, *Papers*).

2. Ibid., 7:20.

3. Ibid., 7:21.

4. Ibid., 7:22.

5. Ibid., 7:23; Varina Davis, *Jefferson Davis, Ex-President of the Confederate States of America: A Memoir by His Wife,* intro., Craig L. Symonds, 2 vols. (1890; reprint, Baltimore: The Nautical and Aviation Publishing Company, 1990), 1:697, 699.

6. Jefferson Davis to Alexander M. Clayton, January 10, 1861, Davis, *Papers,* 7:27–28.

7. James David Barber, *The Presidential Character: Predicting Performance in the White House,* 4th ed. (Englewood Cliffs, N.J.: Prentice-Hall, 1992).

8. Ibid., 4.

9. Ibid., 485.

10. Ibid., 5.

11. Ibid., 9.

12. Ibid.

13. Ibid., 10.

14. Ibid.

15. Ibid.

16. V. Davis, *A Memoir,* 2:18–19.

I. What Manner of Man?

1. Cooper, *Davis,* 8, 11–14. Davis considered 1808 to be the year of his birth, but there is considerable suspicion that he actually was born in 1807. Late in his life he admitted that he did not truly know. The genealogy in Davis, *Papers,* 1: 512, 523, gives both years as possible but suggests that 1808 is most likely correct. There are speculations that his middle name was "Finis," but no evidence exists to corroborate that.

2. Allen, *Davis,* 43.

3. Cooper, *Davis,* 16.

4. Allen C. Guelzo, *Abraham Lincoln: Redeemer President* (Grand Rapids, Mich.: William B. Erdemans, 1999), 5–14.

5. Cooper, *Davis,* 17.

6. Allen, *Davis,* 46.

7. Cooper, *Davis,* 18.

8. Allen, *Davis,* 52.

9. Cooper, *Davis,* 23.

10. Ibid., 25.

11. Ibid., 26.

12. Ibid., 26–28.

13. Ibid., 28.

14. Ibid., 39.

15. Ibid., 30–33.

16. Ibid., 33–34.

17. Ibid., 40.

18. Ibid.

19. Ibid., 44; Allen, *Davis,* 68–69; V. Davis, *A Memoir,* 1: 80–81.

20. Cooper, *Davis,* 46–49.

21. Ibid., 61.

22. Ibid., 50–51, 60.

23. Ibid., 58. Cooper writes that this was Davis's first serious illness, but in this he is incorrect, having failed to note the serious bout with pneumonia in Wisconsin, two winters before this.

24. Allen, *Davis,* 83.

25. Cooper, *Davis,* 65.

26. Ibid., 48; Allen, *Davis,* 82.

27. Cooper, *Davis,* xiv.

28. Ibid., 49.

29. Allen, *Davis,* 91.

30. Ibid., 92, 104.

31. Cooper, *Davis,* xv.

32. Allen, *Davis,* 96–97.

33. Cooper, *Davis,* 81–82.

34. Allen, *Davis,* 112–13.

35. Ibid., 118.

36. Ibid., 123.

37. Cooper, *Davis,* 101.

38. Allen, *Davis,* 128.

39. Cooper, *Davis,* 107.

40. Ibid., 109–10.

41. Allen, *Davis,* 47.

42. Cooper, *Davis,* 140–41.

43. Ibid., 152, 154.

44. Ibid., 157.

45. Ibid., 162–63.

46 Ibid., 168–71.

47. Ibid., 172.

48. Ibid., 250, 254–56.

49. Ibid., 249.

50. Ibid.

51. Allen, *Davis,* 208.

52. Ibid., 215.

53. Ibid., 209.

54. Ibid., 175.

55. Ibid., 176.

56. Jefferson Davis, *The Rise and Fall of the Confederate Government,* 2 vols. (New York: D. Appleton, 1881), 1:135–37.

57. Ibid., 148.

58. Ibid., 152.

59. John Brawner Robbins, "Confederate Nationalism: Politics and Government in the Confederate South, 1861–1865" (Ph.D. diss., Rice University, 1964), 10.

60. Inaugural Address, February 18, 1861, Davis, *Papers,* 7:49–50.

61. Richard Hofstadter, "John C. Calhoun: The Marx of the Master Class," chapter 4, in Hofstadter, *The American Political Tradition and the Men Who Made It* (New York: Knopf, 1948).

62. Cooper, *Davis,* 193.

63. This is in his title, of course, and generally throughout his text.

64. Ibid., 278.

65. W. C. Davis, *Davis,* 269.

66. Grady McWhiney, *Cracker Culture: Celtic Ways in the Old South* (Tuscaloosa: University of Alabama Press, 1988), and Perry D. Jamieson and Grady McWhiney, *Attack and Die* (Tuscaloosa: University of Alabama Press, 1982).

67. Samuel H. Hill, *The South and the North in American Religion* (Athens: University of Georgia Press, 1980), 3–5, 10.

68. See Gabor S. Boritt, ed., *Why the Civil War Came* (New York: Oxford University Press, 1996), and Nina Silber, *The Romance of Reunion: Northerners and the South, 1865–1900* (Chapel Hill: University of North Carolina Press, 1993), 8.

69. Ibid., 21.

70. George C. Rable, *The Confederate Republic: A Revolution Against Politics* (Chapel Hill: University of North Carolina Press, 1966), 2.

71. Ibid.

72. In Alabama, for example, J. Mills Thornton III has shown a hidden alliance between slavery and Jacksonian ideology that made secession possible. White Alabamians, valuing personal freedom—as they perceived it—and political equality, came to believe that their

independence was predicated on the preservation of black slavery (*Politics and Power in a Slave Society: Alabama, 1800–1860* [Baton Rouge: Louisiana State University Press, 1978]).

73. Boritt, ed., *Why the Civil War Came.*

74. Ibid., introduction, xiii–xvii.

2. The Establishment of Government

1. Cooper, *Davis,* 296–99.

2. William Y. Thompson, *Robert Toombs of Georgia* (Baton Rouge: Louisiana State University Press, 1966).

3. Rable, *Confederate Republic,* 64–66; W. C. Davis, *The Union That Shaped the Confederacy,* 90ff.

4. V. Davis, *A Memoir,* 2:18–19.

5. Davis to J. J. Petus, February 12, 1861, in *Jefferson Davis: Constitutionalist,* ed. Dunbar Rowland, 10 vols. (Jackson: Mississippi Department of Archives and History, 1923), 5:46.

6. Cooper, *Davis,* 328.

7. Ibid.

8. W. C. Davis, *Davis,* 304–5; Jefferson Davis to Varina Davis, February 14, 1861, Davis, *Papers,* 7:40–41 n.1; *New Orleans Delta,* February 14, 1861.

9. W. C. Davis, *Davis,* 307.

10. Speech at Montgomery, February 16, 1861, in Rowland, ed., *Davis,* 5:47–49.

11. W. C. Davis, *Davis,* 306; Thomas H. Watts, "Address on the Life and Character of Ex-President Jefferson Davis," Montgomery, Ala., 1889, 14.

12. Barber, *Presidential Character,* 46–47, 82, 85, 121.

13. W. C. Davis, *Davis,* 308.

14. Ibid., 313.

15. Robbins, "Confederate Nationalism," 2.

16. Ibid., 4–5.

17. W. C. Davis, *Davis,* 269.

18. Cobb to wife, February 25, 1861, A. L. Hull, ed., "Correspondence of Thomas Reade Rootes Cobb, 1860–1862," *Publications of Southern History Association* 11 (1907): 241.

19. Richard Beringer, Herman Hattaway, Archer Jones, and William Still, *Why the South Lost the Civil War* (Athens: University of Georgia Press, 1986), 64, 66.

20. Drew Gilpin Faust, *The Creation of Confederate Nationalism: Ideology and Identity in the Civil War South* (Baton Rouge: Louisiana State University Press, 1988), 5.

21. Ibid., 313.

22. Ibid., 14.

23. Ibid.

24. Ibid., 18–19.

25. Ibid., 22–27; the quote is on 27.

26. Frank Moore, ed., *The Rebellion Record: A Diary of American Events,* 12 vols. (New York: Putnam, 1866), 2:277, quoted in Marshal L. DeRosa, *The Confederate Constitution: An Inquiry into American Constitutionalism* (Columbia: University of Missouri Press, 1991), 1.

27. DeRosa, *Confederate Constitution,* 17.

28. Davis, *Rise and Fall,* 1:258.

29. U.S. Congress, Senate, *Journal of the Congress of the Confederate States of America, 1861–1865,* 7 vols. S. doc. 234, 58th Cong., 2d sess., Washington, D.C.: Government Printing Office, 1904–1905. 1:39, 41–42.

30. Ibid., 1:851–96.

31. DeRosa, *Confederate Constitution,* passim.

32. See the parallel texts of the Confederate and U.S. Constitutions in Charles Robert Lee Jr., *The Confederate Constitutions* (Chapel Hill: University of North Carolina Press, 1963), appendix C.

33. DeRosa, *Confederate Constitution,* passim.

34. "An Act declaring the officer who shall act as President in case of vacancies in the offices both of President and Vice President," approved April 19, 1862, in James M. Matthews, ed., *Public Laws . . . Passed at the First Session of the First Congress, 1862* (1862; reprint, Holmes Beach, Fla.: Gaunt, 1970), 46–47.

35. "Proceedings of the Confederate Congress," *Southern Historical Society Papers* (hereinafter SHSP), 4:208, 210, 220–21.

36. DeRosa, *Confederate Constitution,* 5.

37. Robbins, "Confederate Nationalism," 19.

38. W. C. Davis, *The Union That Shaped the Confederacy,* 42–43.

39. Ibid., 91–95.

40. Ibid., 42–43.

41. Speech in Holly Springs, October 25, 1849, Davis, *Papers,* 4:49 (emphasis in original).

42. Ibid.; see also Thomas E. Schott, *Alexander H. Stephens of Georgia: A Biography* (Baton Rouge: Louisiana State University Press, 1988), 87.

43. Davis, *Papers,* 6:xlix; Schott, *Stephens,* 169.

44. Davis, *Papers,* 6:401–2.

45. Reply to Stephen A. Douglas, May 17, 1860, Davis, *Papers,* 6:299; Schott, *Stephens,* 169.

46. Schott, *Stephens,* 331.

47. Ibid., 330.

48. Ibid., 334–35.

49. Davis, *Papers,* 7:116, 121, 127.

50. W. C. Davis, *Davis,* 312.

51. Ibid., 311.

52. W. C. Davis, *The Union That Shaped the Confederacy,* 108–9.

53. Quoted in Rable, *Confederate Republic,* 71.

54. Thompson, *Toombs of Georgia,* 165.

55. E. Merton Coulter, *The Confederate States of America, 1861–1865* (Baton Rouge: Louisiana State University Press, 1950), 7:149–50.

56. Mary Boykin Miller Chesnut, *Mary Chesnut's Civil War,* ed. C. Vann Woodward (New Haven: Yale University Press, 1981), 103 (entry for July 19, 1861). Joe Davis Jr. was Jefferson Davis's nephew.

57. Rembert W. Patrick, *Jefferson Davis and His Cabinet* (Baton Rouge: Louisiana State University Press, 1944), 105–6.

58. Rable, *Confederate Republic,* 72.

59. Ibid.

60. Ibid., 73.

61. Burton J. Hendrick, *Statesmen of the Lost Cause* (Boston: Little Brown, 1939), 104–6.

62. C. Vann Woodward and Elizabeth Muhlenfeld, eds., *The Private Mary Chesnut: The Unpublished Civil War Diaries* (New York: Oxford University Press, 1984), 6–7, 13–14.

63. Quoted from Rable, *Confederate Republic,* 73–74.

64. David L. Yulee to Jefferson Davis, March 1, 1861, quoted in W. C. Davis, *Davis,* 316; cited in Davis, *Papers,* 7:66.

3. Provisional Administration

1. Cooper, *Davis,* 333–34.

2. Ibid., 334–35.

3. See Ezra J. Warner and Wilfred Buck Yearns, eds., *Biographical Register of the Confederate Congress* (Baton Rouge: Louisiana State University Press, 1975).

4. Richard E. Beringer, "A Profile of the Members of the Confederate Congress," *Journal of Southern History* 33 (November 1967):526–38.

5. Warner and Yearns, *Biographical Register,* 1, 18, 50, 73, 84, 88.

6. Ibid., 118, 158, 225, 237, 245–46, 250–51.

7. See William B. Hesseltine, *Confederate Leaders in the New South* (Baton Rouge: Louisiana State University Press, 1950).

8. Beringer, "Profile," 521; Richard E. Beringer, "The Unconscious 'Spirit of Party' in the Confederate Congress," *Civil War History* 18 (December 1972):316 n.19.

9. Beringer, "Profile," 525.

10. Ibid., 539.

11. Thomas B. Alexander and Richard E. Beringer, *The Anatomy of the Confederate Congress* (Nashville: Vanderbilt University Press, 1972), 68, passim.

12. W. C. Davis, *"A Government of Our Own" : The Making of the Confederacy* (New York: Free Press, 1994), 243.

13. Woodward, ed., *Mary Chesnut,* 15–16 (diary entry for March 5, 1861).

14. W. C. Davis, *A Government of Our Own,* 176.

15. Coulter, *Confederate States of America,* 164.

16. Davis, Inaugural Address, February 18, 1861, in *A Compilation of the Messages and*

Papers of the Confederacy, ed. James D. Richardson, 2 vols. (Nashville: U.S. Publishing Company, 1904), 1:34.

17. Ibid., Davis to Howell Cobb, president of the Congress, March 5, 1861, 58.

18. "An Act to raise Provisional Forces for the Confederate States of America, and for other purposes," February 28, 1861, in James M. Matthews, ed., *The Statutes at Large of the Provisional Government of the Confederate States of America* (1864; reprint, Holmes Beach, Fla.: William W. Gaunt and Sons, 1970), 43–44 (hereafter *Statutes*).

19. Ibid., "An Act to provide for the Public Defence," March 6, 1861, 45–46.

20. Ibid., 81.

21. Ibid., "An Act for the Establishment and Organization of a General staff for the Army of the Confederate States of America," passed February 26, 1861, 38–39.

22. Ibid., "An Act amendatory of An Act for the organization of the Staff Departments of the Army, and an Act for the establishment and organization of the Army of the Confederate States of America," passed March 14, 1861, 61–62.

23. See "An Act to abolish supernumerary offices in the Commissary's and Quarter-master's Departments," passed May 1, 1863, in James M. Matthews, ed., *Public Laws of the Confederate States of America, Passed at the Third Session of the First Congress, 1863* (1863; reprint, Holmes Beach, Fla.: Gaunt and Sons, 1970), 134.

24. "An Act to appoint a Second Auditor of the Treasury," March 15, 1861, in Matthews, ed., *Statutes,* 66; "An Act to increase the clerical force of the Treasury Department, in the bureau of the second auditor," May 21, 1861, ibid., 151; and "An Act to organize the clerical force of the Treasury Department," February 13, 1862, ibid., 259.

25. Ibid., "An Act for the establishment and organization of the Army of the Confederate States of America," approved March 6, 1861, 47–52.

26. Robert U. Johnson and Clarence C. Buell, *Battles and Leaders of the Civil War,* 4 vols. (New York: Century, 1887), 1:239.

27. Jerrold Northrop Moore, *Confederate Commissary General: Lucius Bellinger Northrop and the Subsistence Bureau of the Southern Army* (Shippensburg, Pa.: White Mane, 1996), 26, 36.

28. Richard B. Goff, *Confederate Supply* (Durham: Duke University Press, 1969), 6.

29. Ibid., 15–16.

30. Ibid., 16.

31. W. W. Boyce to Jefferson Davis, September 29, 1864, *(Raleigh) Daily Conservative,* October 8, 1864.

32. Jefferson Davis, *Rise and Fall,* 1:249.

4. To Sumter

1. Cooper, *Davis,* 335–36.

2. Ibid., 336, 339.

3. Ibid., 336.

4. W. C. Davis, *A Government of Our Own,* 296.

5. Ibid., 297; Resolutions providing for a digest of laws, March 12, 1861, in Matthews, ed., *Statutes,* 94.

6. Proclamation, March 16, 1861, U.S. Naval War Records Office, *War of the Rebellion: Official Records of the Union and Confederate Navies in the War of the Rebellion,* 30 vols. (Washington, D.C.: U.S. Government Printing Office, 1894–1922), ser. 2, 3:95–96 (hereinafter *ORN*).

7. R. Toombs to William L. Yancey, Pierre A. Rost, and A. Dudley Mann, March 16, 1861, *ORN,* ser. 2, vol. 3:192.

8. Ibid., 3:194–95.

9. W. C. Davis, *A Government of Our Own,* 302; R. Toombs to William L. Yancey, Pierre A. Rost, and A. Dudley Mann, March 16, 1861, *ORN,* ser. 2, vol. 3: 194–95.

10. Richardson, ed., *Messages,* 1:55.

11. W. C. Davis, *A Government of Our Own,* 303.

12. Ibid., 303–4.

13. Herman Hattaway, "Via Confederate Post," *Civil War Times–Illustrated* 15 (April 1976):22–29.

14. Coulter, *Confederate States of America,* 150.

15. W. C. Davis, *A Government of Our Own,* 187, 259.

16. Coulter, *Confederate States of America,* 152–53.

17. W. C. Davis, *A Government of Our Own,* 73, 176.

18. Coulter, *Confederate States of America,* 153.

19. "An Act to continue in force certain laws of the United States of America," adopted February 9, 1861, in Matthews, ed., *Statutes,* 27; Coulter, *Confederate States of America,* 173; Douglas Ball, *Financial Failure and Confederate Defeat* (Urbana and Chicago: University of Chicago Press, 1991), 206.

20. "An Act to raise Money for the support of the Government, and to Provide for the Defense of the Confederate States of America," in Matthews, ed., *Statutes,* 42–43; Coulter, *Confederate States of America,* 174; Richard C. Todd, *Confederate Finance* (Athens: University of Georgia Press, 1954), 25, 82.

21. W. C. Davis, *A Government of Our Own,* 299.

22. *Journal,* 1:464.

23. W. C. Davis, *A Government of Our Own,* 299.

24. Benjamin to L. P. Walker, April 2, 1861, in *The Opinions of the Confederate Attorneys General, 1861–1865,* ed. Rembert W. Patrick (Buffalo, N.Y.: Dennis, 1950), 6–9.

25. W. C. Davis, *A Government of Our Own,* 301.

26. Message to Congress, April 29, 1861, Richardson, ed., *Messages,* 81.

27. Office of the Governor RG 3, Letters Received, John Letcher 1860–1864, Box 15 Folder 6 (Accession 36787) John Letcher to [Jefferson Davis] 3 July 1861, microcopy, State Records Collection, Archives Research Services, The Library of Virginia, Richmond, Virginia. Materials from other depositories that were examined at the Jefferson Davis Association, Rice University, Houston, Texas, will hereafter be designated JDA.

28. "An Act to make further provision for the public defense," May 11, 1861, in

Matthews, ed., *Statutes,* 106; "An Act to increase the Military establishment of the Confederate States, and to amend the 'Act for the establishment and organization of the Army of the Confederate States of America,'" May 16, 1861, ibid., 114–16; "An Act to authorize the President to Confer temporary rank and command, for service with volunteer troops, on officers of the Confederate Army," May 21, 1861, ibid., 127.

29. Robert Barnwell Rhett Sr., to Robert Barnwell Rhett Jr., February 11, 1861, University of South Carolina; typescript in Special Collections Department Bell I. Wiley Papers, Collection 521, Writings of Confederate Congressmen, Box 1, Robert W. Woodruff Library, Emory University.

30. "An Act to provide Munitions of War, and for other purposes," approved February 20, 1861, in Matthews, ed., *Statutes,* 28–29.

31. Ibid., "An Act making appropriations," approved May 21, 1861, 123.

32. Robbins, "Confederate Nationalism," 161, quoting the *Augusta (Ga.) Chronicle,* May 1, 1863.

33. Quoted in Winfred P. Minter, "Confederate Military Supply," *Social Science* 3 (June 1959): 163.

34. We based this and the ensuing five paragraphs on material in two old unpublished Ph.D. dissertations: Herman A. Norton, "The Organization and Function of the Confederate Military Chaplaincy, 1861–1865," Vanderbilt University, 1956; and Frank L. Hieronymus, "For Now and Forever: The Chaplains of the Confederate States Army," University of California, Los Angeles, 1964. But see also Gorrell Clinton Prim, Jr., "Born Again in the Trenches: Revivalism in the Confederate Army," Florida State University, 1982; and Sidney J. Romero, *Religion in the Rebel Ranks* (Lanham, MD: University Press of America, 1983). Romero's unrevised Ph.D. dissertation done some four decades previous at Louisiana State University is little more than a "vanity press.") The topic is quite ripe for a new book-length scholarly treatment, one of which is already under way.

35. "An Act to provide for the appointment of chaplains in the army," approved May 3, 1861, in Matthews, ed., *Statutes,* 99; "An Act to amend an act entitled 'An Act to provide for the appointment of chaplains in the army,' approved May 3, 1861," approved May 16, 1861, ibid., 118; and "An Act to amend the several Acts in relation to the pay of Chaplains in the Army," approved April 19, 1861, in Matthews, ed., *Public Laws, First Session of the First Congress,* 45.

36. See Bruce Allardice, "West Points of the Confederacy: Southern Military Schools and the Confederate Army," *Civil War History* 43 (December 1997):31.

37. John Hope Franklin, *The Militant South: 1800–1861* (Cambridge: Belknap Press of Harvard University Press, 1956), see especially chapter 8.

38. Allardice, "West Points of the Confederacy," 314.

39. Ibid., 321, 330.

40. Richard McMurry, *Two Great Rebel Armies* (Chapel Hill: University of North Carolina Press, 1989).

41. Allardice, "West Points of the Confederacy," 326.

42. Ezra J. Warner, *Generals in Gray: Lives of the Confederate Commanders* (Baton Rouge: Louisiana State University Press, 1959), xxiv–xxv.

43. W. C. Davis, *A Government of Our Own,* 215, quote from 293.

44. Ibid., 293.

45. Ibid., 296.

46. Quoted in ibid., 298.

47. Ibid., 299–300.

48. Ibid., 301.

49. Davis, *A Government of Our Own,* 206; Emory M. Thomas, *The Confederate Nation, 1861–1865* (New York: Harper and Row, 1979), 81.

50. W. C. Davis, *A Government of Our Own,* 209, 303; Allan Nevins, *The War for the Union,* vol. 1, *The Improvised War, 1861–1862* (New York: Charles Scribners Sons, 1959), 40–51.

51. W. C. Davis, *A Government of Our Own,* 210.

52. Ibid., 305.

53. Ibid., 308.

54. Ibid., 308–9.

55. Ibid., 312.

56. Ibid., 283ff.

57. W. C. Davis, *The Union That Shaped the Confederacy,* 123.

58. Cooper, *Davis,* 340.

59. Herman Hattaway, *General Stephen D. Lee* (Jackson: University Press of Mississippi, 1976), 16–17.

60. Quoted in W. C. Davis, *A Government of Our Own,* 306.

61. Hattaway, *General Stephen D. Lee,* 19–20.

62. Ibid., 20.

63. W. C. Davis, *Davis,* 322.

64. Hattaway, *General Stephen D. Lee,* 21.

65. Ibid., 21–22.

66. Ibid., 22–23.

67. Ibid., 24–25.

68. W. C. Davis, *Davis,* 325.

69. W. C. Davis, *A Government of Our Own,* 318.

70. Hattaway, *General Stephen D. Lee,* 26.

71. Charles Royster, "Fort Sumter: At Last the War," in Boritt, ed., *Why the Civil War Came,* 203.

72. Charles W. Ramsdell, "Lincoln and Fort Sumter," *Journal of Southern History* 3 (August 1937): 259–88.

73. Richard N. Current, *Lincoln and the First Shot* (Philadelphia: Lippincott, 1963), 182–208.

74. James M. McPherson, *Battle Cry of Freedom: The Civil War Era,* vol. 6, *The Oxford History of the United States* (New York: Oxford University Press, 1988), 272–74, see especially 272 n.78.

75. Grady McWhiney, "The Confederacy's First Shot," in *Southerners and Other Americans* (New York: Basic Books, 1973), chap. 5, quote from 80.

76. Magill and Fish, quoted in Royster, "Fort Sumter: At Last the War," 206, 211.

5. The Wait for Land Battles

1. Cooper, *Davis,* 351.

2. Ibid., 341.

3. Ibid., 341–42.

4. Mark Neely, *Southern Rights: Political Prisoners and the Myth of Confederate Constitutionalism* (Charlottesville: University Press of Virginia, 1999), 1–2.

5. Ibid., 2, 4.

6. See especially Mark Neely's Pulitzer Prize–winning *The Fate of Liberty: Abraham Lincoln and Civil Liberties* (New York: Oxford University Press, 1991).

7. Neely, *Southern Rights,* 9, 172.

8. Ibid., 173.

9. Ibid., 87–88.

10. Jon Wakelyn, *Pro-Union Confederate Pamphlets* (Columbia: University of Missouri Press, 2000).

11. Neely, *Southern Rights,* 100, 103.

12. Ibid., 136.

13. United States, War Department, *The War of the Rebellion: A Compilation of the Official Records of the Union and Confederate Armies,* 70 vols. in 128. Washington, D.C.: U.S. Government Printing Office, 1880–1901), ser. 2, 2:1369–70 (hereinafter *Official Records*). See also "An Act Respecting Alien Enemies," approved August 8, 1861, in Matthews, ed., *Statutes,* 174–75.

14. Neely, *Southern Rights,* 146.

15. By the President of the United States: A Proclamation, April 15, 1861, *Official Records,* ser. 3, 1:657–68.

16. Davis, *Rise and Fall,* 1:287–98.

17. Ellis to Simon Cameron, April 15, 1861, *Official Records,* ser. 3, 1:72.

18. For complete discussion of the secession procedures in the several states, see Ralph A. Wooster, *The Secession Conventions of the South* (Princeton: Princeton University Press, 1962).

19. Letcher to Simon Cameron, April 16, 1861, *Official Records,* ser. 3, 1:76.

20. Ibid., H. M. Rector to Simon Cameron, April 22, 1861, ser. 3, 1:99.

21. Ibid., Isham G. Harris to Simon Cameron, April 16, 1861, ser. 3, 1:81.

22. W. C. Davis, *A Government of Our Own,* 343.

23. *Journal of the Confederate Congress,* 1:174.

24. Ibid., 1:181; "An Act recognizing the existence of war between the United States and the Confederate States; and concerning letters of marque, prizes and prize goods," approved May 6, 1861, in Matthews, ed., *Statutes,* 100–104; Davis, *A Government of Our Own,* 343.

25. C. F. Jackson to Simon Cameron, *Official Records,* ser. 3, 1:82–83.

26. Ibid., Cameron to Hicks, April 17, 1861, ser. 3, 1:80, and John R. Kenly to Lorenzo Thomas, May 14, 1861, 199.

27. Ibid., William Burton to Cameron, April 25, 1861, ser. 3, 1:114; Patterson to

Cameron, April 25, 1861, ser. 3, 1:110; Cameron to Patterson, April 28, 1861, ser. 3, 1:124–25.

28. Davis, *Rise and Fall,* 1:419–20.

29. Richardson, ed., *Messages,* 1:63–82, quote from 81–82; the scene is described in W. C. Davis, *A Government of Our Own,* 338–41.

30. Joseph L. Harsh, *Confederate Tide Rising: Robert E. Lee and the Making of Southern Strategy, 1861–1862* (Kent, Ohio: Kent State University Press, 1998), 5–7.

31. Ibid., 8, 10.

32. Harsh, *Confederate Tide Rising,* 8; Davis, *Rise and Fall,* 1:292; Proclamation of April 17, 1862, Richardson, ed., *Messages,* 1:60.

33. This is the general thesis in Harsh, *Confederate Tide Rising,* and is reinforced in his *Taken at the Flood: Robert E. Lee and Confederate Strategy in the Maryland Campaign of 1862* (Kent, Ohio: Kent State University Press, 1999).

34. Harsh, *Confederate Tide Rising,* 11.

35. W. C. Davis, *Davis,* 343.

36. W. C. Davis, *A Government of Our Own,* 329.

37. Ibid., 329.

38. Ibid., 330.

39. Speech of Senator James H. Hammond, U.S. Senate, March 4, 1858, *Congressional Globe,* 35th Cong., 1st sess. (Washington, D.C.: John C. Rives, 1858), 961.

40. Coulter, *Confederate States of America,* 420.

41. Bell I. Wiley, "Women of the Lost Cause," chap. 4 in Wiley, *Confederate Women,* Contributions in American History, no. 38 (Westport, Conn.: Greenwood Press, 1975), 140–41.

42. Ibid., 141.

43. Ibid., 132.

44. Ibid., 142.

45. "Gainesville Unconquerables," to Governor Andrew B. Moore, March 30, 1861, Alabama State Archives, in Coulter, *Confederate States of America,* 419–20.

46. Sara Wakeman, *An Uncommon Soldier,* ed. Lauren Cook Burgess (New York: Oxford University Press, 1994).

47. Ladies of Ingleside, to Governor Letcher, April 25, 1861, in Executive Papers, Virginia State Archives, in Coulter, *Confederate States of America,* 420. For more on this general topic, see Elizabeth D. Leonard, *All the Daring of the Soldier: Women of the Civil War Armies* (New York: Norton, 1999).

48. Wiley, *Confederate Women,* 143–44.

49. Coulter, *Confederate States of America,* 421.

50. Glenna R. Schroeder-Lein, *Confederate Hospitals on the Move: Samuel H. Stout and the Army of Tennessee* (Columbia: University of South Carolina Press, 1994), 75 n.38.

51. Ibid., 88.

52. Ibid., 74–75.

53. Ibid., 75–76.

54. Wiley, *Confederate Women,* 145.

55. Ibid.

56. Ibid., 146.

57. Coulter, *Confederate States of America*, 484.

58. W. C. Davis, *A Government of Our Own*, 371–72, 388–91, 399.

59. Cooper, *Davis*, 342–43.

60. W. C. Davis, *The Union That Shaped the Confederacy*, 133 34.

61. Quoted in W. C. Davis, *Davis*, 332–33.

62. Ibid., 335.

63. Coulter, *Confederate States of America*, 150.

64. Todd, *Confederate Finance*, 25, 158–59.

65. Coulter, *Confederate States of America*, 164.

66. W. C. Davis, *The Union That Shaped the Confederacy*, 129.

67. Ibid., 133.

68. Coulter, *Confederate States of America*, 165; Davis, *Papers*, 7:253.

69. Coulter, *Confederate States of America*, 165.

70. Ibid., 164–65, from the *Atlanta Southern Confederacy*, June 25, 1861, and the *Athens Southern Watchman*, July 3, 1861.

71. Coulter, *Confederate States of America*, 165–66; Todd, *Confederate Finance*, 60, 63.

72. "An Act to authorize an issue of treasury notes, and to provide a war tax for their redemption," in Mathews, ed., *Statutes*, 177–83.

73. Coulter, *Confederate States of America*, 175; Todd, *Confederate Finance*, 132.

74. Todd, *Confederate Finance*, 132–35; Ball, *Financial Failure and Confederate Defeat*, 224–25, 227.

75. Coulter, *Confederate States of America*, 175, quoting the *Athens Southern Watchman*, October 16, 1861, and the *Atlanta Southern Confederacy*, August 21, 1861.

76. James A. Rawley, *Turning Points of the Civil War*, Bison Book ed. (Lincoln: University of Nebraska Press, 1966).

77. Michael C. C. Adams, *Our Masters the Rebels* (Cambridge: University of Massachusetts Press, 1974).

78. V. Davis, *A Memoir*, 2:95.

79. Davis, *Rise and Fall*, 1:350–52; Jubal Early, *Jubal Early's Memoirs* (Baltimore: Nautical and Aviation Publishing Company of America, 1989), 27; Edward Porter Alexander, *Fighting for the Confederacy: The Personal Recollections of General Edward Porter Alexander*, ed. Gary W. Gallagher (Chapel Hill: University of North Carolina Press, 1989); quotes from obituary of Leven B. Lane Jr., in the *Baptist Correspondent* (Marion, Ala.), September 11, 1861 (RPR in *Demopolis Times*, n.d.).

80. V. Davis, *A Memoir*, 2:98.

81. J. Davis, *Rise and Fall*, 352–55; Clement Eaton, *Jefferson Davis* (New York: Free Press, 1977), 138.

82. J. B. Jones, *A Rebel War Clerk's Diary at the Confederate State's Capital*, 2 vols. (Philadelphia: J. B. Lippincott, 1866), 1:63–68; Thomas Robson Hay, "Lucius B. Northrop: Commissary General of the Confederacy," *Civil War History* 9, 5 (1963): 6; V. Davis, *A Memoir*, 2:74–75; Thompson, *Toombs*, 171; Davis to C. J. Wright, May 11, 1876, and to V. Davis,

December 7, 1865, in Rowland, ed., *Davis,* 7:514; Alvy L. King, *Louis T. Wigfall, Southern Fire-Eater* (Baton Rouge: Louisiana State University Press, 1970), 128–29; Mrs. D. Giraud Wright, *A Southern Girl in '61* (New York: Doubleday, Page, 1905), 54–55.

83. V. Davis, *A Memoir,* 2:114.

84. Eaton, *Davis,* 138–39.

85. Davis, *Rise and Fall,* 1:442.

86. Quoted in Albert B. Moore, *Conscription and Conflict in the Confederacy* (New York: Macmillan, 1924), 6.

87. Rable, *Confederate Republic,* 84.

88. "An Act to authorize the President of the Confederate States to grant commissions to raise volunteer regiments and battalions, composed of persons who are, or have been, residents of the States of Kentucky, Missouri, Maryland, and Delaware," August 8, 1861, in Matthews, ed., *Statutes,* 174; "An Act to authorize the establishment of recruiting stations for volunteers from the States of Kentucky, Missouri, Maryland, and Delaware," August 30, 1861, ibid., 196–97; "An Act to further provide for the public defence," August 8, 1861, ibid., 176.

89. Ibid., "An Act to provide for local defence and special service," August 21, 1861, and "An Act to authorize the employment of cooks and nurses, other than enlisted men, or volunteers, for the military service," August 21, 1861, 187.

90. "To the Congress of the Confederate States," November 18, 1861, Davis, *Papers,* 7:413.

91. Inaugural Address (as permanent president), February 22, 1862, ibid., 1:186. Actually, the Union army did reach 1 million in size, but not until 1865.

6. In the Aftermath of First Manassas

1. Cooper, *Davis,* 346.

2. Ibid., 346, 350.

3. W. C. Davis, *Davis,* 345.

4. T. R. R. Cobb to wife, February 15, 1861, "Thomas R. R. Cobb . . . Extracts from Letters to His Wife, February 3, 1861–December 10, 1862," ed. A. L. Hull, *SHSP* 28 (1900):282.

5. T. R. R. Cobb to wife, February 28, 1861, in Hull, ed., "Correspondence of Thomas Reade, Rootes Cobb, 1860–1863," *Publications of the Southern History Association,* (1907):243.

6. Woodward, ed., *Mary Chesnut,* 12, entry for February 28, 1861.

7. Robert Barnwell Rhett, "The Confederate Government at Montgomery," in Johnson and Buell, eds., *Battles and Leaders,* 1:104.

8. ——— to Howell Cobb, in "Howell Cobb Papers," ed. R. P. Brooks, *Georgia Historical Quarterly* 6 (1922): 358.

9. Woodward, ed., *Mary Chesnut,* 79, entry for June 27, 1861.

10. Ibid., 138–39, entry for August 8, 1861.

11. Thomas W. Thomas to Stephens, December 31, 1861, in *The Correspondence of Robert Toombs, Alexander H. Stephens, and Howell Cobb,* ed. Ulrich B. Phillips, *Annual*

Report of the American Historical Association for the Year 1911 (Washington, D.C.: U.S. Government Printing Office, 1913), 2:586.

12. Woodward, ed., *Mary Chesnut*, 246, entry for November 28, 1861.

13. W. C. Davis, *The Union That Shaped the Confederacy*, 147.

14. Schott, *Stephens*, 346–47.

15. W. C. Davis, *The Union That Shaped the Confederacy*, 148.

16. Schott, *Stephens*, 347.

17. W. C. Davis, *The Union That Shaped the Confederacy*, 148.

18. " 'Indian' [Alcorn] to My *Dear* Wife," March 16, 1863, in "Letters of James Lusk Alcorn," ed. Percy L. Rainwater, *Journal of Southern History* 3 (May 1937):204.

19. J. H. Hammond to W. W. Boyce, March 17, 1862, in "Boyce-Hammond Correspondence," ed. Rosser H. Taylor, *Journal of Southern History* 3 (August 1937):349.

20. T. R. R. Cobb to ———, in Hull, ed., "Cobb, Extracts," 290–91.

21. Boyce to Hammond, March 17, 1862, in Taylor, ed., "Boyce-Hammond Correspondence," 350.

22. Albert L. Lewis, "The Confederate Congress: A Study in Personnel" (master's thesis, University of Southern California, 1955), 39, from Charles E. Cauthen, *South Carolina Goes to War, 1860–1865,* James Sprunt Studies in History and Political Science (Chapel Hill: University of North Carolina Press, 1950), 213.

23. Stephens to Johnson, April 8, 1864, *Official Records,* ser. 4, 3:279–80; William L. Yancey, debate in Confederate Senate, September 16, 1862, "Proceedings of the Confederate Congress," *SHSP,* 46:153–54.

24. Wigfall to Johnston, August 9, 1863, Papers of Joseph E. Johnston, Box JO 295, The Huntington Library. This item is reproduced by permission of *The Huntington Library, San Marino, California.*

25. V. Davis, *A Memoir,* 2:161–64.

26. See, for example, Clement C. Clay and William Lowndes Yancey to Davis, April 21, 1862, Davis endorsement, April 21, 1862, Davis, *Papers,* 8:150.

27. Robert. G. H. Kean, *Inside the Confederate Government: The Diary of Robert Garlick Hill Kean,* ed. Edward Younger (New York: Oxford University Press, 1957), entry for June 13, 1864, 156.

28. Davis to Varina Howell Davis, May 16, 1862, Davis, *Papers,* 8:179.

29. Akin to wife, January 10, 1865, in *Letters of Warren Akin, Confederate Congressman,* ed. Bell I. Wiley, (Athens: University of Georgia Press, 1959), 75.

30. Davis to J. R. Chalmers, March 17, 1865, in Rowland, ed., *Davis,* 6:513–18; Davis to Mrs. Howell Cobb, March 30, 1865, ibid., 524–25.

31. Hudson Strode, *Jefferson Davis,* 3 vols. (New York: Harcourt, Brace and World, 1955–1964), *Confederate President,* 2:148.

32. Wayne K. Durrill, *War of Another Kind: A Southern Community in the Great Rebellion* (New York: Oxford University Press, 1990), 52–53, 102–3, 107, 166–85, 229.

33. See Nevins, *The Improvised War, 1861–1862,* 129–36.

34. Hattaway had a telephone conversation with Grady McWhiney during the last week of September 2001 in which the latter agreed that he does still believe this and referred us

to the citation in his *Braxton Bragg and Confederate Defeat,* vol. 1, *Field Command* (New York: Columbia University Press, 1969), 307; see also 214, n.18 and 328, n.67.

35. Special Orders no. 88, Adjutant and Inspector General's Office, July 4, 1861, *Official Records,* ser. 1, 4:362; General Orders no. 1, Headquarters Department no. 2, July 12, 1861, ibid., 368; S. Cooper to Polk, June 25, 1861, ibid., 52, pt. 2, 115.

36. Polk to L. P. Walker, July 23, 1861, *Official Records,* ser. 1, 3:613; Wm. T. Withers to L. P. Walker, July 25, 1861, ibid., 4:374.

37. Beriah Magoffin to Jefferson Davis, August [?], 1861, *Official Records,* ser. 1, 4:378. The specific date is unknown, but it is most likely between August 15 and 25.

38. Davis to Magoffin, August 28, 1861, *Official Records,* ser. 1, 4:396–97.

39. Polk to Walker, July 30, 1861, *Official Records,* ser. 1, 4:376; Polk to Walker, August 6, 1861, ibid., 381; C. Wickliffe to Polk, August 6, 1861, ibid., 381; Polk to Magoffin, September 1, 1861, ibid., 179; Joseph H. Parks, *General Leonidas Polk, C.S.A.: The Fighting Bishop* (Baton Rouge: Louisiana State University Press, 1962), 179–80.

40. Thomas Lawrence Connelly, *Army of the Heartland: The Army of Tennessee, 1861–1862* (Baton Rouge: Louisiana State University Press, 1967), 52; Isham G. Harris to Polk, September 4, 1861, *Official Records,* ser. 1, 4:180; Polk to Harris, September 4, 1861, ibid. (emphasis added).

41. Walker to Polk, September 4, 1861, *Official Records,* ser. 1, 4:180; Polk to Davis, September 4, 1861, ibid., 181; Steven E. Woodworth, *Jefferson Davis and His Generals: The Failure of Confederate Command in the West* (Lawrence: University Press of Kansas, 1990), 40, 32 n.38.

42. Davis to Polk, September 4, 1861, *Official Records,* ser. 1, 4:181. Steven E. Woodworth claims the proper date of this message is September 5, which makes chronological sense. Woodworth also believes that the proper wording is as given here, not "the necessity justifies the action," which is the text found in the *Official Records.* See Woodworth, *Davis and His Generals,* 324 n.43.

43. John M. Johnston to Polk, September 9, 1861, *Official Records,* ser. 1, 4:185–86; Polk to Johnston, September 9, 1861, ibid., 186–87; Davis to Polk, September 15, 1861, ibid., 188.

44. Davis to Polk, September 13, 1861, *Official Records,* ser. 1, 4:189.

45. Woodworth, *Davis and His Generals,* 45. Much of this discussion of the violation of Kentucky's neutrality comes from Richard E. Beringer, "Jefferson Davis's Pursuit of Ambition: The Attractive Features of Alternative Decisions," *Civil War History* 38 (March 1992):20–24.

46. Harsh, *Confederate Tide Rising,* 24.

47. Rable, *Confederate Republic,* 112.

48. Ibid., 114; Durrill, *War of Another Kind,* 52–53, 60–66.

49. Davis, *Papers,* 7:413; Harsh, *Confederate Tide Rising,* 28–29.

50. Rable, *Confederate Republic,* 93–94.

51. Ibid., 111–12.

52. Ibid., 112–13; David Donald, "Died of Democracy," in *Why the North Won the Civil War,* ed. Donald (1960; reprint, New York: Collier Books, 1962), 84, 86, 90.

53. W. C. Davis, *Davis,* 389.

54. Joseph T. Durkin, S.J., *Stephen R. Mallory: Confederate Navy Chief* (Chapel Hill: University of North Carolina Press, 1954), 176–77, 248, from Mallory's letter to his son, "Buddy," September 27, 1865, Mallory Papers, Library of Congress (LC), typescript copy of original in Mallory Diary and Reminiscences, Southern Historical Collection (SHC), University of North Carolina Library, Chapel Hill. The letter was written while Mallory was imprisoned in Fort Lafayette.

55. Kean, *Inside the Confederate Government,* entry for June 14, 1863, 72.

56. Jones, *Rebel War Clerk's Diary,* 1:181, entry for November 2, 1862.

57. Kean, *Inside the Confederate Government,* entry for August 9, 1863 (emphasis in original), 90.

58. Ibid., 100–101, entry for August 23, 1863.

59. McMurry, *Two Great Rebel Armies,* 150.

60. Goff, *Confederate Supply,* 4.

61. Coulter, *Confederate States of America,* 240–43, 246.

62. Goff, *Confederate Supply,* 4.

63. Ibid., 4–5.

64. Clement Eaton, *A History of the Southern Confederacy* (New York: Oxford University Press, 1958), 140.

65. Northrop to Davis, August 21, 1861, in Davis, *Papers,* 7:298.

66. Coulter, *Confederate States of America,* 247–48.

67. Allan Nevins, *The War for the Union,* vol. 3 *The Organized War, 1863–1864* (New York: Free Press, 1954), 21.

68. Moore, *Confederate Commissary General,* 110; from Rowland, ed., *Davis,* 5:127–28.

69. Moore, *Confederate Commissary General,* 53.

70. Eaton, *History of the Southern Confederacy,* 252–57.

71. Charles P. Roland, *The Confederacy* (Chicago: University of Chicago Press, 1960), 142; Eaton, *History of the Southern Confederacy,* 253–57.

72. Neely, *Southern Rights,* 30–31, 34, 79.

73. Circular, Quartermaster Generals's Department, November [?], 1861, *Official Records,* ser. 4, 1:767.

74. Coulter, *Confederate States of America,* 269; Richard D. Brown, *Modernization: The Transformation of American Life, 1600–1865* (New York: Hill and Wang, 1976), 143.

75. Emory M. Thomas, *The Confederate Nation, 1861–1865* (New York: Harper and Row, 1979), 201.

76. Brown, *Modernization.*

77. Ibid., 182–86.

78. Moore, *Confederate Commissary General,* 108, 113–14.

79. Ibid., 92.

80. J. B. Benjamin to Joseph E. Brown, September 30, 1861, *Official Records,* ser. 4, 1:634.

81. Ibid., Brown to Benjamin, October 1, 1861.

82. See Coulter, *Confederate States of America,* map between pages 270 and 271 (p. xxiii in this volume).

83. *Journal of the Confederate Congress,* 1:782.

84. Thomas F. Oliver, collector, to Edward Sparrow, December 30, 1861, Southern Historical Collection, University of South Carolina; typescript in Special Collections Department, Bell I. Wiley Papers, Collection 521, Writings of Confederate Congressman, Box 1, Robert W. Woodruff Library, Emory University (emphasis added).

85. A. B. Moore to Gentlemen of the Senate and House of Representatives, October 28, 1861, *Official Records,* ser 4, 1:701–02.

86. Ibid., John Letcher to Gentlemen of the Convention, November 18, 1861, ser. 4, 1:739.

87. Moore, *Confederate Commissary General,* 59–60.

88. L. B. Northrop to L. P. Walker, August 19, 1861, *Official Records,* ser. 4, 1:574–75.

89. Ibid., L. B. Northrop to J. P. Benjamin, January 18, 1862, ser. 4, 1:870–71.

90. Ibid.

91. Ibid., George W. Randolph to Jefferson Davis, April 7, 1862, ser. 4, 1:1050.

92. See Herman Hattaway and Michael Gillespie, "We Shall Cease to Be Friends," *Military History* (August 1984):20–25.

93. Welles to Dupont, October 15, 1861, Papers of Admiral D. D. Porter, PR Box 615, The Huntington Library, San Marino, California.

94. See Norman Ferris, *The Trent Affair: A Diplomatic Crisis* (Knoxville: University of Tennessee Press, 1977).

95. Strode, *Davis,* 2:184–85.

96. Ibid., 2:188.

97. The treaties with the Indian tribes are found in Matthews, ed., *Statutes,* 289–411.

98. Cooper, *Davis,* 369.

7. Forging the Resources of War

1. Cooper, *Davis,* 352–53.

2. Ibid., 353.

3. Ibid., 371.

4. Thomas, *Confederate Nation,* 120–23.

5. John G. Moore, "Mobility and Strategy in the Civil War," *Military Affairs* (now *Journal of Military History*) (summer 1960): 86–77. For a full treatment of logistics in its European historical context, see Martin Van Creveld, *Supplying War: Logistics from Wallenstein to Patton* (Cambridge: University of Massachusetts, 1977).

6. Davis, *Papers,* 8:53.

7. Strode, *Davis,* 2:198–99.

8. Alexander and Beringer, *Anatomy of the Confederate Congress,* 3.

9. Ibid., 3.

10. Ibid., 329.

11. Ibid., 342.

12. Rable, *Confederate Republic,* 125.

13. Robbins, "Confederate Nationalism," 57–58.

14. Richardson, ed., *Messages,* 1:183–88.

15. V. Davis, *A Memoir,* 2:180; Richardson, ed., *Messages,* 1:188.

16. Davis to J. E. Johnston, February 28, 1862, Davis, *Papers,* 8:69; Harsh, *Confederate Tide Rising,* 18.

17. Davis, *Rise and Fall,* 2:101–2.

18. Davis to William M. Brooks, March 15, 1862, Davis, *Papers,* 8:100.

19. Davis to Johnston, March 15, 1862, in Rowland, ed., *Davis,* 5:222.

20. Davis to Braxton Bragg, October 17, 1862, Davis, *Papers,* 8:448.

21. Thomas Bragg Diary, 1861–1862, entry for February 5, 1862, in the Thomas Bragg Papers #3304, microfilm copy of original, frame 456, Southern Historical Collection, Wilson Library, University of North Carolina at Chapel Hill.

22. Ibid., frames 459, 464–71, entries for February 10, 17, 20–21, 26, 1862.

23. Office of the Governor RG 3, Letters Received, John Letcher 1860–1864, Box 20 Folder 7 (Accession 36787) Ths. Bragg to [John Letcher] 24 February 1862, microcopy, State Records Collection, Archives Research Services, The Library of Virginia, Richmond, Virginia, JDA.

24. J. R. Tucker to John Letcher, February 25, 1862, ibid., JDA.

25. "An Act to authorize the suspension of the writ of habeas corpus in certain cases," approved February 27, 1862, in Matthews, ed., *Public Laws, First Session of the First Congress, 1862,* 1.

26. Robbins, "Confederate Nationalism," 64–65.

27. Richardson, ed., *Messages,* 1:219.

28. Ibid., 219–20.

29. Ibid., General Orders no. 8, 220–21.

30. Ibid., General Orders no. 11, 221–22.

31. Ibid., General Orders no. 15, 222–23.

32. Ibid., General Orders no. 18, 223–24.

33. Ibid., General Orders no. 21, 224–25.

34. Ibid., General Orders no. 33, 225–26.

35. Ibid., General Orders no. 19, 226–27.

36. Ibid., 227–28.

37. "An Act to limit the Act Authorizing the suspension of the Writ of Habeas Corpus," approved April 19, 1862, in Matthews, ed., *Public Laws, First Session of the First Congress, 1862,* 40.

38. Robbins, "Confederate Nationalism," 68–70.

39. "An Act for the granting of bounty and furloughs to privates and non-commissioned officers in the provisional army," December 11, 1861, in Matthews, ed., *Statutes,* 223–24.

40. Ibid., "An Act for the recruiting service of the provisional army of the Confederate States," December 19, 1861, 226.

41. Ibid., "An Act to amend an act entitled, 'An act to raise an additional military force to serve during the war,' " approved May 8, 1861, "and for other purposes," January 22, 1862, 248–49.

42. Ibid., "An Act to authorize the President to call upon the several States for troops to serve for three years or during the war," January 23, 1862, 252.

43. Ibid., "An Act to provide for recruiting companies now in the service of the Confederate States for twelve months," January 27, 1862, 254.

44. Ibid., "An Act to amend an act entitled, 'An act to provide for the public defense,' approved March 6, 1861," January 29, 1862, 255.

45. Ibid., "An Act supplemental to an act entitled 'An act providing for the granting of bounty and furloughs to privates and noncommissioned officers in the provisional army,' " February 3, 1862, 256–57.

46. To the Senate and House of Representatives of the Confederate States, February 25, 1862, in Richardson, ed., *Messages,* 1:189–90.

47. Statement of troops in the service of the Confederate States, S. Cooper, Adjutant and Inspector General's Office, March 1, 1862, *Official Records,* ser. 4, 1:962–64. In view of future controversies between Georgia and the Confederate government over conscription, it is worth noting that Georgia had a higher percentage of troops "for the war" than any other state (about two-thirds); Virginia had only about 3 percent.

48. To the Speaker of the House of Representatives, March 4, 1862, in Richardson, ed., *Messages,* 1:194.

49. Ibid., to the Senate and House of Representatives of the Confederate States, March 28, 1862, 1:205–6.

50. Peter Paret, "Justifying the Obligation of Military Service," *Journal of Military History* 57, special issue (October 1993):124.

51. Ibid., 124.

52. Ibid., 125.

53. Ibid., 126.

54. Eric H. Walther, "Fire-Eaters and the Riddle of Confederate Nationalism," paper presented at the annual meeting of the Southern Historical Association, Fort Worth, Texas, 1991, 17.

55. Steven Hahn, *The Roots of Southern Populism: Yeoman Farmers and the Transformation of the Georgia Upcountry, 1850–1890* (New York: Oxford University Press, 1983), 119.

56. H. Flanagin to Jefferson Davis, January 5, 1863, 6MS Am 1649.24 (961), Dearborn Collection, Harvard University, microfilm copy, JDA; R. W. Johnson to Jefferson Davis, June 18, 1863, Clements Library, University of Michigan, microcopy, JDA.

57. "Proceedings," *SHSP,* 45:26.

58. Ibid., 45:27.

59. Hattaway, "Via Confederate Post," 22–29.

60. Coulter, *Confederate States of America,* 156.

61. "An Act to authorize the Issue of Treasury Notes, and to prescribe the Punishment for forging the same, and for forging certificates of Stock, Bonds, or Coupons," March 9, 1861, in Matthews, ed., *Statutes,* 56; "An Act to authorize the issue of Treasury notes, and to provide a war tax for their redemption," August 19, 1861, ibid., 182–83. Counterfeiting postage stamps was evidently less serious; perpetrators were also "deemed to be guilty

of felony" but subject to penalties of only five hundred dollars or five years or both ("An Act to prescribe the Rates of Postage in the Confederate States of America and for other purposes," February 28, 1861, ibid., 35).

62. Coulter, *Confederate States of America,* 156–57; "An Act to punish and repress the importation, by our enemies, of notes purporting to be notes of the Treasury of the Confederate States," October 13, 1862, in James M. Matthews, ed., *Public Laws . . . passed at the Second Session of the First Congress* (1862; reprint, Holmes Beach, Fla.: Gaunt, 1970), 80–81.

63. Coulter, *Confederate States of America,* 158, quoting the *Macon, (Ga.), Daily Telegraph,* February 18, 1864.

64. Coulter, *Confederate States of America,* 159.

65. U.S. Consulate, Liverpool, Official dispatches, Dudley to Seward, May 10, 1862, Thomas Haines Dudley Collection, Box 1, DU-4573, The Huntington Library. This item is reproduced by permission of *The Huntington Library, San Marino, California.*

66. See James D. Bulloch, *The Secret Service of the Confederate States in Europe, or How the Confederate Cruisers Were Equipped,* 2 vols. (New York: Thomas Yoseloff, 1959).

67. Goff, *Confederate Supply,* 33; "An Act concerning the transportation of soldiers, and allowance for clothing of volunteers, and amendatory of the act for the establishment and organization of the army of the Confederate States," May 21, 1861, in Matthews, ed., *Statutes,* 128, and "An Act to amend the second section of 'An act concerning the transportation of soldiers and allowance for clothing of volunteers, and amendatory of the Act for the establishment and organization of the army of the Confederate States,' " August 30, 1861, ibid., 196.

68. Goff, *Confederate Supply,* 33.

69. Ibid., 33–35.

70. Ibid., 35.

71. George W. Randolph to Jefferson Davis, April 7, 1862, *Official Records,* ser. 4, 1:1050.

72. Ibid., L. B. Northrop to George W. Randolph, April 29, 1862, ser. 4, 1:1101.

73. Cooper, *Davis,* 387.

74. Moore, *Confederate Commissary General,* 210.

75. L. B. Northrop to J. P. Benjamin, November 27, 1861, *Official Records,* ser. 4, 1:756–57.

76. Ibid., 37.

77. Moore, *Confederate Commissary General,* 130–31.

78. Joseph E. Johnston to Jefferson Davis, March 13, 1862, photocopy, Davis Papers, Woodson Research Center, Fondren Library, Rice University, Houston, Texas, JDA.

79. Abraham C. Myers to Jefferson Davis, March 7, 1862, photocopy, Davis Papers, Woodson Research Center, Fondren Library, Rice University, Houston, Texas, JDA.

80. Jefferson Davis to Varina Davis, June 11, 1862, microcopy, Davis Family Collection, Box 2, Eleanor S. Brockenbrough Library, The Museum of the Confederacy, Richmond, Virginia, JDA.

81. Moore, *Confederate Commissary General,* 137.

82. "An Act for the Organization of a Corps of Officers for the Working of Nitre Caves and Establishing Nitre Beds," approved April 11, 1862, in Matthews, ed., *Public Laws, First Session of the First Congress,* 27–28.

83. Ibid., "An Act to Encourage the Manufacture of Saltpetre and of Small Arms," approved April 17, 1862, 33–34.

84. Ibid., "An Act Supplementary to the Act entitled, 'An Act to encourage the manufacture of Saltpetre and Small Arms,'" approved April 19, 1862, 38.

85. Ibid.

86. Angus James Johnston, *Virginia Railroads in the Civil War* (Chapel Hill: University of North Carolina Press, 1961), 193.

87. Ibid., 113.

88. Goff, *Confederate Supply,* 41–42.

89. William Blair, *Virginia's Private War: Feeding Body and Soul in the Confederacy, 1861–1865* (New York: Oxford University Press, 1998), 45.

90. John B. Spence to attorney general of the Confederate States, December 4, 1861, *Freedom: A Documentary History of Emancipation, 1861–1867,* ser. 1, vol. 1, *The Destruction of Slavery,* ed. Ira Berlin et al. (London and New York: Cambridge University Press, 1985), 782–83.

91. U.S. War Department, *Journal of the Confederate Congress,* 1:431.

92. Secretary of War L. P. Walker to W. Porcher Miles et al., September 4, 1861, *Official Records,* ser 4, 1:598; August 27, 1861, *Journal of the Confederate Congress,* 1:416.

93. Ibid., 49–50; Jones, *Rebel War Clerk's Diary,* 1:83.

94. Goff, *Confederate Supply,* 50–51.

95. Rable, *Confederate Republic,* 133.

96. Schott, *Stephens,* 348.

97. Ibid., 349–50.

98. Cooper, *Davis,* 382.

99. Ibid.

8. NORTHERN POWER EMERGES

1. Elizabeth Cutting, *Jefferson Davis: Political Soldier* (New York: Dodd, Mead, 1930), 194.

2. Davis, *Papers,* 8:177.

3. Ibid., 131.

4. Ibid., 132 n.2.

5. W. C. Davis, *Davis,* 404.

6. Allen, *Davis,* 306–7.

7. Cooper, *Davis,* 379.

8. Davis to Joseph Davis, April 20, 1862, Davis, *Papers,* 8:147–48.

9. Cooper, *Davis,* 387.

10. Inaugural Address, February 22, 1862, Richardson, ed., *Messages,* 1:186.

11. To the Congress of the Confederate States, February 25, 1862, Davis, *Papers,* 8:58–59.

12. Davis to Johnston, February 28, 1862, Davis, *Papers,* 8:69.

13. Cooper, *Davis,* 387.

14. Ibid., 387–88.

15. Allen, *Davis,* 311–12, and Cooper, *Davis,* 388. These two authors disagree on the precise chronology, but the difference is too trivial for argument here.

16. Davis to William M. Brooks, March 15, 1862, Davis, *Papers,* 8:100.

17. Davis to Johnston, May 11, 1862, Davis, *Papers,* 8:171.

18. Ibid.

19. V. Davis, *A Memoir,* 2:192–93.

20. Allen, *Davis,* 310.

21. Ibid., 312.

22. Davis, *Papers,* 8:168; V. Davis, *Memoir,* 2:269.

23. Davis to Varina Howell Davis, May 13, 1862, Davis, *Papers,* 8:174.

24. Allen, *Davis,* 312; *The Diary of Edmund Ruffin,* ed. William Kauffman Scarborough (Baton Rouge: LSU Press, 1976), 2:460.

25. See, for example, Davis to Johnston, February 28, 1862, Davis, *Papers,* 8:69, and May 17, 1862, ibid., 185.

26. Ibid., Davis to Varina Howell Davis, May 15, 1862, 8:178–79.

27. Ibid., 8:181.

28. Ibid., Davis to Joseph E. Johnston, May 17, 1862, 8:184–85.

29. Ibid., Davis to Varina Howell Davis, May 30, 1862, 8:203–4.

30. Ibid., Varina Howell Davis to Davis, May 30, 1862, 8:205.

31. Cooper, *Davis,* 381.

32. Davis, *Rise and Fall,* 2:128–29; Davis to V. Davis, June 2, 1862, Davis, *Papers,* 8:209; John H. Reagan, *Memoirs, with Special References to Secession and Civil War,* ed. Walter F. McCaleb (New York and Washington, D.C.: Neale, 1906), 141–42. See also Leonne M. Hudson, *The Odyssey of a Southerner: The Life and Times of Gustavus Woodson Smith* (Macon, Ga.: Mercer University Press, 1998), chapter 5.

33. Davis to Varina Howell Davis, June 3, 1863, Davis, *Papers,* 8:217.

34. Harsh, *Confederate Tide Rising,* 50.

35. W. C. Davis, *Davis,* 426–27.

36. Harsh, *Confederate Tide Rising,* 50; Davis to Lee, June 2, 1862, *Official Records,* ser. 1, vol. 11, pt. 3, 569–70.

37. Cooper, *Davis,* 389.

38. Ibid., 391.

39. Harsh, *Confederate Tide Rising,* 55–59; Lee to Davis, June 10, 1863, Robert E. Lee, *Wartime Papers of Robert E. Lee,* ed. Clifford Dowdey and Louis H. Manarin (Boston: Little, Brown, 1961), 507–9; see also Steven E. Woodworth, *Davis and Lee at War* (Lawrence: University Press of Kansas), 1995.

40. Harsh, *Confederate Tide Rising,* 75, 97; Woodworth, *Davis and Lee,* 213–15.

41. Davis, *Rise and Fall,* 2:146–47.

42. W. C. Davis, *Davis,* 429.

43. Allen, *Davis,* 322.

44. V. Davis to J. Davis, July 6, 1862, extract in Davis, *Papers,* 8:282.

45. Davis, *Rise and Fall,* 2:152–53.

46. Davis to Lee, July 5, 1862, Davis, *Papers,* 8:276–77.

47. W. C. Davis, *Davis,* 434.

48. Allen, *Davis,* 326–27.

49. Davis, To the Army of Eastern Virginia, July 5, 1862, in Richardson, ed., *Messages,* 1:229–30.

50. Cooper, *Davis,* 394.

51. Ibid.

52. Ibid., 395.

53. Allen, *Davis,* 318–19.

54. Ibid., 327–28.

55. Ibid., 328.

56. Ibid., 324.

57. W. C. Davis, *Davis,* 451, 454.

58. "An Act to provide for keeping all fire-arms in the armies of the Confederate States in the hands of effective men," April 10, 1862, in Matthews, ed., *Public Laws, First Session of the First Congress,* 24.

59. Francis Pickens to the Confederate governors, March 22, 1862, Circular Letter calling for concerted action on the part of the several states of the Confederacy, Confederate Imprint, #2094-1.

60. "An Act to further provide for the public defense," April 14, 1862, in Matthews, ed., *Public Laws, First Session of the First Congress,* 29–32. The best general survey of Confederate conscription is still Moore, *Conscription and Conflict in the Confederacy.*

61. "An Act to further provide for the public defense," April 16, 1862, in Matthews, ed., *Public Laws, First Session of the First Congress,* 29–32.

62. Ibid., "An Act to further provide for the public defense," April 16, 1862, section 1, para. 2, and sect. 9, 29–31.

63. Ibid., "A Bill [an act] for the enlistment of Cooks in the Army," April 21, 1862, 48.

64. Ibid., "An Act to organize Battalions of Sharp Shooters," April 21, 1862, 51.

65. Ibid., "An Act to amend An Act entitled 'An Act to further provide for the public defense,' passed April 16, 1862," April 21, 1862, 52.

66. Ibid., "An Act to exempt certain persons from enrollment for service in the Armies of the Confederate States," April 21, 1862, 51.

67. "Proceedings," *SHSP,* 45:213.

68. Ibid., 47:205.

69. Emory Upton, *The Military Policy of the United States from 1775* (Washington, D.C.: U.S. Government Printing Office, 1912), 468–69.

9. ESCALATING DEGREES OF WARFARE

1. Cooper, *Davis,* 373.

2. Ibid., 374.

3. W. C. Davis, *Davis,* 608.

4. *National Intelligencer,* July 22, 1862; Allan Nevins, *The War for the Union,* vols. 2, *War Becomes Revolution, 1862–1863* (New York: Charles Scribner's Sons, 1960), 293–94; Ezra J. Warner, *Generals in Blue: Lives of the Union Commanders* (Baton Rouge: Louisiana State University Press, 1964), 511.

5. Charles Royster, *The Destructive War: William Tecumseh Sherman, Stonewall Jackson, and the Americans* (New York: Knopf, 1991), xii.

6. "An Act to regulate the business of Conscription," approved March 7, 1865, in *Laws and Joint Resolutions of the Last Session of the Confederate Congress,* ed. Charles W. Ramsdell, (1941; reprint, New York: AMS Press, 1965), 86–88.

7. To the Senate and House of Representatives of the Confederate States, August 18, 1862, in Richardson, ed., *Messages,* 1:234–37.

8. "An Act to amend an Act entitled 'An Act to provide further for the public defence,' approved April 16, 1862," September 27, 1862, in Matthews, ed., *Public Laws, Second Session of the First Congress,* 61–62.

9. Ibid., "An Act to authorize the establishment of Camps of Instruction and the appointment of officers to command to the same," October 8, 1862, 69.

10. Ibid., "An Act to amend an act entitled 'An Act to further provide for the public defence,'" approved 16 April, 1862, 70.

11. Ibid., "An Act to establish places of rendezvous for the examination of enrolled men," October 11, 1862, 75–76.

12. Ibid., "An Act to amend an Act entitled 'An Act to raise an additional military force to serve during the war,' approved May 8, 1861, and to provide for raising forces in the States of Missouri and Kentucky," October 11, 1862, 76–77.

13. "Proceedings," *SHSP,* 46:20–21.

14. "An Act to exempt certain persons from military duty, and to repeal an 'Act to exempt certain persons from enrollment for service in the army of the Confederate States,' approved April 21, 1862," October 11, 1862, in Matthews, ed., *Public Laws, Second Session of the First Congress,* 77–79.

15. John S. Preston to Hon. J. C. Breckenridge, February [?], 1865, enclosure, "Exemptions," *Offical Records,* ser. 4,3:1102–3, 1110.

16. See Richard E. Beringer, "Confederate Identity and the Will to Fight," in *On the Road to Total War: The American Civil War and the German Wars of Unification, 1861–1871,* ed. Stig Foerster and Jorg Nagler, German Historical Institute (New York: Cambridge University Press, 1997).

17. See Brown, *Modernization,* who argues that the cause of the Civil War was the differing pace of modernization between North and South (see especially chapters 6 and 7).

18. "An Act to relieve the army of disqualified, disabled, and incompetent officers," October 13, 1862, in Matthews, ed., *Public Laws, Second Session of the First Congress,* 85–87.

19. Ibid., "An Act to authorize the formation of volunteer companies for local defense," October 13, 1862, 90.

20. Ibid., "An Act to limit 'An Act authorizing the suspension of the Writ of Habeas Corpus,'" approved April 19, 1862, 40.

21. Speech of Williamson S. Oldham, August 27, 1862, *SHSP* 45 (May 1925):248–49.

22. Ibid., speech of John B. Clark, August 27, 1862, 249.

23. Ibid., speech of Thomas J. Semmes, August 25, 1862, 225.

24. Ibid., speech of Williamson S. Oldham, August 25, 1862, 226.

25. General Order no. 66, Adjutant and Inspector General's Office, September 22, 1862, *Official Records,* ser. 4, 2:83; Robbins, "Confederate Nationalism," 71.

26. Report of the House Committee of the Judiciary, September 13, 1862, *Journal of the Confederate Congress,* 5:375–76.

27. Robbins, "Confederate Nationalism," 72.

28. "An Act authorizing the suspension of the Writ of Habeas Corpus," October 13, 1862, in Matthews, ed., *Public Laws, Second Session of the First Congress,* 84.

29. Moore, *Conscription and Conflict in the Confederacy.*

30. General Orders no. 56, War Department Adjutant and Inspector General's Office, August 1862, *Official Records,* ser.4, 2:39.

31. April 19, 1862, *Journal of the Confederate Congress,* 5:271.

32. Ibid., August 19, 1862, 5:300.

33. Ibid., October 8, 1862, 2:441–42.

34. Jefferson Davis to the Senate of the Confederate States of America, in Richardson, ed., *Messages,* 1:262.

35. Randolph to Lee, October 11, 1862, *Official Records,* ser.4, 2:116.

36. Milton F. Perry, *Infernal Machines: The Story of Confederate Submarine and Mine Warfare* (Baton Rouge: Louisiana State University Press, 1965).

37. Mark Grimsley, *The Hard Hand of War: Union Military Policy Toward Southern Civilians, 1861–1865* (New York: Cambridge University Press, 1995), 4–5.

38. These orders and their role in the switch from conciliation to pragmatic war are discussed in Grimsley, *The Hard Hand of War,* 85–95.

39. Charles Minor Blackford III, ed., and Susan Leigh Blackford, comp., *Letters from Lee's Army, or Memoirs of Life in and out of the Army in Virginia During the War Between the States* (New York: Charles Scribner's Sons, 1947), 86–87.

40. Cooper, *Davis,* 396.

41. Davis to Robert E. Lee, August 30, 1862, Davis, *Papers,* 8:367–68.

42. Davis to Lee, September 2, 1862, *Journal of the Confederate Congress,* 5:339.

43. Ibid., 377.

44. See Harsh, *Confederate Tide Rising,* 162–63.

45. Lee to Davis, September 3, 1862, Davis, *Papers,* 8:373, and Lee to Davis, September 7, 1862, 379.

46. Davis to John Forsyth, July 18, 1862, Davis, *Papers,* 7:293; Harsh, *Confederate Tide Rising,* 19.

47. Davis to Lee and others, September 7 [?], 1862, Roland, ed., *Davis,* 5:338–39; Harsh, *Confederate Tide Rising,* 19; Larry C. Nelson, *Bullets, Ballots, and Rhetoric: Confederate Policy for the United States Presidential Contest of 1864* (Tuscaloosa: University of Alabama Press, 1980), 18.

48. Cooper, *Davis,* 397.

49. Ibid., 400.

50. Davis, *Rise and Fall,* 2:312-43; Rowland, ed., *Davis,* 5:338–39; Dowdey and Manarin, eds., *Wartime Papers of Lee,* chap. 6 (see especially Lee to Davis, September 3, 4, and 5, 1862, 292–94, 295–98); Early, *Memoirs,* 92–161, 403 n.1; Alexander, *Fighting for the Confederacy,* 126–54; Walter H. Taylor, *General Lee: His Campaigns in Virginia, 1861–1865* (Norfolk: Nusbaum Book and News, 1906), 87–139.

51. W. C. Davis, *Davis,* 470.

52. Goff, *Confederate Supply,* 41–42.

53. Cooper, *Davis,* 397–98.

54. Davis to Braxton Bragg, October 17, 1862, Davis, *Papers,* 8:448.

55. Ibid., 452.

56. John W. Crockett and others to Jefferson Davis, August 18, 1862, *Official Records,* ser. 1, vol. 16, pt. 2, 771–72.

57. Ibid., proclamation by Braxton Bragg, September 14, 1862, ser. 1, vol. 16, pt. 2, 822, and also Samuel Jones to Henry C. Wayne, September 16, 1862, 835.

58. Ibid., J. P. McCowan to E. Kirby Smith, September 16, 1862, ser. 1, vol. 16, pt. 2, 836; Kirby Smith to Braxton Bragg, September 18, 1862, 845–46; and Bragg to the Adjutant General, C.S. Army, September 25, 1862, 876.

59. W. C. Davis, *Davis,* 472.

60. Cooper, *Davis,* 402.

61. Ibid., 403.

62. Ibid., 489.

63. Rable, *Confederate Republic,* 156–57.

64. Ibid., 157.

65. Ibid., 165.

66. Schott, *Stephens,* 357, 368.

67. George Green Shackleford, *George Wythe Randolph and the Confederate Elite* (Athens: University of Georgia Press, 1988), 124–25, 129, 132–35, 140–42.

68. Ibid., 145–46; Woodworth, *Davis and His Generals,* 179–80.

69. Cooper, *Davis,* 415.

70. Woodworth, *Davis and His Generals,* 170–71.

71. Cooper, *Davis,* 415–16.

72. Ibid., 416.

73. Ibid.

74. Speech in Jackson, Mississippi, December 26, 1862, Davis, *Papers,* 8:576; ref. to Deut. 32:35 and Rom. 12:19.

75. W. C. Davis, *Davis,* 486.

76. Ibid., 567.

77. Ibid., 567, 569.

78. Ibid., 571, 576.

79. Ibid., 485–88.

80. Cooper, *Davis,* 419.

10. The Threat of Emancipation

1. Cooper, *Davis,* 420,

2. Ibid., 421.

3. James McPherson, "The Whole Family of Man: Lincoln and the Best Hope Abroad," in *The Union, the Confederacy, and the Atlantic Rim,* ed. Robert E. May (West Lafayette, Ind.: Purdue University Press, 1995), 131–32.

4. McPherson, *Battle Cry of Freedom,* 565.

5. Cooper, *Davis,* 408, 421.

6. To the Senate and House of Representatives, January 12, 1863, in Rowland, ed., *Davis,* 5:409.

7. Ibid., Davis to the Confederate Congress, January 12, 1863; Richard H. Wilmer, *The Recent Past from a Southern Standpoint* (New York: Thomas Whittaker, 1887), 223–24; Samuel A. Cartwright, "Alcohol and the Ethiopian," *New Orleans Medical and Surgical Journal* 10 (1853): 161–63; Allen, *Davis,* 342–43.

8. General Orders no. 60, War Department, Adjutant and Inspector General's Office, August 21, 1862, *Official Records,* ser. 1, 14:599.

9. "Proceedings," September 29, 1862, *SHSP,* 47:8.

10. Ibid.

11. *Journal of the Confederate Congress,* October 1, 1862, 5:469.

12. Ibid., October 11, 1862, 5:547.

13. "Proceedings," January 19, 1863, *SHSP,* 47:153.

14. "Joint resolution on the subject of retaliation," approved May 1, 1863, in Matthews, ed., *Public Laws, Third Session of the First Congress,* 167–68.

15. U.S. War Department General Order no. 100, April 24, 1863, *Official Records,* ser. 3, 3:148–64; see especially paragraphs 43, 57, and 67, which are the operative ones in this context. General Order no. 100 also covered many other problems, besides the status of prisoners, and became one of the principal bases of modern rules of warfare.

16. See Dudley Taylor Cornish, *The Sable Arm: Negro Troops in the Union Army, 1861–1865,* new ed. (1956; Lawrence: University Press of Kansas, 1987), 162–80.

17. Allen, *Davis,* 344.

18. Evans to Beauregard, March 17, 1863, quoted in Rable, *Confederate Republic,* 174.

19. Rable, *Confederate Republic,* 174.

20. Quoted in ibid., 174–75.

21. Allen, *Davis,* 346.

22. Ibid., 346–47.

23. Freeman, *R. E. Lee,* 2:483, 499–500; Woodward, ed. *Mary Chesnut,* 477–78; Jones, *Rebel War Clerk's Diary,* 198–200, 231–33; Allen, *Davis,* 347; Davis, *Rise and Fall,* 2:662, 664–65.

24. Todd, *Confederate Finance,* 33; "An Act to authorize a loan and the issue of Treasury Notes; and to prescribe punishment for forging the same, and for forging Certificates of Stock, and Bonds," approved May 16, 1861, in Matthews, ed., *Statutes,* 117–18.

25. Ibid., "An Act to authorize the issue of Treasury notes, and to provide a war tax for their redemption," approved August 19, 1861, 177–83.

26. Todd, *Confederate Finance,* 35.

27. "An Act further supplementary to an act to authorize the issue of Treasury notes, and to provide a war tax for their redemption," approved December 19, 1861, in Matthews, ed., *Statutes,* 225–26.

28. Todd, *Confederate Finance,* 41; "An Act to authorize the exchange of bonds for articles in kind, and the shipment, sale, or hypothecation of such articles," approved April 21, 1862, in Matthews, ed., *Public Laws, First Session of the First Congress,* 47.

29. Todd, *Confederate Finance,* chap. 3, see chart, 119–20.

30. Ibid., 198. In contrast, the legal tender notes issued by the Union rose only to $1.32 by the end of 1862.

31. Coulter, *Confederate States of America,* 176, quoting William M. Browne, Richmond, to Cobb, February 12, 1863, in Howell Cobb Papers; *Augusta Daily Chronicle and Sentinel,* April 2, 1863; *Richmond Daily Examiner,* March 26, 1863, *Richmond Daily Enquirer,* March 2, 1863; Richardson, ed., *Messages,* 1:259; Phillips, ed., *Correspondence of Toombs, Stephens, and Cobb,* 619; and Henry D. Capers, *Life and Times of C. G. Memminger* (Richmond: Everett Waddely, 1893), 445–47; see also Schott, *Stephens,* 367ff.

32. *Journal of the Confederate Congress,* 5:82.

33. Ibid., 5:123; "An Act to provide further means for the Support of the Government," approved April 18, 1862, in Matthews, ed., *Public Laws, First Session of the First Congress,* 28–29, and "An Act authorizing an issue of Treasury notes," approved April 17, 1862, 34.

34. *Journal of the Confederate Congress,* 5:410.

35. Ibid., 367, 426, 480–81.

36. "Proceedings," *SHSP,* 46:219–20.

37. Ibid., 221.

38. Ibid., 47:45; *Journal of the Confederate Congress,* 5:496–99.

39. Davis to the Senate and House of Representatives of the Confederate States, October 8, 1862, in Richardson, ed., *Messages,* 1:259; *Journal of the Confederate Congress,* 5:512, 514.

40. Memminger to Davis, October 6, 1862, Davis, *Papers,* 8:431–32.

41. Todd, *Confederate Finance,* 137–38.

42. To the Senate and House of Representatives, January 12, 1863, in Richardson, ed., *Messages,* 1:293–94.

43. Todd, *Confederate Finance,* 138–39.

44. Coulter, *Confederate States of America,* 177–78.

45. Ibid., 178. For text of the law, see "An Act to lay taxes for the common defense, and carry on the Government of the Confederate States," approved, April 24, 1863, in Matthews, ed., *Public Laws, Third Session of the First Congress,* 115–26. See also the discussion in Todd, *Confederate Finance,* 136–43.

46. Coulter, *Confederate States of America,* 179.

47. Richard F. Bensel, *Yankee Leviathan: The Origins of Central State Authority in America, 1859–1877* (New York: Cambridge University Press, 1990), 170, 170 n.162. Apparently there were no collections in Arkansas, or else records of such have been lost (Todd, *Confederate Finance,* 145).

48. Bensel, *Yankee Leviathan,* 171.

49. Ball, *Financial Failure and Confederate Defeat,* 232.

50. Ibid., 233.

51. Ibid., 236.

52. Ibid., 234.

53. Thomas Hill Watts to Davis, August 8, 1863, in Patrick, *Opinions of the Confederate Attorneys-General,* 311–15.

54. Robbins, "Confederate Nationalism," 74.

55. "An Act to provide and organize Engineer Troops to serve during the war," March 29, 1863, in Matthews, ed., *Public Laws, Third Session of the First Congress,* 98–99.

56. Ibid., "An Act to establish a Volunteer Navy," April 18, 1863, 111–13, and "An Act to create a Provisional Navy of the Confederate States," May 1, 1863, 161–62.

57. Ibid., "An Act to provide for continuing in service seamen and ordinary seamen now in the service of the Confederate States," April 2, 1863, 105.

58. To the Senate and House of Representatives of the Confederate States, January 12, 1863, in Richardson, ed., *Messages,* 1:295.

59. "An Act to repeal certain clauses of an Act entitled 'An Act to exempt certain persons from military service,' &c, approved October 11, 1862," May 1, 1863, in Matthews, ed., *Public Laws, Third Session of the First Congress,* 158–59.

60. Ibid., Joint Resolution relating to the production of provisions, April 4, 1863, 166–67.

61. Address, To the People of the Confederate States, April 10, 1863, in Richardson, ed., *Messages,* 1:331–35.

62. Ibid., To the Senate and House of Representatives, March 18, 1863, 1:312–13.

63. "An Act to exempt contractors for carrying the mails of the Confederate States, and the drivers of post coaches and hacks from military service," April 14, 1863, in Matthews, ed., *Public Laws, Third Session of the First Congress,* 107.

64. Ibid., "An Act to exempt certain persons from military duty, and to repeal an Act entitled 'An Act to exempt certain persons from enrollment for service in the army of the Confederate States,' approved April 21, 1862," October 11, 1862, 77–79.

65. Alexander and Beringer, *Anatomy of the Confederate Congress,* 111; John S. Preston to Hon. J. C. Breckinridge, February [?], 1865, enclosure, "Exemptions," *Official Records,* ser. 4, 3:1102. Virginia exempted only 1,900 state officers and Alabama only

1,300. The fifth largest number of exempt state officers were the 307 from South Carolina, but the report provides no figures for Texas and Arkansas and only partial figures for Tennessee and Louisiana.

66. "An Act to prevent the absence of officers and soldiers without leave," April 16, 1863, in Matthews, ed., *Public Laws, Third Session of the First Congress,* 109.

67. A proclamation, July 15, 1863, in Richardson, ed., *Messages,* 1:326–27.

68. "An Act to Regulate Impressments," passed March 26, 1862, in Matthews, ed., *Public Laws, Third Session of the First Congress,* 102–4.

69. Ibid., "An Act to Regulate Impressments," passed March 26, 1863, 103–4.

70. Blair, *Virginia's Private War,* 43.

71. "An Act to authorize the Governor of the State of Louisiana to press into the service of the State slaves and other property for the public defenses of the State during the present war," January 1, 1863, (Louisiana) *Official Records,* ser. 4, 2:278–79; "An Act to Authorize the impressment of slaves and other personal property for military purposes," January 3, 1863 (Mississippi), ibid., 296–97; "An Act to amend and reenact 'An Act further to provide for the public defense,' passed October 3, 1862," approved March 13, 1863 (Virginia), ibid., 426–28.

72. "An Act to Regulate Impressments," passed March 26, 1863, in Matthews, ed., *Public Laws, Third Session of the First Congress,* 104.

73. Ibid.

74. Alexander and Beringer, *Anatomy of the Confederate Congress,* 140.

75. Confederate States of America, War Department, "Regulations for the Subsistence Department of the Confederate States," regulation 1107 (Richmond, 1862), Rare Book Collection, State Historical Society of Wisconsin, Madison.

76. Ibid.

77. Blair, *Virginia's Private War,* 69.

78. Alexander and Beringer, *Anatomy of the Confederate Congress,* 140.

79. Ball, *Financial Failure and Confederate Defeat,* 231.

80. Ibid., 232; Richard C. Todd, *Confederate Finance,* 198.

81. Eugene Lerner, "Money, Prices, and Wages in the Confederacy, 1861–1865," *Journal of Political Economy* 63 (February 1955):23; see also Todd, *Confederate Finance,* appendix C, which charts the decreasing value of Treasury notes.

82. Ball, *Financial Failure and Confederate Defeat,* 231–32.

83. Moore, *Confederate Commissary General,* foreword, ix.

84. Ibid., 206–7.

85. General Orders no. 104, Adjutant General and Inspector General's Office, December 13, 1862, RG 109, War Department Collection of Confederate Records, M-901, General Orders and Circulars of the Confederate War Department, 1861–1865, roll 1, frame 371, National Archives, JDA.

86. *Journal of the Confederate Congress,* January 15, 1863, 6:23.

87. "Message of the President" to the House of Representatives, January 30, 1863, Confederate Imprint #1265. This message included Seddon's order of December 26, 1862, enclosed in Seddon to Davis, January 28, 1863.

88. Ibid., Frank G. Ruffin and James R. Crenshaw, "Report on the subject of fixing the prices of articles needed by the Bureau of Subsistence," undated, 10.

89. Richardson, ed., *Messages,* 1:293–95.

90. Z. B. Vance to the Honorable General Assembly, November 17, 1862, *Official Records,* ser. 4, 2:181.

91. January 19, 1863, *Journal of the Confederate Congress,* 3:21.

92. "Proceedings," January 15, 1863, *SHSP* 47:126.

93. January 15, 1863, *Journal of the Confederate Congress,* 6:23.

94. "Proceedings," January 15, 1863, *SHSP* 47:127.

95. Ibid., debate of January 28, 1863, 222.

96. Ibid., debate of March 4, 1863, 48:245.

97. Ibid., 246.

98. Ibid., debate of March 5, 1863, 253.

99. Ibid., 255.

100. Ibid., debate of February 13, 1863, 47:122.

101. "An Act to Regulate Impressments," passed March 26, 1863, in Matthews, ed., *Public Laws, Third Session of the First Congress,* 102–4.

102. General Orders no. 31, Adjutant and Inspector General's Office, March 19, 1863, RG 109, War Department Collection of Confederate Records, M-901, General Orders and Circulars of the Confederate War Department, 1861–1865, roll 1, frame 438, National Archives, JDA.

103. Patrick, *Opinions of the Confederate Attorneys' General, 1861–1865,* 217 (emphasis in original).

104. "An Act to Regulate Impressments," passed March 26, 1863, in Matthews, ed., *Public Laws, Third Session of the First Congress,* 102.

105. Ibid.

106. Ibid., 103.

107. Ibid.

108. Ibid.; "An Act to amend an Act entitled 'An Act to regulate impressments by officers of the Army,'" passed April 27, 1863, provided that if the impressment officer disagreed with the results of arbitration he would report his reasons "to the board of appraisers appointed by the President and the Governor of the State, who shall revise the same and make a final valuation," 127. The act of March 26 applied only to the army, but its provisions were extended to the navy the following month (see 131).

109. Coulter, *Confederate States of America,* 252.

110. General Orders no. 65, Adjutant and Inspector General's Office, May 21, 1863, *Official Records* ser. 4, 2:559–62.

111. Ibid., General Orders no. 128, Adjutant and Inspector General's Office, September 30, 1863, 836-38.

112. Davis, *Papers,* 9:105.

113. Ibid., 164–65.

114. Ibid., Davis to Joseph E. Davis, May 7, 1863, 9:166–67.

115. Cooper, *Davis,* 435.

116. Allen, *Davis,* 347–48.
117. Cooper, *Davis,* 435.
118. Rable, *Confederate Republic,* 178–79.
119. Ibid., 179–82.
120. Ibid., 184.
121. Ibid., 186.

11. Union Power Affirmed

1. Davis, *Papers,* 8:575. Emphasis added.

2. Ibid., 577–78.

3. For a full account of the Battle of Chickasaw Bayou, see Herman Hattaway, "Confederate Mythmaking: Top Command and the Chickasaw Bayou Campaign," *Journal of Mississippi History* 33 (November 1970):311–26.

4. Cooper, *Davis,* 437.

5. W. C. Davis, *Davis,* 484.

6. Ibid., 485.

7. Ibid., 498.

8 Davis to Joseph E. Davis, May 31, 1863, Davis, *Papers,* 9:200. See also Davis to Joseph E. Johnston, May 18, 1863, in Rowland, ed., *Davis,* 5:489.

9. W. C. Davis, *Davis,* 503.

10. V. Davis, *A Memoir,* 2:392.

11. W. C. Davis, *Davis,* 504; Davis to Joseph E. Davis, May 7, 1863, Davis, *Papers,* 9:167; Woodworth, *Davis and His Generals,* 206.

12. Cooper, *Davis,* 437.

13. Ibid., 438–39.

14. Ibid., 439.

15. Davis to R. E. Lee, May 31, 1863, Davis, *Papers,* 9:201–203.

16. Ephraim McD. Anderson, *Memoirs: Historical and Personal* (St. Louis: Times Printing, 1868), quoted by Herman Hattaway in *Shades of Blue and Gray* (Columbia: University of Missouri Press, 1997), 134.

17. Ibid., Davis to Reuben Davis, July 20, 1863, 290.

18. Gorgas, *Diary,* 50, entry for July 17, 1863.

19. Davis to Joseph E. Johnston, July 8, 1863, Davis, *Papers,* 9:264.

20. Ibid., editor's commentary on Davis to Joseph E. Johnston, July 8, 1863, 264 n.1.

21. Ibid., Davis to Reuben Davis, July 9, 1863, 291.

22. W. C. Davis, *Davis,* 513. For examples that must have been particularly humiliating to both Jefferson and Varina, see Davis, *Papers,* Jefferson Davis to Sarah Knox Taylor, December 16, 1834, 1:345–46, and Sarah Knox Taylor to Margaret Mackall Smith Taylor, June 17, 1835, 406–7.

23. Rable, *Confederate Republic,* 197; Davis to William M. Brooks, April 2, 1863, Davis, *Papers,* 9:122–24; E. Barksdale to Jefferson Davis, July 29, 1863, in Rowland, ed.,

Davis, 5:580–82; Michael B. Ballard, *Pemberton: A Biography* (Jackson: University Press of Mississippi, 1991), 182–85; Henry, *Story of the Confederacy,* 264.

24. Allen, *Davis,* 361–64.

25. Davis to James M. Howry, August 27, 1863, Davis, *Papers,* 9:357–58.

26. Rable, *Confederate Republic,* 197.

27. Arthur Lyon Fremantle, *Three Months in the Southern States: April–June, 1863* (1864; reprint, Lincoln: University of Nebraska Press, 1991), 205–14; Gorgas, *Diary,* 47, entry for July 2, 1863.

28. Hattaway and Jones, *How the North Won,* 413–14; for a thorough assessment, see pp. 412–421.

29. V. Davis, *A Memoir,* 2:392; W. C. Davis, *Davis,* 506–7.

30. Cooper, *Davis,* 440.

31. This paragraph is a verbatim quote of editorial note, Davis, *Papers,* 9:259.

32. Heth's *Memoirs,* quoted in editor's commentary, Davis, *Papers,* 9:328.

33. This entire paragraph, save for the opening sentence, is a verbatim quote of editor's commentary, Davis, *Papers,* 9:328 n.4.

34. Wigfall to Clay, August 13, 1863, editor's commentary, Davis, *Papers,* 9:311.

35. Davis to Theophilus Holmes, July 15, 1863, in Rowland, ed., *Davis,* 5:555; W. C. Davis, *Davis,* 515.

12. THE MEANING OF THE WAR

1. Davis to Eliza Cannon Cannon, July 18, 1863, Davis, *Papers,* 9:286.

2. Cooper, *Davis,* 442; see also W. C. Davis, *The Union That Shaped the Confederacy,* 198.

3. W. C. Davis, *The Union That Shaped the Confederacy,* 199.

4. Cooper, *Davis,* 443–44.

5. W. C. Davis, *The Union That Shaped the Confederacy,* 203–4.

6. Cooper, *Davis,* 444.

7. Ibid., 447.

8. Proclamation, to the Soldiers of the Confederate States, August 1, 1863, in Richardson, ed., *Messages,* 1:329.

9. W. C. Davis, *Davis,* 516

10. Polk to Bishop Elliott, August 15, 1863, quoted in Parks, *Polk,* 321.

11. Cooper, *Davis,* 455.

12. Quoted in E. B. Long, *The Civil War Day by Day* (Garden City, N.Y.: Doubleday, 1971).

13. Cooper, *Davis,* 456.

14. Quoted in ibid.

15. Ibid., 457.

16. Davis, *Papers,* 10:54–55.

17. Ibid., 90–91.

18. Quoted in Long, *Civil War Day by Day.*

19. Rable, *Confederate Republic,* 215.

20. Ibid., 225.

21. Alexander and Beringer, *Anatomy of the Confederate Congress,* 44–46.

22. *Montgomery Weekly Advertiser,* July 31, 1863, 2.

23. For discussion of the abortive development of political parties in the Second Congress of the Confederacy, see Beringer, "Unconscious 'Spirit of Party,'" 312–33.

24. To the Senate and House of Representatives of the Confederate States, December 7, 1863, in Richardson, ed., *Messages,* 1:347, 369–70.

25. J. C. Shields to S. Cooper, November 6, 1862, *Office Records,* ser. 4, 2:171.

26. To the Senate and House of Representatives of the Confederate States, December 7, 1863, in Richardson, ed., *Messages,* 1:370.

27. "Proceedings," February 24, 1863, *SHSP,* 48:189.

28. Ibid., speech of James L. Orr, 188.

29. Ibid., speech of Edward Sparrow, 187.

30. To the Senate and House of Representatives of the Confederate States, December 7, 1863, in Richardson, ed., *Messages,* 1:370–71.

31. Ibid., 373.

32. "An Act to prevent the enlistment or enrollment of substitutes in the military service of the Confederate States," December 28, 1863, in Matthews, ed., *Public Laws, Third Session of the First Congress,* 172.

33. Ibid., "An Act to put an end to the exemption from military service of those who have heretofore furnished substitutes," January 5, 1864.

34. "An Act to provide an Invalid Corps," approved February 17, 1864, in James M. Matthews, ed., *Public Laws . . . First Session of the Second Congress, 1864* (Holmes Beach, Fla.: Gaunt, 1970), 203.

35. W. C. Davis, *Davis,* 531.

36. Thomas L. Connelly and Archer Jones, *The Politics of Command: Factions and Ideas in Confederate Strategy* (Baton Rouge: Louisiana State University Press, 1973), 195.

37. Strode, *Davis,* 2:331–32.

38. Ibid., 447.

39. Editor's commentary, Davis, *Papers,* 9:289.

40. The black troops have been capably written about by Joseph T. Glatthaar; see *Forged in Battle: The Civil War Alliance of Black Soldiers and White Officers* (New York: Free Press, 1990). An older work by the pioneer student on the subject, Cornish, *The Sable Arm,* still offers rewards to its readers, for it is a classic; look especially for the third edition published with a helpful foreword by Herman Hattaway (Lawrence: University Press of Kansas, 1987). Also significant, if not as much fun to read, is Joseph T[homas] Wilson's *The Black Phalanx: A History of the Negro Soldiers of the United States in the Wars of 1775–1812, 1861–1865* (1890; reprint, New York: Arno Press, 1968). It has been more recently republished with a good introduction by Dudley Cornish. Worthwhile, too, is Versalle F. Washington, *Eagles on Their Buttons: A Black Infantry Regiment in the Civil War* (Columbia: University of Missouri Press, 1999), the inaugural volume in the series "Shades of Blue and Gray for the Modern Reader," edited by Herman Hattaway and Jon Wakelyn.

41. Joint resolution on the subject of retaliation, approved May 1, 1863, in Matthews, ed., *Public Laws, Third Session of the First Congress,* 167–68.

42. William Marvel, *Andersonville: The Last Depot* (Chapel Hill: University of North Carolina Press, 1994), ix, estimates that of the 41,000 prisoners who went to Andersonville, only 26,000 ever reached home again.

43. Robert Knox Sneden, *Eye of the Storm: A Civil War Odyssey,* ed. Charles F. Bryan Jr. and Nelson D. Lankford (New York: Free Press, 2000), passim.

44. Coulter, *Confederate States of America,* 154–55; "An Act to prohibit dealing in the paper currency of the enemy," February 6, 1864, in James M. Matthews, ed., *Public Laws, . . . Fourth Session of the First Congress, 1863–1864* (Holmes Beach, Fla.: Gaunt, 1970), 183.

45. *Richmond Daily Whig,* October 10, 1862, quoted in Coulter, *Confederate States of America,* 405.

46. *Richmond Daily Examiner,* December 21, 1864, and *Richmond Daily Whig,* December 24, 1862, and December 30, 1863; quoted in Coulter, *Confederate States of America,* 405–6.

47. *Richmond Daily Examiner,* February 14, 1863, quoted in Coulter, *Confederate States of America,* 405–6.

48. Coulter, *Confederate States of America,* 406–7.

49. Ibid., 408.

50. Ibid., 410; quote from E. A. Pollard, *Life of Jefferson Davis* (Philadelphia: National Publishing, 1869), 132.

51. See Thomas P. Lowry, M.D., *The Stories the Soldiers Wouldn't Tell: Sex in the Civil War* (Mechanicsburg, Pa.: Stackpole Books, 1994), and Byron T. Stinson, "Civil War Pin-Up Girls," in *Civil War Times–Illustrated* 8 (August 1969): 38–41; Scott Mitchell, "The Bawdy Truth About the Civil War," *Penthouse* [ca. early 1972]: 108–15.

52. Mark Twain, "The Private History of a Campaign That Failed," *Century Magazine* 31 (December 1885):193–204; quote on 204.

53. See Bell I. Wiley, *The Life of Billy Yank, the Common Soldier of the Union* (Indianapolis: Bobbs-Merrill, 1952), 261.

54. See ibid., 259–60.

55. See ibid., 259.

56. See ibid., 262.

57. Ibid., 256; see also Lois Hill, ed., *Poems and Songs of the Civil War* (New York: Fairfax Press, 1990), 228.

58. "An Act to punish drunkenness in the Army," approved April 21, 1862, in Matthews, ed., *Public Laws, First Session of the First Congress,* 47–48.

59. See Bell I. Wiley, *The Life of Johnny Reb, the Common Soldier of the Confederacy* (Indianapolis: Bobbs-Merrill, 1943), chapter 10.

60. See ibid., 38.

61. For an extended discussion of the effect of the war on Southern women, see Donna Rebecca D. Krug, "Women and War in the Confederacy," in Foerster and Stigler, eds., *On the Road to Total War,* 413–48.

62. Wiley, *Confederate Women,* 152.

63. Ibid., 153.

64. Ibid.

65. Coulter, *Confederate States of America,* 418–19.

66. W. C. Davis, *Davis,* 535–36.

67. Malcolm C. McMillan, *The Disintegration of a Confederate State: Three Governors and Alabama's Wartime Home Front, 1861–1865* (Macon, Ga.: Mercer University Press, 1986), 53–57. See also the essays compiled in W. Buck Yearns, ed., *The Confederate Governors* (Athens: University of Georgia Press, 1985).

68. Rable, *Confederate Republic,* 147.

69. Beringer et al., *Why the South Lost,* 208–9; see chapter 10, especially 204–10.

70. General Orders no. 115, August 24, 1863, Adjutant and Inspector General's Office, *Official Records,* ser. 4, 2:743–44.

71. Ibid., General Orders no. 129, October 1, 1863, ser. 4, 2:842–45.

72. Ibid., General Orders no. 145, November 7, 1863.

73. Ibid., General Orders no. 160, December 7, 1863, ser. 4, 2:1049–51.

74. *Montgomery Weekly Advertiser,* August 12, 1863, p. 3.

75. Ibid., January 6, 1864, p. 3.

76. William M. Wadley to General S. Cooper, December 31, 1862, *Official Records,* ser. 4, 2:270–72.

77. William M. Wadley to _____ [circular letter] December 17, 1862, *Official Records,* ser. 4, 2:277–78.

78. Ibid., Special Orders no. 18, Adjutant and Inspector General's Office, January 22, 1863, scr. 4, 2:365; Wadley was replaced by Colonel J. F. Gilmer by Special Orders no. 36, February 12, 1864.

79. Ibid., General Orders no. 85, June 16, 1863, ser. 4, 2:594.

80. Ibid., General Orders no. 10, January 30, 1864, ser. 4, 3:64.

81. Ibid., James A. Seddon to John Milton, July 28, 1865, ser. 4, 3:561.

82. Lee to Davis, January 23, Davis, *Papers,* 9:38–39; *Official Records,* ser. 1, vol. 21, 1110.

83. Myers to Seddon, January 26, 1863, *Official Records,* ser. 4, 2:372.

84. Ibid., William W. Wadley to James A. Seddon, January 26, 1863, ser. 4, 2:373–74.

85. Ibid., General Orders no. 37, Adjutant and Inspector General's Office, April 6, 1863, ser. 4, 2:471.

86. General Orders no. 133, Adjutant and Inspector General's Office, October 5, 1863, Frame 608, RG 109, War Department Collection of Confederate Records, micropublication M-901, General Orders and Circulars of the Confederate War Department, 1861–1865, roll 1, JDA, National Archives.

87. Robert E. Lee to L. B. Northrop, January 13, 1864, *Official Records,* ser. 1, 33:1087.

88. Ibid., G. D. Moore et al. to James A. Seddon, July 2, 1863, ser. 4, 2:616–17.

89. Ibid., James A. Seddon to Joseph E. Brown, October 31, 1863, ser. 4, 2:915.

90. Ibid., Joseph E. Brown to James A. Seddon, November 9, 1863, ser. 4, 2:943.

91. Ibid., Enclosure in M. L. Bonham to James A. Seddon, October 8, 1863, ser. 4, 2:863.

92. Ibid., Enclosure in Z. B. Vance to James A. Seddon, December 29, 1863, ser. 4, 2:1066.

93. Ibid., T. H. Watts to James A. Seddon, January 19, 1864, ser. 4, 3:37.

94. Davis, *Papers,* 10:123.

95. Ibid., 124–25.

96. L. B. Northrop, Report on Subsistence, November 20, 1862, *Official Records,* ser. 4, 2:969.

97. Robert A. Taylor, *Rebel Storehouse: Florida in the Confederate Economy* (Tuscaloosa: University of Alabama Press, 1995), 98.

98. Ibid.

99. Ibid.

100. Ibid., 98–99.

101. Ibid., 102, 104, 120–22.

102. Ibid., 132.

103. For an excellent discussion of Florida's role in the Confederate supply problem, see Taylor, *Rebel Storehouse* (for the problem of meat, particularly, see chapters 5–6). See also George E. Buker, *Blockaders, Refugees, and Contrabands: Civil War on Florida's Gulf Coast, 1861–1865* (Tuscaloosa: University of Alabama Press, 1993).

104. John Milton to James A. Seddon, January 26, 1864, *Official Records,* ser. 4, 3:46; Buker, *Blockaders,* 70.

105. John R. Richards to John Milton, December 30, 1863, *Official Records,* ser. 4, 3:47.

106. Ibid., General Orders no. 39, Adjutant and Inspector General's Office, March 24, 1864, ser. 4, 3:250.

107. Robbins, "Confederate Nationalism," 165, citing *Cunningham v. Campbell et al.,* 33 Ga. 625 (1863).

108. Robbins, "Confederate Nationalism," 167, citing *Alabama and Florida Railroad Company v. Kenney,* 39 Ala. 307 (1864).

109. Coulter, *Confederate States of America,* 252, from Frank Lawrence Owsley, *State Rights in the Confederacy* (1925; reprint, Gloucester, Mass.: Peter Smith, 1961), 219ff; Todd, *Confederate Finance,* 171.

110. Jefferson Davis to the Senate and House of Representatives of the Confederate States, December 7, 1863, in Richardson, ed., *Messages,* 1:373–74.

111. Herschel V. Johnson to Alexander H. Stephens, December 29, 1863, Johnson Papers, Duke University, typescript in Special Collections Department, Bell I. Wiley Papers, Collection 521, Writings of Confederate Congressmen, Box 2, Robert W. Woodruff Library, Emory University.

112. Owsley, *State Rights in the Confederacy,* 270–71.

113. Impressment Certificate, May 25, 1864, Ellis E. Jensen Collection, Civil War, Box 1, Historical State Society of Wisconsin, Madison.

114. "An Act to amend 'An act to regulate impressments,' " approved March 26, 1863, and "to repeal an act amendatory thereof, approved April 27, 1863," approved February 16, 1864, in James M. Matthews, ed., *Public Laws of the Confederate States of America, Passed at the Fourth Session of the First Congress, 1863–1864* (Holmes Beach, Fla.: Gaunt, 1970),

192. A few days later, provision was made for emergency impressment of meat, but the procedures to be followed varied little from those already enacted (see "An Act to authorize the impressment of meat for the use of the army, under certain circumstances," 196).

115. General Orders no. 30, Adjutant and Inspector General's Office, March 7, 1864, *Official Records,* ser. 4, 3:200.

116. General Orders no. 138, Adjutant and Inspector General's Office, October 24, 1863, RG 109, War Department Collection of Confederate Records, micropublication M-901, General Orders and Circulars of the Confederate War Department, 1861–1865, roll 1, frames 613–14, National Archives, JDA.

117. Coulter, *Confederate States of America,* 154.

118. Ibid.

119. Emory M. Thomas, *The American War and Peace 1860–1877* (Englewood Cliffs, N.J.: Prentice-Hall, 1973), 129.

120. Ibid.

121. Emory M. Thomas, *The Confederate Nation, 1861–1865* (New York: Harper and Row, 1979), 176; this section is mainly based on chapter 8 of his book.

122. Editor's commentary, Davis, *Papers,* 9:331.

123. Ibid.; this paragraph, with some scant alteration, is a verbatim quote from editor's commentary.

124. Thomas, *Confederate Nation,* 187; the most important scholarship to date on the Erlanger Loan is by Judith Fenner Gentry and can be found in "A Confederate Success in Europe: The Erlanger Loan," *Journal of Southern History* 36 (May 1970):157–88.

125. Rable, *Confederate Republic,* 239.

126. Cooper, *Davis,* 458–60.

127. Ibid., 461.

128. Ibid., 460–61.

129. *Savannah Republican,* September 11, 1863; *Milledgeville Southern Recorder,* September 8, 22, 29, 1863; Rable, *Confederate Republic,* 239.

130. Mason to Davis, December 24, 1863, in Davis, *Papers,* 10:130–31.

131. Ibid., Davis to Johnston, December 23, 1863, 119.

132. Ibid., 121–22 nn.3, 4.

133. Ibid., 120.

134. Ibid., 122 n.7.

135. Ibid., 119, 122 n.9.

13. WAR LEADERSHIP IN SUPREME TEST

1. Cooper, *Davis,* 461–62.

2. Ibid., 463.

3. Ibid., 464–65.

4. Ibid., 470.

5. W. C. Davis, *Davis,* 540.

6. Johnston to Davis, January 2, 1864, Davis, *Papers,* 10:144–45.

7. Cooper, *Davis,* 472.

8. Cooper, *Davis,* 472; Johnston to Davis, January 15, 1864, Davis, *Papers,* 10: 174–75.

9. Cooper, *Davis,* 470.

10. Davis, *Papers,* 10:246.

11. Ibid., 542.

12. Ibid., 542–43.

13. Richardson, ed., *Messages,* 1:345–82.

14. Rable, *Confederate Republic,* 240–41.

15. Thomas L. Connelly, *Civil War Tennessee: Battles and Leaders* (Knoxville: University of Tennessee Press, 1979), 53; Rowland, ed., *Davis,* 9:522; Seitz, *Bragg,* 410–11; V. Davis, *A Memoir,* 2:462–72, quote 472.

16. Allen, *Davis,* 375.

17. Ibid., 375–76.

18. W. C. Davis, *Davis,* 542–43.

19. V. Davis, *A Memoir,* 2:472.

20. Todd, *Confederate Finance,* 149; from Memminger to T. W. Bocock, December 7, 1863, in *Reports of the Secretary of the Treasury of the Confederate States of America, 1861–1865,* comp. Raphael P. Thian, appendix 3 (Washington, D.C., 1878), 177–94.

21. Todd, *Confederate Finance,* 149.

22. Ball, *Financial Failure and Confederate Defeat,* 236.

23. To the Senate and House of Representatives, December 7, 1863, in Richardson, ed., *Messages,* 1:363–65.

24. Ball, *Financial Failure and Confederate Defeat,* 237.

25. *Journal of the Confederate Congress,* 6:667–68.

26. Ibid., 6:672.

27. Ibid., 6:674, 3:617.

28. Yearns, *Confederate Congress,* 204.

29. *Journal of the Confederate Congress,* 3:739, 741; 6:823–24; Yearns, *Confederate Congress,* 205.

30. Yearns, *Confederate Congress,* 205; *Journal of the Confederate Congress,* 3:763–64, 794.

31. "An Act to levy additional taxes for the common defence and support of the Government," approved February 17, 1864, in Matthews, ed., *Public Law, Fourth Session of the First Congress,* 208–11.

32. Ball, *Financial Failure and Confederate Defeat,* 237; Todd, *Confederate Finance,* 151.

33. "An Act to amend An Act entitled 'An Act to levy taxes for the common defence and carry on the Government of the Confederate States, approved April 24, 1863,' " approved February 17, 1864, in Matthews, ed., *Public Laws, Fourth Session of the First Congress,* 215–27.

34. Ball, *Financial Failure and Confederate Defeat,* appendix C, 279–80.

35. *Huntsville Confederate,* October 8, 1862, 1, from the *Richmond Examiner,* September 26, 1862.

36. Ball, *Financial Failure and Confederate Defeat,* 173.

37. *Huntsville Confederate,* October 8, 1862, 1, from the *Richmond Examiner,* September 26, 1862.

38. *Richmond Dispatch,* January 6, 1864, 2.

39. Ball, *Financial Failure and Confederate Defeat,* 175.

40. Todd, *Confederate Finance,* 198. See also the *Richmond Dispatch,* January 6, 1864, 2, which complained that Treasury notes were really worth only five cents on the dollar, whereas the previous January they had been worth twenty cents on the dollar.

41. Ball, *Financial Failure and Confederate Defeat,* 177.

42. Ibid., 178–79, 181, 182–83, 279–80.

43. Matthews, ed., *Public Laws, Fourth Session of the First Congress,* 183.

44. See the December 1863 debate on this issue in "Proceedings," *SHSP,* 50, especially 102–3.

45. *Richmond Dispatch,* January 1, 1864, 2; Joint Resolution of the Alabama General Assembly, approved December 8, 1863, *Acts of the Called Session, 1863, and of the Third Regular Annual Session of the General Assembly of Alabama* (Montgomery: Safford and Figures, 1864), 218; *Montgomery Weekly Advertiser,* December 16, 1863, 1; *Daily Huntsville Confederate* (Marietta, Ga.), October 21, 1863, 2.

46. Todd, *Confederate Finance,* 73.

47. To the Senate and House of Representatives, December 7, 1863, in Richardson, ed., *Messages,* 1:361, 365, 367–69.

48. "Proceedings," *SHSP* 50:6–8, 10–13, 18–20.

49. *Journal of the Confederate Congress,* 6:579.

50. Ibid., 591.

51. Ibid., 592.

52. Ibid., 593.

53. Ibid., 643–44.

54. Memminger to R. M. T. Hunter, president of the Senate, undated but received January 25, 1864, "Proceedings," *SHSP* 50:295–98; *Journal of the Confederate Congress,* 3:615.

55. *Journal of the Confederate Congress,* 3:616.

56. Ibid.

57. Ibid., 635–36, 656–57, 673, and 6:777–78.

58. Ibid., 6:787–89.

59. Ibid., 3:760–63, and 6:842–43.

60. *Richmond Dispatch,* February 18, 1864, 2.

61. "An Act to reduce the currency and to authorize a new issue of notes and bonds," approved February 17, 1864, in Matthews, ed., *Public Laws, Fourth Session of the First Congress,* 205–8; Todd, *Confederate Finance,* 75; Ball, *Financial Failure and Confederate Defeat,* 188.

62. Coulter, *Confederate States of America,* 160–61.

63. Ibid., 161; Todd, *Confederate Finance,* 75, 113.

64. Coulter, *Confederate States of America,* 161.

65. Charles H. Smith, *Bill Arp, So Called: A Side Show of the Southern Side of the War* (New York: Metropolitan Record Office, 1866), 82 (emphasis in original).

66. Todd, *Confederate Finance,* 113; Yearns, ed., *Confederate Governors,* 208.

67. The *Montgomery Weekly Advertiser,* February 24, 1864, reported that the Richmond prices had gone up 50 to 150 percent.

68. Todd, *Confederate Finance,* 114, 198.

69. Ball, *Financial Failure and Confederate Defeat,* 188.

70. Coulter, *Confederate States of America,* 161–62.

71. Ibid., 162; quoting *Richmond Examiner,* February 16, 1864.

72. Coulter, *Confederate States of America,* 181–82, quoting Memminger to Boyce, March 31, 1864, in Memminger Papers (Division of Manuscripts, LC); Schott, *Stephens,* 407–8; and *Athens Southern Watchman,* June 8, 1864.

73. "An Act to prevent the procuring, aiding and assisting persons to desert from the army of the Confederate States, and for other purposes," January 23, 1864, in Matthews, ed., *Public Laws, Third Session of the First Congress,* 174.

74. To the Senate and House of Representatives of the Confederate States, February 13, 1864, Richardson, ed., *Messages,* 1:404–5.

75. "An Act to provide an Invalid Corps," February 17, 1864, in Matthews, ed., *Public Laws, Fourth Session of the First Congress,* 201.

76. Ibid., "An Act to organize forces to serve during the war," February 17, 1864, 211–15.

77. Ibid., 211.

78. Ibid., 212.

79. *Richmond Dispatch,* January 22, 1864, 2.

80. "An Act to organize forces to serve during the war," February 17, 1864, in Matthews, ed., *Public Law, Fourth Session of the First Congress,* 213–15.

81. To the Senate and House of Representatives of the Confederate States, February 3, 1864, in Richardson, ed., *Messages,* 1:399.

82. *Acts of the General Assembly of the State of Georgia, December 1863,* passed December 14, 1863 (Milledgeville, Ga.: Doughton, Nisbet, Barnes, and Moore, 1864), Title 11, Judiciary, Section 12, p. 45. Notice of this enactment was published in the *Daily Huntsville Confederate,* which then was published in Dalton, Georgia, February 1, 1864, 1.

83. To the Senate and House of Representatives of the Confederate States, February 3, 1864, in Richardson, ed., *Messages,* 1:395–400.

84. To the Senate and House of Representatives of the Confederate States, February, 3, 1864, in Richardson, ed., *Messages,* 1:400.

85. E. G. Reade to William Alexander Graham, February 4, 1864, Private Manuscript Collections, William A. Graham Papers (P.C. 61.6), North Carolina Department of Archives and History, Raleigh, photocopy, JDA.

86. Cooper, *Davis,* 476.

87. Schott, *Stephens,* 392.

88. Cooper, *Davis,* 476–77.

89. Schott, *Stephens,* 397.

90. "An Act to suspend the privilege of the writ of habeas corpus in certain cases," February 15, 1864, in Matthews, ed., *Public Laws, Fourth Session of the First Congress,* 187–89.

91. Ibid., 188–89.

92. Frank L. Owsley, "State Rights in the Confederacy" (thesis no. T11718, Department of Photoduplication, University of Chicago Library); Owsley, *State Rights in the Confederacy.*

93. Robbins, "Confederate Nationalism," 79. By now it will be obvious to discerning readers that we follow Robbins closely on this issue.

94. Allen D. Chandler, ed., *The Confederate Records of the State of Georgia,* 2:610–19, from Robbins, "Confederate Nationalism," 70.

95. Robbins, "Confederate Nationalism," 80–81.

96. Resolutions on the suspension of the habeas corpus, approved March 19, 1864, *Official Records,* ser. 4, 3:234.

97. Ibid., Alexander H. Stephens to H. V. Johnson, April 8, 1864, ser. 4, 3:278–81.

98. "An Act to increase the efficiency of the army by the employment of free negroes and slaves in certain capacities," February 17, 1864, in Matthews, ed., *Public Laws, Fourth Session of the First Congress,* 2:135–36. Black males free under the Treaty of Paris of 1803 or the Florida Treaty of 1819 were excluded from the provisions of this law.

99. Speech of William C. Rives, May 20, 1864, "Proceedings," *SHSP* 51 (March 1959):111.

100. Ibid., speech of Albert Gallatin Brown, May 13, 1864, 60–68.

101. Ibid., Speech of Congressman Henry S. Foote, 104.

102. Kathleen Bailey Davis, "Jefferson Davis and the Mississippi Gubernatorial Contest of 1851, with Selected Letters and Speeches Concerning the Campaign" (master's thesis, Rice University, 1971).

103. Speech of Congressman John P. Murray, "Proceedings," *SHSP* 51 (March 1959):125.

104. *Journal of the Confederate Congress,* 7:58.

105. Jefferson Davis to the House of Representatives, May 20, 1864, in Richardson, ed., *Messages,* 1:452–53.

106. "An Act to increase the efficiency of the army by the employment of free negroes and slaves in certain circumstances," approved February 17, 1864, in Matthews, ed., *Public Laws, Fourth Session of the First Congress,* 235.

107. General Orders no. 32, Adjutant and Inspector General's Office, March 11, 1864, RG 109, War Department Collection of Confederate Records, micropublication M-901, General Orders and Circulars of the Confederate War Department, 1861–1865, roll 1, frame 722, National Archives, JDA.

108. A. L. Rives to James A. Seddon, January 22, 1864, *Official Records,* ser. 4, 3:40.

109. Ibid., John B. Baldwin to Secretary of War, July 20, 1864, ser. 4, 3:547.

110. General Orders no. 9, Adjutant and Inspector General's Office, January 29, 1864, ser. 4, 3:54–55.

111. Ibid., Jno. J. McRae and G. D. Moore, Circular List, April 1, 1864, ser. 4, 3:262–66.

112. Ibid., General Orders no. 41, Adjutant and Inspector General's Office, April 6, 1864, ser. 4, 3:271.

113. *Texas Almanac for 1867* (Galveston: W. D. Richardson, 1866), 213.

114. Ibid.

115. General Orders no. 41, Adjutant and Inspector General's Office, April 6, 1864, ser. 4, 3:271; General Orders no. 47, Adjutant and Inspector General's Office, May 6, 1864, ser. 4, 3:389–92; enclosure dated May 4, 1864, to Special Orders no. 180, Adjutant and Inspector General's Office, August 1, 1864, ser. 1, vol. 42, pt. 2, 1151–55, all in *Official Records.*

116. *Richmond Dispatch,* January 22, 1864, 1. The farmers asked for clarification of this interpretation, but our search for any record of the result turned up nothing.

117. Senate bill 51, May 28, 1864, *Journal of the Confederate Congress,* 4:99.

118. "Proceedings," *SHSP* 51 (March 1959):163, 170; *Journal of the Confederate Congress,* 7:205.

119. "Proceedings," *SHSP* 51(March 1959):163.

120. *Montgomery Weekly Advertiser,* November 13, 1863, 1; General Orders no. 31, Adjutant and Inspector General's Office, March 19, 1863, *Official Records,* ser. 4, 3:441.

121. "Proceedings," *SHSP* 51 (March 1959):163.

122. June 1, 1864, *Journal of the Confederate Congress,* 4:133.

123. Ibid., June 10, 1864, 7:205.

124. *Chattanooga Daily Rebel,* March 22, 1864; Milton F. Perry, *Infernal Machines: The Story of Confederate Submarine and Mine Warfare* (Baton Rouge: LSU Press, 1965), 94–108.

125. Strode, *Davis,* 3:9–10.

126. Ibid., 3:10.

127. Allen, *Davis,* 373; W. C. Davis, *Davis,* 552.

128. Woodward, ed., *Mary Chestnut,* 796.

129. Allen, *Davis,* 374.

130. O. H. Montgomery, *Howell Cobb's Confederate Career* (Tuscaloosa: Confederate Publishing, 1959), 108–9; Davis to JEJ, December 26, 1863, in Rowland, ed., *Davis,* 6:135–37; Davis, *Rise and Fall,* 2:547–50; N. C. Hughes Jr., *General William J. Hardee,* 180; Connelly and Jones, *Politics of Command,* 141–52, 162; Longstreet, *From Manassas to Appomattox,* 544; Seitz, *Bragg,* 414–19; Johnston, *Narrative,* 291–301; John B. Hood, *Advance and Retreat* (1880; reprint, Lincoln: University of Nebraska Press, 1996), 266.

131. Stanley Horn, *The Army of Tennessee* (1941; reprint, Norman: University of Oklahoma Press, 1952), 242; Seitz, *Bragg,* 415–22, and 427–32; Lee, ed., *Pendleton,* 314–20; Davis, *Rise and Fall,* 2:549–52; Albert Castel, *Decision in the West* (Lawrence: University Press of Kansas, 1992), 30–33, 37–38, 73–78, 100–104; JEJ to Wigfall, November 1863, in G. E. Govan and Livingood, *A Different Valor* (Indianapolis: Bobbs-Merrill, 1956), 139.

132. Cooper, *Davis,* 473.

133. V. Davis, *A Memoir,* 2:496.

134. Ibid., 2:487.

135. Allen, *Davis,* 380–81.

136. Allen, *Davis,* 382–383; Emory M. Thomas, *Bold Dragoon: The Life of J. E. B. Stuart* (New York: Harper and Row, 1986), 290–91; Frank H. Alfriend, *The Life of Jefferson*

Davis (Cincinnati and Chicago: Caxton, 1868), 550; Davis to R. E. Lee, May 11, 1864, in Rowland, ed., *Davis,* 6:250.

137. Allen, *Davis,* 382–83; Freeman, *R. E. Lee,* 3:380, 387; Alexander, *Fighting for the Confederacy,* 398–407, 414; W. Taylor, *Four Years with General Lee,* 135–37; McPherson, *Battle Cry of Freedom,* 739–43.

138. Freeman, *R. E. Lee,* 3:380; Alexander, *Fighting for the Confederacy,* 398–407, 417–33; Henry Kyd Douglas, *I Rode with Stonewall* (Chapel Hill: University of North Carolina Press, 1940), 272–74; W. W. Taylor, *Four Years with General Lee,* ed. J. I. Robertson (Bloomington: University of Indiana Press, 1996), 135–37.

139. V. Davis, *A Memoir,* 2:493–94; Davis to Lee, May 15, 1864, in Rowland, ed., *Davis,* 6:252; Lee, ed., *Pendleton,* 326; Freeman, *R. E. Lee,* 3:287–88, 313, 318–21.

140. W. C. Davis, *Davis,* 558.

141. Allen, *Davis,* 384.

142. Davis to Vance, January 8, 1864, 6:143-46, and Davis to Vance, January 8, 1864, 6:143–46, in Rowland, ed., *Davis,* 6:143-46; Yearns, *Confederate Congress,* 174–75; Paul Escott, *After Secession* (Baton Rouge, Louisiana State University Press, 1978), 200–203.

143. Davis, *Rise and Fall,* 2:610–12; Randall, *Civil War,* 615–17; Allen, *Davis,* 384.

14. The Great Hope

1. Cooper, *Davis,* 482.

2. W. C. Davis, *Davis,* 569.

3. Cooper, *Davis,* 487.

4. Ibid., 570.

5. Ibid., 570, 572.

6. W. C. Davis, *Davis,* 573–74; Kean, *Diary,* 175, entry for September 25, 1864.

7. Rable, *Confederate Republic,* 271–72.

8. W. W. Boyce to Jefferson Davis, September 29, 1864, in the *(Raleigh) Daily Conservative,* October 8, 1864.

9. Ibid., Boyce to Davis, September 29, 1864; *Message of His Excellency Joseph E. Brown, to the Legislature of the State of Georgia, Convened in Extra Session at Macon, Georgia, February 15, 1865* (Macon, Ga.: Nisbet, Barnes, and Moore, 1865), 15, 27; "Proceedings," *SHSP* 51 (March 1959):125.

10. Boyce to Davis, September 29, 1864, *(Raleigh) Daily Conservative,* October 8, 1864.

11. Escott, *After Secession* (see, for example, 46–47, 51, 73, 90, 99–104, 115, 127–28, 137, 144, 148–49, 154, 178–81, 184, 196–97, 207–8, 215–16, 219, 221, 223–24, 228, 235–37, 239, 245, 252–57, 259, 262–64, 266–74).

12. Rable, *Confederate Republic,* 274; speech of President Davis in Macon, Georgia, in Rowland, ed., *Davis,* 6:341–44.

13. Speech of President Davis in Montgomery, in Rowland, ed., *Davis,* 6:345.

14. Rable, *Confederate Republic,* 274; speech in Augusta, October 5, 1864, in Rowland, ed., *Davis,* 6:357.

15. Rable, *Confederate Republic,* 275.

16. Ibid., 275–76.

17. Coulter, *Confederate States of America,* 163–64, quoting Memminger to J. P. Boyce, March 31, 1864, in Christopher Gustavus Memminger Papers, 1860–1865 (microfilms in the University of Texas Library, originals in the University of North Carolina Library).

18. Coulter, *Confederate States of America,* 163 n.27.

19. Ibid., 171.

20. J. C. Shields to C. B. Duffield, September 19, 1864, *Official Records,* ser. 4, 3:655, and also endorsement by W. B. Richards Jr., September 12, 1864.

21. Ibid., Special Orders no. 224, September 21, 1864, Adjutant and Inspector General's Office, ser. 1, vol. 42, pt. 2, 1268.

22. Ibid., James A. Seddon to the president of the Confederate States, November 28, 1864, ser. 4, 3:851–53.

23. Ibid., General Orders no. 86, December 5, 1864, Adjutant and Inspector General's Office, ser. 4, 3:897.

24. Ibid., "An Act in Relation to the Public Defense," December 7, 1864, ser. 4, 3:905.

25. Ibid., General Orders no. 309, Adjutant and Inspector General's Office, December 30, 1864, ser. 4, 3:982–86.

26. Ibid., Schedule no. 13, Office Board of Commissioners for Impressment, October 1, 1864, ser. 4, 3:704–6.

27. Lerner, "Money, Prices, and Wages in the Confederacy, 1861–1865," 20–40.

28. Peter W. Gray to Francis Barlow Sexton, September 29, 1863, Eldridge Collection, EG Box 82, The Huntington Library. This item is reproduced by permission of *The Huntington Library, San Marino, California.*

29. Bell to Sterling Price, January 9, 1864, ibid.

30. Charles P. Roland, *The Confederacy* (Chicago: University of Chicago Press, 1960), 174.

31. W. W. Allen to Zebulon Baird Vance, September 26, 1862, in Zebulon Baird Vance, *The Papers of Zebulon Baird Vance,* vol. 1, *1843–1862,* ed. Frontis W. Johnston (Raleigh: State Department of Archives and History, 1963), 230–31.

32. James L. Orr to James A Seddon, probably January 1864, typescript of copy at the University of Texas, location of original unknown; typescript in Special Collections Department, Bell I. Wiley Papers, Collection 521, Writings of Confederate Congressmen, Box 1, Robert W. Woodruff Library, Emory University.

33. John Goode Jr. to James A. Seddon, July 19, 1864, *Official Records,* ser. 4, 3:544.

34. "A Wounded Soldier" to James A. Seddon, July 22, 1864, Letters Received by the Confederate Secretary of War, M-437, roll 118, frames 515–16, JDA, National Archives.

35. Ibid., anonymous to James A. Seddon, July 25, 1864, frames 517–18.

36. Charles W. Ramsdell, *Behind the Lines in the Southern Confederacy* (1944; reprint, New York: Greenwood Press, 1969), 54.

37. Anonymous to Jefferson Davis, May 5, 1864, Letters Received by the Confederate Secretary of War, micropublication M-437, roll 118, frames 443–45, National Archives.

38. Georgia Lee Tatum, *Disloyalty in the Confederacy* (1934; reprint, New York: AMS Press, 1970), 87–88.

39. Ramsdell, *Behind the Lines,* 28.

40. Illegible to Jefferson Davis, September 2, 1864, Letters Received by the Confederate Secretary of War, micropublication M-437, roll 118, frames 687–88, National Archives.

41. Ibid., anonymous to Jefferson Davis, September 1864, frame 749.

42. A proclamation, August 1, 1863, in Richardson, ed., *Messages,* 1:330.

43. Joel Chandler Harris, *On the Plantation: A Story of a Georgia Boy's Adventures During the War* (1892; reprint, Athens: University of Georgia Press, 1980), 138–39.

44. J. E. Joyner to Sidney Smith, August 15, 1863, *Official Records,* ser. 4, 2:721.

45. *Montgomery Weekly Advertiser,* September 16, 1863, 1.

46. Ibid., January 6, 1864, 4. An earlier law to restrict distillation of grain had been passed in 1862. See *Daily Huntsville Confederate* (Dalton, Ga.), June 28, 1864, 1.

47. *Chattanooga Daily Rebel,* April 21, 1864, 1.

48. Many soldiers to Jefferson Davis, September 7, 1864, Letters Received by the Confederate Secretary of War, micropublication M-437, roll 118, frames 702–4, National Archives.

49. Ibid., Armand Auze to G. A. Trenholm, August 25, 1864, frame 707. The chief of engineers reported that although there was no such person as Armand Auze, his workers were indeed destitute.

50. Ibid., Richard G. Anderson, superintendent of the poorhouse, Albemarle County, Virginia, to James A. Seddon, November 11, 1864, frames 839–41.

51. *Huntsville Confederate,* March 26, 1863, 1.

52. *Montgomery Weekly Advertiser,* October 7, 1863, 1.

53. Resolution of October 31, 1863, *Montgomery Weekly Advertiser,* November 13, 1863, 3.

54. Ibid., November 13, 1863, 3.

55. Joint Resolution passed November 28, 1863, *Acts of the Called Session, 1863, and of the Third Regular Annual Session of the General Assembly of Alabama* (Montgomery: Saffold and Figures, 1864), 216.

56. Ibid.

57. A. R. Lawton to J. A. Seddon, August 26, 1863, *Official Records,* ser. 4, 2:755.

58. *Richmond Dispatch,* January 30, 1864, 1.

59. Anonymous to unknown, July 25, 1864, Letters Received by the Confederate Secretary of War, micropublication M-437, roll 118, frames 519–22, JDA, National Archives.

60. Jefferson Davis to Theophilus Holmes, January 28, 1863, microcopy, letterbook (55-D, vol. 1), Louisiana Historical Association Collection, Jefferson Davis Papers, Letterbook I, Manuscripts Department, Tulane University Library, JDA.

61. C. G. Memminger to James A. Seddon, June 2, 1864, *Official Records,* ser. 4, 3:465.

62. Ibid., Seddon to Memminger, June 4, 1864, ser. 4, 3:472.

63. "An Act providing for the establishment and payment of claims for a certain description of property taken or informally impressed for the use of the army," approved June 14, 1864, in Matthews, ed., *Public Laws, Fourth Session of the First Congress,* 271–72; General

Orders no. 54, Adjutant and Inspector General's Office, June 18, 1864, *Official Records,* ser. 4, 3:501–2.

64. Yearns, *Confederate Congress,* 125.

65. James A. Seddon to Howell Cobb, June 27, 1864, *Official Records,* ser. 4, 3:516.

66. Ibid., R. C. Fariss to G. A. Trenholm, August 22, 1864, ser. 4, 3:603–4, and Northrop endorsement of September 16, 1864.

67. Ibid., Special Orders no. 203, Adjutant and Inspector General's Office, August 27, 1864, ser. 4, 3:608.

68. Goff, *Confederate Supply,* 162–64.

69. John S. Preston to John C. Breckinridge, February [?], 1865, *Official Records,* ser. 4, 3:1099–1110. The figure is the total of overseers and agriculturalists enumerated east of the Mississippi River in Table D, Exemptions. Table E indicates another twenty-seven hundred men were detailed from the army to agricultural duty. The exemptions were authorized by Section 10-IV of "An Act to organize forces to serve during the war," approved February 17, 1864, in Matthews, ed., *Public Laws, Fourth Session of the First Congress,* 213–14.

70. L. B. Northrop, circular, September 5, 1864, *Official Records,* ser. 4, 3:623.

71. Ibid., James A. Seddon to Howell Cobb, and others, September 15, 1864, ser. 4, 3:645.

72. Ibid., James A. Seddon to B. H. Hill, September 5, 1864, ser. 4, 3:621.

73. Ibid.

74. Ibid., Richard Morton to I. M. St. John, November 20, 1864, ser. 4, 3:834.

75. *Journal of the Confederate Congress,* November 17, 1864, 4:269.

76. "Proceedings," November 17, 1864, *SHSP* 51 (March 1959):313–14.

77. Ibid., 314.

78. Ibid., January 3, 1865, *SHSP* 52 (July 1959):81.

79. For a much fuller treatment of this topic, and for documentation for quotations used here, see Herman Hattaway, "The General the President Elevated Too High: Davis and John Bell Hood," in *Jefferson Davis's Generals,* ed. Gabor S. Boritt (New York: Oxford University Press, 1999), 84–103.

80. *Journal of the Confederate Congress,* 3:658, 675.

81. Cooper, *Davis,* 486.

82. See Hattaway, "The General"; see also W. C. Davis, *Davis,* p. 547.

83. Allen, *Davis,* 387.

84. Ibid., 388–89.

85. Ibid., 389.

86. Ibid., 390.

87. Richard M. McMurry, *John Bell Hood and the War for Southern Independence* (Lexington: University of Kentucky Press, 1982), 122–23.

88. Nelson, *Bullets, Ballots, and Rhetoric,* 83.

89. B. H. Hill to James A. Seddon, July 14, 1864, *Official Records,* ser. 1, vol. 52, pt. 2, 706.

90. Johnston, *Narrative,* 363.

91. Nelson, *Bullets, Ballots, and Rhetoric,* 83.

92. McMurry, *Hood,* 303.

93. Ibid., 123.

94. Ibid., 137.

95. Cooper, *Davis,* 488–89.

96. Ibid., 489.

97. Ibid., 489–90.

98. Ibid., 490.

99. Cooper, *Davis,* 491–92.

100. Hood, *Advance and Retreat,* 245; Davis speech, Augusta, Georgia, newspaper report, October 10, 1864, in Rowland, ed., *Davis,* 6:356–61, other speeches, 6:341–56; also Davis to E. K. Smith, September 29, 1864, 6:348; Escott, *After Secession,* 219 and n.42.

101. Cooper, *Davis,* 493–94.

102. Ibid., 495.

103. Office of the Governor RG 3, Letters Received, William Smith 1864–1865, Box 4 Folder 1 (Accession 36916) Z. B. Vance to William Smith, 23 September 1864, microcopy, State Records Collection, Archives Research Services, The Library of Virginia, Richmond, Virginia (emphasis in original), JDA.

104. William Smith to Z. B. Vance, September 27, 1864, ibid.

105. To the Senate and House of Representatives of the Confederate States of America, November 7, 1864, in Richardson, ed., *Messages,* 1:484–85.

106. Ibid., 491.

107. Ibid.

108. Ibid., 491–92.

109. Ibid., 492.

110. Woodward, ed., *Mary Chesnut,* 255, entry for December 6, 1861.

111. Craig L. Symonds, *Stonewall of the West: Patrick Cleburne and the Civil War* (Lawrence: University Press of Kansas, 1997), 181–82.

112. Ibid., 183–86.

113. P. R. Cleburne and others to Commanding General, the Corps, Division, Brigade, and Regimental Commanders of the Army of Tennessee, January 2, 1864, *Official Records,* ser. 1, vol. 52, pt. 2, 586–92, quotes on 586, 587, 589; "An Act to organize forces to serve during the war," approved February 17, 1864, in Matthews, ed., *Public Laws, Fourth Session of the First Congress,* 211.

114. P. R. Cleburne and others to Commanding General, the Corps, Division, Brigade, and Regimental Commanders of the Army of Tennessee, January 2, 1864, *Official Records,* ser. 1, vol. 52, pt. 2, 589–90, 592.

115. Symonds, *Cleburne,* 188–89.

116. W. H. T. Walker to Jefferson Davis, January 12, 1864, *Official Records,* ser. 1, vol. 52, pt. 2, 595; Symonds, *Cleburne,* 190.

117. Jefferson Davis to W. H. T. Walker, January 13, 1864, *Official Records,* ser. 1,vol. 52, pt. 2, 596; James A. Seddon to Joseph E. Johnston, January 24, 1864, ibid., 606. How Walker's January 12 letter to Davis, written near Dalton, Georgia, arrived in Richmond

quickly enough for Davis's reply to be dated the next day is uncertain and leads to the conclusion that either Walker misdated his letter, or that the trains were running with most unusual frequency and efficiency, or that Davis had advance knowledge of what was coming. Symonds says the message was hand-carried to Jefferson Davis by Senator Herschel V. Johnson. Even so, one day for reply seems suspiciously quick.

118. Woodward, ed., *Mary Chesnut,* 545, entry for January 19, 1864.

119. Robert F. Durden, *The Gray and the Black: The Confederate Debate on Emancipation* (Baton Rouge: Louisiana State University Press, 1972), chap. 4.

120. Richardson, ed., *Messages,* 1:493–95.

121. Ibid., 495.

122. Davis to Campbell Brown, June 14, 1886, Johnson and Buell, eds., *Battles and Leaders,* vol. 2, facing p. 98, extra-illustrated edition RB 298000, The Huntington Library, San Marino, California.

123. Davis to William Smith, March 25, 1865, *Offical Records,* ser. 1, vol. 46, pt. 3, 1348–49; Smith to Davis, March 30, 1865, ibid., 1366–67.

124. Ibid., Davis to W. H. T. Walker, January 13, 1864, ser. 1, vol. 52, pt. 2, 596.

125. Ibid., Secretary of War James A. Seddon to Major E. B. Briggs, November 24, 1864, ser. 4, 3:846.

126. Ibid., Benjamin to Fred A. Porcher, December 21, 1864, ser. 4, 3:959–60.

127. W. C. Davis, *The Cause Lost: Myths and Realities of the Confederacy* (Lawrence: University Press of Kansas, 1996), 128–29.

128. Ibid., 132.

129. Ibid., 133.

130. Nelson, *Bullets, Ballots, and Rhetoric,* 20.

131. Ibid., 21.

132. Ibid., xii.

133. Ibid., 75–80.

134. Ibid., 99–101.

135. W. C. Davis, *The Cause Lost,* 137.

136. Ibid., 142.

137. Ibid., 146–47.

15. The Winter of Great Discontent

1. Thomas, *Confederate Nation,* 274.

2. Long, *The Civil War Day by Day,* 399.

3. Brooks D. Simpson, "Facilitating Defeat: The Union High Command and the Collapse of the Confederacy," in *The Collapse of the Confederacy,* ed. Mark Grimsley and Brooks D. Simpson (Lincoln: University of Nebraska Press, 2001), 85–86.

4. George C. Rable, "Despair, Hope, and Delusion: The Collapse of Confederate Morale Reexamined," in Grimsley and Simpson, eds., *The Collapse of the Confederacy,* 130–31.

5. Ibid., 132.

6. Ibid., 134.

7. Rable, "Despair, Hope, and Delusion," 142–43.

8. Coulter, *Confederate States of America,* 130ff.

9. Ibid.

10. Ibid., 132.

11. McMurry, *Hood,* 152–53.

12. Ibid., 153.

13. Ibid.; see also June Gow, paper, Southern Historical Association, 1972.

14. Davis to Hood, September 17, 1864, in Rowland, ed., *Davis,* 6:335.

15. McMurry, *Hood,* 155–56.

16. Ibid., 158.

17. Ibid., 157.

18. Davis to Beauregard, October 2, 1864, in Rowland, ed., *Davis,* 6:348–49; Woodworth, *Davis and His Generals,* 291–92.

19. Speech in Columbia, South Carolina, in Rowland, ed., *Davis,* 6:353; Woodworth, *Davis and His Generals,* 293.

20. McMurry, *Hood,* 162; Woodworth, *Davis and His Generals,* 294.

21. Allen, *Davis,* 392–93; Felicity Allen, letter to Herman Hattaway, September 15, 1999, in his possession; Beauregard to Davis, December 6, 1864, in Hood, *Advance and Retreat,* 278–80, which could suggest that Davis had asked Beauregard why he had not countermanded the campaign; J. Davis to Varina Davis, November 3, 1865, which suggests that Davis was "without full information" as to what was going on in the western theater, MS Jefferson Davis Papers, Special Collections and Archives, at Transylvania University Library; Cooper, *Davis,* 499.

22. *Calendar of the Postwar Jefferson Davis Manuscripts* (New York: Burt Franklin, 1943), 100.

23. Lee, ed., *Pendleton,* 380.

24. Woodworth, *Davis and His Generals,* 295, quoting Hood, *Advance and Retreat,* 273; Cooper, *Davis,* 499–500.

25. Woodworth, *Davis and His Generals,* 304; Cooper, *Davis,* 499.

26. Woodward, ed., *Mary Chesnut,* 652–53.

27. Connelly and Jones, *Politics of Command,* 169.

28. Cooper, *Davis,* 502–3.

29. Ibid., 188.

30. W. C. Davis, *Davis,* 576.

31. Cooper, *Davis,* 499.

32. Ibid., 500.

33. McMurry, *Hood,* 187.

34. Ibid., 188.

35. Davis, *Rise and Fall,* 2:579–80.

36. Cooper, *Davis,* 503.

37. Ibid., 504–6.

38. Rable, "Despair, Hope, and Delusion," 136.

39. Ibid., 137.

40. Allen, *Davis,* 396–98; Vandiver, *Tattered Flags,* 295–96; Symonds, *Johnston,* 341–43; Davis, *Rise and Fall,* 2:631; Rable, "Despair, Hope, and Delusion," 139.

41. Benjamin to Robert E. Lee, February 11, 1865, *Official Records,* ser. 1, vol. 46, pt. 2, 1229.

42. Cooper, *Davis,* 501.

43. Samuel Clayton to Jefferson Davis, January 10, 1865, *Official Records,* ser. 4, 3:1000–1001.

44. Ibid., J. H. Stringfellow to Jefferson Davis., ser. 4, 3:1067–70.

45. Josiah Turner Jr., North Carolina, in "Proceedings," *SHSP* 52:241–42.

46. Ibid., Speech of James T. Leach, North Carolina.

47. J. W. Ellis to Jefferson Davis, January 29, 1865, *Official Records,* ser. 4, 3:1041–42.

48. Cooper, *Davis.* 506–7.

49. John T. Lamkin to Mrs. Lamkin, January 3, 1865, Eldridge Collection, EG Box 46, The Huntington Library. This item is reproduced by permission of *The Huntington Library, San Marino, California.*

50. Andrew Hunter to R. E. Lee, January 7, 1865, *Official Records,* ser. 4, 3:1008.

51. Ibid., R. E. Lee to Andrew Hunter, January 11, 1865, 1012–13.

52. Richardson, *Messages,* 1:491–92.

53. Rable, *Confederate Republic,* 283–84.

54. E. G. Reade to William Alexander Graham, February 4, 1864, William A. Graham Papers, Private Manuscript Collections (P.C. 61.6), North Carolina Department of Archives and History, Raleigh, photocopy, JDA.

55. Davis to the Senate and House of Representatives, November 9, 1864, in Richardson, ed., *Messages,* 1:498.

56. Ibid., Davis to the Senate and House of Representatives, March 13, 1865, 1:548–49.

57. Alexander and Beringer, *Anatomy of the Confederate Congress,* 173.

58. Ibid., 199.

59. Robbins, "Confederate Nationalism," 86–87.

60. "An Act to amend an act entitled 'An Act to organize forces to serve during the war,' approved February 17, 1864," approved November 22, 1864, in Ramsdell, ed., *Laws and Joint Resolutions,* 4.

61. Ibid., 23–24.

62. Ibid., "An Act to amend 'an act to provide an Invalid Corps,' approved February 17, 1864," approved January 27, 1865, 27–28.

63. Ibid., "An Act to increase the efficiency of the cavalry of the Confederate States," approved February 23, 1865, 46–49.

64. Ibid., "An Act to authorize the consolidation of companies, battalions, and regiments," approved February 23, 1865, 49–53.

65. Ibid., "An Act for the further organization of the Field Artillery of the Confederate States," approved February 25, 1865, 59–60.

66. Ibid., "An Act declaring certain persons liable to duty in the reserve forces of the respective States," approved March 4, 1865, 79.

67. Ibid., "An Act to regulate the business of Conscription," approved March 7, 1865, 86–88.

68. Richardson, *Messages,* 1:541.

69. Ibid., 1:540–41.

70. Ibid., 543.

71. Williamson S. Oldham, "Last Days of the Confederacy," *DeBow's Review,* 2d ser., 7 (October 1869):860–62.

72. Alexander and Beringer, *Anatomy of the Confederate Congress,* 268; *Journal of the Confederate Congress,* vol. 7.

73. Richardson, ed., *Messages,* 1:547–48.

74. "An Act to diminish the number of exemptions and details," approved March 16, 1865, in Ramsdell, ed., *Laws and Joint Resolutions,* 154.

75. Ibid., "An Act to amend the tenth section of the act entitled 'An act to organize forces to serve during the war,' " approved February 17, 1865, 154.

76. Ibid., "An Act to provide for the employment of free negroes and slaves to work upon fortifications and perform other labor connected with the defenses of the country," approved February 28, 1865, 61–64.

77. Ibid., "An Act to authorize the Secretary of War to negotiate with the Governors of the several States for slave labor," approved March 4, 81.

78. *Message of His Excellency Joseph E. Brown,* 13.

79. Cobb to Seddon, January 8, 1865, *Official Records,* ser. 4, 3:1009.

80. "An Act to increase the military force of the Confederate States," approved March 13, 1865, in Ramsdell, ed., *Laws and Joint Resolutions,* 118–19.

81. Paragraph 4, General Orders no. 14, Adjutant and Inspector General's Office, March 23, 1865, *Official Records,* ser. 4, 3:1161–62.

82. For the slave soldier issue, see Durden, *The Gray and the Black.* The historian at Petersburg National Park has found evidence indicating that at least a few of them did get into a firefight. And there is some anecdotal evidence a few black Confederate units did serve in the final days of the Appomattox Campaign.

83. Northrop endorsement, G. T. Beauregard to S. Cooper, December 23, 1864, *Official Records,* ser. 1, 44:980–81.

84. Trenholm to Davis, January 24, 1865, bMS Am 1649.24 (961), Dearborn Collection, Harvard University, microfilm copy, JDA (by permission of the Houghton Library, Harvard University).

85. Lee to Seddon, February 8, 1865, microcopy, Robert E. Lee Headquarters Papers, Contemporary copy, location of original not known, Virginia Historical Society, Richmond, JDA.

86. Ibid., Davis endorsement, n.d., on Lee to Seddon, February 8, 1865.

87. Ibid., Davis to Seddon, February 8, 1865.

88. Ibid., Proclamation, Moses D. Hoge and others, February 22, 1865, printed, Confederate Imprint, Virginia Historical Society, Richmond, JDA.

89. A. R. Lawton to Secretary of War John C. Breckinridge, March 10, 1865, microcopy, Davis Papers; Rare Books, Manuscript, and Special Collections Library, Duke University, JDA.

90. Circular no. 36, War Department, Bureau of Conscription, December 12, 1864, *Official Records,* ser. 4, 3:933.

91. Ibid., "An Act to repeal all acts and parts of acts heretofore passed by the Legislature of this State on the subject of furnishing slave labor on the coast and fortifications within this State, and otherwise to provide for furnishing such labor," December 23, 1864, ser. 1, 44:983–84.

92. Ibid., John S. Preston to James A. Seddon, December 29, 1864, ser. 4, 3:979, enclosing a copy of "An Act to repeal all acts and parts of acts heretofore passed by the Legislature of this State on the subject of furnishing slave labor on the coast and fortifications within this State, and otherwise to provide for furnishing such labor," December 23, 1864, ser. 1, 44:983–84.

93. Ibid., R. B. Johnson to Governor A. G. Mcgrath, January 10, 1865, ser. 4, 3:1023, forwarded in A. G. Mcgrath to John S. Preston, January 11, 1865, 1020.

94. Ibid., C. D. Melton to John S. Preston, January 14, 1865, ser. 4, 3:1024–25.

95. Ibid., John S. Preston to James A. Seddon, January 15, 1865, ser. 4, 3:1018–19.

96. "An Act to provide for the employment of free negroes and slaves to work upon fortifications and perform other labor connected with the defenses of the country," approved February 28, 1865, in Ramsdell, ed., *Laws and Joint Resolutions,* 61–64.

97. Ibid., "An Act to provide for the more efficient transportation of troops, supplies and munitions of war upon the railroads, steamboats, and canals in the Confederate States, and to control telegraph lines, employed by [the] Government," approved February 28, 1865, 60–61.

98. To the Senate and House of Representatives, March 13, 1865, in Richardson, ed., *Messages,* 1:546.

99. Ibid., 546–47.

100. "An Act to amend the law relating to Impressments," approved March 18, 1865, in Ramsdell, cd., *Laws and Joint Resolutions,* 151–53.

101. Ibid., "An Act to amend an act entitled 'An act to regulate impressments' approved March 26, 1863, as amended by the act approved February 16, 1864," approved March 18, 1865, 151–53.

102. Special Orders no. 72, Adjutant and Inspector General's Office, March 27, 1865, *Official Records,* ser. 4, 3:1169–73.

103. Rable, "Despair, Hope, and Delusion," 146–49.

16. THE BATTLEFIELD REALITIES IN 1865

1. Davis to Hugh Davis, January 8, 1865, in Hudson Strode, *Private Letters, 1823–1889* (New York: Harcourt Brace and World, 1966), 4:140.

2. Richard N. Current, *Lincoln's Loyalists* (Boston: Northeastern University Press, 1992), see especially 214–18.

3. Quoted in Michael J. Ballard, *A Long Shadow: Jefferson Davis and the Final Days of the Confederacy* (Jackson: University Press of Mississippi, 1986), 4–5.

4. Richardson, *Messages,* 1:485.

5. Ballard, *A Long Shadow,* 5.

6. V. Davis, *A Memoir,* 2:536–37.

7. Davis to Lincoln, July 6, 1861, in Richardson, ed., *Messages,* 1:115–16.

8. V. Davis, *A Memoir,* 2:548.

9. Ibid., 2:549.

10. Davis, *Rise and Fall,* 2:597.

11. Arch Fredric Blakey, *General John H. Winder, C.S.A.* (Gainesville: University of Florida Press, 1990), 209–12. See also William Marvel, *Andersonville,* who also exonerates both Captain Wirz and General Winder.

12. Marvel, *Andersonville,* x–xi.

13. Marion B. Lucas, *Sherman and the Burning of Columbia* (College Station: Texas A&M Press, 1976), passim.

14. Davis, *Rise and Fall,* 2:627, 629.

15. W. C. Davis, *Davis,* 581–82.

16. *Journal of the Confederate Congress,* 3:454–55.

17. Ibid., 3:477, 566.

18. Report of the Committee on the Judiciary, on Senate bill no. 150 (Sen. rep. 16), Congressional Documents of the Confederate States of America, 1864–1865, Rare Book Collection, State Historical Society of Wisconsin, Madison.

19. Patrick, *Davis and His Cabinet,* 146–47.

20. Thomas S. Bocock to Jefferson Davis, January 21, 1864 (actually 1865), microcopy, Jefferson Davis Papers, LC; Davis endorsement, n.d., JDA.

21. See Davis's position on Seddon's resignation and the attempt of Congress to reshape the cabinet in *Official Records,* ser. 4, 3:1046–48, a long letter to Seddon accepting his resignation. At that point, of course, Davis really did not have the time to write such letters.

22. W. C. Davis, *Davis,* 582–83.

23. Ibid., 583; Davis to Mrs. Howell Cobb, March 30, 1865, in Rowland, ed., *Davis,* 6:524–25.

24. W. C. Davis, *Davis,* 584.

25. Ibid., 504; "An Act to authorize newspapers to be mailed to soldiers free of postage," in Ramsdell, ed., *Laws and Joint Resolutions,* 28.

26. Barber, *Presidential Character,* 9.

27. Ibid., 148.

28. Brown, *Modernization,* 22, 161, 175.

29. Frank G. Ruffin to William M. Randolph, December 26, 1863, Preston-Radford Papers, Box 3, University of Virginia, quoted in Blair, *Virginia's Private War,* 107.

30. Blair, *Virginia's Private War,* 71.

31. W. C. Davis, *Davis,* 592.

32. Cooper, *Davis,* 511.

33. Stanton to Grant, February 4, 1865, in *The Collected Works of Abraham Lincoln,* ed. Roy F. Basler, 9 vols. (New Brunswick, N.J.: Rutgers University Press, 1953–1955, supplement, 1974 and 1990), 8:258.

34. Cooper, *Davis,* 512.

35. W. C. Davis, *Davis,* 593.

36. Cooper, *Davis,* 512.

37. Ballard, *A Long Shadow,* 19–20.

38. Davis, *Rise and Fall,* 2:608–9.

39. Cooper, *Davis,* 512.

40. Ibid., 513.

41. Ibid.

42. W. C. Davis, *Davis,* 594.

43. William A. Tidwell, with James O. Hall and David Winfred Gaddy, *Come Retribution: The Confederate Secret Service and the Assassination of Lincoln* (Jackson: University of Mississippi Press, 1988), and William A. Tidwell, *April 1865: Confederate Covert Action in the American Civil War* (Kent, Ohio: Kent State University Press, 1995).

44. Cooper, *Davis,* 498.

45. *Daily Chattanooga Rebel* (Selma, Ala.), January 16, 1865, 2.

46. "An Act to amend the fourteenth section of an Act entitled 'An Act to reduce the currency and to authorize a new issue of notes and bonds,' " approved March 1, 1865, in Ramsdell, ed., *Laws and Resolutions,* 73–74.

47. Ball, *Financial Failure and Confederate Defeat,* 296, indicates a debt of about $1.9 billion on October 31, 1864. The *Daily Chattanooga Rebel,* January 16, 1865, estimated it at $1.5 billion, with gold at $20, which meant the debt was worth $75 million in gold, assuming that the editor's information and calculations were correct.

48. To the House of Representatives of the Confederate States of America, February 20, 1865, in Richardson, ed., *Messages,* 1:532–33.

49. John Christopher Schwab, *The Confederate States of America, 1861–1865: A Financial and Industrial History of the South During the Civil War* (New York: C. Scribner's Sons, 1901), 301.

50. Todd, *Confederate Finance,* 154–55; "An Act to levy additional taxes for the year 1865, for the support of the Government," approved March 11, 1865, in Ramsdell, ed., *Laws and Joint Resolutions,* 101–7.

51. Todd, *Confederate Finance,* 155; "An Act to raise coin for the purpose of furnishing necessary supplies for the army," approved March 17, 1865, in Ramsdell, ed., *Laws and Joint Resolutions,* 147–49.

52. Coulter, *Confederate States of America,* 182; Ball, *Financial Failure and Confederate Defeat,* 241.

53. Coulter, *Confederate States of America,* 182.

54. Todd, *Confederate Finance,* 84, 120, 156, 174; Ball, *Financial Failure and Confederate Defeat,* 286–89. Todd's figures are presumably for the entire period of the war, and Ball's cover the period from February 4, 1861, to October 31, 1864. Both Ball and Schwab, *Financial and Industrial History,* 76, indicate that the last Confederate financial

accounting ended in fall 1864; Schwab says October 1 while Ball's tables indicate October 31. In any event, the differences are small, and they are otherwise alike in their demonstration of the inadequacy of Confederate tax policy.

55. Joint Resolution for donations to the Treasury of the Confederate States, approved March 18, 1856, in Ramsdell, ed., *Laws and Resolutions,* 129–30.

56. Coulter, *Confederate States of America,* 171–72, quoting *Richmond Daily Examiner,* March 30, 1865.

57. Coulter, *Confederate States of America,* 172; Ball, *Financial Failure and Confederate Defeat,* 296; Schwab, *Financial and Industrial History,* 77, estimates $1.9 billion on October 1, 1864.

58. "An Act to establish the flag of the Confederate States," in Ramsdell, ed., *Laws and Resolutions,* 74.

59. Quoted in Ballard, *A Long Shadow,* 10.

60. Quoted in ibid.

61. Ibid., 11, quoting D. P. Crook, in *The North, the South, and the Powers.*

62. Cooper, *Davis,* 515.

63. Ballard, *A Long Shadow,* 13.

64. W. C. Davis, *Davis,* 597, 599.

65. Faust, *The Creation of Confederate Nationalism,* 58–59.

66. Ibid., 60.

67. Beringer, Hattaway, Jones, and Still, *Why the South Lost,* 351–61.

68. Faust, *The Creation of Confederate Nationalism,* 63.

69. Ibid., 65–69.

70. Ibid., 69–71.

71. Ibid., 78.

72. Ludwell H. Johnson, "Jefferson Davis and Abraham Lincoln as War Presidents: Nothing Succeeds like Success," *Civil War History* 27 (March 1981): 49–63; Neely, *Southern Rights,* 153–54.

73. David M. Potter, "Jefferson Davis and the Political Factors in Confederate Defeat," in Donald, ed., *Why the North Won the Civil War,* 93–95, 99–100, quote on 100.

74. Potter, "Jefferson Davis and the Political Factors in Confederate Defeat," 101–4, 106, quote on 109.

75. Herman Hattaway and Archer Jones, "Lincoln as Military Strategist," *Civil War History* 26 (December 1980): 295.

76. W. C. Davis, *The Cause Lost,* 148.

77. W. C. Davis, *An Honorable Defeat: The Last Days of the Confederate Government* (New York: Harcourt, 2001), 2.

78. Ibid., 3–4.

79. Ibid., 5.

80. Ibid., 8.

81. Ibid., 21–25.

82. Ibid., 25–27.

83. Ibid., 31–32.

84. Ibid., 33–34.

85. Ibid., 34.

86. Ibid., 38–44.

87. Ibid., 45–46.

88. W. C. Davis, *The Cause Lost*. Emphasis in original.

89. Ibid., 50 (emphasis in original).

17. THE END IN VIRGINIA

1. Cooper, *Davis,* 519.

2. V. Davis, *A Memoir,* 2:579.

3. Ballard, *A Long Shadow,* 26–27.

4. Ibid., 27.

5. Ibid., 26.

6. Ibid., 27.

7. Grimsley and Simpson, eds., *The Collapse of the Confederacy,* 1.

8. Ibid., 1–2.

9. Ibid., 2.

10. Noah Andre Trudeau, *Out of the Storm: The End of the Civil War, April–June 1865* (Baton Rouge: Louisiana State University Press, 1994); Michael Golay, *A Ruined Land: The End of the Civil War* (New York: John Wiley and Sons, 1999); quotes are from the blurb on the back cover of the paperback edition.

11. Jay Wink, *April 1865: The Month That Saved America* (New York: Harper Collins, 2001; and Jay Wink, "They Gave America a Second Chance," in *Parade Magazine*, April 8, 2001.

12. Cooper, *Davis,* 522.

13. V. Davis, *A Memoir,* 2:577.

14. Cooper, *Davis,* 522.

15. W. C. Davis, *Davis,* 601–2.

16. Ballard, *A Long Shadow,* 28.

17. Ibid.

18. W. C. Davis, *An Honorable Defeat,* 54.

19. Ibid., 54.

20. Ibid., 55.

21. Ibid.

22. Ibid., 56.

23. Cooper, *Davis,* 523.

24. Ballard, *A Long Shadow,* 34–35; J. Davis to V. Davis, April 5, 1865, in Rowland, ed., *Davis,* 6:532; Allen, *Davis,* 398; Cooper, *Davis,* 523. Antecommunion is the first part of the communion service, which St. Paul's used as a separate service on first Sundays of the month.

25. Davis, *Rise and Fall,* 2:667; Ballard, *A Long Shadow,* 36–37; Cooper, *Davis,* 523.

26. W. C. Davis, *An Honorable Defeat,* 58.

27. Ballard, *A Long Shadow,* 37–38; Davis, *Rise and Fall,* 2:666–67.

28. Ballard, *A Long Shadow,* 38.

29. W. C. Davis, *An Honorable Defeat,* 59.

30. Ballard, *A Long Shadow,* 40–41, quoting from Davis, *Rise and Fall,* 2:656.

31. Ballard, *A Long Shadow,* 42.

32. Ibid., 42.

33. Davis, *Rise and Fall,* 2:582–83,667-68; Allen, *Davis,* 399; Ballard, *A Long Shadow,* 45.

34. Ballard, *A Long Shadow,* 48.

35. Cooper, *Davis,* 523; W. C. Davis, *An Honorable Defeat,* 63.

36. W. C. Davis, *An Honorable Defeat,* 65.

37. Ballard, *A Long Shadow,* 49; Cooper, *Davis,* 523–24.

38. W. C. Davis, *An Honorable Defeat,* 71.

39. Ibid., 74.

40. Rable, "Despair, Hope, and Delusion," 153; for a general view of this military campaign, see Woodworth, *Davis and Lee at War,* ch. 8.

41. Ballard, *A Long Shadow,* 53; Davis, *An Honorable Defeat,* 75.

42. Ballard, *A Long Shadow,* 53–54.

43. Rowland, ed., *Davis,* 6:533–34.

44. W. C. Davis, *An Honorable Defeat,* 77–78.

45. Ballard, *A Long Shadow,* 56, quoting Davis, *Rise and Fall,* 2:676–77, and To the People of the Confederate States of America, April 4, 1865, in Richardson, ed., *Messages,* 1:569–70.

46. Emory Thomas, *The Confederacy as a Revolutionary Experience* (Englewood Cliffs, N.J.: Prentice-Hall, 1971), 51; W. C. Davis, *Davis,* 608; Ballard, *A Long Shadow,* 56.

47. Cooper, *Davis,* 526–27 (emphasis added).

48. W. C. Davis, *An Honorable Defeat,* 79.

49. J. D. B. DeBow, "Our Danger and Our Duty," *DeBow's Review,* 1st ser., 33 (1862):47–48; To the People of the Confederate States of America, April 4, 1865, in Richardson, ed., *Messages,* 1:569; W. C. Davis, *An Honorable Defeat,* 80.

50. *(Grenada) Mississippian,* August 27, 1863, quoted from *Daily Huntsville Confederate* (Marietta, Ga.), September 9, 1863, 1 (emphasis in original).

51. Ballard, *A Long Shadow,* 57.

52. W. C. Davis, *An Honorable Defeat,* 81–82.

53. William B. Feis, "Jefferson Davis and the 'Guerilla Option,'" in Grimsley and Simpson, eds., *The Collapse of the Confederacy,* 107 (emphasis added).

54. Ibid.

55. W. C. Davis, *An Honorable Defeat,* 84.

56. Ibid., 83.

57. Johnston, *Narrative,* 398–99, 411. See also George M. Fredrickson, *Why the Confederacy Did Not Fight a Guerrilla War After the Fall of Richmond: A Comparative View,*

Thirty-fifth Annual Robert Fortenbaugh Memorial Lecture (Gettysburg, Pa.: Gettysburg College, 1996), who posits that to resort to guerrilla warfare would have brought about social changes that the upper classes were unwilling to risk.

58. W. C. Davis, *Davis,* 600.

59. Eaton, *Davis,* 241.

60. W. C. Davis, *An Honorable Defeat,* 87.

61. W. C. Davis, *Davis,* 610.

62. Ballard, *A Long Shadow,* 61–62.

63. W. C. Davis, *Davis,* 610.

64. W. C. Davis, *An Honorable Defeat,* 93.

65. W. C. Davis, *Davis,* 611.

66. W. C. Davis, *An Honorable Defeat,* 111–12.

67. Cooper, *Davis,* 525.

68. W. C. Davis, *An Honorable Defeat,* 112–13.

69. Ibid., 113–14.

70. Rowland, ed., *Davis,* 6:543.

71. Ballard, *A Long Shadow,* 67–68.

18. THE PSEUDO-CONFEDERACY

1. W. C. Davis, *An Honorable Defeat,* 121.

2. Ballard, *A Long Shadow,* 74–76; W. C. Davis, *An Honorable Defeat,* 126.

3. Ballard, *A Long Shadow,* 77; Cooper, *Davis,* 525; W. C. Davis, *An Honorable Defeat,* 126.

4. W. C. Davis, *An Honorable Defeat,* 127.

5. Ballard, *A Long Shadow,* 78.

6. Ibid., 79.

7. W. C. Davis, *An Honorable Defeat,* 128–29.

8. *Official Records,* ser. 1, vol. 46, pt. 3, 1393; Ballard, *A Long Shadow,* 79.

9. Ballard, *A Long Shadow,* 80; Davis to Joseph E. Johnston, April 11, 1865, in Rowland, ed., *Davis,* 6:543–44.

10. W. C. Davis, *An Honorable Defeat,* 129.

11. Ballard, *A Long Shadow,* 80.

12. W. C. Davis, *An Honorable Defeat,* 130.

13. Ballard, *A Long Shadow,* 81.

14. W. C. Davis, *An Honorable Defeat,* 130–31; Steven E. Woodworth, "The Last Function of Government: Confederate Collapse and Negotiated Peace," in Grimsley and Simpson, eds., *The Collapse of the Confederacy,* 13.

15. Woodworth, "Last Function," 14.

16. Ibid., 33.

17. Ibid., 34.

18. Cooper, *Davis*, 526.

19. W. C. Davis, *An Honorable Defeat*, 133.

20. Ballard, *A Long Shadow*, 81.

21. Reagan, *Memoirs*, 199; Mallory, "Last Days," 240.

22. Ballard, *A Long Shadow*, 82; W. C. Davis, *An Honorable Defeat*, 134.

23. Ballard, *A Long Shadow*, 82; Cooper, *Davis*, 526; W. C. Davis, *An Honorable Defeat*, 135.

24. Ballard, *A Long Shadow*, 82–83.

25. Mark Grimsley, in "Learning to Say 'Enough': Southern Generals and the Final Weeks of the Confederacy," in Grimsley and Simpson, eds., *The Collapse of the Confederacy*, 40.

26. Ibid., 48–49.

27. Ibid., 62.

28. Ibid., 67.

29. *Official Records*, ser. 1, vol. 47, pt. 3, 206–7.

30. Ballard, *A Long Shadow*, 83; W. C. Davis, *An Honorable Defeat*, 137.

31. Ballard, *A Long Shadow*, 84; W. C. Davis, *An Honorable Defeat*, 139.

32. W. C. Davis, *An Honorable Defeat*, 141–42.

33. Ballard, *A Long Shadow*, 84–85.

34. Ibid., 85–86.

35. Ibid., 86.

36. Robert E. Lee Jr., *Recollections and Letters of General Robert E. Lee* (New York: Bramhall House, 1904), 156–57.

37. Ballard, *A Long Shadow*, 86–87; W. C. Davis, *An Honorable Defeat*, 142.

38. Ballard, *A Long Shadow*, 87–88; W. C. Davis, *An Honorable Defeat*, 142.

39. Ballard, *A Long Shadow*, 88.

40. Ibid., quoting from the *Greensboro Patriot*, March 23, 1866.

41. W. C. Davis, *An Honorable Defeat*, 145.

42. Ibid., 147–48.

43. Ballard, *A Long Shadow*, 94–95; W. C. Davis, *An Honorable Defeat*, 149.

44. W. C. Davis, *An Honorable Defeat*, 150.

45. Ballard, *A Long Shadow*, 95; W. C. Davis, *An Honorable Defeat*, 150–52.

46. Ballard, *A Long Shadow*, 98.

47. Ibid.

48. Ibid., 99–100; Cooper, *Davis*, 527.

49. Ballard, *A Long Shadow*, 99–101.

50. Cooper, *Davis*, 528.

51. William Johnston to Jefferson Davis, March 29, 1882, Rowland, ed., *Davis*, 9:158; R. V. Booth, "Last Address of President Davis, C.S.A.," *Confederate Veteran* 22 (July 1914):304.

52. Cooper, *Davis*, 528.

53. Ballard, *A Long Shadow*, 101.

54. W. C. Davis, *Davis*, 620; Cooper, *Davis*, 528–29.

55. A. J. Hanna, *Flight into Oblivion* (Richmond: Johnson, 1938), 47–48; Burton N.

Harrison, "Capture of Davis: Extracts from a Narrative," in Rowland, ed., *Davis,* 9:137; W. C. Davis, *An Honorable Defeat,* 177.

56. W. C. Davis, *An Honorable Defeat,* 175–76.

57. Ibid., 178.

58. *Official Records,* ser. 1, vol. 47, pt. 3, 810, 816; Rowland, ed., *Davis,* 6:556–57; Strode, *Davis, Private Letters,* 153; Ballard, *A Long Shadow,* 102–3.

59. W. C. Davis, *An Honorable Defeat,* 164–65.

60. Ballard, *A Long Shadow,* 104.

61. Ibid., 104–5.

62. Cooper, *Davis,* 529; Jefferson Davis to Varina Davis, April 23, 1865, in Rowland, ed., *Davis,* 6:559-61.

63. Ballard, *A Long Shadow,* 105; Cooper, *Davis,* 529.

64. Ballard, *A Long Shadow,* 106.

65. *Official Records,* ser. 1, vol. 47, pt. 3, 834.

66. Ballard, *A Long Shadow,* 109.

67. I. M. St. John to Jefferson Davis, July 14, 1873, and Josiah Gorgas to Jefferson Davis, undated but probably 1876, in Rowland, ed., *Davis,* 7:355–56, and 8:332 (emphasis added).

68. Ballard, *A Long Shadow,* 110–11; Cooper, *Davis,* 530.

69. W. C. Davis, *An Honorable Defeat,* 167.

70. Ibid., 168.

71. Ibid., 192–93.

72. Ballard, *A Long Shadow,* 112; Mallory, "Last Days," 245–46.

73. Ballard, *A Long Shadow,* 112; W. C. Davis, *An Honorable Defeat,* 200.

74. Ballard, *A Long Shadow,* 117.

75. Rowland, ed., *Davis,* 6:564–65.

76. Ballard, *A Long Shadow,* 117–18.

77. W. C. Davis, *An Honorable Defeat,* 202–3.

78. Ibid., 203.

79. Ballard, *A Long Shadow,* 118.

80. Grimsley, "Learning to Say 'Enough,' " 68.

81. Ibid., 43.

82. Ibid., 43–72, passim; the quotes are on 43, 47, and 72.

83. Ibid., 74.

84. W. C. Davis, *An Honorable Defeat,* 204.

85. Ibid., 204–6.

86. Ballard, *A Long Shadow,* 120; W. C. Davis, *An Honorable Defeat,* 209–10.

87. Ballard, *A Long Shadow,* 120–21.

88. Ibid., 121; Cooper, *Davis,* 530.

89. Cooper, *Davis,* 531; Rowland, ed., *Davis,* 8:172; Ballard, *A Long Shadow,* 122.

90. Ballard, *A Long Shadow,* 122–23; Cooper, *Davis,* 531.

91. Rowland, ed., *Davis,* 8:149, 154, 158, 188; Ballard, *A Long Shadow,* 123; Cooper, *Davis,* 531.

92. Strode, *Davis, Private Letters*, 4:161; Rowland, ed., *Davis*, 6:587–88; Ballard, *A Long Shadow*, 124–25.

93. Ballard, *A Long Shadow*, 125; Cooper, *Davis*, 531; W. C. Davis, *An Honorable Defeat*, 219–20.

94. W. C. Davis, *An Honorable Defeat*, 222–23.

95. Quoted in Ballard, *A Long Shadow*, 126.

96. W. C. Davis, *An Honorable Defeat*, 234–35.

97. Cooper, *Davis*, 531.

98. W. C. Davis, *An Honorable Defeat*, 243–45.

99. Ballard, *A Long Shadow*, 128–29; Warner, *Generals in Gray*, 316–17; the best biography of Benjamin is Eli N. Evans, *Judah P. Benjamin: The Jewish Confederate* (New York: Free Press, 1988); Cooper, *Davis*, 531.

100. W. C. Davis, *An Honorable Defeat*, 244, citing Davis to William Preston Johnston, April 5, 1878, Breckinridge Family Papers, LC.

101. W. C. Davis, *An Honorable Defeat*, 254–55; Cooper, *Davis*, 532.

102. W. C. Davis, *An Honorable Defeat*, 247–51.

103. Ibid., 251–52.

104. Ibid., 257–58.

105. Ibid., 258.

106. Ibid., 258–59.

107. Ibid., 260.

108. Ballard, *A Long Shadow*, 131–32; Cooper, *Davis*, 532.

109. Ballard, *A Long Shadow*, 132–33.

110. W. C. Davis, *An Honorable Defeat*, 263–64.

111. Ibid., 268–69.

112. Ibid., 268; Cooper, *Davis*, 532.

113. Headley, *Confederate Operations*, 437.

114. Ballard, *A Long Shadow*, 137.

115. Harrison, "Capture of Davis," 140–41.

116. Ibid., 226–60; Cooper, *Davis*, 532.

117. Cooper, *Davis*, 533.

118. Only the American Indians have experienced this, since losing the Vietnam War brought no Reconstruction and social restructuring for the American citizens of the 1960s and 1970s.

119. Johnston, *Narrative*, 398–403, 409–15; Davis, *Rise and Fall*, 2:682, 689, 692–96; Davis to "a friend," May 1865, in Robert McElroy, *Jefferson Davis: The Unreal and the Real*, 2 vols. (New York: Harper, 1937), 2:502.

120. Cooper, *Davis*, 534.

121. W. C. Davis, *An Honorable Defeat*, 302–6.

122. Ibid., 310–11.

123. Ibid., 313–91ff.; the quote is on 391.

124. George C. Rable, "Despair, Hope, and Delusion," 154–55.

125. V. Davis, *A Memoir,* 2:648–50; Ada Sterling, ed, *A Belle of the Fifties: Memoirs of Mrs. Clay of Alabama . . . 1853–1866* (New York: Doubleday and Page, 1905), 261–67; *Official Records,* ser. 2, 8:569–71.

126. Silber, *Romance of Reunion,* 19, 22–23, 29, 30–33; W. C. Davis, *An Honorable Defeat,* 352–53.

127. Davis, *Rise and Fall,* 2:704–5.

128. Allen, *Davis,* 422–87; *Official Records,* ser. 2, 8:634, 640, 642, 647, 655–58; McElroy, *Davis,* 2:536–39; Speed to O'Connor, July 6, 1865, in Rowland, ed., *Davis,* 7:37; W. C. Davis, *Breckinridge,* 530.

129. Davis, *Rise and Fall,* 2:705.

130. Allen, *Davis,* 1, 441–42. The photograph is in the Confederate Memorial Hall, 828 Camp Street, New Orleans, Louisiana; Nannie D. Smith, "Reminiscences of Jefferson Davis," *Confederate Veteran* (May 1930):178; in the Davis Family Museum at Beauvoir there is the same picture of Pius IX, with an inscription in the same hand: *Hodie, si vocam Domini audieristis, nolite obdurare corda vostra* (Today if you will hear the voice of the Lord, harden not your hearts), dated December 9, 1866.

131. *Official Records,* ser. 2, 8:773–74, 784–92; Stevenson to Davis, June 7, 1867, in Rowland, ed., *Davis,* 7:11–13; Allen, *Davis,* 453–58, 515–26, 557.

132. Miles to Townsend, December 25, 1865, in *Official Records,* ser. 2, 8:840; Allen, *Davis,* 454.

133. Davis to James Lyons, January 27, 1876, in Rowland, ed., *Davis,* 7:481–85.

134. Allen, *Davis,* 454.

135. V. Davis, *A Memoir,* 2:795; Allen, *Davis,* 488.

EPILOGUE: THE POSTWAR DAVIS

1. Davis, *Papers,* 2:16 n.2; V. Davis, *A Memoir,* 2:800–802; Jones, *Memorial Volume,* 458; Davis to R. S. Guernsey, April 9, 1870, in Rowland, ed., *Davis,* 7:268; Allen, *Davis,* 499–500.

2. Allen, *Davis,* 493.

3. Strode, *Davis,* 3:339–41; V. Davis, *A Memoir,* 2:801; Allen, *Davis,* 491–92.

4. W. C. Davis, *An Honorable Defeat,* 395.

5. Ibid.

6. Davis, *Rise and Fall,* 2:764 ("Esto perpetua" means "it is perpetual").

7. W. C. Davis, *An Honorable Defeat,* 395.

8. Rable, "Despair, Hope, and Delusion," 155.

9. Davis to Mary Stamps, November 10, 1869, in Strode, *Davis, Private Letters,* 321–22, 345; Davis, *Papers,* 5:135 n.14.

10. Charles L. Dufour, *Gentle Tiger: The Gallant Life of Roberdeau Wheat* (Baton Rouge: Louisiana State University Press, 1957), 8, 127, 169; V. Davis, *A Memoir,* 2:915; Allen, *Davis,* 561, 563.

11. This is the general theme of Hesseltine's *Confederate Leaders and the New South.*

12. This is the general theme of Connelly's *The Marble Man: Robert E. Lee and His Image in American Society.*

13. Thomas L. Connelly, *Will Success Spoil Jeff Davis?* (New York: McGraw-Hill, 1963).

14. Rowland, ed., *Davis,* 9:164.

15. Allen, *Davis,* 521, 529–31.

APPENDIX: BARBER'S MODEL OF PRESIDENTIAL LEADERSHIP

1. James David Barber, *The Presidential Character,* 4th ed. (Englewood Cliffs, N.J.: Prentice-Hall, 1992), 5. Barber's third edition was extensively rewritten for the fourth edition. The discussion here is derived from the fourth edition, unless indicated otherwise, and the citation of page numbers from it will be incorporated into the text. There are occasional references to the third edition, however, when they seem consistent with the ideas Barber expressed in 1992. It seems likely that he cut some of the content of the third edition because of space considerations, as he added a discussion of George H. W. Bush and thoroughly reorganized the remainder of the work.

2. James David Barber, *Presidential Character: Predicting Performance in the White House,* 3d ed. (Englewood Cliffs, N.J.: Prentice-Hall, 1985), 524.

3. Barber, *Presidential Character* (4th ed.), 466, 459, 475. The analysis of President Bush is particularly shallow, dismissing the political skill necessary to build the anti-Iraq coalition, and is virtually without consideration that Saddam Hussein might have had something to do with the course of events. And since this edition was published in 1992, Bush's remarkable failure to win reelection could not be examined. The analysis of Bush provides a good example of the reasons to avoid instant history. All in all, Barber would have been well advised to leave him out of the discussion. Even as this note is written, the Iraq story is by no means ended, making it exceedingly difficult to evaluate Bush's leadership objectively.

4. Barber, *Presidential Character* (3d ed.), 302. We refer to this edition at this point because Barber cut much of his analysis of Nixon's "active negativity," as we might call it, when he issued the fourth edition. In it he uses a good deal more space to analyze Nixon's misdeeds than his character or style, and it is therefore less useful for our purposes.

5. Ibid., 313, 314, 341–42.

BIBLIOGRAPHY

Archival Collections

Alabama State Archives.

Clements Library. University of Michigan at Ann Arbor.

Davis, Jefferson. Papers. Louisiana Historical Association Collection. Tulane University Library.

Davis, Jefferson. Papers. Jefferson Davis Association. Rice University.

Davis, Jefferson. Papers. Woodson Research Center, Fondren Library, Rice University.

Dearborn Collection. Harvard University Library.

Dudley, Thomas Haines Collection. Huntington Library. San Marino, California.

Eldridge Collection. Huntington Library. San Marino, California.

Executive Papers, 1860–1865. Archives Branch. Virginia State Library. Richmond.

Fleming Collection. New York Public Library.

Graham, William A. Papers. North Carolina Department of Archives and History. Raleigh.

Jensen, Elles E. Collection. State Historical Society of Wisconsin. Madison.

Johnston, Joseph E. Papers. Huntington Library. San Marino, California.

Lee, Robert E. Headquarters Papers. Virginia Historical Society, Richmond.

National Archives. Record Group 109. War Department Collection of Confederate Records.

Porter, Admiral D. D. Papers. Huntington Library. San Marino, California.

Wiley, Bell I. Papers. Emory University.

Theses, Dissertations, and Unpublished Papers

Davis, Kathleen Bailey. "Jefferson Davis and the Mississippi Gubernatorial Contest of 1851, with Selected Letters and Speeches Concerning the Campaign." Master's thesis, Rice University, 1971.

Hendricks, George Linton. "Union Army Occupation of the Southern Seaboard, 1861–1865." Ann Arbor, Michigan, 1954. Microfilm.

Lewis, Albert L. "The Confederate Congress: A Study in Personnel." Master's thesis, University of Southern California, 1955.

Owsley, Frank L. "State Rights in the Confederacy." Thesis no. T11718, University of Chicago, 1925.

Robbins, John Brawner. "Confederate Nationalism: Politics and Government in the Confederate South, 1861–1865." Ph.D. diss., Rice University, 1964.

Walther, Eric H. "Fire-Eaters and the Riddle of Confederate Nationalism." Paper presented at the annual meeting of the Southern Historical Association, Fort Worth, Texas, 1991.

PRINTED PRIMARY SOURCES

Aiken, Warren. *Letters of Warren Aiken, Confederate Congressman*. Ed. Bell I. Wiley. Athens: University of Georgia Press, 1959.

Alabama General Assembly. *Acts of the Called Session, 1863, and of the Third Regular Annual Session*. Montgomery: Safford and Figures, 1864.

Alexander, Edward Porter. *Fighting for the Confederacy: The Personal Recollections of General Edward Porter Alexander*. Ed. Gary W. Gallagher. Chapel Hill: University of North Carolina Press, 1989.

Basler, Roy F., ed. *The Collected Works of Abraham Lincoln*. 9 vols. New Brunswick, N.J.: Rutgers University Press, 1953–55. Supplements 1974 and 1990.

Blackford, Charles Minor III, ed., and Susan Leigh Blackford, comp. *Letters from Lee's Army, or Memoirs of Life in and out of the Army in Virginia During the War Between the States*. New York: Charles Scribner's Sons, 1947.

Brown, Joseph E. *Message of His Excellency Joseph E. Brown, to the Legislature of the State of Georgia, Convened in Extra Session at Macon, Georgia, February 15, 1865*. Macon: Nisbet, Barnes, and Moore, 1865.

Butler, Benjamin F. *Butler's Book*. Boston: A. M. Thayer, 1892.

Calendar of the Postwar Jefferson Davis Manuscripts. New York: Burt Franklin, 1943.

Chesnut, Mary Boykin Miller. *Mary Chesnut's Civil War*. Ed. C. Vann Woodward. New Haven: Yale University Press, 1981.

———. *The Private Mary Chesnut: The Unpublished Civil War Diaries*. Ed. C. Vann Woodward and Elizabeth Muhlenfeld. New York: Oxford University Press, 1984.

Cobb, Howell. "Howell Cobb Papers." Ed. R. P. Brooks. *Georgia Historical Quarterly* 6(1922).

Cobb, Thomas Reade Rootes. "Correspondence of Thomas Reade Rootes Cobb." Ed. A. L. Hull. *Publications of the Southern Historical Association* 11(1907).

Davis, Jefferson. *Jefferson Davis: Constitutionalist*. Ed. Dunbar Rowland. 10 vols. Jackson: Mississippi Department of Archives and History, 1923.

———. *The Papers of Jefferson Davis*. Ed. Haskell M. Monroe Jr., James T. McIntosh, Lynda Lasswell Crist, and Mary Seaton Dix. 10 vols. to date. Baton Rouge: Louisiana State University Press, 1971–.

———. *The Rise and Fall of the Confederate Government*. 2 vols. New York: D. Appleton, 1881.

Davis, Varina. *Jefferson Davis: A Memoir by His Wife*. 2 vols. Baltimore: Nautical and Aviation Publishing Company of America, 1990.

Douglas, Henry Kyd. *I Rode with Stonewall.* Chapel Hill: University of North Carolina Press, 1940.

Early, Jubal. *Jubal Early's Memoirs: Autobiographical Sketch and Narrative of the War Between the States.* Baltimore: Nautical and Aviation Publishing Company of America, 1989.

Freedom: A Documentary History of Emancipation, 1861–1867. Ser. 1, vol. 1, *The Destruction of Slavery.* Ed. Ira Berlin et al. London and New York: Cambridge University Press, 1985.

Freemantle, Arthur Charles Lyon. *Three Months in the Southern States: April–June 1863.* 1864. Reprint, Lincoln: University of Nebraska Press, 1991.

Gauche, Louis-Hippolyte. *A Frenchman, a Chaplain, a Rebel: The War Letters of Père Louis-Hippolyte Gauche, S. J.* Trans. and ed. Cornelius M. Buckley. Chicago: Loyola University Press, 1981.

Gorgas, Josiah. *The Civil War Diary of General Josiah Gorgas.* Ed. Frank S. Vandiver. University: University of Alabama Press, 1947.

Hood, John B. *Advance and Retreat.* 1880. Reprint, with introduction by Bruce J. Dinges. Lincoln: University of Nebraska Press, 1996.

Johnston, Joseph E. *Narrative of Military Operations.* 1874. Reprint, Bloomington: Indiana University Press, 1959.

Jones, J. B. *A Rebel War Clerk's Diary at the Confederate States Capital.* Ed. Earl S. Miers. Abridgement. New York: Sagamore Press, 1958.

———. *A Rebel War Clerk's Diary at the Confederate States Capital.* 2 vols. Philadelphia: J. B. Lippincott, 1866.

Kean, Robert G. H. *Inside the Confederate Government: The Diary of Robert Garlick Hill Kean.* Ed. Edward Younger. New York: Oxford University Press, 1957.

Lee, Robert E. *Lee's Dispatches: Unpublished Letters of General Robert E. Lee, C.S.A., to Jefferson Davis and the War Department of the Confederate States of America, 1862–1865, from the Private Collection of Wymberley Jones de Renne, of Wormsloe, Georgia.* 1915. Reprint, ed. Grady McWhiney, with 10 new dispatches. Baton Rouge: Louisiana State University Press, 1994.

———. *Wartime Papers of Robert E. Lee.* Ed. Clifford Dowdey and Louis H. Manarin. Boston: Little, Brown, 1961.

Lee, Robert E. Jr. *Recollections and Letters of General Robert E. Lee.* New York: Bramhall House, 1904.

Longstreet, James. *From Manassas to Appomattox: Memoirs of the Civil War in America.* Philadelphia: J. B. Lippincott, 1896.

Matthews, James M., ed. *Public Laws of the Confederate States of America, Passed at the First Session of the First Congress, 1862.* 1862. Reprint, Holmes Beach, Fla.: William W. Gaunt and Sons, 1970.

———. *Public Laws of the Confederate States of America, Passed at the Second Session of the First Congress, 1862.* 1862. Reprint, Holmes Beach, Fla.: William W. Gaunt and Sons, 1970.

———. *Public Laws of the Confederate States of America, Passed at the Third Session of the First Congress, 1863.* 1863. Reprint, Holmes Beach, Fla.: William W. Gaunt and Sons, 1970.

————. *Public Laws of the Confederate States of America, Passed at the Fourth Session of the First Congress, 1863–1864.* 1864. Reprint, Holmes Beach, Fla.: William W. Gaunt and Sons, 1970.

————. *Public Laws of the Confederate States of America, Passed at the First Session of the Second Congress, 1864.* 1864. Reprint, Holmes Beach, Fla.: William W. Gaunt and Sons, 1970.

————. *The Statutes at Large of the Provisional Government of the Confederate States of America.* 1864. Reprint, Holmes Beach, Fla.: William W. Gaunt and Sons, 1970.

Moore, Frank, ed. *The Rebellion Record: A Diary of American Events.* Vols. 1–6, New York: G. P. Putnam, 1861–1863. Vols. 7–12, New York: D. Van Nostrand, 1864–1868.

Patrick, Rembert W., ed. *The Opinions of the Confederate Attorneys General, 1861–1865.* Buffalo, N.Y.: Dennis, 1950.

"Proceedings of the . . . Confederate Congress." (Title varies.) *Southern Historical Society Papers* 44–52 (June 1923–July 1959).

Pryor, Mrs. Roger A. *Reminiscences of Peace and War.* New York: Macmillan, 1924.

Rainwater, Percy L., ed. "Letters of James Lusk Alcorn." *Journal of Southern History* 3(May 1937).

Ramsdell, Charles W., ed. *Laws and Joint Resolutions of the Last Session of the Confederate Congress (November 7, 1864–March 18, 1865), Together with the Secret Acts of Previous Congresses.* 1941. Reprint, New York: AMS Press, 1965.

Reagan, John H. *Memoirs, with Special References to Secession and the Civil War.* Ed. W. F. McCaleb. New York: Neale, 1906.

Richardson, James D., ed. *A Compilation of the Messages and Papers of the Confederacy.* 2 vols. Nashville: U.S. Publishing Company, 1904.

Ruffin, Edmund. *The Diary of Edmund Ruffin.* Ed. William Kauffman Scarborough. Baton Rouge: Louisiana State University Press, 1976.

Sterling, Ada, ed. *A Belle of the Fifties: Memoirs of Mrs. Clay of Alabama, Covering Social and Political Life in Washington and the South, 1853–1866.* New York: Doubleday, Page, 1905.

Taylor, Richard. *Destruction and Reconstruction: Personal Experiences of the Late War.* New York: D. Appleton, 1879.

Taylor, Rosser H., ed. "Boyce-Hammond Correspondence." *Journal of Southern History* 3 (August 1937).

Taylor, Walter H. *General Lee: His Campaigns in Virginia, 1861–1865, with Personal Reminiscences.* Norfolk: Nusbaum Book and News, 1906.

The Texas Almanac for 1867. Galveston: W. D. Richardson, 1866.

Thian, Raphael P., comp. *Reports of the Secretary of the Treasury of the Confederate States of America, 1861–1865.* Washington, D.C., 1878.

Toombs, Robert et al. *The Correspondence of Robert Toombs, Alexander H. Stephens, and Howell Cobb.* Ed. Ulrich B. Phillips. American Historical Association, *Report for the Year 1911*, vol. 2. Washington, D.C.: U.S. Government Printing Office, 1913.

U.S. Congress. Senate. *Journal of the Congress of the Confederate States of America, 1861–1865.* 7 vols. Senate Document no. 234, 58th Cong., 2d sess. Washington, D.C.: U.S. Government Printing Office, 1904–1905.

U.S. Naval War Records Office. *Official Records of the Union and Confederate Navies.* 31 vols. Washington, D.C.: Government Printing Office, 1894–1927.

U.S. War Department. *War of the Rebellion: Official Records of the Union and Confederate Armies.* 70 vols. in 128. Washington, D.C.: Government Printing Office, 1880–1901.

Vance, Zebulon Baird. *The Papers of Zebulon Baird Vance.* Raleigh, N.C.: State Department of Archives and History, 1963.

Wakeman, Sarah Rosetta, a.k.a. Pvt. Lyons Wakeman. *An Uncommon Soldier.* Ed. Lauren Cook Burgess. New York: Oxford University Press, 1994.

Watts, Thomas H. "Address on the Life and Character of Ex-President Jefferson Davis." Montgomery, Ala., 1889.

Wright, Louise [Mrs. D. Giraud]. *A Southern Girl in '61: The Wartime Memories of a Confederate Senator's Daughter.* New York: Doubleday, Page, 1905.

ARTICLES AND EXCERPTS

Allardice, Bruce. "West Points of the Confederacy: Southern Military Schools and the Confederate Army." *Civil War History* 43 (December 1997).

Beringer, Richard E. "Confederate Identity and the Will to Fight." In *On the Road to Total War: The American Civil War and the German Wars of Unification, 1861–1871.* Ed. Stig Foerster and Jorg Nagler. German Historical Institute. New York: Cambridge University Press, 1997.

———. "Jefferson Davis's Pursuit of Ambition: The Attractive Features of Alternative Decisions." *Civil War History* 38 (March 1992).

———. "A Profile of the Members of the Confederate Congress." *Journal of Southern History* 33 (November 1967).

———. "The Unconscious 'Spirit of Party' in the Confederate Congress." *Civil War History* 18 (December 1972).

Booth, R. V. "Last Address of President Davis, C.S.A." *Confederate Veteran* 22 (July 1914).

Cartwright, Samuel A. "Alcohol and the Ethiopian; or the Moral and Physical Effects of Ardent Spirits on the Negro Race, and Some Account of the Peculiarity of That People." *New Orleans Medical and Surgical Journal* 10 (1853).

DeBow, J. D. B. "Our Danger and Our Duty." *DeBow's Review,* 1st ser., 33 (1862).

Donald, David Herbert. Review of W. C. Davis, *Jefferson Davis: The Man and His Hour,* in *New York Times Book Review,* January 12, 1992.

Gentry, Judith Fenner. "A Confederate Success in Europe: The Erlanger Loan." *Journal of Southern History* 36 (May 1970).

George, Joseph Jr. "'Black Flag Warfare': Lincoln and the Raids Against Richmond and Jefferson Davis." *Pennsylvania Magazine of History and Biography* 115 (1991).

Halsey, Ashley Jr. "Who Fired the First Shot?" *Saturday Evening Post*, 1960.

Hattaway, Herman. "Confederate Mythmaking: Top Command and the Chickasaw Bayou Campaign." *Journal of Mississippi History* 33 (November 1970).

———. "The General the President Elevated Too High: Davis and John Bell Hood." In *Jefferson Davis's Generals*, ed. Gabor S. Boritt. New York: Oxford University Press, 1999.

———. "Jefferson Davis and the Historians." In *The Civil War High Command*, ed. Roman J. Heleniak and Lawrence L. Hewitt. Shippensburg, Pa.: White Mane, 1991.

———. Review of W. C. Davis, *Jefferson Davis: The Man and His Hour*, in *Journal of American History* 79 (December 1992).

———. "Via Confederate Post." *Civil War Times–Illustrated* 15 (April 1976).

Hattaway, Herman, and Michael Gillespie. "We Shall Cease to Be Friends." *Military History* (August 1984).

Hattaway, Herman, and Archer Jones. "Lincoln as Military Strategist." *Civil War History* 26 (December 1980).

Hay, Thomas Robson. "Lucius B. Northrop: Commissary General of the Confederacy." *Civil War History* 9 (1963).

Hofstadter, Richard. "John C. Calhoun: The Marx of the Master Class." In Hofstadter, *The American Political Tradition and the Men Who Made It*. New York: Alfred A. Knopf, 1948.

Johnson, Ludwell H. "Jefferson Davis and Abraham Lincoln as War Presidents: Nothing Succeeds Like Success." *Civil War History* 27 (March 1981).

Krug, Donna Rebecca D. "Women and War in the Confederacy." In *On the Road to Total War: The American Civil War and the German Wars of Unification*. Ed. Stig Foerster and Jorg Nagler. German Historical Institute. New York: Cambridge University Press, 1997.

Lerner, Eugene. "Money, Prices, and Wages in the Confederacy, 1861–1865." *Journal of Political Economy* 63 (February 1955).

Little, Robert D. "General Hardee and the Atlanta Campaign." *Georgia Historical Quarterly* 29 (1945).

McMurry, Richard M. " 'The Enemy at Richmond': Joseph E. Johnston and the Confederate Government." *Civil War History* 27 (1981).

McPherson, James. "The Whole Family of Man: Lincoln and the Best Hope Abroad." In *The Union, the Confederacy, and the Atlantic Rim*, ed. Robert E. May. West Lafayette, Ind.: Purdue University Press, 1995.

McWhiney, Grady. "The Confederacy's First Shot." In *Southerners and Other Americans*. New York: Basic Books, 1973.

Minter, Winfred P. "Confederate Military Supply." *Social Science* 3 (June 1959).

Mitchell, Scott. "The Bawdy Truth About the Civil War." *Penthouse* [ca. early 1972].

Moore, John B. "Mobility and Strategy in the Civil War." *Military Affairs* (now *Journal of Military History*) (summer 1960).

Paret, Peter. "Justifying the Obligation of Military Service." *Journal of Military History* 57, special issue (October 1993).

Ramsdell, Charles. "Lincoln and Fort Sumter." *Journal of Southern History* 3 (August 1937).

Royster, Charles. "Fort Sumter: At Last the War." In *Why the Civil War Came,* ed. Gabor Boritt. New York: Oxford University Press, 1996.

Smith, Nannie D. "Reminiscences of Jefferson Davis." *Confederate Veteran* (May 1930).

Stinson, Byron T. "Civil War Pin-Up Girls." *Civil War Times–Illustrated* 8 (August 1969).

Twain, Mark. "The Private History of a Campaign That Failed." *Century Magazine* 31 (December 1885).

Wink, Jay. "They Gave America a Second Chance." *Parade Magazine,* April 8, 2001.

BOOKS

Adams, Michael C. C. *Our Masters the Rebels.* Cambridge: University of Massachusetts Press, 1974.

Alexander, Thomas B., and Richard E. Beringer. *The Anatomy of the Confederate Congress.* Nashville: Vanderbilt University Press, 1972.

Alfriend, Frank H. *The Life of Jefferson Davis.* Cincinnnati and Chicago: Caxton, 1868.

Allen, Felicity. *Unconquerable Heart: Life of Jefferson Davis.* Columbia: University of Missouri Press, 2000.

Andrews, M. M. *Scraps of Paper.* New York: E. P. Dutton, 1929.

Ball, Douglas. *Financial Failure and Confederate Defeat.* Urbana and Chicago: University of Illinois Press, 1991.

Ballard, Michael B. *A Long Shadow: Jefferson Davis and the Final Days of the Confederacy.* Jackson: University Press of Mississippi, 1986.

———. *Pemberton: A Biography.* Jackson: University Press of Mississippi, 1991.

Barber, James David. *The Presidential Character: Predicting Performance in the White House.* Englewood Cliffs, N.J.: Prentice-Hall, 3d ed., 1985; 4th ed., 1992.

Bensel, Richard Franklin. *Yankee Leviathan: The Origins of Central State Authority in America, 1859–1877.* New York: Cambridge University Press, 1990.

Bergeron, Arthur W. *Confederate Mobile.* Jackson: University Press of Mississippi, 1991.

Beringer, Richard E., Herman Hattaway, Archer Jones, and William Still. *Why the South Lost the Civil War.* Athens: University of Georgia Press, 1986.

Black, Robert C. III. *The Railroads of the Confederacy.* Chapel Hill: University of North Carolina Press, 1952.

Blair, William. *Virginia's Private War: Feeding Body and Soul in the Confederacy, 1861–1865.* New York: Oxford University Press, 1998.

Blakey, Arch Fredric. *General John H. Winder, C.S.A.* Gainesville: University of Florida Press, 1990.

The Book of Common Prayer and Administration of the Sacraments, and Other Rites and Ceremonies of the Church, According to the Use of the Protestant Episcopal Church in the United States of America, Together with the Psalter, or Psalms of David. 1850. Reprint, Hartford, Conn.: Thomas Nelson and Sons, 1896.

Boritt, Gabor S., ed. *Why the Civil War Came.* New York: Oxford University Press, 1996.

———. ed. *Why the Confederacy Lost.* New York: Oxford University Press, 1992.

Brown, Richard D. *Modernization: The Transformation of American Life, 1600–1865.* New York: Hill and Wang, 1976.

Buker, George E. *Blockaders, Refugees, and Contrabands: Civil War on Florida's Gulf Coast, 1861–1865.* Tuscaloosa: University of Alabama Press, 1993.

Bulloch, James D. *The Secret Service of the Confederate States in Europe, or How the Confederate Cruisers Were Equipped.* 2 vols. New York: Thomas Yoseloff, 1959.

Butler, Pierce. *Judah P. Benjamin.* 1907. Reprint, New York: Chelsea House, 1980.

Capers, Henry D. *Life and Times of C. G. Memminger.* Richmond: Everett Waddey, 1893.

Castel, Albert. *Decision in the West: The Atlanta Campaign of 1864.* Lawrence: University Press of Kansas, 1992.

Cauthen, Charles E. *South Carolina Goes to War, 1860–1865.* Chapel Hill: University of North Carolina Press, 1950.

Cheshire, Joseph Blount. *The Church in the Confederate States: A History of the Protestant Episcopal Church in the Confederate States.* New York: Longmans, Green, 1912.

Cleveland, Henry. *Alexander H. Stephens: In Public and Private.* Philadelphia: National Publishing Company, 1866.

Connelly, Thomas Lawrence. *Army of the Heartland: The Army of Tennessee, 1861–1862.* Baton Rouge: Louisiana State University Press, 1967.

———. *Civil War Tennessee: Battles and Leaders.* Knoxville: University of Tennessee Press, 1979.

———. *The Marble Man: Robert E. Lee and His Image in American Society.* New York: Knopf, 1977.

———. *Will Success Spoil Jeff Davis?* New York: McGraw-Hill, 1963.

Connelly, Thomas Lawrence, and Archer Jones. *The Politics of Command: Factions and Ideas in Confederate Strategy.* Baton Rouge: Louisiana State University Press, 1973.

Cooper, William Jr. *Jefferson Davis: American.* New York: Knopf, 2000.

Cornish, Dudley Taylor. *The Sable Arm: Negro Troops in the Union Army, 1861–1865.* 1956. New edition, with foreword by Herman Hattaway. Lawrence: University Press of Kansas, 1987.

Coulter, E. Merton. *The Confederate States of America, 1861–1865.* Vol. 7, *A History of the South.* Ed. Wendell Holmes Stephenson and E. Merton Coulter. Baton Rouge: Louisiana State University Press, 1950.

Current, Richard N. *Lincoln and the First Shot.* Philadelphia: Lippincott, 1963.

———. *Lincoln's Loyalists: Union Soldiers from the Confederacy.* Boston: Northeastern University Press, 1992.

Cutting, Elizabeth. *Jefferson Davis: Political Soldier.* New York: Dodd, Mead, 1930.

Dabney, Robert L. *The Life and Campaigns of Lt. Gen. Thomas J. Jackson.* New York: Blelock, 1866.

Dabney, Virginius. *Pistols and Pointed Pens: The Dueling Editors of Old Virginia.* Chapel Hill, N.C.: Algonquin Books of Chapel Hill, 1987.

Davis, William C. *The Cause Lost: Myths and Realities of the Confederacy.* Lawrence: University Press of Kansas, 1996.

———. *"A Government of Our Own" : The Making of the Confederacy*. New York: Free Press, 1994.

———. *An Honorable Defeat: The Last Days of the Confederate Government*. New York: Harcourt, 2001.

———. *Jefferson Davis: The Man and His Hour*. New York: HarperCollins, 1991.

———. *The Union That Shaped the Confederacy: Robert Toombs and Alexander Stephens*. Lawrence: University Press of Kansas, 2001.

DeRosa, Marshal L. *The Confederate Constitution: An Inquiry into American Constitutionalism*. Columbia: University of Missouri Press, 1991.

Donald, David. *Charles Sumner and the Coming of the Civil War*. New York: Knopf, 1960.

———, ed. *Why the North Won the Civil War*. 1960. Reprint, New York: Collier Books, 1962.

Dufour, Charles L. *Gentle Tiger: The Gallant Life of Roberdeau Wheat*. Baton Rouge: Louisiana State University Press, 1957.

Durden, Robert F. *The Gray and the Black: The Confederate Debate on Emancipation*. Baton Rouge: Louisiana State University Press, 1972.

Durkin, Joseph T., S.J. *Stephen R. Mallory: Confederate Navy Chief*. Chapel Hill: University of North Carolina Press, 1954.

Durrill, Wayne K. *War of Another Kind: A Southern Community in the Great Rebellion*. New York: Oxford University Press, 1990.

Eaton, Clement. *A History of the Southern Confederacy*. New York: Oxford University Press, 1958.

———. *Jefferson Davis*. New York: Free Press, 1977.

Escott, Paul. *After Secession: Jefferson Davis and the Failure of Confederate Nationalism*. Baton Rouge: Louisiana State University Press, 1978.

Evans, Eli N. *Judah P. Benjamin: The Jewish Confederate*. New York: Free Press, 1988.

Faust, Drew Gilpin. *The Creation of Confederate Nationalism: Ideology and Identity in the Civil War South*. Baton Rouge: Louisiana State University Press, 1988.

Ferris, Norman. *The Trent Affair: A Diplomatic Crisis*. Knoxville: University of Tennessee Press, 1977.

Franklin, John Hope. *The Militant South: 1800–1861*. Cambridge: Belknap Press of Harvard University Press, 1956.

Frederickson, George M. *Why the Confederacy Did Not Fight a Guerilla War After the Fall of Richmond: A Comparative View*. Thirty-fifth Annual Robert Fortenbaugh Memorial Lecture. Gettysburg, Pa.: Gettysburg College, 1996.

Freeman, Douglas Southall. *Lee's Lieutenants: A Study in Command*. 3 vols. New York: Charles Scribner's Sons, 1942–1946.

———. *R. E. Lee: A Biography*. 4 vols. New York: Charles Scribner's Sons, 1934–1935.

Glatthaar, Joseph T. *Forged in Battle: The Civil War Alliance of Black Soldiers and White Officers*. New York: Free Press, 1990.

Goff, Richard. *Confederate Supply*. Durham, N.C.: Duke University Press, 1969.

Golay, Michael. *A Ruined Land: The End of the Civil War*. New York: John Wiley and Sons, 1999.

Govan, Gilbert E., and James W. Livingood. *A Different Valor: The Story of General Joseph E. Johnston, C.S.A.* Indianapolis: Bobbs-Merrill, 1956.

Grimsley, Mark. *The Hard Hand of War: Union Military Policy Toward Southern Civilians, 1861–1865.* New York: Cambridge University Press, 1995.

Grimsley, Mark, and Brooks D. Simpson, eds. *The Collapse of the Confederacy.* Lincoln: University of Nebraska Press, 2001.

Guelzo, Allen C. *Abraham Lincoln: Redeemer President.* Grand Rapids, Mich.: William B. Erdemans, 1999.

Hahn, Steven. *The Roots of Southern Populism: Yeoman Farmers and the Transformation of the Georgia Upcountry, 1850–1890.* New York: Oxford University Press, 1983.

Hallock, Judith Lee. *Braxton Bragg and Confederate Defeat.* Tuscaloosa: University of Alabama Press, 1991.

Hanna, A. J. *Flight into Oblivion.* Richmond: Johnson Publishing Company, 1938.

Harris, Joel Chandler. *On the Plantation: A Story of a Georgia Boy's Adventures During the Civil War.* Reprint. Athens: University of Georgia Press, 1980.

Harrison, Mrs. Burton [Constance Cary]. *Recollections Grave and Gay.* New York: Charles Scribner's Sons, 1911.

Harsh, Joseph L. *Confederate Tide Rising: Robert E. Lee and the Making of Southern Strategy, 1861–1862.* Kent, Ohio: Kent State University Press, 1998.

———. *Taken at the Flood: Robert E. Lee and Confederate Strategy in the Maryland Campaign of 1862.* Kent, Ohio: Kent State University Press, 1999.

Hattaway, Herman. *General Stephen D. Lee.* Jackson: University Press of Mississippi, 1976.

———. *Shades of Blue and Gray: An Introductory Military History of the Civil War.* Columbia: University of Missouri Press, 1997.

Hattaway, Herman, and Archer Jones. *How the North Won: A Military History of the Civil War.* Urbana and Chicago: University of Illinois Press, 1983.

Headley, John W. *Confederate Operations in Canada and New York.* 1906. Reprint, Alexandria, Va.: Time-Life Books, 1984.

Hendrick, Burton J. *Statesmen of the Lost Cause.* Boston: Little Brown, 1939.

Henry, Robert. *The Story of the Confederacy.* 1931. Rev. ed. with foreword by Douglas Southall Freeman. Gloucester, Mass.: Peter Smith, 1970.

Hesseltine, William B. *Confederate Leaders in the New South.* Baton Rouge: Louisiana State University Press, 1950.

Hill, Lois, ed. *Poems and Songs of the Civil War.* New York: Fairfax Press, 1990.

Hill, Samuel H. *The South and the North in American Religion.* Athens: University of Georgia Press, 1980.

Horn, Stanley. *The Army of Tennessee.* 1941. Reprint, Norman: University of Oklahoma Press, 1952.

Hudson, Leonne M. *The Odyssey of a Southerner: The Life and Times of Gustavus Woodson Smith.* Macon, Ga.: Mercer University Press, 1998.

Hughes, Nathaniel Cheairs Jr. *General William J. Hardee: Old Reliable.* Baton Rouge: Louisiana State University Press, 1965.

Jamieson, Perry, and Grady McWhiney. *Attack and Die*. Tuscaloosa: University of Alabama Press, 1982.

Johnson, Bradley T. *A Memoir of the Life and Public Service of Joseph E. Johnston, Once Quartermaster General of the Army of the United States, and a General in the Army of the Confederate States of America*. Baltimore: R. H. Woodward, 1891.

Johnson, Robert U., and Clarence C. Buell, *Battles and Leaders of the Civil War*. 4 vols. New York: Century, 1887.

Johnston, Angus James. *Virginia Railroads in the Civil War*. Chapel Hill: University of North Carolina Press, 1961.

Johnston, Malcolm, and Richard Hand Browne. *Life of Alexander H. Stephens*. Philadelphia: J. B. Lippincott, 1878.

Johnston, William Preston. *The Life of General Albert Sidney Johnston, Embracing His Service in the Armies of the United States, Republic of Texas, and the Confederate States*. New York: D. Appleton, 1889.

Jones, J. William. *The Davis Memorial Volume, Or our Dead President, Jefferson Davis, and the World's Tribute to His Memory*. N.p.: B. F. Johnson, 1889.

King, Alvy L. *Louis T. Wigfall: Southern Fire-eater*. Baton Rouge: Louisiana State University Press, 1970.

Lash, Jeffrey N. *Destroyer of the Iron Horse: General Joseph E. Johnston and Confederate Rail Transportation, 1861–1865*. Kent, Ohio: Kent State University Press, 1991.

Lee, Charles Robert Jr. *The Confederate Constitutions*. Chapel Hill: University of North Carolina Press, 1963.

Leonard, Elizabeth D. *All the Daring of the Soldier: Women of the Civil War Armies*. New York: Norton, 1999.

Long, E. B. *The Civil War Day by Day: An Almanac, 1861–1865*. Garden City, N.Y.: Doubleday, 1971.

Lowry, Thomas P. *The Story the Soldiers Wouldn't Tell: Sex in the Civil War*. Mechanicsburg, Pa.: Stackpole Books, 1994.

Lucas, Marion B. *Sherman and the Burning of Columbia*. College Station: Texas A&M Press, 1976.

Marvel, William. *Andersonville: The Last Depot*. Chapel Hill: University of North Carolina Press, 1994.

McElroy, Robert. *Jefferson Davis: The Unreal and the Real*. 2 vols. New York: Harper & Brothers, 1937.

McMillan, Malcolm C. *The Disintegration of a Confederate State: Three Governors and Alabama's Wartime Home Front, 1861–1865*. Macon, Ga.: Mercer University Press, 1986.

McMurry, Richard M. *John Bell Hood and the War for Southern Independence*. Lexington: University of Kentucky Press, 1982.

———. *Two Great Rebel Armies: An Essay in Confederate Military History*. Chapel Hill: University of North Carolina Press, 1989.

McPherson, James M. *Battle Cry of Freedom: The Civil War Era*. Vol. 6. *The Oxford History of the United States*. New York: Oxford University Press, 1988.

McWhiney, Grady. *Braxton Bragg and Confederate Defeat*. Volume 1. *Field Command*. New York: Columbia University Press, 1969.

———. *Cracker Culture: Celtic Ways in the Old South*. Tuscaloosa: University of Alabama Press, 1988.

Montgomery, H[enry]. *Howell Cobb's Confederate Career*. Tuscaloosa: Confederate Publishing, 1959.

Moore, Albert B. *Conscription and Conflict in the Confederacy*. New York: Macmillan, 1924.

Moore, Jerrold Northrop. *Confederate Commissary General: Lucius Bellinger Northrop and the Subsistence Bureau of the Southern Army*. Shippensburg, Pa.: White Mane, 1996.

Neely, Mark. *The Fate of Liberty: Abraham Lincoln and Civil Liberties*. New York: Oxford University Press, 1991.

———. *Southern Rights: Political Prisoners and the Myth of Confederate Constitutionalism*. Charlottesville: University Press of Virginia, 1999.

Nelson, Larry E. *Bullets, Ballots, and Rhetoric: Confederate Policy for the United States Presidential Contest of 1864*. University: University of Alabama Press, 1980.

Nevins, Allan. *The War for the Union*. 4 vols. New York: Charles Scribner's Sons, 1959–1971.

Owsley, Frank. *State Rights in the Confederacy*. 1925. Reprint, Gloucester, Mass.: Peter Smith, 1961.

Parks, Joseph H. *General Leonidas Polk, C.S.A.: The Fighting Bishop*. Baton Rouge: Louisiana State University Press, 1962.

Patrick, Rembert W. *Jefferson Davis and His Cabinet*. Baton Rouge: Louisiana State University Press, 1944.

Perry, Milton F. *Infernal Machines: The Story of Confederate Submarine and Mine Warfare*. Baton Rouge: Louisiana State University Press, 1965.

Perry, William Stevens. *The Bishops of the American Church Past and Present: Sketches, Biographical and Bibliographical, of the Bishops of the American Church, with a Preliminary Essay on the Historic Episcopate and Documentary Annals of the Introduction of the Anglican Line of Succession into America*. New York: Christian Literature, 1897.

Polk, William M. *Leonidas Polk: Bishop and General*. 2 vols. New York: Longmans, Green, 1894.

Pollard, E. A. *Life of Jefferson Davis, with a Secret History of the Southern Confederacy*. Philadelphia: National Publishing, 1869.

Rable, George C. *The Confederate Republic: A Revolution Against Politics*. Chapel Hill: University of North Carolina Press, 1994.

Ramsdell, Charles W. *Behind the Lines in the Southern Confederacy*. Reprint. New York: Greenwood Press, 1969.

Randall, J. G., and David Donald. *The Civil War and Reconstruction*. 2d ed., rev. Lexington, Mass.: D. C. Heath, 1969.

Rawley, James. A. *Turning Points of the Civil War*. Bison Book Edition. Lincoln: University of Nebraska Press, 1966.

Roland, Charles P. *The Confederacy*. Chicago: University of Chicago Press, 1960.

Royster, Charles. *The Destructive War: William Tecumseh Sherman, Stonewall Jackson, and the Americans*. New York: Knopf, 1991.

Scharf, J. Thomas. *History of the Confederate States Navy from Its Organization to the Surrender of Its Last Vessel*. New York: Rogers and Sherwood, 1887.

Schott, Thomas E. *Alexander H. Stephens of Georgia: A Biography*. Baton Rouge: Louisiana State University Press, 1988.

Schroeder-Lein, Glenna R. *Confederate Hospitals on the Move: Samuel H. Stout and the Army of Tennessee*. Columbia: University of South Carolina Press, 1994.

Schwab, John Christopher. *The Confederate States of America, 1861–1865: A Financial and Industrial History of the South During the Civil War*. New York: C. Scribner's Sons, 1901.

Seitz, Don C. *Braxton Bragg, General of the Confederacy*. Columbia, S.C.: State, 1924.

Shackleford, George Green. *George Wythe Randolph and the Confederate Elite*. Athens: University of Georgia Press, 1988.

Shaw, Arthur Marvin. *William Preston Johnston: A Transitional Figure of the Confederacy*. Baton Rouge: Louisiana State University Press, 1943.

Shingleton, Royce G. *John T. Wood*. Athens: University of Georgia Press, 1979.

Silber, Nina. *The Romance of Reunion: Northerners and the South, 1865–1900*. Chapel Hill: University of North Carolina Press, 1993.

Smith, Charles H. *Bill Arp, So Called: A Side Show of the Southern Side of the War*. New York: Metropolitan Record Office, 1866.

Sneden, Robert K. *Eye of the Storm: A Civil War Odyssey*. Ed. Charles F. Bryan Jr. and Nelson D. Lankford. New York: Free Press, 2000.

Strode, Hudson. *Jefferson Davis*. Vol. 2, *Confederate President*. New York: Harcourt, Brace, 1959.

———. *Jefferson Davis: Private Letters, 1823–1889*. New York: Harcourt Brace and World, 1966.

Symonds, Craig L. *Joseph E. Johnston: A Civil War Biography*. New York: W. W. Norton, 1992.

———. *Stonewall of the West: Patrick Cleburne and the Civil War*. Lawrence: University Press of Kansas, 1997.

Tatum, Georgia Lee. *Disloyalty in the Confederacy*. Reprint. New York: AMS Press, 1970.

Taylor, Robert A. *Rebel Storehouse: Florida in the Confederate Economy*. Tuscaloosa: University of Alabama Press, 1995.

Taylor, W. H. *Four Years with General Lee*. Ed. J. I. Robertson Jr. Bloomington: University of Indiana Press, 1996.

Thomas, Emory M. *The American War and Peace: 1860–1877*. Englewood Cliffs, N.J.: Prentice-Hall, 1973.

———. *Bold Dragoon: The Life of J. E .B. Stuart*. New York: Harper and Row, 1986.

———. *The Confederacy as a Revolutionary Experience*. Englewood Cliffs, N.J.: Prentice Hall, 1971.

————. *The Confederate Nation, 1861–1865*. New York: Harper and Row, 1979.

Thompson, William Y. *Robert Toombs of Georgia*. Baton Rouge: Louisiana State University Press, 1966.

Thornton, J. Mills III. *Politics and Power in a Slave Society: Alabama, 1800–1860*. Baton Rouge: Louisiana State University Press, 1978.

Tidwell, William A. *April '65: Confederate Covert Action in the American Civil War*. Kent, Ohio: Kent State University Press, 1995.

————, James O. Hall, and David Winfred Gaddy. *Come Retribution: The Confederate Secret Service and the Assassination of Lincoln*. Jackson: University of Mississippi Press, 1988.

Todd, Richard C. *Confederate Finance*. Athens: University of Georgia Press, 1954.

Trudeau, Noah Andre. *Out of the Storm: The End of the Civil War April–June 1865*. Baton Rouge: Louisiana State University Press, 1994.

Upton, Emory. *The Military Policy of the United States from 1775*. Washington, D.C.: U.S. Government Printing Office, 1912.

Van Creveld, Martin. *Supplying War: Logistics from Wallenstein to Patton*. Cambridge: University of Massachusetts Press, 1977.

Vandiver, Frank. *Their Tattered Flags: The Epic of the Confederacy*. 1970. Reprint, College Station: Texas A&M University Press, 1989.

Wakelyn, Jon, ed. *Pro-Union Confederate Pamphlets*. Columbia: University of Missouri Press, 2000.

Warner, Ezra J. *Generals in Blue: Lives of the Union Commanders*. Baton Rouge: Louisiana State University Press, 1964.

————. *Generals in Gray: Lives of the Confederate Commanders*. Baton Rouge: Louisiana State University Press, 1959.

Warner, Ezra J., and Wilfred Buck Yearns. *Biographical Register of the Confederate Congress*. Baton Rouge: Louisiana State University Press, 1975.

Washington, Versalle F. *Eagles on Their Buttons: A Black Infantry Regiment in the Civil War*. Columbia: University of Missouri Press, 1999.

Weddell, Elizabeth Wright. *St. Paul's Church, Richmond, Virginia: Its Historic Years and Memorials*. 2 vols. Richmond: William Byrd Press, 1931.

Wiley, Bell I. *Confederate Women*. Westport, Conn.: Greenwood Press, 1975.

————. *The Life of Billy Yank: The Common Soldier of the Union*. Indianapolis: Bobbs-Merrill, 1952.

————. *The Life of Johnny Reb: The Common Soldier of the Confederacy*. Indianapolis: Bobbs-Merrill, 1943.

Williams, T. Harry. *P. G. T. Beauregard, Napoleon in Gray*. Baton Rouge: Louisiana State University Press, 1955.

Wilmer, Richard H. *The Recent Past from a Southern Standpoint*. New York: Thomas Whittaker, 1887.

Wilson, Joseph T. *The Black Phalanx: A History of the Negro Soldiers of the United States in the Wars of 1775–1812, 1861–1865*. 1890. Reprint, New York: Arno Press, 1968.

Wink, Jay. *April 1865: The Month That Saved America*. New York: HarperCollins, 2001.

Woodworth, Steven E. *Davis and Lee at War.* Lawrence: University Press of Kansas, 1995.

———. *Jefferson Davis and His Generals: The Failure of Confederate Command in the West.* Lawrence: University Press of Kansas, 1990.

Wooster, Ralph. *The Secession Conventions of the South.* Princeton: Princeton University Press, 1962.

Yearns, Wilfred Buck. *The Confederate Congress.* Athens: University of Georgia Press, 1960.

———, ed. *The Confederate Governors.* Athens: University of Georgia Press, 1985.

INDEX